Investigating Cyber Law and Cyber Ethics:

Issues, Impacts and Practices

Alfreda Dudley
Towson University, USA

James Braman
Towson University, USA

Giovanni Vincenti
Towson University, USA

A volume in the Advances in Information
Security, Privacy, and Ethics (AISPE) Book
Series

Information Science REFERENCE

An Imprint of IGI Global

Senior Editorial Director:	Kristin Klinger
Director of Book Publications:	Julia Mosemann
Editorial Director:	Lindsay Johnston
Acquisitions Editor:	Erika Carter
Development Editor:	Myla Harty
Production Editor:	Sean Woznicki
Typesetters:	Lisandro Gonzalez, Adrienne Freeland
Print Coordinator:	Jamie Snavely
Cover Design:	Nick Newcomer

Published in the United States of America by
Information Science Reference (an imprint of IGI Global)
701 E. Chocolate Avenue
Hershey PA 17033
Tel: 717-533-8845
Fax: 717-533-8661
E-mail: cust@igi-global.com
Web site: http://www.igi-global.com

Library of Congress Cataloging-in-Publication Data

Investigating cyber law and cyber ethics: issues, impacts and practices / Alfreda Dudley, James Braman and Giovanni Vincenti, editors.
     p. cm.
  Includes bibliographical references and index.
  Summary: "This book discusses the impact of cyber ethics and cyber law on information technologies and society, featuring current research, theoretical frameworks, and case studies"--Provided by publisher.
  ISBN 978-1-61350-132-0 (hardcover) -- ISBN 978-1-61350-133-7 (ebook) -- ISBN 978-1-61350-134-4 (print & perpetual access) 1. Internet--Law and legislation. 2. Computer crimes. 3. Internet--Social aspects. 4. Internet--Moral and ethical aspects. I. Dudley, Alfreda, 1957- II. Braman, James, 1981- III. Vincenti, Giovanni, 1978-
  K4345.I58 2011
  345'.0268--dc23
                                 2011022933

This book is published in the IGI Global book series Advances in Information Security, Privacy, and Ethics (AISPE) Book Series (ISSN: 1948-9730; eISSN: 1948-9749)

British Cataloguing in Publication Data
A Cataloguing in Publication record for this book is available from the British Library.

All work contributed to this book is new, previously-unpublished material. The views expressed in this book are those of the authors, but not necessarily of the publisher.

Advances in Information Security, Privacy, and Ethics (AISPE) Book Series

ISSN: 1948-9730
EISSN: 1948-9749

MISSION

In the digital age, when everything from municipal power grids to individual mobile telephone locations is all available in electronic form, the implications and protection of this data has never been more important and controversial. As digital technologies become more pervasive in everyday life and the Internet is utilized in ever increasing ways by both private and public entities, the need for more research on securing, regulating, and understanding these areas is growing.

The **Advances in Information Security, Privacy, & Ethics (AISPE) Book Series** is the source for this research, as the series provides only the most cutting-edge research on how information is utilized in the digital age.

COVERAGE

- Access Control
- Device Fingerprinting
- Global Privacy Concerns
- Information Security Standards
- Network Security Services
- Privacy-Enhancing Technologies
- Risk Management
- Security Information Management
- Technoethics
- Tracking Cookies

IGI Global is currently accepting manuscripts for publication within this series. To submit a proposal for a volume in this series, please contact our Acquisition Editors at Acquisitions@igi-global.com or visit: http://www.igi-global.com/publish/.

Titles in this Series

For a list of additional titles in this series, please visit: www.igi-global.com

Theory and Practice of Cryptography Solutions for Secure Information Systems
Atilla Elçi (Aksaray University, Turkey) Josef Pieprzyk (Macquarie University, Australia) Alexander G. Chefranov (Eastern Mediterranean University, North Cyprus) Mehmet A. Orgun (Macquarie University, Australia) Huaxiong Wang (Nanyang Technological University, Singapore) and Rajan Shankaran (Macquarie University, Australia)
Information Science Reference • copyright 2013 • 351pp • H/C (ISBN: 9781466640306) • US $195.00 (our price)

IT Security Governance Innovations Theory and Research
Daniel Mellado (Spanish Tax Agency, Spain) Luis Enrique Sánchez (University of Castilla-La Mancha, Spain) Eduardo Fernández-Medina (University of Castilla – La Mancha, Spain) and Mario Piattini (University of Castilla - La Mancha, Spain)
Information Science Reference • copyright 2013 • 390pp • H/C (ISBN: 9781466620834) • US $195.00 (our price)

Threats, Countermeasures, and Advances in Applied Information Security
Manish Gupta (State University of New York at Buffalo, USA) John Walp (M&T Bank Corporation, USA) and Raj Sharman (State University of New York, USA)
Information Science Reference • copyright 2012 • 319pp • H/C (ISBN: 9781466609785) • US $195.00 (our price)

Investigating Cyber Law and Cyber Ethics Issues, Impacts and Practices
Alfreda Dudley (Towson University, USA) James Braman (Towson University, USA) and Giovanni Vincenti (Towson University, USA)
Information Science Reference • copyright 2012 • 342pp • H/C (ISBN: 9781613501320) • US $195.00 (our price)

Information Assurance and Security Ethics in Complex Systems Interdisciplinary Perspectives
Melissa Jane Dark (Purdue University, USA)
Information Science Reference • copyright 2011 • 306pp • H/C (ISBN: 9781616922450) • US $180.00 (our price)

Chaos Synchronization and Cryptography for Secure Communications Applications for Encryption
Santo Banerjee (Politecnico di Torino, Italy)
Information Science Reference • copyright 2011 • 596pp • H/C (ISBN: 9781615207374) • US $180.00 (our price)

Technoethics and the Evolving Knowledge Society Ethical Issues in Technological Design, Research, Development, and Innovation
Rocci Luppicini (University of Ottawa, Canada)
Information Science Reference • copyright 2010 • 322pp • H/C (ISBN: 9781605669526) • US $180.00 (our price)

www.igi-global.com

701 E. Chocolate Ave., Hershey, PA 17033
Order online at www.igi-global.com or call 717-533-8845 x100
To place a standing order for titles released in this series, contact: cust@igi-global.com
Mon-Fri 8:00 am - 5:00 pm (est) or fax 24 hours a day 717-533-8661

Table of Contents

Section 1
Legal and Jurisdictional Issues Regarding Cyberspace

Section 2
Legal and Ethical Implications Involving Social Networks and Virtual Worlds

Section 3
Legal and Ethical Implications in Cyberspace: An International Perspective

Detailed Table of Contents

Section 1
Legal and Jurisdictional Issues Regarding Cyberspace

Chapter 1
Ugo Pagallo, University of Turin, Italy

As the amount of personal information and data on global networks increase, systems allow for a more granular control over privacy settings by letting users define how much information to divulge. Sometimes the systems suffice for the needs of the users as-is; other times they require a significant tailoring to fulfill one's expectations. The concept of "privacy by design" is built into the majority of IT services today, placing itself at the intersection between the regulations of national legal systems relevant to data protection and personal control. Pagallo's chapter explores in detail the balance between these two realities, focusing on the views generated by the legal systems.

Chapter 2
Gráinne Kirwan, Dun Laoghaire Institute of Art, Design and Technology, Ireland
Andrew Power, Dun Laoghaire Institute of Art, Design and Technology, Ireland

The practice of hacking conceals a large array of motivations, generated by intents that may or may not be malicious in nature. Some argue that this traditionally questionable practice can be very well utilized for positive purposes, when directed towards the welfare of the systems and data by looking for potential vulnerabilities without necessarily exploiting them. The majority of the uninformed population does attach a negative connotation to any form of hacking. This chapter reviews this widespread practice through a wide overview, then approaches the discussion of its ethicality. The authors also offers a perspective given by international legal systems.

A natural consequence to the shifting of every-day operations from a brick-and-mortar paradigm to one that lives completely in cyberspace also entails that the typically associated aspect of crime will also follow this radical change. As more and more crimes committed on Information Systems and computer hardware are reported in the news, affecting sensitive information about millions of people and often involving significant amount of money, the techniques of committing these crimes as well as their counteractions have to evolve continually. This chapter explores the methodologies through which perpetrators often carry on their illegal activities against sensitive data of various natures, focusing especially on the employment of large networks of compromised computers, or botnets. The authors also offer perspectives given by practitioners, law enforcement, and researchers who made cybercrime the focus of their attention.

The variety of computer crimes along with the complexity of the environments in which they take place, compounds the problem of devising a mechanism that can effectively addresses these types of criminal activities. It is extremely important for organizations and governments to understand computer crimes and to establish frameworks and other active measures in order to be proactive in reducing computer based crime. In this chapter the authors discuss these important topics along with a review of academic literature, industry reports, and information from the media, in identifying various types of computer crime and discuss the counter strategies to deal with such crimes in a legal, technological, and organizational context.

Perhaps one of the most profitable applications of a real-life practice carried online, gambling is a phenomenon that affects users across cultures, often reaching pathological levels that cannot be sustained without external help. The significant relevance of this topic becomes even more intricate as we observe the seam that exists in the interaction between gambling in real life and the one that exists on computers alone. This chapter observes the difficulties posed by the variations of the laws, which affect either the physical world or the virtual one. The authors then go on and discuss the possibility of creating systems that embed adherence to laws, providing support for ethics in an effort of protecting unwary or ill-informed users.

Section 2
Legal and Ethical Implications Involving Social Networks and Virtual Worlds

Chapter 6

Miguel A. Garcia-Ruiz, University of Colima, Mexico
Miguel Vargas Martin, University of Ontario Institute of Technology, Canada
Patrik Olsson, University of Ontario Institute of Technology, Canada

The advent of Internet-based technologies has sprung many different initiatives aimed at replicating features of the real world through the cybernetic medium. At times the physical environment in which we live is enhanced through technology through augmented or virtual reality; other times instead it is completely paralleled and often exacerbated. The idea of multi-user virtual environments contains a potential that is barely tapped: few educators still use it; virtual tourism is often limited by the small amount of real-life destinations reproduced through this window. Aspects of sexuality though have been developed significantly enough to also have brought perversions and illegal activities to virtual worlds, sometimes replicating flawlessly the morbidity associated with them. This chapter analyzes child pornography through multi-user virtual environments, reviewing ethical and legal issues that revolve around it.

Chapter 7

Andrew Power, Dun Laoghaire Institute of Art, Design and Technology, Ireland
Gráinne Kirwan, Dun Laoghaire Institute of Art, Design and Technology, Ireland

Any time we wish to visit new places, we usually consider the physical displacement associated with the journey. Often times, in addition to the necessity of reaching the location we wish to visit, we also need to take into consideration aspects that reach different laws and regulations when we decide to cross national borders, visiting new countries. The lines are not so clear, if they are visible at all, when we interact with virtual worlds and virtual spaces. This chapter reviews ethical implications, technical solutions and the privatization of legal remedies of the still underdeveloped realm of the legal system in user-driven virtual environments.

Chapter 8

Ananda Mitra, Wake Forest University, USA

With the increased usage of social networks and the abundance of information we reveal in contributing to our online personas, these narrative bits of information can be used to create a composite of an individual. In this chapter, the author discusses in detail these "narrative bits," or *narbs* that encapsulate measurable attributes - content, authorship, frequency of appearance and spatial information about the user. Certain characteristics of narbs can be measured though a narb weight and matrix for each individual user to reveal certain information. As social networking tools become more common place, it is important to gauge the types of information we reveal and how such information can be used.

Chapter 9

Jean-Philippe Moiny, University of Namur, Belgium

The projection of one's life in cyberspace does not necessarily have to go through 3-dimensional virtual environments. The massive advent of social networking sites has enabled users of any age, culture, and creed to share information about themselves and their lives with anyone who is willing to connect with them. This concept brings a significant stress on the policies that govern what should and shouldn't be shared with others through these social services. The author focuses on four main themes: privacy, data protection, confidentiality of electronic communications, and the unauthorized access to computers. The main subject of this work includes how American and European (in particular Belgian) laws empower users in the process of recovering the control over the global availability of their data through social networks. These two legal systems are compared, utilizing similarities as well as differences as terms of comparison and evaluation.

Section 3
Legal and Ethical Implications in Cyberspace: An International Perspective

Chapter 10

Anne Gerdes, University of Southern Denmark, Denmark

As most aspects of life are moving towards their embedding in the global technological infrastructure offered by the Internet, also dangerous and controversial aspects of life such as terrorism seem to follow. This shift towards a highly technological avenue of information allows for a more capillary distribution of untainted and unaltered credos and documents, potentially increasing the recruiting pool in the eyes of those who actively participate in these practices. This chapter evaluates in detail the strategy of proselytism utilized by Al-Qaeda and potentially other terror-based organizations in modern days. The author points out the essential components that are missing from this campaign, which are inherent characteristics of the Web 2.0 approach to technology and modern diffusion of ideas.

Chapter 11

Richard A. Spinello, Boston College, USA

Tracing the path that information takes from its origin to the end-user is often difficult in today's age of open networks and news services. The process of harnessing, controlling, and filtering such information is yet more complex, as it seriously undermines the freedom that is the basic foundation to the majority of online communications in today's day and age. The mix of these concepts with strict regulations often inflicted to its people by strict governments creates a series of arguments that are of extreme importance. The author analyzes the root causes of disagreements between what should be published and what should be available to the end-user, arguing that a proactive self-regulation may very well establish a firm foundation towards a more successful collaboration between information-providing agencies and government-supervised communications media.

Understanding where the legal regulations of one country end and the other begins is relatively simple in the real world, where we can place physical boundaries between these two different political entities, and monitor the grounds to ensure the enforcement of laws. When we move our discussion to the Internet, we are not as easily able to identify the shifting between governments. This chapter illustrates, through cases and discussion, the importance as well as the difficulties involved in translating rules and regulations typical of the physical world into the digital one represented by websites, flow of information, and services.

The act of defamation is one of the many emergent phenomena associated with social and societal aspects of the Internet's predisposition to world-wide communications. The ease with which messages and information travel over great distances has made the defense against defamation even more crucial. This chapter reviews significant legal achievements such as the Defamation Act and the E-Commerce Directive in light of these new trends, focusing in particular on the case of the United Kingdom's legal system. The discussions here are applicable and important in many contexts where defamation and reputation are involved.

As issues of computer piracy have plagued software developers worldwide, legislators have been faced with the challenge to create regulations in the effort to stop such activities at many levels, both nationally and internationally. This chapter focuses on the presentation of the current Hellenic legal framework on computer program copyright protection following the relative E.U. Directives. Piracy rates, protection of right holders, specific cases, and consequences of copyright infringement are discussed along with recommendations from the author. In a world where software can be easily copied, the topics discussed are important to consider.

Often, when we are exposed to something over and over, we barely pay attention to it any more. In many cases advertising takes this very characteristic, leading us to ignoring it while we really should pay attention, especially if the manner in which it takes place is legal. Internet-based ads, along with all the other kinds of publicity, are subject to regulations that often are not followed entirely or even ignored. This chapter explores in detail the European regulations that affect advertising (in many shapes), prompting for very interesting discussions about these topics well beyond the areas of application discussed here.

Foreword

Everyday each one of us face choices that call for decisions; some major and others minor. These decisions are often influenced by a set of guidelines, adherence to laws, our morals and/or ethics. In most situations these guidelines are straightforward (at least perceivably) for each situation we encounter. In today's information rich and technology dependent culture, many of the lines are blurred when it comes to how we interact and use technology- making informed decisions more difficult. The devices, software and other technology designed to make our lives easier, have in many situations made our lives more complicated when it comes to ethics and laws. Issues that did not exist in the past, now must be addressed and scrutinized, and new laws developed. In many instances however, old crimes and social issues have been reinvented or exacerbated by these new technologies. A cyber criminal can be hiding in one part of the world committing crimes in another part using someone else's identity. Not only does the crime itself need to be analyzed, but also the laws that are being violated and the country. What may be legal or ethically sound for one location may be illegal in another. Other such issues arise from organizations and businesses not fully understanding their vulnerabilities, or computer based crime and/or their responsibilities to protect their data. Social networks have also changed the legal landscape by adding new dimensions of vulnerability and social engineering through the creation of our online digital selves. We spend so much time constructing our online representation, but forget that the information we post online can sometimes be used against us. These types of problems are just a few mentioned in this book as it aims to highlight many mainstream global ethical and legal problems caused or amplified by technology.

With this book, *Investigating Cyber Law and Cyber Ethics: Issues, Impacts and Practices*, observations can be made about the impact of technology, software and the Internet through a legal and ethical point of view. Three main sections provide the framework for the book, which include: Section 1: Legal and Jurisdictional Issues Regarding Cyberspace, Section 2: Legal and Ethical Implications involving Social Networks and Virtual Worlds; and Section 3: Legal and Ethical Implications in Cyberspace – An International Perspective. Through these divisions, a unique collection of articles, research initiatives, essays and discussions are presented with the objective to provided readers with an international view of current trends in these growing areas of importance.

Today cyber technologies have significant impact on privacy, security and individual rights. IT professionals and educators must have a working knowledge of the professional, ethical, legal, security and social issues and responsibilities associated with these technologies. They must be aware of and adhere to the ethical standards of the profession as they formulate solutions to meet user needs in an organizational and societal context. The nature of their involvement with implementing and managing information and communication technologies requires IT professionals to be aware of relevant legal statutes and procedures including computer crime rules of evidence, evidence seizure and handling, as well as court presentation.

Scott Hilberg
Towson University, March 2010

Scott Hilberg *is the Assistant Director for Center for Applied Information Technology (CAIT), the Director of the undergraduate Information Technology program, and Clinical Assistant Professor in the Department of Computer and Information Sciences at Towson University. His academic background includes an Ed.D. in Innovation & Leadership from Wilmington University and a M.A.S. in Management Information Technology from Johns Hopkins University. He has taught programming, system development, and project management. In addition, he has 15+ years of industry experience as a programmer, systems analyst, and IT manager.*

Preface

Computer technologies have continually and rapidly changed and advanced in the last two decades. The impacts of these rapid changes are affecting the use and applications of computer technologies in society. These impacts bring about new focus and scrutiny. One of the fundamental changes in the last decade has been the realization that the context in which computer technologies are used must take into account the ethical implications associated with their use. Examples of computing ethical issues include, but are not limited to: cyberterrorism; security and privacy responsibilities; intellectual property rights; online piracy; blogger litigation; data recovery; data protection; wireless computing; computer crime; et cetera. Another fundamental change is the increased importance of the legal impacts that new computer technologies introduce. However, these changes do not necessarily correspond to the changes in the computer technology itself.

Ethics, when applied to technology-related issues, are also recognized as cyberethics (Tavani, 2010). There is a plethora of viewpoints regarding the subject of cyberethics. For instance, one major question that many professionals both inside and outside the computer community consider: Are cyberethics different from "regular" ethics? Regular ethics are defined as ethics that apply across all contexts (i.e., medical, legal, business, and religious). In some instances, this question can be answered with a definite yes. However, many theorists would state that there are differences between regular ethics and cyberethics. They base their arguments on the fact that cyberethics is based on the impact of computing technologies on individuals and society. However, this does not indicate that computing technologies have introduced new ethical issues. Therefore, some would argue that there are no differences between regular ethics and cyberethics. Their arguments are based on the fact that computing technologies only bring a new dimension to existing ethical issues. A major problem is the practice and application of ethics in computing environments by computing professionals and users.

In the computing culture, professionals and organizations put emphasis on proper or improper design procedures and practices. While this is definitely important, increasing awareness of the ethical behavioral practices of the computing professional and organization is becoming crucial. Computing technology is pervasive in all areas of society; therefore, when considering ethical practices, this component should not be omitted. Computing professionals and organizations are not different species. However, the ethical practices and applications of computing professionals and organizations are becoming suspect in the light of computer crimes, i.e., fraud, identity theft, embezzlement, etc. (Dudley-Sponaugle & Lazar, 2005).

Ethics is a central component in the legal prospectus. However, many legal professionals and academics believe current legal statutes leave much to be desired in regards to computing technologies. In addition, there are further debates regarding the pedagogical structure of the legal curriculum and the inclusion of ethics. "There has been some concern about the growing disjunction between legal educa-tion and the legal profession. While the law schools seem to be moving toward pure theory, the firms are moving toward pure commerce, and both have abandoned the middle ground -ethical practice" (Edwards, 1992). It is the consensus of legal scholars and practitioners that students should be acclimated to the application of ethical principles in law. In doing so, law students will be more adapt in the interpretation and modification of legal doctrine and precedents in the law. It is believed that a good, practical scholar gives due weight to cases, statutes, and other authoritative texts, but also employs theory to criticize doctrine and to propose changes in the law.

Regardless of their views or positions, most ethicists and legal practitioners would agree that ethics and legal knowledge are important in the applications of computer technologies. The issue for many is how to connect ethics and legal knowledge and practice regarding computing technologies implementation. For the past several years, the editors became interested in the ethical behaviors of users in the applica-tion of computer technologies. This lead to several published journal articles and book chapters. While pursuing their ongoing research, the editors were made aware of the lack of publications on how law is being translated and applied to existing computer technologies. This book project became in existence because of the lack or need of different perspectives in these areas. The approach to this book was to discover various viewpoints and issues dealing with the topics of cyberlaw and cyberethics. Moreover, the editors believe the information from this book will provide important insights for future develop-ment and research in these areas.

The book "*Investigating Cyber Law and Cyber Ethics: Issues, Impacts and Practices*" arises from observing the rate of growth registered within the field of technology and the speed at which ethics discussions and legal coverage try to keep up. The difference in advancement offers fertile ground to illegal trades, unethical behaviors, and unmonitored activities in general. Such observation is true for any new endeavor, but it is exacerbated by the high levels of diffusion among the peoples of the world, blurring national boundaries or cultural habits. As the world heads towards a technological global har-monization, the legal systems especially, but also the frames of reference that the field of ethics offers seem to diverge rather than converge. This book's aim represents the summary of the work of many researchers and practitioners who are striving to unite their efforts towards a significant progress. This book is divided into three sections: Section 1, *Legal and Jurisdictional Issues Regarding Cyberspace*, gives an overview of the problem; Section 2, *Legal and Ethical Implications involving Social Networks and Virtual Worlds*, analyzes the above-mentioned gap by focusing on the forefront of technological advancements with the most societal impacts; Section 3, *Legal and Ethical Implications in Cyberspace: An International Perspective*, steps back from the details of technology and approaches the main topic of this work from multiple national angles.

The first set of contributions gathered in Section 1, titled *Legal and Jurisdictional Issues Regarding Cyberspace*, offers a wide perspective on legal and ethical issues related to innovations in technology. In Chapter 1, *Responsibility, Jurisdiction, and the Future of "Privacy by Design,"* Ugo Pagallo analyzes the effects that privacy policies of popular technology-based services have on data protection and personal control. In Chapter 2, titled *Hacking: Legal and Ethical Aspects of an Ambiguous Activity*, Kirwan and Power offer thought-provoking arguments that describe the always controversial practice (or vocation) of hacking. In Chapter 3 the contribution from Zadig and Tejay, titled *Emerging Cybercrime Trends: Legal, Ethical, and Practical Issues*, quantify and qualify through examples some of the new and arising concerns in the expansion of crime into new technological niches. Chapter 4, titled *Law and Technology at Crossroads in Cyberspace: Where Do We Go From Here?* by Ayanso and Herath, analyzes practical aspects of enforcing laws in modern technology-based terrains. Chapter 5, titled *Cyber Law, Cyber Ethics and Online Gambling,* by Gillam and Vartapetiance, concludes the first section by exploring legal and ethical aspects of gambling and addiction, a significant concern that quickly spread from the physical halls of casinos to the online world.

In Section 2, titled *Legal and Ethical Implications involving Social Networks and Virtual Worlds*, we focus the reader's attention on the quickly-rising front of technology that aims at recreating sociality, cultures and societies in cyberspace. Chapter 6 opens this section with the chapter titled *An Overview of Child Abuses in 3D Social Networks and Online Video Games*, by Garcia-Ruiz, Vargas Martin, and Olsson, which analyzes the problem of child abuse in virtual worlds and how it is translated into this new frontier from the physical world. Then Chapter 7, titled *Ethics and Legal Aspects of Virtual Worlds* by Power and Kirwan, focus on legal aspects of virtual worlds in general, offering a broader perspective on the state of ethical and legal progress applied to this virtual representation of life. In Chapter 8, Ananda Mitra discusses *Narbs as a Measure and Indicator of Identity Narratives*, offering a new look to narrative bits and how they may affect our personal (and very real) lives. Jean-Philippe Moiny authored Chapter 9, titled *Cloud Based Social Network Sites: Under Whose Control?* a work that analyzes the implications that cloud-based computing may have over the control, or its lack, of our information, which is still available to us locally, but stored globally.

Finally, we conclude this book by offering the points of view of different social and legal systems in Section 3, titled *Legal and Ethical Implications in Cyberspace: An International Perspective*. Anne Gerdes describes the different approach that terror-centered organizations, such as Al-Qaeda, have developed in order to fully realize their potential in conjunction with innovation-based platforms in Chapter 10, titled *Al-Qaeda on Web 2.0: Radicalization and Recruitment Strategies*. In Chapter 11, titled *Google in China: Corporate Responsibility on a Filtered Internet*, Richard Spinello reviews a case that has made headlines for months, by analyzing the difficult interaction between a population that craves information and the restrictions of a controlling government when it comes to access of a technology that makes of free speech its funding pillar. Jonathan Bishop authored Chapter 12, titled *All's WELL that Ends WELL: A Comparative Analysis of the Constitutional and Administrative Frameworks of Cyberspace and the United Kingdom*, a clear depiction of the lag reported in the process of adapting a national legal system to its Internet-based counterpart. In Chapter 13, Sam De Silva demonstrates through the crime of defamation the gaps that exist in the legal systems that cover the physical and the virtual worlds in his work titled *A UK Law Perspective: Defamation Law as it Applies on the Internet*. Chapter 14 explores the globally sensitive topic of copyright protection, an issue that continues to make headlines any time the legal system identifies a significant discrepancy between what the system should do and how it actually works. This work by Eugenia Alexandropoulou–Egyptiadou is titled *The Hellenic Framework for Computer Program Copyright Protection Following the Implementation of the Relative European Union Directives*. The book is concluded by Radomír Jakab in Chapter 15, titled *Internet Advertising: Legal Aspects in the European Union*, which focuses on the poor regulation of advertising in the digital world as opposed to the laws established within the European Union.

This book brings together a wide range of topics regarding the areas of cyberlaw and cyberethics. In it, readers will find discussions, positions, and information regarding the impacts of these topics across a wide network of disciplines and global perspectives. As new technologies continue to evolve, so too must our understanding of its ethical and legal implications. When a new tool or technology is invented and introduced, what emerges is not always what was originally intended. These new emerging ideas and other advances can have long lasting influences that cannot always be readily foreseeable. It is our desire that this particular book will serve as a both a research and educational tool to encompass knowledge in the growing areas related to technology, ethics and law. It is also our desire that this book will serve to help others see that cyberlaw and cyberethics are important domains in which understanding is key for our future, as our lives become ever further meshed and integrated with the ever growing connected digital world.

Alfreda Dudley
Towson University, USA

James Braman
Towson University, USA

Giovanni Vincenti
Towson University, USA

REFERENCES

Dudley-Sponaugle, A., & Lazar, J. (2005). *Webmasters' perception of ethics within an IT setting.* Information Resources Management Association International Conference, May 15-18, 2005, San Diego, CA.

Edwards, H. (1992). The growing disjunction between legal education and the legal profession. *Michigan Law Review, 91*(1), 34–79. doi:10.2307/1289788

Tavani, H. T. (2010). *Ethics and technology: Controversies, questions, and strategies for ethical computing* (3rd ed.). Danvers, MA: John Wiley & Sons, Inc.

Acknowledgment

This project was the end result of the collaboration of many individuals working together towards a common goal. In a project of this magnitude, many people were involved in its development. The editors are very grateful for all the hard work and dedication by all of the contributing authors who made this book possible. We thank all of the contributors for their time and willingness to share their ideas, experiences, and research efforts. It was our goal to create a volume that consisted of a diverse collection of ideas related to cyberlaw and cyberethics, and through everyone's efforts, that goal has been achieved.. It has been a great pleasure working with such a group of talented individuals.

A special thanks to our Editorial Advisory Board, whose input was valuable. We would also like to thank our Reviewers who volunteered their time helping in the review process and by offering advice and comments for the chapters. Thank you to the IGI staff and publishing team. We wish to thank them for their guidance and patience over this past year .

We would also like to thank and express our gratitude to our families, friends, and colleagues for their encouragement and patience while we have worked on this project. Thank you to everyone who has been involved with this book; without you this book would not have been possible.

Alfreda Dudley
Towson University, USA

James Braman
Towson University, USA

Giovanni Vincenti
Towson University, USA

March 2011

Section 1
Legal and Jurisdictional Issues Regarding Cyberspace

Chapter 1
Responsibility, Jurisdiction, and the Future of "Privacy by Design"

Ugo Pagallo
University of Turin, Italy

ABSTRACT

This chapter focuses on some of the most relevant issues in today's data protection: responsibility and jurisdiction are examined in the light of the principle of "privacy by design." On one hand, both from the substantial and procedural points of view, national legal systems determine differently rights and duties in the field of data protection. On the other hand, these divergences can be overcome to some extent, by preventing privacy infringements through the incorporation of data protection safeguards in information and communication technologies. Although it is unlikely that "privacy by design" can offer the one-size-fits-all solution to the problems emerging in the field, it is plausible that the principle will be the key to understand how today's data protection-issues are being handled. By embedding privacy safeguards in places and spaces, products and processes, such as Information Systems in hospitals, video surveillance networks in public transports, or smart cards for biometric identifiers, the aim should be to strengthen people's rights and widen the range of their choices. On this basis, we can avert both paternalism modelling individual behavior and chauvinism disdaining different national provisions of current legal systems.

INTRODUCTION

Although lawyers may disagree on whether we are in the midst of an "information revolution" (Bynum, 2009; Horner, 2010), most of the time they admit that both the internet and computer networks have deeply changed contemporary legal systems. As stressed by several contributions to *Information Technology Law* (Bainbridge, 2008; Lloyd, 2008; etc.), such a profound transformation has affected not only the substantial and procedural sides of the law, but its cognitive features as well. The impact of technology on today's

DOI: 10.4018/978-1-61350-132-0.ch001

legal systems can be fully appreciated through a threefold perspective.

First, technology has engendered new types of lawsuits or modified old ones. As, for example, the next generation of offences arose within the field of computer crimes (*e.g.*, identity thefts), technology impacted on traditional rights such as copyright (1709) and privacy (1890), turning them into a matter of access, control, and protection over information in digital environments (Heide, 2001; Tavani & Moor, 2001; Ginsburg, 2003; Floridi, 2006).

Secondly, technology has blurred traditional national boundaries as information on the internet tends to have a ubiquitous nature. This challenges the very conception of the law as enforced through physical sanctions in the nation-state. Spamming, for instance, offers a good example: It is transnational par excellence and does not diminish despite harshening criminal laws (like the *CAN-SPAM Act* passed by the U.S. Congress in 2003). No threat of sanctions, in other words, seems to limit spamming.

Finally, technology has deeply transformed the approach of experts to legal information. As Herbert A. Simon pointed out in his seminal book on *The Sciences of Artificial*, this transformation is conveniently illustrated by research in design theory, which "is aimed at broadening the capabilities of computers to aid design, drawing upon the tools of artificial intelligence and operations research" (Simon, 1996). While scholars increasingly insist on the specific impact of design or "architecture" and "code" on legal systems (Lessig, 1999; Katyal, 2002; Zittrain, 2008; van Schewick, 2010), both artificial intelligence and operations research not only further design but, in doing so, affect the structure and evolution of legal systems (Pagallo, 2007; Yeung, 2007).

These three levels of impact have, nonetheless, led some scholars to adopt a sort of techno-deterministic approach, leaving no way open to shape or, at least, to influence the evolution of technology. It is enough to mention that some

have announced "The End of Privacy" (Sykes, 1999), "The Death of Privacy in the 21st Century" (Jarfinkel, 2000), or "Privacy Lost" (Holtzmann, 2006). On this reading, technology would allow these scholars to unveil an already written future: While, in digital environments, spyware, root-kits, profiling techniques, or data mining would erase data protection, FBI programs like Carnivore or some other means like RFID, GPS, CCTV, AmI, or satellites, would lead to the same effect in everyday (or analog) life. However, strongly decentralized and encrypted architectures providing anonymity to their users, as well as systems that permit plausible deniability and a high degree of confidentiality in communications, suggest that rumours of the death of privacy have been greatly exaggerated. Techno-deterministic approaches are in fact liable to the same criticism that John Kenneth Galbraith put forward in his own field: "The only function of economic forecasting is to make astrology look respectable". In order to provide a more balanced picture of the current state-of-the-art, this chapter examines two of the hottest legal topics in data protection, namely, online responsibility and jurisdiction, which are then analyzed in connection with today's debate on the idea of embedding data protection safeguards in ICT and other types of technologies, that is, the principle of "privacy by design". The goal is to shed further light on the aforementioned threefold level-impact of technology on contemporary legal systems, taking leave from all sorts of techno-deterministic drifts. Accordingly, the chapter is presented in five sections.

First, the *background of the analysis* sums up the claims of "unexceptionalism". In its substantial form, it vindicates the analogy between cyberspace and the "real world," that is, between digital and traditional boundaries of legal systems. In the phrasing of Allan R. Stein, "*The Internet is a medium*. It connects people in different places. The injuries inflicted over the Internet are inflicted by people on people. In this sense, the Internet is no different from the myriad of ways that people from one place injure people in other places" (Stein, 1998). In its procedural form, "unexceptionalism" argues that traditional tools and principles of international law can find a solution to the regulatory issues of the digital era. These ideas have been adopted by the European authorities on data protection, *i.e.*, the EU Working Party art. 29 D-95/46/EC. Notwithstanding the ubiquity of information on the internet, the EU WP29 has proposed to solve conflicts of law on the international level through the use of "several alternative criteria for determining extensively the scope of application of national law" (see the WP29 Opinion 5035/01/WP56 from 2002).

There is a paramount difference, however, between cross-border regulations of the internet and the traditional criterion of territoriality, grounded upon the Westphalian paradigm (1648). As remarked in the *section on international conflicts of law*, the right of the states to control events within their territory was originally conceived in a world where cross-border regulations were the exception and not the rule. Vice versa, in a world where virtually all events and transactions have transnational consequences, "unexceptionalism" would result in a form of pan-national jurisdiction covering the entire world (see for instance the aforementioned WP29 Opinion on the regulatory framework for transnational cookies). As I refer in the *section on privacy and design*, such evident drawbacks have pushed scholars and policy makers alike to address issues of responsibility and jurisdiction from another perspective, namely, by embedding data protection safeguards as a default setting in information and communication technologies (ICT). Since the mid 1990s, the overall idea is to bypass otherwise unsolvable issues of transnational jurisdiction and cross-border liability, by totally or partially preventing the impact of harm-generating behaviour in digital environments.

As the *section on future research directions* illustrates, additional work is required. Taking into account current investigations in the field of artificial intelligence (AI) & Law and, more particularly, in the realm of legal ontologies, we should further examine the modelling of highly context-dependent normative concepts like personal data, security measures, or data controllers, as well as the decomposition of the complete design project into its functional components. Yet, we need not rely either on prophetic powers or on divinatory commitments, to reach a workable conclusion: the principle of "privacy by design" ought to be a default mode of operation for both private companies and public institutions, if, and only if, it strengthens individual rights by widening the range of their choices. Whilst the principle is not likely to offer the one-size-fits-all solution to the problems we are dealing with in relation to data protection, it is nonetheless plausible that suggestions coming from the "privacy by design"-debate will be the key to understand most crucial issues of today's legal framework.

BACKGROUND

Legal debate between advocates of the "unexceptionalist" theses and advocates of the uniqueness of the information revolution is not new. The same problem, after all, arose within the field of computer ethics in 1985. On the side of unexceptionalism, Deborah Johnson's idea was that ICT provides for new ways to instrument human actions which raise specific questions that, nonetheless, would only be a "new species of old moral issues" (Johnson, 1985). On the other side, Walter Maner insisted on the new generation of problems which are *unique* to computer ethics: "For all of these issues, there was an essential involvement of computing technology. Except for this technology, these issues would not have arisen, or would not have arisen in their highly altered form. The failure to find satisfactory non-computer analogies testifies to the uniqueness of these issues. (…) Lack of an effective analogy forces us to discover new moral values, formulate new moral principles, develop new policies, and find new ways to think about the issues presented to us" (Maner, 1996; and, previously, Moor, 1985).

A decade later, the ICT revolution forced legal scholars into the debate. In the early 1990s, lawmakers introduced the first global provisions on computer crimes. In 1995, the European Community approved its first general directive on the protection and processing of personal data, *i.e.*, the aforementioned directive 95/46/EC. A year later, in 1996, it was the turn of the exclusivity rights over public communication pursuant to art. 20 of the Berne Convention (1886) to be complemented by two international copyright treaties, namely, the WIPO's *Copyright Treaty* (WCT) and the *Performances and Phonograms Treaty* (WPPT). In 1998, the U.S. Congress amended the *Digital Performance Rights in Sound Recordings Act* from 1995 with both the *Digital Millennium Copyright Act* (DMCA) and the *Sonny Bono Act* on the extension of exclusivity rights. From the standard fourteen-year term of protection granted by the U.S. *Copyright Act* in 1790, copyright was extended to cover twenty-eight years in 1831, a further twenty-eight years of renewal in 1909, fifty years after the author's death in 1976, down to the current seventy years of protection set up in 1998.

In the unexceptionalism vs. uniqueness debate, it is crucial to distinguish the substantial from the procedural side. What the unexceptionalists have indeed been claiming is that we can (and should) handle the new IT law-cases on computer crimes, data protection, or digital copyright, with the settled principles and traditional tools of international law. In the wording of Jack Goldsmith's *Against Cybernarchy*, IT law-problems are "no more complex and challenging than similar issues presented by increasingly prevalent real-space events such as airplane crashes, mass torts, multistate insurance coverage, or multinational commercial transactions, all of which form the bread and butter of modern conflict of law" (Goldsmith, 1998, p. 1234). On this view, traditional legal tools would be capable to resolve the regulatory problems of the ICT revolution because "activity in cyberspace

is functionally identical to transnational activity mediated by other means, such as mail or telephone or smoke signal" (*op. cit.*, p. 1240).

On the side of the uniqueness advocates, however, both the scale and amount of cross-border transactions taking place in cyberspace question this "functional identity". According to David Post's criticism of the unexceptionalist ideas, "border-crossing events and transactions, previously at the margins of the legal system and of sufficient rarity to be cabined off into a small corner of the legal universe (…) have migrated, in cyberspace, to the core of that system" (Post, 2002, p. 1380). Like in other fields of scientific research such as physics, biology, or engineering, scale does matter: "A world in which virtually *all* events and transactions have border-crossing effects is surely not 'functionally identical' to a world in which most do not, at least not with respect to the application of a principle that necessarily requires consideration of the distribution of those effects" (*ibid.*).

To further clarify the terms of the debate, let me go back to the 1998 provisions of the DMCA and, more specifically, to the "safe harbour"-clauses set up by section 512 of the US Code. They define responsibility regimes for copyright liability, in a way that corresponds to the European provisions established by articles 12-15 of directive 2000/31/EC on e-commerce. Theoretically speaking, lawgivers could have chosen one of three different situations in which individuals and corporations find themselves confronted to copyright liability: (i) legal irresponsibility; (ii) strict liability; and (iii) personal responsibility which depends on "fault".

Following the good old idea that "all which is not prohibited is allowed", the first hypothesis of legal irresponsibility is properly illustrated by the immunity provisions for online speech approved by the U.S. Congress in 1996, pursuant to section 230 of the *Communications Decency Act*: "No provider or user of an interactive computer service shall be treated as the publisher or speaker of any information provided by another content provider". The rationale consists in the point that intermediaries should not be considered responsible for what users do or say through their network services, so as to foster people's freedom of speech and the flow of information on the internet. Vice versa, the responsibility of traditional publishers clarifies the hypothesis of liability without fault or strict liability. Notwithstanding eventual illicit or culpable behavior, editors, publishers, and media owners (newspapers, TV channels, etc.), are liable for damages caused by their employees, *e.g.*, pre-digital media's journalists and writers. This mechanism applies to many other cases in which law imposes liability regardless of the person's intention or use of ordinary care, as it occurs with people's responsibility for the behaviour of their pets and, in most legal systems, of their children. Whereas the rationale of the liability involving traditional publishers and editors hinges on the "one-to-many" architecture of pre-digital medias, it seems inappropriate to apply this mechanism of distributing risk to current internet service providers (ISPs), because the architecture of the internet is par excellence "many-to-many".

Still, people are liable mostly for what they voluntarily agree upon through strict contractual obligations and, moreover, for obligations that are imposed by the government to compensate damage done by wrongdoing. There is liability for intentional torts when a person has voluntarily performed the wrongful action prohibited by the law; but legal systems also provide for liability based on lack of due care when the "reasonable" person fails to guard against "foreseeable" harm. This kind of responsibility is neither excluded nor established *a priori*: it is instead grounded on the circumstances of the case. It therefore fits particularly well in this context, as shown by the decision of the European Court of Justice (ECJ) in the *Google v. Louis Vuitton case* from March 23rd, 2010. Although the judgement concerns issues of trademarks, keyword advertising, and search engines, it allows to clarify the third kind of responsibility which depends on personal fault. "In order

to establish whether the liability of a referencing service provider may be limited under Article 14 of Directive 2000/31, it is necessary to examine whether the role played by that service provider is neutral, in the sense that its conduct is merely technical, automatic and passive, pointing to a lack of knowledge or control of the data which it stores" (§ 114 of the decision). The responsibility is thus neither excluded *a priori* (legal irresponsibility), nor established *a priori* (liability without fault), because it depends on "the actual terms on which the service in the cases in the main proceedings is supplied." As a consequence, the Court of Paris should "assess whether the role thus played by Google corresponds to that described in paragraph 114 of the present judgment" (*ibid.*, § 117).

The EU WP29 already remarked this latter point in its 2009 Opinion on social networks. Suggesting some convergences with the legal framework established by section 230(c) of the U.S. *Communications Decency Act*, the EU WP29 affirms that ISPs as well as social network services (SNS) should only be obliged to provide information and adequate warning to users about privacy risks when uploading data: "users should be advised by SNS that pictures or information about other individuals, should only be uploaded with the individual's consent" (WP's Opinion 5/2009). Therefore, users are personally responsible for what they do online via social networks, P2P systems, cloud computing, and the like. This has been confirmed by cases of defamation and privacy or copyright infringements. Conversely, ISPs and SNS should hold responsible only when they fail to remove illegitimate content after having been asked to do so by a judicial or administrative authority. In accordance with this brief account on the principle of online responsibility (Pagallo, 2009), it is thus no surprise that both the American and European legislators, when discussing the responsibility regimes for ISPs' copyright liability, opted for an innovative generation of "safe harbour"-clauses. The new limitations of responsibility cover activities that provide for, among other things, connectivity, cache content, information location tools and search engines. The reason for these novel forms of legal irresponsibility is summed up by the Judiciary Report of the U.S. Senate Committee from 1998 (S. Rep. No. 105-190, p. 8):

Due to the ease with which digital works can be copied and distributed worldwide virtually instantaneously, copyright owners will hesitate to make their works readily available on the Internet without reasonable assurance that they will be protected against massive piracy. (...) At the same time, without clarification of their liability, service providers may hesitate to make the necessary investment in the expansion of the speed and capacity on the Internet. (...) Many service providers engage in directing users to sites in response to inquiries by users or they volunteer sites that users may find attractive. Some of these sites might contain infringing material. In short, by limiting the liability of service providers, the DMCA ensures that the efficiency of the Internet will continue to improve and that the variety and quality of services on the Internet will continue to expand.

Although this general framework has usually improved the efficiency of the internet, these legal provisions present some limits of their own. For instance, the notice and takedown-procedure in section 512 of DMCA has now and then been used to censor legitimate criticism or to silence adversarial political speech. Besides, an empirical study on intermediary immunity under section 230 of the *Communications Decency Act* argues that, while section 230 largely protects intermediaries from liability for third-party speech, this provision does not represent the free pass that many of its critics lament. In a nutshell, "judges have been haphazard in their approach to its application" (Ardia, 2010). Moreover, we should not forget the ubiquitous nature of information on the internet and the unexceptionalist claim that every nation

state has both the "right to control events within its territory and to protect the citizens [which] permits it to regulate the local effects of extraterritorial acts" (Goldsmith, 1998). Even admitting the uniqueness of the information revolution and, thereby, the novelty of its impact on contemporary legal systems, it does not follow that the settled principles and traditional tools of international law are unable to address the new IT law-cases arisen in digital environments. After all, this mechanism was applied to a well-known American company, when an Italian court admitted the responsibility of the internet provider by sentencing some of Google's executives in the *Vividown case*. The executives were, in fact, held liable for "illicit treatment of personal data" pursuant to article 167 of the Italian Data Protection Code, that is, for allowing a video to be posted showing an autistic youth being abused (Tribunal of Milan, decision 1972 from February 24th, 2010). As a matter of legal fact, the court rejected the defendants' idea that data processing performed by Google's servers in California is not governed by Italian law, not even in the case of data transmitted by Italian users. Otherwise – so goes the argument of the court – it would be easy to avoid being subject to Italian and European rules by simply locating the company (and its servers) outside EU borders.

In spite of the noble aim to provide global protection of people's fundamental rights, determining the applicability of national law to cross-borders interaction on the internet ends up in a paradox. In order to understand why scale matters not only in physics or biology, but in legal science as well, let us examine how lawyers deal with issues of jurisdiction and criteria for the international resolution of legal conflicts.

INTERNATIONAL CONFLICTS OF LAW

Jack Goldsmith is probably right when affirming that preliminary issues concerning the applicable law in the international arena represent "the bread and butter" of contemporary lawyers (Goldsmith, 1998). However, what the American scholar apparently missed is that the settled principles and traditional tools of both public and private international law are unable to fully meet the challenges set by the current transnational relationships. The conventional representation of the international legal order as grounded upon the principle of national sovereignty – so that "in the absence of consensual international solutions, prevailing concepts of territorial sovereignty permit a nation to regulate the local effects of extraterritorial conduct" (Goldsmith, 1998, p. 1212) – is criticized because there would be no clear boundaries in cyberspace and, even less so, in today's computer cloud-environments. The ubiquity of information on the internet leads to the illegitimate situation where a state claims to regulate extraterritorial conduct by imposing norms on individuals who have no say in the decisions affecting them (thus jeopardizing the legitimacy of democratic rule of law). In addition, this situation determines the ineffectiveness of state action within the realm of cyberspace for citizens would be affected by conduct that the state is simply unable to regulate (Post, 2002).

In order to further illustrate the drawbacks of unexceptionalism, let me go back to the 2002 Opinion of the European authorities on data protection (5035/01/EN/Final WP 56). On that occasion, examining "alternative criteria for determining extensively the scope of application of national law," the WP29 found a decisive element in today's cookies, *i.e.*, the text-files placed on the computer's hard disk when people access a web site. According to the aforementioned WP29 Opinion 5/2002, cookies should in fact be considered as "equipment" pursuant to art. 4 (1)c of D-95/46/EC: "Each Member State shall apply the national provisions it adopts pursuant to this Directive to the processing of personal data when (…) the controller is not established on Community territory and, for purposes of processing personal

data, makes use of equipment, automated or otherwise, situated on the territory of the said Member State". Moreover, the WP29 argued that the aim of the extensive interpretation of the directive is not only to broaden the range of applicability of EU law. By considering cookies to be a sort of equipment pursuant to the European directive on data protection, the WP29 claimed that the goal is to ensure the protection of people's fundamental rights: "The objective of this provision in Article 4 paragraph 1 lit. c) of Directive 95/46/EC is that an individual should not be without protection as regards processing taking place within his country, solely because the controller is not established on Community territory. This could be simply, because the controller has, in principle, nothing to do with the Community. But it is also imaginable that controllers locate their establishment outside the EU in order to bypass the application of EU law".

Later, on December 1st, 2009, this viewpoint was partially confirmed in a joint contribution by the WP29 and the EU Working Party on Police and Justice (WPPJ). In the document on "The Future of Privacy" (02356/09/EN – WP168), both the WP29 and WPPJ admitted that "article 4 of the directive, determining when the directive is applicable to data processing, leaves room for different interpretation". Nevertheless, in accordance with the previous Opinion from May 30th, 2002, they insisted on the idea that the protection of people's fundamental rights "means that individuals can claim protection also if their data are processed outside the European Union". Could not this noble aim be reached in other ways? In other words, is the protection of people's fundamental rights a good enough reason to bypass the letter and the spirit of the European directive on the protection of personal data? All in all, there are five reasons to surmise that treating cookies as "equipment" according to art. 4 (1)c of D-95/46/EC is legally wrong.

First, the definitions of Art. 2 of D-95/46/EC do not include the meaning of "equipment".

Hence, to consider cookies as a sort of equipment would be more a matter of political choice than of legal interpretation.

Secondly, since many EU provisions apply to non-European companies doing business in Europe, this framework involves issues in the field of consumer law as well. For instance, many of these companies have trouble in excluding EU users from their services because, in order to avoid matters of data protection, they would need to know the residence and the name of the users, clearly entailing potential infringements on data protection law and other issues of jurisdiction. Ultimately, this leads to a vicious circle.

Thirdly, by considering cookies as "equipment" in the processing of personal data, the principal criterion according to which EU Member States should apply the directive would not hinge on the place where the data controller is established. Rather, contrarily to the rationale of the directive, its applicability would depend on the emplacement of the data subject.

Fourthly, by applying EU data protection laws to all the websites employing cookies on the internet, foreign data controllers would be compelled to simultaneously comply with the legislation of every single Member State of the EU, which raises an "impossible burden" (Kuner, 2003).

Finally, there is the paradox which has been mentioned in the introduction of this chapter. Once we admit that cookies are equivalent to "equipment", pursuant to the European directive on the protection of personal data, it follows that every time, for example, a U.S. citizen is accessing a U.S. website during their holidays in Europe, the enforceable norms would be the EU laws on data protection!

Significantly, in the Opinion from July 25th, 2007 (2007/C 255/01), the European Data Protection Supervisor (EDPS), Peter Hustinx, emphasized the limits of this approach insofar as "this system, a logical and necessary consequence of the territorial limitations of the European Union, will not provide full protection to the European data subject in a networked society where physical borders lose importance (…): the information on the Internet has an ubiquitous nature, but the jurisdiction of the European legislator is not ubiquitous". Like other cases put forward by contemporary *lex mercatoria*, corporate governance, or human rights litigation, cyberspace issues show the shortcomings of international approaches based upon the principle of sovereignty and nations' right to unilaterally control events within their territories. As Peter Hustinx stressed in the aforementioned Opinion from 2007, the challenge of protecting personal data at the international level "will be to find practical solutions" through typical transnational measures such as "the use of binding corporate rules by multinational companies." Furthermore, we need to promote "private enforcement of data protection principles through self-regulation and competition," while "accepted standards such as the OECD-guidelines for data protection (1980) and UN-Guidelines could be used as basis" for international agreements on jurisdiction.

However, such international forms of cooperation and integration do not seem to offer the magic bullet. As confirmed by the passenger name record (PNR)-agreements between the U.S. and Europe, along with the hot debate followed within the European institutions, traditionally close allies may engage in often problematic covenants and conventions (Pagallo, 2008; Brouwer, 2009). Besides, practices of censorship, corruption, bribery and filtering, which are unfortunately spread throughout the world, confirm the difficulties to settle most of today's privacy issues through standard international solutions (Deibert *et al.*, 2008). Consequently, in the 2009 document on "The Future of Privacy," it is telling that both the WP29 and the WPPJ have illustrated a different thesis. Indeed, global issues of data protection should be approached by "incorporating technological protection safeguards in information and communication technologies," according to the principle of privacy by design, which "should be binding for technology designers and producers as well as for data controllers who have to decide on the acquisition and use of ICT." In the next section I will examine how far this idea goes.

PRIVACY AND DESIGN

More than a decade ago, in *Code and Other Laws of Cyberspace*, Lawrence Lessig lamented the poverty of research involving the impact of design on both social relationships and the functioning of legal systems (Lessig, 1999). In a few years, however, this gap has been filled by work on privacy (Ackerman and Cranor, 1999); universal usability (Shneiderman, 2000); informed consent (Friedman, Howe, and Felten, 2002); crime control and architecture (Katyal, 2002, 2003); social justice (Borning, Friedman, & Kahn, 2004); allegedly perfect self-enforcement technologies on the internet (Zittrain, 2007); and "design-based instruments for implementing social policy that will aid our understanding of their ethical, legal and public policy complexities" (Yeung, 2007). In particular, Karen Yeung has proposed a theory of legal design, by distinguishing between the subjects in which the design is embedded and the underlying design mechanisms or "modalities of design". On one side, it is feasible to design not only places and spaces, products and processes, but biological organisms as well. This is the case of plants grown through OGM technology or of genetically modified animals like Norwegian salmons, down to the current debate on humans, post-humans, and cyborgs. On the other side, the modalities of design may aim to encourage the change of social behavior, to decrease the impact of harm-generating conducts, or to prevent that those harm-generating conducts may even occur. As an illustration of the first kind of design mechanisms, consider the installation of speed bumps in roads as a means to reduce the velocity of cars (lest drivers opt to destroy their own vehicles). As an example of the second modality of design,

think about the introduction of air-bags to reduce the impact of harm-generating conduct. Finally, as an instance of total prevention, it is enough to mention current projects on "smart cars" able to stop or to limit their own speed according to the driver's health conditions and the inputs of the surrounding environment. In the light of Karen Yeung's taxonomy and its nine possible combinations between subjects (*i.e.*, places, products, organisms) and modalities (*i.e.*, behavioral change and reduction or prevention of harm-generating conducts), what are the relevant scenarios in the field of privacy and design? Leaving aside cases of genetically modified salmons and of OGM plants, what about the most interesting hypotheses for data protection?

In the aforementioned document on "The Future of Privacy," the WP29 and the WPPJ pointed out the goals that should be reached by embedding appropriate technical and organizational measures "both at the time of the design of the processing system and at the time of the processing itself, particularly in order to maintain security and thereby to prevent any unauthorized processing" of personal data (as the recital 46 of directive 95/46/EC establishes). Specifically, the European authorities on data protection claim that the principle of privacy by design "should be binding for technology designers and producers as well as for data controllers who have to decide on the acquisition and use of ICT", so that data minimization and quality of the data should be ensured together with its controllability, transparency, confidentiality, and user friendliness of information interfaces. Among the examples of how the new principle can contribute to better data protection, the EU Working Parties recommend that biometric identifiers "should be stored in devices under control of the data subjects (*i.e.*, smart cards) rather than in external data bases". In addition, the EU authorities suggest that making personal data anonymous both in public transportation systems and in hospitals should be considered a priority. While, in the first case, video surveillance must be designed in such a way that faces of individuals cannot be recognizable, in the case of hospitals' information systems patient names should be kept separated from data on medical treatments and health status.

The soft law-proposal according to which the principle of privacy by design should be applied "as early as possible," namely, at the time of the design of the processing system, does not mean that the exclusive purpose is to prevent any harm-generating behaviour. Most of the time the aim is to encourage changes in the behaviour of the individuals so as to decrease the impact of potential harm generating-conducts through the introduction of friendly interfaces, as confirmed by public complaints against Facebook's data protection policies and the services of Google Buzz. On May 26th, 2010, Facebook announced to have "drastically simplified and improved its privacy controls" which previously amounted to 170 different options under fifty data protection-related settings. The default configuration of the system has therefore been set to record only the name, profile, gender, and networks of the user, while "friends" are no longer automatically included in the flow of information. Moreover, Facebook's platform applications, such as games, social widgets, and the like, can finally be turned off by their *aficionados*. But, how about conceiving design as a means for total prevention? Could it constitute an infallible self-enforcement technology preventing harm generating-conducts overall?

First, attention should be drawn to the technical difficulties of modelling concepts traditionally employed by lawyers, through the formalization of norms, rights, or duties, to fit the processing of a machine. As a matter of fact, "a rich body of scholarship concerning the theory and practice of 'traditional' rule-based regulation bears witness to the impossibility of designing regulatory standards in the form of legal rules that will hit their target with perfect accuracy" (Yeung, 2007). As Eugene Spafford warns, legal scholars should understand that "the only truly secure system is

one that is powered off, cast in a block of concrete and sealed in a lead-lined room with armed guards – and even then I have my doubts" (Garfinkel and Spafford, 1997).

Secondly, privacy is not a zero-sum game between multiple instances of access, control, and protection over information in digital environments. Personal choices indeed play the main role when individuals modulate different levels of access and control, depending on the context and its circumstances (Nissenbaum, 2004). After all, people may enjoy privacy in the midst of a crowd and without having total control over their personal data, whereas total control over that data does not necessarily entail any guarantee of privacy (Tavani, 2007).

Finally, there are ethical issues behind the use of self-enforcement technologies, since people's behaviour would unilaterally be determined on the basis of automatic techniques rather than by choices of the relevant political institutions. A kind of infallible self-enforcement technology, in other words, not only "collapses the public understanding of law with its application eliminating a useful interface between the law's terms and its application" (Zittrain, 2007). What is more, there are instances of self-enforcement technology, *e.g.*, Digital Rights Management (DRM), which enable copyright holders to monitor and regulate the use of their protected artefacts, thus impinging on people's privacy again (Pagallo, 2008).

These various possible applications do not imply that technology is simply "neutral," a bare means to obtain whatever end. Rather, the idea of design, responsibility, and jurisdiction brings us back to the fundamentally political aspects of data protection. As stressed by Flanagan, Howe and Nissenbaum (2008), "some technical artefacts bear directly and systematically on the realization, or suppression, of particular configurations of social, ethical, and political values." Still, we might end up in a vicious circle by embedding values in technology, *e.g.*, through design policies. Consider, for instance, how conflicting values or interpretations thereof may impact on the very design of an artefact. Likewise, regard our need to strike a balance between different goals design can aim at, so that multiple choices of design can result in (another) conflict of values. As a result, is the principle of "privacy by design" replicating the substantial and procedural divergences we find in today's debate among lawyers and policy makers? Was not the principle intended to overcome possible conflicts among values by embedding data protection safeguards in ICT and other types of technology?

My view is that such a paradoxical conclusion can be rejected for two reasons. On the one hand, the variety of interpretations offered of artefacts is counter-balanced by empirical methods of evaluation and verification of the projects. Automated and regression-oriented tests, use of prototypes, internal checks among the design team, users tests in controlled environments, surveys, interviews, and the "generator-test cycle," upon which I insist in the next section, are all devised to limit the range of possible meanings given to the artefact. In the phrasing of Philip Brey, these methods allow us to fully appreciate the distinction between "central" and "peripheral" uses of technological artefacts (Brey, 2010). On the other hand, issues on data protection should be grasped 'by' design, not 'as' design: to conceive data protection 'as design' would mean to aim at some kind of self-enforcement technology eliminating Zittrain's "useful interface" between legal rules and their application (Zittrain, 2008). What is at stake concerns the opportunity of reducing the impact of harm-generating conducts by strengthening people's rights and widening their choices in digital environments. Otherwise, compliance with regulatory frameworks through design policies would be grounded either on a techno-deterministic viewpoint proposing to solve data protection issues 'as' simply matter of design, or on a paternalistic approach planning to change individual behaviour. Consequently, we may claim that "privacy assurance must ideally become

an organization's default mode of operation" (Cavoukian, 2009), if, and only if, in accordance with today's EU legal framework, the principle of privacy by design is devoted to broaden the options of the individuals by letting people take security measures by themselves. Moreover, the principle of privacy by design suggests we prevent some of the conflicts among values and interpretations by adopting the bottom-up approach put forward by the European working parties on data protection, that is, self-regulation and competition among private organizations, within the parameters established by the explicit and often detailed guides of the national authorities. Further conflicts among values and divergent aims of design are mitigated by a stricter (but more effective) version of the principle, according to which the goal is to reinforce people's pre-existing autonomy, rather than building it from scratch.

Open issues persist concerning the technical feasibility of replacing standard international agreements with design patterns so as to prevent online related conflicts over jurisdiction, substantial divergences on the role of people's consent, and the opt-in vs. opt-out diatribe involving the decisions of data subjects. In addition, scholars are confronted with recent developments in artificial intelligence, which are disclosing new perspectives in how we can deal with flows of information in digital environments. A section on future research directions is thus required.

FUTURE RESEARCH DIRECTIONS

Over the last decade and a half privacy commissioners and national authorities have discussed the idea of embedding data protection safeguards in ICT. While the obligation of data controllers to implement appropriate technical and organizational measures was laid down in the first European directive on data protection, namely, in art. 17 of D-95/46/EC, the concept of "Privacy by Design" was further developed by the Ontario's

Privacy Commissioner, Ann Cavoukian, in the late 1990s, to tackle the "ever-growing and systemic effects" of both ICT and large-scale networked data systems. In April 2000, a working paper on "Privacy Design Principles for an Integrated Justice System" was jointly presented by Ontario's Privacy Commissioner and the U.S. Department of Justice (Cavoukian, 2009).

Besides national advisors and working parties on data protection, scholars have dwelled on the topic as well. There has been seminal work on the ethics of design (Friedman, 1986; Mitcham, 1995; Whitbeck, 1996), and privacy (Agre, 1997), and a number of recent publications have focused on data protection issues involved in the design of ICT by the means of value-sensitive design (Friedman and Kahn, 2003; Friedman *et al.*, 2006), and of legal ontologies (Abou-Tair & Berlik, 2006; Mitre *et al.*, 2006; Lioukadis *et al.*, 2007). In addition, the idea of incorporating data protection safeguards in ICT was recently discussed in both "Privacy by Design. The Definitive Workshop" organized in Madrid in November 2009 (Cavoukian, 2010), and the "Intelligent Privacy Management Symposium" held at Stanford University, CA., on March 22nd-24th, 2010 (the program is online at http://research.it.uts.edu.au/magic/privacy2010/schedule.html). The topic being very popular, is there any particular reason why the principle of "privacy by design" is cutting the edge among scholars? All in all, there are three principal motives behind this growing interest.

First, most of the provisions on data protection and design have been disappointing. As frankly stated by the EU WP29 and the WPPJ in their joint document on "The Future of Privacy," a new legal framework is indispensable and it "has to include a provision translating the currently punctual requirements into a broader and consistent principle of privacy by design. This principle should be binding for technology designers and producers as well as for data controllers who have to decide on the acquisition and use of ICT."

Secondly, the call for "a broader and consistent principle of privacy by design" depends on the asymmetry between the ubiquity of information on the internet and the fact that national provisions and jurisdictions are not. A viable solution could thus be to implement privacy safeguards in ICT as default settings, while promoting the enforcement of data protection standards through self-regulation, competition, and the use of binding corporate rules by multinational companies.

Finally, research on the principle of privacy by design is continuously stimulated by developments in the field of artificial intelligence and operations research, which may not only aid the science of design but, in doing so, cast further light on the structure and evolution of legal systems. An interesting example is offered by the ongoing project on the "Neurona Ontology" developed by Pompeu Casanovas and his research team in Barcelona, Spain (Casellas *et al.*, forthcoming). Here, the field of "legal ontologies" is the key to implement new technological advances in managing personal data and providing organizations and citizens "with better guarantees of proper access, storage, management and sharing of files." The explicit goal of the project is to help company officers and citizens "who may have little or no legal knowledge whatsoever," when processing personal data in accordance with mandatory frameworks in force.

Legal ontologies model concepts traditionally employed by lawyers through the formalization of norms, rights, and duties, in fields like criminal law, administrative law, civil law, etc. The objective being that even a machine should comprehend and process this very information, it is necessary to distinguish between the part of the ontology containing all the relevant concepts of the problem domain through the use of taxonomies, and the ontology which includes both the set of rules and constraints that belong to that problem domain (Breuker *et al.*, 2008). An expert system should therefore process the information in compliance with regulatory frameworks on data protection through the conceptualization of classes, relations, properties, and instances pertaining to a given problem domain.

It can nonetheless be argued that data protection regulations not only include "top normative concepts" such as notions of validity, obligation, prohibition, and the like. These rules also present highly context-dependent normative concepts as in the case of personal data, security measures, or data controllers. These notions raise a number of relevant issues when reducing the informational complexity of a legal system where concepts and relations are subject to evolution (Pagallo, 2010). For example, we already met some hermeneutical issues in data protection law, *e.g.*, matters of jurisdiction and definitions of equipment, which can hardly be reduced to an automation process. These technical difficulties make it clear why several projects of legal ontologies have adopted a bottom-up rather than a top-down approach, "starting from smaller parts and sub-solutions to end up with global" answers (Casellas *et al.*, forthcoming). While splitting the work into several tasks and assigning each to a working team, the evaluation phase consists in testing the internal consistency of the project and, according to Herbert A. Simon's "generator test-cycle," involves the decomposition of the complete design into functional components. By generating alternatives and examining them against a set of requirements and constraints, "the test guarantees that important indirect consequences will be noticed and weighed. Alternative decompositions correspond to different ways of dividing the responsibilities for the final design between generators and tests" (Simon, 1996).

Leaving aside criteria such as the functional efficiency, robustness, reliability, elegance, and usability of design projects, the ability to deal with our own ignorance helps us to strike a fair balance between the know-how of current research on privacy by design and its limits. The unfeasible dream of automatizing all data protection does not imply that expert systems and friendly interfaces cannot be developed to achieve such goals as enabling businesses and individuals to take relevant security measures by themselves, while enhancing people's rights and encouraging their behavioural change, so as to restrict the discretion of company officers and public bureaucrats. Waiting for fruitful applications of the principle in, for example, smart environments, online social lending, data loss prevention, wrap contracts, business, digital forensics, and more, it is highly likely that "privacy by design" will represent the privileged understanding of our data protection abilities.

CONCLUSION

This chapter focused on the three level-impact of technology on current legal systems, considering the substantial, procedural, and cognitive features of the subject.

First, I dwelled on the substantial impact examining matters of online responsibility. The main reason why, in the U.S. as in Europe, lawmakers finally opted for a new generation of "safe harbour"-clauses and immunity provisions for copyright liability and freedom of speech, depends on the crucial difference between the "one-to-many" structure of pre-digital medias and the "many-to-many" architecture of the internet.

I took then into account the procedural features of this technological change including issues of jurisdiction as well as different ways to work out traditional international conflicts of law. What used to be the exception has now turned into the rule, in that virtually all events and transactions have transnational effects on the internet. The consequence is a fundamental asymmetry between the ubiquity of information in digital environments and circumscribed territoriality of national jurisdictions, so that tools and settled principles of international law fall short when meeting the challenge of this novel kind of contrast.

Finally, I considered the cognitive implications of technology and how artificial intelligence and operations research help us addressing the new legal issues in the field of privacy by design. Work on legal ontologies and the development of expert systems illustrated some of the automated ways in which it is feasible to process and control personal data in compliance with regulatory frameworks, so as to advise company officers and citizens "who may have little or no legal knowledge whatsoever" (Casellas *et al.*, forthcoming).

Emphasis on this three level-impact of technology, however, does not ignore the mutual interaction through which political decisions influence developments in technology, while technology is reshaping key legal concepts and their environmental framework. Ultimately, the introduction of a new generation of "safe harbour"-clauses and of immunity provisions for copyright liability and freedom of speech makes evident the role of political decisions in, for example, "the future of the internet" (Zittrain, 2008), the improvement of P2P file sharing-applications systems (Pagallo & Durante, 2009), and the like. Still, political decisions have their own limits when it comes to problems of responsibility and jurisdiction concerning data protection. Leaving behind the pitfalls of "unexceptionalism" as well as the panacea of standard international agreements, it is noteworthy that privacy authorities, commissioners, and law makers have suggested to insert data protection safeguards in ICT at the time of design of these processing systems. As an ideal default setting, the principle allows us to remark the most relevant cases of the aforementioned taxonomy on subjects and modalities of design (Yeung, 2007), in the field of data protection.

On one hand, regarding the application of the principle, we should focus on places and spaces, products and processes, rather than other human fellows. (Apart from Sci-Fi hypotheses – remember the scene from *Minority Report* where Tom Cruise acquires eye bulbs at the black market – it would be illegal, and even morally dubious, to redesign individuals so as to protect their personal data. According to today's state-of-the-art, ethical and legal issues of human design involve contemporary debate on cyborgs and robotics, rather than data protection through design policies.) On the other hand, as far as the modalities of design are concerned, the aim to prevent all sorts of harm-generating behaviour and, hence, conflicts of law at the international level, does not seem achievable or desirable through the use of an allegedly infallible self-enforcement technology. While provisions on data protection include highly context-dependent normative concepts, which are hardly reducible to an automation process, the adoption of self-enforcement technologies would unilaterally end up determining people's behaviour on the basis of technology rather than by choices of the relevant political institutions.

Both these practical and ethical constraints do not imply that design policies should lower their goal to just changing the individual behaviour and decreasing the impact of harm-generating conducts. Embedding data protection safeguards in places and spaces, products and processes, such as hospitals' information systems, transports' video surveillance networks, or smart cards for biometric identifiers, is ultimately legitimized by the intention to strengthen people's rights and give a choice or widen the range of choices. Otherwise, combining compliance with regulatory frameworks and design policies would end up in paternalism modelling individual behaviour, or in chauvinism disdaining different national provisions of current legal systems. This stricter version of the principle of privacy by design finally addresses design choices that may result in conflicts among values and, vice versa, different interpretations of values that may impact on the features of design. Since most of the projects have to comply with often detailed and explicit guidance of legislators and privacy authorities, it is likely that the empirical evaluation and verification of design projects are going to play a crucial role in determining whether individual rights have been protected or not.

However, far from delivering any value-free judgement, such an experimental phase of assessment is entwined with the political responsibilities grounding the guidance and provisions of law makers and privacy commissioners. At the end of the day, by insisting on the need to broaden the range of personal choices in digital environments, the stricter version of the principle makes it clear why matters of data protection do not only rely on technology.

REFERENCES

Abou-Tair, D., & Berlik, S. (2006). An ontology-based approach for managing and maintaining privacy in Information Systems. [Berlin/Heidelberg, Germany: Springer.]. *Lecture Notes in Computer Science, 4275*, 983–994. doi:10.1007/11914853_63

Ackerman, M. S., & Cranor, L. (1999). *Privacy critics: UI components to safeguard users'privacy. Extended Abstracts of CHI* (pp. 258–259). New York, NY: ACM Press.

Agre, P. E. (1997). Introduction. In Agre, P. E., & Rotenberg, M. (Eds.), *Technology and privacy: The new landscape* (pp. 1–28). Cambridge, MA: The MIT Press.

Ardia, D. S. (2010). Free speech savior or shield for scoundrels: An empirical study of intermediary immunity under section 230 of the communications decency act. *Loyola of Los Angeles Law Review, 43*(2), 373–505.

Bainbridge, D. (2008). *Introduction to Information Technology law*. London, UK: Pearson.

Borning, A., Friedman, B., & Kahn, P. (2004). Designing for human values in an urban simulation system: Value sensitive design and participatory design. *Proceedings of Eighth Biennial Participatory Design Conference* (pp. 64-67). Toronto, Canada: ACM Press.

Breuker, J., Casanovas, P., Klein, M. C. A., & Francesconi, E. (Eds.). (2008). *Law, ontologies and the Semantic Web: Channelling the legal information flood*. Amsterdam, The Netherlands: IOS Press.

Brey, P. (2010). Values in technology and disclosive computer ethics. In Floridi, L. (Ed.), *Information and computer ethics* (pp. 41–58). Cambridge, UK: Cambridge University Press.

Brouwer, E. (2009). The EU passenger name record (PNR) system and human rights: Transferring passenger data or passenger freedom? *CEPS Working Document, 320*, September.

Bynum, T. W. (2009). *Philosophy and the information revolution*. Paper presented at the Eighth International Conference of Computer Ethics: Philosophical Enquiry, 26-28 June 2009. Corfu, Grece: Ionian Academy.

Casellas, N., Torralba, S., Nieto, J.-E., Meroño, A., Roig, A., Reyes, M., & Casanovas, P. (forthcoming). *The neurona ontology: A data protection compliance ontology*. Paper presented at the Intelligent Privacy Management Symposium, 22-24 March 2010, Stanford University, CA, USA.

Cavoukian, A. (2009). *Privacy by design*. Ontario, Canada: IPC Publications.

Cavoukian, A. (2010). Privacy by design: The definitive workshop. *Identity in the Information Society, 3*(2), 247–251. doi:10.1007/s12394-010-0062-y

Deibert, R. J., Palfrey, J. G., Rohozinski, R., & Zittrain, J. (2008). *Access denied: The practice and policy of global internet filtering*. Cambridge, MA: The MIT Press.

Flanagan, M., Howe, D. C., & Nissenbaum, M. (2008). Embodying values in technology: Theory and practice. In van den Hoven, J., & Weckert, J. (Eds.), *Information Technology and moral philosophy* (pp. 322–353). New York, NY: Cambridge University Press.

Floridi, L. (2006). Four challenges for a theory of informational privacy. *Ethics and Information Technology, 8*(3), 109–119. doi:10.1007/s10676-006-9121-3

Friedman, B. (1986). Value-sensitive design. *Interaction, 3*(6), 17–23.

Friedman, B., Howe, D. C., & Felten, E. (2002). Informed consent in the Mozilla browser: Implementing value-sensitive design. *Proceedings of 35th Annual Hawaii International Conference on System Sciences* (p. 247). IEEE Computer Society.

Friedman, B., & Kahn, P. H. Jr. (2003). Human values, ethics, and design. In Jacko, J., & Sears, A. (Eds.), *The human-computer interaction handbook* (pp. 1177–1201). Mahwah, NJ: Lawrence Erlbaum Associates.

Friedman, B., Kahn, P. H., Jr., & Borning, A. (2006). Value sensitive design and Information Systems. In P. Zhang & D. Galletta (Eds.), *Human-computer interaction in management Information Systems: Foundations* (pp. 348-372). New York, NY: Armonk.

Garfinkel, S., & Spafford, G. (1997). *Web security and commerce*. Sebastopol, CA: O'Reilly.

Ginsburg, J. (2003). From having copies to experiencing works: The development of an access right in US copyright law. *Journal of the Copyright Society of the USA, 50*, 113–131.

Goldsmith, J. (1998). Against cyberanarchy. *The University of Chicago Law Review. University of Chicago. Law School, 65*(4), 1199–1250. doi:10.2307/1600262

Heide, T. (2001). Copyright in the EU and the US: What "access right"? *European Intellectual Property Review, 23*(8), 469–477.

Holtzman, D. H. (2006). *Privacy lost. How technology is endangering your privacy*. New York, NY: Jossey-Bass.

Horner, D. S. (2010). Metaphors in orbit: Revolution, logical malleability, generativity and the future of the Internet. In Arias-Oliva, M., Bynum, T. W., Rogerson, S., & Torres-Corona, T. (Eds.), *ETHICOMP 2010: The "backwards, forwards and sideways" changes of ICT* (pp. 301–208). Tarragona, Spain: Universitat Rovira I Virgili.

Jarfinkel, S. (2000). *Database nation. The death of privacy in the 21st century*. Sebastopol, CA: O'Reilly.

Johnson, D. (1985). *Computer ethics*. Englewood Cliffs, NJ: Prentice-Hall.

Katyal, N. (2002). Architecture as crime control. *The Yale Law Journal, 111*(5), 1039–1139. doi:10.2307/797618

Katyal, N. (2003). Digital architecture as crime control. *The Yale Law Journal, 112*(6), 101–129.

Kuner, C. (2003). *European data privacy law and online business*. Oxford/London, UK: Oxford University Press.

Lessig, L. (1999). *Code and other laws of cyberspace*. New York, NY: Basic Books.

Lioukadis, G., Lioudakisa, G., Koutsoloukasa, E., Tselikasa, N., Kapellakia, S., & Prezerakosa, G. (2007). A middleware architecture for privacy protection. *The International Journal of Computer and Telecommunications Networking, 51*(16), 4679–4696.

Lloyd, I. (2008). *Information Technology law*. Oxford/London, UK: Oxford University Press.

Maner, W. (1996). Unique ethical problems in Information Technology. *Science and Engineering Ethics, 2*, 137–154. doi:10.1007/BF02583549

Mitcham, C. (1995). Ethics into design. In Buchanan, R., & Margolis, V. (Eds.), *Discovering design* (pp. 173–179). Chicago, IL: University of Chicago Press.

Mitre, H., González-Tablas, A., Ramos, B., & Ribagorda, A. (2006). A legal ontology to support privacy preservation in location-based services. [Berlin-Heidelberg, Germany: Springer.]. *Lecture Notes in Computer Science, 4278*, 1755–1764. doi:10.1007/11915072_82

Moor, J. (1985). What is computer ethics? *Metaphilosophy, 16*(4), 266–275. doi:10.1111/j.1467-9973.1985.tb00173.x

Nissenbaum, H. (2004). Privacy as contextual integrity. *Washington Law Review (Seattle, Wash.), 79*(1), 119–158.

Pagallo, U. (2007). Small world paradigm and empirical research in legal ontologies: A topological approach. In Ajani, G., Peruginelli, G., Sartor, G., & Tiscornia, D. (Eds.), *The multilanguage complexity of European law: Methodologies in comparison* (pp. 195–210). Florence, Italy: European Press Academic Publishing.

Pagallo, U. (2008). *La tutela della privacy negli Stati Uniti d'America e in Europa: Modelli giuridici a confronto*. Milan, Italy: Giuffrè.

Pagallo, U. (2009). Sul principio di responsabilità giuridica in rete. *Il diritto dell'informazione e dell'informatica, 25*(4-5), 705-734.

Pagallo, U. (2010). As law goes by: Topology, ontology, evolution. In Casanovas, P. (Eds.), *AI approaches to the complexity of legal systems* (pp. 12–26). Berlin-Heidelberg, Germany: Springer.

Pagallo, U., & Durante, M. (2009). Three roads to P2P systems and their impact on business practices and ethics. *Journal of Business Ethics, 90*(4), 551–564. doi:10.1007/s10551-010-0606-y

Post, D. G. (2002). Against "against cyberspace.". *Berkeley Technology Law Journal, 17*(4), 1365–1383.

Shneiderman, N. (2000). Universal usability. *Communications of the ACM, 43*(3), 84–91. doi:10.1145/332833.332843

Simon, H. A. (1996). *The sciences of the artificial*. Cambridge, MA: The MIT Press.

Stein, A. R. (1998). The unexceptional problem of jurisdiction in cyberspace. *International Lawyer, 32*, 1167–1194.

Sykes, C. (1999). *The end of privacy. The attack on personal rights at home, at work, on-line, and in court*. New York, NY: St. Martin's Griffin.

Tavani, H. T. (2007). Philosophical theories of privacy: Implications for an adequate online privacy policy. *Metaphilosophy, 38*(1), 1–22. doi:10.1111/j.1467-9973.2006.00474.x

Tavani, H. T., & Moor, J. H. (2001). Privacy protection, control of information, and privacy-enhancing technologies. *Computers & Society, 31*(1), 6–11. doi:10.1145/572277.572278

van Schewick, B. (2010). *Internet architecture and innovation*. Cambridge, MA: The MIT Press.

Whitbeck, C. (1996). Ethics as design: Doing justice to moral problems. *The Hastings Center Report, 26*(3), 9–16. doi:10.2307/3527925

Yeung, K. (2007). Towards an understanding of regulation by design. In Brownsword, R., & Yeung, K. (Eds.), *Regulating technologies: Legal futures, regulatory frames and technological fixes* (pp. 79–108). London, UK: Hart Publishing.

Zittrain, J. (2007). Perfect enforcement on tomorrow's Internet. In Brownsword, R., & Yeung, K. (Eds.), *Regulating technologies: Legal futures, regulatory frames and technological fixes* (pp. 125–156). London, UK: Hart Publishing.

Zittrain, J. (2008). *The future of the Internet and how to stop it*. New Haven, CT: Yale University Press.

ADDITIONAL READING

Aarts, E., & Encarnacao, L. K. (Eds.). (2006). *True visions: the emergence of ambient intelligence*. Berlin, Heidelberg: Springer.

De Cew, J. W. (1997). *In pursuit of privacy: law, ethics, and the rise of technology*. Ithaca, NY: Cornell University Press.

Etzioni, A. (2005). Limits of privacy. In Cohen, A. I., & Wellman, C. H. (Eds.), *Contemporary debates in applied ethics* (pp. 253–262). Oxford: Blackwell.

Floridi, L. (2007). A look into the future impact of ICT on our lives. *The Information Society, 23*(1), 59–64. doi:10.1080/01972240601059094

Fried, Ch. (1990). Privacy: a rational context. In Ermann, M. D., Williams, M. B., & Gutierrez, C. (Eds.), *Computers, ethics, and society* (pp. 50–63). New York: Oxford University Press.

Friedman, B. (Ed.). (1997). *Human values and the design of computer technology*. Cambridge, UK: Cambridge University Press.

Gavison, R. (1980). Privacy and the limits of the law. *The Yale Law Journal, 89*(3), 421–471. doi:10.2307/795891

Grodzinsky, F. S., & Tavani, H. T. (2005). P2P networks and the Verizon v. RIAA case: implications for personal privacy and intellectual property. *Ethics and Information Technology, 7*(4), 243–250. doi:10.1007/s10676-006-0012-4

Grodzinsky, F. S., & Tavani, H. T. (2008). Online file sharing: resolving the tensions between privacy and property interest. In Bynum, T. W., Calzarossa, M., De Lotto, D., & Rogerson, S. (Eds.), *Living, working and learning beyond technology: proceedings of the tenth international conference Ethicomp 2008* (pp. 373–383). Mantova, Italy: Tipografia Commerciale.

Hongladarom, S., & Ess, C. (Eds.). (2006). *Information technology ethics: cultural perspectives*. Hershey, Pennsylvania: Idea Publishing. doi:10.4018/978-1-59904-310-4

Hughes, T. (2004). *Human-built world: how to think about technology and culture*. Chicago: University of Chicago Press.

Johnson, D. G., & Nissenbaum, H. (1995). Privacy and databases. In Johnson, D. G., & Nissenbaum, H. (Eds.), *Computers, ethics, and social values* (pp. 262–268). Englewood Cliffs: Prentice Hall.

Katyal, S. (2004). Privacy vs. piracy. *Yale Journal of Law and Technology, 7*, 222–345.

Krug, S. (2005). *Don't make me think*. Indianapolis: New Riders.

Lacy, S. (2001). *Crypto: how the code rebels beat the government – saving privacy in the digital age*. New York: Viking.

Lessig, L. (2002). Privacy as property. *Social Research, 69*(1), 247–269.

Mackenzie, D., & Wajcman, J. (1985). *The social shaping of technology*. Milton Keynes, UK: Open University Press.

Moor, J. H. (1997). Towards a theory of privacy in the information age. *Computers & Society, 27*(3), 27–32. doi:10.1145/270858.270866

Murray, A. (2007). *The regulation of cyberspace: control in the online environment*. Abingdon, UK: Routledge Cavendish.

Nissenbaum, H. (1998). Protecting privacy in an information age: the problem of privacy in public. *Law and Philosophy, 17*(5-6), 559–596.

Norman, D. A. (2007). *The design of future things*. New York: Basic Books.

Pagallo, U., & Bassi, E. (2010). *The future of EU working parties' "the future of privacy" and the principle of privacy by design*. Paper presented at the Third International Seminar of Information Law, 25-26 June 2010, Corfu, Grece: Ionian Academy.

Parent, W. A. (1983). Privacy, morality and the law. *Philosophy & Public Affairs, 12*(4), 269–288.

Pinch, T. J., & Bijker, W. E. (1987). The social construction of facts and artifacts, or, how the sociology of science and the sociology of technology might benefit each other. In Bijker, W. E., Pinch, T. J., & Hughes, T. P. (Eds.), *The social construction of technological systems* (pp. 17–50). Cambridge, MA: The MIT Press.

Prosser, W. (1960). Privacy. *California Law Review, 48*(3), 383–423. doi:10.2307/3478805

Regan, P. M. (1995). *Legislating privacy: technology, social values, and public policy*. Chapel Hill, NC: University of North Carolina Press.

Roessler, B. (2005). *The value of privacy*. Cambridge, UK: Polity Press.

Rosen, J. (2001). *The unwanted gaze: the destruction of privacy in America*. New York: Knopf.

Schön, D. (1983). *The reflective practitioner*. New York: Basic Books.

Slobogin, Ch. (2007). *Privacy at risk: the new government surveillance and the fourth amendment*. Chicago: The University of Chicago Press.

Solove, D. J. (2004). *The digital person: technology and privacy in the information age*. New York: The New York University Press.

Solove, D. J. (2007). 'I've got nothing to hide' and other misunderstandings of privacy. *The San Diego Law Review, 44*, 745–772.

Solove, D. J., Rotenberg, M., & Schwartz, P. M. (2006). *Privacy, information, and technology*. New York: Aspen.

Taipale, K. A. (2003). Data mining and domestic security: connecting the dots to make sense of data. *Columbia Science and Technology Law Review, 5*(2), 1–83.

van den Hoven, J., & Weckert, J. (Eds.). (2008). *Information technology and moral philosophy*. New York: Cambridge University Press.

Volkman, R. (2003). Privacy as life, liberty, property. *Ethics and Information Technology, 5*(4), 199–210. doi:10.1023/B:ETIN.0000017739.09729.9f

Winner, L. (1986). *The whale and the reactor: a search for limits in an age of high technology*. Chicago: University of Chicago Press.

KEY TERMS AND DEFINITIONS

Data Protection: The ideal condition regarding the processing of personal information, in order to assure the protection of the individual right to access, modify, delete, and refuse the processing of data at any given time. Individual rights to data protection entail obligations for the entities processing and controlling personal data, *e.g.*, the duty of processing personal data fairly and lawfully, by informing the data subjects, so that they can give their consent when required by the law.

Design: The traditional act of working out the form of something or someone, which has been broadened by the current capacities of computers to draw upon the tools of artificial intelligence and operations research. Design can aim to encourage the change of social behaviour, decreasing the impact of harm-generating conducts, or preventing harm-generating behaviour from occurring. Spaces and places, processes and products, down to biological organisms like plants, animals, and other human fellows, may be the objects of design.

Jurisdiction: In Ancient Roman law, the power to "say the law" (*dicere ius*); *i.e.*, to interpret and give law to a certain territory over which that power is exercised. In modern private and public international law, several criteria may be adopted to solve conflicts of law between national legal systems. In the absence of consensual international solutions, the state claims a right to control events within its territory so as to regulate the local effects of extraterritorial acts.

Privacy: The old "right to be let alone" that technology has updated by including a need to protect personal data of those who live, work, and interact in digital environments. While, in the U.S., a property standpoint still prevails, making consent the cornerstone in most of the current debate, in Europe privacy is mainly associated with the principle of human dignity and, therefore, considered an inalienable right of the person.

Privacy by Design: The idea of embedding data protection safeguards in ICT and other types of technologies, with the aim to process and control personal data in compliance with current regulatory frameworks. In accordance with today's state-of-the-art, the principle prohibits the redesigning of other human fellows in order to protect their personal data. The goal is rather the implementation of data protection safeguards in places and spaces, products and processes, so as to strengthen people's rights and widen the range of their choices.

Responsibility: The moral force binding people to their obligations and making them respond to their conscience and, eventually, to other fellows' expectations. From a legal viewpoint, we distinguish between legal irresponsibility, strict liability, and responsibility due to personal fault. While people are mostly liable for what they voluntarily agree upon through strict contractual obligations, there are also obligations imposed by the government to compensate for damage caused by wrongdoing or other damaging behaviour, so as to distribute risk among consociates.

Technology: The know-how of tools that *Homo sapiens* have developed over the last hundred thousand years, and that are entwined with our species' capacity to adapt to the challenges of natural environment by reducing its complexity. *Pace* techno-determinism, mutual interaction between values and technological development exists: value concepts influence possible developments of technology, while technology reshapes these values and their environmental framework. Significantly, the Aztecs knew the wheel but preferred not to employ it in the making of their pyramids.

Unexceptionalism: A popular opinion among legal scholars in the mid 1990s, according to which settled principles and traditional tools of international law could successfully grasp the new generation of cases emerging from digital technology (computer crimes, data protection safeguards, and provisions on digital copyright). The overall idea is that "activity in cyberspace is functionally identical to transnational activity mediated by other means, such as mail or telephone or smoke signal" (Goldsmith 1998).

Uniqueness or Exceptionalism-Advocates: Scholars who reckon we are in the midst (or at the very beginning) of an information revolution, so that, contrarily to unexceptionalism, new legal issues are actually arising with the generation of digital cases. While the failure to find satisfactory non-computer analogies confirms the exceptional character of such issues like identity thefts, spamming, or click-and-point contracts, the ubiquity of information on the internet explains why virtually all events and transactions have a transnational impact on current legal systems.

Chapter 2
Hacking:
Legal and Ethical Aspects of an Ambiguous Activity

Gráinne Kirwan
Dun Laoghaire Institute of Art, Design and Technology, Ireland

Andrew Power
Dun Laoghaire Institute of Art, Design and Technology, Ireland

ABSTRACT

Hacking is an activity which has long been tied with ethical and legal complications. The term has evolved to have both ethical and unethical connotations, which can be confusing to the uninitiated. Hacker subculture has a myriad of terminology, sometimes with subtle variations, and this chapter identifies the main subcategories of hackers. The methods used by hackers to infiltrate systems will also be briefly examined, along with the motives for the activities. The question of whether or not hacking can be an ethical activity, and how it should be dealt with by the legal system is considered in this chapter. Consideration is also given to the international legal perspective. The evolving hacker ethic is described and examined, and the justifications provided by hackers are investigated.

INTRODUCTION

The hacking subculture has developed a specific hacker ethic, which has evolved over the course of its lifetime. However, this ethical system is critically flawed in many regards, and its nature tends to be more hedonistic than truly ethical. Even the

nomenclature of hacking culture has significant basis on the ethical position of the hacker, with specific terms (such as 'white-hat'; 'black-hat' and 'grey-hat') assigned to individuals depending on the behaviours they exhibit both during and after the hacking activity. The ethical distinctions within hacking have evolved to such an extent that it is possible to complete Masters level courses in 'Ethical Hacking' (such as that offered by Abertay

DOI: 10.4018/978-1-61350-132-0.ch002

University in Scotland). Realistically, excepting the cases where it is completed by an employee or consultant to benefit their own company or organisation, there are few cases where hacking could truly be considered ethical.

This chapter will introduce several taxonomies of hackers, and illustrate the difficulties in assigning hackers to any one of these classifications. For example, few hackers will consider themselves to be 'black-hat' (or malicious), even though they may engage in illegal activities, or activities which damage websites or computer systems. Further confusion is added by a wide variety of other expressions which are used to describe individuals engaged in various types of hacking activities, such as 'cracker', 'script-kiddies' and 'cyber-punks', to name but a few. To aid in understanding the nature of hacking, a brief overview will be provided of the techniques frequently used by hackers, along with the suspected motives for these actions. The ethical standards of hackers will then be examined, with particular focus on how these principles are ultimately self-serving, with little consideration for others. Finally, an overview will be provided of how hacking is viewed in the legal system, and the types of punishments that can be administrated, along with an evaluation of the likelihood of the success of these. The aims of the chapter are to provide the reader with an understanding of the various types of hacker, both 'ethical' and otherwise, to evaluate the 'hacker ethic' and how it is justified by hackers, and to investigate the legal implications of hacking behavior.

BACKGROUND

There are numerous cases of famous hackers widely available. For example, Gary McKinnon, who hacked into 97 US government computers, including the US Navy and NASA, between 2001 and 2002 using the online name 'Solo'. His declared motive was "to prove US intelligence had found an alien craft run on clean fuel" (BBC News, 28th July 2009, para. 3). McKinnon's hacking became an obsession, and other aspects of his life began to suffer the consequences. He lost his job and girlfriend, stopped eating properly and neglected his personal hygiene. In hindsight he indicated that he "almost wanted to be caught, because it was ruining me" (Boyd, 2008).

Former hacker Kevin Mitnick in particular has made a career from advising on computer security and has authored a number of books on hacking, with a particular focus on social engineering methods (see for example Mitnick & Simon, 2002; Mitnick & Simon, 2005). Mitnick was involved in hacking behaviors from a young age, manipulating telephone systems in order to play pranks and later progressing to infiltrating computer systems. He was apprehended by the police several times, and served time in prison for his hacking. He has since founded a company aimed at improving organisations' IT security, and regularly gives guest lectures based on his hacking experience and security expertise.

Adrian Lamo has also experienced a lot of publicity due to his hacking activities. His 'white-hat' attempts to improve the security of firms led to mixed responses from the companies involved – some were highly appreciative of his efforts, while others filed lawsuits against him (Mitnick & Simon, 2005). He has allegedly hacked into some very high profile companies, including Microsoft, Yahoo!, and Cingular. On managing to hack into the New York Times, he utilized their subscription to *LexisNexis* for three months, before reporting the security hole to the newspaper, via a third party journalist. The New York Times reported the infiltration to the FBI.

Definition and History of Hacking

Hacking began in the late 1950s at a few US universities at a time when computers were rare (Levy, 1984). The original hackers were motivated to use and improve computer technology, and many hackers today indicate that their motives have not changed. Nevertheless, by the early 1960s some hackers' activities had begun to result in financial abuses, examples of which are still common today (such as software piracy and credit card fraud).

The term 'hacker' is a cause for confusion among those wishing to study the field. The media and the vast majority of the general public use it primarily to denote a person who gains unauthorised access to computer systems. However, many online individuals define a 'hacker' as simply a person who is proficient at building and modifying computer systems. The term 'cracker' is often used instead to describe those involved in criminal activity. This term was supposedly coined by hackers ca. 1985 to distinguish themselves from the journalistic misuse of 'hacker'. 'Cracking' normally involves maliciously accessing a network (as per the common perception of 'hacking'). Sterling (1992) indicates that there is considerable lack of consistency in what cybercriminals call themselves. He suggests that most of them choose to call themselves 'hacker'. "Nobody who hacks into systems willingly describes himself (rarely, herself) as a 'computer intruder', 'computer trespasser', 'cracker', 'wormer', 'darkside hacker' or 'high-tech street gangster'. " (p. 56). Sterling indicates that despite numerous attempts to invent terms for the press and public to use in place of the original meaning of 'hacker', few people actually use them. Simpson (2006, as cited in Tavani, 2007) differentiates between the two by defining a hacker as anyone who "accesses a computer system or network without authorization from the owner" and a cracker as a hacker who has "the intention of doing harm or destroying data".

Further confusion is added by the distinction between 'white-hat' and 'black-hat' hackers. 'White-hats' are those who enjoy working with computers, and who may infiltrate the systems of other individuals or groups, but who do not cause malicious damage in the process. Some white-hat hackers can also be termed 'ethical' hackers, and can be company employees or consultants who are specifically tasked with finding exploits in order to make the software more secure. 'Black-hats' are those who hack with the intent of carrying out some form of damaging action. Nonetheless, it should be noted that some 'white-hat hackers' are involved in criminal activity, as they may attempt to gain unauthorised access to the computers or networks of other people or groups. They sometimes justify this action by contacting the individual or group afterwards in an attempt to warn them of the flaw in their security system, as was the case with Adrian Lamo. Despite the differences recognised in cybercultures between white-hat and black-hat hackers (or hackers and crackers), Tavani (2007) suggests that many governments and businesses would view non-malicious hacking as a form of trespass, a view which much legislation supports. A third group are 'grey hat' hackers, a term used to describe hackers who search for exploits, but only disclose these exploits to the system administrators under certain circumstances, often in the hopes of monetary reward. Grey-hat hackers are not affiliated with any specific company or organization, and sometimes distinguish themselves from white-hat hackers on this basis. Chiesa, Ducci and Ciappi (2009) indicate that grey-hat hackers eschew labels, feeling that no single label can define them or what they do.

Other members of the Internet underground include 'phreakers' and 'script-kiddies'. Phreakers are a specific type of hacker, those who participate in hacking telephone systems. Script-kiddies are individuals who are not proficient at hacking, and who download pre-written scripts and tools which are widely available on the Internet in order to carry out their hacking activities (Murphy, 2004). Many hackers start out as script-kiddies, and build their skills from there. They are generally viewed with little respect by the more experienced hackers, and many do not consider them to be true hackers at all. Warren and Leitch (2009) also identify the 'hacker-taggers' – hackers who leave a 'tag' on a website that they have hacked, similar to 'tagging' (leaving a signature mark) by graffiti artists.

The nomenclature of hacking could be of high importance for the individual involved. Bryant and Marshall (2008) suggest that labelling theory may have an application in the terms used by hackers. Labelling theory is one of the sociological theories of crime, suggesting that once a person is named or defined in a certain manner, consequences flow from this, including the possibility that the definition can become a means of defence or adjustment to the societal reaction to them (Rock, 2007). It is therefore possible that once an individual has been assigned the term 'hacker' (or 'cracker' or 'black-hat' or any of the other terms discussed above), then the individual begins to alter their behavior accordingly in order to fit in with the label assigned to them. As such, the media usage of the term 'hacker' to include mainly those who hack for malicious reasons may have an impact on those who term themselves hackers, but whose hacking activities were primarily in the original definition of the term – it is possible that the media usage of the term may alter their behaviors.

In addition to the high level distinctions between hackers and crackers, and white-hats and black-hats, several researchers have suggested further classifications of hackers. Rogers (2000) suggests seven categories of hacker, including 'newbies' (who have limited skills and experience, and are reliant on tools developed by others), 'cyber-punks' (who deliberately attack and vandalise), 'internals' (who are insiders with privileged access and who are often disgruntled employees), 'coders' (who have high skill levels), 'old guard hackers' (who have no criminal intent and high skill levels, and so would most likely equate to 'white-hat' hackers), 'professional criminals' and 'cyber-terrorists'.

Chiesa, Ducci and Ciappi (2009) suggested an alternative and more complex classification system, involving several categories of hackers. These include 'Wannabe lamers', 'script-kiddies', 'crackers', 'ethical hackers', 'quiet, paranoid and skilled hacker', 'industrial spies' and 'government agent'. This classification system shows some overlap with that suggested by Rogers (2000),

for example, 'ethical hackers' are similar to 'old guard hackers' and 'wannabe lamers' would share many of the characteristics of 'newbies'. Most distinctions within many classification systems refer to the experience levels, methods and motives of each type of hacker.

Bearing all this in mind, for the purposes of conciseness, the high level term 'hacker' will be used throughout this chapter, though it should be remembered that the individuals involved may define themselves differently to this, or be described differently by their peers, victims or law-enforcement personnel.

Methods

There are a number of different methods by which hackers infiltrate systems. The international 'Honeynet' project (www.honeynet.org) is designed to monitor hacking attempts by placing computers with limited or no security patches (honeypots) on the Internet and monitoring any hacking attempts on them. Honeynet Projects have been in use since June 2000, and since then have provided considerable data concerning the methods and motivations of hackers.

There are four main methods that hackers use to infiltrate systems (outlined by a hacker named Dustin, in Mitnick & Simon, 2005, p. 126): 'technical entry into the network', 'social engineering', 'dumpster diving' and 'physical entry'. The first, 'technical entry into the network', reflects the common perception held amongst the general public of what hacking is – the individual hacker sitting at their computer at a remote location, gaining access to the network of the target. A hacker may use a variety of tools and techniques to do this (see Furnell, 2010 for descriptions of some of these).

'Social engineering' involves using deception to persuade humans to assist in the penetration of the network. For example, a hacker may call a receptionist at a company, saying they are from an IT support company and need the administrator's password to try to correct a bug in the system. Social engineering could also include eavesdropping on conversations between employees of a company to find out useful information, or 'shoulder surfing' – covertly watching an employee enter their username and password with the intention of using that information in a hacking attempt later. Variations on social engineering include 'phishing' and 'pharming' (Sanders-Reach, 2005), methods which direct users to websites impersonating those of reputable organisations (such as banks and retailers) and are often used for identity theft.

'Dumpster diving' refers to cybercriminals actually searching in the garbage bins of a company for useful articles. This may include scraps of paper with user names and passwords, old computer hard drives which may still have sensitive information on them, or even confidential files that may have been discarded without being properly shredded. Finally, 'physical entry' is just that – where the hacker manages to enter a building directly and carry out the hack from the inside. Sometimes, this could be as simple as getting through a lax security system, and finding a vacant computer terminal which has been left logged on.

These methods indicate that the hacker does not necessarily need to have advanced technical skills in order to complete a successful attack. Social engineering and physical entry tactics do not require any specific computer skills, and can be some of the easiest and most effective means of accomplishing a task. However, Calcutt (1999) suggests that the descriptions of the activities of malicious hackers are regularly over-hyped, fuelling fear and confusion. He indicates that "reports of the threat to society posed by Mitnick and others have been hyped out of all proportion" (p. 57).

Motives for Hacking

Lafrance (2004) proposes that understanding cybercriminals' motivation can help to improve security measures, and describes the motivations that could underlie attacks by insiders in organisations. These include economical profit, revenge, personal interest in a specific file, and external pressure from people or organisations outside of the company (such as organised crime or a family member). Taylor (1999) suggests that some motives cited by hackers for their behaviours include feelings of addiction, the urge of curiosity, boredom with the educational system, enjoyment of feelings of power, peer recognition in the hacking culture and political acts. Schneier (2003) suggests that hackers do not break into systems for profit, but simply to satisfy their intellectual curiosity, for the thrill, and to see if they can.

Fötinger and Ziegler (2004) propose that the hacker may be experiencing a deep sense of inferiority, and that the power they achieve through their hacking activities may increase their self-esteem. They suggest that hackers' main motivations are reputation, respect and acknowledgement, and that the work of hackers fulfils a self-actualisation need (involving personal growth and fulfilment) according to Maslow's (1970) hierarchy of needs. This would indicate that the hacker has already got their lower needs (biological, safety, belongingness and love, and esteem needs) sufficiently catered for. If this is the case, it would suggest that the individual is not hacking for financial needs to survive, nor for emotional attachments, nor to make them accepted among their peer group.

Bryant and Marshall (2008) suggest that the motives of early hackers were to prove themselves against the authorities of the network, with very little malicious intent. Their rewards were self-esteem and peer recognition. However as the number of network users increased, other motives began to appear. When applied to Rogers (2000) taxonomy of hackers, different motives could be assigned to each (for example, cyberterrorists were motivated by ideals, professional criminals were motivated by profit, whereas internals were disgruntled).

Rennie and Shore (2007) reviewed the literature relating to the motives of hacking, and analysed them using Ajzen's (1985, 1991) 'Theory of Planned Behaviour' and Beveren's (2001) 'Flow Theory'. The Theory of Planned Behaviour has been used in a variety of contexts to both explain and predict behaviours, as well as targeting strategies for changing behaviour. Flow theory attempts to explain absorption in a particular activity, where the experience itself is desired, rather than any specific end goal, and is a common explanation for excessive internet activity. When experiencing flow, users feel concentration, curiosity, intrinsic interest and control (Shernoff, Csikszentmihalyi, Schneider & Shernoff, 2003). The emotions reported by hackers are similar to those reported by other people experiencing flow (Rennie & Shore, 2007), and some of the motives offered as explanations by hackers (such as intrinsic interest and curiosity) would also seem to be supported by flow theory. Rennie and Shore (2007) indicate that flow theory therefore explains the progression of the hacker career, but it on its own cannot provide a complete model for computer crime. As such, they propose an advanced model of hacker development, incorporating other factors, such as ideology, vandalism and career, to predict the eventual type of individual which emerges, whether that is an ethical hacker, or a malicious one. They indicate that an important method of dealing with the problem is to address it early, and to reduce the likelihood that teenagers will start hacking behaviours in the first place.

Having considered so many different theoretical approaches, it is worth considering the empirical work in this area, although it is very sparse in comparison to the theoretical writings. Woo, Kim and Dominick (2004) carried out a content analysis of 462 defaced websites, and concluded that about 70% of the defacements could be classified as simple pranks, while the rest had a more political motive. Chiesa, Ducci and Ciappi (2009) describe several motives cited by hackers, including intellectual curiosity, love of technology, fun and games, making the technological world safer, fighting for freedom, conflict with authority, rebelliousness, spirit of adventure and ownership, boredom, fame-seeking, anger and frustration, political reasons, escape from family and/or society and professional reasons. Kirwan (2006) found that the motivations of hackers were very wide-ranging, and little in the way of

consistent patterns could be observed. There were no clear differences between the cited motivations of white-hats and black-hats, despite the fact that discrepancies were expected due to the presence of criminal intent in black-hat hackers. She found that the motivations cited in online interviews with hackers were often quite vague, with hackers often citing 'commendable' reasons for their actions (such as to protect their friends' systems, or because they were passionate about computers), whereas those motives indicated by a content analysis of hacker bulletin boards were much more specific, and included the 'darker' side of hacking related activities, such as unlawfully accessing another person's files.

Based on the literature to date, it appears that hackers have quite a wide range of motivations for their actions. It is unfortunate that we must rely solely on the stated responses of cybercriminals to questions regarding motivation – there is a strong possibility that they are replying in what they perceive to be a socially acceptable way, and as such the results may be quite biased.

HACKER ETHICS

Having considered the nomenclature, methods and motives of hackers, their ethical standards can now be considered. There is a substantial body of literature which considers this topic, spanning a significant length of the history of hacking. Some is complimentary to the hacking community, while much of it does not paint hackers in the highest moral light.

The Hacker Ethic

Many hackers subscribe to a common code of ethics, but this code has changed somewhat over time. In 1984, Levy suggested several key characteristics of the then 'hacker ethic'. These include that:

1. Access to computers, and anything which might teach a person something about the way the world works, should be unlimited and total. *This suggests that hackers feel that computers should not be limited to the wealthy or the privileged, but that all should be able to access them. Given the relative shortage of computers at the time, this was a difficult goal to achieve. Hackers also had a relatively narrow view of this principle – while many felt that they should be allowed access to the computers of others, they were not as eager to allow others access to their own systems;*

2. *All information should be free and available to the public, and secrecy should be avoided.* Evidence of this principle can be seen in the hacking activities of Gary McKinnon, who felt entitled to access confidential government documents;

3. *Mistrust authority – Promote decentralisation.* According to Levy, hackers felt that the best way to support the free dissemination of information was to reduce bureaucracy;

4. *Hackers should be judged by their hacking, and not by any other characteristic that they might exhibit or possess.* This would include characteristics, such as qualifications, race, position, gender or age. Indeed, the very nature of the Internet, and particularly the popular uses of the Internet in the early 1980s, allows an individual to keep these characteristics well hidden;

5. *The creation of art and beauty using computer technology is possible and should be encouraged.* This may include traditional forms of artistic work, for example graphics or music, but a well-written piece of code in itself could be considered beautiful by some hackers. This was especially so at the time, as processing power was limited. If code could be written elegantly, then it allowed more tasks to be achieved by the system;

6. *Computers can change one's life for the better.* They may provide focus, make the hacker more adventurous, or enrich their lives.

While the hacker ethic noted by Levy in 1984 seems admirable on the surface, much of it is oriented to the best interests of the hackers themselves. They indicate that computers and information should be free to all, when it seems unlikely that they would be willing to share some of their own resources in this regard. While the principle indicating that hackers should be judged by their hacking prowess rather than any other criteria seems well intentioned, outsiders cannot help but feel that they are also being judged by their lack of hacking prowess. Regardless, Levy's hacker ethic was not to last.

Mizrach (n.d., circa mid-1990s) carried out a content analysis of twenty-nine online documents in order to determine how widely accepted the hacker ethic was, and if it had changed since Levy's description in 1984. He determined that there was a new hacker ethic, which more current hackers live by, which has some continuity from the previous one. Mizrach indicates that this new hacker ethic evolved like the old one, informally and by processes of mutual reinforcement. He indicates that the new hacker ethic contains some ambiguities and contradictions. The new hacker he identified has ten main principles:

1. "Above all else, do no harm" – similar to the Hippocratic Oath of the medical profession, this suggests that computers and data should not be damaged if at all possible. Mizrach here questions whether there is an ethical dilemma if the hacker inadvertently causes damage to a system;

2. "Protect Privacy" – Mizrach indicates that this in some ways contradicts the original hacker ethic, that all information should be freely available;

3. "Waste not, want not" – that computer resources should not be wasted, and that it is ethically wrong to keep people out of systems when they could be using them. Mizrach here

uses the example of a person's car – if the car is borrowed, filled with fuel, returned with no damage, and perhaps even a few suggestions as to how the performance can be improved, and the owner never misses it, is the act unethical? Mizrach indicates that there is a double-standard here, as most hackers are very possessive over the use of their own systems.

4. "Exceed Limitations" – always attempt to exceed the known limitations of technology or software;

5. "The Communication Imperative" – that people have the right to communicate and associate with their peers freely;

6. "Leave no Traces" – avoid leaving any indication that the hacker was present, and to avoid calling attention to the hacker or their exploits. This is necessary to protect the hacker themselves, the information they have gathered, and other hackers from being apprehended;

7. "Share!" – share information with as many people as possible;

8. "Self-Defence" – against a possible 'Big Brother' situation due to the growing power of government and corporations – the ability to hack effectively reduces the likelihood that these large organisations will affect citizens too much;

9. "Hacking Helps Security" – it is right to find security holes, and then tell people how to fix them. This principle has a number of ethical problems, which are outlined in more detail below;

10. "Trust, but Test" – the hacker must constantly test the integrity of systems and find ways to improve them. This may extend to testing the systems that affect the hacker. So for example if the hacker feels that their confidential information is being held by an agency (perhaps a government department), they feel that they have the right to test the security of that system against

intrusion by others. This principle is again clearly a double-standard – it is likely that other people's information will be held on the same databases and will be available to the hacker if they are successful in their intrusion attempt.

Mizrach also outlines a number of activities that hackers should not engage in according to the new ethic, including profiting from hacking, not adding to the body of hacker knowledge, damaging systems (with or without the use of viruses), excessive selfishness, theft (especially from small organisations), bragging, spying and turning in other hackers to the authorities. He also outlines the consequences of breaking the hacker ethic, indicating that this results mostly in anathema or social ostracization.

Mizrach suggests that the hacker ethic changed for several reasons. Firstly, there was far more computing power available then than when the original hacker ethic was formed. Secondly, a belief that society had changed for the worse. Thirdly, a belief that the computer industry had discarded the original hacker ethic. And finally, that there had been a generational change – that young hackers then were qualitatively different to hackers of a previous generation.

Chiesa, Ducci and Ciappi (2009) summarize the hacker ethic into four main points – do not damage penetrated systems, do not modify the information present on the invaded computer (except the log file to erase evidence of the intrusion), share information and knowledge with other members of the underground, and supply a service by sharing accesses that should be free to all (pp. 171-172). Similarly, Tavani (2007) attempts to summarise the hacker ethic by suggesting that many hackers "have embraced, either explicitly or implicitly, the following three principles" (p. 176) – that information should be free, that hackers provide society with a useful service, and that activities in cyberspace do not harm people in the real world. Tavani goes on to explain the problems with these three principles, at least in theory. For example, he suggests that in many cases, hackers are probably aware that there are limits to the appropriate freedom of information (if all information was free, then privacy would be compromised and the integrity and accuracy of information would be questionable). In addition, while nonmalicious hackers can be beneficial for society, this does not mean that all hacking activity is acceptable. Tavani cites Spafford (2004), who indicates that in some cases, hacking activity could be considered ethical, despite that computer break-ins cause harm. Spafford gives an example of a case where medical data was required in an emergency to save someone's life – in this case Spafford believes that a break-in to this computer would be the ethical thing to do.

Subscription to the Hacker Ethic and Justifications for Breaches

As the hacker ethic appears to be a very dynamic concept, it is difficult to determine exactly whether or not the modern hacker subscribes to it completely. Nevertheless, some hackers (particularly white-hat hackers) do appear to hold their ethical principles in high regard. Lieberman (2003, as cited in Fötinger & Ziegler, 2004) questioned hackers on their subscription to the hacker ethic (as outlined by Levy, 1984), and found that although many hackers agreed with most of the principles involved, only 7% indicated that privacy was not important to them. Lieberman suggests that hackers do not extend that belief to those whose computers they attack, accusing them of a highly hypocritical approach. As with many codes of practice, it is to be expected that some members of the community will not adhere to them. It is evident that at least some hackers do not subscribe to any version of the hacker ethic, and even for those who do, it must be remembered that there are many loopholes within the principles which allow certain unethical and/or illegal behaviours

to be completed without retribution from the hacking community.

Marc Rogers (as cited in Fötinger & Ziegler, 2004) suggests that hackers tend to minimise or misconstrue the consequences of their activities, rationalising that their behaviour is really performing a service to the organisation or society as a whole. Post (also cited in Fötinger & Ziegler, 2004) suggests that hackers share a sense of "ethical flexibility" – the serious consequences of hacking can be more easily ignored as human contact is minimised over the computer. Young, Zhang and Prybutok (2007) also found that the hackers had a high level of moral disengagement, and disregard any negative consequences of hacking by blaming the victims.

So is it possible for ethical hacking to exist? Richard Spinello (2000) indicates that even though many hackers maintain that hacking is for fun and not damaging, and that many of them consider even looking for personal information such as credit card numbers as immoral and unethical, any act of trespassing is unethical, even if there is no attempt to gain personal information. He indicates that "people should not go where they do not belong, either in real space or in cyberspace" (p. 179). He does not argue that searching for personal information is more 'wrong' than simply 'looking around', but that "this does not excuse the latter activity".

When this rationale is extended to the offline world, the ethical implications become clearer. If an individual succeeds in evading all the security guards and precautions which protect the sensitive areas of an important building (for example, the White House), and then proceeds to search through important or confidential documents, but does not actually steal or change anything, it is still clear that their action is unethical, and there would be little hesitation in prosecuting the offender. Even if an intruder makes their way into a person's home, just to have a look around without causing any damage, it is still clearly an unnecessary invasion of privacy. It is also unlikely that the homeowner would forgive that intruder, even if they offer an explanation of how they had managed to overcome the household security, so that the homeowner could then improve their protection measures. Similarly, it is unlikely that the curators of the White House would hire their intruder as a security expert to prevent further invasions. Yet these are common perceptions amongst the hacker community – that it is acceptable to intrude in order to determine the effectiveness of security, and that the victim should be grateful, to the extent of offering financial reward in the form of employment, for the infringement. These beliefs are supported by the evidence that many former hackers have gone on to careers in the IT security field, whether employed by major software developers or freelancing, as in the case of Kevin Mitnick.

So far the evidence would suggest that there is no such thing as ethical hacking. Nevertheless, it is true that if a professional was hired specifically by a company or organisation to test their system security and to report the flaws back to them, then this could be one of the very few circumstances where true ethical hacking exists. This assumes, of course, that the hacker does not attempt to access any files which they are not authorised to do, that they report all security weaknesses to the organisation, and that they make appropriate attempts to work with the organisation to improve their security.

There is another potential set of circumstances within which hacking could be considered ethical. Chiesa et al (2009) cite examples of how 'ethical hackers' have attempted to display the positive sides of hacking, and they use EHAP (Ethical Hackers Against Paedophilia) as an example of this. This organisation uses unconventional, yet legal, tactics to try to combat paedophilia online. Whether or not their activities could truly be considered ethical requires an in-depth evaluation of their techniques. In doing so, it must be remembered that behaviours do not necessarily become ethical because of the person or group

they are being done to, no matter how despicable their actions have been. Similarities can be drawn between this type of behaviour and others where people behave in what may be unethical ways in order to achieve what they feel is an ethical objective, for example the defacement of the websites of research laboratories that engage in animal testing by animal rights activists.

CONSIDERING THE LEGALITY OF HACKING ACTIVITIES

Whether or not hacking behaviours can be considered ethical is not necessarily related to their position legally. Many behaviours that are considered laudable by hackers are not seen as positively by the judicial system. At this point it is useful to consider how common hacking activities are, so that the potential impact on the criminal justice system can be considered.

Rantala (for the US Dept of Justice, Bureau of Justice Statistics; 2008) in a survey of 7,818 businesses that responded to the National Computer Crime Survey in 2005, found that few businesses that detected an incident reported the cybercrime. The proportion of businesses that experienced a cyberattack (such as viruses, denial of service, vandalism or sabotage) or computer security incident (such as spyware, hacking, port scanning, and theft of information) seems to be few, at 6% and 12% respectively.

The Computer Security Institute (CSI) Computer Crime and Security Survey (2009) found that 29.2% of respondents had experienced denial-of-service attacks (up from 21% in 2008); with 17.3% had experienced password sniffing (compared to 9% in 2008). A further 13.5% had experienced website defacement (compared to 6% in 2008). However it is unknown how many companies who had been the target of such attacks did not respond to the survey or report their victimization.

Overall, it is extremely difficult to determine how much hacking activity occurs, partially due to difficulties in completing a methodical survey of the extent of the problem, and partially due to some victims' preference not to admit to being victimised for the sake of avoiding negative publicity. It is also possible that some victims are never aware of the fact that they have been victimised, or if they are, they manage the problem privately (through the use of protection software or fixing/replacing their equipment) and do not report the event. As such, it can be expected that the true extent of hacking activity far exceeds what is recorded and reported by official agencies. The difference between these is termed the 'dark figure'.

In the UK, Garlik (2009) attempts to estimate the dark figure of cybercrime in their annual reports. They estimate that just under 50% of UK businesses experienced a security incident, with 25% experiencing a serious breach. Sixteen percent of businesses experienced an attack from an unauthorised outsider. It is not entirely clear how Garlik reached these figures, and due to the company's interest in selling computer security products, these statistics need to be carefully interpreted. One method of estimating the dark figure is by asking offenders to self-report their activities. The Home Office (2005) report the findings of the Offending, Crime and Justice Survey (OCJS) which was carried out in 2003, and asked participants to self-report their hacking behaviours. They found that 0.9% of Internet users said they had used the Internet to hack into other computers, with males more likely than females (1.3% vs. 0.5%), and younger people (aged 10-25) more likely then older people to admit to hacking behaviors.

How are Hacking Behaviors Tackled Under Law?

Brenner (2006) indicates that according to section 1030 of the US Code, depending on the type of hacking activity engaged in, offenders can be fined, imprisoned for up to ten years, or both.

This imprisonment can be extended to up to 20 years for repeat offenders. Tavani (2007) suggests that most involved would "support legislation that would distinguish between the degrees of punishment handed to those who are found guilty of trespass in cyberspace" (p. 202). Tavani goes on to indicate that in real-world counterparts of these activities (such as breaking and entering), a distinction would normally be made between offenders who have engaged in different degrees of criminal activity (so that the offender who picks a lock but does not enter a premises would normally receive a lesser sentence than the offender who enters the premises but does not steal or damage anything, but who in turn would receive a lesser sentence than the offender who commits burglary).

Brenner (2006) indicates that most US states do tend to use a "two-tiered approach" (p. 84), distinguishing 'simple hacking' (gaining unauthorized access to a computer) from 'aggravated hacking' (gaining unauthorized access to a computer that results in the commission of some further criminal activity). Brenner indicates that these states generally consider "simple hacking a misdemeanor and aggravated hacking a felony" (p. 84). However some states use a single statute for both activities, while others, such as Hawaii, use up to five different classifications.

So there are a variety of means by which hackers can be punished. While imprisonment is one of the most commonly cited punishments, fines can also be implemented. From an international perspective, many countries have extradition treaties, one example of which is the contested extradition of Gary McKinnon from England to the United States of America. In some cases, as was the case with Kevin Mitnick, the hacker's access to technology may be limited. Nevertheless, it has yet to be fully determined if any of these punishments can act as an appropriate deterrent for hackers. Young, Zhang and Prybutok (2007) surveyed hackers and other attendees at a DefCon (a large hacker convention) in Las Vegas. They found that even though hackers perceive that they would be subject to severe judicial punishment if apprehended (thus demonstrating the effectiveness of the US Government in communicating the seriousness of illegal hacking), they continued to engage in illegal hacking activities. However, the hackers felt that there was a low likelihood of this punishment occurring. This is of note as severity of punishment has little effect when the likelihood of punishment is low (Von Hirsch, Bottoms, Burney & Wickstrom, 1999) whereas increased likelihood of punishment has been found to work as a deterrent (Killias, Scheidegger & Nordenson, 2009). Young et al (2007) also found that hackers perceived high utility value from their hacking activities, perceiving the gains from hacking to outweigh the potential losses. It seems likely that until this is reversed hackers are unlikely to reduce their offending behaviours.

Solutions and Recommendations

There are a number of potential actions which could be taken in relation to hacking behaviours, particularly with respect to ethical perspectives. It is not clear yet if hackers truly subscribe to the principles behind the hacker ethic, or if they are simply using it as justification for their actions. In either case, the use of cognitive-behavioural treatment programmes focusing on moral reasoning may reduce recidivism in hackers (see for example Wilson, Allen-Bouffard & MacKenzie, 2005, for a review on the effectiveness of moral reconation therapy with offenders). It may be prudent to extend this tactic to prevent hacking behaviour as well, perhaps by including a class on ethical use of technology during computing courses in schools and universities.

The findings of Young et al (2007) also seem to indicate that it would be more effective to apprehend and punish the majority of hackers than to attempt to deter others by making examples of a few serious offenders. Perhaps the limiting of internet connection speeds for convicted hackers might be a sufficient deterrent for the majority of

prospective offenders. This solution has already been proposed for illegal file-sharers in a number of jurisdictions, and while it would not completely prevent the offender from engaging in hacking behaviour, it would be enough to significantly reduce their potential online behaviors. Admittedly a proficient hacker would be able to find ways around this limited connection, but it could be a suitable punishment for a first-time offender, before resorting to more severe penalties.

FUTURE RESEARCH DIRECTIONS

Despite the significant quantity of literature relating to the ethical positions of hackers, few studies have sought to empirically test if hackers subscribe to the principles outlined above. This is probably due in part to the difficulties in accessing participants – many hackers would not be willing to discuss their behaviors with a researcher for fear that they would be putting themselves at risk of prosecution. In addition, it is difficult for the researcher to ensure that their participants are indeed engaged in hacking behaviours. To date, much research in this area has relied on completing content analysis of hacker bulletin boards, public online spaces in which hackers may not be entirely honest. The hacker ethical principles outlined in this chapter need to be appropriately tested to ensure their validity. Only when this is complete, and the current hacker ethic is established, could intervention programmes such as those outlined above be developed and implemented.

CONCLUSION

Regardless of the arguments presented in the hacker ethics, it seems that true ethical hacking is rare. Even where hacking activities seem to have a higher moral purpose, as with the efforts to thwart paedophiles online, there is still a grey area. While it cannot be disputed that some hackers have higher moral standards than others, to the extent that they feel that the same labels cannot be applied to both groups, it does seem that many hackers hold a distorted ethical perspective. While it is possible that some might genuinely feel that what they are doing is right and for the common good, it would be naïve to believe that no hacker utilises the ethical principles to hide ulterior motives. Many types of offenders provide justifications for their criminal activity, and in most cases society does not recognize these justifications as acceptable excuses for their behaviour, at least not to the extent of waiving punishment. The fact that we would consider doing so for one specific group of offenders (hackers) would therefore be extremely unjust.

REFERENCES

Ajzen, I. (1985). *Action-control: From cognition to behaviour*. New York, NY: Springer-Verlag.

Ajzen, I. (1991). The theory of planned behaviour. *Organizational Behavior and Human Decision Processes*, *50*, 179–211. doi:10.1016/0749-5978(91)90020-T

BBC News Online. *(28th July 2009)*. Hacker's moral crusade over UFO. *Retrieved 24th February 2010 from* http://news.bbc.co.uk/go/pr/fr/-/2/hi/uk_news/8172842.stm

Beveran, J. V. (2001). A conceptual model of hacker development and motivations. *The Journal of Business*, *1*(2). Retrieved from http://www.dvara.net/HK/beveren.pdf.

Boyd, C. (2008, 30th July). Profile: Gary McKinnon. *BBC News Online*. Retrieved 24th February, 2010, from http://news.bbc.co.uk/2/hi/uk_news/7839338.stm

Brenner, S. W. (2006). Defining cybercrime: A review of state and federal law. In Clifford, R. D. (Ed.), *Cybercrime: The investigation, prosecution and defense of a computer related crime* (2nd ed., pp. 13–95). Durham, NC: Carolina Academic Press.

Bryant, R., & Marshall, A. (2008). Criminological and motivational perspectives. In Bryant, R., & Bryant, S. (Eds.), *Investigating digital crime* (pp. 231–248). Chichester, UK: Wiley.

Calcutt, A. (1999). *White noise: An A-Z of the contradictions in cyberculture*. London, UK: MacMillan Press Ltd.

Chiesa, R., Ducci, S., & Ciappi, S. (2009). *Profiling hackers: The science of criminal profiling as applied to the world of hacking*. Boca Raton, FL: Auerbach Publications.

Computer Security Institute. *(2009)*. CSI computer crime and security survey 2009. *Retrieved 8th March, 2010, from* http://gocsi.com/survey

Fafinski, S., & Minassian, N. (2009). *UK cybercrime report 2009*. Published September 2009. Invenio Research. Retrieved 8th March 2010 from http://www.garlik.com/cybercrime_report.php

Fötinger, C. S., & Ziegler, W. (2004). *Understanding a hacker's mind – A psychological insight into the hijacking of identities*. Danube-University Krems, Austria: RSA Security.

Furnell, S. (2010). Hackers, viruses and malicious software. In Y. Jewkes & M. Yar (Eds.), *Handbook of Internet crime* (pp. 173–193). Cullompton, Devon, UK: Willan Publishing.

Home Office. *(2005)*. Fraud and technology crimes: Findings from the 2002/03 British crime survey and 2003 offending, crime and justice survey. *(Home Office Online Report 34/05)*. *Retrieved on 26th July, 2005, from* www.homeoffice.gov.uk/rds/pdfs05/rdsolr3405.pdf

Killias, M., Scheidegger, D., & Nordenson, P. (2009). Effects of increasing the certainty of punishment: A field experiment on public transportation. *European Journal of Criminology, 6*, 387–400. doi:10.1177/1477370809337881

Kirwan, G. H. *(2006)*. An identification of demographic and psychological characteristics of computer hackers using triangulation. *PhD Thesis, Institute of Criminology, College of Business and Law, School of Law. University College Dublin. June 2006*

Lafrance, Y. *(2004)*. Psychology: A previous security tool. *Retrieved on 29th April, 2005, from* http://cnscentre.future.co. kr/resource/security/ hacking/1409.pdf

Levy, S. (1984). *Hackers: Heroes of the computer revolution*. London, UK: Penguin Books.

Maslow, A. H. (1970). *Motivation and personality* (2nd ed.). New York, NY: Harper & Row.

Mitnick, K. D., & Simon, W. L. (2002). *The art of deception: Controlling the human element of security*. Indianapolis, IN: Wiley Publishing Inc.

Mitnick, K. D., & Simon, W. L. (2005). *The art of intrusion: The real stories behind the exploits of hackers, intruders and deceivers*. Indianapolis, IN: Wiley Publishing Inc.

Mizrach, S. *(n.d.)*. Is there a hacker ethic for 90s hackers? *Retrieved on 16th June, 2010, from* http:// www.fiu. edu/~mizrachs /hackethic.html

Murphy, C. (2004, June). Inside the mind of the hacker. *Accountancy Ireland, 36*, 12.

Rennie, L., & Shore, M. (2007). An advanced model of hacking. *Security Journal, 20*, 236–251. doi:10.1057/palgrave.sj.8350019

Rock, P. (2007). Sociological theories of crime. In Maguire, M., Morgan, R., & Reiner, R. (Eds.), *The Oxford handbook of criminology* (4th ed., pp. 3–42). Oxford, UK: Oxford University Press.

Rogers, M. (2000). *A new hacker taxonomy*. University of Manitoba, [Online]. Retrieved on 6th March, 2010, from http://homes.cerias.purdue. edu/~mkr/hacker.doc

Sanders-Reach, C. (2005, May 16). *Beware pharming and other new hacker scams*. New Jersey Law Journal.

Schneier, B. (2003, November/December)... *IEEE Security and Privacy, 1*, 6.

Shernoff, D. J., Csikszentmihalyi, M., Schneider, B., & Shernoff, E. S. (2003). Student engagement in high school classrooms from the perspective of flow theory. *School Psychology Quarterly, 18*, 158–176. doi:10.1521/scpq.18.2.158.21860

Spinello, R. (2000). Information integrity. In Langford, D. (Ed.), *Internet ethics* (pp. 158–180). London, UK: MacMillan Press.

Sterling, B. (1992). *The hacker crackdown: Law and disorder on the electronic frontier*. New York, NY: Penguin.

Tavani, H. T. (2007). *Ethics and technology: Ethical issues in an age of information and communication technology* (2nd ed.). Hoboken, NJ: Wiley.

Taylor, P. (1999). *Hackers*. London, UK: Routledge. doi:10.4324/9780203201503

Von Hirsch, A., Bottoms, A. E., Burney, E., & Wickstrom, P. O. (1999). *Criminal deterrence and sentence severity*. Oxford, UK: Hart.

Wilson, D. B., Allen-Bouffard, L., & MacKenzie, D. L. (2005). A quantitative review of structured, group-oriented, cognitive-behavioural programs for offenders. *Criminal Justice and Behavior, 32*, 172–204..doi:10.1177/0093854804272889

Woo, J. J., Kim, Y., & Dominick, J. (2004). Hackers: Militants or merry pranksters? A content analysis of defaced Web pages. *Media Psychology, 6*, 63–82. doi:10.1207/s1532785xmep0601_3

Young, R., Zhang, L., & Prybutok, V. R. (2007). Hacking into the minds of hackers. *Information Systems Management, 24,* 281–287. doi:10.1080/10580530701585823

ADDITIONAL READING

Brenner, S. W. (2006). Defining Cybercrime: A Review of State and Federal Law. In Clifford, R. D. (Ed.), *Cybercrime* (2nd ed., pp. 13–95). Durham, NC: Carolina Academic Press.

Bryant, R. (2008). *Investigating Digital Crime.* Chichester, England: Wiley.

Cere, R. (2007). Digital undergrounds: alternative politics and civil society. In Jewkes, Y. (Ed.), *Crime Online* (pp. 144–159). Cullompton, England: Willan.

Coleman, E. G., & Golub, A. (2008). Hacker practice: Moral genres and the cultural articulation of liberalism. *Anthropological Theory, 8,* 255–277.. doi:10.1177/1463499608093814

Donato, L. (2009). An Introduction to How Criminal Profiling Could be used as a support for computer hacking investigations. *Journal of Digital Forensic Practice, 2,* 183–195. doi:10.1080/15567280903140946

Ess, C. (2009). *Digital Media Ethics.* Cambridge, England: Polity Press.

Furnell, S. (2010). Hackers, viruses and malicious software (pp. 173 – 193). In Yvonne Jewkes and Majid Yar (2010) *Handbook of Internet Crime (eds).* Cullompton, Devon: Willan Publishing.

Gagon, B. (2008). Cyberwars and cybercrimes. In Leman-Langlois, S. (Ed.), *Technocrime: Technology, crime and social control* (pp. 46–65). Cullompton, England: Willan.

Gunkel, D. J. (2005). Editorial: Introduction to hacking and hacktivism. *New Media & Society, 7,* 595–597. doi:10.1177/1461444805056007

Jordan, T. (2010). Hacktivism: All together in the virtual. In Nayar, P. K. (Ed.), *The New Media and Cybercultures Anthology* (pp. 369–378). Chichester, England: Wiley Blackwell.

McQuade, S. C. III. (2006). *Understanding and Managing Cybercrime.* Boston: Pearson.

Meinel, C. P. (1998). How hackers break in... and how they are caught. *Scientific American, 279,* 98–105. doi:10.1038/scientificamerican1098-98

Taylor, P. (2001). Hacktivism: in search of lost ethics? In Wall, D. S. (Ed.), *Crime and the Internet* (pp. 59–73). London: Routledge.

Taylor, P. A. (2003). Maestros or misogynists? Gender and the social construction of hacking (pp. 126-146). In Yvonne Jewkes (2003) *Dot. cons: Crime, deviance and identity on the Internet.* Cullompton, Devon (UK): Willan Publishing.

Wall, D. S. (2007). *Cybercrime.* Cambridge, England: Polity.

Warren, M., & Leitch, S. (2009). Hacker Taggers: A new type of hackers. *Information Systems Frontiers.* doi:.doi:10.1007/s10796-009-9203-y

Williams, M. (2006). *Virtually Criminal: Crime, Deviance and regulation online.* Abington, England: Routledge.

Woo, H. J. *(2003). The hacker mentality: Exploring the relationship between psychological variables and hacking activities.* Dissertation Abstracts International, 64, 2A, *325.*

Yar, M. (2006). *Cybercrime and Society.* London: Sage.

KEY TERMS AND DEFINITIONS

Black-Hat: A type of hacker who has malicious intent, and may seek to profit from their hacking behaviours, or to intentionally cause damage to a system or website. Another name for a 'cracker.'

Cracker: A type of hacker who has malicious intent, and may seek to profit from their hacking behaviours, or to intentionally cause damage to a system or website. Another name for a 'black-hat'. The term was supposedly coined by the original hacking community in order to distinguish themselves from malicious hackers.

Denial of Service Attack: A type of hacker attack where a system or website is rendered inoperable due to an unusually high number of requests being placed on it.

Dumpster-Diving: A hacking technique which involves searching garbage bins for confidential information which may be useful in gaining unauthorised access.

Ethical Hacking: Hacking in order to test the security of a system or a website with the explicit permission of the owners.

Grey-Hat: A type of hacker who does not have malicious intent, but who only informs their victims of security weaknesses in their system under certain circumstances (for example, when they think that they may be given financial compensation for finding or fixing the security weakness).

Hacker: An individual who gains unauthorised access to computer systems using a variety of means.

Hacker Ethic: An evolving set of ethical practices which some hackers appear to subscribe to.

Social Engineering: A hacking technique which involves manipulating the human element in security to provide confidential information about system security (such as usernames and passwords) to an unauthorised person.

White-Hat: A type of hacker who does not have malicious intent, and who frequently informs their victims of security weaknesses in their system.

Chapter 3
Emerging Cybercrime Trends:
Legal, Ethical, and Practical Issues

Sean M. Zadig
Nova Southeastern University, USA

Gurvirender Tejay
Nova Southeastern University, USA

ABSTRACT

The issue of cybercrime has received much attention of late, as individual and organizational losses from online crimes frequently reach into the hundreds of thousands or even millions of dollars per incident. Computer criminals have begun deploying advanced, distributed techniques, which are increasingly effective and devastating. This chapter describes a number of these techniques and details one particularly prevalent trend: the employment of large networks of compromised computers, or botnets, to conduct a wide variety of online crimes. A typology of botnets is provided, and the supporting infrastructure of botnets and other online crime, including bulletproof hosting providers and money mule networks, are described. The chapter also relates a number of the practical, legal, and ethical challenges experienced by practitioners, law enforcement, and researchers who must deal with these emergent threats.

INTRODUCTION

Cybercrime in the 21st century is rapidly evolving, with new techniques being developed and exploited by criminals worldwide. This new type of crime is no longer the exclusive domain of the Information Systems (IS) security professional; now, every person who interacts with technol-

ogy in some fashion, from the IS manager, to the end user, to the shareholder of a company which utilizes technology, needs to have an awareness of these dangerous new trends. Furthermore, modern cybercrime poses various technical, legal, and ethical challenges to those whose job it is to focus upon it, from scholarly researchers who study cybercrime, to IS security professions who defend against it, and to the law enforcement officers and prosecutors who investigate it.

DOI: 10.4018/978-1-61350-132-0.ch003

Complicating matters significantly is the ever-expanding internationality of the cybercriminals themselves. The advent of the Internet and the diffusion of computer technologies worldwide have resulted in an unprecedented global expansion of computer-based criminal activity (Salifu, 2008). Now, criminals in one country can easily conspire with other criminals in another country to defraud a victim in a third country. Or to complicate matters further, those criminals can rent (or compromise) a server in a fourth country from which to launch their attacks, which may involve compromised victim computers acting as "zombies" in dozens of other countries. In this hypothetical scenario, there are at least four international jurisdictions to deal with, each introducing different legal systems and possibly different languages and diplomatic relations into any attempt to investigate into the activity. This worldwide nature of cybercrime involves significant and unresolved issues related to the application of national laws to international crime, such as differing definitions of criminal conduct in affected countries (Podgor, 2002), making it difficult for law enforcement and prosecutors to apprehend these criminals.

The very nature of these attacks is also shifting. Traditional Internet-based cybercrime once involved attacks by lone hackers against monolithic targets, such as the notable example of British hacker Gary McKinnon in 2001, who conducted attacks against NASA and the Pentagon (Arnell & Reid, 2009). However, many of the attacks which will be discussed in this chapter are instead aimed at individual users, both corporate and residential. These users are also geographically dispersed, like the criminals who target them, and some of these attacks involve millions of victims at a time. For investigators and prosecutors, incorporating the losses experienced by these victims into criminal cases is difficult enough on a national level, but when the victims are foreign, obtaining statements or interviews can often be impossible. Attackers have also become much more focused upon financial motives; while in the past hackers may have attacked for fun, notoriety, or to challenge

themselves (Hoath & Mulhall, 1998; Leeson & Coyle. 2005), more recently, making money from cybercrime victims is a major driving factor (Choo, 2008; Ianelli & Hackworth, 2006).

The remainder of the chapter is organized into five sections. The next section introduces the historical perspective of cybercrime and discusses some of the literature surrounding this perspective. The third section introduces one of the types of malicious software commonly utilized by organized cybercrime groups, botnets, and describes the emerging issues faced by this threat. The fourth section details other common threats, such as bulletproof hosting, mule networks, and other emergent trends. The fifth section describes future research opportunities in the cybercrime field, and the sixth section concludes the chapter.

BACKGROUND

While multiple types of emerging cybercrime will be discussed, the major focus of this chapter will be on the usage of malicious software, or malware, so a brief introduction to malware would be appropriate. The first computer viruses emerged in the 1980's (Cohen, 1987), but spread slowly due to the reliance upon manual disk-to-disk infection (Highland, 1997) as a result of the lack of network connectivity between infected computers. One notable exception to this was the Morris Worm, a fast-spreading computer worm which infected one in twenty computers on the Internet in 1988 (Orman, 2003). The creator of the Morris Worm, once identified, received a sentence of three years of probation and a fine of $10,000, becoming the first individual to be tried by a jury for violating then-new federal hacking laws (Markoff, 1990).

Since the introduction of the World Wide Web in the 1990s (Berners-Lee, et. al, 1994), and the corresponding increased usage of IS by businesses and individuals, the occurrence of malicious software infections and other computer crimes have risen dramatically. For example, the Melissa Virus, a macro virus which infected Microsoft

Office documents and spread using the victims' own email contacts, infected about 1.2 million computers at North American firms in 1999 (Garber, 1999). Despite causing millions of dollars of damages, the creator of the virus received a relatively light sentence of twenty months in prison and a $5,000 fine (USDOJ, 2002). The early 2000's saw a number of destructive viruses cause extensive damage to organizations, including the ILOVEYOU virus of 2000 (Bishop, 2000), whose Filipino creator was identified but could not be prosecuted due to the lack of cybercrime laws in the Philippines, despite causing billions of dollars in damages (Arnold, 2000).

Within the legislative arena, the United States Congress reacted to these early attacks by first passing the Computer Fraud and Abuse Act in 1986, which has since been amended on numerous occasions to keep up with changes in technology (Hong, 1997). The United Kingdom followed suit with its Computer Misuse Act in 1990, and the 2001 Council of Europe's Convention on Cybercrime attempted to set international standards in computer crime law (Bell, 2002). Simultaneously, numerous researchers demonstrated the need for ethical standards as a way to reduce the prevalence of computer crimes (Gardner, Samuels, Render, & Coffinberger, 1989; Harrington, 1996). Despite the presence of these laws and attempts to establish ethical standards in computer usage, and the creation of numerous other laws in foreign jurisdictions, computer crime and in particular targeted attacks from external attackers continue to rise dramatically each year (Richardson, 2008).

Cybercriminals also utilize other tactics aside from self-propagating malware to compromise computer systems. Kevin Mitnick, a hacker who was considered the most wanted cybercriminal of the 1990s, primarily utilized social engineering techniques to compromise over 35 major organizations, costing those organizations a combined total of $300 million (Leung, 2004). Social engineering is "the process by which a hacker deceives others into disclosing valuable data that will benefit the hacker in some way" (Rusch, 1999). The

effectiveness of social engineering techniques in computer intrusions has been documented extensively (Manske, 2000; Damle, 2002; Gupta & Sharman, 2006), and its continued employment by today's cybercriminals will be discussed later in this chapter.

Modern cybercrime has evolved significantly from the early days of computer viruses and malware described above. As the next section will show, today's computer crimes have generally moved away from being orchestrated by a lone hacker towards highly organized and interconnected cybercriminal groups driven by financial motivation. These groups employ highly sophisticated malware to conduct their attacks, often compromising millions of computers without their owners' knowledge or consent. This new breed of cybercriminal poses new challenges for practitioners and researchers, who must defend against and understand the increasingly complex threats that they bring.

A MAJOR THREAT: BOTNETS

One of the most prolific and devastating forms of modern cybercrime comes in the form of botnets, a relatively recent addition to the criminal toolbox. Botnets, or ro*bot net*works, are groups of malware-infected computers, also known as bots or "zombies", which are controlled through a criminal command and control infrastructure (Ianelli & Hackworth, 2006). The criminal controlling the network is known as the "botherder." Estimates on the number of infected computers per botnet vary wildly - for example, one estimate states that 150 million computers, or approximately one quarter of all computers on the Internet, have joined botnets without their owners' knowledge (Weber, 2007). Recent reports have documented botnets of incredible size: 2010's Mariposa botnet had an estimated 13 million victims, including infected computers in half of Fortune 1000 firms (Goodin, 2010); security vendor Finjan published details on a 1.9 million victim botnet in 2009 (Prince,

2009); and 2007's Storm Worm infected between 1 and 5 million computers (Porras, Saidi, & Yegneswaran, 2007), to name a few notable examples. With numbers like these, it is not hard to imagine how a figure of 150 million could be obtained. As will be described later in this section, botnets have a number of criminal applications, ranging from the annoying to the financially terrifying.

A botnet's command and control infrastructure is administered through different means. First came botnets controlled through Internet Relay Chat (IRC), a popular instant messaging service utilized by computer experts and hackers, followed by botnets controlled via the Hypertext Transfer Protocol (HTTP), the protocol which powers the World Wide Web (Ianelli & Hackworth, 2006). In recent years, botnets have also been observed utilizing Peer to Peer (P2P) control mechanisms (Gu, Zhang, & Lee, 2008), or most recently, infrastructure built upon so-called "Web 2.0" services, such as 2009's Twitter botnet (Nazario, 2009). While all types are still in use in today's botnets, as the various control mechanisms evolved, they became progressively more difficult for network defenders and Intrusion Detection Systems (IDS) to identify – for example, IRC is a fairly noisy and easily detected protocol, but HTTP communications blend in with regular web traffic while still contacting malicious IP addresses or domain names. P2P botnets lack a centralized server and instead communicate with infected peers, making IDS rulesets which spot hostile IP addresses less useful, and Web 2.0 botnet traffic is almost indistinguishable from normal user behavior at first glance.

A Typology of Botnets

Modern botnets can perform a number of distributed-computing tasks for the criminals who control them. Some botnets are single-purpose malware, in that they only accomplish one particular task, while other botnets can perform numerous tasks at once. Also common is the use of multiple malware types by a single criminal group, or by numerous groups working in tandem. For example, spam botnets can be used to send victims links to infected websites; the victims unwittingly download malware-loading botnet software, which then installs a botnet designed to steal banking credentials. While three botnets may be involved, operated by three independent cybercrime groups working in concert in an organized fashion, the end goal is financial theft. Refer to Table 1 for a listing of the botnet typology that will be discussed in this section.

Table 1. Common botnet types

Botnet Type	Purpose	Example Botnet
Spam	Delivering unsolicited e-mail	Storm Worm (Porras, Saidi, & Yegneswaran, 2007)
Financial theft	Stealing login credentials to financial websites or credit card numbers	Zeus (Aaron, 2010)
DDoS	Denial of service attacks against websites or servers	BlackEnergy (Nazario, 2007)
Dropper	Installing other types of malware	Bredolab (Bleaken, 2010)
Click fraud	Fraudulent clicks upon online advertisements	Bahama (Hines, 2009)
Intelligence gathering, cyberwarfare	State-sponsored surveillance or destruction for political means	Ghostnet (Everett, 2009), StuxNet (Marks, 2010)
Other	Illegal web hosting (phish, warez), CAPTCHA breaking	Avalanche (Aaron, 2010), Koobface (Baltazar, Costoya, & Flores, 2009)

As mentioned above, spam is a frequent botnet technique. Spam is generally defined as unsolicited electronic messages sent in bulk, and in the botnet world can take the form of email, webpage or forum comments, or instant messages (Banday, Qadri, & Shah, 2009). These messages can be sent for a variety of financially-motivated purposes: for the selling of products, such as pharmaceuticals or counterfeit luxury goods; the recruitment of so-called money mules through "work at home" scams; stock market fraud, where recipients are encouraged to buy certain "penny stocks," thus driving up the price for the shareholders; to direct users to phishing sites, where victims are presented with fraudulent forms for banks and other protected services which collect credentials and other personal information; or simply to spread malware through email, either directly attached to the message or through links to websites hosting malware (Kreibich et al., 2009). Botnets are believed to be responsible for the vast majority of today's spam (Carr, 2008), and numerous spam botnets have been observed operating at one time. The Storm Worm botnet is one of the more noteworthy contemporary examples, both because of its use of P2P and fast-flux techniques (Porras, Saidi, & Yegneswaran, 2007), and because the author remains at large. From a legal perspective, sending spam messages is a criminal violation of the United States' CAN-SPAM Act of 2003 (USFTC, 2004), but is not illegal in other countries such as Russia (Naumov, 2003), which is commonly believed to be a major source of botherders and spammers. This disparity in the criminalization of spam can be a major roadblock in the fight against botnets and online crime.

Some of the most frightening types of botnets are those that target financial information. These botnets may scour the hard drives of infected computers for passwords to banking websites, credit card numbers, or other financial information, or may even intercept victim keystrokes at banking sites and send this data to the attacker, where it can be used immediately or bundled with other victim accounts and sold in underground forums. The prices for stolen bank account credentials, credit cards, and even full identities of victims (such as name, social security number, birthday, and so forth) are set by underground brokers and can be purchased for only a few dollars each (Moore, Clayton, & Anderson, 2009). One extremely successful financial-theft botnet is known as "Zeus," a sophisticated piece of malware distributed by spam which allows criminals to record login credentials sent to online banks, and even utilize the victims' own computers to log into their banking accounts and withdraw funds (Aaron, 2010). These electronic bank robberies have been devastating to small businesses in the United States, whose bank accounts are not insured by the federal government as are individual accounts. Zeus infections at small businesses frequently cost victim organizations hundreds of thousands of dollars per attack, and many attacked companies experience extreme financial distress, such as bankruptcy (Aaron, 2010; Krebs, 2010). Even worse, the Zeus malware is readily available on the criminal underground, and can be purchased as a "kit," which contains all the code and instructions for a criminal to set up his own Zeus botnet, from various criminal forums or websites for a few hundred dollars (Ollman, 2008). These kits are often sold with technical support and warranties, and are "supported by development teams offering guarantees and service-level agreements" (Ollman, 2008, p. 4), revealing how professional and profitable the business creating financial-theft malware has become.

Another common botnet type is one associated with Distributed Denial of Service (DDoS) attacks. In these attacks, large numbers of compromised computers receive instructions to attack particular websites or online services. If enough bots are utilized to conduct the attack, the targeted website may be knocked offline due to the overloading of the server or the saturation of the network connection, or the targeted organization may at least incur significant bandwidth and manpower costs attempting to remediate the attack. These attacks often occur for the purposes of extortion, although paying botherders to avoid attack may be a risky proposition for website owners, as other hackers may learn of the payoff and launch their own attacks (Ianelli & Hackworth, 2006). A frequent target of DDoS botnets are online gambling websites, which are illegal in the US and often incorporate in countries with poor cybercrime investigative capabilities, and whose operators are often reluctant to involve law enforcement or publicize when they are attacked for fear of losing market share (Paulson & Weber, 2006). One popular type of DDoS botnet is known as "BlackEnergy," and, like Zeus, is also sold in kit form, for approximately $40 on underground forums frequented by Russian hackers (Nazario, 2007).

Yet another common botnet purpose is to install other malware. These types of botnets can be termed "loading" or "dropper" botnets, and the criminals who run them can lease or sell infected computers to other criminals who wish to distribute malware or create their own botnets (Bleaken, 2010). This allows cybercriminals to dispense with the onerous task of building a botnet from scratch and to simply pay other criminals to create botnets for them on the fly, using thousands or millions of infected computers ready to receive malware. Also, instead of relying upon chance to distribute malware to victims who may or may not visit a malicious website, purchasers of ready-made botnets may pick and choose the computers they wish to join their criminal network. For example, computers only within a certain country can be infected with a particular banking botnet, or computers on government networks can be joined to an information-stealing botnet. As such, dropper botnet code is often found alongside other, more traditional, botnet malware on infected systems, such as those associated with spam or DDoS attacks. Contemporary examples of dropper botnets

include the "Bredolab" and "Conficker" networks (Bleaken, 2010).

As many Internet users are aware, online advertising provides the engine which drives e-commerce and allows many websites, such as search engines or mapping sites, to be profitable for their operators. When visitors to websites click on advertisements, the sites hosting these ads obtain revenue, often ranging from a fraction of a cent to a few dollars depending upon the type of advertisement, a technique known in the advertising industry as "pay per click." Because this advertising revenue powers much of the Internet, it is not surprising that botnets have been developed to exploit this industry. Many types of malware engage in a practice known as "click fraud," where users' clicks are redirected to advertisements affiliated with the criminals, or where the malware conducts the ad clicking itself. Click fraud can be conducted to either obtain illegally-derived income from legitimate online advertising programs, or as an attack against a competitor advertiser by clicking on their ads and increasing their advertising costs (Jansen, 2007). Significant research efforts have been conducted in an attempt to combat click fraud, including examinations of client authentication (Juels, Stamm, & Jakobsson, 2007), fraud-detection algorithms (Immorlica, Jain, Mahdian, & Talwar, 2005; Zhang & Guan, 2008), and new payment models for use by advertisers (Majumdar, Kulkarni, & Ravishankar, 2007). Numerous examples of click fraud botnets can be found on the Internet, including the "Bahama" botnet, a large network that conducts numerous fraudulent clicks without the victims' knowledge (Hines, 2009).

Another emerging botnet trend includes the state-sponsored use of compromised computers to advance political means, either through surreptitious intelligence gathering or through outright cyberwarfare. As many nations have undoubtedly realized, botnets and malware can be used for other purposes aside from pure financial gain, and armies of thousands or millions of infected computers can be a powerful weapon. One well-publicized example of a suspected state-sponsored information-gathering botnet is known as "GhostNet," a botnet which was operated from the People's Republic of China and obtained classified documents from the government of India and compromised computers belonging to the Office of the Dalai Lama and the United Nations, as well as other organizations conducting business in China (Adair, Deilbert, Rohozinski, Villeneuve, & Walton, 2009). This botnet may have been operated by the government of China itself, or possibly by hackers operating independently and hoping to sell or provide the stolen data to China (Everett, 2009). The botnet known as "StuxNet," which was designed to attack specific industrial control systems, such as the types used to manage power plants, water systems, oil pipelines, and other infrastructure-related systems, has also made headlines recently as a potent cyberwarfare weapon. StuxNet appeared to target Iranian nuclear plants and was created by an apparent professional development team, leading some to suspect that it was sponsored by a nation-state (Marks, 2010). Bringing the individuals or organizations behind cyber-espionage or cyberwarfare botnets is often a difficult proposition, as they may be in fact sponsored by a competing government which will likely not cooperate with a law enforcement investigation.

Finally, botnets can be used for a number of other illegal purposes beyond the types described above. For example, botnets have been observed hosting criminal web content, such as websites devoted to phishing in the case of the Avalanche botnet. This botnet uses compromised computers around the world as a "fast-flux" hosting network, where the phishing domain is hosted on numerous infected computers simultaneously, and was responsible for two-thirds of all phishing attacks in the second half of 2009 (Aaron, 2010). Such a network could conceivably be used to host other illegal content, such as child pornography, malware, or copyrighted works. With such a massive, distributed computing infrastructure in the hands of cybercriminals, only their imaginations limit what can be accomplished. For example, botnets have also been applied to solve computing problems faced by criminals. As many websites utilize CAPTCHA (Completely Automated Public Turing test to tell Computers and Humans Apart) to try to determine if a visitor is a person or a bot by presenting them with distorted text, a botnet known as "Koobface" began presenting CAPTCHA images to users of infected computers, requiring them to solve them as a Windows "security measure" (Baltazar, Costoya, & Flores, 2009). Koobface utilized the solved CAPTCHAs to create additional social networking accounts to spread itself even further, to advance its true purpose of click fraud and malware loading (Villeneuve, 2010).

Botnet Infection Techniques

How are the botnets described above installed on victim computers? This section will introduce a number of common methods of installing malware on the computers of unwitting users. Note that these techniques are in use by many types of malware, not just those belonging in botnets. Many of these installation methods rely upon social engineering techniques, either to trick the user to visit the website containing the malware or to convince the user to install the malware itself.

Oftentimes, searching for questionable items on the Internet, such as pirated software ("warez") or pornography, can be a prelude to infection (Bossler & Holt, 2009). These types of malware frequently pose as "video codec" files, where websites offering often-pornographic movies require that users download and install a codec file to allow them to view the movie. Unbeknownst to the user, this codec file is malicious and often serves as a dropper for other types of malware, including botnet malware (O'Dea, 2009). Downloading files from peer-to-peer filesharing networks, such as BitTorrent or Limewire, is also a common source of malware infection, with software claiming to generate serial keys for pirated programs being one of the most common vectors (Berns & Jung, 2008).

Another type of malware employing social engineering is known as fake antivirus malware. This malicious software poses as legitimate antivirus software and detects a number of non-existent malware files via a webpage after conducting a fraudulent security scan, which, upon download, it offers to remove for a fee. Oftentimes other malware is bundled with the fake antivirus software and is installed unwittingly by the victim, but is not removed after the user pays the fee (Rajab, Ballard, Mavrommatis, Provos, & Zhao, 2010). Fake antivirus malware has grown in popularity, with approximately 148,000 webpages infected with the installation scripts for this attack in 2009, and over one million consumers are believed to have purchased fraudulent antivirus software (Provos, Rajab, & Mavrommatis, 2009).

Other types of sites can also infect visitors, often automatically and without their knowledge, in a technique known as "drive by download," where malicious code hidden within websites is surreptitiously executed and installed. Recent research indicates that 5.9% of webpages on the Internet redirect to malware (Moshchuk, Bragin, Gribble, & Levy, 2006), and 1.3% of search queries to the search engine Google returned at least one result containing malicious software (Provos, Mavrommatis, Rajab, & Monrose, 2008). A 2007 study by Google indicated that approximately 10% of surveyed pages engaged in drive by download activity (Provos, McNamee, Mavrommatis, Wang, & Modadugu, 2007). These websites may have been set up by criminals for the express purpose of infecting visitors or may simply have been poorly-protected sites which were compromised by the attackers. Those sites that are expressly malicious need to find a way to appear in search engine rankings so they can infect users, and they use techniques called "search engine poisoning" or "blackhat search engine optimization (SEO)" to place their malicious links higher in search engine results, where they can be visited by many victims.

Common blackhat SEO techniques include the following: "link stuffing," or creating many fake webpages which all link back to the site containing the malware file, which fools the search engine into believing it is more popular than it really is; "keyword stuffing," where webpages are filled with bogus keywords so they appear to have relevant content to the victim's search; and numerous other techniques (Svore, Wu, Burges, & Raman, 2007). The criminals distributing the malware often use these blackhat SEO techniques to create pages with keywords relating to breaking news or hot trends, sometimes inserting sites into the first page of Google search results on the days following the breaking news story, and sometimes even within the same day (O'Dea, 2009). As an example, for 2010's World Cup, Google searches for terms related to World Cup soccer returned numerous malware results, and in some cases three of the top ten search results returned by Google were malicious (Geide, 2010). In these cases, the infected victim had not done anything wrong, but had merely clicked upon the wrong link returned by the search engine.

Another way cybercriminals often distribute malware is by using malicious advertisements, or "malvertising." These malicious advertisements are inserted into legitimate advertising networks and are displayed on major websites for maximum impact, but instead of showing an online ad, they actually infect the visitor with malware. Even The New York Times was subject to such an attack in 2009, after hackers impersonated a legitimate advertising company and purchased advertising on the website (Johnson, 2009). These malvertisements are a type of drive by download attack, but one which leverages an already-existing infrastructure created and maintained by the advertising networks to distribute their malware. It has become clear through such attacks that these advertising networks, and the sites on which they are hosted, need to do a better job in weeding out malicious advertisements to prevent their infrastructure from being leveraged to further criminal activities.

The above attacks are often extremely successful and frustrating to IT security professionals because they are user-initiated, thus circumventing common security mechanisms such as firewalls. The criminals appear to have realized that conducting attacks against monolithic targets is an expensive and inefficient proposition – now they just need to create a malicious website, conduct black hat SEO or infiltrate an advertising network, and wait for victims to come to them.

Combating Botnets: Problems and Solutions

Now that we have a basic understanding of the types of botnets and their uses by cybercriminals, and how malicious software is often loaded onto victim computers, the question remains: what can be done about them? Due to their hold upon millions of victim computers worldwide, researching and mitigating active botnets presents numerous challenges from both a legal and ethical perspective. This section will briefly discuss some of the approaches utilized by security researchers and law enforcement as well as the advantages and disadvantages of each approach.

In 2009, researchers from the University of California at Santa Barbara infiltrated a botnet known as "Torpig," which steals banking and financial information from victims, similar in many ways to the Zeus botnet described previously. The researchers were able to completely control the botnet for a total of ten days, and recorded sensitive data stolen from approximately 1.2 million victims worldwide. This stolen information provided the researchers with a large amount of data to examine numerous security problems, including rates of IP address change and corresponding impacts upon estimated botnet size, password reuse and complexity in keylogged victims, and analyses of stolen financial information (Stone-Gross et al.,

2009). While the researchers did not conduct any malicious activities with the botnet and did not try to disrupt or destroy the botnet in any way, a number of ethical issues were raised, including how to deal with the collected data, what information should be provided to law enforcement, and whether or not the experiment should have been reviewed by the university's human-subject research review board (Kemmerer, 2009). Furthermore, by controlling the botnet for the short period and capturing the financial credentials of its victims, the researchers may have in fact violated numerous laws, although they mitigated this scenario by coordinating their efforts with law enforcement (Mansfield-Devine, 2009). This example illustrates the wealth of research data which can be obtained from conducting such an infiltration, but had the researchers not coordinated their efforts with law enforcement, they may have encountered legal difficulties.

Also in 2009, researchers from the University of California at Berkeley and Carnegie Mellon University infiltrated the Mega-D spamming botnet and monitored spamming instructions issued by the command and control servers for a period of four months. The researchers developed a special bot which could participate in the network but would not send spam messages – in essence, the researchers were able to "do no harm" through their infiltration (Cho, Caballero, Grier, Paxson, & Song, 2010). Interestingly, while the researchers were conducting their examination of the botnet, the security company FireEye attempted a takedown of the Mega-D botnet by taking a number of the command and control servers and domains offline (Mushtaq, 2009). Mega-D dropped from 11.8% of all spam on the Internet to a mere 0.1% following this takedown (Larkin, 2009). However, the takedown was ultimately unsuccessful, as the Mega-D botnet rebounded after a week, climbing shortly to 17% of all spam (Cho, Caballero, Grier, Paxson, & Song, 2010). The researchers' placement inside of the Mega-D network allowed them to observe the takedown as it occurred and make recommendations for better mitigation methods.

Security researchers utilized a similar approach when examining the Storm botnet, a spam-sending network that was described earlier in this chapter. The researchers, from the University of California campuses at Berkeley and San Diego, infiltrated the Storm botnet and hijacked a portion of it to send out spam messages, in an experiment designed to test the effectiveness of spam campaigns. In this case, the researchers sent out spam messages to Internet users advertising a fake pharmaceutical website and a harmless "dummy" Trojan, to determine the number of sales and infections that a real spam campaign would experience (Kanich et al., 2008). No takedown of the infrastructure was attempted. In this case, no financial information was collected and no systems were infected by the nonfunctional "dummy" malware, which provides less of an ethical dilemma than the previous example. Spam messages were sent out to millions of users as a result of this experiment; however, the researchers argued that the spam would have been sent out anyway, and they merely modified the content of it (Kanich et al., 2008). However, the three previous examples illustrate the ease with which the researchers infiltrated these large and powerful botnets, and there is an ethical dilemma in that the research may inadvertently show more nefarious individuals how to accomplish the same tasks.

Affected organizations have utilized botnet infiltration research to conduct more effective disruption operations. The software vendor Microsoft, fed up with the amount of spam sent to its Hotmail webmail service, utilized a novel approach in combating botnets in early 2010. It filed a civil suit against the operators of the Waledac botnet, a major source of spam messages, and obtained a temporary restraining order which ordered the shutdown of 277 domain names used by Waledac controllers. This prevented hundreds of thousands of infected computers from receiving instructions from the controllers and effectively shut down the

botnet, which had sent approximately 1.5 billion spam messages each day (Whitney, 2010). Researchers from the University of Mannheim and the Technical University Vienna had previously infiltrated the Waledac botnet to analyze its spam-sending techniques (Stock, Gobel, Engelberth, Freiling, & Holz, 2009), and Microsoft contacted these researchers and asked them to assist in the active disruption of the peer-to-peer component of the botnet during the takedown, which resulted in 90% of the infected machines – at least 60,000 computers – falling under the control of the researchers and Microsoft (Kirk, 2010a). Microsoft's methodology, which combined private industry's legal efforts with academic researchers, is a unique solution to the problem of spam and may pave the way forward for future legal actions brought by private companies.

When considering law enforcement efforts, botnet takedowns have been less prevalent. Many of the criminals operating these botnets reside in Russia, the Ukraine, or other Eastern European countries, where extradition is difficult or impossible, and the legal framework to combat online crime is still evolving. Most investigative efforts focus upon the criminals operating the networks and take down the botnet infrastructure through legal means, leaving the infected users to fend for themselves. However, an example of law enforcement actively taking an interest in the infected users can be found in the Dutch National Police's 2010 dismantling of the Bredolab botnet, the dropper botnet described previously. The Dutch Police first took control of 143 command and control servers located at a provider in the Netherlands, thus seizing the botnet by force. Next, they used the botnet to upload a special program to the infected computers, which popped up a window informing the user that they were infected. This technique may have in fact violated computer crime laws, as installing unauthorized software on victim computers is a violation of laws in both the United States and United Kingdom, both of which had infected Bredolab users (Kirk, 2010b). These legislations do not allow for the use of "good" unauthorized software, and as botnets and other malicious software become even more common, the issue of uploading software which alerts the user or even removes the virus completely may need to be revisited.

From an ethical perspective, relatively little attention has been paid to the issue of botnet mitigation. Himma (2004) has addressed the issue of striking back at or simply tracing (so-called "active response") attackers who use compromised machines of infected users and the corresponding impacts that those actions may have upon the innocent victims. Although he addressed the issue of human-directed attacks and not automated malware or botnet attacks, he concluded that such actions are not ethically defensible due to the harm that could be caused to innocent computer users (Himma, 2004). Subsequent research examined the ethicality and legality of active response measures and defended their use, some of which are applicable to the issue of botnet mitigation – including collateral damage, the inadequacy of law enforcement measures, and specific legal statutes in the United States, Canada, and Europe which would likely be violated (Dittrich & Himma, 2005).

Ethics are, however, beginning to be considered when dealing with large numbers of infected victims. The ethical issue of cleaning infected computers was raised by researchers who infiltrated the Kraken spam botnet in 2008 and seized control of the main command and control server; while the researchers argued that removing the malicious software from the 1.8 million infected computers was ethically appropriate, other researchers disagreed, citing the liability that could arise if the removal process goes awry and the fact that the user would be unaware of the decision being made for them (Naraine, 2008). Dittrich, Leder, and Werner (2010) examined the infiltration of the Storm and Conficker botnets from an ethical perspective and considered the ethicality of researchers working with law enforcement, cleaning

up infected computers, and violating the privacy rights of victims to mitigate botnets. While no conclusions were drawn, a number of issues were identified which will need to be worked out within the law enforcement and researcher communities as botnet infiltration by members of these communities becomes more commonplace (Dittrich, Leder, & Werner, 2010).

OTHER CYBERCRIME TRENDS

Bulletproof Hosting Providers

Aside from botnets and malware, numerous other techniques have been active in the cybercrime realm, some of which are new, while some have been in regular use for quite awhile. One major trend worth mentioning is the use of so-called "bulletproof hosting" (BPH) companies by cybercriminals. These companies are usually incorporated in various countries and operate a web hosting and collocation business for criminals, permitting child pornography, spam, viruses, botnets, and other illegal content to be hosted upon their servers, which are located in legitimate datacenters throughout the world. The term "bulletproof" is used because these companies often promise that their customers' sites will remain up and running, even if abuse complaints are received (Stone-Gross, Kruegel, Almeroth, Moser, & Kirda, 2009).

One of the first BPH providers to make headlines was the now-infamous Russian Business Network (RBN). This network, based in St. Petersburg, Russia, hosted many illegal botnets, child pornography, financial-theft Trojans, and other items, and was disconnected from the Internet in 2007 by backbone carriers after media and research reports shined a spotlight on its activities (Bizeul, 2007). Another major BPH, the California-based but Russian-owned McColo Corporation, hosted numerous botnets and was found to cater almost exclusively to cybercriminals. This BPH was taken offline by its upstream providers in late 2008, in an action similar to that taken against RBN, after The Washington Post published an exposé describing the company's activities. This takedown severely crippled a number of major spam botnets, including Srizbi, thought to be the source of 50% of all spam and which never recovered (Bleaken, 2010). Following McColo's shutdown, global spam levels were found to drop by two-thirds, although they recovered soon thereafter (Krebs, 2008). In both of these takedowns, law enforcement was silent, relying instead upon the security community and the media to remove these providers.

A third major BPH takedown, however, did involve law enforcement. In 2009, the US Federal Trade Commission filed suit against another California-based BPH, which was known as Pricewert LLC and Triple Fiber Networks (3FN). The FTC, assisted by federal law enforcement and security researchers, alleged that 3FN protected its criminal clients, who were hosting child pornography, botnets, spam, and spyware, by ignoring abuse notices issued by anti-spam organizations and security researchers. The operators of 3FN also actively participated in the management of botnets, according to transcripts of chats between the senior management of 3FN and botherders obtained by the FTC. The civil suit filed by the FTC also seized and forfeited 3FN's computer servers and other assets, and eventually won a $1.08 million judgment again the firm (USFTC, 2010). Unfortunately, the criminals appeared to learn from the takedown of McColo, and spam levels suffered only a small drop, with some of the affected botnets rebounding the following day (Bleaken, 2010). This indicates that botnet operators have since become more decentralized in their hosting, choosing to host their servers at numerous providers instead of all at one provider like McColo.

Despite these successes, numerous internet service providers still appear to be havens for criminal activity (Stone-Gross, Kruegel, Almeroth, Moser, & Kirda, 2009). This may be because BPH companies can charge premiums for hosting criminal web content, indicating that it is still a lucrative business. Internet service providers also have some legal liability protections from the activities of their customers (Yen, 2000), which may shield them from enforcement action by government agencies. Indeed, to bring criminal or civil charges like in the case of 3FN, the government would need to show knowledge or intent on the part of the provider, which can be difficult without evidence such as chat transcripts which directly implicate the BPH's employees. As the cases of McColo and RBN have shown, however, the BPH companies and their upstream service providers are not immune to the threat of bad press, which may continue to be a useful method for dealing with BPH firms and the criminal activity they enable.

When considering takedowns of BPH providers, some ethical considerations should be taken into account. For example, what did these takedowns actually accomplish? It is true that Srizbi was forced offline, and that loss estimates for the criminals range in the hundreds of thousands to millions of dollars in lost revenues (Bleaken, 2010). Spam levels also dropped temporarily, providing some relief to users and system administrators. However, no known arrests or prosecutions have arisen from any of these takedowns, meaning that the criminals behind both the botnets and BPHs have likely continued their criminal activities. Any botnets which were taken offline, like Srizbi, either recovered or were replaced by new botnets. Furthermore, these shutdowns may actually damage US law enforcement efforts in the long run, by pushing the servers that criminals are using for illegal activity to hosting providers overseas, out of reach of the US legal process. While investigators do have some options for dealing with overseas evidence through the Mutual Legal Assistance Treaty (MLAT) process, these efforts can often be very slow, increasing the risk that the evidence may have disappeared before the host country receives the request. As this discussion has shown, the issue of combating BPH providers is not simple, and like the discussion of the ethics of botnet remediation will require closer study and cooperation between security researchers and law enforcement.

Money Mule Networks

As previously described, a common malware or botnet attack involves financial theft, oftentimes directly from the bank accounts of victims. These accounts may have been accessed by criminals using phished or keylogged banking credentials, or like in the case of Zeus, may have been directly accessed from an infected machine. The mechanics of stealing thousands of dollars from a compromised account introduce some logistical challenges for the criminals. Like a traditional bank robbery, a cybercriminal needs a "getaway driver" – a person who can move money from the stolen account and eventually provide that money to the criminal. This has necessitated the need for networks of "money mules," often unwitting persons who receive stolen funds and then wire them to criminals, or even other money mules to add additional layers of obfuscation.

Money mules are often recruited by answering online job advertisements, either sent by spam or posted online on job recruitment websites. These mules are presented with a work-from-home job as a "transaction processor" or "sales executive." They are told that they will receive money via their bank accounts – payments for goods sold by the nonexistent business they are employed by – and are to wire the money overseas, using services such as Western Union. After they have been sent funds stolen from a compromised account and have wired the money to the criminals, the theft is usually discovered and the money is withdrawn out of their accounts. Unfortunately for the mules, wire transfers via Western Union cannot be recalled, meaning that the mule is often held liable for the stolen funds (Moore, Clayton, & Anderson, 2009).

The networks employed by these money mule recruitment systems are quite sophisticated, employing professionally-designed websites, attention from "supervisors," and daily instructions. The operators often scour online resume sites and contact potential mules directly, offering the mules a commission on the money transferred. One bank account heist may involve dozens of mules working simultaneously, each receiving ten thousand dollars or less (Krebs, 2009). In a very real sense, these mules are often victims themselves, especially considering the fact that they are often liable for the funds they receive, and have not generally been prosecuted due to their lack of criminal intent. While arresting and prosecuting unwitting money mules may have a deterrent effect, the prosecutorial ethics and feasibility of arresting a crime victim are uncertain. However, recent Zeus-related arrests in the US of criminally-complicit money mules, and the operators of mule recruitment networks in the United Kingdom, may increase awareness of the scam (Kaplan, 2010).

West African Scams

The issue of West African, and specifically Nigerian, scams is an old one, dating back to the 1980s, and at first glance may seem to have little applicability to a discussion of emerging cybercrime trends. However, these criminals have continued to evolve with technology, and are now utilizing a number of modern techniques. Historically, victims of Nigerian advance fee fraud scams (or "419" scams – for the applicable section of the Nigerian Criminal Code) receive a solicitation via email informing them of one of a number of claims: that they have won a lottery; that a banker is trying to steal money from the account of a recently-deceased wealthy individual and needs the victim's help in posing as a relative; or that a corrupt government official is stealing from a program or fund and requests that the victim offer their bank account to receive the stolen funds, in exchange for a cut of the proceeds. The scammers then attempt to obtain money from the victim to help facilitate the transaction, starting small but increasing over time (Holt & Graves, 2007). The techniques employed by these scammers, who do indeed often reside in Nigeria, have been well-reported but continue to be successful.

However, Nigerian and other West African cybercriminals have begun to change their tactics, employing modern cybercrime techniques such as phishing for bank credentials and the subsequent theft from online bank accounts (Longe, Ngwa, Wada, Mbarika, & Kvasny, 2009). Nigerian criminals have also begun using money mule "work at home" scams to move money stolen from these accounts (Economic Times, 2010), a process which likely requires collaboration amongst many fraudsters – those who set up phishing sites, those who move money from the bank accounts, those who deal with the mules, and finally, those who pick up the money that the mules wire to them. Finally, Nigerian criminals have also started to branch out into other forms of cybercrime, including identity theft via malware (Gaudin, 2008).

The impact of these crimes upon Nigeria, and other West African nations, has been unprecedented and disastrous. Anticorruption organizations have declared Nigeria as one of the most corrupt countries worldwide, and Nigeria's banking system has been effectively demolished, with other countries refusing to honor its bank drafts or other paper financial instruments. Furthermore, Nigerian service providers have been added to numerous spam blacklists, meaning that many non-Nigerian service providers will not accept email at all from Nigerian customers (Balogun & Obe, 2010). To combat this, the Nigerian government has recently set up a dedicated cybercrime prosecution unit to take Nigerian cybercrime investigations beyond the standard advance fee fraud scams that are regularly investigated (Balal, 2010). Arrests and prosecutions of Nigerian cybercriminals are still relatively rare, but some successes have been observed (Gaudin, 2008), indicating that international law enforcement agencies are increasing their cooperation with Nigerian investigators.

FUTURE RESEARCH DIRECTIONS

Based upon the preceding discussion of cybercrime trends, a number of further research directions are warranted. First, as the description of the interrelatedness of botnets, malware, infection methods, bulletproof hosting companies, and money mule networks above has shown, modern cybercrime is becoming increasingly connected and organized. However, while a large amount of research has been conducted on computer crime and traditional organized crime in general, only basic, exploratory research has been conducted into organized cybercrime groups and their techniques (Choo, 2008), with in-depth ethnographic research still lacking. Furthermore, while there exists a great body of literature regarding the technical aspects of botnets and malware, little research has been conducted regarding the individuals who utilize these tools – there is little understanding of their motivations, organizational structure, and any possible deterrent methods. As the amount of crime which occurs online continues to increase, a greater understanding is needed of ways to de-incentivize the financial impetus which drives individuals to commit these crimes, and there appears to be a need for social, economic, and organizational science research into online cybercrime activities, their causes, and possible solutions.

CONCLUSION

This chapter introduced the IS practitioner and researcher to a number of emergent cybercrime trends, including botnet types and infection methods, bulletproof hosting, money mule networks, and West African cybercrime, and described a number of the technical, legal, and ethical challenges surrounding each. While this chapter did not attempt to describe the entire universe of cybercrime – such a description could easily fill a book – the chapter did detail many of the common techniques employed by cybercriminals, many of which have likely touched the life of the reader in some fashion. Unfortunately, as this chapter has shown, cybercrime is a lucrative business and appears likely to continue to increase. Practitioners and researchers need to be aware of these trends and the impacts they may have upon their businesses and organizations. Furthermore, individuals tasked with protecting organizations from cybercrime, as well as those who investigate it, should remember that there is more to cybercrime than just technical aspects, and that social and economic aspects need to be considered as well.

REFERENCES

Aaron, G. (2010). The state of phishing. *Computer Fraud & Security*, *6*, 5–8. doi:10.1016/S1361-3723(10)70065-8

Adair, S., Deilbert, R., Rohozinski, R., Villeneuve, N., & Walton, G. (2009). *Shadows in the cloud: Investigating cyber espionage 2.0*. Retrieved October 27, 2010 from http: //www.scribd. com/doc/29435784/ shadows-in-the-cloud- Investigating-CyberEspionage-2-0

Arnell, P., & Reid, A. (2009). Hackers beware: The cautionary story of Gary McKinnon. *Information & Communications Technology Law*, *18*(1), 1–12. doi:10.1080/13600830902727822

Arnold, W. (2000, August 22). Philippines to drop charges on e-mail virus. *The New York Times*. Retrieved September 15, 2010 from http: //www. nytimes. com/2000/08/22/business/ technology-philippines-to-drop- charges-on-e-mail-virus. html

Balal, A. (2010, August 20). Nigeria: FG to set up cyber crime prosecution unit. *Daily Trust*. Retrieved October 29, 2010, from http: //allafrica. com/stories/ 201008200780.html

Balogun, V. F., & Obe, O. O. (2010). E-crime in Nigeria: Trends, tricks, and treatment. *Pacific Journal of Science and Technology*, *11*(1), 343–355.

Banday, M. T., Qadri, J. A., & Shah, N. A. (2009). Study of botnets and their threats to Internet security. *Sprouts: Working Papers on Information Systems*, *9*(24). Retrieved from http://sprouts. aisnet.org/9-24

Bell, R. E. (2002). The prosecution of computer crime. *Journal of Financial Crime*, *9*(4), 308–325. doi:10.1108/eb026030

Berners-Lee, T., Cailliau, R., Luotonen, A., Nielsen, H. F., & Secret, A. (1994). The World Wide Web. *Communications of the ACM*, *37*(8), 76–82. doi:10.1145/179606.179671

Berns, A., & Jung., E. (2008). *Searching for malware in Bit-Torrent*. Technical report, University of Iowa, April 24.

Bishop, M. (2000). *Analysis of the ILOVEYOU worm*. Retrieved September 15, 2010, from http: //nob.cs.ucdavis. edu/classes/ecs155-2005-04/ handouts/iloveyou.pdf

Bizeul, D. (2007). *RBN study – Before and after*. Retrieved October 27, 2010, from http: //www. cytrap. eu/files/EU-IST/2007/ pdf/2007-12RussianBusiness NetworkStudy.pdf

Bleaken, D. (2010). Botwars: The fight against criminal cyber networks. *Computer Fraud & Security*.

Bossler, A. M., & Holt, T. J. (2009). On-line activities, guardianship, and malware infection: An examination of routine activities theory. *International Journal of Cyber Criminology*, *3*(1), 400–420.

Carr, J. (2008, March 4). TRACE: Six botnets generate 85 percent of spam. *SC Magazine*. Retrieved October 15, 2010, from http: //www. scmagazineus. com/trace-six-botnets -generate-85-percent-of-spam/ article/107603/

Cho, C. Y., Caballero, J., Grier, C., Paxson, V., & Song, D. (2010). Insights from the inside: A view of botnet management from infiltration. *Proceedings of the Third USENIX Workshop on Large-Scale Exploits and Emergent Threats*, San Jose, CA.

Choo, K. R. (2008). Organised crime groups in cyberspace: A typology. *Trends in Organized Crime*, *11*, 270–295. doi:10.1007/s12117-008-9038-9

Cohen, F. (1987). Computer viruses: Theory and experiments. *Computers & Security*, *6*, 22–35. doi:10.1016/0167-4048(87)90122-2

Damle, P. (2002). Social engineering: A tip of the iceberg. *Information Systems Control Journal, 2*.

Dittrich, D., & Himma, K. E. (2005). Active response to computer intrusions. In H. Bidgoli (Ed.), *The handbook of information security* (664-681). New York, NY: Wiley.

Dittrich, D., Leder, F., & Werner, T. (2010). A case study in ethical decision making regarding remote mitigation of botnets. *Lecture Notes in Computer Science, 6054*, 216–230. doi:10.1007/978-3-642-14992-4_20

Economic Times. (2010, February 17). Money mules on the rise as e-fraud thrives in India. *The Economic Times*. Retrieved October 27, 2010, from http: //economictimes.indiatimes. com/news/news-by-industry/jobs /Money-mules-on-the-rise-as-e-fraud- thrives-in-India/article-show/5584246.cms

Everett, C. (2009). The lucrative world of cyber-espionage. *Computer Fraud & Security*, *7*, 5–7. doi:10.1016/S1361-3723(09)70084-3

Garber, L. (1999). Melissa virus creates a new type of threat. *IEEE Computer*, *32*(6), 16–19.

Gardner, E. P., Samuels, L. B., Render, B., & Coffinberger, R. L. (1989). The importance of ethical standards and computer crime laws for data security. *Information Systems Management*, *6*(4), 42–50. doi:10.1080/07399018908960171

Gaudin, S. (2008, May 1). Nigerian gets 18 months for cyberattack on NASA employee. *Computer-World*. Retrieved October 29, 2010, from http: //www.computerworld. com/s/article/9081838/ Nigerian_gets_18_months_for_cyberattack_on_NASA_employee

Geide, M. (2010, June 21). *World Cup, black hat SEO list*. Retrieved October 29, 2010, from http: //research.zscaler. com/2010/06/world-cup -black-hat-seo-list.html

Goodin, D. (2010, March 2). Authorities dismantle botnet with 13 million infected PCs. *The Register*. Retrieved October 1, 2010, from http: //www.theregister.co. uk/2010/03/02/mariposa_botnet_takedown/

Gu, G., Zhang, J., & Lee, W. (2008). Botsniffer: Detecting botnet command and control channels in network traffic. *Proceedings of the 2008 Network and IT Security Conference*, San Diego, CA.

Gupta, M., & Sharman, R. (2006). Social network theoretic framework for organizational social engineering susceptibility index. *AMCIS 2006 Proceedings*, Paper 408.

Highland, H. J. (1997). A history of computer viruses – Introduction. *Computers & Security*, *16*, 412–415. doi:10.1016/S0167-4048(97)82245-6

Himma, K. E. (2004). The ethics of tracing hacker attacks through the machines of innocent persons. *International Journal of Information Ethics*, *2*, 1–13.

Hines, M. (2009, October 23). Botnet click fraud problem growing. *eWeek Security Watch.* Retrieved October 15, 2010, from http: //security-watch.eweek. com/click_fraud/botnet_clickfraud _problem_growing.html

Hoath, P., & Mulhall, T. (1998a). Hacking: motivation and deterrence, part I. *Computer Fraud & Security*, *4*, 16–19. doi:10.1016/S1361-3723(97)86611-0

Holt, T. J., & Graves, D. C. (2007). A qualitative analysis of advance fee fraud e-mail schemes. *International Journal of Cyber Criminology*, *1*(1), 137–154.

Hong, H. (1997). Hacking through the Computer Fraud and Abuse Act. *U.C. Davis Law Review*, *31*, 283–308.

Ianelli, N., & Hackworth, A. (2006). Botnets as a vehicle for online crime. *Proceedings of the International Conference on Forensic Computer Science*, Brasila, Brasil.

Immorlica, N., Jain, K., Mahdian, M., & Talwar, K. (2005). Click fraud resistant methods for learning click-through rates. *Lecture Notes in Computer Science*, *3828*, 34–45. doi:10.1007/11600930_5

Jansen, B. J. (2007). Click fraud. *IEEE Computer*, *40*(7), 85–86.

Johnson, B. (2009, September 25). Internet companies face up to malvertising threat. *The Guardian*. Retrieved October 27, 2010, from http: //www.guardian.co. uk/technology/2009/sep/ 25/ malvertising

Juels, A., Stamm, S., & Jakobsson, M. (2007). Combating click fraud via premium clicks. *Proceedings of the 16th USENIX Security Symposium*, Boston, MA.

Kaplan, J. A. (2010, September 30). FBI charges dozens in global computer virus scam. *Fox News*. Retrieved October 28, 2010, from http: //www. foxnews. com/scitech/2010/ 09/30/fbi-charges-dozens-global-virus-scam/

Kemmerer, R. A. (2009). How to steal a botnet and what can happen when you do. *Proceedings of the 11th International Conference on Information and Communications Security*, Beijing, China.

Kirk, J. (2010a, February 25). Microsoft recruited top notch guns for Waledac takedown. *PCWorld*. Retrieved October 15, 2010, from http: //www. pcworld. com/businesscenter/article/190234/ microsoft_recruited_top_notch_guns_for_wale-dac_takedown.html

Kirk, J. (2010b, October 26). Did Dutch police break the law taking down a botnet? *PCWorld*. Retrieved October 29, 2010, from http: //www. pcworld. com/businesscenter/article/208825 / did_dutch_police_break_the_ law_taking_ down_a_botnet.html

Krebs, B. (2008, November 12). Spam volumes drop by two-thirds after firm goes offline. *The Washington Post*. Retrieved October 27, 2010, from http: //voices.washingtonpost. com/securi-tyfix/2008/11/spam_volumes_drop_by_23_after. html

Krebs, B. (2009, September 24). Money mule recruitment network exposed. *The Washington Post*. Retrieved October 27, 2010, from http: // voices.washingtonpost. com/securityfix/2009/09/ money_ mule_recruitment_101.html

Krebs, B. (2010, February 24). N.Y. firm faces bankruptcy from $164,000 e-banking loss. *KrebsOnSecurity*. Retrieved September 15, 2010, from http: //krebsonsecurity. com/2010/02/n-y-firm-faces-bankruptcy-from -164000-e-banking-loss/

Kreibich, C., Kanich, C., Levchenko, K., Enright, B., Voelker, G. M., Paxson, V., & Savage, S. (2009). Spamcraft: An inside look at spam campaign orchestration. *Proceedings of the 2nd USENIX Workshop on Large-scale Exploits and Emergent Threats*, Boston, MA.

Larking, E. (2009, December 27). Good guys bring down the Mega-D botnet. *PC World*. Retrieved October 1, 2010 from http: //www.pcworld. com/article/185122/ good_guys_bring_down_ the_megad_botnet.html

Leeson, P. T., & Coyne, C. J. (2005). The economics of computer hacking. *Journal of Law, Economics, &. Policy, 1*, 511–532.

Leung, R. (2004, October 20). Kevin Mitnick: Cyberthief. *60 Minutes*. Retrieved September 1, 2010, from http: //www.cbsnews. com/stories/2004/10/ 20/60II/main650428.shtml

Longe, O., Ngwa, O., Wada, F., Mbarika, V., & Kvasny, L. (2009). Criminal uses of information & communication technologies in sub-Saharan Africa: Trends, concerns, and perspectives. *Journal of Information Technology Impact, 9*(3), 155–172.

Majumdar, S., Kulkarni, D., & Ravishankar, C. V. (2007). Addressing click fraud in content delivery systems. *Proceedings of the 26th IEEE International Conference on Computer Communications*, Anchorage, AK.

Mansfield-Devine, S. (2009). Hacking the hackers. *Computer Fraud & Security, 6*, 10–13. doi:10.1016/S1361-3723(09)70073-9

Manske, K. (2000). An introduction to social engineering. *Information Systems Security, 9*(5), 53–59. doi:10.1201/1086/43312.9.5.20001112/ 31378.10

Markoff, J. (1990, May 5). Computer intruder is put on probation and fined $10,000. *The New York Times*. Retrieved September 1, 2010, from http: //www.nytimes. com/1990/05/05/us/computer-intruder-is-put-on-probation -and-fined-10000. html

Marks, P. (2010, October 12). Why the Stuxnet worm is like nothing seen before. *The New Scientist*. Retrieved October 20, 2010, from http: // www.newscientist. com/article/dn19504 -why-the-stuxnet-worm -is-like-nothing-seen- before. html?full=true

Moore, T., Clayton, R., & Anderson, R. (2009). The economics of online crime. *The Journal of Economic Perspectives, 23*(3), 3–20. doi:10.1257/ jep.23.3.3

Moshchuk, A., Bragin, T., Gribble, S. D., & Levy, H. M. (2006). A crawler-based study of spyware on the web. *Proceedings of the 13th Annual Network and Distributed System Security Symposium*, San Diego, CA.

Mushtaq, A. (2009, November 6). *Smashing the mega-D/Ozdok botnet in 24 hours*. FireEye Malware Intelligence Lab. Retrieved October 20, 2010, from http: //blog.fireeye. com/research/2009/11/ smashing-the-ozdok.html

Naraine, R. (2008, May 1). Kraken botnet infiltration triggers ethics debate. *eWeek*. Retrieved October 15, 2010, from http: //www.eweek. com/c/a/Security/ Kraken-Botnet- Infiltration-Triggers-Ethics-Debate/

Naumov, V. (2003). Legal aspects of spam in Russia. *Legal Russia*. Retrieved October 1, 2010, from http: //www.law.edu. ru/doc/document. asp?docID=1237554

Nazario, J. (2007). *BlackEnergy DDoS bot analysis*. Technical report, Arbor Networks, October 2007.

Nazario, J. (2009). *Twitter-based botnet command channel*. Retrieved September 20, 2010, from http: //asert.arbornetworks. com/2009/08/ twitter- based-botnet-command- channel/

O'Dea, H. (2009). The modern rogue – Malware with a face. *Proceedings of the 2009 Virus Bulletin Conference*, Geneva, Switzerland.

Ollman, G. (2008). The evolution of commercial malware development kits and colour-by-numbers custom malware. *Computer Fraud & Security*, (9): 4–7. doi:10.1016/S1361-3723(08)70135-0

Orman, H. (2003). The Morris Worm: A fifteen year perspective. *IEEE Security & Privacy, 1*(5), 35–43. doi:10.1109/MSECP.2003.1236233

Paulson, R. A., & Weber, J. E. (2006). Cyberextortion: An overview of distributed denial service attacks against online gaming companies. *Issues in Information Systems, 7*(2), 52–56.

Podgor, E. S. (2002). International computer fraud: A paradigm for limiting national jurisdiction. *U.C. Davis Law Review, 35*, 267–317.

Porras, P., Saidi, H., & Yegneswaran, V. (2007). A multi-perspective analysis of the Storm (Peacomm) Worm. Technical report, SRI International (October 2007).

Prince, B. (2009, April 22). Finjan reveals 1.9 million-strong botnet at RSA. *eWeek.com*. Retrieved October 1, 2010, from http: //www.eweek. com/c/a/Security/ Finjan-Reveals-19-million-Strong-Botnet-at- RSA-502336/

Provos, N., Mavrommatis, P., Rajab, M. A., & Monrose, F. (2008). All your iFRAMES point to us. *Proceedings of the 17th USENIX Security Symposium*, 1-15, San Jose, CA.

Provos, N., McNamee, D., Mavrommatis, P., Wang, K., & Modadugu, N. (2007). The ghost in the browser: Analysis of Web-based malware. *Proceedings of the First Workshop on Hot Topics in Understanding Botnets*, Cambridge, MA.

Provos, N., Rajab, M. A., & Mavrommatis, P. (2009). Cybercrime 2.0: When the cloud turns dark. *Communications of the ACM, 52*(4), 42–47. doi:10.1145/1498765.1498782

Rajab, M. A., Ballard, L., Mavrommatis, P., Provos, N., & Zhao, X. (2010). The nocebo effect on the Web: An analysis of fake anti-virus distribution. *Proceedings of the 3rd USENIX Workshop on Large-Scale Exploits and Emergent Threats*, San Jose, CA.

Richardson, R. (2008). *2008 CSI computer crime & security survey*. Retrieved October 8, 2009, from http: //i.cmpnet. com/v2.gocsi.com /pdf/ CSIsurvey2008.pdf

Rusch, J. J. (1999). The social engineering of Internet fraud. *Proceedings of the Internet Global Summit (INET99)*, San Jose, CA. Retrieved from http: //www.isoc. org/inet99/proceedings/ 3g/3g_2.htm

Salifu, A. (2008). The impact of Internet crime on development. *Journal of Financial Crime, 15*(4), 432–443. doi:10.1108/13590790810907254

Stock, B., Gobel, J., Engelberth, M., Freiling, F. C., & Holz, T. (2009). Walowdac – Analysis of a peer-to-peer botnet. *Proceedings of the 2009 European Conference on Computer Network Defense*, (pp. 13-20). Milano, Italy.

Stone-Gross, B., Cova, M., Cavallaro, L., Gilbert, B., Szydlowski, M., & Kemmerer, R. ... Vigna, G. (2009). Your botnet is my botnet: Analysis of a botnet takeover. *Proceedings of the 16th ACM Conference on Computer and Communications Security*, (pp. 635-647). Chicago, IL.

Stone-Gross, B., Kruegel, C., Almeroth, K., Moser, A., & Kirda, E. (2009). FIRE: Finding rogue networks. *Proceedings of the 2009 Computer Security Applications Conference*, (pp. 231-240). Honolulu, HI.

Svore, K. M., Wu, Q., Burges, C. J. C., & Raman, A. (2007). Improving Web spam classification using rank-time features. *Proceedings of the 2rd International Workshop on Adversarial Information Retrieval on the Web*, (pp. 9-16). Banff, Canada.

US Department of Justice. (2002, May 1). *Creator of Melissa virus sentenced to 20 months in federal prison*. Retrieved September 1, 2010, from http://www.justice. gov/criminal/cybercrime/ melissaSent.htm

US Federal Trade Commission. (2004, April 29). *FTC announces first Can-Spam Act cases*. Retrieved September 15, 2010, from http://www. ftc. gov/opa/2004/04/ 040429canspam.shtm

US Federal Trade Commission. (2010, May 19). *FTC permanently shuts down notorious rogue Internet service provider*. Retrieved October 18, 2010, from http://www.ftc. gov/opa/2010/05/ perm.shtm

Villeneuve, N. (2010). *Koobface: Inside a crimeware network*. Retrieved January 10, 2011, from http://www.infowar-monitor. net/reports/ iwm-koobface.pdf

Weber, T. (2007, January 25). Criminals may overwhelm the Web. *BBC News*. Retrieved October 3, 2010, from http://news.bbc.co. uk/2/hi/business/ 6298641.stm

Whitney, L. (2010, February 25). With legal nod, Microsoft ambushes Waledac botnet. *CNet News*. Retrieved October 20, 2010, from http://news. cnet.com/ 8301-1009_3-10459558-83.html

Yen, A. C. (2000). Internet service provider liability for subscriber copyright infringement, enterprise liability, and the First Amendment. *The Georgetown Law Journal, 88*, 1–56.

Zhang, L., & Guan, Y. (2008). Detecting click fraud in pay-per-click streams of online advertising networks. *Proceedings of the 28th International Conference on Distributed Computing Systems*, (pp. 77-84). Beijing, China.

KEY TERMS AND DEFINITIONS

Botnet: A ro*bot net*work, or a network of compromised computer systems linked together for a common purpose.

Bulletproof Hosting Provider: An internet service provider which caters exclusively to cybercriminals, and shields them from legal requests.

Cybercrime: Also referred to as computer crime, or computer-based criminal activity.

Distributed Denial of Service Attack (DDoS): An attack, often orchestrated by a botnet, which targets websites or computer servers with floods of requests, in order to overwhelm the targeted system and drive it offline.

Malware: Also referred to as malicious software, or software which is installed without authorization upon a victim computer that has a malicious or criminal purpose.

Malvertisement: A malicious advertisement, placed by criminals, which redirects visitors to malware. These advertisements are often placed into legitimate online advertising networks and may be displayed on unwitting third-party websites.

Virus: A type of malware, which spreads in an automated fashion between vulnerable computers, much like a biological virus does with living creatures.

Chapter 4
Law and Technology at Crossroads in Cyberspace:
Where Do We Go From Here?

Anteneh Ayanso
Brock University, Canada

Tejaswini Herath
Brock University, Canada

ABSTRACT

Historical incidents have taught organizations several key lessons on computer crimes. The complexity of the current technology environment dictates that no one mechanism can effectively address computer crimes. Investing in the most sophisticated counter-technologies alone is not enough to fight cyber threats. Thus it has become increasingly important for organizations and governments to establish control frameworks that incorporate proactive measures in the technological, legislative, and administrative dimensions. While it is government's role to keep up with the legislative rules, organizations need to have the right security policies and guidelines in place as well as develop awareness in the legal front to combat computer crimes. With the review of the academic literature, industry reports, and the media, this chapter identifies various kinds of computer crimes and discusses the counter strategies to tackle such crimes in the legal, technological, and organizational dimensions.

INTRODUCTION

Computer crime has evolved to be a serious problem that deserves attention. The Internet enabled environment facilitates many flexible work opportunities for employees allowing them to work away from their desks. Telecommuting, working from home, remote computing while travelling is becoming common occurrence in many organizations. Thus organizations are subjected to a wide range of computer crimes through their personnel that are directed towards organizations as well as public mass in general. Employees as well as managers need to be aware of these issues and have a clear understanding of the various types

DOI: 10.4018/978-1-61350-132-0.ch004

of cyber threats in the current environment and how they could be controlled.

Computer crime varies significantly from one context to another depending on what scope (individual, organization, or society) it focuses on or even which country it refers to. Today, the Internet influences every activity of our life. As the number of transactional, communicative and distributional aspects of our lives goes online, higher is our vulnerability to cybercrime. The kind of crimes that are committed in the cyberspace are several and diverse, capable of causing serious damages to both person and property ranging from reputational harm, privacy violations, cyber stalking to intellectual property violations, economic fraud and security breaches, to name only a few. Worst still, detecting the cyber criminal in the online environment is subject to technological sophistication and knowledge which not all law enforcement agencies have the capacity to do. With the multitude of advantages that the Internet brings with it, this represents the darker side of this marvelous technology.

The evolution of the Internet to the current state of social media further complicates the ethical and legal conundrums that arise in various settings. The issue with WikiLeaks exemplifies how far the Internet can expose the world and the complexity of the social, ethical and legal debates that arise. For example, how do we maintain a balance between the right to information and the right to privacy? How much does copyright as an intellectual property right have a meaning in the current social media environment? Where does one draw the line between free speech and online defamation given that Internet allows one to reach a mass audience with little or no cost and almost anonymously? Thus, technology and law have a very complex relationship. Law attempts to closely observe the ways and means by which technology can be used to achieve unethical ends and outlaws the same by codifying such practice. However, technology moves at too fast a pace that the legal statutes cannot always catch up to it in time. New genre of crimes is being discovered on

the Internet and accordingly we have to update our statutes and develop alternative mechanisms to overcome these threats. The list of cybercrimes is also in a nascent stage and continues to evolve as the bridge between our physical world and cyber world shrinks at an increasingly rapid pace. Thus, the challenge for managers today is to monitor progress and update the measures in all angles – technological, organizational, and legal. This chapter attempts to contribute towards this direction and provides an overview of computer crimes, examines the possible impacts of computer crimes at various contexts, and discusses alternative control mechanisms.

COMPUTER CRIME: AN OVERVIEW

The term computer crime has been given several labels, such as cybercrime, e-crime, hi-tech crime, electronic crime, etc. Today there are a variety of computer crimes at different scopes and contexts, and there is a lack of standardized classifications or definitions for many of the activities that could be considered illegal. Computer crime brings tremendous harm to both the public and organizations. For individuals, computer crimes can attack privacy, identity, and personal property. For the public and government, computer crimes can destroy infrastructure and administrative systems and can threaten national security.

Definition

Given the complexity and diversity of computer crimes in the current environment, no definition can comprehensively describe it (Gordon & Ford, 2006; Goodman, 2010). Gordon and Ford (2006) define computer crime as "any crime that is facilitated or committed using a computer, network, or hardware device".

According to the U.S. Department of Justice (DOJ), computer crime is defined as "any violations of criminal law that involve knowledge of computer technology for their perpetration, investigation, or prosecution" (Volonino & Robinson, 2004, p. 155).

According to the 2002 report by Statistics Canada, there was no single definition of cybercrime that the majority of police departments used (Kowalski, 2002). Cybercrime is a broadly used term to describe criminal activity committed on computers or the Internet. Canadian law enforcement agencies accepted the definition: "a criminal offence involving a computer as the object of the crime, or the tool used to commit a material component of the offence." In similar vein, Foreign Affairs and International Trade Canada discusses cyber crime as consisting of specific crimes dealing with computers and networks (such as hacking) and the facilitation of traditional crime through the use of computers (child pornography, hate crimes, telemarketing /Internet fraud). They also discuss "computer-supported crime" which covers the use of computers by criminals for communication and document or data storage, the activities which might not be illegal in and of themselves, but are often invaluable in the investigation of actual crimes. (Foreign Affairs and International Trade Canada, n.d.)

Classification

In an attempt to classify the cybercrimes, Gordon and Ford (2006) describe them as Type I and Type II. According to their classification, the characteristics of Type I crime include the following:

- It is generally a singular or discrete event from the perspective of the victim.
- It often is facilitated by the introduction of crimeware programs such as keystroke loggers, viruses, rootkits or Trojan horses into the user's computer system.
- The introductions can, but may not necessarily be, facilitated by vulnerabilities.

Type I crimes require that data be protected from common threats such as viruses and worms, but also that users be aware of the risks or "vulner-

abilities". Examples include phishing attempts, theft or manipulation of data or services via hacking or viruses, identity theft, and bank or e-commerce fraud based upon stolen credentials (Gordon & Ford, 2006).

The description of Type II cybercrime, on the other hand, includes activities such as cyberstalking and harassment, child predation, extortion, blackmail, stock market manipulation. The key characteristics of Type II crime are the following:

- It is generally facilitated by programs that do not fit under the classification crimeware. For example, conversations may take place using IM (Instant Messaging) clients or files may be transferred using the FTP protocol.
- There are generally repeated contacts or events from the perspective of the user.

Gordon and Ford (2006) also emphasize that cybercrime presents a continuum ranging from crime which is almost entirely technological in nature and crime which is entirely people-related. Thus, very few events can be purely Type I or Type II, representing either end of a continuum.

While computer crime encompasses a broad range of potentially illegal activities, broadly, it may be divided into one of two types of categories: (1) crimes that target computer networks or devices directly – computer is an object of attack; (2) crimes facilitated by computer networks or devices – where computer is a subject of an attack and the primary target of which is independent of the computer network or device (Whitman & Mattord, 2008).

New technologies have created criminal opportunities by creating new types of crimes as well as by new ways of committing the crimes which had existed before the Internet. Most cybercrimes involve attack on information about individuals, corporations, or governments (Cybercrime, 2010). These attacks do not take place on a physical or terrestrial space; rather the personal or corporate virtual body composed of a set of informational attributes that define individuals or institutions on the Internet. On individual level, in the digital age our virtual identities have become an essential element of everyday life. These identities which embody a package of numbers and identifiers exist in multiple computer databases owned by governments and corporations. As the privacy advocates alarm us, we often give out our names, address and phone numbers without a second thought (Office of the Privacy Commissioner of Canada, 2001). This can have devastating impact not only on individuals, but also on corporations. New scams such as spear phishing, where employees may give out their logon credentials and thus inadvertently giving a free pass to cyber criminals, have become a real concern for security managers. Thus, examples of crimes that merely use computer networks or devices would include: cyber stalking, fraud, identity theft, phishing scams as well as information warfare, whereas examples of crimes that primarily target computer networks or devices would include: computer viruses, worms, malware (malicious code), and denial-of-service attacks etc.

In general, organizations are plagued with a variety of threats that arise from internal sources as well as external sources, from deliberate human acts or naive mistakes, from natural sources or human failures of designs in hardware or software. Forces of nature such as floods, ice storms, earthquakes etc. are among the most disruptive threats which disturb not only individual lives, but also information systems and storages. There are various types of technical failures related to hardware, software, services and power. Technical hardware failures may occur because of manufacturing flaws that can cause system to perform outside of expected parameters, resulting in unreliable or poor service. Hardware failures such as hard drive failures are examples of this type of threat. While some of the failures are intermittent; some can be terminal. Potential deviations in the Internet service as well as power irregularities can dramatically affect availability of information and systems. Technical software failures often occur due to software bugs that result from inadequate

attention in software development stages. To be prepared and counter act, organizations must implement controls to limit damage and prepare contingency plans for continued operations. In today's ever-changing digital environment, another facet that managers are often concerned about is technological obsolescence. Antiquated or outdated infrastructure can lead to unreliable systems and inadequate services for employees or customers. Thus, proper managerial planning should be undertaken to prevent technology obsolescence. While security managers must account for all these threats, the threats that are deliberate acts are more pertinent to the context in this chapter. These include deliberate acts of trespass, theft, sabotage or vandalism, deliberate software attacks, compromises to intellectual property, and human errors or failures (Whitman & Mattord, 2010). We discuss these below and provide a glossary of the different types of computer-related crimes in the Key Terms and Definitions section.

- **Deliberate Acts of Theft:** Theft is the taking of another's property illegally. Within an organization, that property can be physical, electronic, or intellectual. The value of information can suffer substantially when it is copied and taken away without the owner's knowledge. Physical theft such as theft of computer and networking equipment can also be harmful and cause substantial losses. For instance, recent news reported that the theft of computers from a medical clinic one of which contained patient numbers and names resulted in Department of Health to give out new health insurance numbers to all the affected patients (Weston, 2011). But theft of physical devices can be controlled quite easily. A wide variety of measures can be used from simple locked doors to trained security personnel and the installation of alarm systems. Electronic theft, however, is a more complex problem to manage and control because organizations usually may not even know it has occurred.

- **Deliberate Acts of Espionage, Trespass, Sabotage or Vandalism:** These threats pertain to unauthorized access to data or destruction of systems or information. These threats represent a broad category of electronic and human activities that breach the confidentiality of information. When an unauthorized individual gains access to the information an organization is trying to protect, that act is categorized as a deliberate act of espionage or trespass. Recent news reported one such incident. Rival company was accused by K&W Tire for spying on company secrets through emails accessed by K&W employees that were also employed by the rival company (Smart, 2011). Similar trespass can also occur in instances of shoulder surfing at computer terminals, desks, ATM machines, public phones, or other places where a person is accessing confidential information. The threat of trespass can lead to unauthorized real or virtual actions that enable information gatherers to enter premises or systems. An organization can implement controls to mark the boundaries of its virtual territory which indicate to trespassers that they are encroaching on the organization's cyberspace. The classic perpetrator of deliberate acts of espionage or trespass is the hacker. A hacker may use skill, guile, or fraud to attempt to bypass the controls placed around information or systems. The hacker frequently spends long hours examining the types and structures of target systems.

- **Deliberate Software Attacks:** Deliberate software attacks are probably the most known set of attacks which occur when an individual or group designs software to attack unsuspecting systems. Most of this software is referred to as malicious code or malicious software, or sometimes malware. These software components or programs are designed to damage, destroy, or deny service to the target systems. Some of the more common instances of malicious code are viruses, worms, trojan horses, logic bombs, back doors, and denial-of-services attacks.

  - **Computer Viruses** are segments of code that perform malicious actions by attaching to another computer program. This code behaves very much like a virus pathogen attaching itself to the existing program and takes control of that program's access to the targeted computer. The virus-controlled target program then carries out the virus's plan by replicating itself into additional targeted systems. The macro virus is embedded in the automatically executing macro code, common in office productivity software like word processors, spread sheets, and database applications. The boot virus infects the key operating systems files located in a computer's boot sector.

  - **Worm** is a segment of computer code that spreads by itself and performs malicious actions without requiring another computer program. These malicious programs replicate themselves constantly without requiring another program to provide a safe environment for replication. Worms can continue replicating themselves until they completely fill available resources, such as memory, hard drive space, and network bandwidth. Some of the viruses and worms can infect boot sectors while some may hide in the root of the system, known as rootkit. A recent outbreak of Stuxnet is an example of a very sophisticated malware which had rootkit that infected SCADA devices (Falliere, 2010).

○ **Trojan Horses** are software programs that, like in Greek mythology, hide their true nature and reveal their designed behavior only when activated. Trojan horses are frequently disguised as helpful, interesting, or necessary pieces of software, such as readme.exe files often included with shareware or freeware packages. A typical behavior of a Trojan horse is to capture sensitive information such as passwords, account numbers, etc. and send them to the creator of the Trojan horse.

Another example of malicious code is a *logic bomb*. It is a segment of computer code that is embedded within an organization's existing computer programs and is designed to activate and perform a destructive action at a certain time and date. To impose the most impact, these are often activated during nights or during the time when systems personnel are away from work and system monitoring is low.

Some other types of malicious software that relate to the internet use include spyware, and keyloggers, among others. *Spyware* collects personal information about users without their consent. Two types of spyware are keystroke loggers (keyloggers) and screen scrapers. *Keystroke loggers* record your keystrokes and your Web browsing history. *Screen scrapers* record a continuous "movie" of what you do on a screen.

Often these types of threats are dealt with antivirus programs which work with the signatures of known malicious software. However polymorphism, a threat that changes its apparent shape over time, represents a new threat not detectable by techniques that are looking for a preconfigured signature. These threats actually evolve, changing their size and appearance to elude detection by antivirus software programs, making detection more of a challenge.

Other types of threats that target the organizational servers include denial-of service type attacks. In a *denial-of-service* (DoS) attack, the attacker sends a large number of connection or information requests to a target. So many requests are made that the target system cannot handle them successfully along with other, legitimate requests for service. This may result in a system crash or merely an inability to perform ordinary functions. In a special kind of DoS attack known as mail bombing, an attacker routes large quantities of e-mail targeting the email servers. A related attack known as *distributed denial-of-service* (DDoS) is a coordinated stream of requests launched against a target from many locations simultaneously. For example, the main Web site of MasterCard was a target in a large distributed denial of service (DDoS) attack in retaliation for the credit card company's decision to cut off services to WikiLeaks (Vijayan, 2010). In this type of attack, the attacker first takes over many computers. Often this is done through creating a back door which is gaining access to system or network using known or previously unknown/newly discovered access mechanism. A virus or worm can have a payload that installs a back door or trap door component in a system which allows the attacker to access the system at will with special privileges. These computers are called zombies or bots and together in a network these bots form a botnet. When these computers are not being used by users, an attacker can use them to send DoS requests or spam. Reports suggest that millions of computers can be infected with these kinds of malwares and often majority of home users are not even aware that their computers have been exploited (BBC News, June, 2007). Botnets of this size are also used in information warfare tactics, also known as cyberwar, bringing the government information systems or infrastructure down. Some of the well publicized attacks include an attempt to take down the internet infrastructure of most wired country in Europe, Estonia (Davis, 2007) as well as internet infrastructure of Gerogia more recently (Danchev, 2008).

- **Potential Acts of Human Error or Failure**: The losses due to insider threats continue to be a significant threat to organizations. It is well accepted that the biggest threat to the security of an organization's information assets are the company's employees due to their proximity to the organizational data. Recent surveys of security breaches suggest that many security incidents are the result of staff errors and misdemeanors (Hejazi & Lefort, 2009; PriceWaterHouseCoopers, 2004; Privacyrights.org, 2005, 2006). Although, sometimes the insider attacks can be intentional assaults carried out by disgruntled employees, often the insider threats are the result of unintentional acts. Employee mistakes can easily lead to revelation of classified data, entry of erroneous data, accidental deletion or modification of data, storage of data in unprotected areas, and failure to protect information.

In related attacks known as social engineering attacks, attackers use social skills to convince employees to reveal access details or other valuable information. Kevin Mitnick, known as the "King of Social Engineering", served several years in a federal prison as a result of this crime against several major corporations and their networks. "People are the weakest link. You can have the best technology; firewalls, intrusion-detection systems, biometric devices... and somebody can call an unsuspecting employee"— Kevin Mitnick (Abreu, 2000)

Inexperience, improper training, the making of incorrect assumptions, and other circumstances can cause problems. Tailgating, shoulder surfing, carelessness with laptops and portable computing devices, opening questionable e-mails, careless Internet surfing, responding to phishing emails, poor password selection and use are some of the threats that employees are subjected to. Many threats can be prevented with organizational controls, ranging from simple procedures, such as requiring the user to type a critical command twice, to more complex procedures, such as the verification of commands by a second party.

COUNTER-ACTING COMPUTER CRIMES: CONTROL MECHANISMS

The most difficult aspect of computer crime is the inability on the part of an individual or an orga-

Figure 1. Approaches to controlling computer crime

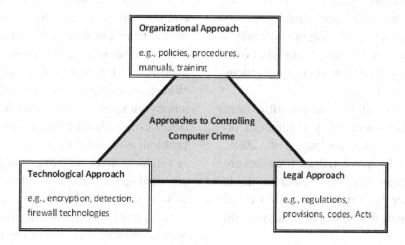

nization to spot it on time. The technology trends in network speeds, mobility, and storage further increase the vulnerability as well as the impact of computer crime. Although, there are no universal guidelines or solutions for all types of computer crime, organizations and nations have tried different mechanisms that fall mainly in three major areas: government legislation, organizational policy, and technological protections (see Figure 1).

Although the growing danger from crimes committed against computers, or against information on computers, is beginning to claim attention from global community leaders, in most countries around the world, however, existing laws are likely to be unenforceable against such crimes (Cybercrime Law, 2010). This lack of legal protection means that businesses and governments must rely solely on other measures to protect themselves from the variety of cybercrimes (McConnell International, 2000).

The Legal Approach and Critical Challenges

Individuals and organizations have become victims of various types of computer crime, such as identity theft, loss of financial transactions or accounts, virus attacks from cyber criminals, etc. U.S. Government Accountability Office (GAO) (2007), in its cyber-crime report GAO-07-075, mentions four major legal challenges that this epidemic faces: ensuring cyber-crime is reported; ensuring adequate analytical and technical capabilities for law enforcement; working in a borderless environment with laws of multiple jurisdictions; and implementing information security practices and raising awareness.

To evade the possibility of liabilities and negative public exposure, many companies do not report the breaches (Gordon *et al.*, 2006; Richardson, 2008). Even when these breaches are reported, in most cases there are no clear standards to trace and penalize the criminals since they could be located anywhere in the world or they could be computer programs designed to act on behalf of these criminals.

While in many of the cyber threats above, activity can easily be identified as inappropriate there are many difficulties with holding the perpetrators responsible for their actions. In addition to the challenge with defining and categorizing the cyber crime, one of the main challenges with these activities lies in different organizations and nations applying different standards to label an activity as illegal or unethical. An activity that is considered normal or not controlled at all in one nation could be a serious crime in another nation. A review of cybercrime laws (Cybercrime Law, 2010) shows many countries across the globe do not have regulations to deal with internet crime. Even within a country, different states or provinces have different regulations or appetite for dealing with such activities. For many multi-national companies which operate beyond their organizational boundaries and across nations, it is becoming increasingly difficult to apply consistent legal standards to safeguard themselves from illegal computer activities, which could easily translate to millions of dollars.

One of the important aspects of cybercrime is its rather global character: actions can occur in jurisdictions separated by vast distances. This poses severe problems for law enforcement since previously local or even national crimes now require international cooperation. For example, if a person accesses information located on a computer in a country which explicitly bans such access from a country where such activity is not explicitly banned, is that individual committing a crime in a nation where such act is illegal? Where exactly does cybercrime take place? As a network spanning the entire globe, the Internet offers criminals multiple hiding places. Another problem with holding a perpetrator responsible is catching them. Although, just as criminals in physical space leave cues that skilled people can follow, cybercriminals leave clues as to their identity and location; in order to follow such clues across national boundaries, though, international cybercrime treaties must be ratified. International laws, however, suffer from many problems including: lack of universal cooperation, differences in interpretations of laws, outdated laws against fraud, problems with evidence admissibility, extradition, and low priority.

There have been many international efforts in this regard (Whitman & Mattord, 2008). In 1996, the Council of Europe, together with government representatives from the United States, Canada, and Japan, drafted a preliminary international treaty covering computer crime. On November 23, 2001, the Council of Europe Cybercrime Convention was signed by 30 states. The Convention on Cyber-Crime is the first international treaty on crimes committed via the Internet and other computer networks, dealing particularly with infringements of copyright, computer-related fraud, child pornography and violations of network security. It also contains a series of powers and procedures such as the search of computer networks and interception. Agreement on Trade-Related Aspects of Intellectual Property Rights, created by World Trade Organization (WTO), is a significant international effort to protect intellectual property rights. This agreement covers five issues: application of basic principles of trading system and international intellectual property agreements, giving adequate protection to intellectual property rights, enforcement of those rights by countries in their own territories, settling intellectual property disputes, and transitional arrangements while new system is being introduced. United Nations Charter to some degree provides provisions for information security during information warfare.

Despite the many convenient features and advantages of online services both in the private and public domains, the privacy of personal information has always been the main concern to citizens and consumers. To protect citizens and consumers as well as help businesses conduct their operations, several nations have taken various initiatives and developed guidelines and legislations. These guidelines and legislations focus on the collection, storage, accessing and

sharing of personal information by companies. In the absence of proper organizational policy and control, the privacy and security of individuals is always a target by cybercriminals. Thus, the role of government legislation is to guide organizations and hold them accountable and responsible for the consequence of violating rules pertaining to the collection, storage, access and distribution of personal information.

Europe is recognized for its strong information privacy laws (The European Directive on Data Protection) that all member states adhere to (Baltzan *et al.*, 2008). This directive grants member states the right to know the source of personal data processing and the purposes, the right to access and/or rectify inaccuracies in one's own personal data, and the right to disallow the use of personal data. These rights are based on several key principles concerning the collection or storage of personal data that every organization processing personal data has to comply with. One of these key principles restricts the flow of personal information outside the European Union unless the country offers an equivalent level of privacy protection. This, for example, necessitated the establishment of a "safe harbour" program for organizations in the United States to show evidence of compliance with the directive and conduct business in Europe.

In the United States, although much has been done to improve legislation, information privacy is not highly legislated or regulated (Baltzan et al., 2008). One major problem is the conflict with existing laws such as the first amendment on free speech. There is also significant variation across states. Some of the initiatives at the federal level include Children's Online Privacy Protection Act (COPPA) and the Health Insurance Portability and Accountability Act (HIPAA). Established in 1998, COPPA applies to the collection of personal information from American children under 13 years of age. This also requires companies in other countries selling children products to the United States to comply with COPPA. Enacted by the United States Congress in 1996, HIPAA establishes national standards for the electronic data interchange of health care-related transactions between providers, insurance plans, and employees.

In Canada, privacy laws closely match the European directive (Baltzan et al., 2008). Its modern privacy law is the Personal Information Protection and Electronic Documents Act (PIPEDA). Although PIPEDA was established in 2001, like its precursor (i.e, The Privacy Act of 1983), it was applicable only to federally regulated organizations. However, in 2004, PIPEDA was extended to all other organizations and brought Canada in compliance with the European Union's Directive. Similar to the European Directive, PIPEDA has several guiding principles based on the Canadian Standards Association's Model Code for the Protection of Personal Information.

Furthermore, piracy and copyright infringements have become frequent cases in the current online environment where ownership of data and application cannot be easily traced. Thus, government legislation can play an important role in the area of intellectual property through provisions governing trademarks, copyrights, and patents.

Another major aspect of criminal investigations of these kinds of activities, however, relates to collection, storage, preservation, and presentation of evidence. In presenting the evidence in a court of law there are several barriers to admissibility. There are concerns that computer evidence can be readily altered or deleted, it can be invisibly and undetectably altered, it can be stored in a different format to that when it is printed or displayed, it is generally difficult for the layman to understand among others. As Giordano (2004) explains, the presentation of electronic evidence:

- Depends on the relative sophistication and computer friendliness of jurists.
- Requires those jurists to make fine distinctions between evidence generated by computer and evidence generated by computer that contains embedded statements.
- The manner in which the evidence is retrieved (beyond chain of custody issues)

is not subject to the same level of judicial scrutiny as that of other evidence.

- The idea that since anything digital is subject to manipulation, the possibility exists that the evidence was tampered with or even fabricated.
- No industry standards exist for imaging data from a hard drive. Rather, several methods have gained acceptance as ways of performing this function.
- The software that images or copies hard drives is not usually required to pass an evidentiary hearing.
- The collector of the evidence often acts as a quasi-expert and is asked to render an opinion with respect to the implications of the data.

Organizational Approach

In spite of difficulties associated with the legal actions against the perpetrators, organizations are expected to pay due attention to evade such situations. To minimize liabilities and reduce risks from electronic, physical threats and reduce the losses from legal action, the information security practitioner must understand the current legal environment, stay current as new laws and regulations emerge, and watch for issues that need attention. Thus security managers in demonstrating due care must ensure that employees know what constitutes acceptable behaviour and know the consequences of illegal or unethical actions.

Different people play different roles in the organization; as such their responsibilities with securing the data may vary. For instance, data owners are responsible for the security and use of a particular set of information. Data owners usually determine the level of data classification associated with the data, as well as changes to that classification required by organizational change. Data custodians are responsible for the storage, maintenance, and protection of the information. The duties of a data custodian often include overseeing data storage and backups, implementing the specific procedures and policies laid out in the security policies and plans, and reporting to the data owner. Data Users are the end systems users who work with the information to perform their daily jobs supporting the mission of the organization. Everyone in the organization is responsible for the security of data, so data users are included here as individuals with an information security role.

In addition, in conducting due diligence, organizations should make a valid effort to protect the assets continually maintaining a level of effort. Due care and due diligence are important in organizations part to show that they had taken effort in securing their assets. Organizational controls ranging from physical control to application-level control, involve methods, policies, and procedures that ensure protection of organizational assets as well as ensure accuracy and reliability of records, and operational adherence to management standards. Security professional suggest using 'defense in depth' by implementing security in layers. This requires that organization establish sufficient security controls and safeguards so that an intruder faces multiple layers of controls. These layers of security can be envisioned as:

- **Physical security:** this entails protection of physical items, objects, or areas of an organization from unauthorized access and misuse. Some of the measures include locks and doors for the premises, locks for network cabinets and server rooms, video surveillances, chains and locks for physically securing servers, laptops, and many other such controls.
- **Data and Operations security:** to protect the data and details of a particular operation or series of activities. These may include the access control to manage rights and responsibility for access to particular set of data, may also the processes put in place to ensure the integrity of data such as how changes should be made to system or data, how they should be documented, and many other such controls.

- **Network and Communications security:** to protect an organization's communications media, technology, networking components, connections, and contents. This entails appropriate network configurations, use of internal and external firewalls, proxy servers, demilitarized zones with more secured internal networks, use of cryptography etc.
- **Personnel security:** individual or group of individuals who are authorized to access the organization and its operations are trustworthy, capable, and operationally safe individuals to secure and operate an organization's control systems (Idaho National Engineering and Environmental Laboratory, 2004). Although many specifications are given for the security or systems personnel, many guidelines for hiring, new employee orientations, security training and awareness, accountability, termination policies and procedures are applicable and necessary for all personnel who use or have access to computers in their daily work routines.

In general, security policies and procedures within an organization should be broad enough to incorporate such critical issues as privacy, acceptable or ethical use of hardware and software, email, the Internet, as well as social media.

Technological Approach

There are several ways to deal with computer crime using technologies. Management needs to consider the appropriate technologies that should be in place to support the successful implementation of security policies. The security technologies in place and the policies and procedures for acceptable use should be integrated components of any security strategy within an organization. The most commonly used protection measures using technology include:

- **Authentication and Authorization:** provides a system of tracking access to network resources. Authentication provides the mechanism to verifying and confirming users' identities, and granting the user access privileges to system and network resources. Authentication involves the use of user ID and password, a smart card, or in some sensitive areas, the use of unique physical characteristics, such as a fingerprint, voice recording, or retinal scan.

- **Firewall:** a security gateway in the form of hardware and/or software placed between an organization's internal network and external network to prevent outsiders from invading private networks. Firewalls track and control communication, deciding whether to pass, reject, encrypt or log information and ensure that all communication and transmission conform to the organization's security policy (www.sofaware.com).

- **Intrusion Detection System (IDS):** an application designed to *detect* network-based attacks, such as Denial of Service (DoS) attacks (www.sofaware.com). Once an attack is detected, attack details are logged and the system administrator is notified. The main role of IDS is to detect attacks, not preventing them. Prevention is supported by Intrusion Prevention System (IPS).

- **Intrusion Prevention System (IPS):** an application designed to *prevent* network-based attacks, such as Denial of Service (DoS) attacks ((www.sofaware.com). Once an Intrusion Detection System (IDS) detects an attack, an IPS will take actions to cease the current, and prevent future, attacks. Actions include terminating offending connections and reconfiguring firewalls to intercept the attack.

- **Encryption:** provides a method of encoding messages before transmission in a network, then decoding them at the receiving end so that recipients can read or hear them. In public key (asymmetric) encryption, two mathematically-related keys combine to form a key pair, one to encrypt and the other to decrypt. In particular, the use of wireless networks requires significant management attention in this area of protection. Wireless networks are more vulnerable than cabled networks. Retail businesses are an ideal target on such networks. One major example is the attack on the U.S.-based The TJX Companies due to security holes in the stores' wireless networks, which cost the company more than $171.5-million (Lopez-Pacheco, 2010). TJX's financial and personal identification customer data was the main target. TJX detected suspicious software in its computer system in December 2006 and immediately began investigating. The company found that Cyber intruders, who had gained access to TJX's system in the summer of 2005 via the wireless LANs at two of its stores in Miami, Fla., had been able to access more than 45 million payment cards in Canada, the United States, Puerto Rico, the United Kingdom and Ireland. In addition to credit card information, the intruders had also obtained the drivers' licenses, names and addresses of hundreds of people who had provided the company's stores with the information for unreceipted merchandise-return transactions a few years earlier. Reports indicated that even as TJX was investigating, the intruder continued to have access to the system for some time. Organizations should always update the security levels in their encryption technology as cyber criminals use many different tactics and match the technology constantly.

- **Technologies for secure remote connections and transactions:** this includes a host of technologies that provide secure communications and transmission of data across networks or the Internet (www.so-faware.com):

- **Secure Hyptertext Transfer Protocol (S-HTTP):** a security-enhanced version of HTTP providing a variety of mechanisms to enable confidentiality, authentication and integrity.
- **Secure Socket Layer (SSL):** a protocol standardized for secure communications for HTTP. It combines encryption and the services of a Certificate Authority to provide a secure environment for electronic commerce and communications and provides authentication between servers and browsers, as well as a method for encryption and validation of client-server communications.
- **Virtual Private Network (VPI):** an inexpensive and flexible network that is configured within a public network to provide data integrity and confidentiality through authentication and encryption. With a VPI, data can be securely transmitted between two branch locations across the Internet or be encrypted between a server and a client within a Local Area Network (LAN).

SOCIAL MEDIA AND CYBERCRIME

Social media sites pose several challenges ranging from defamation, copyright infringements, to national interests. Several anti-social activities have attracted the attention of law enforcement agencies, violated privacy, and created copyright problems and piracy issues. Instances of a major anti-social practice "cyber bullying" have been observed on several social media sites. For example, Youtube was accused of hosting a video showing a gang of twelve boys sexually abusing a 17-yer-old Victorian girl (Smith, 2007). As a result of this, the Victorian Government in Australia blocked access to YouTube from school property. In response to increased concerns on this issue, YouTube has launched its own anti-cyberbullying

initiative – the Beatbullying channel (BBC News, November, 2007).

In June of 2007, Flickr, a popular photo sharing Web site, expanded its operations into seven additional languages. However, users were restricted to photos that were deemed safe by Flickr's filtering system (Shankland, 2007). The largest outcry over this issue of censorship occurred in Germany. According to Flickr, the decision to change the Flickr experience in Germany was to ensure that Yahoo Germany was in compliance with local legal restrictions, because Germany has much more stringent age-verification laws than its neighbouring countries and specifies much harsher penalties, including jail time, for those with direct responsibility (Shankland, 2007). Thus, the strict age verification laws in Germany and a few other countries forced Flickr to enforce restrictions on user's accounts to avoid any legal ramifications.

In 2009, Facebook, the popular social networking website, agreed to make changes to better protect the personal information of its users as a result of negotiations with Canada's privacy commissioner (Hartley, 2009). The commissioner's involvement started because of complaints received from a concerned citizen, Harley Finkelstein, a third-year law student at the University of Ottawa and an intern with the Canadian Internet Policy and Public Interest Clinic. Mr. Finkelstein set out to help protect his 14-year-old sister, Lindsey, who loved Facebook and the various games and quizzes relating to Hannah Montana and the Jonas Brothers that she would download. Worried about the personal details the makers of those applications were collecting from the profiles of his sister and the estimated two million other Canadian Facebook users under the age of 18, Mr. Finkelstein and fellow intern Jordan Plener began digging into the privacy practices of Facebook in January 2008, and whether its policies complied with privacy laws. Five months later, their work led to a complaint lodged against Facebook with the Office of the Privacy Commissioner of Canada. The complaint prompted the office to investigate, which resulted in Facebook's sweeping changes to its privacy and security policies that will bring its practices in line with Canadian law, the Personal Information Protection and Electronic Documents Act (PIPEDA). The key areas of concern include Facebook's practice of indefinitely storing personal information of its users even after they deactivate their accounts or die, how the personal information of non-users is handled, confusing or incomplete privacy information on the site, and the way Facebook shares the personal information of its users with third-party software developers who create games, quizzes and other applications that run on its network.

Social media also poses several challenges to organizations in their internal as well as external communications. In its sixth annual study of outbound email and data loss prevention issues, Proofpoint, Inc. found that US companies are increasingly concerned about a growing number of data leaks caused by employee misuse of email, blogs, social networks, multimedia channels and even text messages (Marketwire, 2009). According to the 2009 study, 43 percent of US companies surveyed had investigated an email-based leak of confidential or proprietary information in the previous 12 months. Nearly a third of them, 31 percent, terminated an employee for violating email policies in the same period (up from 26 percent in 2008). With respect to blogs, 18 percent had investigated a data loss event via a blog or message board in the previous 12 months. 17 percent disciplined an employee for violating blog or message board policies, while nearly nine percent reported terminating an employee for such a violation (both increases from 2008, 11 percent and six percent, respectively). With respect to video and audio sharing sites like YouTube, the survey found that more US companies reported investigating exposure events across these channels which is 18 percent, up from 12 percent in 2008. As a result, 15 percent have disciplined an employee for violating multimedia sharing / posting policies in the previous 12 months, while eight percent reported terminating an employee for such a violation. Concerning social networks,

the survey found that US companies are experiencing more exposure incidents involving sites like Facebook and LinkedIn as compared to 2008 which is 17 percent versus 12 percent. The companies are also taking more serious measures on offending employees where eight percent reported terminating an employee for such a violation as compared to only four percent in 2008. Furthermore, the survey found risks associated with even short message services like SMS texts and Twitter where 13 percent of US companies investigated an exposure event involving mobile or Web-based short message services in the previous 12 months.

Such alarming statistics and trends clearly indicate the need to pay serious attention to security measures towards new technologies. The above statistics are indicative of the need for a policy framework towards social media and related activities. Information management policies concerning communications both within and outside of organizations should extend to embrace all the channels employees are exposed to. In some cases, employees are unaware of the implications of engaging in social media activities. Policies must be clearly communicated to employees to avoid serious consequences. Simply terminating employees is not an effective solution as employees may engage in retaliatory activities after they leave the companies. In fact, the same survey found that 18 percent of US companies investigated a suspected leak or theft of confidential or proprietary information associated with an employee leaving the company through voluntary or involuntary termination in the previous 12 months.

Although existing laws apply equally to online and offline conduct, social media activities raise serious legal issues around content use and infringement, and defamation (Ossian, 2009). Ossian (2009) discusses some of the key legal issues that may arise as a result of social media activities:

- **Third Party Content:** Organizations must make sure that publishing content such as text, graphics, photos or other media on a social media sites comply with applicable copyright laws. In addition, organizations must secure the right to post all third party content before posting them. For example, Getty Images, Inc., the world's leading provider of visual content, established a partnership with PicScout, a company that uses sophisticated crawling and image recognition technology to track down unauthorized use of Getty Images' copyrighted works online. Following this, Getty pursues statutory damages under the U.S. Copyright Act based on each separate occurrence of infringement, such as each use of a single image on multiple web pages (Ossian, 2009).

- **Content Ownership/Control:** When organizations develop profile pages on social media sites, they should verify terms of use regarding content ownership even when accounts are deleted. Organizations should be also careful not to disclose any sensitive or proprietary information in this process.

- **Defamation/Other Torts:** Care should be taken to avoid contents that could be defamatory to a third party and potentially be the basis for other tort liability, such as intentional infliction of emotional distress, interference with advantageous economic relations, fraud or misrepresentation.

- **Criminal Activity:** In some circumstances, contents posted on social media sites can become evidence of criminal activity as well as a catalyst for offline criminal activities and charges. Although social networking sites prohibit the use of their sites for illegal purposes, the convenient tools and features available on these sites may prompt criminal activities.

- **Employment Practices:** Hiring practices based on social media contents and information are raising legal issues in many places. One controversial issue is discrimination by employers during online recruit-

ment processes, such as not accepting invitations from online contacts of a specific race, gender, or religion (Abramson, 2009).

- **Litigation Impact:** This relates to the use of social media tools by litigants, witnesses and jurors and its impact on the fairness of a trial. For example, if jurors access information about the subject matter of the trial outside of the court proceedings, it can interfere with the jurors' obligation to deliberate based solely on the evidence presented by the parties.

Fayle (2007) discusses some recent developments pertaining to the legal obligations that arise out of the use of social networks in the U.S. legal framework. He emphasized that the two most important statutes to consider when discussing the legal liabilities and obligations of the social networking sites are Section 512(c) of the Digital Millenium Copyright Act and Section 230 of the Communications Decency Act:

- **Section 512(c) of the Digital Millennium Copyright Act:** Removes liability for copyright infringement from websites that allow users to post content, as long as the site has a mechanism in place whereby the copyright owner can request the removal of infringing content. The site must also not receive a financial benefit directly attributable to the infringing activity. For example, YouTube has claimed a 512(c) defense against the copyright infringement accusations by several content owners.

- **Section 230 of the Communications Decency Act:** Immunizes website from any liability resulting from the publication of information provided by another. For example, if a user posts defamatory or otherwise illegal content, Section 230 shields the social network provider from any liability arising out of the publication. However, websites that, in whole or in part, create or develop contested information are deemed "content providers" that do not benefit from the protections of Section 230.

- **State Laws:** In addition to the above federal statutes, several states have also enacted or proposed laws that would create requirements for social networking sites, particularly in regards to monitoring the presence and activities of sexual predators using the sites.

Thus, given such immunities granted to social media sites, individuals and organizations should take extra precautions, particularly in posting defamatory content or content that infringes on intellectual property rights (Fayle, 2007). Despite such developments on the legal side of social media activities, strong legal statutes require significant commitments from governments, courts, content providers, as well as users.

CONCLUSION

In general, from highly advanced societies to least developed nations, various governments have attempted to encourage better computer laws and establish, within their boundaries, what they consider "acceptable practices". However, what makes computer crime different from traditional laws is that it has no geographic or national boundaries. The number and types of computer crimes will grow at a rapid pace and become more serious with the advancement of technology in the future. Therefore, the legal solution demands regional and international collaborations and the modification of existing national and international laws that may conflict with desired laws at an international setting.

The lack of well-developed legal statutes requires organizations to tie the technological, organizational, and legal mechanisms closer and provide more integrated control strategy. While the law provides guidelines on the rights and obligations of individuals, companies, and busi-

ness partners, organizations need to support the law with information management policies that should be outlined and communicated clearly to every member of an organization. The law requires interpretations within each organization's context. Thus, management has the responsibility to contextualize the legal implications of computer-related activities within and outside of an organization.

Establishing a well-integrated control framework involves several initiatives in all three angles. The most important step, however, is awareness. Awareness involves understanding the various types of internal as well as external threats. This requires budget and scheduled training of individuals involved in the various roles within an organization. It also involves identifying the areas and the activities that are prone to any kind of computer crime and the associated risks. These initial steps are often ignored, but they represent the foundation to any security strategy. Given this foundation, legal implications need to be translated into policies and procedures that can range from company-wide policies to policies for individual applications. In the absence of clear policies, even well-trained technology managers are not free from cyber threats. On the technology side, initial investment and constant updates are required to provide effective solution for monitoring and detecting threats. Therefore, by having all the technology, policies, and legal provisions work together, organizations can minimize the threats, if not possible to totally eliminate the risks.

REFERENCES

Abramson, F. (2009). *Social networks, employees and anti-discrimination laws*. Retrieved December 20, 2010, from http: //nylawblog. com/2009/10/ social-networks -employees-and-anti-discrimination-laws/

Abreu, E. (2000). Kevin Mitnick bares all. *The Industry Standard*. Retrieved December 15, 2010, from http://www.networkworld. com/news/2000/0928mitnick.html

Baltzan, P., Phillips, A., & Detlor, B. (2008). *Business driven Information Systems* (Canadian Edition). Toronto, Canada: McGraw-Hill Ryerson Limited.

Cybercrime. (2010). *Encyclopædia Britannica*. Encyclopædia Britannica Online. Retrieved December 15, 2010, from http: //www.britannica. com/EBchecked/topic/ 130595/cybercrime

Cybercrime law.(2010). *Cybercrime laws from around the world*. Retrieved December 15, 2010, from http: //www.cybercrimelaw. net/Cybercrimelaws. html

Danchev, D. (2008). Coordinated Russia vs Georgia cyber attack in progress. *ZDNet*. Retrieved December 15, 2010, from http: //www. zdnet. com/blog/security/ coordinated-russia-vs-georgia-cyber-attack-in-progress/1670

Davis, J. (2007). Hackers take down the most wired country in Europe. *Wired Magazine*. Retrieved December 15, 2010, from http://www.wired. com/politics/ security/magazine/ 15-09/ff_estonia.

Falliere, N. (2010). Stuxnet introduces the first known rootkit for industrial control systems. Retrieved December 15, 2010, from http://www.symantec.com/ connect/blogs/stuxnet-introduces-first- known-rootkit-scada-devices

Fayle, K. (2007). Understanding the legal issues for social networking sites and their users. *Find Law*. Retrieved December 20, 2010, from http: //articles.technology.findlaw. com/2007/Sep/18/10966.html

Foreign Affairs and International Trade Canada. (n.d.). *CyberCrime – overview*. Retrieved December 15, 2010, from http: //www.international.gc. ca/crime/cyber_crime- criminalite.aspx

Giordano, S. M. (2004). Electronic evidence and the law. *Information Systems Frontiers, 6*(2), 161–169. doi:10.1023/B:ISFI.0000025783.79791.c8

Goodman, M. (2010). International dimensions of cybercrime. In Ghosh, S., & Turrini, E. (Eds.), *Cybercrimes: A multidisciplinary analysis, part 7* (pp. 311–339). Berlin/Heidelberg, Germany: Springer-Verlag. doi:10.1007/978-3-642-13547-7_17

Gordon, L. A., Loeb, M. P., Lucyshyn, W., & Richardson, R. (2006). *2006 CSI/FBI computer crime and security survey: Computer Security Institute*.

Gordon, S., & Ford, R. (2006). On the definition and classification of cybercrime. *Journal in Computer Virology, 2*(1), 13–20. doi:10.1007/s11416-006-0015-z

Hartley, M. (2009). How one Canadian changed Facebook forever. *National Post*. Retrieved December 20, 2010, from http://www.ottawacitizen. com/Canadian+changed+Facebook+forever/1939365/story.html

Hejazi, W., & Lefort, A. (2009). *2009 Rotman-Telus joint study on Canadian IT security practices*. Rotman School of Management and TELUS.

Idaho National Engineering and Environmental Laboratory. (2004). *Personnel security guidelines*. Control Systems Security and Test Center. Retrieved December 15, 2010, from http: //www.us-cert. gov/control_systems/ pdf/personnel_guide0904.pdf

Kabay, M. E. (2008). *Glossary of computer crime terms*. Retrieved December 20, 2010, from http: //www.mekabay. com/overviews/ glossary.pdf

Kowalski, M. (2002). *Cyber-crime: Issues, data sources, and feasibility of collecting police-reported statistics*. (Statistics Canada Catalogue no. 85-558-XIE). Retrieved December 15, 2010, from http: //dsp-psd.pwgsc.gc. ca/Collection/Statcan/ 85-558-X/85-558-XIE2002001.pdf

Lopez-Pacheco, A. (2010). Cyberthreats to the retail industry. *Financial Post*. Retrieved December 20, 2010, from http://www.vancouversun.com/business/smart-shift/fp/Cyberthreats+retail+industry/3935446/story.html

Marketwire. (2009). *Proofpoint survey says: State of economy leads to increased data loss risk for large companies*. Retrieved December 20, 2010, from http://www.marketwire.com/press-release/Proofpoint-Inc-1027877.html

McConnell International. (2000). *Cyber crime... and punishment? Archaic laws threaten global information*. Retrieved December 15, 2010, from http://www.witsa.org/papers/McConnell-cybercrime.pdf

Milhorn, H. T. (2010). *Cybercrime: How to avoid becoming a victim*. Universal Publishers Cybercrime Glossary. Retrieved December 20, 2010 from http //cybercrimeglossary.netfirms.com/#a

News, B. B. C. (June 14, 2007). *FBI tries to fight zombie hordes*. Retrieved December 15, 2010, from http://news.bbc.co.uk/2/hi/6752853.stm

News, B. B. C. (November 19, 2007). *YouTube tackles bullying online*. Retrieved December 20, 2010, from http://news.bbc.co.uk/2/hi/uk_news/education/7098978.stm

Office of the Privacy Commissioner of Canada. (July 2001). *Protecting your personal information*. Retrieved December 15, 2010, from http://www.priv.gc.ca/fs-fi/02_05_d_12_e.cfm

Ossian, K. L. (2009). *Legal issues in social networking*. Miller Canfield Paddock and Stone PLC, Institute of Continuing Legal Education. Retrieved December 20, 2010 from http://www.millercanfield.com/publications-articles.html

PriceWaterHouseCoopers. (2004). *Information security breaches survey 2004.*

Privacyrights.org. (April 20, 2005). *A chronology of data breaches*. Retrieved December 15, 2010, from http://www.privacyrights.org/ar/ChronDataBreaches.htm

Privacyrights.org. (2006). *2006 disclosures of U.S. data incidents*. Retrieved December 15, 2010, from www.privacyrights.org/ar/ChronDataBreaches

Richardson, R. (2008). *2008 computer crime & security survey*. Computer Security Institute.

Shankland, S. (June 15, 2007). *Flickr curtails German photo sharing*. Retrieved December 20, 2010, from CNet News: http://news.cnet.com/8301-10784_3-9730348-7.html

Smart, G. (January 29, 2011). *Rivals accused of spying by e-mail: Former K&W Tire employees, employed by another firm, face hearing that they accessed information*. Retrieved February 02, 2011, from Lancaster News: http://articles.lancasteronline.com/local/4/344888

Smith, B. (March 2007). Schools ban YouTube Sites in cyber-bully fight. *The Age*. Retrieved December 20, 2010, from http://www.theage.com.au/articles/2007/03/01/1172338796092.html

SofaWare Technologies. (2010). *Security glossary*. Retrieved December 20, 2010, from http://www.sofaware.com/glossary.aspx?boneId=189&Letter=A

United States Government Accountability Office. (2007). *CYBERCRIME: Public and private entities face challenges in addressing cyber threats*. (GAO-07-075). Retrieved December 15, 2010, from http://www.gao.gov/new.items/d07705.pdf

Vijayan. J. (2010). MasterCard, Visa others hit by DDoS attacks over WikiLeaks. *Computerworld*. Retrieved January 28, 2011, from http://www.computerworld.com/s/article/9200521/

Volonino, L., & Robinson, S. R. (2004). *Principles and practice of information security*. Upper Saddle River, NJ: Pearson Prentice Hall.

Ward, M. (2006). Hi-tech crime: A glossary. *BBC News*. Retrieved December 20, 2010, from http://news.bbc.co. uk/2/hi/uk_news/ 5400052.stm

Weston, G. (2011). *Province to issue new medicare numbers in wake of computer theft.* Retrieved February 2, 2011, from http://dailygleaner.cana-daeast. com/cityregion/ article/1372944

Whitman, M. E., & Mattord, H. J. (2008). *Principles of information security.* Boston, MA: Thompson Course Technology.

ADDITIONAL READING

Cybercrime. (2010). Encyclopædia Britannica. Encyclopædia Britannica Online. http://www. britannica. com/EBchecked/topic/ 130595/cybercrime

http://news.bbc.co. uk/2/hi/uk_news/ 5400052. stm

http://www.mekabay. com/overviews/ glossary. pdf

http://www.sofaware. com/glossary.aspx ?boneId=189&Letter=A

Kabay, M.E. (2008). Glossary of Computer Crime Terms.

Milhorn, H. T. (2010). *Cybercrime: How to Avoid Becoming a Victim*, Universal Publishers, Cybercrime Glossary. http://cybercrimeglossary. netfirms. com/#a

SofaWare Technologies, Security Glossary. (2010).

Ward, M. (2006). Hi-tech crime: A glossary, BBC News website.

KEY TERMS AND DEFINITIONS

Advanced Fee Fraud: Any scam that promises a sum of money with an upfront fee (e.g., The 419 or Nigerian fraud).

Adware: Advertising-supported software that periodically pops up advertisements on a user's computer based on key words entered in search engines and the types of websites the user visits. Adware is usually downloaded as part of free online applications and programs users download.

Charity Scam: A bogus charity that collects money from people online.

Child Pornography: Illegal use of children in pornographic pictures or films via the Internet.

Credit Card Fraud: Unauthorized and illegal use of someone's credit card for purchases or adding charges to a card for goods or services not received.

Credit Repair Scam: Bogus claim to repair credit problem for fees.

Cyber Bullying or Cyber Stalking: This occurs when one person or a group of people harasses another individual over the Internet. This act is becoming increasingly common with the proliferation of social media. It often occurs in chat rooms, newsgroups, or through hate e-mails to interested parties.

Cyber Defamation: This occurs when someone publishes defamatory matter about someone on a website or sends e-mails containing defamatory information.

Cyber Terrorism: An act of terrorism committed through the use of cyberspace or computer resources towards a government, group, or organization.

Cyber Warfare: Cyber attacks that are feared to become the norm in future warfare among nation.

Data Diddling: Modifying or altering data for fun and profit; e.g., modifying grades, changing credit ratings, altering security clearance information, fixing salaries, or circumventing bookkeeping and audit regulations.

Data Leakage: Uncontrolled, unauthorized transmission of classified information from a data centre or computer system to the outside. It may include physical removal of data storage devices, computers, or other devices and materials containing data.

Dating Scam: Making contact with another person for money through an online dating agency and pretending to be looking for romance or marriage.

Denial-of-Service Attack (DoS Attack) or Distributed Denial-of-Service Attack (DDoS Attack): A method of crashing an Internet server by flooding it with continuous bogus requests so as to deny legitimate requests. DDoS involves several computers in different locations to intensify the attack.

Diploma/Degree Mill: Online "colleges" or "universities" which offer fraudulent or virtually worthless degrees in exchange for payment.

Drive-by Download: When a spyware installed while a user visits a malicious website.

Drug Trafficking: Selling illegal substances through encrypted e-mail and other Internet Technology. Virtual exchanges allow more intimidated individuals to more comfortably purchase illegal drugs and avoid physical risks in the process of exchanging.

Dumpster Diving: The physical act of looking through trash containers for access codes or other sensitive information.

Gambling Fraud: Online casino scams and sports betting scams.

Hacking: An activity of breaking into a computer system to gain an unauthorized access. Hacker's original meaning refers to trained professionals. As a result, the term "Cracker" is often used to refer to individuals who gain unauthorized access to computer systems with malicious intent.

Hoaxes: A purposeful act of presenting or sending false statements so convincingly that the readers believe it and proceed to actions that could open doors to unauthorised users to compromise confidential information in a computer network or

cause other loses. Popular social networks such as Facebook are currently the primary target of this.

Identity Theft: Involves stealing money and obtaining other benefits through the use of a false identity. It is the act of pretending to be someone else by using someone else's identity as one's own.

Illegal Alien Fraud: Charging an illegal alien for paperwork and transportation into another country, but not delivering on the promise after the money is paid.

Intellectual Property crimes, Copyright infringement, Trademarks Violations: Include software piracy, illegal copying of programs, distribution of copies of software or the unauthorized use of copyrighted material or trademarks in a manner that violates one of the owner's exclusive rights, such as the right to reproduce or perform the copyrighted work.

IP Spoofing: An attack where the attacker disguises himself as another user by means of a false IP network address.

Keystroke Logger (Keylogger): A program that allows recording every character typed on a keyboard by a computer user.

Loan Scam: Promising a loan for an upfront fee, regardless of one's credit history.

Logic Bomb: Malicious code that is designed to be event dependent. When the designated event occurs, it crashes the computer, release a virus or any other harmful possibilities.

Lottery Scam: Scam emails that instructs the recipient to keep the notice secret and to contact an agent named in the email and pay money as fees, but never receive any lottery payments.

Mouse-Trapping: Setting up websites in such a way that users can't leave the sites by clicking on the "back" or "home" button. This happens often on pornographic sites. When users attempt click, they may be connected to another pornographic site.

Online Sales Fraud: Happens when someone orders and pays for an item online and then the item is never delivered.

Pagejacking: Webpage hijacking is stealing content from a website and copying it into another website to drain off some of the original site's traffic to the copied webpage.

Password Sniffing: Examining data traffic for the purpose of finding passwords and using them for masquerading attacks.

Pharming: Misdirecting traffic from one Website to a Website controlled by a criminal hacker by altering the domain name system or by altering configuration files on a victim's computer.

Phishing: An Internet scam designed to trick an email recipient into revealing his or her credit card number, passwords, Social Security number, and other personal information to individuals who intend to use them for fraudulent purposes. The emails usually instruct the recipient to verify or update account information by providing the recipient with a link to a website where the information can be entered.

Piggybacking: Entering secure premises by following an authorized person through the security grid. It also refers to unauthorized access to information by using a terminal that is already logged on with an authorized ID (identification).

Salami Attack: A financial crime that involves removing negligible amounts and accumulating larger sum of money.

Social Engineering: An attack where the attacker uses social skills to trick a legitimate employee into providing confidential company information such as passwords.

Spamming: Sending unsolicited mass email messages to many users at a time, with the usual intention of advertising products to potential customers or defrauding them.

Spoofing: Disguising one computer as another via a fake website or email address to send information through the Internet. A spoofed email is one in which e-mail header is forged so that mail appears to originate from one source but actually has been sent from another source.

Spyware: Programs that gather information about a user's Web surfing habits and sends this information to a third party, usually without the user's permission or knowledge. These programs often change system settings, install keystroke loggers, collect and report personal information without the user's notice and consent.

Travel Scam: Happens when victims are told by email that they have won a free or incredibly cheap trip and the recipients are required to make extra reservations through a specific company which involve costs that are much higher than market price. The tricks may change forms depending on the context of the offers.

Trojan Horse: A program that appears legitimate, but disguised to do damage once installed or run on a computer. When opened on one's computer, it can do silly and annoying actions or cause serious damage by deleting files in a computer system. Trojans can also open a backdoor that gives unauthorised users access to confidential or personal information.

Virus: A malicious code that attaches itself to a program or executable file in order to spread from one computer to another and cause damages that can range from simple effects severe damage to software or files. A virus spreads and infects a computer with a human action, such as when one runs or opens a malicious program. The common causes are sharing infected files or sending e-mails with viruses as attachments.

Web Jacking: Gaining access and control over the website of another, and changing the content of the website for fulfilling political objective or for money.

Wiretapping: Eavesdropping on data or voice transmissions by attaching unauthorized equipment or software to the communications medium (in the case of wires, coaxial metal cables and optical cables) or by intercepting and interpreting broadcast data (in the case of wireless phones, cellular phones, and wireless networks).

Worm: Similar to a virus, but it does not need the host to attach themselves and spread from computer to computer. A worm takes advantage of file or information transport features on one computer and can travel to another computer unaided. A worm is has the ability to replicate itself on one system and send out several copies of itself.

Chapter 5
Cyber Law, Cyber Ethics and Online Gambling

Lee Gillam
University of Surrey, UK

Anna Vartapetiance
University of Surrey, UK

ABSTRACT

Cyberspace offers up numerous possibilities for entertainment and leisure, and can be a rich source for information. Unfortunately, it can also be a dangerous place for the unwary or ill-informed. In this chapter, we discuss some of the legal and ethical issues that can arise in the interface between cyberspaces and real places for virtual tourists. We mention the difficulties posed by variations in laws in the physical world, and how these make for problems in the virtual world. We discuss how it is possible to create systems that embed adherence to laws and provide support for ethics in order to avoid harm to the unwary or ill-informed. We show how we have applied such principles in a machine ethics system for online gambling.

INTRODUCTION

Cyberspace. A consensual hallucination experienced daily by billions of legitimate operators, in every nation, by children being taught mathematical concepts... A graphic representation of data abstracted from the banks of every computer in the human system... (Gibson, 1984, p.51)

DOI: 10.4018/978-1-61350-132-0.ch005

The advent of "cyberspace" has led to traditional geographical boundaries being transcended. Cyberspace also creates the illusion for people that most things are available cheaper or for free, and all actions undertaken are acceptable everywhere. Sitting in front of a computer, a person accessing the internet is virtually relocated to a "generalized elsewhere" of distant places and "non-local" people (Jewkes, 2003). While the person inhabits this generalized everywhere, they may be incorrectly extending the rules and social norms that are applicable in their own physical location across the geographical boundaries, or believing there is a relaxation of regulations and restrictions. They may also be erroneously enlarging their personal security perimeter, acting under a false impression that the limit of communication is with the computer screen itself, or is restricted to specific intended set of interested people. In this generalized elsewhere, people can be whoever, whatever, and wherever they wish, presenting themselves and re-inventing themselves as they desire. Unfortunately, this also offers the opportunity for those with fewer scruples to pretend to be people who already exist, based on information they have managed to obtain from unsuspecting users who are under such illusions and who become susceptible to such problems.

A key difficulty for cyberspace users is in this rapid but undistinguished crossing of boundaries that include legal, ethical and religious, amongst others. For tourists in the physical world, there are often certain clear indications of when geographical boundaries have been crossed, and other symbols may identify such a difference. In cyberspace, one can rapidly move across boundaries of geography without ever being aware of the fact. This can create significant difficulties for software designers and internet users alike in understanding what applies, where it applies, when it applies, and, most difficult of all, why.

Over time, geographical entities have introduced, updated, replaced and even discarded laws that enforce or supplement societal and cultural norms. As technologies have emerged, lawmakers have attempted to keep pace. Unfortunately, reinterpreting through legal cases and through the crafting of new legislation where old was insufficiently encompassing can be awkward and appear ill-informed. During such processes, typically elongated if anything remotely useful is to emerge, the technology has usually moved on: the present pace of technological innovation is vastly outstripping the ability of the majority to keep up with new products, let alone for lawmakers to keep up with problems created by new products. If laws are found wanting, those developing such technologies have to make reference to ethics and professional standards while the gaps are closed, and must hope for the best outcomes when courts decide whether their use of new technologies is acceptable or not. The jurisdictional framing of laws introduces yet another issue: the illusion of the generalized everywhere is not reflected in any kind of generalized law. Cyberspace has no set of unified laws governing all actions, enabling the fight against the crimes, or for promoting the wellbeing of society and prevention of harm. There may be some degree of commonality in law, for example when European Union member states implement certain directives, but these can happen over varying time spans, and even the transfer to a national implementation may be considered incomplete (Ashford, 2010).

Cyberspace offers up many benefits, but many more substantial risks. It may be possible to trust in well-known brands, but there are many others attempting to deceive through masquerading as these trusted brands using, for example, phishing attacks. By compromising weakly secured systems, it is possible to construct botnets (Weber, 2007) that can coordinate attacks against yet other systems, act as spam generators to catch the unwary, deploy ransomware (Net-Security, 2010) or obtain and distribute personal data contained within such systems. By the time such systems are detected and blocked, yet further such botnets will have been spawned. Meanwhile, those who compose phishing emails or construct such systems are difficult to identify and bring to justice. Personal data obtained via such approaches can include credit card numbers, bank account details, and potentially even DNA profiles (Vartapetiance & Gillam, 2010). Such personal data is becoming increasingly valuable because it can be used fraudulently for purposes of identification. With such data, it becomes possible to obtain credit in another person's name, and consequently to impact on their credit records. The first that an affected, and innocent, party knows of this is when they genuinely approach an organization to obtain credit, are refused, and have to uncover reasons why.

Such problems as outlined above raise the need for combined consideration of ethics, law and professionalism. Jurisdiction-based legislation seems ill-formed for problems that cross geographical boundaries, potentially with vast physical separation of these boundaries. Professional and ethical standards may transcend boundaries, but these also require systematic adoption by a majority in order to be effective. Conversely, acting legally may not guarantee that the actions are ethically or professionally acceptable.

In this chapter, we explore some of the legal difficulties that emerge in cyberspace and activities directly related to it. Our motivation is the development of computer systems that can embody ethical support and prevent unfortunate consequences due to a lack of, or incorrect, legal knowledge. Prevention of harm is key. In the second section, we explore examples of legal problems that relate strongly to cyberspace in order to emphasize the existence of certain differences due to geographical variations in laws. Section three makes consideration for Machine Ethics as involving the embodiment of legal, ethical and professional standards in computer programs for various purposes. In Section four, we discuss how online gambling offers difficulties that span the legal, ethical and religious. We explore the argument that companies might not (knowingly) infringe laws, yet in attempting to increase their profits by allowing certain behaviors, can give rise to addiction, which is certainly unethical. In Section five, we describe a system we have designed and implemented, EthiCasino, that demonstrates how to promote legally and ethically acceptable online gambling. Some sections are reproduced from our previous publication on "Machine Ethics for Gambling in the Metaverse: an "EthiCasino"", featured in Volume 2, Issue 3 of the Journal of Virtual Worlds Research (JVWR) and recontextualized in this chapter. They are included here by kind permission of the Editor in Chief of JVWR. We conclude by suggesting future directions for this work and identify areas which need more specific attention.

BACKGROUND

As discussed, people who believe in the supposed liberty afforded by cyberspace must take care in what they do. While there is nothing necessarily sinister in the technology itself, the actions that technologies facilitate may not always be harmless. Most cybercrimes are reasonably common offences and computer technologies have simply provided new ways to commit old crimes (Jewkes, 2003). However, laws have often been found wanting when considering what new technologies provide for. In real places, a person can only be in one place at one time; in cyberspaces, a person will be in a single physical location but can be simultaneously undertaking actions that link them with systems located in disparate locations, each of which has implications for laws, acceptable behaviors, and so on. In addition, the usual markers of identity are missing: cyberspace makes possible the creation of an identity so fluid and multiple that it strains the very limits of the notion (Jewkes, 2003). Those who can hide or fake an identity can act without fear of reprisal, surveillance, or legal intervention, and there is much supporting software for doing this. The powerful tools of investigation and identification, including surveillance cameras, fingerprints and DNA databases, can be as impotent in cyberspace as laws based on physical borders of countries being applied to people who are physically elsewhere. Additionally, for honest citizens, knowing the rules of one's own country provides insufficient coverage.

The 'Terms of Use' on websites bears testament to the need to understand the location of the servers being used, and this implies knowing the relevant laws of the country being virtually visited by making use of these servers. These terms of use can be many pages long if printed, and typically comprise legal-like phrasing that makes it something of a challenge for an everyday user to understand. This is brought into sharp focus when 'clickwrap' software is prevalent, and companies have opportunities for mischief here (Richmond, 2010; Fox News, 2010). The physical correlate is apparent whenever people travel abroad, and some are occasionally surprised to find themselves incarcerated for violating laws or traditions that they claim no knowledge of (BBC News, 2010).

With some 192 registered countries, according to the United Nations, understanding all of these legal systems across the various languages would be a substantial undertaking. Yet even variations amongst countries apparently close in spirit can be stark. We demonstrate this by two relatively simple examples: the first relating to Copyright Law, the second to Computer Crime and additional legislation which can be brought to bear.

COPYRIGHT LAW

Are you allowed to download the songs from your CD to your MP3 player in America? What if you do this same in the UK? What if you do this in America and travel to the UK?

The well-documented case of the file sharing website Napster (Baase, 2008) shows how technological advances can lead to new "old" crimes. The UK Copyright Act 1988 contains clauses relating to providing the apparatus for copyright infringement (secondary infringement), so would likely have been a starting point against a UK-based Napster. In its application, this law may well have needed to be reinterpreted as it appears the US law was. Since file sharing websites became a principal focus, those in cyberspace would be expected to be generally wary of the dangers, and typically huge fines, involved with large-scale distribution of music tracks. However, the very act of 'ripping' tracks from a CD into different formats in order to create shareable music files, may or may not

be legal depending on your location. A visitor to the UK may be surprised to find that, at the time of writing, the same law also makes it illegal to make such copies. A survey by Consumer Focus in 2010 showed that almost three in four (73%) of the UK population did not know that it was illegal to convert from CD to MP3. A majority would think that copying songs from the CD they own, having paid for it, is entirely legal: a CD can be played by an individual for their own listening pleasure on any suitable device and is readily portable, and it could be argued that this simply extends the range of suitable devices.

In America, the Recording Industry Association of America (RIAA) suggests that is acceptable to copy music if the CD is legitimately owned and it's for personal use only.

- *It's okay to copy music onto an analog cassette, but not for commercial purposes.*
- *It's also okay to copy music onto special Audio CD-R's, mini-discs, and digital tapes (because royalties have been paid on them) – but, again, not for commercial purposes.*
- *Beyond that, there's no legal "right" to copy the copyrighted music on a CD onto a CD-R. However, burning a copy of CD onto a CD-R, or transferring a copy onto your computer hard drive or your portable music player, won't usually raise concerns so long as:*
- *The copy is made from an authorized original CD that you legitimately own*
- *The copy is just for your personal use. It's not a personal use – in fact, it's illegal – to give away the copy or lend it to others for copying.*
- *The owners of copyrighted music have the right to use protection technology to allow or prevent copying.*
- *Remember, it's never okay to sell or make commercial use of a copy that you make.*
Source: RIAA

RIAA includes over 1.600 record companies, representing over 85% of the US market, so it has some considerable influence. However, it is unclear how much of RIAA's advice is provided for by the Digital Millennium Copyright Act 1998, and how much is RIAA-specific and may invite interest from the remaining 15% who RIAA do not represent. However, that is probably of lesser concern that would be the case if present UK legislation were to become more robustly enforced: the unwary American tourists, visiting the UK with CDs and, on RIAA advice, converting these for use on their MP3 players and laptops could find themselves in trouble.

In this discussion, the problems of cyberspace became amplified through focus on Napster, and in that process the importance of an act that also breaches copyright law in the UK is forgotten about. We suggested, above, that a person may be incorrectly extending the rules and social norms that are applicable in their own physical location, or believing there is a relaxation of regulations and restrictions, while inhabiting the generalized everywhere. This example demonstrates that people may even take such apparent relaxation back to the real world from cyberspace, and this may have its own attendant problems.

COMPUTER CRIME

You live in the UK and hack into a system in America. Whose laws apply?

Hacking into computers is generally a crime. When UK citizen Gary McKinnon, an "unemployed system administrator" was caught having hacked into 97 United States military and NASA computers, including US Army, US Navy, Department of Defense and the US Air Force (McKinnon v. U.S.), it was likely that legal proceedings would follow. However, the nature of the proceedings has been highly controversial.

In 2002, he was interviewed by the UK National Hi-Tech Crime Unit (NHTCU)[1], and was indicted by a federal grand jury in the Eastern District of Virginia in November 2002 on seven counts of cybercrime (U.S. v. McKinnon). It was claimed that he caused damages costing over $700,000, and had deleted US Navy weapons logs on about 300 computers after September 11th attacks. However, he denied most of the charges and argued that he was only interested in UFOs and believed that such information should be publicly accessible. Furthermore, as there was little or no security in placed on these systems, he thought what he did wouldn't be considered as hacking. McKinnon committed his hacking activities from his home computer in London. Here, the Computer Misuse Act 1990, section 1, would be applicable as he had caused "a computer to perform any function with intent to secure access to any program or data held in any computer", which was his intention, and technically he was not authorized to do so.

On 7th October 2004, an extradition request was made so that McKinnon could be prosecuted in America (US v. McKinnon). It was convenient that the Extradition Act 2003 had provided for such an action without needing *prima facie* evidence; asymmetric provisions relating to this Act would not allow the same in the opposite direction. Nor was this the first instance of the application of this law: following the collapse of Enron in late 2001, the Natwest Three (US v. David Bermingham, et al.) were indicted in 2002, arrested in the UK in 2004, and extradited to the US in 2006 using this 2003 law. Arguably, this represents an *ex post facto* relaxation on the requirement for evidence; retrospective application of law is frowned upon in some places, and simply unacceptable in others. After many years, at the time of writing (October 2010), McKinnon is still waiting for a decision on whether he is to be extradited (Kennedy, 2010). A timeline of events in the McKinnon and Natwest Three cases is shown in Table 1.

Here, the focus is on the prioritization of real world laws in relation to problems that have oc-

Table 1. Timeline of McKinnon and NatWest three cases

Gary McKinnon		Year	Natwest three	
Interviewed by police	March 19, 2002	**2002**	2002	Indicted on seven counts of wire fraud by Huston, Texas
Interviewed by NHTCU	August 8, 2002			
Indicted of seven counts of computer crime by a federal grand jury in the eastern	November 2002			
Extradition Act 2003 (early 2004)				
Subject to bail conditions	June 2005	**2005**	2002-2006	Series of courts in UK
US began extradition proceedings	Later in 2005			
Extradition approved by UK	July 2006	**2006**	2006	Extradition to US
Appeal to the High Court in London	February 2007	**2007**	November 2007	Plead guilty
House of Lords agree to hear the appeal	July 2007			
Case presented in House of Lords	June 16, 2008	**2008**	February 22, 2008	Sentenced to 37 months in prison
Rejected	July 2008			
Appeal to European Court of Human Rights against extradition - rejected	August 2008		November 2008	To spend the rest of their sentences in the UK
Won permission from High Court to apply for judicial review against extradition	January 23, 2009	**2009**	End of 2009	Released
Lost the appeal	July 31, 2009			
Case still open and being reviewed by new coalition government		**2010**	Free	
NB: this table has been constructed based on well known news websites (e.g. BBC News and Guardian). Imprecise dates due to lack of readily available information.				

curred in cyberspace. Gary McKinnon is trying to imply relaxations of laws into cyberspace to support his own ends. The unwary must be careful that the targets of their crimes do not try to apply unexpected, and even *ex post facto*, laws in such situations to try to bring the perpetrators to justice.

Machine Ethics

No sensible decision can be made any longer without taking into account not only the world as it is, but the world as it will be (Asimov, 1983, p.5).

Given the difficulty for everyday users in interpreting laws, there are two related possibilities: (i) to have incredibly well-specified, unambiguous, and highly readable laws so that they are readily understood by all users of cyberspaces; (ii) to codify laws into location-aware computer programs such that users are protected from attendant harms. Very long documents are very likely not going to be read, limiting the entire purpose of (i), so this brings us towards computerization of laws. Computerized laws need not be fully explicable, but they must allow for certain behaviours, warn about certain others, and deny yet others in certain locations, for certain users, and at certain times. The key principle being embodied here is the avoidance of harm to users, and this indicates ethics generally and, for us, Machine Ethics specifically.

Machine ethics is concerned with defining how machines should behave towards human users and other machines, with emphasis on avoiding harm and other negative consequences of autonomous machines, or unmonitored and unmanned computer programs. Researchers in machine ethics aim towards constructing machines whose decisions and actions will honor privacy, protect civil rights and individual liberty, and further the welfare of others (Allen, Wallach & Smit, 2005). However, the study of machine ethics is still undertaken by a relative minority, despite its apparent importance as autonomous machines become more prevalent. To produce ethical machines, it is necessary to understand how humans deal with ethics in decision making, and then try to construct appropriate behaviors within machines, or autonomous avatars, which with continuous availability and unemotional responses might start to replace human (ethical) advisors in a near future.

Steps towards ethical machines have been taken that focus on medical ethics, attempting to ensure human safety and social health. Such systems are intended towards understanding, and possibly reducing or avoiding, the potential for harm to an individual from, for example, unnecessary or incorrect medical intervention or in considering the kinds and nature of treatments being administered and any limiting factors that may consequentially emerge. In these systems, the final decision remains one of a human decision-maker, who becomes informed by such ethical considerations. The mainstream literature largely discusses using Case-Based Reasoning and machine learning techniques to implement systems that can mimic the responses of the researchers (Anderson, Anderson & Armen, 2005; McLaren & Ashley, 2000). A machine-based ethical advisor apparently has the following advantages, many of which are familiar arguments in the development of intelligent systems:

- Always available
- Unemotional
- Employ mixture of ethical theories
- Can explain reasoning
- Capacity for simulations
- Capacity for range of legal considerations
- No hypothetical limits on the number of situations assessed

A synthesized overview of many of the systems reported in the literature as ethical machines is shown in Table 2. Each of these systems has a specific ethical approach and related techniques that provide for solutions to ethical dilemmas, targeted at particular audiences and challenges for those audiences. The majority of these existing systems focus on medical ethics, with limited coverage for other applications of ethics.

To develop a machine-based ethical advisor, we must make reference to such systems, but need not be constrained in our thinking by them. The problem with systems inherently based on cases and rules is that adaptation to other domains requires a new set of domain-specific rules or cases to be developed or captured; this is a well-known bottleneck in artificially intelligent systems and it may be more appropriate to attempt to avoid such constraints. Further, we need to determine the key ethical and legal points which are being embodied within such a system so that there is more than simply an informing approach: the ethical advisor must also be able to intervene when the need arises. Essentially, such a system must offer the best approach grounded in ethics and law, rather than simply offer up its reasoning. We explore this in the following sections in relation to online gambling.

ONLINE GAMBLING

Are you allowed to gamble online in America? What if you go to UK or any other country in the world?

Table 2. Evaluation of existing applications

Name	Developed By:	Ethical Approach	Techniques	Suitable	Ethical Area
Ethos	Searing, D.	Moral DM	Not AI Some ethical samples	Engineering Students	Practical- ethical problems
Dax Cowart	Multiple writers	Moral DM	Not AI	Students, Teachers	Biomedical ethics, Right to die
Metanet	Guarini, M.	Particularism Motive consequential-ism	Pair case (SRN), Case base, Neural network (training), Three layers	Problems in flag-ging	Killing or allowing to die
	Robins, R. And Wallach, W.	Desire-intention	Multi-agent	Not implemented	
Truth-Teller	McLaren, B. M.	Casuistry	Pair case, Case-Based Reasoning,	Ethical advice	Pragmatic or hypo-thetical cases
HYPO	Ashley, K. D.	Legal- reasoning	Case base	Legal advice	Hypothetical cases
SIROCCO	McLaren, B. M	Casuistry	Pair case, Case-Based Reasoning, Simulating "moral imagination"	Ethical device	NSPE Code of Ethics
Jeremy	Anderson, M. Anderson, S. Armen, C.	Hedonistic act utilitari-anism	"Moral arithmetic"		Rule generalization
W.D.	Anderson, M. Anderson, S. Armen, C	Prima facie duty, Casuistry	Inductive-logic pro-gramming, Learning algorithm, Reflective equilibrium		Rule generalization
MedEthEx	Anderson, M. Anderson, S. Armen, C.	W.D. Medical ethics, Casuistry, Prima facie duty	Inductive-logic program-ming, Machine learning, Re-flective equilibrium	Health care work-ers	Biomedical ethics
EthEl	Anderson, M. Anderson, S.	Prima facie duty, Casu-istry, W.D., Medical ethics	Inductive-logic pro-gramming, Learning algorithm, Reflective equilibrium	Eldercare	Biomedical ethics

In Section 2, we discussed two examples in which differences in international laws were key. We could also have explored these situations from the perspective of a number of ethical theories, although the ethical dimensions are less obviously relevant in contrast to the question posed above. In gambling, and in online gambling in particular, gamblers should be "responsible". Some can become addicted, lose large amounts of money and be used by others as a means to earn money to support their addiction or resort to crime. Meanwhile, those providing for online gambling are making substantial revenues: online casinos alone are due to reach $4.7 billion by end of 2010 (iGambling Business, n.d.), and it has been estimated that the gambling business generally will hit $125 billion by 2015 (Young, 2006).

In cyberspace, gambling may or may not be a crime; it may or may not be taboo; knowing which it is and when is the first challenge. Prevention of harm then becomes important. In this section, we discuss gambling, its issues in general, and the reality for those seeking to gamble in cyberspace.

Gambling Ethics

Gambling is described as:

... betting or staking of something of value, with consciousness of risk and hope of gain, on the

outcome of a game, a contest, or an uncertain event whose result may be determined by accident. Commercial establishments such as casinos... may organize gambling when a portion of the money wagered by patrons can be easily acquired by participation as a favoured party in the game, by rental of space, or by withdrawing a portion of the betting pool (Gilmne, n.d.).

This simple definition leads to further observations about people's behaviour in relation to possibility of winning extra money or goods:

1. People may play for money not for fun
2. The odds of losing are much higher than wining and outcome is uncertain
3. People may chase the game to win back the money they lost
4. People may lose the sense of their own "will" because they are playing a game in which "will" is not an element
5. They do not feel they need to gain the knowledge about how to play before they begin because they consider it just a "GAME"

Such observations can lead towards corruption, addiction and organized crime. To reduce the risk of harm both to players and society, different countries have (different) regulations for the industry – in the UK, this is the Gambling Act 2005. Although each country approaches these issues differently, many have taken steps to raise public awareness about such problems. For example, the UK's law discusses limiting the number of casinos and forcing members of the industry to demonstrate their plans for contributions to research, for raising public awareness about the problems gambling can cause, and for helping to treat those affected (Russell, 2006). America has approached awareness issues by introducing The National Gambling Impact Study Commission Act 1996 (NGISCA; H.R.5474), which included a comprehensive legal and factual study of the social and economic impacts of gambling. Other steps

for raising awareness have been taken by NGOs, promoting the idea that players should be aware of the time and money that they spend on gambling, and the consequences and risks involved.

According to "Ethical Corporation" there are three reasons the online gambling industry should take its responsibilities seriously (Saha, 2005):

- To clear up the industry's traditional image
- To attract potential customers who otherwise steer clear because of this image, and
- To comply with regulations

However, often when gambling websites are demonstrating that they are being "responsible", such a demonstration may simply be encapsulated in a document containing the kinds of rhetoric presented below:

- We are there to help whenever you realize that you need a control over the money that you spend
- We can decrease the amount of money you can put into your account if you ask.
- You can increase it again if you feel you are in control.
- If you think you need a break from gambling, you can use self-exclusion tool
- If you suspect that you may have a gambling problem, you may seek professional help from the following links
- Make sure gambling does not become a problem in your life and you do not lose control of your play.
- Make sure that the decision to gamble is your personal choice.

Such statements require individuals who may be experiencing addiction to be aware of the fact, and to be in sufficient control to do something about it. The "problem" is for the end user to deal with, and the organization has effectively absolved itself of responsibility. Gambling addiction is identified as one of the most destructive addictions which is not physically apparent - an "invisible addiction" (Comeau, 1997). Psychologists believe that online gamblers are even more prone to addiction because they can play without distraction or recognition.

Internet gambling, unlike many other types of gambling activity, is a solitary activity, which makes it even more dangerous: people can gamble uninterrupted and undetected for unlimited periods of time (Price, 2006).

Furthermore, the capability for adopting multiple false identities in cyberspace means that simply blocking user accounts is going to be ineffective. It is unlikely, then, that self-control could be exerted or easily enforced for online gambling.

Websites such as gambleaware.co.uk offer potential players and gamblers information about the odds of winning, the average return to players, "house edge", a gambling fact and fiction quiz, and more, to offer increased awareness. Gambleaware (n.d.) define a responsible gambler as a person who:

- Gambles for fun, not to make money or to escape problems.
- Knows that they are very unlikely to win in the long run.
- Does not try to 'chase' or win back losses.
- Gambles with money set aside for entertainment and never uses money intended for rent, bill or food.
- Does not borrow money to gamble.
- Does not let gambling affect their relationships with family and friends.

Defining measures to differentiate between responsible players and addicted gamblers would certainly help to prevent addiction, corruption and crime, but what do such measures look like?

Gambling Laws and Regulations

Though countries do have laws relating to gambling, people tend to ignore such laws in cyberspace. Huge growth in online gambling[2] often brings it in line with physical forms of gambling. Some countries have created new laws for online gambling, while others extended old laws to cover it. Interestingly, America has a restrictive law in the Unlawful Internet Gambling Enforcement Act 2006. This law has reportedly had a detrimental impact on its economy: it has been estimated that US could have created between 16,000 and 32,000 jobs and generated a total gross expenditure in the nation's economy of $94 billion over the first five years and $57.5 billion in domestic taxation (H2 Gambling Capital, 2010).

Such new and extended laws include:

- US: The Unlawful Internet Gambling Enforcement Act 2006 (UIGEA, H.R.4411): Prohibits financial institutions from approving transactions between U.S.-based customer accounts and offshore gambling merchants.
- US: Internet Gambling Regulation and Enforcement Act 2007 (IGREA, H.R.2046): "Providing a provision for licensing of internet gambling facilities by the Director of the Financial Crimes enforcement network"
- US: Skill Game Protection Act 2007 (SGPA, H.R.2610): "Legalize internet skilled games where players' skills are important in winning or losing games such as poker, bridge and chess"
- US: Internet Gambling Regulation and Tax Enforcement Act 2007 (IGRTEA, HR 2607): "Legalize internet gambling tax collection requirements"
- US: Internet Gambling Regulation, Consumer Protection, and Enforcement Act 2009 (H.R. 2267): (under discussion) provide licensing of Internet Gambling

activities, consider consumer protection and tax enforcement. If passed, it will create a an exception to the Unlawful Internet Gambling Enforcement Act of 2006 (UIGEA) for poker

- Australia: Interactive Gambling Act 2001 (IGA): Provides protection for Australian players from the harmful effects of gambling
- UK: Gambling Act 2005 (c. 19): "it is not illegal for British residents to gamble online and it is not illegal for overseas operators to offer online gambling to British residents (though there are restrictions on advertising)"

Variation leads towards three principal divisions:

1. Countries where gamblers are free to play online, or there is no specific regulation, e.g. UK
2. Countries where gamblers are not allowed to play online, e.g. USA (GAO, 2002), and
3. Countries where gambling of any kind is prohibited, e.g. Islamic countries (Lewis, 2003)

A glimpse of the legality of online gambling in 100 countries is shown in Table 3:

Where gambling of any kind is legal, or not legislated against, it may also be age-restricted. Mostly, the gambling age – whether in cyberspaces or in real places - varies between 18 and 21; specific exceptions are Greece and some provinces in Portugal with minimum ages of 23 and 25 respectively, where online gambling is not currently allowed but a government might wish to allow it if it could improve the economic situations of either countries. So, whilst in one country, it may be perfectly possible for you to gamble online; go to another country and visit the same website, and you might not be allowed to or might be age restricted when doing so.

The cyberspace problems of online gambling are wider still. Suppose that a US company was operating an online gambling website from UK servers, allowing gamblers to play from all over the world with terms of use that say that if security breaches occur then the company is responsible and American courts are primary. A time later, a UK citizen on holiday on a Caribbean Island hacks the system and takes credit card numbers and information about gamblers from Saudi Arabia and the US. The hacker obtains large amounts of money from players and disappears.

1. Can the company report a cybercrime? And if so, who to?
2. Can Saudi Arabian and U.S. gamblers report the crime? Gambling of any kind is prohibited for Saudis and online gambling is forbidden for US players.
3. Can players claim their money back from the company in America, based on the terms of use?
4. For the hacker, which laws should be applicable? How does this compare to the Gary McKinnon case?

Companies who have not taken full account of the applicable laws will end up paying the consequences. One well-known example relates to casinos in the Second Life (SL) virtual world. All casinos were forced to close, effectively overnight, in SL by the FBI. Companies that had invested substantially in their virtual world presence suddenly lost revenues, and the virtual world itself lost users as a consequence. The country of origin of the gambling companies was irrelevant since the servers were operating in the US. Players from all over the world had been gambling in online casinos in SL, making it one of the strongest businesses in that virtual environment, and therefore having the most significant impact on the associated virtual world economy.

Inevitably, it will be suggested that universal legislation should be required for online gambling,

Table 3. Online gambling regulations in different countries

Countries and territories where online gambling is legal							
1	Aland Islands	19	Dominican Republic	37	Lithuania	55	Seychelles
2	Alderney	20	Estonia	38	Luxembourg	56	Singapore
3	Antigua	21	Finland **	39	Macau	57	Slovenia
4	Argentina	22	France ***	40	Malta	58	Solomon Islands
5	Aruba	23	Germany	41	Mauritius	59	South Africa
6	Australia *	24	Gibraltar	42	Monaco	60	South Korea
7	Austria	25	Grenada	43	Myanmar	61	Spain
8	Bahamas	26	Hungary	44	Nepal	62	St. Kitts and Nevis
9	Belgium	27	Iceland	45	Netherlands Antilles	63	St. Vincent
10	Belize	28	India	46	Norfolk Island	64	Swaziland
11	Brazil	29	Ireland	47	North Korea	65	Sweden
12	Chile	30	Isle of Man	48	Norway	66	Switzerland
13	Colombia	31	Israel	49	Panama	67	Taiwan
14	Comoros	32	Italy	50	Philippines	68	Tanzania
15	Costa Rica	33	Jamaica	51	Poland	69	United Kingdom
16	Czech Republic	34	Jersey	52	Russia	70	US Virgin Islands
17	Denmark	35	Kalmykia	53	Sark	71	Vanuatu
18	Dominica	36	Latvia	54	Serbia	72	Venezuela
Countries where online gambling is illegal							
1	Afghanistan	8	Greece	15	New Zealand	22	Taiwan
2	Algeria	9	Hong Kong	16	Nigeria	23	Thailand
3	Bahrain	10	Indonesia	17	Pakistan	24	The Bahamas
4	Brunei	11	Iran	18	Portugal	25	The Netherlands
5	China	12	Japan	19	Saudi Arabia	26	Turkey
6	Cyprus	13	Jordan	20	South Korea	27	United States
7	Dubai	14	Libya	21	Sudan	28	Vietnam

* For Australia, different laws might be applied in different states.
** Must be a Finnish resident with a Finnish bank account to play.
***FRANCE'S National Assembly has voted in favour of a bill to legalize online gambling. Approval is still needed by the European Union and France's Conseil d'Etat (Supreme Court) and Conseil Constitutionnel (Constitutional Council). Previously, France did not allow such companies within its borders, but its citizens could gamble from other companies internationally.

Note: the regulations might be changed by the time its printed (updated 10/2010)

but this will favour those with the most restrictive practices and therefore be readily unacceptable to large numbers of people. There may be the argument that users should take responsibility for knowing whether or not to play based on their country's laws. However, it might be considered unreasonable to ask users or potential users to read the regulations from all over the world in order to know whether or not they are affected. This, then, leads back to controls that must be put in place by the online gambling providers (Price, 2006). These responsibilities can be implemented by ensuring that servers are sensibly located, and controlling who enters on the basis of country of request and acceptable age for gamblers (both of which can change). There remains, then, the need to prevent harm, and here we also propose the embedding of such prevention in computer programs. We discuss such embedding in the next section.

MACHINE ETHICS FOR ONLINE GAMBLING

Machine ethics has not yet been applied by others for avoidance of harm in relation to online gambling. Alongside a number of other pursuits, and because gambling has potential for addiction, it could be claimed that a system for ethical gambling may be as effective for humans and social health as medical ethics. Machine ethics may not cure addiction, but it may be able to act to reduce the likelihood of addiction. Our consideration here is how Machine Ethics may support responsible gambling and lead towards an Ethical Corporation.

We base the design of EthiCasino on prior literature and systems in Machine Ethics as shown in Table 2. We have been inspired in particular by three of these systems, W.D., MedEthEx and EthEl, that have used Ross' *prima facie* duties (1930), extended by Garrett (2004). Ross introduced seven "prima facie duties" as guidelines for solving ethical dilemmas but these are not rules without exception. If an action does not satisfy a "duty", it is not necessarily violating a "rule"; however if a person is not practising these duties then he or she is failing in their duties. Garrett (2004) believed there to be aspects of human ethical life

not covered by Ross, and extended this list with three further duties. MedEthEx uses a series of questions with a three responses, "Yes", "No" and "Don't know", to decide the outcome in relation to three of Ross' and Garrett's duties: *non-injury*, *beneficence* and *freedom* (autonomy). By weighting outcomes between -2 and +2, the application explains the likely impact on the patient ability to clarify the areas in which decisions will be made. EthEl takes two kinds of actions based on decisions made: (i) reminding users; (ii) notifying overseers. A system using Ross' and Garrett's duties for responsible gambling should consider the potential for the duties not being satisfied and act accordingly.

While MedEthEx and EthEl concentrate on three main duties of non- injury, beneficence and freedom, EthiCasino considers a wider range of duties; in particular, EthiCasino employs 6 of Ross' 7 duties and all 3 duties defined by Garret in different stages (Table 4). Using these Prima facie duties enables the system to learn from users' behaviour even if they might not match exactly the original definition of the duties.

EthiCasino takes certain actions that support the performance of these duties in order to assure users' safety and wellbeing by minimizing possibilities of problematic and addictive behaviour, providing ethically-acceptable support, and meeting the requirements of mimicking action of human ethical advisors. This aims at ensuring fair

Table 4. Duties of Ross and Garret in each stage

Stage	Name	Ross's duties involved
Stage 1: Legal considerations	Legal issues	Justice, Harm prevention, Non-injury, Beneficence, Self-improvement
Stage 2: Knowledge of Risk	Ethical issues	Justice, Harm prevention, Non- injury
Stage 3: Boundaries for time and money	Boundaries	Justice, Harm prevention, Respect of freedom, Fidelity, Gratitude
Stage 4: Appropriate reminders: "nagware"	VIKIs reminders	Non-injury, Beneficence, Self-improvement, Care
Stage 5: Boundary conditions	VIKIs alert	Justice, Harm prevention, Non-injury, Beneficence

actions for both virtual gambler and virtual casino:

1. Gambler:
   a. Clarify the possible risks of gambling online
   b. Choose playing hours and amount of money they wish to gamble
   c. Remind the users of their playing hours and the amount money they are losing
2. Casino:
   a. Take decisions about whether or not to let specific persons play based on their answers
   b. Notify the company if a user is going over their own limitation
   c. Log the user off if they don't take action after being reminded by the system

We discuss the 5 main, often inter-dependent, stages involving legal and ethical considerations below:

Stage 1: Legal considerations

Consideration of legal issues involves variations in acceptability of online gambling and associated age restrictions in 100 countries, as presented above. Here, system can attempt to capture the geographical location (DNS lookup) of the end user, and act accordingly, but because of the capacity for technological circumvention the gambler needs to self-certify. Self-certification is required, also, for confirming the age of the end user. Should the location of the end user change over time from the original registration, the legal situation may change accordingly and location information must be captured and verified for each session.

Stage 2: Knowledge of Risk

Decisions related to financial risks may be taken in a number of business environments, especially in relation to stock markets and world economies. Those involved in taking such decisions are usually considered well-informed and have a number of checks and balances against which to validate their decisions or off-set their risks and/or losses. The person's knowledge is the effective tool in making the final decision. Unfortunately, because of the purported "entertainment" aspect of gambling, it is less important for users to have such knowledge or to consider how to off-set risks and losses and more favorable to revenues if users are less well-informed.

To evaluate the risk behaviours of end users, we designed a questionnaire comprising 12 questions related to gambling fact and fiction and 8 related to risk and loss aversion. We offered L\$$10^3$ to participants, equivalent to around 2½ hours camping, and obtained 61 responses to this questionnaire from Second Life users within a week. On average, 12.22 questions were correctly answered, with 7 and 17 as minimum and maximum. We *a priori* weighted questions based on our own perceptions of associated risk or negative impact on users in the absence of knowledge, leading to a division of questions into four categories:

1. **Low risk:** users should be able to learn quickly or lack of knowledge will not have much negative impact. e.g. Q3: "Some people are luckier than others" (fact or fiction)
2. **Medium risk:** users may believe in luck. e.g. Q6: "My lucky number will increase my chance of winning the lottery" (fact or fiction)
3. **Medium-high risk:** questions relate to calculations and predictability of results e.g. Q14: "Assume you bet \$1 on the toss of a coin the chances of heads or tails are 50/50. If you win and 'house edge' is 10% how much you will be paid? (10c, 50c, 90c, \$1)"
4. **High risk:** question regards perceptions of earning money and realistic facts of gam-

Figure 1. Risk groups based on responses to questions on gambling

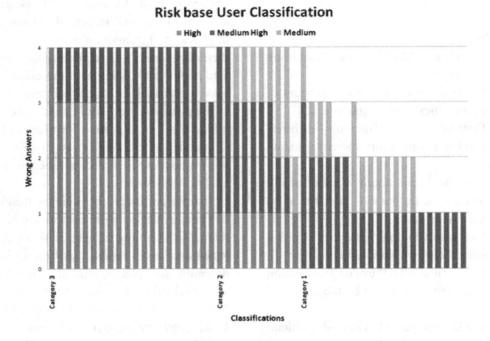

bling. e.g. Q1: "Gambling is an easy way to make money" (fact or fiction)

User answers and weightings led to three distinct classes of users (Figure 1), important so that the system can help them to avoid negative impacts of incorrect decisions:

- **Group one:** Those who may only need additional information about the games (low and medium risk questions)
- **Group two:** Those who need to be reminded about the facts (medium-high risk questions), and
- **Group three:** Those who need full monitoring and potential intervention because they are less informed and might be more prone to addiction (high risk questions)

To evaluate these behaviour profiles, we analysed the correlations between the 20 questions for 50 users (Table 3), hoping that diversification

would exist across the various responses. The resulting correlation matrix showed maximum correlation between 18 of the questions of less than 0.5 (-1/+1), suggesting that the questions themselves had a reasonable degree of independence. On this basis, the risk classification becomes the important factor since the individual questions themselves do not act as a reliable predictor for others in the same class.

Stage 3: Boundaries for time and money

For a user to stay in control, part of the main challenge of gambling, the system should allow them to opt for boundaries. Considering that each user background and experience is different, and that there is such variation across responses to 20 questions about gambling, it could be unethical to enforce boundaries without end user permissions. Users are asked to define their own boundaries both for the amount of time and the amount of

Figure 2. Maximum boundaries for each category

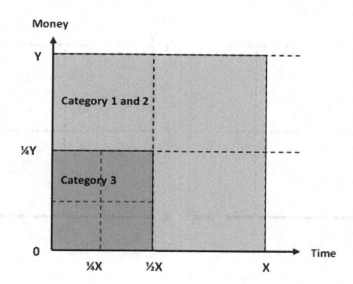

money they plan to spend: these two elements are core in addiction and harm. The user's choice of boundaries is checked against their apparent riskiness. For users with profiles in Groups 1 and 2, the system will allow users to participate with limited interference; users in Group 3 will receive a moderated limit as the maximum boundary (Figure 2).

Stage 4: Appropriate reminders: "nagware"

In EthiCasino, to minimize the potential for destructive behaviours, we adopt the idea of "nagware"[4] as used by a number of software providers to remind users of specific actions, e.g. that they should pay for the software they have been using. In EthiCasino, this nagware has been called **VIKI**[5] and undertakes specific responsibilities:

- **Artificial ethical conscience:** suggestions allied to risk taking and user's circumstances, e.g. "high risk of losses, do you still what to bet?"
- **Educational:** providing access to information about each game, risks and odds as-

sociated to it, e.g. "roulette, your odds are 35 to 1"
- **Nagging:** Regularly reminding users, depending on their risk profiles, about the time and money spent, as both head towards the limits they have set.

Users receive reminders depending on how they approach their own specified limits. Those identified as having riskier behaviours will receive fewer reminders compared to other users. Those who have spent their money more quickly may be tempted to spend more, sometimes chasing losses. Those who manage not to make losses within the initial time period may be encouraged to continue and to make assumptions over the likelihood of larger future wins. Of course, user profiles may change over time depending on the increased or decreased risky behaviour of the end user (Figure 3).

Stage 5: Boundary conditions

After users receive their final reminder from VIKI, they will be prevented from further gambling. The purpose here is to ensure the user's

Figure 3. Possible users' behavior

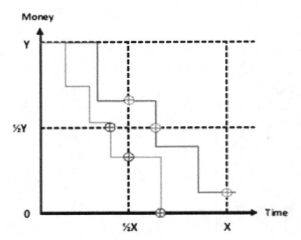 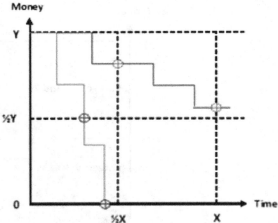

own boundaries are enforced and to ensure the risky behaviours do not lead to harm; that is, EthiCasino acts to prevent behaviours that might lead to addiction. Those continuing beyond their own time and financial limits may also be going beyond their own limits of rational behaviour. A virtual doorman who ejects non-conforming end users is a possible future consideration.

FUTURE RESEARCH DIRECTIONS

This chapter offers several avenues for future work, both with a narrow focus on ethical and legal online gambling and wider focus on ethical and legal cyberspace. Some are directly driven from the principles of EthiCasino, while others emerge from the concepts of machine ethics for cyberspace. Examples are:

1. **Ethical data mining:** An artificial agent can be designed to deal with data and rules which not only will increase the accuracy of the system but its ethicality (fairness) as well.

2. **Ethical gambling websites:** the framework of EthiCasino could be adopted for online gambling of all kinds.

3. **Ethical and legal advisors:** formulated around specific ethical and legal problems in other domains, and grounded in applicable laws. For example, advisors for business ethics could act to prevent unethical actions (some of which may be similar to gambling) or promote adherence to codes of ethics and professional practice.

In all of these, ethics fill the gaps between laws, technologies, and what people know and/ or are allowed to do and/or should be prevented from doing for their own good.

CONCLUSION

In this chapter we have discussed the difficult interplay between cyberspaces and real places, the relationship of laws to both, and how the consideration of ethics can help to avoid some of the inherent problems. Cyberspace can be a dangerous place for ill-informed virtual tourists since they are rapidly crossing legal, typically geographic, boundaries without being aware of this fact. In so doing, the virtual tourist may be inappropriately projecting local laws and customs into cyberspace, or believing that such laws and customs are related. We provided examples of how specific laws related to cyberspace in different ways, and in particular how crime investigations become contentious. We then introduced the importance of Machine Ethics and applied this to Online Gambling. The motivation here is to prevent legal problems as would arise due to variations in international law, for example relating to acceptability and age for online gambling. In doing so, we assumed that the "sophisticated verification systems"[6] of extant online gambling companies were already sufficiently capable of verifying a user's age so did not warrant further investigation. The importance of reducing the likelihood of addiction and therefore improving, at least, the autonomy of users gives rise to the system discussed acting as an ethical advisor which can intervene when necessary. Our offered ethical framework, via EthiCasino[7], is a prototype created in the Second Life virtual world. EthiCasino implements specific ethical theories and learns about the risky behaviour and (lack of) knowledge of its users. While most other ethical systems considered in this paper are either conceptual or prototype conceptual models, never tested with actual users, or are otherwise unavailable or have been discarded by their creators, the ethical principles behind EthiCasino have undergone limited testing with users.

With the substantial revenues estimated for online gambling, a system such as EthiCasino may help to ensure that the ethical side of gambling remains to the fore by addressing issues relating to the impulse to gamble (Cutter & Smith, 2008). Reactive and non-intervening systems may be ineffective as people may not be aware of their lack of knowledge of odds, can adopt alternate identities to work around being restricted, and because problem gamblers may not realize that they have a problem. EthiCasino requires users to demonstrate their levels of gambling knowledge

in order to assess their likely risk profile, and also requires them to provide limits before they become caught up in the actions. If their risk profile increases, or they exceed their self-imposed limits, intervention should occur; those who demonstrate low levels of gambling knowledge may be unable to increase their limits. The design of such a system may lead some to want to discuss privacy issues in relation to monitoring. It is important to note that gambling companies will already have a large amount of information about their customers and their gambling habits, so would be readily capable of invading their privacy if minded to, and could infer, post hoc, an overall risk profile for a user. The purpose of EthiCasino is to help *users* to avoid unfortunate consequences, and to assist through provision of limits. If it were unethical to ask people about their competency and knowledge in relation to potential dangers, and to build in definable alters, both driving tests and alarm clocks would be deemed unethical.

We claim that EthiCasino demonstrates how users can be helped to avoid problems with addiction. The prototype framework of EthiCasino is relatively well-developed, and EthiCasino has been evaluated by a number of machine ethicists and experts in philosophy, computer science and business. A larger-scale evaluation is needed, but offering this in Second Life would entail allowing for online gambling, ruling out such an effort. The move to an alternative virtual world, the creation of a private virtual world, or the transference of the principles to web-based gambling system may allow for such an evaluation. Such considerations as these, if applied within virtual worlds, might help to reverse the substantial decline in turnover seen due to the hosting of online gambling systems being illegal in the US; more widely, this could offer up new opportunities for the advent of gambling, ethically, elsewhere.

REFERENCES

Allen, C., Wallach, W., & Smit, I. (2006). Why machine ethics? *IEEE Intelligent Systems, 21*(4), 12–17. doi:10.1109/MIS.2006.83

Anderson, M., Anderson, S., & Armen, C. (2005). Towards machine ethics: Implementing two action-based ethical theories. *Proceeding of AAAI 2005 Fall Symposium on Machine Ethics,* (pp. 1-7). AAAI Press.

Ashford, W. (2010, June 9). Data Protection Act is out of kilter with EU law, warns privacy lawyer. *Computer Weekly*. Retrieved from http: //www.computerweekly. com/Articles/2010/06/09/241513/ Data-Protection-Act-is-out-of-kilter- with-EU-law-warns-privacy.htm

Asimov, I. (1983). *Asimov on science fiction.* London, UK: Granada.

Baase, S. (2008). *Gift of fire: Social, legal, and ethical issues for computing and the Internet* (3rd ed.). Cambridge, MA: Pearson.

Boyd, C. (2008). Profile: Gary McKinnon. *BBC News*. Retrieved from http: //news.bbc.co. uk/1/hi/technology/ 4715612.stm

Comeau, S. (1997). Getting high on gambling. *McGill Reporter*. Retrieved from http: //reporter-archive.mcgill. ca/Rep/r3004/ gambling.html

Consumer Focus. (2010). *Outdated copyright law confuses consumers*. Retrieved from http: //www. consumerfocus.org. uk/news/outdated-copyright-law-confuses-consumers

Cutter, C., & Smith, M. (2008, April). Gambling addiction and problem gambling: Signs, symptoms and treatment. *helpguide.org*. Retrieved from http: //www.helpguide. org/mental/gambling_addiction.htm

FoxNews. (2010, April 15). 7,500 online shoppers unknowingly sold their souls. *Fox News*. Retrieved from http: //www.foxnews. com/scitech/2010/ 04/15/online-shoppers- unknowingly-sold-souls/

Gambleaware. (n.d.). Responsible gambling. *Gambleaware*. Retrieved from http ://gambleaware.co.uk/ responsible-gambling

GAO. (2002). *Internet gambling: An overview of the issues*. United States General Accounting Office. Retrieved from http: //www.gao. gov/new. items/ d0389.pdf

Garrett, J. (2004). *A simple and usable (although incomplete) ethical theory based on the ethics of W. D. Ross*. Western Kentucky University. Retrieved from http: //www.wku. edu/~jan.garrett/ ethics/rossethc.htm

Gibson, W. (1984). *Neuromancer*. New York, NY: Ace Books.

Glimne, D. (n.d.) Gambling. *Encyclopaedia Britannica*. Retrieved from http://www.britannica.com

H2 Gambling Capital. (2010). *United States Internet gambling: Job creation – Executive summary*. H2 Gambling Capital. Retrieved from www. safeandsecureig. org/news/InternetGamblingStudy _04_15_2010.pdf

iGambling Business. (n.d.). *Rosy future for online casino industry*. iGambling Business. Retrieved from http: //www.igamingbusiness. com/content/ rosy-future- online-casino-industry

Jewkes, Y. (Ed.). (2003). *Dot.cons: Crime, deviance and identity on the internet*. Cullompton, UK: Willan.

Kennedy, M. (2010, September 08). Extradition treaties to be reviewed. *The Guardian*. Retrieved from http: //www.guardian.co. uk/law/2010/ sep/08/ extradition-treaties-to-be-reviewed

Lewis, E. (2003). *Gambling and Islam: Clashing and co-existing*. Brigham Young University. Retrieved from http: /www.math.byu. edu/~jarvis/ gambling /student-papers/eric-lewis.pdf

McKinnon (Appellant) v Government of the United States of America (Respondents) and Another. (2008). UKHL 59. House of Lords.

McLaren, B. M., & Ashley, K. D. (2000). Assessing relevance with extensionally defined principles and cases. *Proceedings of the 17th National Conference of Artificial Intelligence,* AAAI press, Austin, Texas. (pp. 316-322).

Net-Security. (2010). Botnets drive the rise of ransomware. *Net Security*. Retrieved from http: //www.net-security. org/secworld. php?id=9095

News, B. B. C. (2010, April 04). Jailed Dubai kissing pair lose appeal over conviction. *BBC News*. Retrieved from http: //news.bbc.co. uk/1/ hi/uk/ 8602449.stm

Pasick, A. (2007). FBI checks gambling in Second Life virtual world. *Reuters*. Retrieved from http: //www.reuters. com/article/technologyNews/ idUSHUN43981820070405

Price, J. (2006). *Gambling - Internet Gambling*. The Ethics and Religious Library Commission. Retrieved from http://erlc. com/article/gambling-internet-gambling

RIAA. (n.d.). *Piracy: Online and on the street*. Recording Industry Association of America (RIAA). Retrieved from http://www.riaa.com/ physicalpiracy.php

Richmond, S. (2010, April 17). Gamestation collects customers' souls in April Fools gag. *Telegraph*. Retrieved from http: //blogs.telegraph. co. uk/technology/shanerichmond/ 100004946/ gamestation-collects- customers-souls-in-april-fools-gag/

Ross, W. D. (1930). *The right and the good*. Oxford, UK: Oxford University Press.

Russell, J. (2006). Europe: Responsible gambling: A safer bet? *Ethical Corporation*. Retrieved from http: //www.ethicalcorp. com/content.asp? ContentID=4291

Saha, P. (2005). Gambling with responsibilities. *Ethical Corporation*. Retrieved from http: //www. ethicalcorp. com/content.asp? ContentID=3774

United States of America v. David Bermingham, et al., 18 U.S.C. §§ 1343 & 2. CR-02-00597.

United States of America v. Gary McKinnon. 18 U.S.C. §§ 1030(a)(5)(A) & 2 Indictment.

Vartapetiance, A., & Gillam, L. (2010). DNA dataveillance: Protecting the innocent? *Journal of Information. Communication and Ethics in Society,* 8(3), 270–288. doi:10.1108/14779961011071079

Weber, T. (2007, January 25). Criminals may overwhelm the Web. *BBC News*. Retrieved from http: //news.bbc.co. uk/1/hi/business/ 6298641.stm

Young, A. (2006). *Gambling or gaming, entertainment or exploitation?* Ethical Investment Advisory Group of the Church of England. Retrieved from http: //www.cofe.anglican. org/info/ethical/policystatements/ gambling.pdf

ADDITIONAL READING

Anderson, M., & Anderson, S. (2006). Computing an Ethical Theory with Multiple Prima Facie Duties, Proccedings of the 10th international Conference on the Simulation and Synthesis of Living Systems, Indiana University

Anderson, M., & Anderson, S. (2008). EthEl: Toward a Principled Ethical Eldercare Robot *Robotic Helpers: User Interaction, Interfaces and Companions in Assistive and Therapy Robotics Workshop at the Third ACM/IEEE Human-Robot Interaction Conference.* ACM/IEEE. Amsterdam, NL, 33-39

Arkin, R. C. (2008). "Governing Lethal Behaviour: Embedding Ethics in a Hybrid Deliberative/Reactive Robot Architecture - Part I: Motivation and Philosophy", *Robotic Helpers: User Interaction, Interfaces and Companions in Assistive and Therapy Robotics Workshop at the Third ACM/IEEE Human-Robot Interaction Conference.* ACM/IEEE. Amsterdam, NL

Bentham, J. (1948). *Introduction to the Principles of Morals and Legislation,* Oxford, UK, (origial work published at 1781). Retrieved from http: //socserv.mcmaster. ca/econ/ugcm/3ll3/bentham/morals.pdf

Bringsjord, S. And Arkoudas, K. And Bello, P. (2006). Toward a General Logicist Methodology for Engineering Ethically Correct Robots. *IEEE Intelligent Systems, 21*(4), 38–44. doi:10.1109/MIS.2006.82

Carlson, D. (2007). Internet gambling law a success, but faces scrutiny. *The Ethics and Religious Library Commision.* Retrieved from http: //erlc.com/article/ internet-gambling-law-a -success-but-faces-scrutiny

EETL. (n.d.). Engineering Ethics Transcription Exercise. *University of Pittsburgh.* Retrieved from http://www.pitt.edu/~bmclaren/ethics/

Guarini, M. (2006). Particularism and Classification and Reclassification of Moral Cases. *IEEE Intelligent Systems, 21*(4), 22–28. doi:10.1109/MIS.2006.76

Kilcullen, R. (1996). Rawls, A Theory of Justice. *Macquarie University.* Retrieved from http: //www.humanities.mq.edu. au/Ockham/y6411.html

McCarty, L. T. (1997). Some Arguments About Legal Arguments, *Proceeding of the Sixth Internationa Conference of Artificial Intelligence and Law,* ACM, New York, 215-224

McLaren, B. M. (2003). Extensionally Defining Principles and Cases in Ethics: an AI Model. *Artificial Intelligence Journal, 150*(November), 145–181. doi:10.1016/S0004-3702(03)00135-8

McLaren, B. M. (2006). Computational Models of Ethical Reasoning: Challenges, Initial Steps, and Future Directions. *IEEE Intelligent Systems, 21*(4), 29–37. doi:10.1109/MIS.2006.67

Moor, J. H. (2006). The Nature, Importance and Difficulty of Machine Ethics. *IEEE Intelligent Systems, 21*(4), 18–21. doi:10.1109/MIS.2006.80

Power, T. M. (2006). Prospects for a Kantian Machine. *IEEE Intelligent Systems, 21*(4), 46–51. doi:10.1109/MIS.2006.77

Robbins, R. W., & Wallace, W. A. (2006). Decision Support for Ethical Problem Solving: A Multi-agent Approach. *Decision Support Systems, 43*(4), 1571–1587. doi:10.1016/j.dss.2006.03.003

Sharkey, N. E. (2007). Automated Killers and the Computing Profession. *IEEE Computer Society Press, 40*(11), 122–127.

SIROCCO. (n.d.). System for Intelligent Retrieval of Operationalized Cases and COdes (SIROCCO). *SIROCCO home page.* Retrieved from http: //sirocco.lrdc.pitt. edu/sirocco/index.html

UVA Video Library. (2002). Dax's Story: A Severely Burned Man's Thirty-Year Odyssey. *University of Virginia.* Retrieved from http: //www.researchchannel. org/prog/displayevent.aspx?rID=3619

KEY TERMS AND DEFINITIONS

Cyberspace: Introduced by William Gibson in Neuromancer (1984) as "*A consensual hallucination experienced daily by billions of legitimate operators*". Now used interchangeable with World Wide Web as it meets criteria mentioned by Gibson.

Cybercrime: Or crime mediated by computer.

Machine Ethics: A research area concerned with defining how machines should behave towards human users and other machines, with emphasis on avoiding harm and other negative consequences of autonomous machines, or unmonitored and unmanned computer programs.

Second Life: A multi-user virtual environment developed by Linden Labs.

Online Gambling: Using online websites, virtual worlds, and other such software to gamble, a opposed to physically entering a casino or betting shop.

Responsible Gambling: Gambling whilst being fully aware of the facts of gambling, and staying in control of both money and time.

EthiCasino: Our prototype system for demonstrating ethical and legal approaches to online gambling.

ENDNOTES

[1]   Note: NHTCU has been moved under SOCA e-crime unit

[2]   Internet gambling revenue for offshore companies was estimated to be $5.4 billion in 2009 from players in the United States and $25.8 billion from players worldwide, according to H2 Gambling Capital.

[3]   This is the Second Life Currency of Linden Dollars (L$) which has a published rate of exchange with other currencies.

[4]   The idea to describe this as "nagware" was introduced by Prof. Allen, Indiana University (private correspondence, 16/6/2008)

[5]   Virtual interactive Kinetic Intelligence (VIKI) is a fictional computer introduced by Isaac Asimov. She serves as a central computer for robots to provide them with a form of "consciousness" recognizable to humans

[6]   For example: 888.com, vanguardcasino.co.uk, slotpower.co.uk, luckycreek.com

[7]   The prototype has been built on Surrey Island http://slurl.com/secondlife/Surrey%20Island/144/149/25

Section 2
Legal and Ethical Implications Involving Social Networks and Virtual Worlds

Chapter 6
An Overview of Child Abuses in 3D Social Networks and Online Video Games

Miguel A. Garcia-Ruiz
University of Colima, Mexico

Miguel Vargas Martin
University of Ontario Institute of Technology, Canada

Patrik Olsson
University of Ontario Institute of Technology, Canada

ABSTRACT

It appears that child pornography distribution and child abuses on the Internet have permeated to massively multiplayer online role-playing video games (MMORPG) and 3D social networks, such as Second Life (SL), a compelling online virtual world where millions of users have registered. Although SL is intended for general entertainment in its adult (over 18) version, cases of simulated pedophilia have been reported inside SL's virtual world, generated by some of its users, employing SL communication capabilities to trade and show child pornography images to exchange related text messages. This chapter provides a literature review on child pornography in MMORPGs and other 3D social networks including SL, as well as policy and network approaches for overcoming child abuse. A review on ethical and legal issues of dealing with child pornography and other types of child abuse in 3D social networks and MMORPGs is also addressed in this chapter.

INTRODUCTION

Child pornography has been defined as "any visual depiction of sexually explicit conduct involving children under the age of 18" (Kierkegaard, 2008), and is a persistent form of social deviation con-flicting with the established social norms in any society (Schell et al., 2007). Social or humankind deviations can be defined as actions, behaviors, or thoughts that are carried out by individuals or group of persons in irresponsible, immoral, un-ethical, and/or illegal manners (Gomme, 2002). The trading of child pornography is presumably

DOI: 10.4018/978-1-61350-132-0.ch006

an underground multi-billion Internet industry worldwide, and in February 2009 alone, almost 1900 cases of child pornography and other types of child sexual abuse were reported weekly at the National Center for Missing & Exploited Children of the U.S. (Cybertipline, 2009). Law enforcement agencies and Non-governmental Organizations (NGOs) of a number of countries have started to track down and catch pedophiles (both child pornography producers and consumers) and child stalkers, mainly doing manual search on Web search engines and with the help of specialized software or by providing services where the public can alert them on child abuse and other disturbing content (Hansen, 2005). However, this is an enormous and complex task, due to the increasing number of producers and consumers of child pornography (Shell et al., 2007), and the ever increasing number of child pornography images and other materials on the Internet (Beech et al., 2008). This increase may, to a significant extent, be attributed to low-cost and technologically advanced digital photography and video cameras that have facilitated child pornography production, as well as easy and fast Internet accesses for persons who exploit and consume child pornography (Taylor et al., 2001), not to mention novel ways to conceal child pornography from law enforcement agencies (Farid, 2004).

Child pornography on the Internet and its underground revenues are not the only issues regarding child pornography. Psychology and social studies have shown that a number of people who are exposed to child pornography on the Internet do suffer psychological disorders, such as the so-called cybersex addiction, and other disinhibited and inappropriate sexual, from the norm, deviating behaviors (Quayle & Taylor, 2001; Quayle, & Taylor, 2002).

The purpose of this chapter is twofold. While we implicitly raise awareness by outlining misuses of technology that pose Internet threats, we touch upon a number of technical scenarios which may fall into cracks of legal systems at both international and in a number of countries due to the

fast pace of information technology development (see e.g., Future Crimes, 2010). Furthermore, we discuss how some massively multiplayer online role-playing games (MMORPGs) and 3D social networks have been used to exploit and molest children, and provide a perspective of future trends.

It is arguable whether crimes against children are increasing or not. While the US National Center for Missing and Exploited Children (Wolak et al. 2006) found a smaller proportion of youth Internet users receiving sexual solicitations from 2001 to 2006, and the US Department of Justice (Department of Justice, 2009) reports lower trends of children victimization in recent years (homicide, rape, robbery, and both simple and aggravated assault are included in the report), these numbers refer to the US only, however the problem of child exploitation deserves global perspectives. From a global perspective, data is not as encouraging as UNICEF (UNICEF Child Protection Information Sheet, 2006) has reported alarming numbers of children involved in commercial sexual exploitation in developing countries. Our position, here, is from a neutral point of view, in light of recent documented events that have used MMORPGs and 3D social networks as a channel to perpetrate sexual crimes against children. We do not argue whether these incidents are "significant" enough to make a case that deserves attention, but we focus on the facts from an information technology perspective, and comment on the dangers these misuses of technology may pose should they become significantly persistent.

MISUSE OF VIDEO GAMES AND 3D SOCIAL NETWORKS

In this section we review some documented and hypothetical incidents that have happened or could happen in MMORPGs and 3D social networks, and use these cases to build a table where we classify and compare different virtual environments and their incidence of child abuse under different scenarios.

Child Abuse in MMORPGs

People that produce, trade, and consume child pornography generally use web pages, emails, and peer-to-peer (P2P) file sharing programs, among other Internet services, for carrying out this illegal activity. More recently, pedophiles have been trading child pornography material through blogs, micro blogs, and other recent types of web 2.0 social networks, and are taking advantage of video games in the form of online 3D virtual worlds, called MMORPG (Garcia-Ruiz et al., 2009). This type of videogame runs on personal computers, as well as on "game boxes" (also called "consoles"), which are dedicated computers for playing video games, running the games either as stand-alone or online for multi-participant use. There have been reported cases of pedophiles using MMORPGs for committing child abuse. For instance, a man in the US was sentenced to jail because he met a minor through an online MMORPG game called Warhawk that runs on a popular brand of game box. After forming a trusting relationship with the child, the stalker convinced the minor to take nude pictures of herself, and later he traded these images to other pedophiles (Ruiz, 2007). This illegal activity of convincing a child on the Internet is also called child luring or grooming (Kierkegaard, 2008). A similar case happened in a popular MMORPG game called World of Warcraft; this time sexual assault to a minor was involved, after the stalker made contact with the child through this video game and met the child in person (McKinnon, 2008).

Child Abuse in 3D Social Networks

A number of child pornography issues have also been found in Second Life (SL), a very popular 3D social network (a 3D social network is an online and collaborative virtual world where its users socialize via avatars), which has experienced great growth in the number of users since it was created in 2003 by Linden Lab, a San Francisco-based company. SL consists of a huge online 3D

virtual world called Metaverse. The Metaverse world contains designated areas called islands, where its users can purchase or rent from Linden Lab or from other users for a fee. Millions of users have registered at SL, where they meet, socialize, play, and do almost anything they want as in the real world through virtual personifications of themselves called avatars. SL users can communicate through their avatars employing voice over IP (VoIP) technology, text messages, and gestures. Users can contribute to SL by developing and uploading graphical 3D objects to SL's virtual world, such as buildings, houses, plants, cars, etc. It is also possible to upload, show and trade images and video files in SL. In addition, a compelling option of SL is that its users can personalize many of its features. For example, they can change their avatar's garments to use "designer" clothes, as well as sell goods and services using SL's own money, called Linden Dollars (about 250 L$ per one US dollar at the time of writing this chapter), which can be acquired at Linden Lab's dollar exchange web site using a real credit card (Linden Dollars, 2010). However, it has been found that 3D social networks like SL pose potential risks on fraud, exploitation of users' data, and other illegal and malicious activities that hackers may commit (Miller, 2008), due to their limited terms of use and network data security schemes.

Bell (2008) estimates that about 15% of SL's islands contain legal and illegal mature material, including child pornography images and videos, and a small number of child pornography traders have been already identified and banned at SL by Linden Lab, following previous users complaints. Some of the SL pornography traders have already been processed in Germany, through German police and Linden Lab joint cooperation. There have been other reported cases of illegal images showing child abuse in SL (Duranske, 2008), and it seems that there are many more unreported cases of this type. In addition, some SL users have created childlike avatars present in SL, simulating acts of pedophilia with other avatars (Connolly, 2007).

Another example of social deviation present in SL, besides trading child pornography, includes role playing child molestation scenarios. There have been cases in the adult version of SL where a number of participants act with their respective avatars in simulations of child abuse, where one or more users use representations of abused child-like avatars, and some SL users have created and represented their avatars appearing as child-like characters wearing provocative clothes (Connolly, 2007). Moreover, there are documented reports of a person that created an eight-year old avatar who sold sex to other avatars (McNeil, 2007). A major problem with SL is that user registration is unverified, allowing any people (even underage people) to register in the adult version practically anonymously (Twohey, 2008), thereby facilitating illegal activities, even though in the adult version users have to pay for goods and services with their credit cards, thus somewhat reducing the need for user identification. Another child pornography issue present in SL (and presumably in some MMORPGs) is that Hentai (Japanese cartoon pornography) and other kinds of childlike-porn animated characters have been present in SL (McNeil, 2007), although it has been reported that SL's creators are continuously banning and removing them from SL's Metaverse.

The presence of child pornography and chat rooms about child pornography has been also denounced in other 3D social networks like Imvu (2009). Imvu is a recently popular network based on 3D scenarios where people communicate through text messages, including those from Microsoft's Messenger. It seems that emerging 3D social networks are tainted rapidly with child pornography.

Types of Child Pornography and Child Abuse on the Internet

We have conducted a non-exhaustive summary of the problems on child pornography and child abuse in general that have appeared on Internet services, social networks, and MMORPGs, shown in Table 1.

As we can see from Table 1, almost all the child pornography-related problems present in conventional Internet services are also present in 3D social networks. Since MMORPGs and social

Table 1. Child pornography and related problems present in Internet services and social networks.

Problem	Does it happen in conventional (2D) social networks, web pages, email, P2P, etc.?	Does it happen in MMORPGs, SL and other online virtual worlds?
Uploading and downloading child pornography images and videos	Yes	Yes
Minors accessing child pornography material	Yes	Yes
3D graphic (avatar) simulating sexual assault to minors	No	Yes
Illegal Hentai (Japanese porn cartoons) and other types of animated characters representing child pornography	Yes	Yes
Sexual offenders stalking minors (child grooming or luring)	Yes	Yes
Communications and online meetings among pedophiles and sexual offenders related to child pornography	Yes	Yes
Text messages related to child pornography, including dedicated chat rooms	Yes	Yes

networks in the form of online virtual worlds are of recent and widespread use, there is little research and few applications today on how to prevent and overcome this problem worldwide.

We believe that one of the causes of having child pornography present on 3D social networks is that some of them are not moderated in a responsible and adequate manner, or not moderated at all, either manually or automatically. While we acknowledge that this is a huge task to achieve in large MMORPGs played by thousands of users at one time, we believe that this is not impossible to do in a social network. For instance, take the example of the moderators that control the uploading of videos at the popular www.youtube.com web site. Table 2 shows a non-exhaustive list of popular online 3D social networks (including MMORPGs) that are moderated (or not). Some of them are immensely popular, like RuneScape, which has been the most popular free MMORPG in the world, according to the 2008 Guinness World Records, with more than 100 million registered users. Phantasy Star Universe is also a popular commercial MMORPG for game consoles. It is important to note that some video games work as stand-alone but can be played by a small number of users at the same game console. Thus, this type of games does not present the threat of online child pornography. Some MMORPGs do not allow avatar customization. This way, childlike avatars cannot be used for role playing depicting child molestation scenarios.

The MMORPGs in Table 2 are representative of PC and console-based video games, respectively. Second Life creators have already taken strong measures against child pornography content, and it seems that in the future there will be more action from its moderators in this respect. Most, if not all, MMORPGs can be difficult to moderate, in general, because of the way their games and roles are structured, but mainly because of the great number of users accessing these types

Table 2. A list of popular 3D social networks and MMORPGs.

Name	Type of online virtual world	Platform used	Has it presented cases of child pornography and other child abuses?	Does it pose any difficulty to implement moderators against child pornography?
Second Life	3D social network	Personal computers	Yes	No. SL has already imposed strong measures and ongoing moderation, but it is not very efficient
Active Worlds	3D social network	Personal computers	?	No
Imvu	3D social network	Personal computers	Yes	No. Users communicate through text messages, they should be relatively easy to moderate
World of Warcraft	MMORPG	Personal computers	Yes	Yes, too many users play it online
RuneScape	MMORPG	Personal computers	?	Yes, too many users play it online
Phantasy Star Universe	MMORPG	Game consoles	?	Possibly
Halo 3	MMORPG	Game consoles	?	Possibly, easy to upload and download images almost anywhere in the game, although not many participants playing at the same time
Warhawk	MMORPG	Game consoles	Yes	Yes, too many users play it online

of 3D social networks. In addition, practically all the MMORPGs and 3D social networks allow for text messaging and/or voice communication among participants (Bell, 2008). This already has been exploited by pedophiles to exchange messages on child pornography and by stalkers to lure children (Ruiz, 2007).

SOCIAL AND LEGAL ASPECTS

In this section we describe the similarities of incidents in the real and the virtual world. We then outline some important international efforts to address the problem from a global and socio-legal perspective. Finally we briefly analyze the position adopted by one of the most widespread 3D social networks.

Child Exploitation in the Converged Online/Offline Environments

The disturbing occurrence and complex nature of child abuses in 3D social networks and MMOR-PGs is a result of the convergence of the offline and online environments (Bloomfield & Duranske, 2009). By interpreting the use or misuse of technology in the online environments as a reflection of what has/is actually taken place in the offline environment e.g. the society in general, we recognize that measures need to be taken to fight this criminal behavior. Child exploitation and abuse are violations that are taking place on a daily basis in the offline environment and have been transferred to the online environment by its perpetrators, and consequently the child exploitation and abuse have also moved to the Internet.

Sexual exploitation of children is by all means a sensitive matter that has been seriously discussed within the United Nations and consequently led to the formation of a Special Rapporteur on critical child rights areas like preventing and combating the sale of children, child prostitution and child pornography. The First World Congress against Commercial Sexual Exploitation of Children took place in 1996 in Stockholm and has since then been followed by various major congresses to put focus on this critical and complex problem.

The exploitative use of children in prostitution and pornography as well as sale of children and child trafficking is covered by articles 34 of the United Nations' Convention on the Rights of the Child (2010):

Article 34

States Parties undertake to protect the child from all forms of sexual exploitation and sexual abuse. For these purposes, States Parties shall in particular take all appropriate national, bilateral and multilateral measures to prevent:

(a) The inducement or coercion of a child to engage in any unlawful sexual activity;

(b) The exploitative use of children in prostitution or other unlawful sexual practices;

(c) The exploitative use of children in pornographic performances and materials.

Law enforcement agencies and child rights organizations, among many others, are increasingly disturbed with the growing accessibility to Internet based forums providing pornographic photographs of children and also the growth of virtual child pornography. The difference between the two is that the latter corresponds to technologically-generated images where no actual child is involved, but as Eneman, Gillespie, and Stahl (2009) accentuate in their article *Criminalising Fantasies: The Regulation of Virtual Child Pornography,* the growth and also the very subsistence of virtual child pornography put emphasis on important ethical and legal issues. Eneman, Gillespie, and Stahl (2009) inform us that *"there is an ongoing debate whether the possession of virtual child pornography should be criminal-*

ized", and provide insight on the controversy of criminalizing such images.

One problem lies in the fact that it is difficult to define what virtual child pornography really signifies (Wilson, 2009). If we look into The UN Optional Protocol to the Convention on the Rights of the Child on the Sale of Children, Child Prostitution and Child Pornography, it has a fairly broad definition when discussing any representation "by whatever means" of a sexual representation of a child. As Eneman, Gillespie, and Stahl (2009) argue *"this could conceivably include non-visual depictions, for example text or audio files."* The reason for this broad definition seems to be that The UN Optional Protocol is striving to get as many Member States of the United Nations as possible to sign this protocol to move the positions forward in this sensitive and complicated subject area.

There are other significant International instruments that have a more rigid and specialized focus on visual depictions like the Council of Europe Convention on Cyberspace, Council Framework Decision 2004/68/JHA on Combating the Sexual Exploitation of Children and Child Pornography and the Council of Europe Convention on the Protection of Children Against Sexual Exploitation and Sexual Abuse. Eneman, Gillespie, and Stahl (2009) point out that *"further problems with the definition of child pornography include the age of a child which has traditionally differed between jurisdictions (usually based on the age at which a child can consent to sexual intercourse. Whilst some international instruments continue to adopt this approach, others (most notably the UN Optional Protocol and Council Framework 2004/68/JHA) reject this approach and suggest that "child" should mean any child under the age of majority (universally set at 18 under the UN Convention on the Rights of the Child)".*

This is an important issue from a socio-legal point of view due to the fact that as many as 191 Member States of the United Nations have ratified the UN Convention on the Rights of the Child from 1989 and consequently obliged themselves to promote and respect the articles that constitute this convention. The first article in the UNCRC states that; *"a child means every human being below the age of 18 years unless, under the law applicable to the child, majority is attained".*

Socio-Legal Issues

We have shown at the beginning of this chapter a definition on child pornography, as well as related social deviations and some of their consequences. We are not going to address any of these questions as this chapter refers to child abuses in 3D social networks and online video games without abounding on legal, moral, or philosophical definitions of child pornography. In this section we limit ourselves to providing a concise literature review on legal aspects.

Most countries have not established the legal framework necessary to determine the status or punishments regarding child pornography and illegal online pornography, let alone legal issues about child pornography in online virtual worlds such as Second Life or MMORPGs. Nevertheless, the Netherlands and Germany already have established and enforced punishments of various years of jail and hefty fines for people involved in the production and distribution of child pornography on the Internet, including child pornography trading in Second Life (Johnson & Rogers, 2009).

However, child pornography is unclear for other countries' laws, although there are general concerns about the development and use of graphic 3D avatars in online virtual worlds to simulate child abuse (Johnson & Rogers, 2009). Despite this concern, U.S. jurisprudence has established that virtual (graphic) child pornography that does not use real children or real images of children is not punishable by U.S. Law (Meek-Pietro, 2008).

Another legal issue regarding online virtual worlds (including SL and MMORPGs) is their possible banning and filtering from the Internet. Documented evidence shows that some countries' governments are filtering and restricting Internet accesses to certain type of information, and especially banning access to some web pages and other Internet services (Delbert et al., 2008). They often block information about politics, but also relating to sexuality, culture, or religion—that their governments deem too sensitive for their citizens. This can be eventually applied to blocking online virtual worlds as well, overlooking freedom of speech and other legal matters.

The terms of use agreements of some popular MMORPGs and 3D social networks do warn their users not to use sexual contents in the virtual world (for instance, see World of Warcraft (2009)), but almost none of them refer specifically to banning child pornography or related contents (for example, childlike cartoons or avatars) used for indecent activities. The creators of Second Life have already declared the following on banning child pornography in its online virtual world (Linden, 2007):

"Under our Community Standards policy, real-life images, avatar portrayals, and other depictions of sexual or lewd acts involving or appearing to involve children or minors are not allowed within Second Life. When detected, individuals and groups promoting or providing such content and activities will be subject to sanctions, which may include termination of accounts, closure of groups, removal of content, and loss of land or access to land."

There are three key aspects, which are considered in breach of the community standards:

(1) participation by residents in lewd or sexual acts in which one or more of the avatars appears to represent minors (or the depiction of such acts in images, video, textures, or text) is a violation of the community standards;

(2) promoting or catering to such behavior or representations violates our community standards.

For instance, the placement of avatars appearing to represent minors in proximity to "sex beds" or other sexualized graphics, objects, or scripts, would violate our community standards, as would the placement of sexualized "pose balls" or other content in areas depicting playgrounds or children's spaces;

(3) the graphic depiction of children in a sexual or lewd manner violates our community standards."

This statement from Linden Lab sets a precedent that will serve to revise and amend the terms of use agreements of many 3D social networks and MMORPGs in the future.

Although users of online virtual worlds have the right to express, act, and look the way they like with their avatars, the ethical, moral, and legal issues regarding free speech and free will in online virtual worlds is beyond the scope of this chapter.

As concluded in the World Congress III against Sexual Exploitation of Children and Adolescents (2010), there is a scarcity of specific national plans of action (NPA) against commercial sexual exploitation of children and trafficking in several countries of the world. To effectively combat this complex area of violations against children and their rights there is a need for further collaboration between the financial sector, NGOs, law enforcement and Internet service providers (ISPs) to stop online sexual abuse. Today the collaboration is limited and needs to be reinforced with constructive initiatives and legislative responses to come to terms with the exploitation and cruelty. A harmonization of legislations with international standards/provisions/substantive policies are of importance to fill out the gaps in the criminalisation of the various acts related to sexual exploitation, particularly when connected to the use of new information and communication technologies (ICT) (World Congress III against Sexual Exploitation of Children and Adolescents, 2010).

PREVENTION AND PROTECTION APPROACHES

Prevention and protection approaches must come from different fronts, including social, legal, and technological. This section discusses technical aspects by extrapolating existing solutions already implemented in social networks and the situation in their MMORPG counterparts. Furthermore, we outline what we believe to be the main obstacles in implementing protection mechanisms in virtual environments, and provide a brief explanation of possible ways to overcome these obstacles.

Possible Ways to Prevent and Override Online Child Pornography

Law enforcement agencies and researchers worldwide already have designed and applied measures to counter child pornography on the Internet in general. Some of those measures are summarized in Table 3.

As we can see in Table 3, specific methods and techniques to prevent, mitigate, and counter child pornography in 3D social networks, and customized methods for SL and MMORPGs, are largely unexplored. We consider that SL and other 3D social networks present special characteristics, where some of the real-world or general Internet measures against child abuse may not efficiently or easily apply for different reasons, including technical issues and privacy protection laws, among others. Moreover, given the realistic characteristics of some online 3D social networks, it is possible to develop and use a credible human-like 3D avatar bot in SL for monitoring image and video trafficking, and thus automating this task. A bot can be defined as a computer program that accomplishes automated tasks on the Internet, sometimes using Artificial Intelligence algorithms, such as searching for information trends or patterns on a number of web sites or chat rooms (Bell et al., 2004). However, the use of bots in some MMORPGs like World of Warcraft is forbidden (World of Warcraft, 2009) mainly because bots can interfere with the general users' activities and game rules, whereas in some 3D social networks the use of bots is allowed, as in Active Worlds (Active Worlds bots, 2009).

CHALLENGES ON TACKLING CHILD PORNOGRAPHY IN ONLINE VIRTUAL WORLDS

There are important technical and legal issues for countering child pornography in MMORPGs, SL, and other types of online virtual worlds. Some of these issues are described in Table 4.

As shown in Table 4, a number of technical issues are concerned with user identification for registering and logging in to online virtual worlds. As can be seen from Table 4, there are a number of issues on child pornography and online virtual worlds that need to be further researched and implemented.

Table 3. Measures implemented to counter pornography.

Measures implemented on traditional social networks (web pages, blogs, etc.)	Measures already implemented (or not) in online 3D social networks and MMORPGs
Honeypots (decoy websites and chat rooms to attract and identify pedophiles)	Not yet efficiently implemented or used
Automated analysis of images	Not yet efficiently implemented or used
Denounces made by general users	Denounces made by general users
Manual search done by law enforcement agencies	Manual search done by law enforcement agencies.
Artificial Intelligence bots to identify pedophiles	Not yet efficiently implemented or used.

Table 4. Technical and legal issues for countering child pornography in online virtual worlds.

Type of challenge	Possible ways to overcome the challenge
Users do not declare themselves properly when registering.	Implement efficient and safe registration through Artificial Intelligence, biometrics, or other types of methods
Unrestricted exchange of images and videos	Automated filtering can be implemented, or some users act as vigilantes, but privacy and legal issues may apply
Minors can register in adults version of MMORPGs and some 3D social networks, like SL's over 18 version	Develop and apply parental filters
There is no easy way of denouncing child abuse in most online virtual worlds	Virtual world developers should implement a special feature where any user or Internet visitor can easily identify or record the exact place where the child pornography trade or action is taking place in that virtual world. Also, developers should set up a particular email account or web site to report suspected cases of pedophilia.
MMORPGs and other virtual worlds' legal issues are not well defined, or not defined at all, in some countries' laws.	Strengthen and amend laws to deal with child pornography in online virtual worlds.

CONCLUDING REMARKS

As new technologies enhance our daily life and facilitate automation of efficient processes, users not always make the best use of technology. While this chapter is product of a continuing comprehensive study currently undergoing, we now try to capture our view on the problem, and provide some guidelines for future work.

Our Vision

To counter child pornography, short, medium, and long-term measures can be applied. Short-term measures to help prevent child abuse in MMORPGs include the following:

One strong short-term measure is to strengthen moderator activities against child pornography in online virtual worlds, as analyzed in this chapter. Another one is to establish clearly and concisely in the Terms of Use Agreements the banning of child pornography and child abuse, including childlike avatars and indecent behaviors using childlike characters or real images, and that further legal actions will be taken should this occur.

Skelton (2009) provides a number of useful suggestions for parents about monitoring and preventing children from making contact with obscene material present in MMORPGs, such as:

1. Activate parental chat profanity filters. A number of games include this option. Also, install third-party chat filters.
2. Monitor children constantly about what they are typing and doing in the MMORPG.
3. Implement third-party programs that monitors the time-limits of MMORPG usage.
4. Children should join family-friendly guilds only (a guild is a type of special interest group of gamers inside MMORPGs). Parents should also join that guild, to monitor what is being said and shown there.
5. Parents should take time to explain improper behaviors and obscene material that they may find in the MMORPG to their children.
6. Establish trust with children on MMORPG usage, displaying honest communication with them.

Past literature has shown other efforts to prevent child abuse in social networks, such as peer-monitoring groups composed of informed youths that protect themselves (Staunton, 2009), which certainly can be applied to MMORPGs and other types of online virtual worlds as well.

Medium and long-term approaches (because of their complexity to develop and implement) to countermeasure child pornography in 3D social networks and MMORPGS include automatic software searches and identification of child pornography images, such as Ibrahim's approach (2009).

We believe that child pornography and other child abuses can be efficiently identified in 3D social networks and online MMORPGs by employing a mixed approach, by combining manual and automatic searches, done by both law enforcement and specialized computer programs (i.e. Artificial Intelligence bots, image processing and analysis, etc.), provided that legal punishments against child pornography creators and consumers are implemented in countries that do not have these types of punishments at the moment.

DIRECTIONS AND TRENDS FOR FUTURE WORK

It appears that one of the factors that will shape the future of child pornography on the Internet, including child abuse in online virtual worlds, and video games, is the misuse of new technologies, and particularly ICT, to keep producing, distributing, and consuming child pornography. According to the trends on pedophiles and technology adoption analyzed elsewhere, it seems that the more accessible and reliable technology will be, the more unscrupulous users will make use of it to trade child abuse images and videos. It is possible that in the near future consumers and distributors of child pornography may extensively use Worldwide Interoperability for Microwave Access (WiMAX) technology (Kumar, 2008), a recent type of fast and long-range wireless network that is already available in some countries. WiMAX is a wireless communication medium to provide up to 72 Mbit/s symmetric broadband speed, suitable for transmitting multimedia information, including online streaming video (Halepovic et al., 2009), and it can also be employed for collaborative virtual environments.

WiMAX is used for point to point Internet access, based on the IEEE 802.16 broadband

wireless access standard protocol, and users can access a wireless WiMAX network through mobile computing, using it wherever the users like (they can be tens of kilometers away from the WiMAX base station), with high and reliable bandwidth, and not only using nearby wireless access points as it happens with current WiFi wireless technology. However, child pornography on WiMAX may bring new dimensions to the problem as WiMAX supports wide coverage and its users will be using mobile computing, possibly affecting the identification of the exact physical location of persons involved in trafficking child pornography using WiMAX.

Medium and long term measures include the development of artificial intelligence programs, combined with human searches and analyses, to help counter this problem.

The countering of child pornography in 3D social networks should be an integral and multidisciplinary activity, since it is necessary to coordinate efforts from different fields, such as computer networks, psychology, criminology, etc.

Recent research has demonstrated the effectiveness of virtual world-based role plays to train college women resist sexual attacks on campus (Jouriles et al., 2009). Jouriles et al. showed that realistic virtual world scenarios were useful to teach young women rape-resistance and sexual coercion skills and to have them practice these skills in a controlled situation. Further research may point to using virtual worlds in a controlled environment to teach children about child abuse and its prevention in online virtual worlds.

CONCLUSION

This chapter has attempted to raise a certain degree of awareness by outlining misuses of technology that pose Internet threats, technical scenarios in 3D social networks and MMORPGs which may fall into cracks of legal systems at both international and in a number of countries. Furthermore, this chapter described how a number of social networks and computer applications have been used to perpetrate crimes against children, and provide a perspective of future trends.

Online virtual worlds in 3D such as Second Life or World of Warcraft are not only MMORPGs. They resemble real life in many senses, containing live communities that carry out rich social and commercial activities. An ever increasing number of participants are enrolling in MMORPG every day. In addition, some 3D social networks have important applications in training and education that need to be ready to prevent pornography abuse. However, child pornography trading and other types of child abuse have permeated 3D social networks, and it seems that this will be increasing in the future, perhaps tainting other untouched 3D social networks by illegal pornography as well. To tackle this, it is necessary to conduct research on more efficient methods for detecting child pornography in social networks. Conversely, real-world measures may need to be adapted and utilized to efficiently function in online virtual worlds.

Moreover, researchers and practitioners that develop hardware and software to effectively prevent, filter and detect child pornography in 3D social networks and MMORPGs should be aware of privacy, ethical, and legal issues on countering Internet child abuse. In addition, researchers and practitioners should also be aware about novel and evolving hardware and software technologies that pedophiles and other sexual offenders may use in the future.

It is important to raise awareness about child pornography present in 3D social networks and MMORPGs among network administrators, policy makers, law enforcement agencies, educators, and public in general, to take further strong technical and legal measures. Possible measures in the short term on the risks of child pornography in 3D and other types of social networks include adequate parent measures to prevent children

and adults from accessing child pornography at home, planned and educated warnings in blogs and web pages, talks with students and teachers, and especially encouraging children and other types of users to denounce abusive practices of social networks to the network and virtual world administrators.

ACKNOWLEDGMENT

All trademarks, trade names, service marks, and logos referenced in this chapter belong to their respective companies. M.A.G.R. acknowledges partial support from the National Council of Science and Technology (CONACYT) of Mexico, grants no. FOMIX Colima-2008-C01-83651 and 94140, and participated in the preparation of this chapter while he was a Visiting Professor at the Faculty of Business and IT, University of Ontario Institute of Technology, Oshawa, Canada. M.A.G.R. and M.V.M. acknowledge the support of a Canadian Foundation (name withheld upon the Foundation's request).

REFERENCES

Active Worlds Bots. (2009). *AW contents guidelines*. Retrieved December 27, 2009, from http://www.activeworlds. com/community/ terms.asp

Beech, A. R., Elliott, I. A., Birgden, A., & Findlater, D. (2008). The Internet and child sexual offending: A criminological review. *Aggression and Violent Behavior*, 13.

Bell, D., Loader, B. D., & Pleace, N. (2004). *Cyberculture: The key concept*. New York, NY: Routledge.

Bell, E. (2008). *Theories of performance*. Thousand Oaks, CA: Sage Publications.

Bengel, J. (2004). ChatTrack: Chat room topic detection using classification. *Lecture Notes in Computer Science*, 3073.

Bloomfield, R., & Duranske, B. (2009). Protecting children in virtual worlds without undermining their economic, educational, and social benefits. *Washington and Lee Law Review*, 66.

Connolly, K. (2007, May 9). Second Life in virtual child sex scandal. *The Guardian, UK*. Retrieved December 27, 2009, from http: //www.guardian. co. uk/technology/2007/may/09 /secondlife. web20

Convention on the Rights of the Child. (2010). *Convention on the Rights of the Child*. United Nations. Retrieved May 25, 2010, from http: // www2.ohchr. org/english/ law/crc.htm

Cybertipline. (2009). *Cybertipline fact sheet, National Center for Missing & Exploited Children (U.S.)*. Retrieved December 27, 2009, from http://www.missingkids. com/en_US/documents/ CyberTiplineFactSheet.pdf

Deibert, R., Palfrey, J. G., Rohozinski, R., & Zittrain, J. (2008). *Access denied: The practice and policy of global Internet filtering*. Cambridge, MA: MIT Press.

Department of Justice. (2009). *Violent victimization rates by age, 1973-2008*. Retrieved December 27, 2009, from http: //www.ojp.usdoj. gov/bjs/ glance/ tables/vagetab.htm

Duranske, B. T. (2008). *Virtual law: Navigating the legal landscape of virtual worlds*. Chicago, IL: American Bar Association.

Eneman, M., Gillespie, A. A., & Carsten Stahl, B. (2009). *Criminalising fantasies*. Conference paper ECIS 2007, The 15th European Conference on Information Systems, St. Gallen, Switzerland.

Farid, H. (2004). *Creating and detecting doctored and virtual images: Implications to the Child Pornography Prevention Act*. (Technical Report no. TR2004-518), Department of Computer Science, Dartmouth College, USA.

Future Crimes. (2010). *Future crimes: Anticipating tomorrow's crime today*. Retrieved June 29, 2010, from http: //www.futurecrimes. com/ category/ virtual-world-crime/

Garcia-Ruiz, M. A., Vargas Martin, M., Ibrahim, A., Edwards, A., & Aquino-Santos, R. (2009). *Combating child exploitation in Second Life*. 2009 IEEE Toronto International Conference – Science and Technology for Humanity (TIC-STH).

Gomme, I. M. (2002). *The shadow line: Deviance and crime in Canada*. Scarborough, Ontario, Canada: Thomson/Nelson.

Halepovic, E., Ghaderi, M., & Williamson, C. (2009). Multimedia application performance on a WiMAX network. In *Proceedings of SPIE, the International Society for Optical Engineering, Multimedia Computing and Networking Conference*.

Hansen, C. (2005). Catching potential Internet sex predators. *Dateline NBC News*. Retrieved December 27, 2009, from http: //www.msnbc. msn. com/id/9927253/

Ibrahim, A. A. (2009). *Detecting and preventing the electronic transmission of illegal images*. Unpublished Master's thesis. Faculty of Engineering and Applied Science, University of Ontario Institute of Technology, Oshawa, Canada.

Imvu. (2009). *Imvu and virtual sex*. Retrieved December 27, 2009, from http: //community. blogsafety.liveworld. com/topic/Connectsafely-Forum-Archive/Imvu-And-Virtual/1200000449? &messageID=1200003361

Johnson, M., & Rogers, K. M. (2009). Too far down the yellow brick road – Cyber-hysteria and virtual porn. *Journal of International Commercial Law and Technology, 4*(1).

Jouriles, E. N., McDonald, R., Kullowatz, A., Rosenfield, D., Gomez, G. S., & Cuevas, A. (2009). Can virtual reality increase the realism of role plays used to teach college women sexual coercion and rape-resistance skills? *Behavior Therapy*, 40.

Kherfi, M. L. (2004). Image retrieval from the World Wide Web: Issues, techniques, and systems. *ACM Computing Surveys, 36*(1), 35–67. doi:10.1145/1013208.1013210

Kierkegaard, S. (2008). Cybering, online grooming and ageplay. *Computer Law & Security Report, 28*, 41–55. doi:10.1016/j.clsr.2007.11.004

Kumar, A. (2008). *Mobile broadcasting with WiMAX: Principles, technology, and applications.* Boston, MA: Focal Press.

Linden, K. (2007). *Clarification of policy disallowing "ageplay."* Retrieved December 27, 2009, from https: //blogs.secondlife. com/community/features/ blog/2007/11/14/clarification-of-policy-disallowing-ageplay

Linden Dollars. (2010). *Currency exchange.* Retrieved May 25, 2010, from http: //secondlife. com/whatis/ currency.php

McCullagh, D. (2008). *FBI posts fake hyperlinks to snare child porn suspects.* Retrieved December 27, 2009, from http://news.cnet.com/8301-13578_3-9899151-38.html

McKinnon, J. (2008). Police: Man, girl met in World of Warcraft, had sex. *Pittsburgh Post-Gazette.* Retrieved December 27, 2009, from http: //www.post-gazette. com/pg/09037/947352 -100.stm

McNeil, J. (2007). Virtual child porn: The Second Life for pervs? *Doublethink Online.* Retrieved December 27, 2009, from http: //www.americas-future. org/doublethink/2007/04/ 04/virtual-child-porn-the- second-life-for-pervs/

Meek-Prieto, C. (2008). Just age playing around? How Second Life aids and abets child pornography. *North Carolina Journal of Law & Technology, 88.*

Miller, C. (2008). Virtual worlds, real exploits. *Network Security*, May.

Ohzahata, S., Hagiwara, Y., Matsuaki, T., & Kawashima, K. (2005). A traffic identification method and evaluations for a pure P2P application. *Lecture Notes in Computer Science* (LNCS), *3431.* Heidelberg, Germany: Springer.

Quayle, E., & Taylor, M. (2001). Child seduction and self-representation on the Internet. *Cyberpsychology & Behavior, 4*(5). doi:10.1089/109493101753235197

Quayle, E., & Taylor, M. (2002). Child pornography and the Internet: Perpetuating a cycle of abuse. *Deviant Behavior, 23*(4). doi:10.1080/01639620290086413

Ropelato, J. (2009). *Internet pornography statistics.* Retrieved December 27, 2009, from http: //internet-filter-review.toptenreviews. com/internet-pornography- statistics.html

Ruiz, R. (2007). Police: Ky. man got humble girl to send him nude photos. *The Houston Chronicle.* Retrieved December 27 2009, from http: //www. chron. com/disp/story.mpl/ front/6311073.html

Schell, B. H., Vargas Martin, M., Hung, P. C. K., & Rueda, L. (2007). Cyber child pornography: A review paper of the social and legal issues and remedies—And a proposed technological solution. *Aggression and Violent Behavior, 12*, 45–63. doi:10.1016/j.avb.2006.03.003

Skelton, J. (2009). Monitoring your child's on-line gaming. *Salt Lake MMORPG Examiner*. Retrieved December 27, 2009, from http: //www. examiner. com/x-8040-Salt-Lake-MMORPG-Examiner~y2009m4d18- Monitoring-your-childs-online-gaming

Staunton, T. (2009). *Safeguarding cyberworld, keeping children and young people safe online*. Plymouth, UK: Plymouth Safeguarding Children Board.

Taylor, M., Quayle, E., & Holland, G. (2001). Child pornography, the Internet and offending. *Canadian Journal of Policy Research*, 2(2), 94–100.

Twohey, M. (2008, May 6). Kirk: Second Life dangerous to kids Says online social network is vulnerable to predators. *Chicago Tribune*. Retrieved December 27, 2009, from http: //archives.chicagotribune. com/2008/may/06/news/ chi-online-predator-alert-06-may06

UNICEF. (2010). *The World Congress III against Sexual Exploitation of Children and Adolescents*, Rio de Janeiro Brazil, from 25-28 November 2008, UNICEF. Retrieved May 25, 2010, from http: // www.unicef. org/infobycountry/ brazil_46520. html

UNICEF Child Protection Information Sheet. (2006). *Commercial sexual exploitation*. Retrieved December 27, 2009, from http: //www.unicef. org/ protection/files/ Sexual_Exploitation.pdf

Wilson, R. F. (2009). Sex play in virtual worlds. *Washington and Lee Law Review*, 66, 1127–1174.

Wolak, J., Mitchell, K., & Finkelhor, D. (2006). *Online victimization of youth: Five years later*. Retrieved December 27, 2009, from http: //www. missingkids. com/en_US/publications/ NC167. pdf

World of Warcraft. (2009). *World of Warcraft terms of use agreement*. Retrieved December 27, 2009, from http: //www.worldofwarcraft. com/ legal/ termsofuse.html

ADDITIONAL READING

Benford, S., Greenhalgh, C., Rodden, T., & Pycock, J. (2001). Collaborative virtual environments. *Communications of the ACM*, 44(7), 79–85. doi:10.1145/379300.379322

Bogost, I. (2007). *Persuasive Games – the expressive power of videogames*. Cambridge, MA: MIT Press.

Burdea, G., & Coiffet, P. (2003). *Virtual reality technology* (2nd ed.). New York, NY: John Wiley and Sons.

Fraser, M., Glover, T., Vaghi, I., Benford, S., Greenhalgh, C., Hindmarsh, J., & Heath, C. (2000). Revealing the realities of collaborative virtual reality. *In Proceedings of the Third international Conference on Collaborative Virtual Environments* (San Francisco, California, United States). E. Churchill and M. Reddy, Eds. CVE '00. ACM, New York, NY, 29-37.

Garcia-Ruiz, M. A., Vargas Martin, M., & Ibrahim, A. (2009). Combating Child Exploitation in Second Life. In *Proc. 2009 IEEE Toronto International Conference – Science and Technology for Humanity*, pp. 761-766, September 26 – 27, Toronto Canada.

Howe, N., & Strauss, W. (2000). *Millennials Rising: The Next Generation*. New York: Vintage Books.

Ibrahim, A., & Vargas Martin, M. (2009). Addressing Privacy Constraints for Efficient Monitoring of Network Traffic for Illicit Images. In *Proc. 2009 IEEE Toronto International Conference – Science and Technology for Humanity*, pp. 302-308, September 26 – 27, Toronto, Canada.

Jackson, R. L., & Fagan, E. (2000). Collaboration and learning within immersive virtual reality. In *Proceedings of Collaborative Virtual Environments*. San Francisco, CA: ACM. doi:10.1145/351006.351018

Juul, J. (2005). *Half-Real: video games between real rules and fictional worlds*. Cambridge, MA: MIT Press.

Meadows, M. (2007). *I, avatar: The culture and consequences of having a second life* (1st ed.). Thousand Oaks, CA: New Riders Publishing.

Messinger, P. R., Stroulia, E., Lyons, K., Bone, M., Niu, R. H., Smirnov, K., & Perelgut, S. (2009). Virtual worlds - past, present, and future: New directions in social computing. *Decision Support Systems, 47*(3). doi:10.1016/j.dss.2009.02.014

Ondrejka, C. (2006). Finding common ground in new worlds. *Games and Culture*, January.

Sherman, W. R., & Craig, A. B. (2003). *Understanding virtual reality*. San Francisco, CA: Morgan Kauffman.

Stoup, P. (2008). The development and failure of social norms in Second Life. *Duke Law Journal, 58.2*, 311(34).

Theil, S. (2008). Tune in tomorrow. *Newsweek*, August 18-25 issue.

Yee, N., Bailenson, J. N., Urbanek, M., Chang, F., & Merget, D. (2007). The unbearable likeness of being digital: The persistence of nonverbal social norms in online virtual environments. *The Journal of CyberPsychology and Behavior, 10*, 115–121. doi:10.1089/cpb.2006.9984

KEY TERMS AND DEFINITIONS

Child Pornography: Any visual depiction of sexually explicit conduct involving persons under the age of 18.

Collaborative Virtual Reality: A shared virtual world using a local network or the Internet as a communication medium, where its users interact to work, learn, train, and carry out other activities together.

Game Box: Also called "console", it is a dedicated computer for playing video games, running the games either as stand-alone or online for multi-participant uses.

MMORPG: Multiplayer online role-playing video games, also considered as a kind of 3D social network.

Second Life: A social network in the form of 3D virtual world shared by millions of registered users, using the Internet as a communication medium.

Social Networking Site: A particular collaborative software used on the Internet by a set of persons, used mainly as a communication medium to interact and share common interests in it.

Three-Dimensional Social Network: A 3D social network is an online and collaborative virtual world where its users socialize via avatars.

Three-Dimensional Virtual Environment: A computer-generated 3D space, also called virtual world, where 3D graphical objects and sounds reside. Its user is represented in the virtual environment by an avatar (a graphical personification) and can interact with the virtual objects and its environment.

Virtual Reality: Computer technology capable of generating a three-dimensional space called virtual environment, which is highly user interactive, multimodal, and immersive.

Chapter 7
Ethics and Legal Aspects of Virtual Worlds

Andrew Power
Dun Laoghaire Institute of Art, Design and Technology, Ireland

Gráinne Kirwan
Dun Laoghaire Institute of Art, Design and Technology, Ireland

ABSTRACT

The development of a legal environment for virtual worlds presents issues of both law and ethics. The cross-border nature of online law and particularly law in virtual environments suggests that some lessons on its formation can be gained by looking at the development of international law, specifically the ideas of soft law and adaptive governance. In assessing the ethical implications of such environments the network of online regulations, technical solutions and the privatization of legal remedies offer some direction. While legal systems in online virtual worlds require development, the ethical acceptability of actions in these worlds is somewhat clearer, and users need to take care to ensure that their behaviors do not harm others.

INTRODUCTION

Virtual worlds are becoming a more important and prevalent part of our real world with each passing month. Shirky (2010, p37) argues that the old view of online as a separate space, cyberspace, apart from the real world is fading. Now that computers and other internet enabled devices (such as smartphones) have been so broadly adopted there is no

separate cyberworld, just a more interconnected 'new' world. The internet augments real world social life rather than providing an alternative to it. Instead of becoming a separate cyberspace, our electronic networks are becoming embedded in real life (Shirky, 2009, p196). According to Adams (2010, p2) the virtual interactive worlds of *Second Life* (with 15,464,773 residents as of October 13, 2008) and *World of Warcraft* (with over 10,000,000 players) have populations larger than Sweden. The reason for this growth is in

DOI: 10.4018/978-1-61350-132-0.ch007

part, due to the natural inclination of humans to want to form groups and interact with each other, combined with the increasing simplicity of the technology to allow it. As Shirky (2009, p105) states *"Communications tools don't get socially interesting until they get technologically boring. [The tool] has to have been around long enough that most of society is using it. It's when a technology becomes normal, then ubiquitous, and finally so pervasive as to be invisible, that the really profound changes happen"*.

Crime in a virtual world can take a number of forms. Some activities such as the theft of goods are relatively clear-cut whereas private law issues such as harassment or commercial disputes are more complex. Online crime has been defined as, *"crime committed using a computer and the internet to steal a person's identity or sell contraband or stalk victims or disrupt operations with malevolent programs"* (Princeton University, n.d.). The IT security company Symantec (n.d.) defines two categories of cybercrime, *"Type I, examples of this type of cybercrime include but are not limited to phishing, theft or manipulation of data or services via hacking or viruses, identity theft, and bank or e-commerce fraud. Type II cybercrime includes, but is not limited to activities such as cyberstalking and harassment, child predation, extortion, blackmail, stock market manipulation, complex corporate espionage, and planning or carrying out terrorist activities"*. Types of crime can be categorized as internet enabled crimes, internet specific crimes and new crimes committed in a virtual world. The first two categories of online crime have been observed for many years and the third, which coincided with the growth in online virtual environments, is a more recent development. Internet enabled crimes are those crimes which existed offline but are facilitated by the Internet. These include credit card fraud, defamation, blackmail, obscenity, money laundering, and copyright infringement. Internet specific crimes are those that did not exist before the arrival of networked computing and more specifically the

proliferation of the internet. These include, hacking, cyber vandalism, dissemination of viruses, denial of service attacks, and domain name hijacking. The third category of crimes committed in a virtual world arises when individuals are acting through their online avatars or alternate personas (the Sanskrit word avatara means incarnation). In computing an avatar is a representation of the user in the form of a three-dimensional model. Harassing another individual through their online representation may or may not be criminal but it is at the very least antisocial. It is also the case that that online activities can lead to very real crimes offline.

This chapter aims to introduce some of the types of crimes which can occur in virtual worlds through a series of examples of actual virtual crimes, such as virtual sexual assault, theft, and child pornography. It should be noted that while the term 'crimes' will be used to describe these acts throughout the chapter, and the term 'criminals' assigned to the perpetrators, the actions are not necessarily criminal events under any offline legal system, and the perpetrators may not be considered criminal by a court of law. In some cases there have been offline consequences of the actions which are real criminal events, but in many cases no criminal prosecution is currently possible. Nevertheless, this is not to say that these virtual criminal behaviors are actually ethical, and the chapter also considers the impact of the behavior on the individuals involved. Finally it is aimed to determine what the implications are for law formation in virtual worlds, along with an examination of how these should be implemented.

VIRTUAL WORLDS AND ONLINE CRIMES

A number of cases of online crime have been presented in the media. The case of Mr. Bungle as described by Julian Dibbell in 1993 is probably the most famous case of crime in a virtual world.

In this case a series of sexual assaults were carried out in the text-based online world LambdaMOO by a character called Mr. Bungle. The controller of this character carried out the assaults on other players using 'voodoo dolls', subprograms that attribute actions to other players' characters that they did not intend. Mr. Bungle was actually controlled by several university students acting as one to direct the attacks (Dibbell, 1998). The Bungle case is interesting because of the reported after-effects on the victims. One reported severe distress in the aftermath of the attack. Several other players reported their anger at the events, to the extent that many called for Mr. Bungle to be 'toaded' (banned from the virtual world, with the character itself deleted). The calls to toad Mr. Bungle led to debates within the world, with some arguing that in the virtual world, rape had not been criminalized, and so it could not be considered punishable. It was also queried if the university students who had created the character of Mr. Bungle could be punished in the real world, perhaps under laws concerning obscene phone calls or punishment from the university authorities, although this course of action did not seem to be popular amongst the players involved. While no final decision was made by the players, eventually a 'wizard' (an administrator in the virtual world) acted alone and toaded Mr. Bungle independently. As such, those who played Mr. Bungle were punished in the virtual world, where their 'crimes' took place, but not the real world, where the effects were experienced by the victims. Eventually LambdaMOO developed a ballot system, where players could vote for the toading of a 'criminal' character, and if sufficient votes were received, then the wizards would complete the request.

Internet child pornography is a topic which is eliciting greater attention from society and the media, as parents and caregivers become more aware of the risks to their children and law enforcement agencies become more aware of the techniques and strategies used by offenders.

Sheldon and Howitt (2007) indicate that at least in terms of convictions, internet child pornography is the major activity that constitutes Internet related sex crimes. An example of the kind of ethical controversies this subject can produce is the Wonderland area of Second Life which provided a place for role play of sexual activity with "child" avatars. This drew out many questions which are dealt with by Adams (2010) and also by Kirwan and Power (2011). These include examining when the fantasy of illegality becomes illegal, the verification of participant's age, and the definition of harm in a virtual world. Online activity may be an outlet for harmful urges or an encouragement toward them; it may have a therapeutic role or alternatively promote the normalization of unacceptable behaviours. These and other questions are explored by Adams (2010) in particular. In the case of Wonderland, Linden Labs initially defended the existence of Wonderland in Second Life on the basis that it did not violate the rules of Second Life, although in time it did close down (Adams, 2010, p56). It is, however, one of a number of such sites many which continue to carry similar abuse images, altered photographs, or textual descriptions relating to children and sex.

Online theft of virtual goods has led to serious crimes offline. In 2008 a Russian member of the Platanium clan of an MMORPG (Massively Multiplayer Online Role-Playing Game) was assaulted in the Russian city of Ufa by a member of the rival Coo-clocks clan in retaliation for a virtual assault in the game. The man died of his injuries en route to hospital (Truta, 2008). Even if the activity does not spill over into the real world but remains online it is clear that crime can occur. In August 2005 a Japanese man was arrested for using software 'bots' to 'virtually' assault online characters in the computer game *Lineage II* and seal their virtual possessions. Bots, or web robots, are software applications that run automated tasks over the Internet. He was then able to sell these items through a Japanese auction website (Knight, 2005). In October 2008, a Dutch court sentenced two teenagers to 360 hours of community service for 'virtually' beating up a classmate and stealing his digital goods (Irish Times, 2008). In 2007 a Dutch teenager was arrested for stealing virtual furniture from 'rooms' in *Habbo Hotel*, a 3D social networking website; this virtual furniture was valued at €4,000 (BBC, 2007).

In Britain a couple are divorcing after the wife discovered her husband's online alter-ego was having an affair online with another, virtual, woman (Guardian, 2007). This is interesting in that the "affair" was virtual and involved a relationship between the avatar of the husband and the avatar of another woman. Is it possible to be unfaithful to your real world partner by having your alter ego have an online only relationship? Clearly in the view of this man's wife it is and it hurt just as much, she said *"His was the ultimate betrayal. He had been lying to me."* Was this a question of trust, ethics, or just a lack of a shared understanding about the rules of a game vs. the rules of life?

ETHICS IN A VIRTUAL WORLD

The question of ethics in virtual worlds can draw some lessons from ontological theory and value pluralism. In other words our view of what is ethical is informed by our world view in the first instance and secondly that more than one system of values can exist simultaneously. Isaiah Berlin (1980) argued against the logical positivism which had come to dominate the study of politics and governance. His argument was that it could never account for questions such as 'what is justice'. When it comes to questions like this there is never a single answer so this leads to a variety of answers depending on the value systems in a given time and place. There can be no one value system that can accommodate all that is valuable. So there will be competing value systems even within the same community and at a given point in time. There is also no objective system to evaluate which is right and which is wrong (or less right!). Value systems are essential to the models through which we see ourselves and the world around us and they embody deeply held convictions. John Rawls (1973, 1996) sought to develop a theory of justice suitable for governing political communities in the light of irreconcilable moral disagreements. It was based on the basic conditions governing human behavior.

These debates are crucial in considering the governance of online societies. Social networks will emerge in different ways and for different purposes and as such will require different value systems by which to construct governance systems. Constructing systems of variable ethics and providing choice in online value systems will pose increasing challenges to states, individuals and systems of justice. To give one example, the behavior considered correct and moral in an environment such as Grand Theft Auto will, one hopes, be quite different to that of Club Penguin. The world of Grand Theft Auto consists of a mixture of action, adventure, driving, and shooting and has gained controversy for its adult nature and violent themes. Club Penguin in contrast is aimed at young children who use cartoon penguins as avatars to play a series of games in a wintery environment. Both in terms of the activities engaged in and the nature of the language used these environments could not be more different from an ethical perspective. However both conform to their own internal rule set for player behavior.

Online identities are not restricted by reality. They 'need not in any way correspond to a person's real life identity: people can make and remake themselves, choosing their gender and the details of their online presentation' (Mnookin, 1996). When a person is online, their identity does not need to reflect their offline identity. It is possible to change our gender, make ourselves younger, thinner and more attractive than we really are, or even change our species (for example, the various supernatural creatures that inhabit online games such as 'World of Warcraft'). Impression management is the process of controlling the impressions that other people form, and aspects of impression management normally outside our control in face-to-face interactions, can be controlled in online environments (Chester & Bretherton, 2007). In the online context, we can easily manage and alter how other people see us in ways that were never before possible.

Given this reality, can a personal attack against an avatar be construed as the equivalent of an attack against the person whom the avatar represents? The 'humanity' or otherwise of avatars in virtual worlds is important. Can they be considered equal to human victims of crimes? Has harm really been done? The answer to this lies both in the degree of separation the creator of the avatar has between their online and offline personas and their degree of attachment to their avatar. Spending a large amount of time 'in the skin' of our avatar can lead to strong feelings of association to the point where an attack on the avatar can feel like an attack on self. The degree to which a person experiences a strong sense of presence within a virtual world is discussed in detail by Kirwan (2009). It is also true that as we spend greater amounts of time online the differences between our online and offline personalities are becoming closer. In part this is because it is just too much trouble to maintain two different personae but also because the distinction between the 'real' world and our online world are no longer meaningful. Shirky (2009, p196) outlines the problem of treating the internet as some sort of separate space or cyberspace when he states; *"The internet augments real-world social life rather than providing an alternative to it. Instead of becoming a separate cyberspace, our electronic networks are becoming deeply embedded in real life"*. We only live in one world it is just that an increasing portion of our time is spent interconnected to others though technology. It is not an alternative world it is just part of our new world.

If this position is accepted then the question of the ways in which offline norms apply to vir-

tual worlds is important. The ability to engage in unethical behavior in virtual worlds may impact on the psychology of the individual. The impact of violent films on behavior has been disputed for years (Möller, 2009; Anderson, 1997; Parke et al, 1977) as has the impact of computer games with some supplies offering advice online (Toys Advice, n.d.). The greater immersive reality of virtual worlds may have a stronger impact on participants but more research is needed to draw firm conclusions. In the case of the 'Wonderland' area of Second Life referred to earlier, arguments were made (Adams, 2010) to support both sides of this particularly contentious example. On the one hand, users were more likely to engage in unethical behaviors offline, having been exposed to such behaviors online and conversely that it may permit the user to express these desired behaviors in a 'safe' environment, thus preventing them from engaging in these behaviors offline.

Impact on Victims of Virtual Crime

There are a number of reactions that are evident in victims of crime, as outlined by Kirwan (2009). These vary according to both the type of crime and the coping strategy and personality of the individual victim, but can include Acute Stress Disorder (ASD) or Post-Traumatic Stress Disorder (PTSD), self-blaming for victimization, victim blaming (where others put all or partial blame for the victimization on the victim themselves), and a need for retribution. Virtual victimization, either of property crime or a crime against the person, should not be considered as severe as if a similar offence occurred in real life. There can be no doubt that a victim of a real-life sexual assault experiences post-victimization symptoms that are far more severe than those of an online victim. However, it would be an error to believe that an online victimization has no effect on the victim at all.

Victim blaming appears to be particularly common for virtual crime. It has been argued that victims of virtual crime could easily escape. In Second Life, it is possible to engage in rape fantasies, where another player has control over the "victim's" avatar, but this is usually given with consent. There are suggestions that some individuals have been tricked into giving their consent, but even bearing this in mind, there has been widespread criticism by Second Life commentators of anyone who allows an attack to take place, as it is alleged that it is always possible to 'teleport' away from any situation. Even if teleportation fails, it is still possible for the victim to exit the game, disconnect from the network connection or turn off their computer and thus end the event. It is clear that victims of virtual crime do seem to experience some extent of victim blaming by others – they are in ways being blamed for not escaping their attacker. Those victims who experience the greatest degree of presence – those who are most immersed in the game - are probably those who are least likely to think of closing the application to escape. It should also be considered that a victim may experience discomfort at being victimized, even if they do escape relatively quickly. As in a real life crime, the initial stages of the attack may be confusing or upsetting enough to cause significant distress, even if the victim manages to escape quickly.

There is also some evidence of self-blaming by various victims of virtual crimes. Some victims refer to their relative naivety in the online world prior to victimization (Jay, 2007), and indicate that if they had been more experienced they may have realized what was happening sooner. A victim may also feel that they should not have experimented in the virtual world at all, or that they should have researched the types of events which can occur in virtual worlds more thoroughly before exploring the world. There are also suggestions that a victim who is inexperienced with the virtual world's user interface may inadvertently give control of their avatar to another user. It is certain that empirical study needs to be completed on this topic before a definitive conclusion can be reached as to the degree of self-blaming which occurs.

There is also some evidence of limited symptoms of ASD in victims of virtual crimes, such as some anecdotal accounts of intrusive memories, emotional numbing and upset from victims of virtual sexual assault (see for example Dibbell, 1993, 1998). While it is impossible to make an accurate judgment without a full psychological evaluation, it seems very unlikely that these victims would receive a clinical diagnosis of either ASD or PTSD. This is because there is no mention of either flashbacks or heightened autonomic arousal (possibly due to the lack of real danger to the victim's life), nor does it appear that the symptoms lasted for very long. There are also several accounts of individuals who have experienced online victimization, but who do not see it as a serious assault and do not appear to experience any severe negative reaction. Those most at risk appear to be those who have previously experienced victimization of a real-life sexual assault, where the online attack has served to remind the victim of the previous attack. As such, while not a major risk, the possibility of developing ASD or PTSD is a factor that should be monitored in future victims of serious online assaults, especially those who have been previously victimized in real life.

Finally, there is substantial anecdotal evidence of a need for retribution in victims of virtual crimes, such as the calls for the toading of Mr. Bungle. Similar reactions have been noted by other victims of crimes in virtual worlds, to the extent that in some cases victims have approached real world police forces seeking justice. This is possibly the strongest evidence that victims of virtual offences experience similar psychological reactions to victims of real life offences, although again, empirical evidence is lacking to date. As victims begin to seek justice, it seems necessary to consider the legal position of crimes in virtual worlds.

The Evolving Law Online

Law online is inevitably international in nature given the cross boarder nature of the internet. International law developed through the work of Austin (1832) who defined law as, 'the command of the king'. This was 'depersonalized' by Hart (1997) who defined it as, 'law is a set of rules'. Dworkin (1986) evolved this further to introduce the concept of judgment and saw law as a matter of interpretation and thus in the hands of the judiciary. This separation of law from the king or state in turn allowed for the possibility of non-State or supra-State law making bodies. As law making moved from the sole preserve of the state to supra-State bodies such as the European Union and to entities such as the United Nations (UN), the International Monetary Fund (IMF), the World Bank, and the World Trade Organization (WTO), there was a move away from systems of command and control. As these changes occurred individual states had less autonomy the importance of non-state actors grew and governance by peer review became important.

Another influence on the development of online law is the concept of soft law. Soft laws are those which consist of informal rules which are non-binding but due to cultural norms or standards of conduct, have practical effect (Burgess, 2002). These are distinct from hard laws which are the rules and regulations that make up legal systems in the traditional sense. In the early days of the internet the instinct of governments was to solve the perceived problems of control by hard law. In the US the Clinton administration tried on many occasions to pass laws to control pornography online. The Communications Decency Act (CDA) was followed by the Child Online Protection Act (COPA) which was followed by the Children's Internet Protection Act (CHIPA). All were passed into law and all were challenged in the courts under freedom of speech issues.

One of the changes in our society brought about by the connectivity and interaction of the internet is the need to shift from prevention to reaction. Society simply has less control over what kind of values they can confer on their members, and this in turn means a loss of prevention as a strategy for reducing harm (Shirky, 2009, p308). For example, governments have to increase surveillance and punishment of pedophiles, now that the pedophiles are able to gather online and trade tips on earning the trust of children. This requires a move from a strategy of prevention to one of monitoring and reaction, as a side effect of more control of media slipping into the hands of citizens (Shirky, 2009 p309).

Soft law offers techniques for compromise and cooperation between States and private actors. Soft law can provide opportunities for deliberation, systematic comparisons, and learning (Schäfer, 2006). It may not commit a government to a policy but it may achieve the desired result by moral persuasion and peer pressure. It may also allow a state to engage with an issue otherwise impossible for domestic reasons and open the possibility for more substantive agreements in the future.

In considering the appropriate legal framework for the international realm of the internet the nature both of the activities taking place and the individuals and organizations using it need to be considered. The legitimacy or appropriateness of hard versus soft laws depends on the society they are seeking to legalize. In the context of online social networks soft laws have a power and potential for support which may make them more effective than the hard laws that might attempt to assert legitimacy. The confluence of States, individuals, businesses, and other non State actors that make up the legal, regulatory and technical web of behaviors that constitute the internet make it somewhat unique.

There are a number of views about the need for 'cyberlaws'. One is that rules for online activities in cyberspace need to come from territorial States (Goldsmith, 1998). The other is that there is a case for considering cyberspace as a different place where we can and should make new rules (Johnson & Post, 1996). A third option is to look at the decentralization of law making, and the development of processes which do not seek to impose a framework of law but which allows one to emerge.

This could involve the creation of in-world systems of governance (controlled by software engineers, users, administrators, or a combination of these). Service providers would develop their own systems of governance and ethics. The law would come from the bottom up as users select the services, products and environment that match their own standards of behavior and ethics. This would constitute a system of variable ethics. For example a user may chose to abide by the ethical norms in Grand Theft Auto and be quite comfortable with the notion of violent behavior as a norm. Another user may be more comfortable in the ethical environment of Club Penguin. The ethical world is thus no longer normative but adaptable, variable or "fit for purpose". A similar approach is suggested by Cannataci and Mifsud-Bonnici (2007, p.60), who make the case that 'there is developing a mesh of private and State rules and remedies which are independent and complementary'. The internet community can adopt rules and remedies based on their 'fitness for purpose'. State regulation may be appropriate to control certain activities, technical standards may be more appropriate in other situations, and private regulation may be appropriate where access to State courts or processes are impossible. In the example cited above of Mr. Bungle in LambdaMoo, internal governance through user agreed ethical norms and technical restrictions provided the 'victim' with some opportunity for redress and punishment through exclusion. This may have been sufficient to address the sense of loss and helplessness that occurred. Our understanding of justice may change as we see what emerges from un-coerced individual choice (Post, 1996). The appropriate legal or ethical framework on one context or virtual environment may be quite different in another.

Some aspects of what can and cannot be done, or even what may be considered right or wrong, will be determined by software engineers. They will find ways to prevent file sharing, illegal downloading or many other elements of our online activities. The blocking or filtering software that has largely removed the need for states to struggle with issues of censorship is being improved and refined all the time. This raises the question of the ethical landscape which results from coding. If the rules of the environment are set in part by programmers are we confident that the ethical norms of, for example, a young, male, college educated, Californian, software engineer will necessarily match the needs or desires of all users? Private regulations also exist in the realm of codes of behavior agreed amongst groups of users or laid down by commercial organizations that provide a service or social networking environment. The intertwining of State and private regulation is both inevitable and necessary to provide real-time solutions to millions of online customers and consumers.

Another part of the framework for considering law on the internet can be taken from the writing of Cooney and Lang (2007). They describe the recent development of learning-centered alternatives to traditional command-and-control regulatory frameworks, variously described as 'experimentalist' governance, 'reflexive' governance, or 'new' governance. Elements of these approaches contribute to what Cooney and Lang call adaptive governance. In this way all the sources of governance; user choice, code, private and state regulation, are all in constant flux as they both influences each other and improve and change overtime.

Policing, Punishment and Victim Support

Online crimes with real world impact and risks should be under the remit of the traditional and appropriate enforcement agencies. This would include child pornography, online grooming of children, identity theft and appropriate hacking activities. However, in many cases the line is blurred, such as if a virtual attack is interpreted as an actual threat against the victim in real life (where both the victim perceives it as a threat against their real self and the perpetrator intends it as a real life threat). If an item is stolen in a virtual world, and the item can be judged to have an actual monetary value in real life, then it may also be possible to prosecute the thief in real life (Hof, 2006). However, the line between a real life crime, and one which is purely virtual, is less coherent when the damages caused to the victim are emotional or psychological in nature, without any physical or monetary harm being caused. It is for these cases in particular that legal systems need to consider what the most appropriate course of action should be.

Policing of virtual worlds would most likely need to be unique to each world, if only because different worlds have differing social norms and definitions of acceptable and unacceptable behaviors. For example, players in an online war game such as Battlefield are unlikely to need a legal recourse if their avatar is killed when they lose, especially when the avatars come back to 'life' after a short time. However, if the same virtual murder occurred in an online world aimed at young children, it would obviously be much less acceptable. With this in mind, should it be obligatory for the creator of each virtual world to put in place a strict set of laws or regulations outlining what is and is not acceptable in the world, and ensuring that the virtual world is patrolled sufficiently well to ensure that all wrongdoings are observed and punished appropriately? This is probably particularly appropriate if the creators of the virtual world are profiting financially from its users, although Linden Labs has shown reluctance to embrace this approach (Holahan, 2006). This 'big brother' approach to life online is strongly opposed by many cyber-citizens. An alternative is to make cybersocieties mirrors of the real world, where the

police rely greatly on the citizens of the relevant society to report misconduct. On the other hand, this approach may also be open to abuse as one or more players could make unfounded allegations against another. In extreme cases, there may be a market for 'cyber-lawyers' who defend avatars against allegations by others or mount a case for cyber-prosecutions in virtual worlds.

The punishment of virtual crime is often framed by a restorative justice approach. This refers to processes involving mediation between the offender and the victim (Howitt, 2009). Rather than focusing on the criminal activity itself, it focuses on the harm caused by the crime, and more specifically, the victims of the crime. It often involves a mediated meeting between the victim and the offender, where both are allowed to express sentiments and explanations, and the offender is given the opportunity to apologize. The aims of restorative justice are a satisfied victim, an offender who feels that they have been fairly dealt with, and reintegration of the community, rather than financial compensation or specific punishment. If the mediation does not meet the satisfaction of all involved, alternative punishments can then be considered. It would appear that the restorative justice approach is ideally suited for many virtual crimes as it allows the victim to feel that they have been heard, while allowing the community to remain cohesive. However, it should be noted that not all victims of real life crimes have felt satisfied by the process (Wemmers, 2006), and so in some online cases it may be inadequate or fail to satisfy those involved. As was seen in the Mr. Bungle case, banishment from an online community is often considered the most severe punishment possible in virtual worlds. Nevertheless, it is easily overcome by creating a new avatar. It has been argued that virtual punishment is the appropriate recourse for crimes which occur in an online community (McKinnon, 1997). In theft cases where the item has a 'real world' value, then it may be possible in some jurisdictions to enforce a 'real world' punishment also – perhaps a fine or a prison term. But to prosecute cases such as Mr. Bungle in the real world, it would require that laws are rewritten, perhaps to include malicious infliction of emotional distress using computer mediated communication (Brenner, 2001).

The reactions described by victims of virtual crime suggest that it may be useful if some form of victim aid was put in place to assist them with the process of dealing with their difficulties. This aid could take a number of different forms, including help with reporting the offence, emotional, financial and legal assistance, and the possible introduction of restorative justice. Victims of real-life offences normally have relatively straightforward procedures available to them for the reporting of criminal offences. Police helplines, patrols and stations are often the initial ports of call for a recent victim of real-life crime. In online worlds, the reporting procedure is less clear, and the user may need to invest time and energy to determine how to report their experience. Although many online worlds have procedures for reporting misconduct, these are not always found to be satisfactory by victims if they wish to report more serious offences (Jay, 2007). Similarly, reporting the occurrence to the administrators of the online world alone may not meet the victim's need for retribution, especially if they feel that they have experienced real-world harm because of the virtual crime. In those cases, the victim may prefer to approach the real-world authorities. To aid victims in this regard, many online worlds need to be clearer about their complaints procedures, and the possible outcomes of this. They may also need to be clearer about the possible repercussions of reporting virtual crimes to real world authorities.

Victims of real world crimes receive varying degrees of emotional, financial and legal aid, depending on the offence which occurred. In some cases, this aid is provided through charitable organizations, such as Victim Support, sometimes through government organizations, and also through informal supports such as family and friends. Financial aid is probably the least applicable to victims of virtual crime, as although theft of property can occur, it is unlikely to result in severe poverty for the victim. Also, because items with a designated real-world value are starting to be considered by real-world authorities, there is some possibility of financial recompense. Legal aid, both in terms of the provision of a lawyer and in terms of help in understanding the court system, can also be provided to real world victims. The legal situation is somewhat less clear for victims of virtual crimes, particularly where the punishment is meted out in the virtual world, as in the Mr. Bungle case. In that event, the victims and other users were required to effectively set up a legal system themselves. But from the cases which have been publicized to date, it appears that the greatest need for assistance that online victims have is for emotional support. In some cases victims have sought this from other members of the online community, but the evidence of victim-blaming for virtual crimes which is apparent to date may result in increased upset for victims, instead of alleviating their distress.

FUTURE RESEARCH DIRECTIONS

Further research needs to be conducted in order to determine how widespread virtual crime actually is, and to establish how severely most victims react to it. The factors which lead to more severe reactions should then be identified. If virtual crime is determined to be a serious problem, with substantial effects on victims, then a greater focus needs to be placed on how online communities deal with this problem, and if legislation needs to be changed to reflect the psychological and emotional consequences of victimization. It should also be established if there are distinct or unique motives for online crime which do not apply to offline crime and how can these be combated.

Further work into the 'humanity' or otherwise of avatars in virtual worlds and the connection a user feels towards their avatar is important to considering the ethical response of users to each other. In the case of unethical behavior, does the ability to engage in it in the relative anonymity of a virtual world impact on the psychology of the individual? Further, what aspects of virtual worlds cause a shift in ethical standards in the individual? It may be that the disinhibition noted with online interactions is a primary factor.

CONCLUSION

Online virtual worlds have become more common in recent years, yet they have largely been making the rules up as they go. In many cases, the administrators of the virtual world are left trying to deal with individual cases of virtual crime or anti social behavior, often without the action being criminalized in the community beforehand. In some cases this has been relatively successful, but in others victims of virtual offences appear to undergo quite serious emotional reactions to their victimization, suffering symptoms similar to those experienced by victims of offline offences. Nevertheless, there is often limited acceptance of the legitimacy of this emotional reaction from others. With increasing numbers of both children and adults joining multiple online communities, it is important that adequate protection is provided to the cybercitizen. However, the cybercitizen also requires education, so that they are better informed as to what is ethically acceptable in online virtual worlds.

These ideas of variable ethics (providing choice in online value system), soft law and adaptive governance offer lessons to the notion of a structure of laws for virtual worlds. Systems of informal rules could be implemented which may not be binding but have effect through a shared understanding of their benefits. Law could be introduced which is flexible and open to change as knowledge and the online experience develop. Such laws should be developed through agreements which include State and non-state actors, and which involve both citizens and businesses. Soft law offers lessons on continuous learning in a changing environment, resulting in an evolving system of law and ethics. This will be one of the principle challenges for states, individuals and systems of justice as we move more of our lives online.

REFERENCES

Adams, A. A. (2010). Virtual sex with child avatars. In Wankel, C., & Malleck, S. (Eds.), *Emerging ethical issues of life in virtual worlds* (pp. 55–72). Charlotte, NC: Information Age Publishing.

Anderson, C. A. (1997). Effects of violent movies and trait hostility on hostile feelings and aggressive thoughts. *Aggressive Behavior*, *23*, 161–178. Retrieved from http: //www. psychology.iastate. edu/faculty/caa/abstracts/ 1995-1999/97A.pdf. doi:10.1002/(SICI)1098-2337(1997)23:3<161::AID-AB2>3.0.CO;2-P

Austin, J. (2000). *The province of jurisprudence determined*. New York, NY: Prometheus Books.

BBC. (2007). *Virtual theft leads to arrest*. Retrieved August 1, 2010, from http: //news.bbc. co. uk/2/hi/technology/ 7094764.stm

Berlin, I. (1980). *Concepts and categories: Philosophical essays*. Oxford, UK: Oxford University Press.

Brenner, S.W. (2001). Is there such a thing as virtual crime? *California Criminal Law Review, 4*.

Burgess, P. (2002). What's so European about the European Union? Legitimacy between institution and identity. *European Journal of Social Theory*, *5*, 467. doi:10.1177/136843102760513866

Cannataci, J., & Mifsud-Bonnici, J. P. (2007). Weaving the mesh: Finding remedies in cyberspace. *International Review of Law Computers & Technology, 21*(1), 59–78. doi:10.1080/13600860701281705

Chester, A., & Bretherton, D. (2007). Impression management and identity online. In Joinson, A., McKenna, K., Postmes, T., & Reips, U. (Eds.), *The Oxford handbook of Internet psychology* (pp. 223–236). New York, NY: Oxford University Press.

Cooney, R., & Lang, A. (2007). Taking uncertainty seriously: Adaptive governance and international trade. *European Journal of International Law, 18,* 523. doi:10.1093/ejil/chm030

Cybercrime. (n.d.). *Princeton WordNet*. Retrieved August 1, 2010, from http: //wordnetweb.princeton. edu/perl/webwn?s= cybercrime

Dibbell, J. (1993). *A rape in cyberspace*. Retrieved August 1, 2010, from http: //loki.stockton.edu/~kinsellt/stuff/ dibbelrapeincyberspace.html

Dibbell, J. (1998). *A rape in cyberspace*. Retrieved August 1, 2010, from http: //www.juliandibbell. com/texts/ bungle.html

Dworkin, R. (1986). *Law's empire*. Oregon: Hart Publishing.

Goldsmith, J. L. (1998). Against cyberanarchy. *The University of Chicago Law Review. University of Chicago. Law School, 65,* 1199. doi:10.2307/1600262

Guardian. (2008) *Second Life affair leads to couple's real-life divorce*. Retrieved August 1, 2010, from http: //www.guardian.co. uk/technology/ 2008/nov/14/second-life- virtual-worlds-divorce

Hart, H. L. A. (1997). *The concept of law*. New York, NY: Oxford University Press.

Hof, R. (2006). *Real threat to virtual goods in Second Life*. Retrieved August 1, 2010, from http: //www.businessweek. com/the_thread/techbeat/ archives/2006/11/ real_threat_to.html

Holahan, C. (2006). *The dark side of Second Life*. Retrieved August 1, 2010, from http: //www. businessweek. com/technology/ content/nov2006/ tc20061121_727243.htm

Howitt, D. (2009). *Introduction to forensic and criminal psychology* (3rd ed.). Pearson.

Jay, E. (2007). *Rape in cyberspace*. Retrieved August 1, 2010, from https: //lists.secondlife. com/ pipermail/educators/ 2007-May/009237.html

Johnson, D., & Post, D. (1996). Law and boarders – The rise of law in cyberspace. *Stanford Law Review, 48*(5), 1367–1402. doi:10.2307/1229390

Kirwan, G. (2009, November). Presence and the victims of crime in online virtual worlds. *Proceedings of Presence 2009 – the 12th Annual International Workshop on Presence, International Society for Presence Research*, November 11-13, Los Angeles, California. Retrieved from http: // astro.temple. edu/~tuc16417/papers/ Kirwan.pdf

Kirwan, G., & Power, A. (2011). *The psychology of cybercrime: Concepts and principles*. Hershey, PA: IGI Global. doi:10.4018/978-1-61350-350-8

Knight, W. (2005). *Computer characters mugged in virtual crime spree*. Retrieved August 1, 2010, http: //www.newscientist. com/article/dn7865

McKinnon, R. C. (1997). Punishing the persona: Correctional strategies for the virtual offender. In Jones, S. (Ed.), *The undernet: The Internet and the ither*. Sage.

Mnookin, J. (1996). Virtual(ly) law: The emergence of law in LambdaMOO. *Journal of Computer-Mediated Communication, 2*(1). Retrieved August 1, 2010, from http: //www.ascusc. org/ jcmc/vol2/issue1/ lambda.html

Möller, I., & Barbara, K. (2009). Exposure to violent video games and aggression in German adolescents: A longitudinal analysis. *Aggressive Behavior*, *35*, 75–89. Retrieved from http: // videogames.procon. org/sourcefiles/ Germanado-lescents.pdf. doi:10.1002/ab.20290

Parke, R. D., Berkowitz, L., Leyens, J. P., West, S. G., & Sebastian, R. J. (1977). some effects of violent and nonviolent movies on the behavior of juvenile delinquents. In L. Berkowitz (Ed.), *Advances in experimental social psychology,* vol. 10. Academic Press. Retrieved from http: //books.google. com/books?hl=en&lr=&id=lEgM5N6rIKw C&oi=fnd&pg=PA135&dq= violent+films&o ts=mtgWqOnCf1&sig=yV- zZDu_SK8j3XRz-W7WfbnR6L7 E#v=onepage&q=violent%20 films&f=false

Post, D. (1996). Governing cyberspace. *Wayne Law Review*, *43*(1), 155–171.

Rawls, J. (1973). *A theory of justice*. Oxford, UK: Oxford University Press.

Rawls, J. (1996). *Political liberalism*. New York, NY: Columbia University Press.

Schäfer, A. (2006). Resolving deadlock: Why international organizations introduce soft law. [Oxford, UK: Blackwell Publishing Ltd.]. *European Law Journal*, *12*(2), 194–208. doi:10.1111/j.1468-0386.2006.00315.x

Sheldon, K., & Howitt, D. (2007). *Sex offenders and the Internet*. Chichester, UK: Wiley.

Shirky, C. (2009). *Here comes everybody*. London, UK: Penguin.

Shirky, C. (2010). *Cognitive surplus*. London, UK: Penguin.

Symantec. (n.d.). *What is cybercrime?* Retrieved August 1, 2010, from http: //www.symantec. com/ norton/cybercrime/ definition.jsp

The Irish Times. (2008). *Woman faces jail for hacking her virtual husband to death*. Retrieved August 1, 2010, from http: //www.irishtimes. com/news-paper/frontpage/2008/1025/ 1224838828960. html

Toys Advice. (n.d.). *Impact of computer games on child development*. Retrieved August 1, 2010 www. toysadvice.co. uk/impact-computer-games-child-development.html

Truta, F. (2008). *Russia - Gamer kills gamer over gamer killing gamer... Er, in-game!* Retrieved August 1, 2010, from http: //news.softpedia. com/ news/Russia-Gamer-Kills -Gamer-over-Gamer-Killing -Gamer-Er-In-Game-76619.shtml

Wemmers, J. A., & Cyr, K. (2006). Victims' perspectives on restorative justice: How much involvement are victims looking for? *International Review of Victimology*, *11*, 259–274.

ADDITIONAL READING

Bailenson, J. N., & Segovia, K. Y. (2010). Virtual Doppelgangers: Psychological effects of avatars who ignore their owners. In Bainbridge, W. S. (Ed.), *Online Worlds: Convergence of the Real and the Virtual* (pp. 175–186). London: Springer-Verlag. doi:10.1007/978-1-84882-825-4_14

Bainbridge, W. S., Lutters, W., Rhoten, D., & Lowood, H. (2010). The Future of Virtual Worlds. In Bainbridge, W. S. (Ed.), *Online Worlds: Convergence of the Real and the Virtual* (pp. 289–302). London: Springer-Verlag. doi:10.1007/978-1-84882-825-4_23

Barnett, J., Coulson, M., & Foreman, N. (2010). Examining Player Anger in World of Warcraft. In Bainbridge, W. S. (Ed.), *Online Worlds: Convergence of the Real and the Virtual* (pp. 147–160). London: Springer-Verlag. doi:10.1007/978-1-84882-825-4_12

Bente, G., Rüggenberg, S., Krämer, N. C., & Eschenburg, F. (2008). Avatar-Mediated networking: Increasing social presence and interpersonal trust in net-based collaborations. *Human Communication Research*, *34*, 287–318. doi:10.1111/j.1468-2958.2008.00322.x

Boellstorff, T. (2010). A typology of ethnographic scales for virtual worlds. In Bainbridge, W. S. (Ed.), *Online Worlds: Convergence of the Real and the Virtual* (pp. 123–134). London: Springer-Verlag. doi:10.1007/978-1-84882-825-4_10

Ducheneaut, N. (2010). Massively Multiplayer Online Games as Living Laboratories: Opportunities and Pitfalls. In Bainbridge, W. S. (Ed.), *Online Worlds: Convergence of the Real and the Virtual* (pp. 135–146). London: Springer-Verlag. doi:10.1007/978-1-84882-825-4_11

Ess, C. (2009). *Digital Media Ethics*. Cambridge, England: Polity Press.

Guest, T. (2007). *Second Lives: A Journey Through Virtual Worlds*. London: Random House.

Hickey-Moody, A., & Wood, D. (2010). Ethics in Second Life: Difference, Desire and the Production of Subjectivity. In Wankel, C., & Malleck, S. (Eds.), *Emerging Ethical Issues of Life in Virtual Worlds* (pp. 153–176). Charlotte, NC: Information Age Publishing.

Hoyle, C., & Zedner, L. (2007). Victims, Victimization, and Criminal Justice. In Maguire, M., Morgan, R., & Reiner, R. (Eds.), *The Oxford Handbook of Criminology* (4th ed., pp. 461–495). Oxford University Press.

Maher, M. L. (2010). What people talk about in virtual worlds. In Bainbridge, W. S. (Ed.), *Online Worlds: Convergence of the Real and the Virtual* (pp. 201–212). London: Springer-Verlag. doi:10.1007/978-1-84882-825-4_16

Meadows, M. S. (2008). *I, Avatar: The Culture and Consequences of Having a Second Life*. Berkeley, CA: New Riders.

Pasquinelli, E. (2010). The illusion of reality: Cognitive aspects and ethical drawbacks: The case of Second Life. In Wankel, C., & Malleck, S. (Eds.), *Emerging Ethical Issues of Life in Virtual Worlds* (pp. 197–216). Charlotte, NC: Information Age Publishing.

Pearce, C. (2006). *Seeing and being seen: Presence & Play in Online Virtual Worlds. Online, offline and the concept of presence when games and VR collide*. USC Institute for Creative Technologies.

Prisco, G. (2010). Future evolution of virtual worlds as communication environments. In Bainbridge, W. S. (Ed.), *Online Worlds: Convergence of the Real and the Virtual* (pp. 279–288). London: Springer-Verlag. doi:10.1007/978-1-84882-825-4_22

Sicart, M. (2010). This War is a Lie: Ethical Implications of Massively Multiplayer Online Game Design. In Wankel, C., & Malleck, S. (Eds.), *Emerging Ethical Issues of Life in Virtual Worlds* (pp. 177–196). Charlotte, NC: Information Age Publishing.

Soraker, J. H. (2010). The Neglect of reason: A plea for rationalist accounts of the effects of virtual violence. In Wankel, C., & Malleck, S. (Eds.), *Emerging Ethical Issues of Life in Virtual Worlds* (pp. 15–32). Charlotte, NC: Information Age Publishing.

Tavani, H. T. (2007). *Ethics and Technology: Ethical Issues in an Age of Information and Communication Technology* (2nd ed.). Hoboken, NJ: Wiley.

Wall, D., & Williams, M. (2007). Policing diversity in the digital age: maintaining order in virtual communities. *Criminology & Criminal Justice*, *7*, 391–415. doi:10.1177/1748895807082064

Wall, D. S. (2007). *Cybercrime*. Cambridge, England: Polity.

Wankel, C., & Malleck, S. (2010). Exploring New Ethical Issues in the virtual worlds of the twenty-first century. In Wankel, C., & Malleck, S. (Eds.), *Emerging Ethical Issues of Life in Virtual Worlds* (pp. 1–14). Charlotte, NC: Information Age Publishing.

Whitson, J., & Doyle, A. (2008). Second Life and governing deviance in virtual worlds. In Leman-Langlois, S. (Ed.), *Technocrime: Technology, crime and social control. Cullompton, Devon: Willan* (pp. 88–111).

Williams, M. (2006). *Virtually Criminal: Crime, deviance and regulation online*. Oxon, England: Routledge.

Williams, M. (2010). The virtual neighbourhood watch: netizens in action. In Jewkes, Y., & Yar, M. (Eds.), *Handbook of Internet Crime* (pp. 562–581). Cullompton, England: Willan.

Yee, N. (2010). Changing the Rules: Social Architectures in Virtual Worlds. In Bainbridge, W. S. (Ed.), *Online Worlds: Convergence of the Real and the Virtual* (pp. 213–224). London: Springer-Verlag. doi:10.1007/978-1-84882-825-4_17

KEY TERMS AND DEFINITIONS

Adaptive Governance System: A system of governance that can adapt to the needs of the governed. It is flexible, collaborative and learning based.

Avatar: In computing, a representation of the user in the form of a three-dimensional model.

Cybercrime: Crimes that occur in online environments. These can be subdivided into internet enabled crimes, internet specific crimes and new crimes committed in a virtual world.

Cybersociety: An online community of users who have formed an either implicit or explicit society, possibly with a set of social norms, rules and etiquette.

Soft Law: A concept of law that is developed by agreement, laws which consist of informal rules which are non-binding but due to cultural norms or standards of conduct, have practical effect.

Variable Ethics: The concept that ethics are not fixed but vary depending on the nature of the virtual world you are in and the accepted norms of that world.

Virtual World: Virtual representations of three-dimensional spaces, often online.

Chapter 8
Narbs as a Measure and Indicator of Identity Narratives

Ananda Mitra
Wake Forest University, USA

ABSTRACT

Social media systems allow individuals to create a discursive identity for themselves using different tools all of which function as narrative bits of information, or "narbs," which in unison create a composite identity of an individual. The narbs possess certain specific measurable attributes - type of content, authorship, frequency of appearance and spatial information. Each of these attributes offer bits of information about the individual and careful examination and enumeration of these attributes of the narbs produce a narb weight and a narb matrix which can be examined numerically to provide a preliminary understanding of how granulated an identity narrative would be when narbs are examined for a particular individual.

INTRODUCTION

The growing number of people who have began to subscribe to social networking sites (SNS) in the early part of the Twenty-first century has been a phenomenon that has attracted significant attention from scholars, popular media, and the general population as people have embraced the SNS system as a tool of communication (Kirkpatrick, 2010; Lenhart, 2009). This growth has also resulted in concerns over the way in which

SNS information could be used by individuals and institutions to learn about each other. The two concerns that are addressed in this chapter deal with first, finding a way to systematically enumerate and analyze the information on SNS and secondly using the enumeration system to better manage the way in which narrative bytes or "narbs," are produced and used (Mitra, 2010). To begin with, it is useful to consider the place of SNS in a larger context of creating a presence for an individual or institution when the "real" object disappears from sight to be substituted by a discursive presence.

DOI: 10.4018/978-1-61350-132-0.ch008

The phenomenon of creating a digital discursive presence on SNS is an example of the increasing digitization of everyday life activities as an increasing number of people are creating social media profiles or micro-blogging their every single mundane activity. However, the process of creating a presence via technological mediation existed before digitization became the driving force behind much of modern tools. Consider for instance the phenomenon of creating the "party line". This was a popular use of the familiar telephone technology that would allow many people, often women, to connect with each other in a synchronous manner and talk over the phone for long periods of time and share a variety of information about each other, and most importantly, about others in the form of gossip (Rakow, 1988). The telephone allowed individuals to transcend the barrier of space and create a "telephonic presence" where the telephonic glue held together the people even if they were not "there" in the real. This idea was extrapolated when digitization allowed for the creation and circulation of the "digital presence" through tools such as such as listserves and Usenet groups that were popular in the late 1980s and early 1990s[1]. The technology was not sufficiently sophisticated to allow for sharing of much beyond written texts that would create the discursive space where the virtual communities would be formed (Mitra, 1996, 1997).

A crucial common element in all the different networks was the way in which a person would choose to present themselves within the network independent of the technology used to connect the people. Bracketing out the real networks, where the "flesh and blood" person would actually interact with another "real" person, the specific networking technology had an impact on the specific presence that would be created. The telephone only allowed for the voice to be the vehicle for creating the presence whereas the multi-media options provided by Web sites such as Chatroulette (Kreps, 2010) can allow for the production of a more detailed and variegated presence based

primarily on the content of the connection. This chapter examines the ways in which the existing and emergent tools are producing opportunities for creating the presence that brings with concerns around deciphering the identity of an individual based on the digital presence that is created for and by the individual. The key objective is to develop a systematic way of understanding how the presence is created around different elements such as content, authorship, place and frequency at which the discourses are produced. The specific form of digital tool is what has been labeled as SNS[2] and it is useful to consider the idea of social networking where presence exists and identity is constructed.

OVERVIEW OF SOCIAL NETWORKING

The transformation from the virtual communities based around text-intensive discussion boards to the SNS was made possible because of two major developments in the technological sphere – availability of powerful digital machines, and the wide-spread penetration of high-speed data connections. The first component of the change refers to the proliferation of digital tools, from computers to smart cell phones, that are able to rapidly process the large amounts of data produced by the digitization[3] of audio and image information. The second component of the change refers to the way in which the digital tools are able to connect to central repository of data files which can store extremely large amounts of data that can be rapidly transmitted from a centralized location to a digital tool. These two technological developments led to the emergence and popularity of a class of Web-based applications that quickly came to be known as SNS. As pointed out in the articles in the special theme section of the *Journal of Computer Mediated Communication* compiled by Boyd and Ellison (2007) there were numerous SNS forums that came and went in the latter

1990s and the early 2000s, with different SNS providing different kinds of functionality and attracting different levels of following among users. Independent of what the nature and purpose of the SNS was, what remained common across these systems is the fact that users of these networks had to create a digital presence of themselves to be a part of the network. To be sure, the very process of becoming a member of the network involved the act of selecting a set of personal attributes that would become the "profile" of the person creating the presence.

The process of creating presence is, however, neither novel nor unique to SNS. For instance, the replacement of the "real" person by the "virtual" presence was witnessed with the emergence of the early virtual communities based on text based exchanges. Given the available technological sophistication of the CMC of the 1980s and 1990s, most of the interactions that made up the virtual communities were based on textual discourse made up by people who would use the computer to present a virtual self to other members of the group[4]. The replacement of the real person by the virtually available discourse also created a condition where the discourse became the primary mode of creating a presence of the person. This presence was removed from the real because it might have been impossible to ever have a clear understanding of the real entity since the entity was always already produced by discourses. This phenomenon produced specific issues related to the authenticity of the entity that would be available in discourse (Mitra, 2002). First, it would be impossible to be sure that what was being presented in a discursive form was indeed what the entity was. This phenomenon extends to all entities that have a digital presence – from a person to an institution – and the presence is often the careful construction of a "face" that is visible to the World (Hyde & Mitra, 2000). The user of the information must decide if the presence is authentic and trustworthy so that the observer can make specific attributions about

the real entity that is depicted online. Secondly, the matter, naturally, is simpler if the observer has some *a priori* information about the real entity. For example, if one were to know that a person is likely to exaggerate, then this prior information would attenuate the interpretation of whatever is reported in an online situation. In such cases, the real and the virtual coalesce to produce a specific cybernetic presence where both the real and the virtual are considered together to understand who a person is[5]. The authentic identity of a person or institution was the product of the ways in which an entity would manufacture specific images in the realm of cybernetic space. Much of identity production in the synthetic digital-real realm was done by the careful selection and propagation of discourse by the person or institution creating the representation. Consider for instance the way in which a "home page" is created where specific and carefully selected images and discourse is used to describe the face of a person or an institution so that in combination with the real face of the entity a complete image of the unit is manufactured for global consumption.

The situation changes somewhat with the SNS where the primary method used to speak about an individual is through the use of tiny narrative bits, abbreviated into the term 'narbs' that the individual along with the numerous friends can place in the digital space called the profile of an individual (Mitra, 2010). These narbs become the building blocks of the profile page of a person as they are constantly added to the profile page of an individual. Visiting the profile of an individual is tantamount to examining the narbs of the person and the narbs, in their summation, offers a notion of what the person is like. Making attributions of the "real" person thus begins with the careful examination of the narbs that produce the digital presence of the person on a SNS. The narbs become the building blocks of the digital and cybernetic presence of the individual and it is important to consider a systematic way of enumerating the narbs so that the composite narrative identity can be judged for its authenticity and validity for presenting an accurate image of the real person. The process begins by examining a set of specific attributes of all narbs.

There are four significant attribute for each narb. To begin with, it is important to consider the person who is the author of the narb. There are two possibilities that exist here – either the individual retains agency and authorship in producing the personal narb or it is a friend of the person who actually produces the narb that is placed on an individual's profile page. Another attribute of a narb that is important to consider is the content of the narb, which could vary from simple text to an elaborate video with commentary or connections with other texts via hyperlinks from the profile page. A third attribute of narbs is the frequency with which narbs are updated and the chronological characteristics of the narbs. Finally, a fourth way to consider the narbs is their relationships with real life space and place, since narbs can be used to indicate where a person is placed in the real world. It is important to note that these attributes do not represent independent and distinct forms of narbs, but using these attributes allow for the examination of any narb from all these different perspectives. Thus, for any narb it is possible to ask four specific questions – Who produced it? What is it made up of? When was it produced? And where was it produced? Answering these questions about the numerous narbs can begin to create an image of an individual which then becomes the locus of debate about the authenticity of the image.

NARB ATTRIBUTES

Agency

There are two major kinds of narbs that can be identified on the basis of agency – those that are produced by an individual and those that are produced for the individual by someone else. The first kind is a "self narb" where an individual is able to retain control on the information that is produced and circulated amongst the community of friends within a SNS. The second kind is the "other narb" where an individual has little control on the information that is produced and circulated within the group of friends within a SNS. Both these narbs play a role in the production of the digital presence of an individual where an observer would study both set of narbs to put together the digital image. Unless the observer is especially careful in distinguishing between the self and the other narbs the composite image of the digital presence could have internal contradictions and inconsistencies that could produce a confusing image.

The process is best illustrated with a hypothetical example. Consider, for instance, a profile page from any popular SNS. Generally the information on the profile page is populated with updates from the numerous friends who are on SNS as well as the updates of personal status of the individual. A person can choose to update status at a rapid pace offering details of the flow of everyday life by recording simple events in one's life. These self narbs could become a chronicle of the person's real life existence. In that spirit, a person on vacation with friends might simply be recording the places visited over a span of time. However, a friend travelling with the individual could be chronicling specific events during the trip with the use of photographs that are tagged with name of the individual. As soon as a picture is tagged, that information usually appears on the profile page of the individual and a person observing the profile page is able to see the picture that has been tagged. The picture could reveal information that could be quite contrary to what the updated status claims. While the individual's self narb - the personal updates - might claim that the trip is educational, the other narb - the tagged picture - could represent an evening at a nightclub. These two narbs might not tell one consistent story leading to a conflicted image of the individual, and consequently call into question the authenticity and the trustworthiness of the different narbs. Yet, this is not necessarily a new phenomenon. In real life, a person is evaluated both in terms of the real face the person presents as well as the way in which a person is described. Consider for instance the importance of letters of recommendation in the context of evaluating the worth of a person. For example, when a person might seek higher education opportunities it is not uncommon for an university to seek a "statement of purpose" authored by the applicant and a set of letters of recommendation authored by trustworthy individuals who can present an authentic description of the person within the context of the application to an institution of higher education. The combination of this information offers the evaluators some basis to come to a decision about the person's worth. This principle is immensely scaled up in the case of SNS. It is no longer the case that three to five people are offered the agency to remark on an individual but any one of the hundreds of friends that encrust an individual are agents who can comment on the identity of an individual. Unlike the letter of recommendation that is sought from trustworthy agents, the hundreds of friends could say what they please about an individual and contribute to the production of the face of the individual.

The conflict is the result of the fact that different people act as authors of the narbs. Authorship and agency are closely related (Mitra & Watts, 2001). The agent is the person who has an interest in producing a specific image through carefully selected discourse. The agent carefully selects the voice that would be utilized in telling a story. In the case of the self narbs an individual is able to retain the control on agency and be thoughtful about the narrative that the self narbs produce. Also, as in the case of most agents, there is a certain internal consistency in the narrative, as suggested

in seminal work of scholars like Walter Fisher (1987) and Paul Ricouer (1984) on narratives. Others have also demonstrated the way in which identity is often constructed around specific narratives that a person might create for oneself (Autio, 2004; Bers, 1999; Hall, 1992; Jones, et. al., 2008; Redman, 2005; Whitebrook, 2001). However, on SNS, there are hundreds of other potential agents, with about the same authoring powers as any of the other agents, who can contribute to the digital image of the individual. There is no guarantee that these agents and their other narbs would have any consistency with the self narbs – leading to the condition of confusion that an observer might experience in developing a composite image of a digital person. Furthermore, the confusion is exaggerated by the different kinds of content – from simple texts to elaborate applications – that are used to produce the digital image. The next section examines the different kinds of content that make up the narbs encountered.

Content

The process of digitization reduces any form of information into a series of binary codes eventually represented by '0' and '1.' The outcome of this process is the fact that the code can be used to represent any form of information: from written text to elaborate video; these different forms of content can be combined to produce a composite narrative about what the content refers to. The idea of multi-media presentation is built on the construct that different kinds of content produce an overall depiction of the subject matter of a presentation. Narb content also operates in a similar fashion. Most SNS allow the inclusion of different kinds of content that can be accessed from the primary page allotted to a member of a SNS. The simplest form of content is the text 'update' of personal status produced by a self narb. These messages are usually short and provide rudimentary information about what a person might be doing at a particular point in time. These simple updates of one's status have become ubiquitous elements for most SNS, and some have actually promoted these updates so aggressively that users might be producing these short messages at a very rapid interval. This type of content is usually only textual and can only be authored by the owner of the SNS account. These updates can also be traced over time to examine to the different status narbs that have been offered by an individual, virtually creating a narrative time line of the person using the text narbs.

These text narbs are supplemented in many SNS by another series of textual content where the narb represents a publicly available message sent to an individual by others. These textual narbs compose a narrative that shows what others are telling an individual and display information that might have been unknown to many of the observers who read these text narbs. Consider for instance the way in which a person is offered birthday wishes using text narbs that show one person wishing another a happy birthday. Such a textual narb often creates a cascade of messages as others are reminded of the day and in a short time numerous text narbs populate the primary page of an individual. As in the case of any textual content, the stories told by these narbs remain embedded in the few words that can be used for the updates and messages.

The details of the message change when narbs are made up of visual content in the form of pictures and videos. Such content is becoming increasingly popular with the rapid penetration of different tools that can easily collect and distribute visual information. Commonly used smartphones are equipped with digital still and video cameras and tiny computer programs, often called 'apps,' on these tools allows the user to instantly send a picture or video to a SNS Web site where the visual content becomes a narb. The process of "mobile uploads" that is offered by some smart-phones also allows the user to annotate the picture with a textual narb creating a composite story that includes the visual and textual content. The

relatively inexpensive way of doing these updates allows individuals to quickly add numerous narbs to a profile presenting a fairly detailed story of oneself using pictures and words.

It is also possible to create video and audio narbs where the user is able to present such information as a part of the story one creates about oneself. The fact that both audio and video content are technologically more difficult to handle produces specific challenges for using them as narbs. In most cases, this type of content is provided as a hyperlink to a different digital resource that resides on the Internet. Especially for SNS that are not built around the audio/video platform, the audio/video form of content becomes a little bit more challenging to use as a narb and also somewhat more difficult to use for the observer. Part of the difficulty arises from the fact that it takes a little longer to consume the audio and video narbs, and by definition, the narb is a "bit" of information that creates a very quick image of a person. Since narbs often function as the tiniest bit of personal information that can be read quickly, the audio/video information is not as well suited to serve as narbs making the process of creating the composite narrative somewhat more challenging when the audio/video content is included in the production of narbs.

While the audio/video content is less suitable for a large group of SNS, it must be noted that there are some SNS that are designed around video. These SNS focus only on video content (which also contains the audio content) provided by its numerous users and the image of the user is produced around the video information connected to an individual[6]. These Web resources serve as SNS because these connect together many individuals whose relation to each other is built around the video content each person provides. Furthermore, the video content provided by an individual is potentially available to anyone else with access to the Web resource. A commercial example of the video SNS is YouTube where content is built completely around audio/video information complemented by some text accompanying the video content. However, such content do not qualify as narbs as in the case of other SNS where the networking component is considered to be very important.

In summary, the mainstream SNS resources are built largely around images and words whereas the video and audio content is somewhat less utilized in the traditional SNS. The ease of producing the text and images also leads to a variation in the frequency at which narbs are made available by individuals and that is another component of the narb that is worthy of consideration.

Frequency and Flow

One of the significant differences between the way in which Web sites operate and narbs do is the frequency with which information is updated using narbs. Generally, Web sites do not change too often unless the Web site belongs to organizations that are in the business of reporting news or information that must remain current. Personal Web sites could change to show specific changes in real life events, but the process of altering a Web site is more complex than creating a small narb and reporting that to the SNS. The success of SNS lies precisely in the fact that individuals habitually provide narbs that populate the SNS page of the all the people connected to that individual. These updates make up the primary content of SNS. However, it is also possible to consider the frequency with which different individuals would provide new narbs. There is a good amount of variation in the frequency of updates with some people updating so rapidly that the traditional SNS was not considered to the be the best forum of such updates, and new forums called micro-blogging system became popular to accommodate those who would compulsively report changes to their personal status as soon as the change happened (McCarthy, 2009). On the other hand, there are some who completely disappear from sight because their infrequent updates

get lost amongst the narbs provided by those who are regular in updating.

The frequency of updates provide a sense of commitment to keep others informed of the life story of an individual as new narbs appear so that observers get an opportunity to see what exactly might be happening in the life of another individual. However, the frequently updated narbs also embody a sense of flow of narbs where the frequently updated narbs, when observed in the correct chronological sequence, tells a specific story about the way in which a person's life might have changed over time. These narbs become the living story of an individual and presents for others an opportunity to see what has gone on in one's life, but could also provide the incentive to follow the narbs of any particular individual as new things are anticipated in the person's life. As in the case of all good narratives the narbs that flow in a specific and observable manner over a period of time offer the continuity that a good story must always have (Fisher, 1987). The continuity over time is also complemented by the way in which narbs are able to demonstrate movement through space as well. There are increasing numbers of tools that allow users to report their position in space as they continue to provide narbs over time.

Place

Most narratives are located in specific places and happen within a spatial context. At the same time, at a personal level, one of the most common queries about a new acquaintance is, "where are you from?" Knowing the spatial origins of a person and the current spatial location provides a specific set of attributes for the person. Yet, in creating the digital presence of an individual the place where a person is becomes relatively inessential (Mitra, 2008). A person is in the virtual place called cyberspace, and the fact that the person is constantly updating personal status via narbs was considered sufficient to create a narrative about the person, even though the spatial information can offer significant additional information to better construct the identity narrative of an individual. The increasing adoption of the technology offered by the Global Positioning System (GPS) has begun to offer the place information as part of the narrative produced by SNSs.

The GPS technology allows a person to know where one is with great deal of accuracy[7]. If a person has a GPS-enabled smartphone with mapping software installed on the phone then a person only needs to be in clear view of the sky and one would appear as a dot on a digital map. However, since smartphones are devices that also allow for SNS narb updates, it is possible to provide a spatial narb that reports the location of a person's smartphone at any point in time. As long as one assumes that the smartphone is with the individual it is possible to know where the person is. Having that information can add to the image of the person as different components of narbs build the composite narrative about the individual. Indeed, some of the smartphones and SNS have made the place narb a ubiquitous tool where the user only needs to activate a simple feature and the place narb would automatically report on the location of the individual's smartphone without the individual actually having to do anything special to report the location. This is a passive process that recedes into the background where an individual might not have to do much more than a simple key press to create a narb that immediately reports the location of the person's smartphone as a narb on SNS (Miller, 2010).

The place narb has also been a part of an active system where individuals would actively and deliberately report their location to create a specific narrative. Most SNS offer "third party" applications that allow a user to perform a large range of functions like report special kinds of information about oneself or play multi-player games with their friends. One such application offers the user the opportunity to indicate the number of places one has visited using a map of the World. Here the user can actually build a complete narrative based on the pins that indicate specific place narbs. In this case, the place information is shared not only as the immediate location of the individual based on GPS coordinates, but by participation in an application that allows an observer how an individual has moved through space over time or the different places an individual has been over a length of time. This spatial information does not rely on automated systems such as GPS, but are products of deliberate work by an individual to share specific information related to the places one has been to, or the place one occupies at the time of producing the narb by making a statement like, "just landed in Chicago."

The place narb thus operates in two different ways. It is possible to have a digital tool such as a smartphone or GPS-enabled digital camera automatically record and report the spatial information. Such information can accompany a mobile upload of a picture where there is metadata about the place where the picture was taken. The second way a place narb appears is when a person reports a place using specific applications that are built to offer spatial information or by a personal status update that contains explicit spatial information. One primary difference between these two modes lies in the frequency with which these narbs appear. The automatic method could happen constantly whereas the method using the applications or status update would only occur when the individual chooses to provide the update. The place narb becomes a good example of how the different components discussed in this essay offer an analytic framework and every narb could indeed possess all the different components.

Components of a Narb

Based on the discussion above it is possible to claim that any particular narb possesses characteristics that include different elements in different amounts. Because any narb contains different portions of the four components identified here it is possible to tag a specific narb with its different characteristics. The categorization of a narb is based around the answer to the following questions:

- Who creates the narb?
- What is the content of the narb?
- How long after the previous narb does the narb under scrutiny appear?
- What spatial location is specified in the narb?

It is then possible to tag any specific narb along these vectors where the answers indicate the quality of the narb. When this analysis is applied to a collection of narbs available on a person's profile page in any SNS it is possible to calculate a numerical value for a set of narbs. That value can provide an indication about the usefulness of SNS narbs in composing the identity narrative of the person. In some cases, the numerical value could have characteristics that would call into question the authenticity of the identity narrative composed from the narbs. In such cases it would be wise not to rely on narbs to offer an authentic identity narrative and look elsewhere to find such narratives. The numerical value of a narb, or a set of narbs, is based on the weight of any narb with respect to the four questions indicated earlier.

Each of the questions described here can have responses that can be translated to specific numerical values that provide a specific narb with very specific quantitative values as described in Figure 1. Each narb is considered to have four contributing elements that make up the total weight of the narb. Each contributing factor can provide up to one unit towards the weight making the maximum weight for any narb to be 4.0. This represents the summative value for the narb. For instance it is possible to claim that a self-narb that is simply textual and presents location information within three hours of the earlier posting would have a summative weight of 3.05 (see Figure 1). Over

a fixed length of time it would be possible to compute the total narb weight for an individual.

As also shown in Figure 1, a second numerical value is obtained by creating a narb matrix which is made up of a two by two matrix where each of the four numbers in the matrix represent the different values attached to the four elements of the narb. Using the principles of matrix mathematics, it is then possible to create a composite matrix for numerous narbs over a fixed period of time. Thus any narb could produce a narb weight and a set of narbs yield a narb matrix both of which can play an important role in the process of creating an identity narrative for an individual.

Creating a number from a narb allows an analyst to move beyond the condition that narbs usually do not lend themselves to very careful textual, critical or rhetorical analysis because narbs are, by definition, bits of information and not lengthy passages about an individual. Consequently narbs could be considered somewhat banal and not truly worthy of analysis. At the same time, in a somewhat internally inconsistent manner, there are instances when individual narbs sometimes become the focus of attention and the entire identity of an individual could become crystallized around only a small number of narbs among the hundreds the person might have on the profile page of a SNS (see e.g., Frazier, 2010). There are thus two opposing threats related to the analysis of narbs – either the content could be ignored because narbs are considered inconsequential or a single narb could receive undue attention creating an unreliable narrative. Both these issues are addressed when specific numeric values can be produced about a single or set of narbs.

The process would begin with the selection of a threshold of narbs that would be used for the analysis. This threshold could be a certain length of time. For instance, it could be argued that narbs that have been produced within the past twelve months are worthy of analysis, or only the last 100 narbs need be analyzed. Once a defensible threshold has been established it is possible to

Figure 1. Computing the narb weight and narb matrix

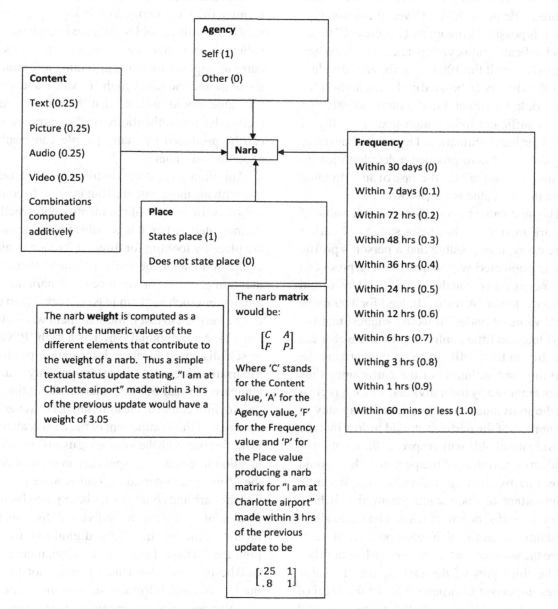

begin to create the set of numbers related to the narbs. Consider, for instance, an individual who has 100 narbs available for analysis. Each of the narbs is represented as a narb matrix which also allows for the computation of the narb weight. The first point of focus is the 'C' value of the matrix (see Figure 1). It has been argued in the realm of discourse analysis that more information is contained in a message that is made up of different discursive components. A photograph with written annotation and a brief audio element would be considered more elaborated than a simple textual update. Furthermore, the more complex content becomes a more trustworthy message given that it contains greater depth which makes it more difficult to 'fake.' Given these assumptions, it is possible to claim that a higher 'C' value would indicate a more variegated message. When summed over all the 100 narbs, for an individual who offers highly elaborated narbs, the highest 'C' value could be 100 and that would indicate that there is sufficient information that is worthy of careful further examination. That careful narrative analysis would help produce a detailed identity narrative as compared to the case of an individual where the 'C' value is much lower.

The next value to consider is the 'A' value of the narb matrix. As has been suggested earlier in the essay, it is possible that a person's profile page is populated with narbs that are produced by someone other than the individual. This would produce a lower 'A' value. Indeed for 100 narbs an 'A' value of under 30 would suggest that the individual has little control on the narbs that are available on the profile page problematizing the reliability and authentic of the narbs since they are not authored by the individual. Once it is clear that the individual has a low level of agency in the creation of the narbs, it should follow that the narbs are unreliable with respect to the creation of the identity narrative of the person. Others could present narbs about an individual and it would be important to understand the motive behind the 'other narbs' before much can be made about the identity narrative that relies on a set of narbs where the summative 'A' value has a low number.

The third part of the matrix, the 'F' value carries important information about the level of activity of an individual in the arena of digital social networking. Those who frequently update their status could yield a more detailed identity narrative compared to those who do not use the system as much. Therefore, a higher value for this would indicate that there is a larger amount of

information to be used to construct the composite identity from the narbs. Yet, being a part of the matrix this value could be balanced against the 'A' value to ensure that the updates are indeed self-narbs as opposed to others providing information about an individual. A high 'F' value and a low 'A' value would indicate that there is a need to reconsider the authenticity of the narrative that can be produced by many people commenting about an individual.

The final part of the matrix, the 'P' value is one with the most potential but is yet to become a very significant part of the identity construction. As indicated earlier, it is possible to get a sense of the place by looking for direct reference to place in the content of the narb. If indeed there is a mention of place, for instance in the narb making a statement such as "I am in New York," then that can be verified to test if the statement was indeed truthful. An individual who has a high 'P' value in self-disclosed location information produces a narrative identity whose authenticity can be compared to real life information about the patterns of movement of the individual. However, the potential of this component of the matrix also lies in the fact that with the increasing use of ubiquitous location information, especially in smartphones, the 'P' information might get automatically coded into the narb and could always be expected to have a value of '1' unless the individual disables that location functionality of the digital tool used to produce the narb. In such a situation, there could well be questions about the reason for not disclosing the location information. In some ways, the 'P' value becomes a surrogate measure of privacy about location with a lower 'P' value indicating a desire on the part of the individual to keep the location information undisclosed. That information can help in building a composite narrative identity of an individual.

DISCUSSION AND CONCLUDING REMARKS

There is sufficient evidence to suggest that information from SNS is being used to make attributions about individuals. Consider for instance the situation with a waitress who lost her job because of an impulsive status update on a popular SNS or the case of a college professor who was placed on "administrative leave" because of a few narbs posted on a SNS site (Frazier, 2010; Roper, 2010; Stripling, 2010). In such instances, these attributions can have long-ranging effects on the lives of people whose narratives are produced out of the SNS information since these narratives "become" authoritative and authentic based on the discursive appeal of a single entry on the profile page of a person (Budden & Budden, 2008; Clark, 2006; Finder, 2006). In such situations, there is little desire and attempt to examine the discourse for its various components, and in relation to the other type of information that is available at the profile page. Unfortunately, as demonstrated in the few cases cited here, and numerous others that go unreported, it is the limited number of discourses that often gain precedence when narratives are produced from narbs. Yet, these are indeed narbs, i.e., bits of information that must be combined to create the larger identity narrative. This pitfall would be avoided when the numeric system described here is applied to the analysis, before leaping to conclusions on the basis of a single narb.

Creating a numeric rubric to examine narbs is surely fraught with the danger of losing sight of the discursive nature of the narbs. This essay is not about reducing the importance of a careful discursive analysis of narbs. Indeed, that process is a necessary part of the creation of identity narratives and attributions about individuals. However, the process of textual and discursive analysis of specific narbs is a laborious and resource-intensive task. It would make much more sense to create the summated narb matrices before selecting what

set of narbs would yield useful information. For instance, consider the hypothetical summated narb matrices over a fixed period of time of two individuals:

$$\begin{bmatrix} 2.5 & 3 \\ 0.50 & 0 \end{bmatrix} \text{(X)} \quad \begin{bmatrix} 2.5 & 10 \\ 0.75 & 3 \end{bmatrix} \text{(Y)}$$

Even though they are posting similar type of content as evidenced from the 'C' value of the matrices, the narbs of person 'Y' could yield much more authentic information given the higher value for both 'A' and 'P,' and because the narb matrix of person 'Y' represent a more active person on the SNS who holds agency over the narbs that are available. It is therefore more likely that the discursive analysis of the narbs of person 'Y' would yield more authentic identity narrative. Consequently, when large number of identity narratives might be sought, it would make more sense to examine the discourses of person 'Y' as compared to the person 'X.' Such comparisons can begin to simplify two major concerns related to SNS – privacy and profiling.

The concerns of privacy and profiling are linked to each other in certain instances where status updates that produce narbs become the source of private information that results in the production of profiles of individuals. Much of this concern, as stated in popular media, results from the fact that specific narbs are used to create profiles as in the case of colleges which would use the narbs of high school students when they apply for admission into a college (Hechinger, 2008; Livingstone, 2008). That approach often relies on single or very few narbs to create grand narratives about the identity of an individual. However, as suggested here, it is first important to get a sense of the type of narbs that are actually available at the personal SNS site of an individual. The first step before creating narrative profiles ought to be enumerating the narbs using the numeric system suggested here. For instance, if the narb weight over a fixed period of time is low, it is relatively safe to claim that the profile that can be obtained from the narbs is weak and incomplete because the individual does not offer sufficient narbs to create a useful profile. If the narb weight is high then it would be important to compute the narb matrix for the individual and examine the various cells of the narb matrix to decide if an authentic and reliable profile narrative can be obtained from the narbs. This systematic approach could eliminate the need to look at the narb in detail if some sets of narbs can be screened out on the basis of the narb matrix. With millions of people maintaining different kinds of narbs on multiple SNS sites the automated production of narb matrices could reduce the burden of looking at large amounts of narb content to find useful information.

Looking at narbs from the numeric perspective also offers individuals an opportunity to produce a systematic way of managing narbs. If a particular cell, such as the 'A' value appears to be low compared to the overall narb weight, it would indicate to an individual that other people are contributing to an individual's identity narrative compared to the person himself or herself. Such checks based on the ongoing computation of a narb matrix could offer a simple and systematic way to see how an individual's profile is developing in the large SNS space. Knowing those values could allow an individual to change the kinds of narbs being produced and become more mindful of the way in which narbs populate the identity narrative being produced.

The use of SNS is no longer a novelty, and is increasingly becoming a mainstay of the identity of people. This increasing use of narbs requires a more systematic way to manage narbs, and that can be done with the use of narb weights and matrices. This chapter offers a way to do the computations in a standardized manner that can be applied to many different SNS systems because the four elements of a narb identified here remain common across most SNS systems. It is important to manage the narbs that create the identity narrative and management begins with a better understanding the nature of the narbs, as suggested here.

REFERENCES

Autio. (2004). Finnish young people's narrative construction of consumer identity. *International Journal of Consumer Studies, 28*(4), 388-398.

Bers, M. (1999). Narrative construction kits: Who am I? Who are you? What are we? In *Proceedings of "Narrative Intelligence" Fall Symposium*, AAAI'99.

Boyd, D., & Ellison, N. (2007). Social network sites: Definition, history, and scholarship. *Journal of Computer-Mediated Communication, 13*(1). doi:10.1111/j.1083-6101.2007.00393.x

Budden, C. B., & Budden, M. C. (2008). The social network generation and implications for human resources. *2008 ABR & TLC Conference Proceedings*.

Clark, A. S. (June 20, 2006). Employers look at Facebook, too. *CBS Evening News*.

Finder, A. (June 11, 2006). For some, online persona undermines a résumé. *The New York Times*.

Fisher, W. R. (1987). *Human communication as narration: Toward a philosophy of reason, value, and action*. Columbia, SC: University of South Carolina Press.

Frazier, E. (2010). Facebook post costs waitress her job. *Charlotte Observer*. Retrieved from http: //www.charlotteobserver.com/2010/05/17/1440447/ facebook-post-costs-waitress-her.html

Hall, S. (1992) Cultural identity and diaspora. In Rutherford (Ed.), Identity: Community, culture, difference. London, UK: Sage.

Hechinger, J. (2008). College applicants, beware: Your Facebook page is showing. *Wall Street Journal*. Retrieved from http: //online.wsj. com/article/ SB122170459104151023.html

Hyde, M., & Mitra, A. (2000). On the ethics of creating a face in cyberspace: The case of a university. In Berdayes, V., & Murphy, J. (Eds.), *Computers, human interaction and organizations* (pp. 161–188). New York, NY: Praeger.

Jones, R., Latham, L., & Betta, M. (2008). Narrative construction of the social entrepreneurial identity. *International Journal of Entrepreneurial Behavior & Research, 14*(5), 330–345. doi:10.1108/13552550810897687

Kirkpatrick, M. (2010). Facebook's Zuckerberg says the age of privacy is over. *Read Write Web.* Retrieved from http: //www.readwriteweb. com/ archives/facebooks_ zuckerberg_says_the_age_ of _privacy_is_ov.php

Kreps, D. G. (2010). Foucault, exhibitionism and voyeurism on Chatroulette. *Cultural Attitudes Towards Technology and Communication, 6,* 17–21.

Lenhart, A. (January 14, 2009). *Social networks grow: Friending mom and dad.* Pew Internet & American Life Project.

Livingstone, S. (2008). Taking risky opportunities in youthful content creation: Teenagers' use of social networking sites for intimacy, privacy and self-expression. *New Media & Society, 10,* 393–411. doi:10.1177/1461444808089415

McCarthy, C. (2009). Twitter hits 5 billion tweets. *cNet News.* Retrieved from http: //news.cnet. com/8301-13577_3- 10378353-36.html

Miller, P. (2010). How to use Facebook places. *PC World.* Retrieved from http: //www.pcworld. com/ article/203819/ how_to_use_facebook_places. html

Mitra, A. (1996). Nations and the Internet: The case of a national newsgroup, "soc.cult. indian. *Convergence (London), 2*(1), 44–75. doi:10.1177/135485659600200106

Mitra, A. (1997). Virtual commonality: Looking for India on the Internet. In Jones, S. (Ed.), *Virtual culture.* Newbury Park, CA: SAGE.

Mitra, A. (2002, March). Trust, authenticity and discursive power in cyberspace. *Communications of the ACM, 45*(3). doi:10.1145/504729.504748

Mitra, A. (2008). Using blogs to create cybernetic space. *Convergence, 14*(4), 457–452.

Mitra, A. (2010). Creating a presence on social networks via narbs. *Global Media Journal, 9*(16).

Mitra, A., & Watts, E. (2002). Theorizing cyberspace: The idea of voice applied to the Internet discourse. *New Media & Society, 4*(4), 479–298. doi:10.1177/146144402321466778

Rakow, L. (1988). Women and the telephone: The gendering of a communication technology. In Kramarae, C. (Ed.), *Technology and women's voices: Keeping in touch* (pp. 207–228). New York, NY: Routledge.

Redman, P. (2005). The narrative formation of identity revisited. *Narrative Inquiry, 15*(1), 25–44. doi:10.1075/ni.15.1.02red

Ricoeur, P. (1984). *Time and narrative, I (trans. Kathleen McLaughlin and David Pellauer).* Chicago, IL: University of Chicago Press.

Roper, M. F. (2010). The bosses who snoop on Facebook. *The Guardian.* Retrieved from http: // www.guardian.co. uk/commentisfree/2010/mar/ 24/bosses-snoop-facebook-twitter-blogs

Stripling, J. (2010). Faculty on Facebook: Privacy concerns raised by suspension. *USA Today.* Retrieved from http: //www.usatoday. com/news/education/ 2010-03-02-facebook-professors_N.htm

Whitebrook, M. (2001). *Identity, narrative and politics.* New York, NY: Routledge.

ENDNOTES

[1] The adoption of these technologies led to a flurry of academic discussion about the creation of "virtual communities" as demonstrated in anthologies such as *Virtual Culture* compiled by Jones (1997) where scholars examined the ways in which special communities could be imagined around shared discourses on the Internet. In many ways, the ideas developed in the late-90s allowed for the contextualization of the phenomenon of social networking that came to the forefront nearly a decade later.

[2] The term "social network" which was best defined by Barnes (1954) around a continuum of stability and function of the networks where a network was made up of a limited number of spatially adjacent people who would create a connection to achieve a particular purpose. In the case of Barnes, his focus was on a small Norwegian community where he noted that the networks were of three major types: Stable organizations with formalized modes of interaction, unstable connections that were created for specific functions, and networks based on interpersonal connections where other social phenomenon like class would play a critical role in the creation and maintenance of the network. To be sure, all these connections were based on spatial proximity limiting the number of participants in any network.

[3] Digitization refers to the process by which analog information like the electrical modulations produced by sound waves can be converted to binary data made up of only two digits – '0' and '1.' The digitization process produces large sets of number made up of the two digits, and complex information like videos produce extremely large amounts of digital data that need to be processed by the digital tools.

[4] The recognition of the disappearance of the "real" person and the accompanying cues that modify interpersonal communication continues to be an area of focus for scholars as there is a continuing desire to understand the way in which the process of communication changes when some of non-verbal cues are replaced by textual elements like "smiley faces" or emoticons that remains a popular and standard set of symbols in much of CMC (see, e.g., Walther, 2001).

[5] The idea of a "cybernetic space" refers to a unique condition where the real and the virtual come together to produce a condition where neither is privileged. The real is influenced by the virtual and the virtual conditions the real offering the opportunity to carve out a space where both are important (Mitra, 2003)

[6] This is typically the case with commercial Web sites such as Yahoo and Flickr that allow individuals to store videos and pictures on serves that can be accessed by a community permitted by the user.

[7] The use of the Global Positioning System (GPS) is quickly becoming ubiquitous as smartphones are equipped with GPS receivers and mapping programs that allows an individual to know where the person is, and since the phone is a communication device, the individual can also announce the location to a community of friends. This has been commercialized by corporations such as Foursquare and Facebook that allows "friends" to share their locations with each other.

Chapter 9
Cloud Based Social Network Sites:
Under Whose Control?

Jean-Philippe Moiny
University of Namur, Belgium

ABSTRACT

In studying Social Network Sites (SNSes), this chapter starts from the identification of a loss of users' control over personal information. It briefly defines what SNSes are and links them to "cloud computing." Its purpose is to identify how American and European (or as the case may be, Belgian) laws empower users to recover some control where they lack technical means to control information related to them. It will be shown that user's consent is central to numerous legal dispositions. To this end, four legal themes are studied: privacy, data protection (consent and right of access), confidentiality of electronic communications, and the prohibition of unauthorized access to computers (hacking). Through these reflections, the American and European perspectives are compared, and the differences between these inevitably lead to a final title underlying the importance of rules governing prescriptive and adjudicative jurisdictions concerns. These rules are finally sketched, before the conclusion finally summarizes the whole purpose.

As the author of this chapter is a European jurist, European law constitutes the point of departure of the reflections, and can be sometimes (titles I and IV) the sole legal framework of the discussion. The information in this chapter is current up to January 28, 2010, save as otherwise stipulated. It should be noted that the information that is studied in context is constantly changing.

DOI: 10.4018/978-1-61350-132-0.ch009

INTRODUCTION

Two quotations illustrate a claim for control coming from the users of Social Network Sites (SNSes). From the US civil liberties association, before the American Federal Trade Commission [FTC], "EPIC urges the Commission to [...] require Facebook to give users meaningful control over personal information" (EPIC v. Facebook 1, 2009, no. 3)[1], "[c]ompel Facebook to make its data collection practices clearer and more comprehensible and to give Facebook users meaningful control over personal information provided by Facebook to advertisers and developers" (EPIC v. Facebook 1, 2009, no. 118)[2]. Actually, "users desire control over the collection and use of information about them" (UC Berkeley, School of Information [UCBSI], 2009, p. 5). More recently, a modification of Facebook's privacy settings lead to a new complaint of EPIC noticing that users are now forced to make public data they could formerly keep restricted (EPIC v. Facebook 3, 2010). It has notably been claimed that Facebook "Converted Facebook Users' Private Information into "Publicly Available" Information" (EPIC v. Facebook 3, 2010, nos. 35 and ff.) and "Discloses the Personal Information of Facebook Users without Consent" (EPIC v. Facebook 3, 2010, nos. 65 and ff.). As regards the European Union and the group known as the Berlin Working Party, SNSes providers were already advised to "[i]mprove user control over use of profile data" (International Working Party on Data Protection [IWGDPT], 2008, pp. 6-7).

In the context of SNSes (I), Internet surfers seem to partially lose the legitimate[3] *ownership* of data relating to them. They suffer a *loss of control*[4] (II). To some extent, law – at least, the fields studied here – faces this concern. But how is and should it be done (III)? American and European regulatory systems both need to be referred to, and their differences brought into focus. While individuals are not generally bothered by these differences,

these SNSes often have a foot in Europe and the other in the United States – frequently California (Facebook, LinkedIn, and Second Life). But which law and which judges are in control (IV)?

This chapter defines what SNSes are, legally and technically. It also suggests some consideration related to the SNSes market. For the needs of the whole purpose, Facebook is taken as a recurrent example. SNSes generally constitute information society services pertaining to cloud computing technology. Therefore, some ideas can be extended to cloud computing in general. The technology used and the functioning of SNSes lead to identifying a certain loss of control over their personal data by users. Some legal issues related to this loss are therefore addressed. Moreover, privacy and data protection are studied in this chapter. A legal conception of privacy which empowers users is chosen as regards American and European perspectives. In this respect, the horizontal effect of the fundamental right to privacy is discussed. The focus then moves to specific concerns related to data protection. The quality of consent of the data subject, apparently omnipresent in the context of SNSes, is discussed. The data subject has to be informed by SNS providers. His consent should be separated from his consent to the general terms and conditions of the SNS. And finally, such consent has to be freely given. This last point requires to be linked with the considerations related to the SNS market. The relevance of the data subject's right of access in the context of SNSes is then examined, before the confidentiality of electronic communications is brought into focus. The use of cookies by the SNS provider is specifically discussed in this framework. And some reflections relate to the qualifying an SNS as an electronic communications service. Mainly, this chapter identifies which communications are protected. The interest then moves to the protection of the user's terminal. The prohibition of hacking is discussed in the context of SNSes. It is questioned if a breach of the terms of use of an SNS by a user in fact makes them a "hacker." Other specific developments related to cookies are scrutinized. Finally, the text briefly discusses European private international law from the prescriptive and adjudicative jurisdictions[5] viewpoints. Due to the differences between American and European law, the question of the applicable law becomes particularly relevant in a context where different legal systems and cultures collide.

THE CONTEXT OF SOCIAL NETWORK SITES

This section describes what SNSes are from the technical and legal viewpoints. It also tries to describe the relevant market of SNSes. This latter will then reveal relevant as regards the consent of SNSes users. To these ends, only European law is taken into account.

Social Network Sites and Cloud Computing

Briefly and technically, an SNS "can be defined as [a] website whose main purpose is to act as a connector among users" (Levin & Sánchez Abril, 2009, p. 1017) [6]. In particular, we could call Facebook and similar SNSes[7] "meta-SNS." This means SNSes that relate to indeterminate contexts. Through them, users can share whatever kind of information they want, from individualized and, generally, nominative profiles. Data – whether personal or not – and their exchange, are essential attributes of SNSes[8]. Providers host and manage the profiles completed by users, and what these users share. Applications can sometimes also be added to the profiles[9]. This constitutes the principal business promoted by SNS providers: Hosting and making available data to members of the social network[10], according to the sharing rules chosen by these users among a range of options (*e.g.* Facebook's privacy settings) defined by SNS providers.

SNSes also use what is called "cloud computing." Cloud computing is "a different form of IT infrastructure" (Joint, Baker, & Eccles, 2009, p. 270). SNSes usually embed different kinds of cloud computing services[11]. They consist of applications utilized by users from their browser, on remote third-party servers. In this respect, an SNS is "software as a service." Users' data (texts, images, videos, etc.) are also stored in datacenters, generally located abroad (*e.g.* in the U.S. as regards Facebook[12]), and not on the users' own personal computers. These datacenters are managed by the SNS provider (or their subcontractor) who then provides "data storage as a service" (or, more generally, "infrastructure as a service"). Finally, looking at Facebook-like SNSes, a "platform as a service", the application programming interface [API] is also provided to developers. Such API enables them to create applications (software) running through the SNS[13].

In European legal terms, these kinds of services are Information Society Services in the sense of the E-commerce Directive[14]. In fact, SNSes are normally "provided for remuneration." Their providers pursue an economic activity[15]. Indeed, SNSes "are usually for-profit businesses" (Levin et al., 2009, p. 1019)[16]. In the case of Facebook, advertisement banners and the targeted advertisement service *Ads* (and its variants *Social Ads* and *Engagement Ads*[17]) secure an economic counterpart for Facebook Inc. These applications, for which you have to pay, are integrated to the social network. *Ads* offers companies – or anyone – the ability to target a defined audience of the network, according to criteria they choose – e.g. sex, age, location or other criteria corresponding to certain fields of the user's profile –, to promote services or products. The *Insights* tool can be cited too. It permits the assessment of the effectiveness of the ordered targeted ads. The *Gifts* application can also be noted, enabling people to send gifts ($1 per gift) to friends. Finally, *Polls*, to carry out polls through the network, is also for a charge. Facebook is not the only one

SNS with advertisement functionalities. Indeed, LinkedIn and MySpace also offer a user targeted advertisement function (Office of Privacy Commissioner of Canada [OPCC], 2009, pp. 22 and 30). Moreover, licenses granted by users to SNS providers allow the latter to commercially use the copyrighted content of the former. Some of these licenses go beyond the sole technical needs for the functioning of the provided service. In this respect, these licenses might also constitute this kind of economic counterpart[18].

This chapter will discuss the consent of an SNS user is usually central to the legal rules that are identified to empower users to recover control over their personal data in the abovementioned context. Since the free character of the users' consents will partially depend on the SNSes market, this latter is then now discussed.

The Market of Social Network Sites

European competition law and the economic tools it relies on are useful to give an insight into the SNS market. Taking Facebook as a point of departure, the SNS relevant market has first to be identified. This leads "to identify in a systematic way the immediate competitive constraints faced by an undertaking" (EC DG Competition, 2005, no. 12). If there are a lot of SNSes providers in the relevant market of the SNS, the user will be free to choose one or another, depending on his preferences as regards, for instance, price, functionalities, data processing, etc. However, it would still be necessary that these providers compete as regards these elements – e.g. data protection.

After the relevant market has been identified, it is interesting to observe if a SNS provider has a dominant position on this market. Because of this situation a dominant position could make this provider insensitive to the claim of control arising from society[19]. Such a situation can prevent the web surfers to effectively choose. Moreover, competition law would prohibit the dominant SNS provider from abusing his position[20]. That is

to say that the company could be forbidden from adopting certain conduct that other companies are free to adopt. For instance, could a dominant SNS provider prevent an application developer from building an application on the SNS API (refusal to supply) offering the users the possibility to easily retrieve all their data from the SNS, in a convenient format, to easily leave the network? Could the SNS provider rely on targeted advertising and processing of personal data of its users (or even the sale of personal data) to finance its service and offer them for "free" to its users (predatory pricing)? Although these questions are interesting, the purpose only concentrates on the definition of the relevant market and the potential identification of a dominant position.

In regards to the relevant market, SNS is a wide concept that covers different services that can generally be qualified as "multi-sided platform." "A multi-sided platform provides goods or services to two or more distinct groups of customers who need each other in some way and who rely on the platform to intermediate transactions between them" (Evans, 2008, pp. 8-9). For instance, Facebook proposes targeted advertisement services to businesses (*Ads*), services to those who promote political, businesses, etc. (*Pages*), services to "friends" (the average user Profile), an application programming interface [API] for any developer of application, etc. To some extent, these groups of customers are dependant. The more users there are users, the more companies are interested in advertising over the network. The more there are applications on the network, the more users want to join the network, and vice versa. The more companies advertise through the network, the more the provider earns money, the longer the service remains free for its users and can be permanently innovating, the more users will be inclined to join and remain on the network, etc. As D.S. Evans (2008, p.10) writes, "many multi-sided platforms make their money from one side and make access to the platform available to another side for a price that does not cover the cost of provision. Facebook, for example, is free to users and makes money by selling advertising." The functionalities of Facebook for which we have to pay will therefore lead to the providing of free users profiles.

A priori, there is no one global market for SNSes. And the purpose does not delimit the *markets* of SNSes. It only gives some elements for reflection. For instance, one division could be made between what would be called a *large or narrow thematic centered SNS* – e.g. a network related to movies (Flixster), to business (LinkedIn), to sexuality, etc. – and *meta-SNS,* unrelated to specific topics – e.g. Facebook, Netlog, Bebo, MySpace, etc. SNSes can also be targeted to a particular geographic region or to the whole world. Another division could follow from the functionalities, the "tools", provided by the SNS. For instance, YouTube is content broadcasting oriented, while Twitter was more a text messages communication tool. Facebook is at once a text messages communication tool, a content broadcasting tool and a platform for third party applications. If Twitter and Facebook are not thematic-centered, they nonetheless diverge as regards the functionalities provided.

But whatever the case, the *network of users* is critical in regards to the success and the lure of the SNS concerned. This is true from a *quantitative* viewpoint – *how many* users does the network involve and *how much* are they involved? What could be called the *quantitative users network*? This is extremely relevant in regards to YouTube-like SNS and meta-SNS such as Facebook. Moreover, the network of users can be relevant from a more subjective *qualitative* viewpoint – *Who* is in the network (e.g. are my friends there)? What could be called the *qualitative users network*? From this last viewpoint, the *temporal dimension* is particularly relevant, as the following scenario shows: The more a user uses an SNS, the more he is captive of this SNS. Because, on the one hand, he brings his own individual network in the SNS; and, on the other hand, he creates a network

of individuals he wants to keep alive. Then, to leave the SNS – for example to search for better data protection[21] –, he will have to convince his relational network to do the same. Knowing that in the latter situation, they would not necessarily wish to migrate. Such *qualitative users' network* would be more important (i.e., Facebook-like SNSes than YouTube-like ones).

These three identified elements – the purpose(s) of the network, the offered functionalities and, specifically, the network of users – lead to the possibility that SNSes are *not substitutable* or *interchangeable* goods (or services) from the consumers' viewpoint. "This approach to product market definition uses a 'functional interchangeability' yardstick based on the 'qualitative' criteria of characteristics, price and intended use" (Jones & Sufrin, 2008, p. 62). Therefore, different SNSes in the broad sense of the concept can pertain to different relevant markets[22]. For instance, Facebook and YouTube (purchased by Google, Inc. in 2006) are clearly not in the same market. The launch of Google Buzz demonstrated it. Facebook and eBay are not in the same relevant market[23]. Due to their different purposes, Facebook and LinkedIn could arguably be deemed to pertain to different relevant markets, despite the fact that Facebook offers the possibility to join a "work" network. Arguably, Facebook and Twitter are not in the same relevant market, diverging as regards their functionalities. Twitter was originally oriented to the sharing of short messages. While Facebook gives a wider range of functionalities. T. Eisenmann, G. Parker and M. Van Alstyne (2009, pp. 12 and 14) identify Facebook and Twitter as "weak substitutes." That is to say that they "serve the same broad purpose but satisfy different sets of user needs because they rely on different technologies." They also provide another example:

Monster.com and LinkedIn.com use different approaches in helping users find and fill jobs: searchable listings and social networking, respectively. These approaches offer different advantages: listings are valuable when parties wish to conduct a comprehensive search, whereas social networks provide a mutually trusted third party's assessment of fit.

Anyway, it needs to be underlined that the offered functionalities and the offered websites can quickly evolve. What "matters is that a sufficiently large number of consumers do consider that a product is a good substitute for the product supplied by the undertaking concerned" (EC DG Competition, 2005, no. 18)[24]. The purpose here is not to say that each SNS equals a specific relevant market. For instance, YouTube and Dailymotion are direct competitors. They share the same purpose and propose similar functionalities. Facebook and MySpace could also be deemed to pertain to the same relevant market. But if these two latter are both intended to (notably) socialize, how taking into account what we called the *qualitative users network*? If too much importance is given to the fact that the friends and contacts of a particular user are located only on one SNS and not on another, this could lead to a too narrow definition of the relevant market. But if no importance is given to such a question, the risk would be then to miss the fact that there is no concrete alternative for a particular user. And that this latter has therefore no real possibility to choose.

In any case, the "demand substitutability"[25] can be low since, notably, SNSes produce positive and direct (and indirect) network effects. "A network effect, as defined in [Spulber's] discussion, refers to the dependence of a consumer's benefit on the consumption of another consumer. In short, "network effects are mutual benefits of consumption" (Spulber, 2008, p. 10)[26]. This is directly linked to the multi-sided platform markets above-mentioned. And this also implies, on the one hand, that users bear high switching costs if they want to migrate. Their profile, data and network are anchored in a particular SNS[27]. On the other hand, new entrants in a SNSes market are confronted

with a huge barrier to entry. However, these latter are not necessarily irremediably closed to the market. Entering the market – or even, creating a new market – by elaborating a new functionality and being really innovative (e.g. Twitter) is a solution[28]. As T. Eisenmann, G. Parker and M. Van Alstyne (2009, p. 1) write, "revolutionary functionality" is a path to enter the market. Moreover, the authors pointed out that "platform envelopment" is another way[29]. A new entrant could also try to leverage the position he has in a second market (e.g. webmail such as Gmail) in the SNS market (Google Buzz). In so doing, the entrant is able to profit from the network of users it has in this second market, simply adding a new functionality to the platform he manages. Of course, SNS providers inspire each other. A company can also enter the market by purchasing an incumbent firm. For example, Google bought Youtube and Facebook tried to buy Twitter[30]. Finally, free data portability – and more generally, interoperability of cloud computing services, *would* contribute to making it easier to enter a market. However, this is not the case. Indeed generally, "[o]ne of the most pressing issues with respect to cloud computing is the current difference between the individual vendor approaches, and the implicit lack of interoperability" (Jefferey & Neidecker-Lutz, 2010, p. 31). Anyway, the data portability seems possible even in the present technology context as was stated in a workshop organized by the W3C[31]. It would permit the migration from one SNS, reinforcing individuals' freedom. However, it could also be a threat for privacy and data protection if it is not well designed – what about the export of privacy settings (Grimmelmann, 2009)[32]?

These elements show that the SNSes market is not so easy to draw, and that it can rapidly change. This is not without consequences as regards the potential dominant position of an SNS provider. While alone today in his own market, he could tomorrow face numerous new competitors. To remain in a dominant position, the SNS provider,

Facebook for instance, should have significant market power[33] in the relevant market of "meta-SNS." In other words, Facebook will have to be able to act "independently" of its customers, its competitors and of consumers[34]. It constitutes "the largest social network service in the United States"[35] and its significant presence in the European market cannot be ignored. But while its market share could be high, an oligopoly could exist (e.g. Facebook, MySpace, Bebo and Netlog). And the difficulty to enter the market might also be relative. It has moreover to be noted that in the "new economy"[36], "[d]ominant positions are often temporary and fragile" (Jones & Sufrin, 2008, p. 429), and "[c]ompetition is dynamic", taking place "*to satisfy* the market." Firms compete "to dominate the market" and are "fragile monopolists" that have to continuously innovate (Ahlborn, Evans, & Padilla, 2001, p. 160). So, even assuming that Facebook has a high market share, the dynamics of the new economy lessens the relevance of this observation (Ahlborn, Evans, & Padilla, 2001, p. 163)[37]. "[C]urrent market shares may overstate or understate probable future competitive significance" (Antitrust Modernization Commission, 2007, p. 40). Moreover, it shouldn't be ignored that "competition to *obtain* a monopoly is an important form of competition" (Posner, 2001, p. 117)[38].

These considerations sketched the SNSes markets and underlined a potential lack of choice – of liberty – that users could suffer. These elements have to be kept in mind each time law takes into account the consent of the SNS user.

USERS' LOSS OF CONTROL

A users' loss of control in SNSes can be noticed at three levels: The creation of personal data, their accessibility and their deletion. Facebook will be the principle example used in this section. The focus of this examination is the "average user" of the SNS. The "average user" of the SNS is someone who does not develop applications (developers), does not order targeted ads, etc. Although, there exist other users of the services provided through the network.

Initially, a user controls the production of personal data relating to him/herself on an SNS. The user decides which data they reveal. However this primary control over personal data is limited. First, other users can disseminate data through the network; or more insidiously, for instance, when they synchronize their iPhone with Facebook[39]. Second, SNSes providers could spontaneously and automatically collect data from other sources, such as other websites (e.g. via Facebook *Beacon*[40]), cookies[41], data brokers, etc., pursuing "enhancement" to get more accurate profiles (UCBSI, 2009, p. 9). SNSes providers can also compel users to disclose data such as their real name, date of birth and email address[42]. The user in question does not have any practical control over this production of data. Admittedly, as regards what they have to disclose, users can lie… The cookie method[43], contested in DoubleClick (2001)[44], and the recording of clickstream data "generated by our cyber-activity" (Kang, 1998, p. 1119)[45] (also known as "clicktrail" (Kang, 1998, p. 1227)) are good examples. The SNS provider is able to record the user's use of – or his behavior on – the social network. What the users do when logged on and when they are not; provided the fact that the use of a cookie is necessary in this latter case[46]. For instance, Facebook's privacy policy[47] permits Facebook to record clickstream data relating to its users[48]. So it could store which pages the users consulted, which searches have been made, the groups they joined[49], etc.

Subsequently, by choosing privacy settings, SNS members have the feeling they control the dissemination of personal data related to them. However, again, this control is limited. First and foremost, users cannot control personal data they didn't personally disclose. Then, the privacy settings are themselves limited. In fact, users do not define their content. Their options are set out by the SNS provider and can evolve as the provider wishes (e.g. modifying the functionalities of the website or directly changing the settings). The infrastructure where users socialize can transform out of their control, even against their wishes. This lack or loss of control is reinforced by the use of cloud computing technologies[50]. In addition, the content of the privacy settings have to be technically secure[51]. Furthermore, privacy settings generally concern the communication of data between users and not as concerns the SNS provider. This means that "once information is 'out', forget about maintaining exclusive control over it" (Kang & Buchner, 2004, p. 242). Once data are accessed by other users, an individual cannot control subsequent uses of the data by them. Facebook's evolution illustrated the relativity of privacy settings and their fluctuations. Originally, only the name of the members and the sub-networks they joined (professional, geographic, etc.) had *necessarily to be shared* through the global Facebook network[52]. But thereafter, the user's profile photo, their friends list, the 'Pages' they are a fan of, their sex and geographical location[53] were considered by Facebook to be public information. But this has again evolved[54]. Anyway, this was crucial as regards Facebook Platform and Applications. Indeed, according to Facebook's former privacy policy: "Applications will always be able to access your publicly available information (name, Profile picture, gender, current city, networks, friend list and pages) and information that is visible to everyone." EPIC's recent complaint before the FTC illustrates the importance of the modification[55]. As a matter of interest, this previous modification of the privacy settings seemed to have gotten Mark Zuckerberg, Facebook's CEO, into trouble when his own photos were publicized… (EPIC v. Facebook 1, 2009, no. 41). But for all that, positive evolutions cannot be denied. In this respect, a user can now, admittedly to a limited extent, control Facebook's use of their name as regards Social Ads and the affixing of this name to advertisements delivered to their friends, telling them the

'Pages' they are a fan of. Moreover, the user can also specify to which friends are addressed the posts they make on their 'Wall'. The complaint of EPIC also had effect over Facebook since, for instance, users are now able again to make their friend list confidential[56]. A huge concern is that in a short period of time, due to the processing capabilities of today's computers, vast amounts of data can be extracted from the network. No matter if the privacy settings come back later to their original status.

Finally, the user's last means to control the proliferation of data related to them is outright deletion, which is equally limited as regards data not directly produced by the user. Moreover, SNS providers sometimes reserve the right to keep data after the deactivation of the user's account or during a certain period of time in backup copies. Once again, when data are downloaded by other users, they cannot be deleted. This SNSes practice illustrates the lack of control over the deletion of data. For instance, the reactivation option of Hi5 suggests that data will be kept (OPCC, 2009, p. 17)[57]. In regards to LinkedIn when a user wishes to terminate his account and permanently delete their data, they must send an email to LinkedIn (OPCC, 2009, p. 24)[58]. LiveJournal keeps a users' data thirty days after the suppression of their account (OPCC, 2009, p. 29)[59]. And finally, concerning Facebook, originally a member couldn't delete their account, while now they can choose between deactivation and permanent suppression of their account; the bleeding occurred and is not reversible.

USERS EMPOWERED TO CONTROL

When a specific loss of control has been identified, law – but not only law – might bring a solution. Hearing that the present paper is focused on law, how does the law – or specific parts of it – deal with the identified loss of control? Privacy and Data Protection are first studied, from general

U.E. and U.S. perspectives. Then, two specific topics are evoked: Consent and contract, and the data subject's right of access. The confidentiality of electronic communications is discussed secondly, in general and as regards more specifically cookies. Finally, the protection of Internet surfers' computer terminals is approached as regards hacking in general, a specific concern related to cookies being then addressed.

PRIVACY AND DATA PROTECTION

General Discussion

This section examines users' loss of control, users' understanding of privacy, and addressing these concerns from EU and US perspectives. Solove (2002) interestingly pointed out that: "Not all privacy problems are the same and different conceptions of privacy work best in different contexts. Instead of trying to fit new problems into old conceptions, we should seek to understand the special circumstances of a particular problem." Such conceptions of privacy will empower the user to recover some control. (Solove 2002, p. 1147)

European Union

Numerous legal instruments relate to privacy and data protection. The main rules the purpose takes into account are Article 8 of the European Convention for the Protection of Human Rights and Fundamental Freedoms [ECHR] and the directives 95/46/EC and 2002/58/EC[60]. Without defining privacy – one cannot[61] and others have already studied this concept in depth[62] –, the purpose is focused on a useful understanding of privacy. The latter ensures individuals, using data protection rules, a certain power of control in the context of SNSes. They receive control such as regards their "informational environment" and the "circulation of their image", the processing activities of the data controller being then restricted (Poullet,

2008, p. 41). Privacy, under the view suggested by Y. Poullet and A. Rouvroy, can be defined as the right to "informational self-determination", as identified in 1983 by the German *Bundesverfassungsgerichtshof* (Poullet & Rouvroy, 2009/1, pp. 52-58). According to the authors (2009/1, p. 75), one of the facets of privacy is that we have a certain control over a number of aspects of our personalities that we project to the world.

Data protection can be seen as an evolution of privacy due to the new challenges raised in our information society and the new privacy threats (Poullet, 2008, p. 38). It is aimed at ensuring the respect of privacy (Docquir, 2008, p. 84) – but not only privacy[63] –, and the EHR Court links data protection directly to the human right to have their private and family life respected[64]. As we will see, data protection notably proceeds to the "horizontalization" of privacy. "[D]ata protection and privacy are clearly substantially overlapping concepts" (Walden, 2007, p. 461). But data protection has its own legal regime (Docquir, 2008, p. 86). And "the right to data protection is recognized as an autonomous fundamental right in Article 8 of the Charter of Fundamental Rights of the European Union" (Working Party 29, WP168, p. 5). It provides data subjects with legal means to exercise a control over personal information. It also frames the activities of the data controllers. In this respect, the fundamental purpose[65] and data quality[66] principles, enshrined in directive 95/46/EC, are crucial. And to some extent, they mirror H. Nissembaum's conception of privacy as "contextual integrity" (Dumortier, 2009, p. 13), discussed later. As regards the relations between privacy and data protection, according to P. De Hert and S. Gutwirth (2006, pp. 67-69 and 71-76), privacy could be viewed as an "opacity tool", protecting individuals against public and private actors' interference in their individual matters. While data protection would be a "transparency tool" aimed at compelling these actors to use good practice, focusing on the transparence of their procedures and acts (De Hert & Gutwirth,

2006, pp. 69-70 and 76-82). In this respect, privacy has a prohibitive nature and data protection offers various procedural guarantees, channeling powers to protect the individual's privacy and to promote accountability. Consistent with this model, privacy would restrict the reduction of the control that individuals enjoy as regards personal data. While data protection would determine the terms according to which such reductions could be accepted. As a working rule, we could retain that data protection implements privacy in practical terms, within the context of computing and Internet technologies, arming data subjects with specific subjective rights against data controllers. This partly answers a question that now needs to be briefly addressed, that is, the horizontal effect of Article 8 ECHR. And this also avoids some speculative reflections about what the ECHR could impose on the States as regards the private relations involved in the (contractual) context of SNSes.

The human rights enshrined in the ECHR – and more precisely Article 8 ECHR [67] – can have a horizontal effect[68]. It is also referred to as the German theory of "*Drittwirkung*" ("third party effect of human rights"). Originally human rights only concerned the relations between, on the one hand, individuals, and on the other hand, the State. This is the "vertical effect" of Human rights. Nowadays, it is well established that they also concern interpersonal relations. This is their "horizontal effect." The State has an "obligation to protect human rights" and, in this respect, "to avoid human rights violations by private person" (Nowak, 2003, p. 50). Generally, the horizontal effects of the ECHR are brought in by legislative measures of the Member States of the Council of Europe protecting fundamental rights (data protection rules could be an example as regards Article 8 ECHR, criminal law as regards Articles 2 and 3, etc.). *Before a national Court*, the horizontal effect of the ECHR – or, more generally, of constitutional rights – can manifest itself in two general ways: directly horizontal or indirectly horizontal. And

this latter can be subdivided into different subcategories. For instance in the UK, R. Clayton and H. Tomlinson (2001, pp. 204-207 and 223-238) identify five "horizontal" impacts that the Human Rights Act (1998) can have on disputes between private litigants. To sum up, a right of the ECHR has a *direct horizontal effect*[69] when a Court can deduce from the ECHR's pronouncements, the legal effects directly applying to private legal relations. Whereas the same disposition of the ECHR would have an *indirect horizontal effect* if the Court had to rely on previously existing private law applying to the particular case at stake, then construing these rules in the light of the ECHR[70]. For instance, in the UK, the ECHR has an indirect horizontal effect (Clayton & Tomlinson, 2001, pp. 217-218; Phillipson, 1999). This is also the case in Germany, and more or less the case in Belgium, the situation in The Netherlands and in France being less clear (van der Plancke & Van Leuven, 2008, pp. 201-202)[71].

A crucial question is to determine to what extent a State is *obliged* under ECHR to ensure that private relations are compatible with human rights (van der Plancke & Van Leuven, 2008, p. 210) and, in particular as regards the present point, the right to privacy. Horizontal effect is clearly linked with the positive obligations falling to the States. "[P]ositive obligations are a *source* of horizontal effect" (Gardbaum, 2006, p. 770). However, "the actual extent to which the state [(*i.e.* its organs including the Courts[72])] is to protect private persons is highly controversial and unclear in theory and practice as yet" (Nowak, 2003, p. 50). And the States have a margin of appreciation to this end, the proportionality principle also applying[73]. It can here be referred to what is called the "diagonal effect" of the ECHR (Dickson, 1999, pp. 59 and ff.)[74]. In this respect, *the State* can be held responsible by the European Court of Human Rights for the violation of rights enshrined in the ECHR *by private parties* if such a violation is permitted by its *inaction*[75], "by tolerating the occurrence of the prohibited acts" (Meron, 2000, no. 11). And such inaction could be the fact of *a court* denying, for instance, the right to privacy of an individual vis-à-vis another individual, and failing to remedy a violation of the ECHR. In such case, the violation of the ECHR by an individual could then be only *indirectly* (Zwaak, 2006, p. 29) brought to the European Court of Human Rights, which would give a ruling as regards the state responsibility[76].

A good example arises from the SNSes context – and more generally cloud computing – to illustrate the usefulness of the *judicial* (before a Court) potential of the indirect (or direct) horizontal effect of Article 8 ECHR. Let's take as the premise that the directive 95/46/EC – and its implementation in a particular Member State – does not apply to a particular user subscribing to an SNS, due to a domestic use exemption[77]. In such a case, the European regime related to transborder data flows will then not apply. Though, this user could send personal data concerning other individuals (data subjects) to a foreign State where the facilities – data centers – of the SNS provider are located, no matter if the data protection afforded by this State is or is not adequate. If this provider then processes the data for its own purposes or subsequently discloses the data collected in any way, the "data subjects" could suffer damage, just as the privacy of the subscriber to the SNS himself could be threatened. If it were the case, Article 8 ECHR and its horizontal effect would ensure the protection of the data subjects and the privacy of the user at stake. For instance, in Belgium, a lawsuit could be initiated on the basis of Article 1382 of the Belgian Civil Code (general rule as regards extra-contractual liability) coupled with Article 8 ECHR. In other words, the horizontal effect of Article 8 ECHR could help to fill the gaps in data protection rules in the SNSes – or cloud computing – context, ensuring the data subject the recovery of control.

To sum up, data protection and privacy give the users of SNSes a certain legal control over their personal information, empowering them, to some extent, to prevent or limit what can be done

as regards personal data related to them when they are not technically able to do so themselves. And if data protection rules do not apply for any reason, the indirect horizontal effect of Article 8 ECHR could be invoked.

United States of America

Originally in the United States[78], privacy was conceptualized in common law from S. Warren and L. Brandeis's paper (1890). Privacy was identified as the "right to be let alone." Later, it was systematized by W. Prosser, in four privacy torts: Intrusion Upon Seclusion, Appropriation of Name or Likeness, Publicity Given to Private Life (also known as Public Disclosure of Private Facts) and Publicity Placing Person in False Light (Richards & Solove, 2007, pp. 146-156; Dunne, 2009, pp. 195-197)[79]. Among these torts, confirmed in the Second Restatement of Torts, the purpose essentially focuses on the Public Disclosure of Private Facts Tort, preventing the disclosure of data. The torts relate to inter-individual relations. The American federal Constitution enshrines the right to privacy. The Fourth Amendment is notably a cornerstone to this end[80]. Some constitutions of federated States also enshrine the right to privacy. But "the state charters, like the federal constitution, do not regulate interactions among citizens" (Schwartz & Reidenberg, 1996, pp. 9-10). In other words, "[t]he state constitutions emphasize the powers of government and the limits on them, rather than the regulation of relations between citizens" (Schwartz & Reidenberg, 1996, pp. 9-10). They primarily concern relations between States and individuals (vertical effect), requiring a "state action" to apply. Nonetheless, "the development of 'state action' doctrine shows that even where the constitutional rights are defined in vertical terms, the courts will extend constitutional guarantees to some relationships between private individuals" (Clayton & Tomlinson, 2001, p. 208). The American Constitution can in fact be considered to have an indirect horizontal effect (Gardbaum, 2005, p. 415)[81]. In California for instance, the "constitutional right to informational privacy has been found to apply to both the public and the private sector" (Schwartz & Reidenberg, 1996, pp. 133-134). Referring to the common law (privacy tort) and the Californian Constitution, the Supreme Court of California, in Hernandez v. Hillsides (2009), recently underlined that these "two sources of privacy protection 'are not unrelated' under California law." Citing another decision, the Court recalled that the right to privacy in the California Constitution "creates at least a limited *right of action* against *both private and government* entities"[82] (emphasis added by the author). However that may be, under the American Constitutional system, States do not have any "positive obligations" according to the Constitution (Schwartz & Reidenberg, 1996, p. 35). In this respect, constitutional systems generally reject positive obligations; "like in the United States, are thereby rejecting an important source of indirect horizontal effect", (Gardbaum, 2005, p. 770).

Privacy suffers substantial weaknesses in the context of SNSes. The only one that holds our attention is its dependence on the well-known "reasonable expectation of privacy" [83 84]. If technological progress sometimes creates such expectations, it often erodes them (Sprague, 2008, p. 89)[85]. The more technologies are used to monitor individuals, the less they have expectations of privacy (Solove, 2002, p. 1142). In the same sense, "[w]ith every click of the mouse on the Internet, the expectation of privacy diminishes and a voyeuristic society expands" (Kane & Delange, 2009, p. 347). Informing individuals about data processing could also have the same pernicious effect[86]. So, a *duty* to inform could, in this respect, be problematic. "The problem [...] is that [the] protection [of privacy] dissipates as technology develops and enters general public use" (Sprague, 2008, p. 121). In other words, "[e]xpectations of privacy are established by social norms" (Sprague, 2008, p. 129)[87]. In City of Ontario v. Quon (2010),

the US Supreme Court did not hesitate, recently, to watch for the setting of these social norms before deciding on the question of reasonable expectation in the context of work and communication technologies[88]. It explicitly avoided the discussion. And M. Zuckerberg claiming that "privacy is no longer a 'social norm'" (EPIC v. Facebook 2, 2010, no. 10) might be accepted.

Because of the necessity of a reasonable expectation of privacy, what is "knowingly exposed to the public" is not protected (Sprague, 2008, p. 125)[89]. So "there will be no cause of action if [the plaintiff] happened to reveal this information in cyberspace often regarded as public" (Purtova, 2009, p. 511). And yet, as we wrote above, the sharing of data – personal and otherwise – is at the core of SNSes. As an example, the U.S. Court of Appeals for the Ninth Circuit held, in USA v. Forrester (2007), that there is no reasonable expectation of privacy as regards "Internet Protocol ("IP") addresses of the websites the defendant visited", "and the total volume of data transmitted to and from the defendant's account"[90]. This reasoning has also already been transposed in the context of "electronic bulletin boards" where data are delivered to a huge number of users:

In Guest v. Leis, 255 F.3d 325, 333 (6th Cir. 2007), we concluded that users of electronic bulletin boards lacked an expectation of privacy in material posted on the bulletin board, as such materials were "intended for publication or public posting." Of course the public disclosure of material to an untold number of readers distinguishes bulletin board postings from e-mails, which typically have a limited, select number of recipients. (Steven Warshack v. USA, 2007) (Emphasis added by author).

Anyway, users have reasonable expectations of privacy as regards the content of their emails and email accounts, as it is illustrated by Steven Warshack v. USA (2007). So, useless to say that choosing privacy settings is a minimum a user *has to* do if he/she hopes to be protected.

So what place is left for privacy in SNSes? SNS providers and users seem to have a great deal of latitude with the personal data they can access. However, Warren and Brandeis (1980, p. 198) have already argued that "common law secures to each individual the right of determining, ordinarily, to what extent his thoughts, sentiments, and emotions shall be communicated to others." And the US Supreme Court judged that "both the common law and the literal understandings of privacy encompass the individual's control of information concerning his or her person" (U.S. Dept. of Justice v. Reporters Committee, 1989). "[I]nformation privacy" was thus already anticipated in the oldest American conceptualization of privacy. "Information privacy is 'an individual's claim to control the terms under which personal information – information identifiable to the individual – is acquired, disclosed, and used'" (Kang, 1998, p. 1205, quoting the Principles for Providing and Using Personal Information produced by the Clinton administration's Information Infrastructure Task Force)[91].

Does American data protection fill the gap we identified? Its application is sectoral[92] and a general statute law related to "commercial data brokers"[93] – or the profiling industry – and "behavioral advertising"[94] is lacking. It can be pointed out incidentally, that the private sector is supposed to be virtuous when self-regulating. "Self-regulation, after all, is simply the ability to decide for oneself what the term 'reasonable' means" (Killingsworth, 1999, p. 71)[95]. That contrasts sharply with EU perspective where mandatory rules generally apply[96]. Therefore, "e-socialization" is regulated through privacy policies. These policies are mandatory under the Safe Harbor Principles[97] [SHP] and, sometimes, under State law[98]. But it has to be underlined that, more generally, different elements "have all recently converged to create a new environment in which implementing a privacy policy is a business necessity for most, and legally advisable for all" (Killingsworth, 1999, p. 59). Unfortunately,

they suffer from vagueness as regards SNSes[99], and even as regards the Web more generally[100].

Commercial practices are also framed by FTC enforcement actions against unfair or deceptive practices within/or affecting commerce[101] which leads to a "growing 'common law' of privacy" (UCBSI, 2010, p. 10)[102]. As regards SNSes, Twitter has already had to deal with the FTC (In the Matter of Twitter Inc., FTC, 2010), as Facebook might do in the context of the EPIC et al. complaints (EPIC v. Facebook 1, 2 & 3, 2009, 2010). Finally, even if the SHP, (their weaknesses put aside) incorporate a limited "system of consumer control" (Manny, 2003, p. 6), these only relate to personal data coming from EU.

WHAT HELP CAN BE FOUND TODAY?

The concept of "limited privacy" could help. According to L. Strahilevitz (2004, p. 18),

Limited privacy" is the idea that when an individual reveals private information about themselves to one or more people, they may retain a reasonable expectation that the recipients of the information will not disseminate it further. (Strahilevitz, 2004, pp. 18-22).

An "expectation of limited privacy" would then be at stake. The prime example quoted by the L. Strahilevitz (2004, pp. 18-22) in this respect, in California, is based on the intrusion upon seclusion tort, other cases involving the public disclosure of private facts tort. But the courts unfortunately not necessarily accept it (Strahilevitz, 2004, pp. 22-25).

Some researchers have suggested remedies as regards privacy and data protection. One would be to create a specific "model of propertized personal information" that constitutes a "hybrid inalienability" model (Schwartz, 2004). Another solution would be to adapt trade secrecy default rules "to the licensing of personal information" (Samuelson, 2000). Still another way would be to rely on a dynamic theory of informational privacy, being an "autonomy-based approach to data privacy protection" focusing on the meaningful autonomy of the individual (Cohen, 2000). According to L. Strahilevitz (2004), a possibility would result in defining reasonable expectations of privacy according to the "Social Network Theory" (Strahilevitz, 2004). Privacy would then depend on people to whom the data have been communicated.

Next to these interesting propositions, two other solutions seem particularly relevant in the context of SNSes. As a new "path" to take to enhance users' privacy protection, American common law and English common law could be linked (Richards & Solove, 2007, pp. 156-158). The English common law focused on the development of the breach of confidentiality[103] tort – highlighted by Warren, Brandeis and Prosser. Indeed, this latter tort takes into account the "limited purpose" for which data have communicated to third-parties, focusing on the "nature of the relationship" at stake, in spite of the "nature of the information" which has a main role as regards the American privacy tort. An "expectation of trust" would be protected (Richards & Solove, 2007, pp. 174-175). In this respect, it could be helpful to give the users of an SNS the ability to construct their own privacy policy they could contractually oppose other users when they access their profiles. For instance, before viewing the profile of a user – or before becoming a friend of this user –, another user could have to accept a preliminary page, clicking "I accept" and concluding a clickwrap contract with the user whose profile is going to be consulted. Such a privacy policy could also be opposed to applications developers, etc. However, to this aim, SNS providers would have to modify the software they offer. Another concern would then arise, that is to say: how far such contract could go as regards limitations to the freedom of expression of the user consulting the profile[104]?

The theory of H. Nissenbaum (2004), conceptualizing privacy as "contextual integrity", seems also particularly relevant concerning SNSes. According to her, privacy would ensure individuals a right to maintain the contextual integrity of the information at stake[105]. In this same sense, F. Dumortier (2009, p. 15) underlines that "European authorities could impose less multi-contextual content for SNSes by demanding the operators of such sites to limit their architecture in accordance with each user's specific intents." Both theories fit best the cases of "meta-SNS" like Facebook, where lots of contexts intertwine and when the service is offered with the so highly praised opportunity for users to control information related to them[106] – though it is still requested.

It is interesting to note that, to some extent, both theories focus on the *purpose* of the communication of data. Like the European general data protection directive 95/46/EC enshrines the fundamental purpose principle of the processing.

However, whatever theory is chosen to overstep the classically required reasonable expectation of privacy, concerns remain. On Facebook-like SNSes, the "misleading notion[s] of "community"" and "friends" (IWGDPT, 2008, p. 2) are "nebulous at best" (Kane & Delange, 2009, p. 319). Indeed, "OSNs have loosened traditional notions of intimacy and friendship and their respective nomenclature" (Levin & Sánchez Abril, 2009, p. 1018). This remains a practical hurdle to better privacy. This is all the truer when third-party applications are able to extract personal data from SNS databases. We conclude finally with N. Purtova (2009, p. 514), that "*the current US data protection law offers virtually no tools to return control of personal data to individuals*" (emphasis added by author). But it is necessary to add that a positive evolution could occur thanks to privacy scholars and civil liberties associations. And this would necessarily be through statute law or through a groundbreaking case-law.

SPECIFIC TOPICS

To confront SNSes with data protection and privacy does constitute a huge task. Therefore, this section focuses on two relevant concerns relating to data protection: Consent and contract, and the right to access. We discussed elsewhere the material applicability of directive 95/46/EC to SNSes providers, and take as a premise that it applies[107].

Consent and Contract

The Trade of Personal Data: Without explaining further the issues raised by the conclusion of a contract between SNS providers and their users – this was seen previously[108] –, a meeting of the SNS user's and SNS provider's minds can occur. Indeed, the former adheres to the latter's offer of a contract of adhesion[109]. This contract seems to be the place where, and above all the *means* by which, consent is given by data subjects – users of the SNS – to the SNS provider's processing of personal data related to them[110]. The economy of the proposed deal looks straightforward: "Let me process your data in order to deliver and target advertisements, I'll give you a "free" access to my network and I'll delete the data if you delete your account." Or, following a worst-case scenario, "let me do what I wish with your data (including selling it to data brokers, government agencies, potential employers, etc.), I'll give you access to my network that I can deny for any reason, and I reserve the right to keep your data even if you deactivate your account"[111].

In other words, using an SNS could lead to consent to the sale of personal data. It is well known that "[i]ntangible information has become a basic asset, the fuel driving the "Information Economy", and personal data comprises a substantial share of such information assets" (Walden, 2007, p. 459). Advertisements and behavioral advertisements – notably having recourse to the use of cookies and web beacons – drive a significant part of the web industry. This use of, for instance, cookies, is so common that, according to P. Polański (2007, p. 323), it could join the ranks of Internet customs[112]. Answering a complaint directed against Facebook, the Assistant Privacy Commissioner of Canada has recognized that, "[o]ur views with respect to advertising have adapted to the social networking site business model. We have accepted that a certain amount of advertising is something users have to agree to since use of the site is free and the company needs to generate revenue." (Denham, 2009, no.14)[113]

The very question is how far the freedom of contract can go. How to market personal data if one accepts that it can be marketed? Since one's image can be exploited[114], what about other personal data[115]? The answer lies between two extremes defining how one perceives personal data: "Ordinary commodity" or "absolute intangibility"[116]. A median path should be found *in concreto*, taking into account the place afforded by data protection to consent, the different subjective elements and the interest of the collectivity. In this respect, perceptions can vary significantly. Some think that "[t]he sanctity of personality is inconsistent with selling privacy in the marketplace, for baubles", and others not concerned about, "transform themselves into commercialized entertainment packages to satisfy their own exhibitionism and other people's voyeurism" (Kang & Buchner, 2004, p. 230). Taking Facebook as an example, if targeted advertising is necessary to the economic viability of the SNS – without any doubt, a valuable service for its users –, and limited to the possibility, for companies, to select some criteria to define an audience, without any access to personal data and any other transfer of personal data[117], this seems acceptable.

However that may be, beyond the "privacy prohibiting limits"[118], such marketing needs to be led according to data protection rules. Because data protection rules pertain to public order, they restrict the parties' autonomy. According to Belgian contract law, if the contract between the SNS provider and its user has an effect of creating or maintaining a processing operation contrary to these rules, it is void[119]. It is true that consent has a limited value as legitimate ground for data processing (Poullet & Rouvroy, 2009/1, pp. 72-74). Anyway, as far as SNS providers recourse to the data subject's consent, this consent has to be a "freely given, specific and informed indication of his wishes" (Article 2, h) Directive 95/46/EC). It has to be "unambiguously given" (Article 7 a) Directive 1995/46/EC). A *qualified* consent is required. Moreover and notably, it can only relate to processing aimed at "specified, explicit and legitimate purposes" (Article 6.1, b) Directive 95/46/EC), and involving "adequate, relevant and non excessive data" (Article 6.1, c) Directive 95/46/EC) in relation to the purposes of the processing, data which can only be kept "for no longer than is necessary" for these purposes (Article 6.1, e) of directive 95/46/EC). This "qualified" consent is also limited as regards its objective[120]. The purpose next only focuses on the fact that consent is *qualified*, that is to say: Informed, specific and free. This latter point also directly echoes with our brief analysis of the SNS market.

A Qualified Consent: Consent has to be *informed*. SNSes and cloud computing technologies can seem impenetrable – where are the data?[121] While the purposes of the processing have to be specified and explicit. As far as targeted advertisements are concerned, better information is needed as E. Denham pointed it out (2009, nos. 134 and 139)[122]. It has been noted however above that privacy policies are usually vague, which is incompatible with directive 95/46/EC. Explanatory screens related to data protection – how privacy settings work?; what data are processed for which purposes?, etc. – could be of help before the user subscribes to an SNS. Although Facebook has already answered that such a process would dissuade web surfers from joining the network (Denham, 2009, no. 66). As E. Denham (2009, nos. 13 and 51) suggested, a real time information process, anterior to the processing of any personal data, could be useful. In cases like Facebook, the

function of the API Platform has to be clearly explained to users. Indeed, personal data can be retrieved via such a platform; any developer of applications could be located anywhere in the world. This reinforces the density (complexity) and opacity of the "SNS cloud" at stake. Users should know where their personal information is or at least, where it *may be* processed (stored, made available, etc.)[123]. Moreover, no matter where data are collected (from the data subject or a third-party) information duties enshrined in directive 95/46/EC should have to be fulfilled *before* any contract is concluded[124]. This may be crucial due to the practice of clickwrap and browsewrap contracts. Such information is decisive as regards the will to enter into a contract and to use the service.

Consent has also to be *specific*. As regards SNSes, it is given, notably, when the user subscribes to the service and creates an account, clicking on "Create my account", "I accept" or similar formulations. When he clicks, he is considered to consent to terms of use and the privacy policy[125]. Firstly, consent can only target specific processing operations. Data subjects cannot concede a "thematic general power" to process personal data. "Consent in bulk for any future processing without knowing the circumstances surrounding the processing cannot be valid consent" (WP171, 2010, p. 14). Consent must be "limited." Secondly, and although consent to the processing of personal data is clearly linked with the concluded contract between the user and the SNS provider, it should be technically dissociated from the expression of the "blanket assent" to the general terms of use and privacy policy of the SNS in question[126]. It is here referred to about how consumers conclude (e-)contracts. " 'Blanket assent' is best understood to mean that, although consumers do not read standard terms, so long as their formal presentation and substance are reasonable, consumers comprehend the existence of the terms and agree to be bound to them" (Hillman & Rachlinski, 2001, pp. 33-34). " 'Blanket assent' means only that, given the realities of mass-market contracting, the consumer chooses to enter a transaction that includes a package of reasonable, albeit mostly unfavorable to her, boilerplate terms" (Hillman & Rachlinski, 2001, pp. 33-34). In another but similar context, Working Party 29 declared itself in favor of such a procedural dissociation (WP115, 2005, p. 5)[127]. "[C]onsent means active participation of the data subject prior to the collection and processing of data" (Working Party 29, WP171, 2010, p. 15). It is not tacit acquiescence. And in the United States, the FTC (In the matter of Sears, 2009) might deem, in some particular cases, that the practice of a company is deceptive when it promotes its business without informing users *before they consent* to any terms of use and privacy policy, and outside these documents, about their practices related to personal data processing[128]. Irrespective of the fact that the processing occurs later, after that the individual has expressed consent.

The data subject's will, must finally be freely given. As stated O. De Schutter, studying the renunciation to fundamental rights, what is suspicious in a particular deal, is the commercial exploitation ("*marchandisation*") of the right at stake, specific constraints arising from trade banking on the individuals' needs (De Schutter, 2005, p. 457). Individuals' behaviors are dictated by their need of a material advantage or by financial incentives (De Schutter, 2005, p. 463). In the SNSes context, for instance, "the introduction of a fee should be considered as an additional option at the choice of the user for financing the service instead of the use of profile data for marketing" (IWGDPT, 2008, pp. 6-7). This is possible with LiveJournal[129]. But it has to be kept into mind that, "the interest in privacy is like the interest in receiving access to the electoral franchise, clean air, or national defense: it should not depend on socioeconomic status" (Schwartz, 2004, p. 2086). Behind any doubt, competition within the SNS market is relevant and could be decisive in regards to commercial use of personal data. If a user has no real choice, his consent is not free. With no possible alternative, the user can only accept to

use the offered technology (SNS) or reject it. This directly refers to the short analysis of the SNSes market suggested above. It is impossible here to go into economic details of the "meta-SNS" market. It can only be emphasized that the history of Facebook shows that this latter has acted relatively independently from its customers – having then seemed to be dominant –, modifying the website, the privacy policies and the terms of use several times[130]. However, it cannot be denied that users' (often represented by American civil liberties unions) protests have also influenced the website and its policy. The intervention of public authorities has also had the same effect. Practically, the combination of both interventions had effect. Although "dominance is fleeting" (Evans, 2008, p. 17) in such markets, the KnowPrivacy (UCBSI, 2010, pp. 11-12) study underlined, as regards web privacy in general, that "there is not enough market differentiation for users to make informed choices [...; b]ecause [privacy policies] are all equally poor, users have no viable alternatives. This is a *market failure*" (emphasis added by the author). And "the argument that users should simply avoid certain websites is unrealistic [; m]ore and more of our social and political discourse is taking place on these popular websites" (UCBSI, 2010, p. 31) where we are unceasingly urged to be. So it has to be emphasized that consent expressed in the use of SNSes is often not free.

This is all the truer when the SNS provider proceeds to unilateral modifications to the privacy settings – or functionalities – of the network that have to be accepted if the user wants to continue using the network in the same way. This occurred several times as regards Facebook[131]. In such cases, if the user as no other alternative than leaving the network if he does not agree to changes, his consent is not free. Direct or indirect (through the evolution of the service) modifications of privacy settings restricting the original panel of choices the user could make are forbidden by data protection rules. With the exception that if the further processing implied by the modification is compatible with the original processing, which is not the case when the *degree* of accessibility to users' personal data over an SNS is increased. Indeed, if a user originally can limit the accessibility to such data, he cannot reasonably expect that such fundamental characteristic of the offered service will later be modified. Another exception is if the processing is based otherwise than on the data subject's consent. An archetype of such forbidden evolution of privacy settings would precisely be to consider as public information, information whose access to could originally be restricted by users.

Conclusion and Thoughts About the Safe Harbor Principles

Keeping the previous points in mind, it can be argued that an SNS provider like Facebook, as a data controller, often cannot legally rely on the consent of its users to process personal data related to them. Users are not clearly and willingly informed, their consent is usually non specific, and not free enough. Of course, it is impossible to suggest a conclusion as regards every possible case. Each processing operation requires particular study. And if consent is void, however, this does not mean that the processing involved is illegal for this reason. Indeed, their legitimacy can be founded on, for instance, Article 7, f) of directive 95/46/EC[132].

Across the Atlantic, Facebook and LinkedIn have adhered to the SHP[133]. According to the choice principle of the SHP, an SNS provider has to inform (European) data subjects "about the purposes for which it collects and uses information about them." What it does when they decide to access the offered service, therefore consenting to the processing operations at stake. Under SHP, a *qualified* consent is not required. In this respect and without an in-depth analysis, SHP does not directly seem to permit the aforementioned reasoning.

DATA SUBJECT'S RIGHT OF ACCESS

Article 12 of Directive 95/46/EC grants to every data subject "three fundamental rights" (Leberton, 2009, p. 320)[134] relating to the personal data processing at stake and towards the data controller: A right of access, a right of rectification and a right of erasure or blocking. These rights constitute a legal means afforded to data subjects against the previously mentioned lack of control they suffer in the SNS context. They are equipped against unlawful processing of personal data concerning them. They can seek out who is processing the data (the SNS provider, another user[135] (application developer or anyone else) or a third-party to the network), claiming the deletion of the data at stake if the data are conserved for too long a period of time, depending on the purposes of the processing (e.g. if the SNS provider keeps a user's data after this latter has chosen to delete his account). If the "average" user of an SNS falls within the scope of directive 95/46/EC – which is not necessarily the case[136] –, it has to be noted however that the right of access of the data subject could conflict with his right to the confidentiality of his electronic communications[137] and, as may be the case, with his right to the secrecy of his correspondence. But these concerns are not addressed here.

According to directive 95/46/EC (Article 12, a)), the data subject has a right to be informed, by the controller, about the recipients (or categories of recipients) to whom the data are and *have been* disclosed or communicated. The European Court of justice has recently ruled that, to ensure the aforementioned rights (rectification, erasure and blocking), the right of access must of necessity *relate to the past*. If that were not the case, the data subject would not be in a position effectively to exercise his right to have data presumed unlawful or incorrect rectified, erased or blocked or to bring legal proceedings and obtain compensation for the damage suffered." (College van burgemeester en wethouders van Rotterdam v. M.E.E. Rijkeboer 2009, no. 54) (Emphasis added by author.)

Needless to say, the right of access is a cornerstone of data protection as regards the transparency of processing operations and the effectiveness of data protection rules – that is to say, of data subjects' control over personal data. Thus, as a rule, SNS providers would have to store information about people who have had access to personal data related to their users physical persons[138], when they have been involved in such transfers as data controllers. Admittedly, as far as the past is concerned, the right of access can be limited. Limiting it, different factors can be taken into account: The possible exercise of the aforementioned rights implies an appreciation of: the length of time the personal data are to be stored; the obligation following from Article 6 (e); the more or less sensitive nature of the data; the risks represented by the processing; the number of recipients; and, finally, the burden (having regard to the state of the art and the cost of their implementation) that such a storage represent for the data controller (College van burgemeester en wethouders van Rotterdam v. M.E.E. Rijkeboer 2009, nos 57-59)[139]. A balance has to be struck[140]. So to some extent, this fundamental right of access empowers the data subject to "track" the personal data related to them in and outside an SNS.

In the US, how the right of access has been enacted by the SHP can be deplored. Indeed, it is indirectly dependent on American privacy regulation:

[I]ndividuals must have access to personal information about them that an organization holds and be able to correct, amend or delete that information where it is inaccurate, except where the burden or expense of providing access would be disproportionate to the risks to the individual's privacy in the case in question, or where the legitimate rights of persons other than the individual would be violated. (Access Principle and FAQ no. 8)[141] (Emphasis added by author.)

Moreover, it must be noted that "U.S. law will apply to questions of interpretation and compliance with the SHP." Therefore, if there is no risk for the individual's privacy, it is tempting to conclude that any burden supported by the data controller would be disproportionate. And as it has been mentioned above, in the SNS context, American courts could deem that the user of an SNS cannot have a reasonable expectation of privacy[142] – or reasonable expectation for "limited privacy." His privacy will thus not be threatened. Therefore, following American law, the right of access enshrined in the SHP could have shrunk to virtually nothing in the SNSes context.

It is finally of great interest, as the study KnowPrivacy – based on the fifty most consulted websites in the United States at the time of the study – has shown, to mention the sharing of information between affiliates (here, the SNS provider and its affiliated companies). Such sharing is usually foreseen in the privacy policies of websites. The study emphasized in this respect that "[b]ased on our experience, it appears that users have no practical way of knowing with whom their data will be shared" (UCBSI, 2009, p. 28) – what the European right of access can do. It notably underlined that "MySpace, one of the most popular social networking sites (especially among younger users), is owned by NewsCorp, which has over 1500 subsidiaries" (UCBSI, 2009, p. 28)[143]. And the study did not include "subsidiaries of subsidiaries." The European right of access could be especially useful and helpful to identify if such sharing of personal data occurred. It would also be useful if the SNS provider and the application developers were deemed to be joint controllers of the processing involved by the applications. As regards Facebook, is the pure creation of a platform permitting the access by an application to the data of the users who accept this application enough to make of Facebook and the developer joint controllers? If Facebook *compels the users* (technically or by contract) to share a minimum of information with such an application – i.e.

through the platform –, to be able to use it – and other application, making the access to the API Platform functionality conditional to the sharing of personal data –, it is a co-controller at least as regards these data. What about if Facebook does not compel users to share any personal information, the application developer having to require a specific authorization of the users adding his application? In this case, Facebook would seem not to be a data controller. When applications can access to data of an SNS, the question of joint control will depend on the particular functioning of the platform at stake and is crucial as regards the applicability of data protection rules. Anyway, if the SNS provider and an application developer were deemed joint controllers, they would be both compelled to monitor the applications. For instance, they would store a "log" of the personal data these applications accessed. And if the SNS provider is able to store the clickstream of its average users, it should be able to record this "access stream."

CONFIDENTIALITY OF ELECTRONIC COMMUNICATIONS

This section tries to identify in European (III.2.1.) and American (III.2.2) law, which communications are protected and when under the confidentiality of electronic communications protected by both laws.

European Law

According to Article 5.1 of directive 2002/58/EC, Member States have to ensure the confidentiality of electronic communications – exceptions of course existing[144]. This "e-Privacy" directive applies "to the *processing of personal data* in connection with the provision of *publicly available electronic communications services* in *public communications networks* in the Community"[145] (Article 3.1 of directive 2002/58/EC) (emphasis

added by author). If the material scope of the directive[146] is circumscribed in such a manner, some of its dispositions nonetheless apply beyond, such as Articles 5.1, 5.3 and 13[147]. As regards the confidentiality of communications, the protected communications must be realized by means "of a public communications network and publicly available electronic communications services." Both concepts are defined by directive 2002/21/EC (Article 2, d) and c)) which definitions apply as regards directive 2002/58/EC (Article 2). To be public, the network and the electronic communication services have to be "available to all members of the public on the same basis" (EC Communication, 1998), "as opposed to use in a private or corporate network" (EC staff working document, 2004, no. 4.2); the Directive 2002/58/EC "focuses on public electronic communications networks and services, and does not apply to closed user groups and corporate networks" (Recital 55 of directive 2009/136/EC).

To apply the above-mentioned rule in the context of SNSes firstly requires identifying which electronic communication services and public networks are at stake. In this respect, our little knowledge of computers science inevitably limits the scope of the discussion. Secondly, the communications that are protected under directive 2002/58/EC are specified. And thirdly, the implementation of the latter directive in Belgian law is confronted to the analysis.

Electronic Communications Service(s) and Network(s)

When an individual uses an SNS, he first connects to and uses the Internet – a "public communications network" [PCN][148] – with his computer[149] through his own Internet access provider – a classical "electronic communications service" [ECS][150] provider[151]. By these means, he is able to use the software (as a service) provided by the SNS provider. He clicks on the relevant buttons and writes messages or selects files in the relevant fields to make the application work and do what it is expected to do (send a message, join a group, chat, share a video, modify a birth date, change privacy settings, etc.). For instance, he writes a message in a specific field, selects the names of the contact (or friend) he wants to write to, and then clicks on "send." According to the terminology of the Working Party 29, the SNS provider would be its own Internet Service Provider[152] when it hosts the social network (the application and its web interface – the website) and users' data (there profile, what they share, etc.), and replies to users' requests (WP37, 2001, p. 24). It provides content: the application and its web interface connected to a giant database. The content broadcasted in the relevant fields of the Website constantly changes according to users' wishes, these latter being able to share and access to others' information through a framework designed by the SNS provider. Design which is more or less modifiable by members depending on the SNS[153], and can therefore also change. Finally, we assume that the SNS provider most probably subscribes to an Internet access service which enables him to connect to and make available its website on the Internet.

However, could *the SNS provider himself* be considered as the provider of an ECS (the SNS)? Or, even as a PCN provider (the technical infrastructure necessary for the working of the SNS)?

What is central in regards to the qualification as an ECS is "the *conveyance* of signals on *electronic communications network* [CN[154]]" (emphasis added by author). This is, for instance, clearly done by an Internet access provider [IAP] (the one of the SNS provider, and the one of the user at stake). The definition is neutral from a technological viewpoint[155], and the IAP is the archetype of the ECS provider in the context of Internet. An SNS provider should most probably operate an electronic communications network [CN] in the sense of directive 2002/21/CE – which provides a large definition[156]. Indeed, it should have (or at least rent[157]) computers, computers

servers, switches and routers linked with cables, maybe at one place in the world or maybe at different interconnected via the Internet locations in the world. As private companies, for instance, have sometimes their own private network. These facilities are used to provide the SNS website, to answer users' requests, to store users' data and make them available, etc. However, it is true that the "computers" used by the SNS providers to offer its service could be deemed not to constitute a CN under the definition of Directive 2002/21/EC. It would only be considered as equipment[158]. In such a case, it would then be clear that the SNS provider could not be a PCN provider, since it would even not operate a CN. And hearing that the network at stake would then be the Internet, the IAPes would be the only ECS providers, because they would be the only ones to *convey* data on the PCN at stake. The exchange of information between users permitted by the SNS provider on its own computers and database would then happen outside any CN.

If it is taken as premise that the SNS provider operates his own CN, which seems correct in technique, it conveys signals on this particular network to answer users' requests and give them the web pages with content they asked. These web pages are the visible lay out of the SNS and its functionalities. In this perspective, the SNS provider would seem to provide an ECS. However, services providing, or exercising editorial control over, *content* transmitted using CN – *e.g.* Internet – and ECS – *e.g.* Internet access – are explicitly excluded from the definition of ECS; Information society services which do not consist *wholly or mainly* in the conveyance of signals on CN are not ECS (Article 2, c), of directive 2002/21/EC). In other words, directive 2002/21/EC "does not cover services such as broadcast content, or electronic commerce services" (Proposal for a Directive on a common regulatory framework for electronic communications networks and service, 2000). The recital 10 of Directive 2002/21/EC specifies that the "provision of web-based content" is not covered by this Directive. And in our view, it can be considered that the SNS provider mainly provides *content*: an application giving access to a wide database through a website with different functionalities. Therefore, the SNS provider is not an ECS provider. And the SNS is not an ECS. The *conveyance* evoked above is nothing else than an *incidental* activity necessary to deliver the content asked by users of the SNS. With other words, the service provided by the SNS provider do not consist mainly in the conveyance of signals, which processing operations are only incidental due to the fact that the SNS provider hosts and operate himself its website[159]. A web hosting service provider could to the contrary be an ECS because its main activity would consist in the conveyance of signals. Its task is to answer and send the right pages requested by users, not to provide any specific content of his own. Taking as a premise that the SNS is not an ECS, the CN of the SNS provider could neither be considered as a PCN because it would not be mainly used for the provision of ECSes. And the only one ECS-PCN layer that exists in the context of SNSes is the IAPes-Internet one.

However, the Working Party 29 (WP148, p. 12) has already considered that "publicly accessible email service" is an electronic communication service, and Recital 10 of Directive 2002/21/EC underlined that "voice telephony and electronic mail *conveyance* services are covered by this Directive" (emphasis added by author), while the provision of "web-based content" is not. In our view, this reasoning cannot apply to webmail or "webmail-like" services such as the "send a message" functionality that SNSes, such as Facebook, could offer, or such as different forums over the Web. Indeed, in the same sense as above, a Web-mail service would not constitute an ECS because what is provided is mainly content: an application offering people the possibility to communicate through mails and back up these latter. It is clear that both services, Webmail and SNS, permit the exchange of information between their users, but

technically, data packets are in principle conveyed on the Internet by the IAPes, and that is on this conveyance that directive 2002/21/EC focus. The fact that the provided service has an *interpersonal communicative ambit* (webmails and even SNSes and Forums) does not prevent that content is offered, relying on the IAPes conveyance services to finally deliver webpages to users. In this respect, it does not matter that an application can retrieve data from the databases at stake[160].

To sum up, in our view, the SNS provider is considered not to operate a CN, and then only the IAPes provide a conveyance service over the Internet. Or, the SNS is considered to operate a CN; however, does not offer an ECS because the offered service consists mainly in offering content. And the reasoning is coherent despite the interpersonal communicative ambit of SNSes which will be nonetheless taken into account as regards the protected communications. Not to consider SNSes provider as ECS and/or PCN providers is not without consequences as regards, of course, telecom regulation, but also, data retention duties[161]. As regards the SNS context and directive 2002/58/EC, the publicly available ECS and CN at stake are Internet access services and the Internet. To some extent, this view reflects the reasoning held by the Austrian Regulatory Authority for Broadcasting and Telecommunications ([ARABT], 2005, p. 5) as regards voice over IP[162]. The protected communications have now to be identified.

Protected Communications under Directive 2002/58/EC

Directive 2002/58/EC provides that Member States "shall prohibit listening, tapping, storage or other kinds of interception or surveillance of *communications and the related traffic data* by persons other than users, without the consent of the users concerned" (Article 5.1 of directive 2002/58/EC) (emphasis added by author). A communication is "any information *exchanged or conveyed* between a *finite number of parties* by means of a *publicly available electronic communications service*" (Article 2, al. 2, d) of directive 2002/58/EC) (emphasis added by author). Such a communication (its content and its traffic data) is protected to ensure the respect of fundamental rights as recalled by Recitals 2 and 3 of directive 2002/58/EC[163]. In this respect, the interpersonal communicative ambit or function of the service provided by the SNSes is relevant, contrary to what has been suggested as regards the qualification as an ECS.

To identify which pieces of information are protected and in the context of SNSes; it is taken as a point of departure that a user wants to share data (text, image, sound or video) with other users of the SNS. To be protected, a communication needs to satisfy a technical criterion – the means by which it is exchanged –, and an "audience" one – who are pieces of information intended to? In our view, the appreciation of these criterions can vary according to the fact that the communication is in transmission or is, after the transmission, in storage in the SNS. Any piece of information exchanged between SNS users is conveyed through the Internet *and* subsequently, via the SNS provider through its own facilities[164].

During a first stage, as already noted, information users want to share on SNSes are conveyed by IAPes, through the Internet, to the SNS provider. Any communication arising in this first *transmission* stage between the SNS provider and the SNS user is exchanged between those two parties and protected against any interference of a third party. But data are not directly conveyed *between users* by their IAPes, since the SNS is always a necessary intermediary mean to access such data[165]. The other user who is addressee has also to use his own IA service to be able to connect to Facebook and retrieve data. In other words, when data are exchanged between users of an SNS, the above-mentioned first stage of communication occurs for each user: then sender

and the recipient both use their IA to connect to the SNS an use its functionalities.

Data are, during a second stage, *stored* by the SNS provider who makes them available according to the privacy settings or the functionality of the SNS chosen by users[166]. Here, it is not clear if the protection afforded by Article 5 of directive 2002/58/EC goes further than the first *transmission* stage identified above. It neither provides that it doesn't apply *after* the transmission of the communication. In our view, some communications should remain protected after their transmission through the Internet. Specifically, users who first conveyed to the SNS provider are intended *to a finite number of users of the SNS* and stored on the SNS provider servers. In regards to these communications, the SNS works as a "technical storage" necessary to the conveyance of data between SNS users. Without the SNS provider, there is no communication. So, if during a first stage data are transmitted to the SNS, it usually occurs for a "technical storage" purpose. Information is generally not intended to SNSes provider[167]. And in our view, even when communications are conserved as back up by their parties, they could nonetheless remain protected under Directive 2002/58/EC. Even if it is true that the prohibition of hacking will protect stored information, the confidentiality of communications affords to users' protection of their communications vis-à-vis the SNSes providers and, as the case may be, vis-à-vis application developers and other users who are authorized to access the computers at stake[168]. Users usually let their communications stored somewhere, either for their ongoing transmission, either for pure convenience as backup. For example, in regards to web mail, users may wish to save their mails as backup on the servers of the webmail (which usually is a default option): Even if users bring them back to their computers using web mail software (i.e., Microsoft Outlook or Apple Mail). Users also sometimes act this way to be able to consult these mails everywhere in the world. Not to protect such stored communication would risk ruining the confidentiality of electronic communications, limiting this latter to a very short first transmission stage.

Taking Facebook as an example, the purpose can be illustrated and some nuances can be brought. The electronic communications involved by the use of the "send a message" (to one or more friends) functionality of the SNS are clearly protected. Even after messages are not deleted by users having received and saw them, they should also remain protected. Indeed, either they are kept for back up reason, either for ongoing discussion because it works as a kind of "recording chat." Instant messaging conversations are also protected (they can be made between two friends). As it would also be the case of the chat (or "video chat") communications on "Chatroulette" for instance[169]. Invitations to events sent to a limited number of friends are also protected. The list of webpages *visited* by a Facebook user, would these pages be profiles, Facebook pages or groups, is also generally protected. Indeed, the subjacent communications only occur between the user at stake and Facebook[170] – the requests are only intended to Facebook. In all these instances, the addressee of the pieces of information are limited and do not fluctuate.

To the contrary, wall posts and data shared on the SNS with all the users of the SNS – or even any web surfer when the relevant data are publicly available from the web –, are not protected communications[171]. Admittedly, strictly speaking, the number of members of an SNS is *finite*. Nonetheless, if *anybody can join* an SNS (just as in the case of Facebook), data which are available to the whole community are clearly public. It would then be excessive to consider that such a sharing involve protected electronic communications. The audience of the network is *fluctuating* between an unrealistic minimum of two users (if we take as a premise that a communication occurs) and a maximum of nearly the whole world…

But what about information exchanged through private groups, and restricted access profiles or parts of such profiles (*e.g.* Walls)? For example, on Facebook, a group can be "open", "closed" or "secret." Open, a group is public. Anybody can join and consult the discussion board, the group's Wall, etc. In such a case, to join a group doesn't involve a protected electronic communication, as it is the case of posting text, images, etc. However, the pure information resulting in the *consultation* of the group's wall, discussion board, etc., remains a protected communication because it is only exchanged with Facebook. If a group is closed, only members approved by the administrators of the group can see the discussion board and the wall and join it. However, the group description is visible by non members, while what is shared through the pages of the group is not. Finally, if the group is secret, it doesn't appear in the members' profiles, or in the search results of the SNS. An invitation has to be sent to the potential future member. As regards profiles, the accessibility to data can also be limited, when the wall of a user is restricted to his friends or to a particular list of friends. In such context, communications seems to appear between a finite number of parties, and *a priori,* it could arguably be considered that the confidentiality of electronic communications applies.

However, how to take into account the fact that a group, a part of a profile, or any other part of the network, can be restricted to *selected* members but nonetheless *numerous* members *and of different contexts* (work, sport, education, sexuality, etc.) and whose number is *fluctuating*? In our view, if in fact, access to the particular part of the profile, to the group, etc., at stake is systematically given to the general public on the same basis[172], or given to a lot of people from really different contexts[173] or, more generally, fluctuating, it can then be argued that the communications at stake are not protected. Indeed, in these cases, the communication has an *indeterminate* or *irrelevant* audience which composition is *fluctuating*. Even if this audience, at a certain times share pieces of information, it is a *finite* sharing, which parties can be numbered. Pieces of information are posted and their accessibility can vary. To deem it otherwise could threaten the Freedom of expression[174], notably ensured by the ECHR which, as already noted, can have a diagonal indirect effect. Therefore, such communications would be protected during the first transmission stage – still occurring between two parties. But not during the second technical storage stage where they are intended to an indeterminate or irrelevant audience which composition is fluctuating.

It has now to be evaluated if such reasoning can be transposed as regards the implementation of directive 2002/58/EC, taking Belgium as an example.

Protected Communications under Belgian Implementation of Directive 2002/58/EC

If the above-mentioned reasoning seems defendable as regards Article 5 of Directive 2002/58/EC, how it is implemented in Belgian law and does this reasoning remain valid? The confidentiality of electronic communications is protected through both rules that existed before directive 2002/58/EC: one is enshrined in the Belgian Penal Code [PC][175] and the other one is in the Law on Electronic Communications [LEC] (Article 124). According to the LEC, *no one* can, if he is not authorized by *all* the persons *directly or indirectly* involved in the electronic communication, intentionally acquaint himself with the *existence* of this electronically transmitted and not sent to him communication, intentionally identify the persons concerned by the transmission of the information and its content, or still use in anyway the identification or the data obtained (intentionally or not). To break this rule is criminally punished[176]. According to Article 314bis of the Belgian PC, shall notably be punished the one who, with any apparatus, intentionally listen (or make listen), acquaint himself or tape *private*[177]*communications* to which he is not a participant, *during their transmission*, without the consent of each participant to the communica-

tion. In this respect, communications are private when they are not intended to "every man jack" ("*tout un chacun*") (Proposition of Data Privacy Act, Belgium, 1992, p. 7).

Some scholars argue that the protection afforded by the LEC goes further the pure transmission of the communication (de Terwangne, Herveg, & Van Gyseghem, 2005, pp. 50 and 91; Lambert, 1999, pp. 203-204). Indeed, this transmission condition is not required under the LEC while it is explicitly needed in Article 314 bis of the Belgian PC[178]. Nonetheless, other scholars argue that the LEC only applies during the transmission of the communication (Docquir, 2008, pp. 81-82; de Corte, 2000, p. 12)[179]. As regards Article 314 bis of the Belgian PC, its aim is not to protect communications when they are "at destination", for instance as shown by the *travaux parlementaires*, when mails are stored on the computer of the addressee (LEC, preparatory act, 1992, p. 6), but during their transmission. In this respect, it has been judged, by the Leuven Court of first instance (N.V.G.P.G. v. C.P., 2007), that an e-mail not already read or downloaded from the server is still in transmission and therefore still protected by the PC.

How to apply both dispositions? For instance, it has been argued that the PC protected the content of the communication, while the LEC protected other pieces of information such as the existence of the communication and its parties – traffic data. However, to acquaint oneself with the content of a communication also implies to acquaint oneself of the existence of the communication. In our view, P. De Hert's reasoning related to e-mails gives a good solution and permits the interpretation above mentioned related to Article 5 of directive 2002/58/EC and the context of SNSes. According to the author, the protection of PC lasts until the emails are taken in and until the addressee has knowledge of the emails, which is to say during their transmission[180]. And then the LEC can still apply after the transmission of the e-mail (De Hert, 2001, pp. 124-125 and footnote no. 86).

Conclusion

Finally, the fate of the protected communications and their traffic data is under the control of the qualified consents of the parties to these communications, even when they are stored. This means that to acquaint himself of protected communications, a third party needs the consent, as defined by directive 1995/46/EC[181] and exposed in the first part of this chapter, of each party to the communication. And such a third-party could be an advertiser, an application developer, the SNS provider[182], etc. We suggested that this qualified consent protect whole the communications occurring between a user and the SNS provider, during a first transmission stage. Then, during the second technical storage stage, are only protected those communications which are intended to a finite number of parties and when such parties do not constitute an indeterminate or irrelevant audience whose composition is fluctuating.

AMERICAN LAW

In the United States, the Electronic Communications Privacy Act [ECPA] ensures the confidentiality of the electronic communications. "Title I of the ECPA, known as the Wiretap Act [(18 USC §§ 2701-2712)], protects wire, oral, and electronic communications while *in transit*. Title II, also known as the Stored Communications Act (SCA) [(18 USC §§ 2701-2712)], protects data while held *in storage*" (Kane & Delange, 2009, p. 324)[183] (emphasis added by author). And the definitions of the terms of the Wiretap Act also apply to the Stored communications Act (18 USC § 2711 (1)).

In both Acts, what is protected is an electronic communication. Electronic communication is a wide concept. It means "any transfer of signs, signals, writing, images, sounds, data, or intelligence of any nature transmitted in whole or in part by a wire, radio, electromagnetic, photoelectronic or photooptical system that affects interstate or foreign commerce" (18 USC § 2510 (12))[184]. For example, the First Circuit held that an email and the "[t]ransmission of completed online forms [...]" (Pharmatrak, Privacy Litigation, 2003) constitute such communications. In the case of SNSes, messages sent from one profile to another one or more, or instantaneously sent via Chat functionalities should be considered as electronic communications. Even if such a definition seems to show that the spectrum of the protected communications is broader than according to directive 2002/58/EC, the next developments will show that restrictions related to the audience of the communications at stake also exist.

The Wiretap Act is first very briefly discussed, because it will reveal less relevant as regards SNSes. The Stored Communications Act requires more developments. Then, the consent of the user of the SNS is studied as a potential exception to the application of both acts.

Wiretap Act

According to the Wiretap Act[185], it is notably forbidden to intentionally intercept any wire, oral, or electronic communication (18 USC § 2511 (1) (a)). Hearing that "a contemporaneous interception – *i.e.*, an acquisition during "flight" – is required to implicate [this Act]" (USA v. Steiger, 2003)[186]. Therefore, as regards the context of SNSes, the Wiretap Act will only apply to the first transmission stage we identified – communications occurring between the SNS user and the SNS provider. And the Stored Communications Act directly focuses on communications that are stored for short or long term – once data are on the SNS servers, they are stored.

Stored Communications Act

The Stored Communications Act "provides privacy protection to communications held by two types of providers": The provider of public electronic communication services[187] [ECS] and the ones of public remote computing services [RCS][188] (Kerr, 2004, p. 7). The principle is that they cannot knowingly divulge to any person or entity the content[189] of the users' electronic communications (18 USC § 2702 (a) (1) (2)). However, they can divulge non-content information to private entities (but not to a governmental entity) (18 USC § 2702 (a) (1) (3))[190]. If the services they provide are not public[191] – which is generally not the case of SNSes –, the Stored Communications Act does not apply. The Act also provides that, except in some cases, nobody can "intentionally [access] without authorization a facility through which an electronic communication service is provided" or "intentionally [exceed] an authorization to access that facility" when the electronic communication is "in electronic storage in such system" (18 USC § 2701 (a) (1) and (2)).

As O.S. Kerr (2004, p. 9) points out, the "classifications of ECS and RCS are context sensitive: The key is the provider's role with respect to a particular copy of a particular communication, rather than the provider's status in the abstract." In this respect, O.S. Kerr (2004, p. 10) writes that "files held in intermediate "electronic storage"[192] are protected under the ECS rules", while files held for "long-term storage by that same provider are protected by the RCS rules." So, the "traditional view" is that an email, not opened – or not retrieved from the webmail server – falls under the ECS rules, while an opened one – or a retrieved from the webmail server one – falls under the RCS rules (Kerr, 2004, pp. 10-11).

But it has to be underlined in this respect that, according to the Court of Appeals for the Ninth Circuit (Theofel v. Farey-Jones, 2003), such non-retrieved mails can be deemed to be stored for backup purposes and then still falling under the ECS rules. It has to be recalled that the Ninth Circuit rules California where numerous SNS are established (*e.g.* Facebook and Twitter). The Ninth Circuit decided the following:

An obvious purpose for storing a message on an ISP's server after delivery is to provide a second copy of the message in the event that the user needs to download it again – if, for example, the message is accidentally erased from the user's own computer. The ISP copy of the message functions as a "backup" for the user. Notably, nothing in the Act requires that the backup protection be for the benefit of the ISP rather than the user. Storage under these circumstances thus literally falls within the statutory definition. (Theofel v. Farey-Jones, 2003)

The regimes related to both types of stored communications substantially differ as regards the access to the communications by the Government[193]. For our purpose, as regards the disclosure of information to private entities, one discrepancy has to be pointed out. Indeed, it could reveal important in the context of SNSes. As regards the RCS, the communications are protected "if the provider is not authorized to access the contents of any such communications for purposes of providing any services other than storage or computer processing" (18 USC § 2702 (a) (2) (b)). It is therefore still useful to qualify the SNS provider.

The traditional ECS provider is an Internet service provider, a phone company or even a webmail provider. But Courts have already deemed that an electronic bulletin board fits the definition of an ECS (Kaufman v. Nest Seekers, 2006)[194]. In addition, it has been the case of a "web-based forum where parties could communicate" (Inventory Locator v. Partsbase, 2005). Therefore, SNSes groups, profiles, etc., could be at stake. In this respect, not all electronic bulletin boards or forums would be protected. Indeed, as it was stated by the Eleventh Circuit in Snow v. DirectTV (2006), in "order to be protected by the [Stored Communications Act]; an Internet website must be configured in some way so as to limit ready access by the general public"[195]. And according to the Court's judgment referring to Konop v. Hawaiian Airlines (2002), the simple need of a registration *without any screening* could be insufficient for the application of the Stored Communication Act. The Court underlined that:

[A] short simple statement that the plaintiff screens the registrants before granting access may have been sufficient to infer that the website was not configured to be readily accessible to the general public. However, Snow failed to make this or any remotely similar allegation. Instead, Snow's allegations describe, in essence, a self-screening methodology by which those who are not the website's intended users would voluntarily excuse themselves. Because this is insufficient to draw an inference that the website is not readily accessible to the general public, Snow's complaint fails to state a cause of action and it was proper to dismiss it. (Snow v. DirectTV, 2006)

And in Konop v. Hawaiian Airlines (2002):

"Konop controlled access to his website by requiring visitors to log in with a user name and password. Konop provided user names to certain Hawaiian employees, but not to managers or union representatives. To obtain a password and view the site, an eligible employee had to register and consent to an agreement not to disclose the site's contents."

Since "Anyone can join" Facebook and also other SNSes, a user's content available to any member of the network (e.g. Wall posts of "public" profile but nonetheless restricted to the members of the SNS) will not be protected under the Stored Communications Act and the ECS rules. To the contrary, the content which will only be disclosed to the user's friends ("private" profile), who have been screened because they have been individually accepted by the user at stake, could be protected. The suggested reasoning above as regards communications occurring between a finite number of parties could be transposed here. Of course and *a fortiori,* the public parts of the profile that

are accessible from the Web without subscribing to the SNS will not be protected. Of course, the present reasoning would only apply insofar as Courts accept to make an analogy between an SNS and a Forum or a webmail depending on the communications at stake.

The RCS rules target longer storage of data – beyond the backup storage. It requires processing services, and these services originally concerned an "outsourcing function" needed, originally, where companies do not have the technological resources to have their own IT infrastructure to process data themselves (Kerr, 2004, pp. 26-27). Clearly, SNSes permit their users to store data for a long term, as they also provide data storage as a service. For instance, YouTube has already been deemed to constitute a RCS (Viacom v. YouTube, 2008). Of course, the same considerations as above mentioned related to the public or private character of the service will apply. Most probably, and putting aside Theofel v. Farey-Jones (2003), SNS will usually be considered as RCS because users outsource the processing of their data and store them on the SNS provider's servers for an indeterminate period of time.

Therefore the following question arises: If Theofel v. Farey-Jones (2003) does not apply, SNS provider being considered as RCS providers and not ECS providers, how far the access, to provide other services, to the data claimed by the SNS provider in the privacy policy and terms of use affects the protection afforded to its users by the Stored Communications Act? For instance as regards Facebook, Facebook Inc. can access the data to deliver targeted advertisements, how does this have to be taken into consideration? In other words, when and how far is an access "in connection" with the provision of the service? For example in Viacom v. Youtube (2008), the Court decided that the authorization of YouTube to "access and delete potentially infringing private videos is granted *in connection with*" YouTube's provision of storage services (emphasis added by author). It is impossible here to answer that question which seems close to the question of the users' consents that can lead to an exception to the Stored Communications Act and the Wiretap Act. This question can be addressed now.

Consent and Stored Communications Act and Wiretap Act

The consent to terms of service and privacy policy of SNSes websites could lead to an exception to the prohibitions set in the Stored Communications Act[196] and in the Wiretap Act[197]. To this respect, there is a substantial difference between American law and European law. In other words, communications can be intercepted when they are transmitted or disclosed when they are stored with the consent, to sum up, of *one of the parties* to the communication. For "example, the sender (originator) of an e-mail as well as any intended recipients may give consent to disclose the communication" (Ackermann, 2009, p. 43). Under the Stored Communication Act, according to the federal rules protecting electronic communications, a "one party consent" is then only required (Schwartz & Reidenberg, 1996, p. 226).

Some States, such as California, have however adopted a "two-party consent rule" (Schwartz & Reidenberg, 1996, p. 227) requiring the consent of each party to the communication at stake. But for instance, the relevant Californian rule, related to the eavesdropping or recording of communications, is of little help here. Indeed it does not lead to the same result we could plead for under directive 2002/58/EC. In the case of communications realized through the Internet, the Californian Penal Code § 632 (a) would apply. According to this disposition:

"[e]very person who, intentionally and without the consent of all parties to a confidential communication, by means of any electronic amplifying or recording device, eavesdrops upon or records the confidential communication, whether the communication is carried on among the parties in the presence of one another or by means of a telegraph, telephone, or other device, except a radio, shall be punished..."

Therefore, only the confidential communications are protected, that is to say the communications "carried on in circumstances as may reasonably indicate that any party to the communication desires it to be confined to the parties thereto." And in any case, such a communication is not "a communication made in […] any other circumstance in which the parties to the communication may reasonably expect that the communication may be overheard or recorded" (California Penal Code § 632 (c)). Moreover, the "person" targeted by the offence "excludes an individual known by all parties to a confidential communication to be overhearing or recording the communication" (California Penal Code § 632 (b)).

The lawfulness of the collection of clickstream data through cookies has been discussed in regards to the Stored Communications Act and the Wiretap Act. These Acts illustrate the consequences of a "one party consent" rule. In DoubleClick Privacy Litigation (2001)[198], the Court applied the same reasoning as regards the consent in the Stored Communications Act and in the Wiretap Act. It noted that contracts existed between DoubleClick and the websites involved in the use of cookies for the DoubleClick's advertisement program. Due to these contracts, electronic communications between these websites and their web surfers – their clickstream – could lawfully be communicated to DoubleClick[199]; "because plaintiffs' GET, POST and GIF submissions to DoubleClick-affiliated Web sites are all "intended for" those Web sites, the Web sites' authorization is sufficient to except DoubleClick's access under § 2701 (c)(2)." As regards the identification number of the cookie, that is not communicated to the Web sites at stake, the Court considered that, even if it were protected – *quod non* according to the Court –, DoubleClick's access is authorized because:

In every practical sense, the cookies' identification numbers are internal DoubleClick communications – both "of" and "intended for" Double-Click. DoubleClick creates the cookies, assigns them identification numbers, and places them on plaintiffs' hard drives. The cookies and their identification numbers are vital to DoubleClick and meaningless to anyone else. In contrast, virtually all plaintiffs are unaware that the cookies exist, that these cookies have identification numbers, that DoubleClick accesses these identification numbers and that these numbers are critical to DoubleClick's operations. (DoubleClick Privacy Litigation, 2001) (emphasis added by author)[200]

While an application of directive 2002/58/EC would have required, in addition, the consent of the web surfers.

As regards the consent itself and the Wiretap Act, if a party has knowledge or notification of the interception, her consent does not need to be express and can only be "inferred from the surrounding circumstances" (Garrie & Wong, 2009, p. 146, footnote no. 88). A *qualified* consent as what is required under directive 95/46/EC is not needed. The First Circuit Court of Appeals considered, still as regards the Wiretap Act, that,

Consent may be explicit or implied, but it must be actual consent rather than constructive consent"; it requires an "actual notice" or that "the surrounding circumstances convincingly show that the party knew about and consented to the interception. (Pharmatrak, Privacy Litigation, 2003)

Finally, in Viacom v. YouTube (2008), where the YouTube RCS and the Stored Communications Act were at stake, the Court addressed, in some extent, the question of the scope of the user consent to the terms of use and privacy policy of the website. It had been argued that users of YouTube have consented to the disclosure of data by assenting to the YouTube website's Terms of Use and Privacy Policy, which contain provisions licensing YouTube to distribute user submissions (such as videos) in connection with its website and business, disclaiming liability for disclosure of user submissions, and notifying users that videos they divulge online in the public areas of the website may be viewed by the public (Viacom v. YouTube, 2008)

And the Court answered that,

[N]one of those clauses [could] fairly be construed as a grant of permission from users to reveal to plaintiffs [(notably Viacom, claiming that it owned copyrights in television programs, etc., broadcasted by YouTube users)] the videos that they have designated as private and chosen to share only with specified recipients (Viacom v. YouTube, 2008) (emphasis added by author)

It is interesting to see that the Court directly takes into account the fact that the users at stake have defined privacy settings.

Conclusion

The protection of the confidentiality of communications seems more elaborated in the United States than in Belgium where the transposition of directive 2002/58/EC as regards this topic is relatively brief. But directive 2002/58/EC gives Member States enough margin to establish a well balanced framework. The ECPA and, more precisely, the Stored Communications Act should offer the SNSes users a mean to control, by their consents, the protected communications. However and some interpretation concerns put aside, only the consent of one party to the communication at stake is required. And such consent does not need to be qualified as it has to be as regards directive 2002/58/EC. This shows two substantial differences between the American and European regimes of confidentiality of electronic communications.

PROTECTION OF COMPUTERS

Judge Kleinfeld, who dissented in USA v. Micah Gourde (2006), underlined that:

[F]or most people, their computers are their most private spaces. People commonly talk about the bedroom as a very private space, yet when they have parties, all the guests — including perfect strangers — are invited to toss their coats on the bed. But if one of those guests is caught exploring the host's computer, that will be his last invitation. There are just too many secrets on people's computers, most legal, some embarrassing, and some potentially tragic in their implications [...] a married mother of three may be carrying on a steamy email correspondence with an old high school boyfriend. Or an otherwise respectable, middle-aged gentleman may be looking at dirty pictures. (USA. v. Micah Gourde, 2006)

Without any doubt, the web surfer's terminal – computer or mobile phone, etc. – is a very private space. So much that Y. Poullet (2008, pp. 62-65) has already suggested that it should be at the core of a third generation of data protection rules, making it closer to a "private electronic space", a "virtual domicile" (Y. Poullet, 2010). The author also refers to Germany that knows a new fundamental right to the confidentiality and the integrity of the technological information systems, based on the general right to personality[201]. In our view, the user should have the complete ownership of its terminal, controlling to which other terminals this latter "speaks" and what it "tells" them. For instance, everybody should have a *user-friendly* mean to monitor (and, need be, to block) the electronic communications coming from its computer terminal to the Internet and

coming from this latter, to the former. It should be pointed out that, particularly as regards SNSes, the user's computer terminal is more than a *place* where personal information is stored[202] and life happens. It is also, and above all, a *mean to behave*, a necessary extension of the individual to "e-socialize" with others and, more generally, to "e-act."

Whatever can be the links between privacy, data protection and the computer terminal, the purpose focuses on the prohibition of hacking (III.3.1). It then underlines the consequences that directive 2002/58/CE could have as regards the use of cookies. Indeed, cookies imply the access to the computer of a web surfer (III.3.2). In this context, the user's consent is still a key mean of control.

HACKING AND SNSES

Hacking is internationally prohibited, like it is in Belgian and American law. The unauthorized access to a computer is forbidden. As regards SNSes, it seems particularly interesting to determine if a breach of a contract (terms of use), concluded between the user and the SNS provider as regards the use of the website, could lead to a hacking. Indeed, the access to the provider's servers would then occur contrary to what is authorized to users.

The Prohibition of Hacking

Thanks to the prohibition of hacking, the SNS user is empowered to control the access to his personal computer, the writing of data on it and the extraction of data from it. As the SNS provider is empowered to do the same as regards his own servers. In the Internet, the use of cookies, for instance, involves accessing to and writing data on the web surfer's personal computer. As the use of a SNS implies writing on the computers of the SNS provider. The Council of Europe's Covenant on Cybercrime (Budapest Convention,

2001) compels its Member States[203] to establish a criminal offence forbidding hacking[204]. It targets the intentional access, "without right", to computer systems (Article 2 of the Budapest Convention, 2001). A scholar emphasized that since "in order to be considered an offence, the conduct must be committed intentionally and unlawfully, i.e. "without right"", "there are acts which, if duly [...] *accepted as lawful commercial practices*, will not be considered a criminal offence under the Convention" (Csonka, 2006, p. 483) (emphasis added by author). Indeed, according to the Explanatory Report of the Budapest Convention (no. 38): "legitimate and common activities inherent in the design of networks, or legitimate and common operating or commercial practices should not be criminalized."

For instance as regards cookies, the explanatory report follows:

The application of standard tools provided for in the commonly applied communication protocols and programs, is not in itself 'without right', in particular where the rightholder of the accessed system can be considered to have accepted its application, e.g. in the case of 'cookies' by not rejecting the initial installment or not removing it (no. 48)

Therefore, it seems implicitly that to define the parameters of a browser or to let the default rules play is enough to authorize access to a computer. Although the actual widespread browsers – Safari, Internet Explorer and Firefox – do not integrate a really user-friendly tool to easily and practically manage the cookies coming from the different websites. And although numerous websites – like SNSes, e.g. Facebook – technically compel web surfers to accept cookies to access the website.

The Belgian PC protects everyone against an unauthorized access to his computer (Article 550 bis CP)[205]. In the Code's words, will be punished anyone who, *knowing* that he is *not authorized, access* to a computer system or remains in such

a system – external hacking –, a *malicious intent* being an aggravating circumstance (Article 550 bis, § 1, CP). Will also be punished anyone who, with a fraudulent intent, *exceeds his power to access* to such a computer system – internal hacking (Article 550 bis, § 1, CP). Therefore, the *mens rea* varies depending on the qualification as an "external hacking" (to access without authorization) or an "internal hacking" (to exceed rights of access). The internal hacking requires a fraudulent or malicious intent. That is to say the lure of illegal profit or malice (*Projet de Loi*, 2000, p. 16). In each case, the breaking of a protection system is not a constitutive element of the offence (*Projet de Loi*, 2000, p. 17)[206]. Of course, if such protection systems have been broken or by-passed, it is then impossible, for the individual at stake, to argue that he ignored he was not authorized to access to the computer at stake[207].

In American federal law[208], the Computer Fraud and Abuse Act (18 USC § 1030 [CFAA])[209] forbids hacking. Who "intentionally accesses a computer without authorization or exceeds authorized access, and thereby obtains" (18 USC § 1030, (a) 2°) "information from any protected computer[210]" will be punished (18 USC § 1030 (a), 2° (C)). Like in the Belgian PC, the breaking of a protection system is not required. But contrary to this Code, the *mens rea* is the same in both cases of hacking (internal or external). Coming back to the example of cookies, in the aforementioned matter DoubleClick Privacy Litigation (2001), the Court applied this statute. However, the lessons it provides are limited for the purpose, since DoubleClick did not question that it had not had the authorization to access web surfers' computers. The debate focused on the kind of damage at stake and the threshold victims had to demonstrate for the success of their suit. This is precisely what they failed to do, leading them to the failure of their lawsuit[211]. This case nonetheless shows that the use of cookies could lead to hacking.

American case law provides some answers to an interesting question that could be decisive in the SNSes context and that needs now to be addressed: Could a breach of a contract – if there is actually a contract between an SNS provider and its users[212] – amount to an unauthorized access to a computer, constituting therefore a criminal offence?

Hacking and Breach of a Contract

In the United States, different cases show that "[t]he extent of authorization may turn upon the contents of an employment agreement or similar document, a terms of service notice, or a log-on banner outlining the permissible purposes for accessing a computer or computer network" (Computer Crime and Intellectual Property Section, Criminal Division ([CCIPS], 2007, pp. 6-10). Courts have had to decide if the knowingly breach of a website's terms of service (AOL) (AOL v. LCGM, 1998), and even those of an SNS (MySpace) (USA v. Lori Drew, 2009) could lead to hacking. Indeed, the access to an SNS necessarily implies the access to the computer systems of its provider (or of the provider's subs contractors). As regards internal hacking and the CFAA, a conscious behavior, without any malicious intent, suffices to be punished as it has been noted. In AOL v. LCGM (1998), where unsolicited bulk emails were at stake, the defendant was deemed guilty of hacking[213]. The Court decided that,

Defendants have admitted to maintaining an AOL membership and using that membership to harvest the e-mail addresses of AOL members. Defendants have stated that they acquired these e-mail addresses by using extractor software programs. Defendants' actions violated AOL's Terms of Service, and as such were unauthorized. (AOL v. LCGM, 1998)

Whereas, in the matter of USA v. Lori Drew, the defendant was found not guilty (2009). In this latter case, the defendant was a mother who harassed a young girl using MySpace. To this aim,

she falsely represented herself as a young boy (with a photo). She knowingly violated MySpace terms of use compelling users to provide real information. The American government, suing her, pleaded that such a behavior constituted a hacking – without specifying if it was an internal or an external one – of MySpace's servers[214].

Judge Wu concluded that the government wrongly charged her because of the "void-for-vagueness doctrine"[215]. Although he specified that "within the breach of contract approach, most courts that have considered the issue have held that a conscious violation of a website's terms of services/use will render the access unauthorized and/or cause it to exceed authorization"[216]. As stated by Judge Wu, "[t]o avoid contravening the void-for-vagueness doctrine, the criminal statute must contain "relatively clear guidelines as to prohibited conduct" and provide "objective criteria" to evaluate whether a crime has been committed" (USA v. Lori Drew, 2009). He deemed in particular that if any breach of terms of use constituted a criminal offense of hacking, the "fair warning requirement" would not be satisfied[217]. Which means that an average individual would not be able to identify what is forbidden and what is not.

Not to follow Judge Wu's point of view in the context of SNSes would lead to potentially sentence for internal hacking anyone who, breaching – without any bad intent – the terms of use requiring its identification, would act under a pseudonym. Such "an interpretation that criminalizes routine computer use would give the government the power to arrest any typical computer user" (Kerr, 2010, p. 17). Terms of use are potentially really vague and "[v]iolating the [terms of service] is the norm; complying with them the exception" (Kerr, 2010, 21). Terms of use can be so vague that any illegal *intent* – from a civil or a penal viewpoint – in the use of the website – or service – at stake would lead to a breach of these terms[218]. This would therefore make the web surfer guilty of hacking. The reasoning can be pushed to an absurd result taking an IAP as an example. If an

CloudBasedSocialNetworkSites

IAP contractually forbids that his customer pursues any illegal purpose using the Internet access services provided[219], any use of the Internet with an illegal intent would then imply an unauthorized access to the IAP's computer infrastructure, and would therefore constitute a hacking. This is clearly an unpredictable result.

Transposed in Belgian law, the reasoning of Judge Wu would lead to consider that the proposed interpretation is contrary to the "legality principle" ("*prinicpe de légalité*") of criminal law[220]. It has to be recalled that, according to the Belgian PC and contrary to the CFAA, an internal hacking requires a fraudulent or malicious intent (*Projet de Loi*, 2000, p. 16). If the defendant, in USA v. Lori Drew (2009), had such a malicious intent since she wanted to harass a young user of the social network[221], would she be for all that guilty of hacking according to Belgian law? Clearly, the considerations evoked above can be recalled here, *mutatis mutandis*. She shouldn't have been sentenced for hacking. Moreover, focusing on the classification made by the Belgian legislator, computers are here only a mean to commit another offence (harassment), a *modus operandi,* and not the aim of the criminality as it is normally the case as regards hacking (*Projet de Loi*, 2000, pp. 6-7). In this second category of offences, where computers are the target of the criminality, the legislator focused on behaviors infringing the confidentiality, the integrity and the availability of computers or of data stored in them or processed or transferred through them (*Projet de Loi*, 2000, pp. 6-7). In USA v. Lori Drew (2009), to harass by means of a simulated flirt and under a false identity is something else.

Maybe the conclusion would be different if the harasser mother had wished to obtain access to the private profile of the MySpace user to retrieve data from this profile, knowing that the young girl would never have given access to her profile if the harasser didn't act under a false name. In this case, it could be argued that the mother would have tried to by-pass the technical protections that ensure the private character of the profile at stake, by deceiving the holder of the profile, exploiting her credulity.

However that may be, the disputed reasoning in U.S.A. v. Drew (2009) could prove to be a very powerful legal mean to protect SNS users against the wrongful transfer and use of personal information relating to them. This would be particularly true as regards the application programming interfaces [API] provided by SNSes and the applications developed by third-party developers. For instance on Facebook, as explained, an application can access personal data through the Facebook platform. If technical measures are not carried out by the SNS provider, and if the applications developers breach the terms of use related to the processing of users' personal data, would they become hackers? Facebook constitutes a case in point, as one looks at what the assistant to the Canadian Privacy Commissioner wrote in her report:

In the absence of any evidence of technological safeguards, I can only assume that, when Facebook speaks of limits on access to users' information, it speaks of contractual limits. In other words, as means of limiting access, it is relying mainly upon certain prohibitions stated in policy documents, and upon trust in the application developers' acknowledged agreement to abide by those prohibitions. (Denham, 2009, no. 199)

However Facebook contested this statement (Denham, 2009, no. 197). The security measures taken by Twitter have also been criticized when Twitter has been hacked by hacker taking administrative control of the website and accessing to (private) personal data. This finally led to a settlement between Twitter and the FTC (In the Matter of Twitter Inc., FTC, 2010).

The same question would arise if SNSes providers gave their users the possibility to define their own rules of diffusion of personal data in a privacy policy they could transform into a binding contract, as suggested above. In this latter case, the "authorization" to access to the SNS servers would be directly defined by the users.

Therefore, the question is: When could a contractually forbidden access to the servers of an SNS provider, not prevented by technical measures, – the developer at stake only having reasonable notice of the additional developer terms of use – lead to an internal hacking under Belgium Penal Code and/or CFAA[222]? In particular, *quid* if this behavior would have constituted such a hacking if the contractual terms had been technically concretized? In our view, the precedent developments related to USA v. Lori Drew (2009) are still relevant in such a case. But some elements could moderate the previous conclusions. Indeed, on the one hand, a specific vigilance is waited from the application developer. He controls the development of his application and knows the working of the API on which he grafts his product if he wants that this latter works. And on the other hand, the developer would infringe the confidentiality of the SNS's systems in the extent that he would access and retrieve data he can not access or retrieve. Contrary to what happened as regards MySpace. Anyway, the potential responsibility – or irresponsibility – of the application developer would not prevent in any manner the responsibility of the SNS provider himself who would not provide the users adequate protection measures to protect their profiles and personal data.

Conclusion

The American and Belgian prohibitions of hacking are close[223]. This is logical hearing that both States ratified the Budapest Convention. They diverge nonetheless to some extent, for instance as regards the *mens rea* required for an internal hacking: no malicious intent is required according to American law. Anyway, the CFAA and the Belgian PC empower users to control the access to their computer, and SNSes providers to control the access to their servers. In our view, the pure

breach of a contract (terms of service) concluded with a SNS provider, if such a contract is valid, should generally not lead to hacking. Even if it could be argued for the contrary as regards applications developers as suggested. Therefore, where no technical protection measures are put in place, the confidentiality of electronic communications remains an important guardrail.

DIRECTIVE 2002/58/ EC AND COOKIES

Directive 2002/58 could have a specific role to play as regards cookies which are, as already noted, written on users' computers. Its former Article 5.3[224] provided for that "the use of electronic communications networks to store information or to gain access to *information stored in the terminal equipment* of a subscriber or user" was "only allowed on condition that the subscriber or user concerned is provided with" due *information according to Directive 95/46* "and is offered *the right to refuse* such processing by the data controller" (emphasis added by author). A purely technical storage or access was nonetheless permitted to facilitate the transmission of electronic communications or if it was necessary, in order to provide an information society service explicitly requested by the subscriber or user (Article 5.3 of directive 2002/58/EC)[225]. In this respect, the user of cookies or web beacons – e.g. a SNS provider – can comply with its duties at once and for their future use during the user's next connections (Recital 25 of directive 2002/58/EC).

Since the recent modification of directive 2002/58/EC, for the use of cookies in the context of the processing of personal data to be permitted, the user (or subscriber) has henceforth to give his or her "consent" as defined according to directive 95/46/EC (Article 2, al. 2, f) of directive 2002/58/EC). The old opt-out[226] process becomes on opt-in one. In other words, the use of cookies requires what was previously named a qualified consent. However, the French version of Directive 2009/136/EC modifying Directive 2002/58/EC requires that the user or the subscriber has given his or her "*accord*" –not defined by these directives – in place of "*consentement*" – referring to Directive 95/46/EC. The use of the word "*accord*" is most probably a simple formal mistake.

But the study of the legislative history of the Directive 2009/136/EC and the policy that could be behind recital 25 of Directive 2002/58/EC could show that it would not be the case. On the one hand, in his first lecture, the European Parliament proposed to modify Article 5.3 in such a way that the prior consent of the user or the subscriber would be first and foremost required to use cookies, "taking into account that *browser settings constitute prior consent*", and that then, this user or subscriber was offered "the right to refuse such processing by the data controller" (Article 2.5 of European Parliament legislative resolution, 2008) (emphasis added by author). This would mean that, following the European Parliament, defining the browser settings – or letting the default rules play – constitutes a "qualified" consent under directive 95/46/EC despite what has been noted about the widespread browsers[227] – lobbyism[228]? For the record, the Working Party 29 (WP171, 2010, pp. 13-15) recently considered that browser settings generally do not raise to the expression of valid consent[229]. And it declared itself in favor of a prior opt in consent mechanism (WP171, 2010, pp. 16-17). However that may be, this amendment has been rejected by the Commission that was then followed by the common position of the Council.

On the other hand, the consent required as regards cookies does not seem to have to be "as free" as the "qualified" consent, since recital 25 of directive 2002/58/EC, *in fine*, reads as follows: "Access to specific website content may still be made conditional on the well-informed acceptance of a cookie or similar device, if it is used for a legitimate purpose." Admittedly, directive 95/46/EC does not necessarily forbid a website provider – e.g. an SNS provider – to make the

access to his service depending on the consent of the web surfer to the processing of personal data related to him[230], basing his processing operation on such consent.

Anyway, if one of the objectives of the Commission was to "[ensure] a high level of protection of consumers' and users' rights, including the right to privacy and data protection in electronic communications", to "[enhance] the protection of individuals' privacy and personal data in the electronic communications sector, in particular through strengthened security-related provisions" (COM/2007/0698 final, no. 1), and if the Parliament wanted "[s]trengthened provisions on protection against spyware and placing of cookies on users' devices"(COM/2009/0421 final, no. 3.1), having regard to the actual state of the art concerning basic and widespread browsers, the simple settings of such a browser cannot constitute the "assent" or "*accord*" needed by the data controller to use cookies or other tracking web beacons[231].

To sum up, if an SNS provider chooses to use cookies, he can only act under the control of the user's qualified consent he has to obtain before the placement of the cookie (e.g. by checking a specific box authorizing this processing). Except if he uses cookies for a purely technical purpose.

WHICH LAW AND WHICH JUDGE ARE IN CONTROL?

Given the differences identified above, between American and European rules related to privacy, data protection, confidentiality of electronic communications and hacking, it is interesting to discuss, admittedly briefly and without any in depth analysis, the question of the applicable law (prescriptive jurisdiction). As a premise, the question of the competent judge (adjudicative jurisdiction) has to be sketched. Without any doubt, these concerns need further assessment. They are only evoked from the European – if required, Belgian – perspective.

First and foremost, it has to be noted that a contractual choice of law made by the SNS provider – California law being often chosen[232] –, and of a jurisdiction – California jurisdiction as regards Facebook – is probable. In this respect, the SNS provider does not necessarily pursue the goal of avoiding the user's empowerment to control what happens. Although excessive limitations on liability clauses are a clue of the contrary... For instance, California law, in the United States, is one of the most developed as regards privacy[233]: "California [...] has the most comprehensive approach to data protection", and "[a]s a result of a series of important judicial opinions, California has the strongest constitutional scheme of data protection in the United States" (Schwartz & Reidenberg, 1996, pp. 132 and 135). To choose Californian jurisdictions is therefore not to try to avoid privacy. Although it has been noticed that privacy and data protection suffer significant limitations in the United States in general. However that may be, European law limits the autonomy of the parties as regards conflict of laws, for instance when consumers – concerning applicable law and jurisdiction[234] – or distance contracts – concerning applicable law[235] – are at stake. The rest of the purpose takes as a premise that there is no choice of law and no choice of judge.

If a user of the SNS suffers harm due to the violation of data protection or privacy rules, the extra-contractual liability of SNSes providers – need be, other users – could be staked. The "courts for the place where the harmful event occurred or may occur" would then have jurisdiction (Article 5.3 of regulation 44/2001/EC). However as regards applicable law, data protection and privacy have their own legal regimes. Courts of a Member State should normally apply the data protection rules of this State if the data controller is therein established, and if the processing operation occurs in the context of the activities of this establishment. Or, if the data controller, not established within the territory of the European Union, uses equipment[236] on the territory of this Member State, to the purpose of the processing operation at stake. Admittedly, the debate is here simplified[237].

According to Belgian private international law[238], the obligation resulting from a threat to privacy would be governed by the law of the State where the harmful behavior took place *or* where the harm occurred or *may occur*, unless that the person responsible demonstrate that she could not foreseen that the harm would occur in this State (Article 99, §2, 1 of the Belgian Private International Law Code). When a Belgian user of an SNS is at stake, it is reasonable to foresee that the harm he could suffer through the SNS can occur in Belgium, where he usually lives.

In addition, Article 8 ECHR could influence conflict of laws, *in concreto*, in a particular case. Indeed, insomuch as a foreign law would be to apply according to the national conflicts of law rules of a Court, the judge could have to discard the application of this foreign law – e.g. via a public order exception – if such an application thereof would create a situation conflicting with Article 8 ECHR, in the particular matter brought before him[239]. For the record, Article 8 ECHR includes, to some extent – but which precisely? –, data protection rules. In this respect, it still has to be determined when Article 8 ECHR could have to prevail over a foreign law in international cases. That is to say: which link with the territories of the contracting States would have to be satisfied as regards Internet in general, and which rights – if not all – enshrined in Article 8 ECHR cannot be tempered by the international characteristics of the situation at stake.

Concerning contracts concluded by consumers and contractual litigations, the Courts of the State where the SNS user is domiciled could have jurisdiction in cases where the SNS provider *directs its activities* notably *to* that Member State (Article 15 of regulation 44/2001/EC). And then even if there is a choice of law provision in the contract at stake, the consumer could not be deprived "of the protection afforded to him by provisions that cannot be derogated from by agreement by virtue of the law" of the concerned Member State. Given that absent this choice of law, the whole law of this Member State would apply (Article 6 of regulation 593/2008/EC)[240]. Facebook, for instance, indisputably directs its activities to the UK, to France, Belgium, etc., in general, to the territory of the European Community[241], just as Hi5 precisely targeted international markets (OPCC, 2009, p. 15). Another example could be the website "Chatroulette" that began locally and is now worldwide used and, most probably, targeted[242]. To the contrary, MySpace originally excluded users located outside the United States, screening them by means of their IP addresses (OPCC, 2009, p. 15).

Still as regards consumer protection, directive 93/13/EC forbids unfair terms in consumer contracts notwithstanding a choice of law electing a foreign State law if the contract has a close connection with the territory of the Member States[243]. Which should be the case, for instance, when a user of an SNS has its habitual residence in a Member State, usually uses the SNS on its personal computer located in this Member State – the SNS being put on its market –, when cookies are placed on his personal computer and when this user is a data subject whose personal data are processed after transborder data flows from the Community territory.

Concerning Belgian criminal law, the adjudicative and prescriptive jurisdictions depend, as a rule, on the place where the offence has been committed. Criminal law is territorial, although it could exceptionally be extraterritorial[244]. To apply Belgian law and bring a criminal case before a Belgian court, it suffices that one of the constitutive elements of the offence occurred, in whole or in part, in Belgium (Kuty, 2009, p. 365). Which refers to the "subjective and objective territorial principles" (Hayashi, 2006, p. 286). Hacking can be taken as an example. In a case admittedly limited to the Belgian territory, a Court of first instance (OM v. P.K., 2008) find itself competent while the

responsible of the hacking realized his unlawful behavior from its domicile, in a place were this Court was not competent. An unlawful access to an MSN account was notably at stake, and the Court decided that the victim, who was domiciled in the area of its jurisdiction, could bring her case before it. It was the Court of the place where the victim couldn't access her Hotmail account.

As regards the confidentiality of electronic communications, the Belgian LEC could apply to the unlawful use of cookies by SNSes providers who could be sued in Belgium. In such case, the acquaint of the communications at stake happens through the cookies located on the computer terminal of the concerned individual, thus, as the case may be, in Belgium. Given that the LEC does not define its territorial scope[245], the general above mentioned rule of Belgian criminal law should apply to determine the applicable law (Article 100 CP). Concerning the adjudicative jurisdiction, a criminal prosecution would occur according to the same rules of criminal law. And a civil claim for damages could be introduced before the "courts for the place where the harmful event occurred or may occur" (Article 5.3 of regulation 44/2001/EC), or before the court seized for the criminal prosecution (to the extent that that court has jurisdiction under its own law to entertain civil proceedings) (Article 5.4 of regulation 44/2001/EC)[246].

Finally without going into details, even European competition law could apply to SNS providers established outside the territory of the Community according to the effects doctrine. This doctrine has been applied in the United States and, in some extent, in European competition law[247]. In this respect, the global character of the market at stake will be particularly relevant in the analysis. For the record, European competition law has been evoked in the context of SNSes notably as regards the potential refusal of an SNS provider to access his platform of application. And it has been asked if providing a SNS free of charge in exchange of targeted advertising could not constitute a predatory pricing practice.

Now, which conclusion taking out of this brief outline of private international law? A kind of convergence arises as regards the possible applicability of European – Belgian – law as regards many legal concerns – consumer protection, privacy, hacking, confidentiality of electronic communications, competition – to a same SNS provider who would be established outside the territory of the European Union. Aside from data protection, that seems to follow an own regime leading to another conclusion. Put aside the Facebook's offices established in Europe[248] – given that their activities could be deemed distinct from those of Facebook, Inc. in California –, as Facebook Inc. processes personal data, it is a data controller established in the United States. A complicated and questionable interpretation of data protection rules seemed required to subject Facebook to the integrality of European data protection law – i.e. not only the transborder data flows regime[249]. Now, the discussion is probably more straightforward. Indeed, the clause 18.1 of the last version of the Statement of Rights and Responsibilities (October 4, 2010) specifies that "[i]f you are a resident of or have your principal place of business in the US or Canada, this Statement is an agreement between you and Facebook, Inc. Otherwise, this Statement is an agreement between you and *Facebook Ireland Limited*" (emphasis added by author). But the question remains subjected to the determination of the activities of the Irish office of Facebook.

Anyway, put aside the clause and the role of the Irish company, a Facebook-like SNS presents a lot of connections with the European Union as it was shown. Wouldn't it be useful to think again conflicts of law rules as regards data protection in this context, giving these rules, if it were deemed opportune – and we think it is – another territoriality[250]? Data protection could take profit of rapprochement with consumer contracts conflicts of law rules. After all, a software as a service is offered to European web surfers – final consumers –, free of charge hearing that their personal data can be used by the SNS provider. The criteria of applicability of data protection rules could take into account the data protection obligations at stake, the habitual residence of the individual concerned, the fact that the service provider directs its activities to the territory of the European Union, the fact that the Foreign State where the data controller is established only ensures an adequate protection[251] – or no adequate protection –, the place of establishment of this data controller, etc. Given that the localization of the equipments could not be relevant in the context of SNSes[252]. Article 4 of directive 95/46/EC has to be improved[253] to ensure better legal certainty. And the previous considerations should matter to this end.

As the case may be, the territoriality of the data protection rules could vary depending on what they impose to the data controllers or, *if an evolution of the is this sense is desirable and happens*, depending on the fact that they impose duties to the data controller *or to "data processors"* (SNS providers and, more generally, cloud computing service providers). Of course, in this respect, the question would be to determine if it is desirable and useful, or even required, to impose specific duties to cloud computing service providers when they are not data controllers. These rules could be useful, for instance, when the user of the service falls outside of the scope of Directive 95/46/EC (e.g. domestic use exemption) but nonetheless process personal data.

However that may be, nowadays, the international character of SNS and more generally cloud computing and Internet services requires an international discussion[254], at the end of which, on the one hand, data subject's rights must not be sacrificed to the profit of emergent technologies and on the other hand, this emergence must not be suffocated to death due to an unrealistic and unworkable conception of data protection.

CONCLUSION

In the context of cloud based SNSes, users claim more control over personal information. In fact, users lose some control. Principally, on the one hand, as regards the creation of personal data related to them and, on the other hand, concerning their spread and secondary use. It has been shown clearly that European and American law empower them, to a certain extent, to recover ownership over such data. Even if these laws differ and are not easy to apply to the SNSes environment.

Privacy, defined as "information self-determination" in European law, and as "contextual integrity" or "informational privacy" in the United States constitutes a first users' mean of control over information related to them. However, we noted that American privacy suffers weaknesses in SNSes due to its subordination to reasonable expectation of privacy. Admittedly, from a theoretical point of view, the interpretation of this requirement can evolve and compensate for the present weaknesses. Anyway, it has been suggested that contracts between users could help to solve the problem. European privacy is generally not subordinated to reasonable expectation of privacy. At the present time, European and American law diverge. But American law offers a conceptual framework permitting an evolution that would make both laws closer.

European privacy is "horizontalized" through data protection rules. While, at the present time, American law does not offer a general data protection framework. As regards European law, the purpose firstly brought into focus the interconnections between contract law and the qualified consent of the data subject. In this respect, it underlined that when using SNSes, the consent of users often does not satisfy the conditions required by data protection rule. Yet, SNSes providers usually rely on such consent. Even if no general conclusion can be proposed, users generally lack information as regards the processing of personal data.

Their consents usually are not specific and only implied by the global assent to terms and conditions. And, finally, they are not often free insofar as the SNSes market is characterized by strong network effects – even if the market is dynamic –, and as they have no other choice that consenting to subsequent modifications of the service and the relevant terms if they want to remain on the social network. As far as the American Safe Harbor Principles are concerned, these do not require such a qualified consent. We also noted that the European individuals' right of access gives user a powerful mean to follow the spread of personal data and, as the case may be, stamp it out. While the right of access enshrined in the Safe Harbor Principles depends on the American privacy conception.

The confidentiality of electronic communications and the prohibition of hacking have been identified as two other means to control information. Concerning both these sets of rules, American law and European law are still different to some extent. For instance, the confidentiality of electronic communications is protected by a two-party consent rule in Europe. While in the United States, a one-party consent rule is established. And concerning hacking, both laws diverge concerning the *mens rea* required for internal hacking. Both laws also suffer interpretation concerns. As regards the confidentiality of electronic communications, it revealed difficult to identify which "actors" are concerned and which communications are protected. An interpretation ensuring users the protection of numerous communications occurring, on the one hand, between them and the SNS provider and, on the other hand, between themselves through the Internet and the network of the SNS provider himself has been suggested. Anyway, law appears difficult to apply in the SNSes context. As regards hacking, things seem less complicated at first sight. But they become more difficult when it has to be decided if the breach of a contract (terms of use) can lead to hacking. It has been concluded that it should not be the case, even if, as regards application platform interfaces, it could be argued to the contrary.

The discrepancies between American and European laws lead us to a brief discussion related to adjudicative and prescriptive jurisdictions rules. These latter should bring legal certainty where SNSes involve inevitably and permanently both regulatory framework. The supply of popular SNSes comes from the United States (Facebook, LinkedIn, Twitter, etc.), and a significant part of the demand lies in Europe. We pointed out that European – as the case may be, Belgian – consumer protection law, privacy law, criminal law and competition law could apply to American based SNSes providers such as Facebook, when European judges are competent to give a ruling on a case. However, this is less evident as regards data protection rules whose territoriality could be thought again depending on the services at stake.

In any case, our purpose was not to eclipse the individual's responsibility. As B. Kane and B.T. Delange (2009, p. 345) wrote: "the ultimate guardian of privacy is the individual." The SNS user lies amongst the first people accountable of what becomes of personal data related to him. Nonetheless, when he is urged to get into a storm cloud where he thinks he is on cloud nine, he can then fall again on the grim reality, lacking control; in the "SNS-cloud", not everybody is a weather forecaster. Then, the legal means we presented come on stage.

NOTE

Jean-Philippe Moiny is a Research fellow FRS-FNRS in the *Research Centre on IT and Law (CRID) at the University of Namur, Belgium.*

REFERENCES

Ackermann, T. G. (2009). Consent and discovery under the Stored Communications Act. *The Federal Lawyer, 200,* 43–46.

Ahlborn, C., Evans, D. S., & Padilla, A. J. (2001). Competition policy in the new economy: Is European competition law up to the challenge?. *European Competition Law Review, 22.*

Antitrust Modernization Commission. (April, 2007). *Report and recommendations.* Retrieved on January 30, 2010, from http: //govinfo.library. unt. edu/amc/

Austrian Regulatory Authority for Broadcasting and Telecommunications. (April, 2005). *Guidelines for VoIP service providers.* Consultation Document. Retrieved on January 30, 2010, from http: //www.eadp. org/main7/position / VoIP_Guidelines_2005 _AUSTRIA.pdf.

Berman, G. A. (2006). *The constitution, international treaties, and contracts.* In Convergence in legal systems in the 21st century, General Reports delivered at the XVIth International Congress of Comparative Law, Brisbane, 2002. Brussels, Belgium: Bruylant.

Boyd, D. M., & Ellison, N. B. (October, 2007). *Social network sites: Definition, history, and scholarship.* Retrieved January 30, 2010, from http://www.danah.org/papers/

Bucklin, R. E., & Sismeiro, C. (2008). *Click here for Internet insight: Advances in clickstream data analysis in marketing.* Retrieved on January 30, 2010, from http://www.ssrn.com

Buya, R., Yeo, C. S., & Venugopal, S. (2008). *Market-oriented cloud computing: Vision, hype, and reality for delivering IT services as computing utilities.* Retrieved on January 30, 2010, from http://arxiv.org/pdf/0808.3558

Byrnside, I. (2008). Six clicks of separation: The legal ramifications of employers using social networking sites to research applicants. *Vanderbilt Journal of Entertainment and Technology Law, 10.*

Ciocchetti, C. A. (2007). E-commerce and information privacy: Privacy policies as personal information protectors. *American Business Law Journal*, 44.

Clayton, R., & Tomlinson, H. (2001). *The law of human rights*. Oxford, United Kingdom: Oxford University Press.

Cohen, J. E. (2000). Cyberspace and privacy: A new legal paradigm? *Stanford Law Review*, 52.

Computer Crime and Intellectual Property Section. Criminal Division, & Eltringham, S. (principal ed.), (2007). *Prosecuting computer crimes*. United States of America: Office of Legal Education, Executive Office For United States Attorneys. Retrieved on January 30, 2010, from http: // www.justice. gov/criminal/ cybercrime/ccmanual/ccmanual.pdf

Couillard, D. A. (2009). Defogging the cloud: Applying fourth amendment principles to evolving privacy expectations in cloud computing. *Minnesota Law Review*, 93.

Csonka, P. (2006). The council of Europe's convention on cyber-crime and other European initiatives. *International Review of Penal Law, 77*, 3–4.

Dalsen, W. (2009). Civil remedies for invasions of privacy: A perspective on software vendors and intrusion upon seclusion. *Wisconsin Law Review*, 1059–1091.

de Corte, R. (2000). E-mails taboe voor de werkgever of niet. *Juristenkrant, 7.*

De Hert, P. (2001). Internetrechten in het bedrijf. Controle op e-mail en Internetgebruik in Belgisch en Europees perspectief. *Auteurs & Média,* 1.

De Hert, P., & Gutwirth, S. (2006). Privacy, data protection and law enforcement. Opacity of the individual and transparency of power. In Claes, E., Duff, A., & Gutwirth, S. (Eds.), *Privacy and the criminal law. Antwerpen, Belgium & Oxford.* United Kingdom: Intersentia.

De Hert, P., de Vries, K., & Gutwirth, S. (2009). Note d'observation sous Cour constitutionnelle fédérale allemande, 27 February 2008. *Revue du Droit des Technologies de l'Information, 34.*

Denham, E. (Assistant Privacy Commissioner of Canada). (July 16, 2009). *Report of findings into the complaint filed by the Canadian Internet Policy and Public Interest Clinic (CIPPIC) against Facebook Inc. under the Personal Information Protection and Electronic Documents Act*. Retrieved on January 30, 2010, from http: //www. priv.gc. ca/cf-dc/2009/ 2009_008_0716_e.pdf

De Schutter, O. (2005). La renonciation aux droits fondamentaux, La libre disposition du soi et la règne de l'échange. In Dumont, H., Ost, F., & Van Drooghenbroeck, S. (Eds.), *La responsabilité, face cachée des droits de l'homme*. Brussels, Belgium: Bruylant.

de Terwangne, C., Herveg, J., & Van Gyseghem, J.-M. (2005). *Le divorce et les technologies de l'information et de la communication. Introduction à la protection des données dans la preuve des causes de divorce*. Brussels, Belgium: Kluwer.

de Villenfagne, F., & Dusollier, S. (2001). La Belgique sort enfin ses armes contre la cybercriminalité: à propos de la loi du 28 novembre 2000 sur la criminalité informatique. *Auteurs & Média, 1.*

Dhont, J., & Pérez Asinari, M. V. (2003). New physics and the law. A comparative approach to the EU and US privacy and data protection regulation. In *Usage of methodology in European law*. Namur, Belgium: Presses Universitaires de Namur.

Dhont, J., & Rosier, K. (2003). Directive vie privée et communications électroniques: Premiers commentaries. *Revue Ubiquité – Droit des technologies de l'information, 15.*

Dickson, B. (1999). The horizontal application of human rights law. In Hegarty, A., & Leonard, S. (Eds.), *Human rights, an agenda for the 21st century.* London, United Kingdom & Sydney, Australia: Cavendish Publishing.

Dinant, J.-M. (2000). Les traitements invisibles sur Internet. In Montero, E. (Ed.), *Droit des technologies de l'information, Regards prosepctifs: à l'occasion des vingt ans du C.R.I.D. Cahiers du C.R.I.D. Brussels.* Belgium: Bruylant.

Docquir, B. (2008). *Le droit de la vie privée.* Brussels, Belgium: Larcier.

Dreier, T. (2010). Opt in and opt out mechanisms in the Internet era – Towards a common theory. *Computer Law and Security Review, 26.*

Dumortier, F. (2009). *Facebook and risks of decontextualization of information.* Retrieved on January 2010, from http://works.bepress.com/franck_dumortier/1

Dunne, R. (2009). *Computers and the law, an introduction to basic legal principles and their application in cyberspace.* Cambridge, United Kingdom: Cambridge University Press.

Economic and Social Committee. (2000). *Opinion on the proposal for a directive of the European Parliament and of the Council on a common regulatory frame work for electronic communications networks and services.* COM(2000) 393 final – 2000/0184 COD.

Edwards, L. (2009). Consumer privacy law: Online direct marketing. In Edwards, L., & Waelde, C. (Eds.), *Law and the Internet.* Oxford, United Kingdom & Portland, OR: Hart.

Eisenmann, T., Parker, G., & Van Alstyne, M. (July 30, 2009). *Platform envelopment.* Retrieved on January 30, 2010, from http://www.ssrn.com

European Commission. (1997). Commission notice on the definition of relevant market for the purposes of community competition law. *Official Journal, C, 372.*

European Commission. (1998). Communication, status of voice communications on Internet under community law and, in particular, pursuant to directive 90/388/EEC. *Official Journal, C, 6.*

European Commission. (2000). *Proposal for a Directive of the European Parliament and of the Council on a common regulatory framework for electronic communications networks and services.* Explanatory memorandum. COM/2000/0393 final - COD 2000/0184.

European Commission staff working document. (June 14, 2004). *The treatment of Voice over Internet Protocol (VoIP) under the EU Regulatory Framework* (information and consultation document). Retrieved on January 30, 2010, from http://ec.europa.eu/information_society/policy/ecomm/doc/library/working_docs/406_14_voip_consult_paper_v2_1.pdf

European Commission. DG Competition. (December, 2005). *DG Competition discussion paper on the application of Article 82 of the Treaty to exclusionary abuses.* Retrieved on January 30, 2010, from http://ec.europa.eu/competition/antitrust/art82/discpaper2005.pdf

European Network and Information Security Agency, & Hogben, G. (Ed.). (October, 2007). *Position paper no. 1 - Security issues and recommendations for online social networks.* Retrieved on January 30, 2010, from http://www.enisa.europa.eu

European Network and Information Security Agency. Catteddu, D., & Hogben, G. (Eds.). (November, 2009). Cloud computing, benefits, risks and recommendations for information security. Retrieved on February 20, 2010, from http: //www.enisa.europa. eu/act/rm/files/deliverables/cloud-computing-risk-assessment

European Regulators Group. (December, 2007). *ERG common position on VoIP.* Retrieved on January 30, 2010, from http: //www.irg. eu/streaming/erg_07_56rev2_cp_ voip_final.pdf?contentId=543022&field=ATTACHED_FILE

Evans, D. S. (2008). Antitrust issues raised by the emerging global internet economy. *Northwestern University Law Review*, 102.

Gardbaum, S. (2003). The horizontal effect of constitutional rights. *Michigan Law Review*, 102.

Gardbaum, S. (2006). Where the (state) action is, a review essay on the Constitution in private relations: Expanding Constitutionalism. In Sajó, A., & Uitz, R. (Eds.), *International Journal of Constitutional Law, 4.* Eleven International Publishing.

Garrie, D. B., Armstrong, M. J., & Harris, D. P. (2005). Voice over Internet Protocol and the Wiretap Act: Is your conversation protected? *Seattle University Law Review*, 29.

Garrie, D. B., & Wong, R. (2006). Demystifying clickstream data: A European and U.S. perspective. *Emory International Law Review*, 20.

Garrie, D. B., & Wong, R. (2009). Privacy in electronic communications: The regulation of VoIP in the EU and the United States. *Computer Telecommunications Law Review, 6.*

Gindin, S. E. (2009). Nobody reads your privacy policy or online contract? Lessons learned and questions raised by the FTC's action against Sears. *Northwestern Journal of Technology and Intellectual Property, 8.*

Grimmelmann, J. (2009). Saving Facebook. *Iowa Law Review*, 94.

Hammje, P. (1997). Droits fondamentaux et ordre public. *Revue Critique de Droit International Privé,* 1.

Hayashi, M. (2006). Objective territorial principle or effects doctrine? Jurisdiction and cyberspace. *In Law,* 6.

Herveg, J., & Gayrel, C. (2009). Décisions de la Cour européenne des droits de l'homme relative à l'article 8 de la Convention européenne des droits de l'homme. In de Terwangne, C., & Dussollier, S. (Eds.), *Chronique de jurisprudence en droit des technologies de l'information (2002-2008), Revue du Droit des Technologies de l'Information, 35.* Brussels, Belgium: Larcier.

Hillman, R. A., & Rachlinski, J. J. (2001). *Standard-form contracting in the electronic age.* Retrieved on January 30, 2010, from http://www/ssrn.com

International Working Group on Data Protection in Telecommunications (Berlin Working Group). (March 4, 2008). Report and guidance on privacy in social network services. Rome Memorandum. Retrieved January 30, 2010, from www. datenschutz-berlin.de

Jefferey, K., & Neidecker-Lutz, B. (Eds.). (2010). *The future of cloud computing, opportunities for European cloud computing beyond 2010.* Report written for the European Commission, Information Society and Media, public version 1.0. Retrieved on February 10, 2010, from http://cordis.europa.eu/fp7/ict/ssai/docs/cloud-report-final.pdf

Joint, A., Baker, E., & Eccles, E. (2009). Hey, you, get off of that cloud? *Computer Law & Security Review, 25.*

Jones, A., & Sufrin, B. (2008). *EC competition law.* Oxford, United Kingdom: Oxford University Press.

Kane, B., & Delange, B. T. (2009). A tale of two Internets: Web 2.0 slices, dices, and is privacy resistant. *Idaho Law Review, 45*, 2009.

Kang, J. (1998). Information privacy in cyberspace transactions. *Stanford Law Review*, 50.

Kang, J., & Buchner, B. (2004). Privacy in Atlantis. *Harvard Journal of Law & Technology*, 18.

Katz, M. L., & Shapiro, C. (1994). Systems competition and network effects. Retrieved on January 30, 2010, from http://www.utdallas.edu/~liebowit/knowledge_goods/k&sjel94/jel94.html.

Kéfer, F., & Cornelis, S. (2009). L'arrêt *Copland* ou l'espérance légitime du travailleur quant au caractère privé de ses communications. *Revue Trimestrielle des Droits de l'Homme, 79.*

Kerr, O. S. (2004). A user's guide to the Stored Communications Act, and a legislator's guide to amending it. *The George Washington Law Review, 72.*

Kerr, O. S. (2010). (forthcoming). Vagueness challenges to the Computer Fraud and Abuse Act. [from http://www.ssrn.com]. *Minnesota Law Review*. Retrieved on March 20, 2010.

Keustermans, J., & Mols, F. (2001-2002). De wet van 28 november 2000 inzake informaticacriminaliteit: een eerste overzicht. *Rechtskundig Weekblad, 21.*

Killingsworth, S. (1999). Minding your own business: Privacy policies in principle and in practice. *Journal of Intellectual Property Law, 7.*

King, N. J. (2008). Fundamental human right principle inspires U.S. data privacy law, but protections are less than fundamental. In Pérez Asinari, M. V., & Palazzi, P. (Eds.), *Défis du droit à la protection de la vie privée: perspectives du droit européen et nord-américain. Cahiers du C.R.I.D. (no. 31).* Brussels, Belgium: Bruylant.

Korff, D., Brown, I., et al. (2010). *Comparative study on different approaches to new privacy challenges, in particular in the light of technological developments.* Final report delivered in the framework of contract JLS/2008/C4/011, European Commission, Directorate-General Justice, Freedom and Security, 20 January 2010. Retrieved on September 15, 2010, from http: // ec.europa. eu/justice/policies/ privacy/docs/studies/ new_privacy_challenges/ final_report_en.pdf

Kuner, C. (2010). Data protection law and international jurisdiction on the Internet (Part 1 & 2). *International Journal of Law and Information Technology, 2 & 3.*

Kuty, F. (2009). Principes généraux du droit pénal belge: *Vol. I. La loi pénale.* Brussels, Belgium: De Boeck & Larcier.

Labrusse, C. (1974). Droit constitutionnel et droit international privé en Allemagne fédérale. *Revue Critique de Droit International Privé*, 1-46.

Lambert, P. (1999). Bescherming van prive-(tele) communicatie. In J. Dumortier (Ed.), *Recente ontwikkelingen in informatica- en telecommunicatierecht.* Brugge, Belgium: die Keure.

Leberton, G. (2009). *Libertés publiques et droits de l'Homme.* Paris, France: Dalloz.

Le Métayer, D., & Monteleone, S. (2009). Automated consent through privacy agents: Legal requirements and technical architecture. *Computer Law & Security Review, 25.*

Léonard, T. (2001). *E-commerce* et protection des données à caractère personnel, quelques considérations sur la licéité des pratiques nouvelles de *marketing* sur *internet*. In Byttebier, K., Feltkamp, R., & Janssens, E. (Eds.), *Internet en Recht*. Antwerpen, Belgium: Maklu.

Levin, A., & Sánchez Abril, P. (2009). Two notions of privacy online. *Vanderbilt J. of Ent. And Tech. Law, 11*, 1017.

Levinet, L. (2008). *Théorie générale des droits et libertés*. Brussels, Belgium: Bruylant, Nemesis.

Lind, R. C., & Muysert, P. (2003). Innovation and competition policy: Challenges for the new millennium. *European Competition Law Review, 24.*

Lobe, B., & Staksrud, E. (Eds.). (2010). *Evaluation of the implementation of the safer social networking principles for the EU part ii: testing of 20 providers of social networking service in Europe*. Report written for the European Commission under the Safer Internet Programme. Luxembourg, January 2010, (p. 24). Retrieved January 30, 2010, from http: //ec.europa. eu/information_society/ activities/social_networking/ eu_action/implementation_princip/index_en.htm

Louveaux, S., & Pérez Asinari, M. V. (2008). Introduction. Directive 2002/58: The Need of Specific Legislation. In Pérez Asinari, M. V., & Palazzi, P. (Eds.), *Défis du droit à la protection de la vie privée: perspectives du droit européen et nord-américain. Cahiers du C.R.I.D. (no. 31)*. Brussels, Belgium: Bruylant.

Madrid Resolution. (November 5, 2009). *Joint proposal for a draft of international standards on the protection of privacy with regard to the processing of personal data*. 31st International Conference of Data Protection and Privacy Commissioners. Retrieved on October 15, 2010, from http: //www.privacyconference2009. org/ media/Publicaciones/common/ estandares_resolucion_madrid_en.pdf

Manny, C. H. (2003). Personal privacy-transatlantic perspectives, European and American privacy: commerce, rights and justice – part 1. *Computer Law & Security Report*, 19.

Mantouvalou, V. (2008). Human rights and unfair dismissal: Private acts in public spaces. *The Modern Law Review*, 71.

Mayer, P. (1991). La Convention européenne des droits de l'homme et l'application des normes étrangères. *Revue Critique de Droit International Privé, 4.*

Mercado Kierkegaard, S. (2005). Lobbyism and the opt in/opt out cookie controversy: How the cookies (almost) crumbled: Privacy & lobbyism. *Computer Law & Security Report*, 21.

Meron, T. (April 26, 2000). *The implications of the European Convention on Human Rights for the development of public international law*. Ad Hoc Committee of Legal Advisers on the International Public Law (CAHDI). Retrieved on January 30, 2010, from https: //wcd.coe.int/ ViewDoc.jsp?id=348429 &Site=COE&BackC olorInternet=DBDCF2 &BackColorIntranet= FDC864&BackColorLogged=FDC864

Moine, I. (1997). *Les choses hors commerce: Une approche de la personne humaine juridique*. Paris, France: Librairie Génrale de Droit et de Jurisprudence.

Moiny, J.-P., & De Groote, B. (2009). Cyberconsommation et droit international privé. *Revue du Droit des Technologies de l'Information, 37.*

Moiny, J. P. (2010). Facebook au regard des règles européennes de protection des données. *European Journal of Consumer Law, 2.*

Moiny, J.-P. (2010/1). Contracter dans les réseaux sociaux: Un geste inadéquat pour contracter sa vie privée. *Revue de la Faculté de Droit de l'Université de Liège, 2.*

Moreno, O., & Van Koekenbeek, S. (2008). Les enjeux de la vie privée au travail et sa dynamique dans l'entreprise. In Docquir, B., & Puttemans, A. (Eds.), *Actualités du droit de la vie privée*. Brussels, Belgium: Bruylant.

National Institute of Standards and Technology. Information Technology Laboratory, Mell, P., & Grance, T. (July 10, 2009). *The NIST definition of cloud computing*, version 15. Retrieved on February 10, 2010, from http: //csrc.nist. gov/ groups/SNS/ cloud-computing/

Nissenbaum, H. (2004). Privacy as contextual integrity. *Washington Law Review (Seattle, Wash.)*, 79.

Nowak, M. (2003). *Introduction to the international human rights regime*. Leiden, The Netherlands & Boston, MA: Martinus Nijhoff.

Office of Privacy Commissionner of Canada, & Barrigar, J. (February, 2009). *Social network site privacy: A comparative analysis of six sites*. Retrieved on January 30, 2010, from http: //www.priv. gc. ca/information/pub/sub_comp_200901_e.pdf

Phillipson, G. (1999). The Human Rights Act, horizontal effect and the common law: A bang or a whimper. *The Modern Law Review*, 62.

Polański, P. P. (2007). *Customary law of the Internet: In the search for a supranational cyberspace law*. La Haye, The Netherlands: T.M.C. Asser Press.

Posner, R. A. (November, 2000). *Antitrust in the new economy*. Retrieved on January 30, 2010, from http://www.ssrn.com

Poullet, Y. (2008). Pour une troisième génération de réglementation de protection des données. In Pérez Asinari, M. V., & Palazzi, P. (Eds.), *Défis du droit à la protection de la vie privée: perspectives du droit européen et nord-américain. Cahiers du C.R.I.D. (no. 31)*. Brussels, Belgium: Bruylant.

Poullet, Y., & Rouvroy, A. (2009). Le droit à l'autodétermination informationnelle et la valeur du développement personnel. Une réévaluation de l'importance de la vie privée pour la démocratie. In *Etat de droit et virtualité*. Montréal, Canada: Thémis.

Poullet, Y., & Rouvroy, A.(2009/1). The right to informational self-determination and the value of self-development: Reassessing the importance of privacy for democracy. In Gutwirth, S., Poullet, Y., De Hert, P., de Terwangne, C., & Nouwt, S. (Eds.), *Reinventing data protection*. Springer Verlag.

Poullet, Y. (2010). About the e-privacy directive: Towards a third generation of data protection legislation. In Gutwirth, S., Poullet, Y., & de Hert, P. (Eds.), *Data protection in a profiled world*. Springer. doi:10.1007/978-90-481-8865-9_1

Purtova, N. (2009). Property rights in personal data: Learning from the American discourse. *Computer Law & Security Review, 25*.

Richards, N. M., & Solove, D. J. (2007). Privacy's other path: Recovering the law of confidentiality. *The Georgetown Law Journal*, 96.

Rigaux, F. (1980). La loi applicable à la protection des individus à l'égard du traitement automatisé des données à caractère personnel. *Revue Critique de Droit International Privé, 444-478*.

Rigaux, F. (1998). *La protection de la vie privée et des autres biens de la personnalité*. Brussels, Belgium: Bruylant.

Rosier, K. (2008). La directive 2002/58/CE vie privée et communications électroniques et la directive 95/46/CE relative au traitement des données à caractère personnel: comment les (ré)concilier? In Pérez Asinari, M. V., & Palazzi, P. (Eds.), *Défis du droit à la protection de la vie privée – Perspectives du droit européen et Nord-américain, coll. Cahiers du C.R.I.D. (no. 31)*. Brussels, Belgium: Bruylant.

Samuelson, P. (2000). Privacy as intellectual property? *Stanford Law Review*, 52.

Schwartz, P. M., & Reidenberg, J. R. (1996). *Data privacy law. United States of America*. Virginia: Michie.

Schwartz, P. M. (2004). Property, privacy, and personal data. *Harvard Law Review*, 117.

Scolnik, A. (2009). Protections for electronic communications: The Stored Communications Act and the Fourth Amendment. *Fordham Law Review*, 78.

Shin, D., & Lopes, R. (2009). *Enabling interoperable and selective data sharing among social networking sites*. In CollaborateCom 2008, The 4th International Conference on Collaborative Computing: Networking, Applications and Work-sharing. Springer.

Simmons, J. L. (2009). Buying you: The government's use of fourth-parties to launder data about the people. *Columbia Business Law Review, 3*.

Soghoian, C. (August, 2009). Caught in the cloud: Privacy, encryption, and government back doors in the Web 2.0 era. Retrieved on February 20, 2010, from www.ssrn.com

Solove, D. J. (2002). Conceptualizing privacy. *California Law Review*, 90.

Solove, D. J., & Hoofnagle, C. J. (2006). A model regime of privacy protection. *University of Illinois Law Review*, 2.

Sorosky, S. B. (2008). United States v. Forrester: An unwarranted narrowing of the fourth amendment. *Loyola of Los Angeles Law Review*, 41.

Sprague, R. (2008). Orwell was an optimist: The evolution of privacy in the United States and its de-evolution for American employees. *The John Marshall Law Review*, 42.

Spulber, D. F. (2008). Consumer coordination in the small and in the large: Implications for antitrust in markets with network effects. Retrieved on January 30, 2010, from http://www.ssrn.com

Strahilevitz, L. J. (December, 2004). *A social networks theory of privacy*. Retrieved on January 30, 2010, from http://www.ssrn.com

Sudre, F. (2008). *Droit Européen et international des droits de l'homme*. Paris, France: Presses Universitaires de France.

Sudre, F. (2009). *Les grands arrêts de la Cour européenne des Droits de l'homme*. Paris, France: Presses Universitaires de France.

Berkeley, U. C. School of Information, Gomez, J., Pinnick, T., & Soltani, A. (June 1st, 2009). *KnowPrivacy*. Retrieved January 30, 2010, from http://knowprivacy.org/

Vandermeersch, D. (1997). Le droit pénal et la procédure pénale confrontés à Internet (les apprentis surfeurs). In H. Bartholomeeusen, e.a. (Eds.), *Internet sous le regard du droit*. Brussels, Belgium: Editions du jeune barreau de Bruxelles.

van der Plancke, V., & Van Leuven, N. (2008). La privatization du respect de la convention européenne des droits de l'homme: faut-il reconnaître un effet horizontal generalisé? In *Entre ombres et lumières: cinquante ans d'application de la convention européenne des droits de l'homme en Belgique* (pp. x–x). Brussels, Belgium: Bruylant.

Van Linthout, P., & Kerkhofs, J. (2008). Internetrecherche: informaticatap en netwerkzoeking, licht aan het eind van de tunnel. *Tijdschrift voor Strafrecht, 2*.

Van Overstraeten, T., Bruyndonckx, B., Szafran, E., & Rousseau, S. (2005). Belgium finally adopted the Electronic Communications Act transposing the EU telecom Package. *Computer and Telecommunication Law Review, 11*.

Vaquero, L. M., Rodero Merino, L., Caceres, J., & Lindner, M. (2009). A break in the clouds: Towards a cloud definition. *Computer Communication Review*, 50. Retrieved on February 20, 2010, from http: //ccr.sigcomm. org/drupal/files/p50-v39n1l-vaqueroA.pdf

Veljanovski, C. (2001). E.C. antitrust in the new European economy: Is the European Commission's view of the network economy right?. *European Competition Law Review, 22.*

Volokh, E. (2000). Freedom of speech, information privacy, and the troubling implications of a right to stop people from speaking about you. *Stanford Law Review*, 52.

W3C. (2009). *Workshop on the Future of Social Networking*. Final report, Barcelona, 15-16 January 2009. Retrieved on January 15, 2010, from http: //www.w3. org/2008/09/ msnws/report.

Walden, I. (2007). Privacy and data protection. In Reed, C., & Angel, J. (Eds.), *Computer law, the law and regulation of Information Technology*. Oxford, United Kingdom: Oxford University Press.

Warren, S. D., & Brandeis, L. D. (1890). The right to privacy. *Harvard Law Review*, 4.

Wong, R. (October, 2008). *Social networking: Anybody is a data controller!* Retrieved on January 30, 2010, from http://papers.ssrn.com/

Working Party 29. (November 21, 2000). *Privacy on the Internet – An integrated EU approach to online data protection*. WP37. Retrieved on January 30, 2010, from http: //ec.europa. eu/justice/ policies/ privacy/workinggroup/ index_en.htm

Working Party 29. (November 25, 2005). *Opinion on the use of location data with a view to providing value-added services*. WP115. Retrieved on January 30, 2010, from http: //ec.europa. eu/justice/ policies/ privacy/workinggroup/ index_en.htm

Working Party 29. (April 4, 2008). *Opinion 1/2008 on data protection issues related to search engines*. WP148. Retrieved on January 30, 2010, from http: //ec.europa. eu/justice/policies/ privacy/ workinggroup /index_en.htm

Working Party 29. (June 12, 2009). *Opinion 5/2009 on online social networking*. WP163. Retrieved on January 30, 2010, from http: // ec.europa. eu/justice/policies/ privacy/working-group/ index_en.htm

Working Party 29. (December 1st, 2009). *The future of privacy*. Joint contribution to the Consultation of the European Commission on the legal framework for the fundamental right to protection of personal data. Retrieved on January 30, 2010, from http: //ec.europa. eu/justice/policies/ privacy/working-group /index_en.htm

Working Party 29. (February 16, 2010). *Opinion 1/2010 on the concepts of controller and processor*. WP169. Retrieved on May 20, 2010, from http: //ec.europa. eu/justice/policies/ privacy/ workinggroup /index_en.htm

Working Party 29. (June 22, 2010). *Opinion 2/2010 on online behavioural advertising*. WP171. Retrieved on September 3, 2010, from http: // ec.europa. eu/justice/policies/ privacy/docs/wp-docs/ 2010/wp171_en.pdf

Working Party 29. (December 16, 2010). *Opinion 8/2010 on applicable law*. WP179. Retrieved on January 5, 2010, from http: //ec.europa. eu/ justice/policies /privacy/docs/wpdocs/ 2010/ wp179_en.pdf.

Youseff, L., & Butrico Dilma Da Silva, M. (2009). *Toward a unified ontology of cloud computing*. Retrieved on February 20, 2010, from http: // www.cs.ucsb.edu/~lyouseff/CCOntology/ Cloud-Ontology.pdf

Zwaak, L. (2006). General survey of the European Convention. In P. van Dijk, F. van Hoof, A. van Rijn & L. Zwaak (Eds.), *Theory and practice of the European Convention on Human Rights*. Antwerpen, Belgium & Oxford, United Kingdom: Intersentia.

ENDNOTES

1   *See also* no. 105. This complaint has been supplemented, *see* EPIC v. Facebook 2 (2010).

2   *See also* Lobe & Staksrud, 2010, p. 24. Here Facebook's declaration to adhere to the Safer Social Networking Principles for the EU has been deemed partially compliant, notably with, principle 3 ("empower users through tools and technology"), and so are the measures implemented on the SNS as regards the self-declaration.

3   The present paper does not study conflicts that could exist between, on the one hand, privacy and data protection and, on the other hand, the freedom of expression or other fundamental rights or liberties.

4   As regards the analysis of consumer complaints, the *KnowPrivacy* study concludes that "[t]he biggest concern among the complaints we coded was the *lack of control*" (UCBSI, 2009, p. 32).

5   As regards the concepts of prescriptive and adjudicative jurisdictions, *see* Kuner, 2010, p. 185.

6   For a more complete definition, *see* Boyd & Ellison, 2007, p. 2. *See also* Working Party 29, WP163, pp. 4-5).

7   The purpose principally takes Facebook into consideration – and therefore, any "Facebook like" SNS –, sometimes approaching other SNSes. *See infra* for considerations related to the SNS market.

8   "Web 2.0 capitalizes on advances made in the ability to share information through the Internet" (Kane & Delange, 2009, p. 322).

9   As a rule, Facebook only hosts its own applications.

10   As regards common characteristics of SNS, *see* European Network and Information Security Agency [ENISA], 2007, p. 5.

11   About "cloud computing", *see* Buya, Yeo & Venugopal, 2008; Jefferey & Neidecker-Lutz, 2010, pp. 9-10; National Institute of Standards and Technology, 2009; ENISA, 2009, pp. 14-15; Soghoian, 2009, pp. 5-12; Vaquero, Rodero Merino, Caceres & Lindner, 2009, p. 50; Youssef & Butrico Dilma Da Silva, 2009.

12   *See e.g.* http://www.datacenterknowledge. com/archives/2009/04/17/a-look-inside-facebooks-data-center/, last visited on January 10, 2010.

13   These applications can be hosted on the servers of the developer of the application (or, of course, its subcontractor's servers). An application constitutes software as a service.

14   *See* Article 1, 2), a) Directive 98/48/EC, and Article 14 Directive 2000/31/EC. Later in the paper, the potential qualification of SNSes as electronic communication services, at least as regards some services, will shortly be discussed.

15   Whether they are directly remunerated or not by users, *see* Recital 18 Directive 2000/31/EC.

16   "Advertising is key to the business model of most SNS", Office of Privacy Commissioner of Canada [OPCC], 2009, p. 41.

17   *See* http://www.facebook.com/advertising/?src=awgl01&v=ntl1, http://www.insidefacebook. com/2008/10/30/facebook-advertising-resources-the-6-types-of-ads-on-the-new-home-page/; http://www.insidefacebook. com/2009/01/27/facebook-relaunches-polls-as-new-home-page-engagement-ad/, http://www.insidefacebook. com/2009/09/23/facebooks-new-sampling-engagement-ads-now-available-for-brands/, last visited on January 10, 2010.

18   E.g. "you grant [Facebook] a non-exclusive, transferable, sub-licensable, royalty-free, worldwide license to use any IP content that you post on or in connection with Facebook

("IP License")", notably stipulates the Statement of Rights and Responsibilities – formerly called "Terms of Use."

[19] *See supra* the introduction.

[20] *See* Article 102 of the Treaty on the Functioning of the European Union. The prohibition provided for in this Article applies when five elements are established: one or more undertakings, a dominant position, the dominant position being held within the common market or a substantial part of it, an abuse (the acts detailed in the Article only being examples) and an effect on inter-State trade (Jones & Sufrin, 2008, p. 298).

[21] If tomorrow I leave Facebook, will my friends follow me? I don't think so. Maybe if their friends (our common friends and their exclusive friends) follow them. Then what about the friends of these friends? Which critical mass of "friends" will I have to convince?

[22] *See* Nederlandsche Banden Industrie Michelin v. Commission of the European Communities (1983), no.37: "The possibilities of competition must be judged in the context of the market comprising the totality of the products which, with respect to their characteristics, are particularly suitable for satisfying constant needs and are only to a limited extent *interchangeable* with other products" (emphasis added by author). *See also* EC Commission, 1997, no.7, for instance recently quoted by the Court of First Instance in Microsoft Corp. v. Commission (2007), no.484. The question of the relevant geographic market is put aside taking as a premise that SNS such as Facebook are targeted to the whole Community market. However, an SNS could be limited to a Country, *see infra*. Also, a SNS could *de facto* be geographically limited by the use of particular languages (such as Japanese, *see* http://mixi.jp). Furthermore, it can be underlined that the "Small but Significant and Non-Transitory Increase in Price" test

for the market definition (as regards this concept, *see* DG Competition discussion paper nos. 14-17.) can be less relevant "when competition is based on drastic innovations leading to the replacement of the current dominant firm, not on price competition between competitors" (Lind & Muysert, 2003, p. 88). As regards SNS, usually, users do not have to directly pay any price in coin money. As previously explained, in the context of multi-sided platforms like Facebook, the functionalities of Facebook for which we have to pay will lead to the providing of free users profiles. Therefore, it will generally make no sense for an SNS provider to charge its average users. Except sometimes (*e.g. see infra* as regards Hi5), when the SNS provider proposes to pay a fee in place of publishing advertisements on the website, or some SNS could usually be paying (dating SNS, etc.). If the SSNIP-Test is applied to Facebook, the website then becoming paying, most probably, users will move, for instance, to MySpace or Netlog. Most probably also, if other Facebook-like SNS didn't exist, web surfers would stop using the SNS, coming back to traditional instant messaging networks (such as MSN Messenger, Yahoo Chat, etc.), which would lead to the "cellophane fallacy." In this respect, if Facebook, with Facebook Chat, is arguably also on the market of instant messaging, MSN Messenger doesn't pertain to the market of Facebook-like SNS.

[23] But we could wonder if, as regards the Marketplace application coupled to the Facebook network through the API platform, Facebook would not be on the same relevant market than eBay.

[24] Another viewpoint could be taken, for instance as regards the market of e-advertising or even the one of targeted advertising.

[25] As regards this concept, *see* Jones & Sufrin, 2008, pp. 65-78.

26   *See also* Katz & Shapiro, 1994. Network effects are also called network externalities or economies of scale in consumption, *see* (Posner, 2000, p. 2).

27   The switching costs would still be higher if users, relying on cloud computing technologies (SNS providers generally providing data storage as a service), deleted their data from their own personal computers and then had to bring them back from the cloud provider.

28   Admittedly, according to what has been suggested, this could also lead to the creation of a new market.

29   The authors "define platform envelopment as entry by one platform provider into another's market, combining its own platform's functionality with the target's in a multi-platform bundle that leverages shared user relationships and common components" (Eisenmann, Parker, & Van Alstyne, 2009, p. 1).

30   *See* http://kara.allthingsd.com/20081124/when-twitter-met-facebook-the-acquisition-deal-that-fail-whaled/, last consulted the May 7, 2010.

31   "Given the growing number and maturity of data interoperability formats and protocols, there is a significant opportunity for social networks to reduce the detrimental effects of architectural silos by opening their closed communities for the benefit of users. Totally distributed social networking is a possible future scenario" (W3C Workshop, 2009, p. 5). The report however underlined that the "difficulty of sharing users' assets (i.e. the user generated content posted on a given social network) across social networks was mentioned as a potential area where further work would be beneficial" (p. 7). *See for instance* Shin & Lopes, 2009, pp. 439-450. *See also* the Webpage of the W3C Social Web Incubator Group whose mission "is to understand the systems and technologies that permit the description and identifica-

tion of people, groups, organizations, and user-generated content in extensible and privacy-respecting ways" (http://www.w3.org/2005/Incubator/socialweb/, last visited on September 3, 2010).

32   The author emphasized that, "[a]s social-network-site data becomes more portable, it also becomes less secure – and thus less private. The supposedly privacy-promoting solution so badly misunderstands the social nature of relationships on social network sites that it destroys the privacy it means to save" (Grimmelmann, 2009, pp. 1194-1195). It could be imagined that the migration of data to another SNS is depending on the redefining of the privacy settings on the new SNS. Given that before any choice of privacy settings, data would be totally inaccessible by defaults.

33   "Market power is the power to influence market prices, output, innovation, the variety or quality of goods and services, or other parameters of competition on the market for a significant period of time" (EC DG Competition, 2005, no.24).

34   "The dominant position thus referred to relates to a position of economic strength enjoyed by an undertaking which enables it to prevent effective competition being maintained on the relevant market by affording it *the power to behave to an appreciable extent independently of its competitors, its customers and ultimately of the consumers*" (emphasis added by author) (Hoffmann-La Roche & Co. AG v Commission of the European Communities (1979), no.38).

35   EPIC Before the FTC supp., 2010, no.1. For October 2009 statistics, *see* for instance http://www.hitwise.com/index.php/us/press-center/press-releases/2009/social-networking-sept-09/, last visited August 15, 2010. This reference puts Facebook, MySpace and Twitter in the same market.

36 Which "has become almost synonymous with the information technology industries including computer software, hardware, internet-based businesses and associated technologies such as wireless communications", but "also includes biotechnology, medical devices, pharmaceuticals, aerospace and others" (Lind & Muysert, 2003, p. 87).

37 The authors underline that "market contestability" would be a better indicator of market power. As regards Facebook-like SNS, it could be argued that Facebook does not enjoy a "position of dominance because potential entry imposes an effective competitive constraint on its conduct." Putting into perspective the impact of network effect, C. Veljanovski (2001, p. 117) writes that "[p]arts of the new economy, even though subject to a process of "serial monopolization", do not inflict the harmful effects attributed to static monopolies."

38 Posner underlines that "the prospect of a network monopoly should thus induce not only a high rate of innovation but also a low-price strategy that induces early joining and compensates the early joiners for the fact that eventually the network entrepreneur may be able to charge a monopoly price."

39 About the Facebook iPhone application, *see* EPIC et al. before the FTC, 2009, nos 26-44. In this case, the contacts list of an iPhone user (identities and phone number) are communicated to Facebook, while "[s]ome Facebook users and non-Facebook users have consciously chosen *not* to provide Facebook with their contact information" (EPIC et al. before the FTC, 2009, no.39).

40 This application makes it possible to inform user's friends of what the latter did on other websites insofar as these websites subscribe to the Facebook Beacon application). This is at present litigated in the United States, Facebook having proposed (*see*http://www.beaconclasssettlement.com/, last visited on

October 10, 2010), which has been approved in March 2010 (*see*http://www.wired.com/threatlevel/2010/03/facebook-beacon-2, last visited on October 21, 2010).

41 *See*http://www.facebook.com/policy.php, last visited on January 10, 2010; EPIC v. Facebook 3, 2010, no.89.

42 For instance, the terms of use of Facebook, LinkedIn and MySpace notably compel users to provide their real names during the subscribing process.

43 As regards "tracking cookies" and "flash cookies", *see* WP171, 2010, pp. 6-7.

44 About this case, *see notably* Edwards, 2009, pp. 512-515 and 528-531.

45 *See also* Dinant, 2000, pp. 278-282; Mercado Kierkegaard, 2005, pp. 314 and ff.; Working Party 29, WP37, 2000, p. 16.

46 This hypothesis makes sense when the social network can be publicly consulted (*e.g.* MySpace, some parts of profiles on Facebook and LinkedIn, YouTube, etc.).

47 Users can read, in the second title of the Privacy Policy (last revised on December 22, 2010), what follows:
Information we collect when you interact with Facebook: Site activity information. We keep track of *some of the actions you take on Facebook, such as* adding connections (including joining a group or adding a friend), creating a photo album, sending a gift, poking another user, indicating you "like" a post, attending an event, or connecting with an application. In some cases you are also taking an action when you provide information or content to us. For example, if you share a video, in addition to storing the actual content you uploaded, we might log the fact that you shared it. Access Device and Browser Information. When you access Facebook from a computer, mobile phone, or other device, we may collect information from that device about your browser type,

location, and IP address, as well as *the pages you visit.*" (Emphasis added by author).

48   *Clickstream* data consists of information about the Internet activity of a web surfer due to his browsing through a website. *See* Garrie & Wong, 2006, pp. 565-567; Bucklin & Sismeiro, 2008.

49   In this case, it is necessary for Facebook to store which group a user has joined. If this were not the case the user would have systematically join each group he wants to consult again, etc.

50   Facebook modifies the service it offers, on its servers (or those of its subcontractors) and the user does not have any control over such evolutions and they *have to* consent if they want to continue to use the website.

51   It can be noted that, in the United States, a "data security breach incident" is typically one that draws the U.S. Federal Trade Commission's [FTC] attention (Ciocchetti, 2007, pp. 94-95). The Twitter case recently illustrated it (In the matter of Twitter Inc., 2010).

52   The use of applications however requires greater disclosures of information.

53   Formerly, a user could join a Region network. Users can no longer join such networks but they can specify a location in their profile.

54   Most probably due to the EPIC complaint before the FTC and the users' opposition.

55   *See supra.*

56   To this respect, the website has been last tested on October 15, 2010.

57   *See* OPCC, 2009, p. 17.

58   "To request that we close your account and remove your information from the LinkedIn website, please send your request to customer_service@linkedin.com. Please send your request using an email account that you have registered with LinkedIn under your name. You will receive a response to requests sent to customer_service@linkedin.com within five business days of its receipt"

(http://www.linkedin.com/static?key=privacy_policy, last visited on January 15, 2010). It has to be noted that according to the new privacy policy (last consulted on October 15, 2010), the deletion of the account seems easier.

59   *See* OPCC, 2009, p. 29.

60   *See also* at the European level, Article 7 (privacy) and 8 (data protection) Charter of Fundamental Rights of the European Union, 12 December 2007, which has now the same legal value as the Treaties, *see* Article 6.1 of the Treaty on European Union; Convention for the Protection of Individuals with regard to Automatic Processing of Personal Data, adopted in Strasbourg, 28 January, 1981, hereinafter referred to as "ETS 108", and its Additional Protocol regarding supervisory authorities and transborder data flows, adopted in Strasbourg, 8 November 2001. At an international level, *see* Article 17, International Covenant on Civil and Political Rights, adopted by General Assembly resolution 2200A (XXI) of 16 December 1966; O.E.C.D. Recommendation of the Council concerning guidelines governing the protection of privacy and transborder flows of personal data, 23 September 1980. And at the Belgian level, *see* Article 22 of the *Constitution coordonnée*, 17 February 1994 and the Belgian Privacy Act hereinafter referred to as "LVP."

61   The concept of privacy is "*contingent au contexte sociétaire dans lequel nos capacités autonomiques en tant qu'individus doivent être protégées*" (Poullet & Rouvroy, 2009, p. 190).

62   D.J. Solove identifies six conceptions of privacy: "The Right to Be Let Alone", "Limited Access to the Self", "Secrecy", "Control Over Personal Information", "Personhood", "Intimacy" (Solove, 2002, pp. 1099-1124). As regards privacy, *see generally and notably*

Docquir, 2008; Poullet, 2008, pp. 35-38; Rigaux, 1998.

63. I.e. it is, to some extent, a shield against discrimination.

64. *See* Herveg & Gayrel, 2009, pp. 104-105.

65. Article 6.1, b) Directive 95/46/EC.

66. Article 6.1, b) and c) Directive 95/46/EC.

67. As regards Article 8 ECHR specifically, *see* Zwaak, 2006, pp. 729 and 743; Sudre, 2008, pp. 191-204 and 245-258; Moreno & Van Koekenbeek, 2008, pp. 44-47 and 49-52.

68. *See notably* Berman, 2006, pp. 1080-1085; Zwaak, 2006, pp. 28-32; Levinet, 2008, p. 61; Nowak, 2003, p. 53. L. Zwaak (2006, p.29) writes that two views of the *Drittwirkung* can be identified, one stating that human rights "*apply*" to the legal relation between private parties, and another one enabling the individual to *enforce* the rights against another individual.

69. As an example of direct horizontal effect, R. Clayton and H. Tomlinson (2001, pp. 217-218) write that "in Ireland it is well established that constitutional guarantees have direct horizontal application to litigation between private individuals", the Irish constitution itself directly imposing obligations on private individuals. But in the UK, G. Phillipson (1999, pp. 824 and ff.) and V. Mantouvalou (2008, pp. 916-917) state that the Human Rights Act (1998) – and privacy in particular – does not have a direct horizontal effect because it does not create a cause of action between private parties.

70. *See* van der Plancke & Van Leuven, 2008; Gardbaum, 2003, pp. 394-411.

71. *See* van der Plancke & Van Leuven, p. 205, for examples as regards Belgium. As regards France and a possible direct horizontal effect of the ECHR, *see* Sudre, 2009, pp. 31-32. F. Sudre underlines that before a national Court, the question of the direct horizontal effect coincides with that of the "direct effect" or "self-executing", which originally is not the same since it refers to ability of a Covenant to have effects in domestic law – and the differences between monism and dualism. As regards the direct applicability of treaties, *see notably* Berman, 2006, pp. 1093-1095.

72. For instance in the UK, the Human Rights Act (1998) explicitly stipulates that "it is unlawful for a public authority to act in a way which is incompatible with a Convention right" (s.6 (1)), understood that the concept of public authority includes a court or a tribunal (s.6 (3)(a)).

73. The measures that a State could be obliged to take due to the positive obligations it has can not be disproportionate as regards the individual interests to protect.

74. *See* van der Plancke & Van Leuven, 2008, p. 212, who borrow the words from B. Dickson (1999, pp. 59 and ff.).

75. And of course, if this violation also results from its *actions or encouragements*. "This accountability on the one hand depends on the type of human right concerned, and on the other, what measures the state has taken to protect against violations by private persons in general, and in individual cases" (Nowak, 2003, p. 53). *See* van der Plancke & Van Leuven, 2008, pp. 215-218).

76. Of course, it is impossible for any individual to introduce a recourse before the European Court of Human Rights *against another individual*. This would be contrary to the *ratione personae* competence of the Court, *see notably* Article 34 ECHR.

77. *See infra* footnotes nos. 135 and 136.

78. About U.S. privacy law, *see generally* Purtova, 2009, pp. 508-514.

79. As regards these torts, *see notably* Dunne, 2009, pp. 195-197.

80. For a summary about the Constitutional Right to Privacy, *see* Sprague, 2008, pp. 103-110; Purtova, 2009, pp. 512-513; Dunne, 2009, pp. 197-237.

[81] S. Gardbaum (2003, p. 415) wrote that the American Constitution has a "strong indirect horizontal effect", referring to the conceptualization of the indirect horizontal effect suggested by Phillipson (1999). According to S. Gardbaum, this means that "all law – including, of course, all private law – is directly and fully subject to constitutional rights and may be challenged in private litigation. This, in turn, means that constitutional rights fully protect the individual whether it is another individual or the government that seeks to rely on an unconstitutional law", (Gardbaum, 2006, p. 766). The indirect effect results from the hierarchy of the norms and from the fact that the government, the courts (adjudicating litigations), etc., are subject to the Constitution. As regards UK, *see* footnote nr 72.

[82] Referring to the common law (privacy tort) and the Californian Constitution, the Supreme Court of California, in Hernandez v. Hillsides (2009), recently underlined that these "two sources of privacy protection 'are not unrelated' under California law." Citing another decision, the Court recalled that the right to privacy in the California Constitution "creates at least a limited *right of action* against *both private and government* entities" (emphasis added by the author). In the case submitted to the Court, both the common law and the Constitution were invoked. Therefore, it seems that the Californian right to privacy could even have a *limited* direct horizontal effect. Admittedly as regards this Californian constitutional right to privacy, the Court stated that the individual must possess a "legally protected privacy interest" […] "determined by established social norms *derived from such sources as the common law and statutory enactment*" (emphasis added by the author). But the Court nevertheless refers to two causes of action.

[83] Regarding other weaknesses, *see* Richards & Solove, 2007, pp. 175-176; Sprague, 2008, pp. 101-102; King, 2008, p. 97; Strahilevitz, 2004, pp. 9-10; N. Purtova, 2009. As regards the intrusion upon seclusion tort, *see* Dalsen, 2009, pp. 1071-1075.

[84] The European Court of Human Rights has already taken into account the reasonable expectations of privacy of the individual who claims a violation of his privacy, for instance, in the work context, *see* Kéfer & Cornelis, 2009, p. 784.

[85] *See also* Poullet & Rouvroy, 2009/1, p. 48.

[86] As regards the monitoring of the activity of Internet users, *see* Sorosky, 2008, p. 1137.

[87] It has to be pointed out that reasonable expectation of privacy is only subjective as far as torts are concerned, but should be objective (i.e. that society will accept them) as regards constitutional rights (Strahilevitz, 2004, p. 13, footnote no.29; Sprague, 2008, p. 106). W. Dalsen (2009, pp. 1071-1075) however also refers to an objective expectation for privacy as regards the intrusion upon seclusion tort. *See* Hernandez v. Hillsides.

[88] The Supreme Court (City of Ontario v. Quon, 2010, pp. 10-12) decided that: "The judiciary risks error by elaborating too fully on the Fourth Amendment implications of emerging technology before its role in society has become clear." "At present, it is uncertain how workplace norms, and the law's treatment of them, will evolve." "A broad holding concerning employees' privacy expectations vis-à-vis employer-provided technological equipment might have implications for future cases that cannot be predicted. It is preferable to dispose of this case on narrower grounds."

[89] R. Sprague (2008, p. 125) writes: "[u]nder the *Florida v. Riley* plurality's approach, the expectation of privacy is defeated if a single member of the public could conceivably position herself to see into the area in question without doing anything illegal."

"According to Webster's initial definition, information may be classified as 'private' if it is 'intended for or restricted to the use of a particular person or group or class of persons: not freely available to the public'" (U.S. Dep. of Justice v. Reporters Committee, 1989).

90   For a criticism, *see* Sorosky, 2008, pp. 1121-1142. This case is an application of the "third-party doctrine." While the author correctly points out that "individuals have no viable choice but to reveal information to a third party"; "the third-party argument should not apply when a defendant relies on a mode of communication and has no choice but to continue using that mode, despite the existence of a third-party intermediary", (Sorosky, 2008, pp. 1133-1134). For a discussion related to the Fourth Amendment and cloud computing, *see* Couillard, 2009, pp. 2205 and ff.

91   J. Kang (1998) identifies, under the word "privacy", three "clusters" of ideas, functionally interconnected and often concomitantly involved in a same situation: "space, decision and information." He focuses on the third concept.

92   *See notably* the Privacy Act (1974), the Fair Credit Reporting Act (1970), the Cable TV Privacy Act (1984), the Children's Online Privacy Protection Act (1998) and the Video Privacy Protection Act (1988). About these acts, *see* Solove & Hoofnagle, 2006, pp. 359-368. As regards the Video Privacy Protection Act, *see* Viacom v. YouTube (2008), where the District Court for the Southern District of New York refused to extend its scope to videos watched through YouTube.

93   "An entire industry devoted primarily to processing and disseminating personal information", (Solove & Hoofnagle, 2006, p. 359.

94   *See* Gindin, 2009, pp. 28-35.

95   Nonetheless our purpose is not to ignore or diminish the potential huge benefits to which self-regulation can lead.

96   For a comparison between U.E. and U.S. perspectives, *see* Dhont & Pérez Asinari, 2003, pp. 79-96.

97   *See* http://www.export.gov/safeharbor.

98   *See for example,* in California, the Online Privacy Protection Act of 2003 – Business and Professions Code sections 22575-22579.

99   As regards Facebook, LinkedIn, LiveJournal, MySpace, Hi5 and Skyrock (skyblogs), *see* OPCC, 2009, p. 43.

100   In this respect, "the policies are often vague about actual practices, and contain statements that are contradictory or misleading" (UCBSI, 2010, p. 33, *see also* pp. 11-12).

101   *See* FTC Policy Statement on Unfairness, December 17, 1980, and FTC Policy Statement on Deception, October, 14, 1983.

102   For an overview of documents published by the FTC, *see* Gindin, 2009, pp. 1-36.

103   *See* as regards English law, Walden, 2007, pp. 462-463.

104   Contractual limitations would satisfy those who protest against rules about data protection due to free speech protection considerations, *see* Volokh, 2000, pp. 7-11.

105   Once information is produced, it is in a context linked with "informational norms", i.e.: "norms of appropriateness" and "norms of flow or distribution." If later these rules are not respected by the individuals involved by the production of the information at stake, there is a violation of privacy, regardless of this violation is or not justified (and then, lawful). For instance, in the friendship context – word for word targeted on Facebook (where you have "friends"), but in practical terms distorted –, H. Nissenbaum (2004) explains that the norms of appropriateness are loose – we tell ourselves a lot –, while norms of flow are much more strict – zip it, lock it, put it in your pocket. For an ap-

plication of this theory in the SNS context, *see*Dumortier (2009).

106 "Privacy is built around a few key ideas: You should have control over what you share. It should be easy to find and connect with friends. Your privacy settings should be simple and easy to understand" (http://www.facebook.com/privacy/explanation.php?ref=pf, last visited on February 13, 2010).

107 *See* Moiny, 2010, pp. 247-250; Wong, 2008; Working Party 29, WP163, pp. 5-7; Working Party 29, WP169, pp. 21 and 23.

108 *See* Moiny, 2010/1. In this paper, we discussed the contract formation in the context of SNS as regards American and Belgian laws.

109 In the United States, choice of law clauses generally electing California law, *see notably*, as regards SecondLife, True.com and MySpace where a contract has already been considered concluded: Bragg v. Linden Research (2007); Cohn v. Truebeginnings (2007); as an obiter dictum, in a footnote, USA v. Lori Drew (2009).

110 Even if consent is not always necessary to the lawfulness of a processing operation (*see notably* Article 7, f) Directive 95/46), the SNS provider generally relies on such a basis (which is normal as regards Safe Harbor Principles). In this respect, consent is supposed to be expressed at the moment of the subscription (the user agreeing to the terms of use and privacy policy) and later by defining privacy settings and spontaneously communicating data.

111 In some extent, it has to be noted that Facebook was originally not so far from this doomsday scenario. Users could not permanently delete their accounts and the privacy policy was (and is still to some extent) unclear about the purposes of the processing operations Facebook could realize. Moreover, a terms of use modification seemed – but has been challenged by users and finally avoided – to give Facebook extensive rights as regards the conservation of users' data, *see*http://consumerist.com/2009/02/facebooks-new-terms-of-service-we-can-do-anything-we-want-with-your-content-forever.html, last visited on March 15, 2010.

112 P. Polański (2007, pp. 305-306 and 323) aims at "signal[ing] the emergence of potential customary norms in global Internet-based commerce" and identifies "the most important Internet common practices." He cites as an "Internet-specific custom", the "Right to explore user's behaviour", and underlines that "[i]t is also a global practice of website operators to employ cookies or web beacons for the purpose of tracking user behaviour or storing important personal data to personalise a website. The whole online advertising industry relies on the legal permissibility of this practice."

113 *See also* nos. 130 and ff.

114 In Belgium, *see for instance* a judgment of the Tribunal du commerce of Liège, Real de Madrid et al. v. Hilton Group Plc. et al. (2006).

115 Our societies admit the validity of the exploitation of the "goods of the personality" ("*biens de la personnalité*") (Léonard, 2001, p. 437 and the references cited in footnote no.55).

116 *See generally* about this topic Moine, 1997, pp. 352-366; Kang & Buchner, 2004, pp. 230 and ff; Samuelson, 2000, pp. 1125 and ff; Schwartz, 2004, pp. 2056 and ff.

117 Such as the selling of personal data to the American government, *see* Simmons, 2009, pp. 984-999.

118 *See supra* as regards privacy and data protection.

119 *See notably* as regards nullity due to violation of the public order, the decision of the Belgian Cour de cassation no. C980042F (1999). *See also* Rigaux, 1980, p. 473.

[120] *See also* Article 8.1 of directive 95/46/EC.

[121] As regards the servers of the cloud computing service provider: "The location of these servers can be spread all over the world, with the data changing and moving continuously between the provider's servers" (Joint, Baker, & Eccles, 2009, p. 271).

[122] Facebook's privacy policy explicitly reveals that information is used for advertising purpose: "4. How We Use Your Information... To serve personalized advertising to you."

[123] "[O]ne of the practical implications of cloud-sourcing is that its cost-efficiencies are driven by a freedom a provider has to move the data/application/operating system to the most efficient location for them" (Joint, Baker, & Eccles, 2009, p. 272).

[124] Without prejudice to a latter real-time information.

[125] And for instance, as regards Facebook, LinkedIn, MySpace, Twitter and SecondLife, these documents are not displayed, they are only accessible through hyperlinks.

[126] It is here referred to about how consumers conclude (e-)contracts. " 'Blanket assent' is best understood to mean that, although consumers do not read standard terms, so long as their formal presentation and substance are reasonable, consumers comprehend the existence of the terms and agree to be bound to them." " 'Blanket assent' means only that, given the realities of mass-market contracting, the consumer chooses to enter a transaction that includes a package of reasonable, albeit mostly unfavorable to her, boilerplate terms" (Hillman & Rachlinski, 2001, pp. 33-34).

[127] Following Working Party 29 (WP115, 2005, p. 5), as regards the use of location data with a view to providing value-added services, the definition of consent "explicitly rules out consent being given as part of accepting the general terms and conditions for the electronic communications service offered."

See Le Métayer & Monteleone, 2009, pp. 137-138.

[128] The F.T.C. compelled Sears to inform its users "[c]learly and prominently, and *prior to* the display of, *and on a separate screen from*, any final "end user license agreement," "privacy policy," "terms of use" page, or similar document" (In the Matter of Sears, 2009, p. 3). Concerning this particular case and what could be learned from it, *see* Gindin, 2009.

[129] "LiveJournal offers six different types of accounts, with the extent of advertising, size of account, and access to services defined by the type of account selected" (OPCC, 2009, p. 25).

[130] EPIC, in its recent complaint against Facebook (EPIC v. Facebook 3, 2010, no. 121) underlined that "Facebook Has a History of Changing Its Service in Ways that Harm Users' Privacy", and enumerated the different substantial revisions of the website's terms of use and privacy policy that occurred in spite of users protestations (nos. 121-132).

[131] *See* footnote no. 130.

[132] If the "processing is necessary for the purposes of the legitimate interests pursued by the controller or by the third party or parties to whom the data are disclosed, except where such interests are overridden by the interests for fundamental rights and freedoms of the data subject which require protection under Article 1 (1)."

[133] Facebook and LinkedIn also bear the TrustE label. Originally, MySpace did the same but doesn't bear this label anymore.

[134] *See* Article 8, b) and c) ETS 108 and Article 8.2 Charter of Fundamental Rights of the European Union.

[135] But a user who is a legal or natural person that has to comply with Directive 95/46/EC, and therefore do not fall (if natural person) within the domestic use exemption of Article 3.2, second dash Directive 95/46/EC.

136 It could be argued that a user having a non-publicly accessible profile, only accessible to a definite number of contacts he accepted, fall outside the scope of Directive 95/46/EC. *See* as regards this question Working Party 29, WP163, 2010, pp. 5-7; Moiny, 2010, pp. 250-254. In this case, the data subject would suffer a lack of protection (e.g. how would he be protected against transborder data flows to countries lacking an adequate data protection law, how the security of the processing operations would be ensured, etc.). Another question is to know if he needs a specific protection in this case. We think so in the elusive context of cloud computing. The following questions arise if we wonder about an evolution of data protection rules. If a very strict interpretation of the domestic use exemption is adopted, it could be opportune to impose to a natural person data controller and using SNS or cloud computing services for a personal purpose, a "diet" data protection regime. In our view, the solution to intrusive data protection rules for an individual socializing over the Internet, lays in a lighter data protection regime, and not in an exclusion of the scope of the regulation.

137 *See infra.*

138 Legal persons could use SNS to promote their business (with a Page on Facebook or an account on LinkedIn that has a clearly professional purpose), and it leads to the question of a potential extension of data protection rules to such legal persons – but, if desirable, which ones (S.M.Es?) and when?

139 College van burgemeester en wethouders van Rotterdam v. M.E.E. Rijkeboer (2009), nos. 57-59.

140 The limits Member States would fix have to result from
a fair balance between, on the one hand, the interest of the data subject in protecting his privacy, in particular by way of his rights to rectification, erasure and blocking of the data in the event that the processing of the data does not comply with the Directive, and rights to object and to bring legal proceedings and, on the other, the burden which the obligation to store that information represents for the controller. (College van burgemeester en wethouders van Rotterdam v. M.E.E. Rijkeboer (2009), no.64)

141 Compare with Article 13, §2 Directive 95/46/EC.

142 *See supra.*

143 More generally, the study underlined that "[o]ur review of the policies showed that only 23 of the top 50 affirmatively stated that users could have access to some portion of the information the website had collected about them. The remaining 27 policies lacked mention of access or their statements about access were unclear. However, none of the policies specified that a user could access *all* the data that had been gathered" (UCBSI, 2009, p. 30). The first recommendation of KnowPrivacy relates to the right of access, (UCBSI, 2009, p. 32).

144 Some technical storage remains permitted (Article 5.1, *in fine,* of Directive 2002/58/EC), so does the "legally authorized recording of communications and the related traffic data when carried out in the course of lawful business practice for the purpose of providing evidence of a commercial transaction or of any other business communication" (Article 5.2 of Directive 2002/58/EC). Moreover, Member States can adopt some exceptions according to Article 15. Finally, Directive 2006/24/EC mustn't be forgotten.

145 See Working Party 29, WP148, p. 14.

146 Concerning this topic, *see* Working Party 29, WP37, 2000, pp. 22-23; Working Party 29, WP148, 2008, pp. 12-13; Rosier, 2008, p. 339.

147 *See* Dhont & Rosier, 2003, pp. 10-12 and pp. 15-16; Rosier, 2008, pp. 327-354 and

pp. 339 and 341; Louveaux & Pérez Asinari, 2008, p. 323.

[148] Public communications network "means an electronic communications network used wholly or mainly for the provision of electronic communications services available to the public which support the transfer of information between network termination points", Article 2, d) of Directive 2002/21/EC. *See* the Belgian transposition of this disposition, Article 2, 3° *Loi relative aux communications électroniques* [LEC]. About this law, *see* Van Overstraeten, Bruyndonckx, Szafran, & Rousseau, 2005, pp. 203-208.

[149] The use of an SNS from a mobile phone through the GSM network (not via Airport) is not taken into consideration. This case does not change the reasoning related to the SNS provider.

[150] Electronic communications service "means a service normally provided for remuneration which consists wholly or mainly in the conveyance of signals on electronic communications networks, including telecommunications services and transmission services in networks used for broadcasting, but exclude services providing, or exercising editorial control over, content transmitted using electronic communications networks and services; it does not include information society services, as defined in Article 1 of Directive 98/34/EC, which do not consist wholly or mainly in the conveyance of signals on electronic communications networks" (Article 2, § 1 of Directive 2002/58 and Article 2, c) of Directive 2002/21). *See also* Article 2, 5° of LEC

[151] "There is no doubt that connecting Internet users to an *ISP*, providing Internet services to Internet users and routing requests and replies from Internet users to website servers and back are telecommunications services. So, Directive 97/66/EC applies to telecommunications providers, *Internet Service Providers* and providers of *routers* and lines for Internet traffic", (Working Party 29, WP37, 2001, p. 23).

[152] "The *Internet Service Provider (ISP)* provides services to individuals and companies on the Web. It owns or hires a permanent TCP/IP connection and uses servers permanently connected to the Internet. Classically, it will offer web hosting (web pages stored on its web server), access to newsgroups, access to an FTP server and electronic mail. This involves one or more servers using the HTTP, NNTP, FTP, SMTP and POP3 *protocols*" (Working Party 29, WP37, 2001, p. 12).

[153] For instance, each Facebook profile, group and page are provided in a uniform presentation. While MySpace users can modify the presentation of their pages.

[154] Which "means transmission systems and, where applicable, switching or routing equipment and other resources, including network elements which are not active, which permit the conveyance of signals by wire, radio, optical or other electromagnetic means, including satellite networks, fixed (circuit- and packet-switched, including Internet) and mobile terrestrial networks, electricity cable systems, to the extent that they are used for the purpose of transmitting signals, networks used for radio and television broadcasting, and cable television networks, irrespective of the type of information conveyed" (Article 2, (a) of Directive 2002/21).

[155] Which has been underlined by the Economic and Social Committee which "particularly welcomed the commitment to base the proposed regulatory evolution on: *technology neutrality, including no Internet-specific measures. Technologically neutral regulation should not, however, lead to stronger regulation of new services, but rather to the roll back of existing specific regulation of*

traditional services", (Economic and Social Committee, 2000).

156   *See* footnote no. 154.

157   As an example, Facebook rents data centers and plan to have its own one, *see* http://gigaom.com/2010/01/21/facebook-matures-will-build-its-own-data-center/, last consulted on 3 June 2010.

158   This question would depend on the material facilities of the SNS provider at stake.

159   A web hosting service provider could to the contrary be an ECS because its main activity would consist in the conveyance of signals. Its task is to answer and send the right pages requested by users, not to provide any specific content of his own.

160   As regards webmails, applications like Microsoft Outlook, Mozilla Thunderbird or Apple Mail enable the user to retrieve his emails from the server and download them on its own computer. As regards SNSes, an application should be imagined to retrieve photos, videos, etc. from the website's database.

161   Indeed, Directive 2006/24/EC applies to "the obligations of the providers of *publicly available electronic communications services* or of *public communications networks* with respect to the retention of certain data which are generated or processed by them" (emphasis added by author), Article 1.1. Coming back to the example of the webmail, in our view, a webmail provider does not provides any ECS and therefore does not have to retain any data, even if the Directive 2006/24/EC targets Internet e-mail (Article 5.1 (a)(2°), (b)(2°), (c)(2°), (d)(2°) and (e) (3)). In this respect, the Directive imposes that data are retained "to the extent that those data are generated or processed *by providers of publicly available electronic communications services or of a public communications network* [...] *in the process of supplying the communication services*

concerned" (Article 3.1). That is to say that, for instance, data must be retained as regards Internet e-mail provided by IAPes, because data related to the Internet e-mail are then processed by providers of ECS (Internet access) in the process of supplying this Internet access. In practical terms, the Internet e-mail is provided with the Internet access, both services being linked and provided at once. But as regards webmail providers, hearing that these latter do not provide ECS such as Internet access, no Internet e-mail data has to be retained under Directive 2006/24/EC. If the webmail provider offers an ECS such as hosting websites, the provision of Internet e-mail is another service and data generated in providing this latter do not appear to be generated in the process of supplying hosting. It could be deemed otherwise if specific e-mail accounts were provided to the ones who would subscribe to the hosting service.

162   The reasoning of the Austrian Regulatory Authority for Broadcasting and Telecommunications ([ARABT], 2005, p. 5) as regards voice over IP is the following:

The key Internet service enabling the global transport of data packets is Internet Connectivity. Internet Connectivity, as provided by Internet Backbone Providers (on wholesale level) and ISPs, (on retail level) undoubtedly is a classic ECS. On top of this basic ECS "Internet Connectivity" within the "Internet Access" product of ISPs numerous intelligent Internet services and applications are provided by third party providers, e.g. based on corresponding application servers. Both third party service provider and the end customer have to be connected to the Internet and be able to use the Internet Connectivity without restrictions. For classification of such an intelligent service (e.g. a server based VoIP service) as ECS or non-ECS it has to be investigated if the service offered to the end customer by a specific third party service provider wholly or mainly comprises the ECS Internet Connectivity or not. In typical Internet-only VoIP applications (i.e. without access to the PSTN) the VoIP provider in essence provides to his subscriber the called party's IP-address only and has no function or responsibility with regard to the transport of the IP voice packets between VoIP users. Therefore it would not be reasonable if a VoIP subscriber complains to his VoIP provider in case of poor voice quality, as the transmission of IP voice packets (i.e. the ECS part of the combination of the two generally totally independent products used by the VoIP subscriber) is not part of the VoIP service. Transmission of voice packets is the technically and contractually independent service of the VoIP user's ISP on request of the user's terminal software. If therefore the transmission of IP voice packets between the calling party and the called party is not part of the VoIP service (no corresponding cost elements within the VoIP service price, no (re)selling of Internet Connectivity) it has to be recognized, that such a VoIP service does not mainly consist in the conveyance of electronic signals (i.e. IP voice packets in this case) which would be the necessary prerequisite for a classification as ECS according to the European framework and the TKG 2003.

However, again as regards voice over IP and more precisely, as regards voice over IP services where "E.164" telephone numbers are not provided and from which there is no access to or from the Public Switched Telephone Network, the European Regulators Group ([ERG], 2007, p. 4) noticed that this "case […] includes different implementations: from pure peer-to-peer, based simply on a VoIP software which uses users' computers as nodes of the connection to more centralized architectures based on call management servers, data bases and

routers provided by the VoIP operator." It then underlined in footnote that "different regulatory approaches are adopted by the Member States due to an uncertainty on the regulatory treatment of such services: it is not clear whether this case should be considered an electronic communication service." In this respect, it could be argued that if the SNS provider operates an CN, it provides such a "more centralized architecture", which could plead in the sense that it provides an ECS and a PCN

163 According to these recitals: "This Directive seeks to respect the fundamental rights and observes the principles recognized in particular by the Charter of fundamental rights of the European Union. In particular, this Directive seeks to ensure full respect for the rights set out in Articles 7 and 8 of that Charter", and "Confidentiality of communications is guaranteed in accordance with the international instruments relating to human rights, in particular the European Convention for the Protection of Human Rights and Fundamental Freedoms, and the constitutions of the Member States."

164 Even if users not *only* use an ECS.

165 As regards instant messaging (chat), for instance, data could be however directly transmitted between users, without going through the SNS servers.

166 This second storage stage does not occur as regards chat, when communications are delivered immediately and in real time.

167 Some data are however *intended to* the SNS provider. That is for instance the case as regards pieces of information users have to give to the SNS provider when subscribing to the network (name, age, gender, etc.).

168 *See infra* as regards hacking.

169 Chatroulette (http://chatroulette.com/) is not really a social network, in the extent that users do not have profiles. It is what we would call a "video chat" website randomly

linking people through webcam, microphone and traditional chat. *See* http://www.spiegel.de/internation-al/0,1518,681681,00.html, http://bits.blogs.nytimes.com/2010/02/13/chatroulettes-founder-17-introduces-himself/, last visited on March 20, 2010. Even if, generally, the user doesn't know with who he is going to be connected (this individual is indeterminate), the communication nonetheless happens between a finite number of parties, that is to say, two parties. At least, two computers are involved even if more individuals are behind the webcams. And these communications seem always in the first transmission stage identified above.

170 The "the Working Party thinks that surfing through different sites should be seen as a form of communication and as such should be covered by the scope of application of Article 5" of the old Directive 97/66 (Working Party 29, WP37, 2001, p. 50).

171 *See infra* where such communications would be considered to be intended to an "indeterminate" or "irrelevant" audience with fluctuating accessibility.

172 *E.g.* if a user or a group accept no matter who as a friend or member and, in fact, has really a lot of friends or members (e.g. 500 people).

173 As regards Facebook-like SNS for instance, lots of contexts intertwine through the profile of a user. *See* Moiny, 2010, p. 252.

174 If communications were deemed protected, another solution to safeguard the freedom of expression would be for Member States to provide for a "one-party consent rule" (*see infra*) as regards the second stage of transmission. The consent of one party to the communication would then be enough for the divulgation of the communications.

175 The knowingly use of an information obtained in such a way is also punished. *See*

Article 314bis, §1, 1°, and §2 Belgium PC, *see also* Article 259 bis PC.

176 *See* Article 145, §1 LEC

177 Communications are private when they are not intended to "every man jack" ("*tout un chacun*"), *See* (Proposition of Data Privacy Act, Belgium, 1992, p. 7).

178 *See notably* Vandermeersch, 1997, pp. 247-255, discussing the condition of "during transmission" in the context of Internet.

179 R. de Corte (2000, p. 12), writing about the former Telecom Law, underlines that both Articles protect different kinds of information: one protects the content of the communication (Penal Code) and the other "telecommunication data" (Telecom Law). However, since the implementation of Directive 2002/58/EC, content is now protected under the LEC, according to the wording of its Article 125. Anyway, it could also be argued that to know the content of a communication implies to know its existence. Both disposition could and still can apply at the same time.

180 The interpretation of the transmission stage can be refined. From the Criminal point of view, as regards the requiring of "during transmission" (in the context of Article 90 ter of the Belgian Criminal Procedure Code), some scholars propose to presume that the transmission occurs between the sender and the "*a priori* expected terminus of the transmission" ("*geïndiceerd noodzakelijk eindstation*", the authors considering that "*geïndiceerd*" means what can reasonably be expected *a priori*). In this sense, on the one hand, they consider that the "terminus" of the transmission is the personal computer of a user when "popmail" (normally provided by the Internet Access Provider) are used (i.e. when the mails are retrieved through a software such as Safari or Thunderbird). Even if the IAP gives the possibility to use the "popmail" as a "webmail" through a

website. And on the other hand, the transmission ends as regards webmails, when the mails are in the "webmailbox." Even if the webmail can be used as a "popmail" (Van Linthout & Kerkhofs, 2008, pp. 86-88).

[181] *See* Article 2 Directive 2002/58.

[182] Of course, as it has been shown, the SNS provider can acquaint himself of each protected communication occurring through the SNS but strictly for the sole technical purpose of their transmission (including their backup).

[183] *See also* Killingsworth, 1999, pp. 75-76.

[184] However, the Act specifies that this concept does not include: "(A) any wire or oral communication; (B) any communication made through a tone-only paging device; (C) any communication from a tracking device (as defined in section 3117 of this title); or (D) electronic funds transfer information stored by a financial institution in a communications system used for the electronic storage and transfer of funds."

[185] As regards the Wiretap Act, *see notably* Garrie, Armstrong, & Harris, 2005, pp. 115-117.

[186] The Court notably quotes Konop v. Hawaiian Airlines (2002).

[187] According to 18 USC § 2510 (15), ""electronic communication service" means any service which provides to users thereof the ability to send or receive wire or electronic communications."

[188] According to 18 USC § 2711 (2), the term "remote computing service" means the provision to the public of computer storage or processing services by means of an electronic communications system."

[189] For example, the text of a message and the subject line, *see* § 2510 (8); Kerr, 2004, p. 24.

[190] "For example, a company can disclose records about how its customers used its services to a marketing company" (Kerr, 2004, p. 15).

[191] 18 USC § 2702 (a)(1) and (2) target services provided "to the public." The service will be public if the provider offers it to "the public at large", "for a fee or without cost", where "anyone can sign up and pay for an account", etc. The service is not public if it involves a special relationship between the provider and the user (e.g. a university and its students, an employer an his employees) (Kerr, 2004, pp. 22-23).

[192] Following 18 USC § 2510 (17), ""electronic storage" means— (A) any *temporary, intermediate storage* of a wire or electronic communication incidental to the electronic transmission thereof; and (B) any storage of such communication by an electronic communication service for purposes of *backup protection* of such communication" (emphasis added by author).

[193] For a summary of the difference, *see notably* Scolnik, 2009, pp. 376-377.

[194] *See also* USA v. Steiger, 2003.

[195] *See also* Kaufman v. Nest Seekers, 2006: only "electronic bulletin boards which are note readily accessible to the public are protected under the Act."

[196] According to 18 USC § 2702 (b) (3), "a provider described in subsection (a) may divulge the contents of a communication", "with the lawful consent of the originator or an addressee or intended recipient of such communication, or the subscriber in the case of remote computing service." According to § 2701 (c) (2), § 2701 (a) does not apply if the access to the communication stored in a facility through which an ECS is provided is authorized "by a user of that service with respect to a communication of or intended for that user."

[197] 18 USC § 2511 (2) (d): "it shall not be unlawful under this chapter for a person not acting under color of law to intercept a wire, oral, or electronic communication where such person is a party to the communica-

tion or where one of the parties to the communication has given prior consent to such interception unless such communication is intercepted for the purpose of committing any criminal or tortious act in violation of the Constitution or laws of the United States or of any State."

198 *See in the same sense* Pharmatrak Privacy Litigation (2002), reversed by the First Circuit (Pharmatrak, Privacy Litigation, 2003), deeming that the clients of Pharmatrak did not consent to the collection of personal data; Chance v. Avenue (2001).

199 The Court considered that ""Internet Access" is the relevant electronic communications service", provided by the Internet Service provider, and that "Web Sites are "users" under the ECPA" (DoubleClick Privacy Litigation, 2001).

200 It has to be noted that other class action suits had been filed against DoubleClick for privacy violations and led to a settlement, *see* Mercado Kierkegaard, 2005, p. 315.

201 As regards the decision, *see* De Hert, de Vries, & Gutwirth, 2009, pp. 87-92.

202 In the context of SNSes, data can (and is) even be stored elsewhere, in data centers due to the use of cloud computing technologies.

203 Including the United States having signed and ratified this Convention.

204 *See also* Council Framework Decision 2005/222/JHA.

205 *See* concerning this rule, Keustermans & Mols, 2001-2002, pp. 725-728; De Villenfagne & Dusollier, 2001, pp. 69-71.

206 Article 2 of the Budapest Convention provides that "A Party may require that the offence be committed by infringing security measures." The Belgian legislator has not required this condition deeming that this would cause "complications" such as the need to identify the level of protection required and to reveal the protection systems for evidence considerations. It also considered that protec-

tion systems are standardized. The purpose will show that the absence of this condition causes interpretation difficulties to identify when access is authorized.

207 Except maybe if he is a student in computer science realizing an exercise in a teaching framework, and non-intentionally going further than what is required by his professor...

208 Hacking is also punished under States Law. For instance in California, and without going into the details of the California Penal Code, shall be punished who "[k]nowingly and without permission uses or causes to be used computer services" (California Penal Code § 502, (c), (3)), that is to say, notably, "computer time, data processing, or storage functions, or other uses of a computer, computer system, or computer network" (Californian Penal Code § 502, (a), (4)).

209 18 USC, § 1030.

210 "In a nutshell, "protected computer" covers computers used in interstate or foreign commerce (e.g., the Internet) and computers of the federal government and financial institutions" (Computer Crime and Intellectual Property Section, Criminal Division [CCIPS], 2007, p. 3).

211 Plaintiffs had to demonstrate that the harm they suffered corresponds to one of the categories included in the 18 USC, § 1030, (g) and (c) (4), (A), i), I to VI. In Doubleclick Privacy Litigation (2001), it was about demonstrating a "loss to 1 or more persons during any 1-year period (and, for purposes of an investigation, prosecution, or other proceeding brought by the United States only, loss resulting from a related course of conduct affecting 1 or more other protected computers) aggregating at least $5,000 in value."

212 *See* Moiny, 2010/1, pp. 6-96.

213 "Defendants have admitted to maintaining an AOL membership and using that member-

ship to harvest the e-mail addresses of AOL members. Defendants have stated that they acquired these e-mail addresses by using extractor software programs. Defendants' actions violated AOL's Terms of Service, and as such was unauthorized" (AOL v. LCGM, 1998).

214   More exactly, it would be about exceeding access rights, in place of accessing without authorization, *see* in the same sense LVRC Holdings v. Christopher Brekka (2009).

215   This doctrine is made up of two tests: "fair notice" and "discriminatory enforcement." "The fair notice test asks whether the law is so vague and standardless that it leaves the public uncertain as to the conduct it prohibits." "If a law is so vague that a person cannot tell what is prohibited, it leaves judges and jurors free to decide, without any legally fixed standards, what is prohibited and what is not in each particular case." The second test is focused on "how much discretion the law gives the police" (Kerr, 2010, p. 14).

216   As regards scholars and, for instance, the case of employers using SNSes to investigate jobs applicants, *see* Byrnside, 2008, p. 468.

217   Judge Wu also underlines that the SNS provider would not necessarily forbid the access to the website in the case of breach of the terms of use. Therefore, such a breach would not necessarily lead to an access without authorization.

218   The hypothesis is not insane. For instance, Article 5.2 of Gmail's terms of service (last visited on April 5, 2010) specifies that: "You agree to use the Services only for *purposes* that are permitted by (a) the Terms and (b) *any applicable law, regulation or generally accepted practices or guidelines in the relevant jurisdictions* (including any laws regarding the export of data or software to and from the United States or other relevant countries)" (emphasis added by author).

219   The Belgacom (a Belgian IAP) Acceptable Use Policy, as regards Internet services (including Internet access), prohibits, in its Article 2.1, "to use the Service for any purposes other than those which are legal", *see* http://www.belgacom.be/private/gallery/content/documents/conditions/aup_v1_fr.pdf, last visited on April 5, 2010.

220   *See* as regards this topic Kuty, 2009, pp. 70 and ff.

221   After having flirted under the avatar of a young boy, the defendant told the deceived young girl that the boy "no longer liked her", and that "the world would be a better place without her in it."

222   As regards Belgian law, the developer would act "fraudulently", pursuing an unlawful benefit resulting from an unlawful processing operation.

223   Hearing that we did not study the sentences, which is not relevant for the purpose.

224   Implemented in Belgium in the Article 129 of the LEC

225   *See also* Article 129, al. 1, 1° and 2° LEC

226   *See* Mercado Kierkegaard, 2005, p. 320, *see* pp. 315-316 as regards the concepts of opt-in and opt-out. Concerning these latter, *see also* Dreier, 2010, pp. 144 and ff.

227   *See supra.*

228   About the pressure from industry lobbyists as regards the adoption of the old version of Directive 2002/58/EC and cookies, *see* Kierkegaard, 2005, pp. 318-321.

229   It considered that: "Browsers or other applications which default reject 3rd party cookies and which require the data subject to engage in an affirmative action to accept both the setting of and continued transmission of information contained in cookies by specific web sites may be able to deliver valid and effective consent" (WP171, 2010, p. 14).

230   *See supra.*

231   *See* Recital 24 of Directive 2002/58/EC as regards the concerned devices.

[232] E.g. SecondLife, LinkedIn, Facebook, Twitter and YouTube (worldwide).

[233] *See* Strahilevitz, 2004, p. 18.

[234] *See* Moiny & De Groote, pp. 5 and ff. *See notably* Articles 15 to 17 of Regulation 44/2001/EC and Article 6 of Regulation 593/2008/EC.

[235] *See* Article 12.2 of Directive 97/7/EC.

[236] As regards cloud computing, the localization of equipments needed to the processing of personal data could be automatically assigned owing to the technical effectiveness of the offered service.

[237] If the data controller is established in another Member State, this Member State has to apply its data protection rules. The Directive then does not precise what the Member State of the place of establishment has to do, given that the applicability of its data protection rules can not restrict the free flow of personal data. The applicable law to data protection will depend on the national implementation of Article 4 of directive 95/46/EC. *E.g. see* Article 3bis of the Belgian Data Protection Act (1992). For a brief discussion about conflicts of law and directive 95/46, especially in the context of SNSes, *see* Moiny, 2010. *See also* for more details Workin Party 29, WP179, 2010, and Kuner, 2010.

[238] For the record, Regulation 864/2007/EC on the law applicable to non-contractual obligations does not apply to "non-contractual obligations arising out of violations of privacy and rights relating to personality, including defamation" (Article 1.2, g)). Therefore, it has to be referred to national conflicts of laws rules.

[239] It still remains necessary to further identify in which cases the application of the foreign rule contrary to the ECHR is justified by the "foreignness" ("*extranéité*") of the situation, Mayer, 1991, p. 664; P. Hammje (1997, pp. 14-18) suggests a "public order exception" with the development of public order specific to the defense of fundamental rights. *See also* Labrusse, 1997.

[240] Admittedly, this Article only applies if the consumer has its "habitual residence" in the concerned Member State. While the concept of "domicile", relevant as regards "Brussels I" Regulation, is something else. For the needs of the purpose, we consider that the consumer at stake has its domicile – which has to be determined according to the law of the State where the domicile is claimed to be – in the State where he has his habitual residence.

[241] *See* Moiny, 2010. The only geographical exclusion is the following: "[i]f you are located in a country embargoed by the United States, or… you will not engage in commercial activities on Facebook (such as advertising or payments) or operate a Platform application or website."

[242] *See* footnote no. 169.

[243] "Member States shall take the necessary measures to ensure that the consumer does not lose the protection granted by this Directive by virtue of the choice of the law of a non-Member country as the law applicable to the contract if the latter has a close connection with the territory of the Member States", Article 6.2 of Directive.

[244] *See,* Kuty, 2009, pp. 382 and ff.

[245] It is not discussed here if Directives 95/46/EC and 2002/58/EC have the same territorial scope due to their connections. If it were the case, Belgian law having to be interpreted in accordance whit European law, the LEC, as far as it implements Directive 2002/58/EC, would have had to be territorially limited according to Articles 4 and 1 of Directive 95/46/EC.

[246] Article 5.4 "Brussels 1" Regulation.

[247] As regards this doctrine and the extraterritoriality of competition law, *See* Jones & Surfin, 2008, pp. 1356-1387.

248 An SNS provider directing its activities to the worldwide market does not necessarily has offices in Europe. For instance, does Twitter has any office in Europe? Anyway, lots of European citizens subscribed to Twitter.

249 *See* Moiny, 2010; WP148, 2010.

250 The Working Party 29 recently noted that "there are situations which fall outside the scope of application of the directive. This is the case where non-EU established controllers direct their activities to EU residents which result in the collection and further processing of personal data" ... "If they do so without using equipment in the EU, then Directive 95/46/EC does not apply" (WP168, 2009, no. 27).

251 As regards the Convention no. 108 of the Council of Europe, the processing of personal data for criminal purposes is involved in the adequacy assessment, while it is not as regards Directive 95/46/EC. Could it be tempered through conflicts of law rules? Or, according to Article 8 ECHR, *does it have to be* tempered in such a manner, or by a public order exception, etc.?

252 *See* footnotes nos. 121 and 123. For instance, an American Company, having processing facilities on the European territory, could use these facilities, due to technical effectiveness considerations, to process personal information related to American data subjects. It is tenable to consider that, as regards opportunity, European data protection law should not apply in such a case. But the place of these equipments could be a clue of the will of a company to direct its activities toward a specific market or toward the worldwide market. For instance, the creator of Chatroulette – a seventeen years old boy (does he know anything about data protection?) –, with the expansion of use of its website, seems now to use servers in Germany, *see* http://bits.blogs.nytimes.com/2010/02/13/chatroulettes-founder-17-introduces-himself/, last visited on March 15, 2010.

253 In the same sense and for suggestions, *see* Korff & Brown, 2010, pp. 24-26.

254 *See* for instance the Madrid Resolution (2009).

APPENDIX

Legislation and Preparatory Acts (Chronological Order)

Convention of the Council of Europe for the Protection of Individuals with regard to Automatic Processing of Personal Data (ETS 108), adopted in Strasbourg, January 28,1981.

FTC Policy Statement on Deception, October 14, 1983, retrieved on January 15, 2010, from http://www.ftc.gov/bcp/policystmt/ad-decept.htm.

Belgian Privacy Act, Loi relative à la protection de la vie privée à l'égard des traitements de données à caractère personnel, December 8, 1992, *M.B.*, March 18, 1993. Preparatory Acts, *Doc. parl.*, Sén., sess. ord. 1992-1993, no. 843/1.

Council Directive 93/13/EEC of 5 April 1993 on unfair terms in consumer contracts, *O.J.*, L 95, April 21, 1993.

Directive 95/46/EC of the European Parliament and of the Council of 24 October 1995 on the protection of individuals with regard to the processing of personal data and on the free movement of such data, *O.J.*, L 281, November 23, 1995.

Directive 97/7/EC of the European Parliament and of the Council of 20 May 1997 on the protection of consumers in respect of distance contracts - Statement by the Council and the Parliament re Article 6 (1) - Statement by the Commission re Article 3 (1), first indent *O.J.*, L 144, June 4, 1997.

Directive 98/48/EC of the European Parliament and of the Council of 20 July 1998 amending Directive 98/34/EC laying down a procedure for the provision of information in the field of technical standards and regulations, *O.J.*, L 217, August 5, 1998.

Projet de loi relatif à la criminalité informatique, Commentaire des articles, *Doc. parl.*, Ch. repr., sess. ord. 1999-2000, no. 0213/001.

Directive 2000/31/EC of the European Parliament and of the Council of 8 June 2000 on certain legal aspects of information society services, in particular electronic commerce, in the Internal Market, O.J., L 178, July 17, 2000.

Convention of the Council of Europe on Cybercrime (ETS 185), signed at Budapest, November 23, 2001.

Council Regulation (EC) No 44/2001 of 22 December 2000 on jurisdiction and the recognition and enforcement of judgments in civil and commercial matters, *O.J.*, L 12, January 16, 2001.

Directive 2002/21/EC of the European Parliament and of the Council of 7 March 2002 on a common regulatory framework for electronic communications networks and services (Framework Directive), *O.J.*, L 108, April 24, 2002.

Directive 2002/58/EC of the European Parliament and of the Council of 12 July 2002 concerning the processing of personal data and the protection of privacy in the electronic communications sector, *O.J.*, L 201, July 31, 2002

Belgian Private International Law Code, Loi portant le Code de droit international privé, 16 July 2004, *M.B.,* July 27, 2004.

Council Framework Decision 2005/222/JHA of 24 February 2005 on attacks against information systems, *O.J.,* L 69, March 16, 2005.

Belgian Law on Electronic Communications, Loi relative aux communications électroniques, June 13, 2005, *M.B.*, June 20, 2005. Preparatory Acts, *Doc. parl.*, Sén., sess. ord. 1992-1993, no 843/1.

Directive 2006/24/EC of the European Parliament and of the Council of 15 March 2006 on the retention of data generated or processed in connection with the provision of publicly available electronic communications services or of public communications networks and amending Directive 2002/58/EC, *O.J.*, L 105, April 13, 2006.

Proposal for a Directive of the European Parliament and of the Council amending Directive 2002/22/EC on universal service and users' rights relating to electronic communications networks, Directive 2002/58/EC concerning the processing of personal data and the protection of privacy in the electronic communications sector and Regulation (EC) No 2006/2004 on consumer protection cooperation, COM/2007/0698 final - COD 2007/0248.

Regulation (EC) No 864/2007 of the European Parliament and of the Council of 11 July 2007 on the law applicable to non-contractual obligations (Rome II), O.J., L 199, July 31, 2007.

European Parliament legislative resolution of 24 September 2008 on the proposal for a directive of the European Parliament and of the Council amending Directive 2002/22/EC on universal service and users" rights relating to electronic communications networks, Directive 2002/58/EC concerning the processing of personal data and the protection of privacy in the electronic communications sector and Regulation (EC) No 2006/2004 on consumer protection cooperation, COM(2007)0698 – C6-0420/2007 – 2007/0248(COD) – T6-0452/2008.

Regulation (EC) No 593/2008 of the European Parliament and of the Council of 17 June 2008 on the law applicable to contractual obligations, *O.J.*, L 177, July 4, 2008.

Directive 2009/136/EC of the European Parliament and the Council of 25 November 2009 amending Directive 2002/22/EC on universal service and users' rights relating to electronic communications networks and services, Directive 2002/58/EC concerning the processing of personal data and the protection of privacy in the electronic communications sector and Regulation (EC) No 2006/2004 on cooperation between national authorities responsible for the enforcement of consumer protection laws, *O.J.*, L 337, December 18, 2009.

FTC Policy Statement on Unfairness, December 17, 1980, retrieved on January 15, 2010, from http://www.ftc.gov/bcp/policystmt/ad-unfair.htm.

Case Law (Chronological Order)

Hoffmann-La Roche & Co. AG v Commission of the European Communities, Case 85/76, *Rec.* 1979, p. 461 (ECJ, February 13, 1979).

Nederlandsche Banden Industrie Michelin v. Commission of the European Communities, Case 322/81, *Rec.* 1983, p. 3461 (ECJ, November 9, 1983).

U.S. Dept. Of Justice et al. v. Reporters Committee for Freedom of the Press et al., 489 U. S. 749 (US Supreme Court, March 22, 1989).

America Online Inc. v. LCGM et al.), 46 F. Supp.2d 444, Civ. Act. No. 98-102-A (ED Virginia, November 10, 1998.

Case no. (*role*) C980042F, *Droit des Affaires – Ondernemingsrecht*, 2001, pp. 356 and ff (Belgian Cour de cassation, April 8, 1999).

In re Doubleclick Inc. Privacy Litigation, 154 F. Supp.2d 497, 00 Civ. 0641 (SD New York, March 28, 2001).

Dane Chance, et al. v. Avenue A, Inc. 165 F.Supp. 2d 1153, No. C00-1964C, 2001 US Dist. Lexis 17503 (WD Washington, September 14, 2001).

In re Pharmatrak, Inc. Privacy Litigation, Civ. Act. No. 00-11672-JLT (District of Massachussets, August 13, 2002).

Konop v. Hawaiian Airlines, Inc., 302 F.3d 868 (9th Cir., August 23, 2002).

United States of America v. Steiger, 318 F.3d 1039 (11th Cir., January 14, 2003).

In Re Pharmatrak, Inc. Privacy Litigation, 329 F.3d 9 (1st Cir., May 9, 2003).

George Theofel et al. v. Alwyn Farey-Jones, 359 F.3d 1066 (9th Cir., August 28, 2003).

United States of America v. Micah J. Gourde, 382 F.3d 1003, (9th Cir., September 2, 2004).

Inventory Locator Serv., LLC v. Partsbase, Inc., 2005 WL 2179185 (WD Tennessee, October 19, 2005).

Michael Snow v. Directtv, INC., et al., 450 F.3d 1314 (11th Cir., June 1st, 2006).

Allen Kaufman v. Nest Seekers, LLC, 2006 WL 2807177 (SD New York, September 26, 2006).

Real de Madrid et al. v. Hilton Group Plc. et al., *Auteurs & Média*, 5, 2007 (Tribunal du Commerce, Liège, November 24, 2006).

Bragg v. Linden Research, Inc., and Philip Rosedale, 487 F. Supp. 2d 593 (ED Pennsylvania, May 30, 2007.

Steven Warshack v. USA, 490 F.3d 455 (6th Cir., June 18, 2007).

United States of America v. Mark Stephen Forrester, Dennis Louis Alba, 495 F.3d 1041 (9th Cir., July 25, 2007).

Cohn v. Truebeginnings, LLC et al., B190423 (California Court of Appeal, July 31, 2007).

Microsoft Corp. v. Commission, Case T-201/04, *Rec.* 2007, p. II-03601 (CFI, September, 17, 2007).

N.V. G.P.G. v. C.P., *Tijdschrift voor Strafrecht,* 3, 2008 (Tribunal Correctionnel de Louvain, December 4, 2007).

Viacom International, Inc. v. Youtube, Inc., and Google, Inc., 540 F.Supp.2d 461 (SD New York, March 7, 2008).

OM v. P.K., *Tijdschrift voor Strafrecht,* 2009, 2 (Tribunal correctionnel de Dendermonde, September 29, 2008).

LVRC Holdings LLC v. Christopher Brekka et al., No. 07-17116 (9th Cir., March 13, 2009). Retrieved from http://www.ca9.uscourts.gov/opinions/ view_subpage.php?pk_id=0000009960.

College van burgemeester en wethouders van Rotterdam v. M.E.E. Rijkeboer, Case C-553/07, *Rec.* 2009, p. I-03889 (ECJ, May 7, 2009).

Abigail Hernandez et. al. v. Hillsides, Inc., (Supreme Court of California, August 3, 2009). Retrieved on January 30, 2010, from http://www.courtinfo.ca. gov/opinions/ archive/S147552.PDF.

United States of America v. Lori Drew, no. CR 08-0582-GW (CD California, August 28, 2009).

City of Ontario et al. v. Quon et al. (US Supreme Court, June 17, 2010). Retrieved on October 10, 2010, from http://www.supremecourt.gov/opinions/09pdf/08-1332.pdf.

FTC Consent Orders and Complaints (Chronological Order)

In the Matter of Sears Holdings Management Corporation (August, 31, 2009), U.S.A. Federal Trade Commission, retrieved on January 30, 2010, from
http://www.ftc.gov/os/caselist/0823099/090604searsdo.pdf.

EPIC et al. v. Facebook, Before the FTC, December 17, 2009, Complaint, Request for Investigation, Injunction, and Other Relief (EPIC v. Facebook 1). Retrieved on January 30, 2010, from
http://epic.org/privacy/inrefacebook/EPIC-FacebookComplaint.pdf.

EPIC et al. v. Facebook before the FTC supp., January 14, 2010, Supplemental Materials in Support of Pending Complaint and Request for Injunction, Request for Investigation and for Other Relief (EPIC v. Facebook 2). Retrieved January 30, 2010, from
http://epic.org/privacy/inrefacebook/EPIC_Facebook_Supp.pdf.

In the Matter of Facebook, Before the FTC, May 5, 2010, Complaint, Request for Investigation, Injunction, and Other Relief (EPIC v. Facebook 3). Retrieved on October 10, 2010, from http://epic.org/privacy/facebook/EPIC_FTC_FB_Complaint.pdf.

In the matter of Twitter Inc., Agreement Containing Consent Order, no. 0923093, June 24, 2010. Retrieved on October 10, 2010, from http://www.ftc.gov/os/caselist/0923093/100624twitteragree.pdf.

Section 3
Legal and Ethical
Implications in Cyberspace:
An International Perspective

Chapter 10
Al–Qaeda on Web 2.0:
Radicalization and Recruitment Strategies

Anne Gerdes
University of Southern Denmark, Denmark

ABSTRACT

This chapter investigates al-Qaeda's use of Web 2.0 as a tool for radicalization and recruitment. The media network of al-Qaeda is described in order to demonstrate the impact of their well structured media strategy for harnessing the power of the Web. They use a strategy that makes them stand out from other extremist groups, who in most cases lack an overall approach towards branding and Web communication. It is shown why this strategy works and enables al-Qaeda to set the agenda for online global jihadism and cultivate virtual communities of engaged jihobbyists. Finally, a virtue ethical perspective demonstrates the shortcomings of the al-Qaeda Web 2.0 strategies, by which it is suggested that their Achilles' heel is exactly the ideas inherent to Web 2.0, which are reflected in a bottom up participatory perspective. Thus, the Al-Qaeda online social movement does allow for engaged user participation, but without providing opportunities for free spirited critical reflection and self articulation of goals.

INTRODUCTION

In what follows, the main focus will be on al-Qaeda's use of the Web as a base for recruitment and as an effective tool of radicalization, and to a minor degree, as a base of operations. In the first part, I outline the professionalism which surrounds the al-Qaeda media machine, followed by an analysis of al-Qaeda's media strategy, emphasizing how effective use of persuasive online strategies (Fogg, 2003, Fogg, 2008) has enabled them to cultivate online communities of practices for scaffolding the Al-Qaeda identity. Here, with reference to virtue ethics, Benkler and Nissenbaum report findings from successful online collaboration among large groups of volunteers (Benkler

DOI: 10.4018/978-1-61350-132-0.ch010

& Nissenbaum, 2006). Following this line, I elaborate on their findings and seek to understand the motivation of extremist online activities from a virtue ethical perspective, in which I nevertheless takes the position that it is a contradiction in terms to speak about a virtuous terrorist. As such, virtue ethic (MacIntyre, 1999, 2000; Foot, 1978) is introduced to illustrate the shortcomings of the al-Qaeda strategy wherein self-selection of goals is only acceptable as long as participants do not question the religious interpretation contained in global jihadism. This is probably going to be the main reason for the future break down of al-Qaeda; the fact that no movement, so far, has in the long run been able to maintain a practice which suppresses critical reflection. Hence, I will elaborate on the notion of critical reflection with reference to Hannah Arendt's phenomenological investigation of the importance of a thinking experience, and whether this faculty prevents us from acting morally wrong (1964, 1971, and 1973).

BACKGROUND

The wave of uprisings in the Middle East underlines the fact that al-Qaeda's overall impact has been rather small. Young Arabs like everybody else want to live in free societies. Thus, al-Qaeda has not been able to convert the public at large. Nevertheless, the global online jihad movement will still be able to initiate self-radicalization among young people with extremist attitudes.

According to the recognized specialist on al-Qaeda strategy, ideology and media, Dr. Jarret Brachman, al-Qaeda - the most famous practitioners of jihadist ideology - nowadays conceptualizes itself as a media group who uses terrorism, rather than a terrorist group that uses the media.

Today's global jihadist movement cannot be classified with reference to a single al-Qaeda, since Al-Qaeda consists of interrelated networks (MI5 Security Service, 2010). Hence, there is the al-Qaeda high command (founded by late Osama bin Laden), al-Qaeda affiliate groups, individuals, and groups and cells, which are supported by Al-Qaeda (London 7/7 bombers, Istanbul bombers), as well as groups and cells inspired by Al-Qaeda. Against all odds, the movement is still going strong, and Brachman points to three reasons for this (Brachman, 2008, pp. 10-21): First, global jihadism implies a religious ideology which finds resonance among radical groups of Muslims who fell a global lack of justice. Secondly, al-Qaeda is a social online movement, where everybody sympathetic to their case can participate. Consequently, as will be illustrated in more detail later, the significance of the movement is reflected in its Web activities, which are characterized by lively, dynamic many-to-many communication and production of user generated content among eager participants. As such, the global jihadist movement has become a Web directed phenomenon, which develops through strategic use of online communication, global social networking platforms, discussion boards and online learning initiatives. Thirdly, Brachman points to the fact that al-Qaeda uses war zones as real life training settings for experimenting with attack strategies, which afterwards can be transferred to civilian areas. These arguments are also supported in findings by Weinberg and Perliger in an investigation of the history of 430 terror groups (Weinberg & Perliger, 2010). In a comparison of ways in which al-Qaeda differs from previous terror organizations, they too point to three similar reasons, and elaborate on the religious component by directing attention to the fact that a movement driven by religion is often stronger than a purely political movement, since the last mentioned is rationally structured and therefore to a lesser degree capable of taking advantage of the power to stir emotions. They conclude that most terror groups have life cycles of five to ten years and the use of terrorism has not proved to be a successful enterprise in order to obtain long term goals. All though Al-Qaeda is more than twenty years old by now, Weinberg and Perliger argue that there is reason to be optimistic regarding the future elimination of Al-Qaeda, since the movement is vulnerable when leading members are neutralized. For instance, the death of Abu Musab al-Zarqawi and Shamil Basayev destabilized their organizations in Iraq and Chechnya.

The prospects of al-Qa`ida creating a new caliphate remain in the realm of the fantastic. In short, while the end may not be near, it might not be far off either. As a result, while no "silver bullet" will bring an end to al-Qa`ida, a combination of external pressure exerted by the relevant authorities and internal decay brought on by organizational woes should reduce the threat to a manageable level (Weinberger & Perliger, 2010, p. 18).

All though Weinberg and Perliger stress the role of terrorists' access to the internet, they are skeptical regarding the overall impact of the Web, holding that experience shows us how extremist groups in North America and Europe have not been able to obtain anything else but endless arm-chair discussions among a minority of participants (Weinberger & Perliger, 2010, p. 17). But, contrary to most extremist groups, which lack critical mass of followers and content, the al-Qaeda media strategy includes branding management, enabling them to utilize the persuasive power of the internet on all levels. Hereby, they are proficient at sustaining ongoing momentum and enthusiasm in virtual communities, in which jihobbyists (a term coined by Jarret Brachman: Brachman, 2008, p. 19) can engage in vivid discussions, sometimes as a first step towards taking their mission into the real world. Thus, the rhetoric in forums centers around how to take action; and the story of the Jordanian doctor Human al-Balawi (also called Abu Dujana al-Khurasani) reflects an example of an apparently theatrical jihobbyist who nevertheless ended up as a suicide bomber, when blowing himself up at a Central Intelligence Agency base in Afghanistan on the orders of the Pakistani Taliban (Kohlmann, 2010, p. 4). Like-

wise, after the 7/7 London bombers, a member of an al-Qaeda related forum asked for advice to take action, and other users encouraged him to establish a virtual cell with two or three people: "Once harmony and mutual trust are established, training conducted and videos watched, then you can meet in reality and execute some operations in the field" (Cool & Glasser, 2005, pp. 5-6). Examples like these do of course not by themselves serve as sufficient reasons for stating that online activities foster real life terror engagement. When analyzing terror actions, the reasons for carrying out suicide missions can only be uncovered with reference to richly faceted causal complexes. But the affordance of the Web to a certain extend minimizes the element of risk in connection to terrorist activities; watching training videos is not as demanding as real life training, and of course not as effective, but the option still represents an invitation to initial low level action. Likewise, cyberspace provides a rather secure environment for negotiation of plans, which can be carried out by using encrypted internet channels instead of throwing face to face meetings:

"Al Qaeda's innovation on the Web "erodes the ability of our security services to hit them when they're most vulnerable, when they're moving," said Micahel Scheuer, former chief of the CIA unit that tracked bin Laden. "It used to be they had to go to Sudan, they had to go to Yemen, they had to go to Afghanistan to train," he added. Now even when such travel is necessary, an al-Qaeda operative "no longer has to carry anything that's incriminating. He doesn't need his schematics, he doesn't need his blueprints, he doesn't need formulas." Everything is posted on the Web or "can be sent ahead by encrypted Internet, and it gets lost in the billions of messages that are out there" (Cool & Glasser, 2005, p. 2).

In what follows, I will refrain from discussing al-Qaeda's covert use of the Internet as a base of operation, and primarily focus on al-Qaeda's visible presence on the Web, stressing the organizations Web strategy in its movement from Web 1.0 to Web 2.0 use of the internet (O'Reilly, 2005). Gradually, the al-Qaeda media strategy has shifted from using static homepages, which implies information transfer and one-to-many communication, towards a dynamic use of the internet, implying many-to-many communication and interaction among participants, who forms communities around social networking platforms, such as Facebook and YouTube (Conway, & McInerney, 2008). As everybody else on Web 2.0, jihobbyists are not just passive browsers but active participants, engaged in the production of user generated content in the form of discussion posts, propaganda videos or learning objects including instruction manuals for virtual training of future terrorists. Above all, the themes of their contributions are staged by an agenda setting controlled brand management strategy shaped by the al-Qaeda top.

The international shutdown of vital militant al-Qaeda homepages by authorities (in autumn 2008), as part of a strategy for fighting the spread of al-Qaeda propaganda, has further forced al-Qaeda to reshape their media strategy. Sites, such as al-Ekhlaas, al-Boraq, al-Firdaws, al-Hesbah and Absar al-Mujahediin were closed down because they were considered to play significant roles for terror related groups. These sites were password protected and accessible to a small inner circle of users (CTA: Center for Terror Analysis. The Danish Security Intelligence Service, 2010, p. 2). From such sites it was possible to distribute violent material as well as training videos and instruction manuals for preparation of bombs; in addition some of these sites were used for online terror planning activities. The initiative by Western countries to shut off sites with extremist Islamic propaganda made it difficult for al-Qaeda to spread their ideas, but only shortly. In fact, fixed homepages had for long posed a problem for al-Qaeda,

due to the fact that these sites were vulnerable to hacker attacks from authorities or volunteer campaigners. As such, they routinely made use of the internet in a protected, anonymous, nomadic sense (Cool & Glasser, 2005, p. 4). Their user habits included regularly change of Web addresses on sites and forums; likewise they would urge users to download material immediately after release.

As a consequence of the banning strategy towards militant homepages, al-Qaeda and so called jihadist Internet Brigades began to invade global social networking platforms, like Facebook, as well as popular moderate Islamic forums. Thus, the spread of jihad-promoting content continues, and more over, it now reaches a broader audience (CTA: Center for Terror Analysis. The Danish Security Intelligence Service, 2010, p. 3), (Bermingham, Conway, McInerney, O'Hare & Smeaton, 2009). Also, several jihadist themed Web forums, managed by independent actors, continue to flourish and play vital roles as tools of radicalization.

In the following section, I will describe the established media network of al-Qaeda in order to illustrate the impact of their media strategy for harnessing the power of the Web. A strategy, which makes them stand out from other extremist groups, who in most cases lack an overall approach towards branding and Web communication. Subsequently, I analyze the mechanisms which enable al-Qaeda to cultivate virtual communities with active hard working user groups on all levels from graphic designers and translators of Arabic texts to training cells, which prepare for terror missions. Finally, I elaborate on my argument regarding the shortcomings of the al-Qaeda Web 2.0 strategies, in which I suggest that their Achilles' heel is exactly the ideas inherent to Web 2.0, which are reflected in a bottom up participatory perspective (O'Reilly, 2005). Hence, their global online social movement does allow for engaged user participation, but without providing opportunities for free spirited critical reflection and self articulation of goals.

THE AL-QAEDA MEDIA NETWORK

The global jihadist Web continues to undergo changes, but one of the leading forces on the al-Qaeda media scene is the official media production group, as-Sahab, which makes al-Qaeda sovereign, not having to depend solely on news organizations, such as Al-Jazweera, in speaking their case or covering activities from the jihad fronts (Brachmann 2008, p. 126). Originally, As-Sahab was part of a media department established back in 1988, when al-Qaeda formed (Seib, 2008, p. 75). It was from this platform Bin-Laden called for war against the U.S and spread the call for jihad. Since 2003, as-Sahab has turned into a jihadist media empire, which releases major professional productions on a regularly basis. As-Sahab is a media brand, with its own logo on everything from microphones to coffee mugs and video productions, last mentioned featuring expert senior al-Qaeda personalities, appearing in front of bookshelves with impressive titles, including both religious writings as well as scientific writings, some or all of which are written by the "celebrity" in question. Ayman Al-Zawahiri oversees the overall direction and operations of as-Sahab, and he frequently appears in its video productions (Brachman, 2008, p. 131). Thus, al-Qaeda puts great effort in brand-name management; the as-Sahab name and brand logo signals credibility and authenticity. By this media strategy, al-Qaeda gives the impression of being just like any modern social movement with potential appeal to moderate Muslim Web users.

In complete contrast to this smooth approach, the overall media strategy in the early 00'es was heavily influenced by Abu Musab al-Zarqarwi, the popular operational commander and self-announced head of al-Qaeda in Iraq (who was killed 2006 by a U.S. Air strike). He used media work to distribute violent videos, first in Iraq in 2004 with the beheading of the businessman Nicholas Berg. The video was downloaded more than 500,000 times within 24 hours. In 2004, Zarqawi released an online magazine *Zurwat al-Sanam* and

a homepage with videos, including a variety of download options (Seib, 2008, pp. 75-76).

Since 2003, the al-Qaeda favorite strategist Ayman al-Zawahiri, was overshadowed by Zarqarwi, as Brachman phrases it:" the new posterboy of global jihadism" (Brachman, 2008, p. 101). This forced Zawahiri to modify his public rhetoric, and he increasingly engaged in discussion of social and cultural topics. Furthermore, in 2005, al-Qaeda's senior leadership disagreed with Zarqawi's, even to their taste, extremely violent methodology both in real life as well as in cyberspace. The two sides and their respective supporters actually competed in forming arguments against each others. Thus, if one media outlet broadcasted a video with Zarqawi, others would quickly release a bin Laden and Zawahiri video (Brachman, 2008, p. 109).

The disagreements between the parties were brought to a sudden end with the death of Zarqawi in 2006, and the overall media image of al-Qaeda, as presented by as-Sahab, now appears to be less violent, offering persuasive experiences through pleasing rhetorics as opposed to violent beheadings.

Zawahiri reconsolidated his power within the network as a top leader and member of the al-Qaeda High Command, and he is now in charge of and emphasizes the importance of having a media strategy for worldwide recruiting, which enables Muslims to understand *Shaira* and to see through the American propaganda. Thus, as-Sahab represents technically and rhetorically quality video production with high credibility in the jihadist communities.

The distribution of as-Sahab productions is coordinated by al-Fajr media center, which, since 2006, has been responsible for online logistics and managed to build up a trusted network in cyberspace. Al-Fajr is the primary distribution vehicle used by different media groups associated with regional commands; such as the Islamic State of Iraq, al-Qaeda in the Arabian Peninsula, al-Qaeda in the land of the Islamic Maghreb and al-Qaeda's High Command, which uses the media production group as-Sahab. Media productions are transmitted to Al-Fajr, which approve them for dissemination and coordinate when and on which forums to bring the different productions (Brachman, 2008, pp. 134-135). Thus, Al-Fajr scaffolds the legitimacy and credibility of al-Qaeda media productions. With support from al-Fajr and their skills for timing, Zawahiri and as-Sahab set the agenda for hot topics to be discussed among jihobbyists in online forums.

As a further support of proof of al-Qaeda's ability to make intelligent use of the Web, Zawahiri, in 2007, participated in an online interview including a chat session with questions from individuals and news organizations (Seib, 2008, p. 79). This maneuver in cyberspace made the authorities, who have hunted Zawahiri for years, look ridiculous, and moreover, throwing a news conference, made al-Qaeda appear authorized, operating like any other political or governmental organization.

Similarly, recruiting efforts are sustained by using persuasive design, which even takes into consideration whether the message has to be delivered with appeal to European and American Muslims or supporters. Besides "simple" translation's tasks, also more sophisticated rhetorical strategies are considered. Thus, in order to target the German audience, jihad-promoting content are framed by emphasizing a rhetorical style, which relays on logical arguments as opposed to emotional or purely religious arguments.

In one of the most famous propaganda video productions *The Power of the Truth*, clever use of remix, from both Western and Muslim sources, underscores the need for global jihad by using the West's own words to pass judgment on it (Brachman, 2008, p. 103, 108). In addition, justification for the jihadist arguments can be collected from sites such as WikiLeaks, who describes itself as a: "multi-jurisdictional public service designed to support whistleblowers, journalists and activists who have sensitive materials to communicate to the public" (WikiLeak.org). Among its many

whistleblower releases, Wikileaks has from time to time released classified US Military material, which provides evidence of the cruelty of the Iraq and Afghan war. For instance, in April 2010, WikiLeaks released a military video depicting the slaying of a dozen people, including two Reuter's reporters, in the Iraqi suburb of Bagdad (Wikileaks, 2010); and late July 2010, WikiLeaks released over 77,000 classified U.S. military records regarding the last six years of the Afghan war, some of which tells another story of the war than the official American and Western worlds versions. In this sense, the Western world sometimes appears to be its own worst enemy in fighting terrorism.

Radicalization via Jihadist Online Forums

The established al-Qaeda media machine is a catalyst and inspiration to many jihobbyists on the Web, who participate in jihadist themed online activities on blogs, discussion boards and social networking platforms, which are either strictly jihadist oriented or mainstream sites, such as Facebook and YouTube. The banning-strategy of al-Qaeda Websites has advanced the transfer of the movement from static Web 1.0 use of the internet - which relay on one-way communication, focusing on passive acquisition of information - into Web 2.0 use modes, characterized by participation via bottom up activities and many-to-many communication, in which users take part in the building up of vivid communities.

As an example, the Ansar Al-Mujahideen Forum (Ansar Al-Mujahideen Network, 2010) was created in 2008 by ordinary members from the closed down al-Ekhlass forum (Kohlman, 2010, p. 2). The Web forum organizes Islamic knowledge sharing and serves as a platform for discussion of topics regarding Islam, Muslims, jihad and the Mujahideen. It exemplifies the decentralized bottom up participatory approach to the Web, in which idealistic Web entrepreneurs make virtual communities flourish. In this sense, the organization of the jihadist Web does not differ from that of ordinary online communities.

The decentralization of Web activities sometimes stirs up conflicts between the established al-Qaeda media groups and creative Web initiatives. Thus, at the beginning, the al-Fajr media center questioned the credibility of the Ansar Al-Mujahideen Forum. But it is still going strong and instead of turning to the established al-Qaeda media network for assistance, the forum depends on volunteer efforts and encourage everybody active on the forum to participate:

"...It's not just about copying and pasting...we need to develop our media skills, produce more videos and audio releases in arabic and also in english, and other languages if it is possible. Doing this is gonna improve the quality and the professionality [sic] of the brothers and sisters and you know very well how important media is" (Kohlman, 2010, p. 3).

Despite the fact that online jihadist propaganda is increasingly decentralized, it is still orchestrated by the overall al-Qaeda narrative. In this sense it matters less if forums, such as Ansar Al-Mujahideen, from time to time make mistakes. The competitive jihadist media market furthermore encourages forum builders to do their best in order to catch the attention of users. Thus, the established al-Qaeda media network allows room for a participatory form of cyber terrorism. Here, self selection of goals and boosting of online activities plays an important role for fostering engagement. These prerequisites go hand in hand in encouraging people to take part on all levels in order maintain momentum.

In addition, Benkler and Nissenbaum (2006) analyse collaboration among groups on the Internet, who effectively coordinate a joint enterprise, such as open-source software development, the Wikipedia project, and research tasks in which ordinary people relieve researchers by volunteering to carry out standard tasks. They notice that

individuals might engage in online collaboration if it is organized such as to allow for smaller or larger grained contributions, thereby elucidating the fact that even minor contributions make a difference (Benkler & Nissenbaum, 2006, p. 401). This kind of online peer production grants people an opportunity to engage in practices which promote virtuous actions and engagement that further provide for additional virtuous character formation. Volunteerism and self-articulation of goals seem to be important preconditions for forming productive environments, which create room for the flourishing of virtues such as autonomy, creativity, independence and liberation. Hence, the development of such communities constitutes an alternative to the established managerial and contract-based production surrounding activities in both education and work life, and offers instead an opportunity for self-decision in carrying out tasks. Independence of institutional rules and roles implies that self-motivation and commitment from the very beginning goes into the formation of collaboration and production – "No matter what other demands constrain their lives; participation in peer production constitutes an arena of autonomy, an arena where they are free to act according to self-articulated goals and principles" (Benkler & Nissenbaum, 2006, p. 405). In a jihadist perspective, this kind of self selection allows for self-radicalisation and recruitment on a step by step basis in which involvement in the jihadist movement gradually increases.

Radicalization via Jihadist Invasion of Facebook.com

The Facebook invasion took off in 2008 with the purpose of reaching out to a wide crowd of Muslims using Facebook. On the al-Falooja forum, a poster suggested that seven "brigades" should invade social networking platforms, like Facebook, in order to spread jihad- and matyr-promoting content (Shactman, 2010). Official Facebook administrators frequently seek to remove militant groups and users with extremist Muslim attitudes, but as a counteraction, these groups share information about how to avoid having user profiles deleted. The jihadist Facebook strategy includes forming groups with radical positions in seeking to congregate users with "the right" attitude (CTA: Center for Terror Analysis. The Danish Security Intelligence Service, 2010, p. 3).

In this way, al-Qaeda supporters harness Facebook's potential for large scale persuasion. Using Facebook as a platform for radicalization and recruitment initiatives seems obvious; as a small example consider the overwhelming amount of occasions, in which you have been prompted by Facebook friends and asked to join Facebook groups. You probably click to learn more about the group and maybe you decide to join it; since your Facebook friends have asked you, and they are all part of a trusted network of people you either know personally or people you "know" via trusted friends. Of course, the jihadist invasion of Facebook is not costless, since it also provides Western intelligence agencies with an observable map for tracking activities and networks. Still, the price to be paid for exposure on a platform which affords surveillance, has to be measured up against the advantages of being present on a platform, which allows for mass persuasion. Moreover jihadist user strategies for Facebook differ among radical Muslims, some of which have formed groups like any other Facebook groups, while others work under cover with false identities and seek to exploit existing Facebook groups and networks, which are hostile towards their opinions.

Contrary to an ordinary Web forum, which grows into a mature community by passing through certain developmental stages in establishing critical mass of users and content; Facebook represents a community of friends, in which new groups can easily launch their ideas and foster engagement among friends. Apart from offering an easy set up framework for groups, Facebook also enables a new type of mass interpersonal persuasion, which might sustain radicalisation.

These points can be further elaborated on by bringing attention to B. J. Fogg's work on persuasive technology, which emphasizes the use of interactive technologies in changing human behavior (Fogg, 2003). Consequently, Fogg has coined the term "Captology" in referring to the study of computers as persuasive technologies. In the article *Mass Interpersonal Persuasion: An Early View on a New Phenomenon* (2008), Fogg throws light on mechanisms involved when individuals change attitudes and behaviors on a mass scale (MIP). Here, Fogg appoints Facebook in particular to be an outstanding example of a large scale persuasive technology.

Mass persuasion is not a new notion, but by means of global social networking platforms, ordinary users have the power to influence and reach a broad audience via interpersonal relations. In accounting for this phenomenon, Fogg lists six components, which go into the formation of mass interpersonal persuasion, and he furthermore stresses that these components had never been present altogether in one place until the launching of Facebook Platform in 2007, which allowed for a new way for third parties to distribute Web applications. For instance, the application ILike obtained over one million users within a week with an application, who persuaded people to give up personal information about their taste in music (later on, people were persuaded to buy concert tickets with friends. By now, this new form of persuasion has become main stream on Facebook and other social networking services (Fogg, 2008, p. 26).

According to Fogg, it is the combination of a *persuasive experience* (element no. 1) and social dynamics, which makes persuasion on Facebook unique. Moreover, the computer mediated *automated structure* (element no. 2) of the persuasive experience allows for repeating the persuasive experience over and over again, and makes it easy for people to share an experience with others. In distributing or joining a persuasive experience, simplicity is a core issue; if people can participate without too much trouble, just by one or two mouse clicks, they are likely to do so. By means of *social distribution* (element no. 3) the persuasive experience can spread easily and quickly via a *rapid cycle* (element no. 4). Hereby it wins credibility because it stems from a trusted network of friends and the rapid cycle of the persuasive experience builds up momentum and enthusiasm. Furthermore, mass interpersonal persuasion implies a *huge social graph* (element no. 5), ensuring a critical mass of users. Facebook provides for this by allowing millions of people to interact with each others. In addition, a movement might take off in Facebook and travel to other affiliated social graphs. Finally, Fogg mentions *measured impact* (element no. 6), which refers to statistical measurements reported. This enables Facebook users (and of course Facebook. com, as well as other parties, such as companies and application developers) to keep track of the effects of their interventions, and ordinary users are likely to be affected by the fact that a lot of other users have joined up for this or that group (Fogg, 2008. pp. 26-30).

"Mass interpersonal persuasion matters because this new phenomenon gives ordinary individuals the ability to reach and influence millions of people. This is new. Over the past century, mass media has been the primary channel for persuasion. These channels were controlled by powerful people and organizations. They used mass media largely to achieve their own goals. Now, the landscape is changing. I believe the power to persuade will continue to become less centralized, thanks to MIP. For early evidence of decentralization, we can see how much impact ordinary individuals have had with blogs and online videos. This is just the beginning. Individuals will have even more impact in the world as we continue creating tools that enable MIP. We are at the start of a revolution in how individuals and cultures make decisions and take action" (Fogg, 2008, p. 33).

To briefly sum up, the official al-Qaeda media network is highly successful in setting the agenda for global online jihadism: An effective brand-management strategy guarantees the credibility of media productions. Likewise, the use of Web 2.0 tools, such as Web forums and Facebook, creates a context that is conducive to engaged user involvement on all levels, allowing for different levels of participation ranging from the posting of a few messages to the production of advanced jihad-promoting video footages. Also, utilization of Web 2.0 tools simply makes it possible to reach out to a broad audience. With this as a background, the following section offers further clarification of the phenomenon behind the engaged practice surrounding al-Qaeda and global jihadism on the Web.

A Virtue Ethical Perspective on Al-Qaeda and Global Jihadism

In what follows, I explore ways in which motivation and engagement can be fostered and maintained among jihadist participants in online communities. As previously mentioned, Benkler and Nissenbaum (2006) discuss findings from studies of online communities, which successfully manage a joint endeavor, partly due to the organization of the projects, which allows room for variously sized contributions; partly because of peer review moderation of performance in the shape of electronic ranking systems or online pad on the backs among users, who praises each other's work (Benkler & Nissenbaum, 2006, pp. 400-401). In addition, from a virtue ethical outlook, they argue that online peer production is particular motivating since it provides an opportunity to engage in practices which endorse virtuous actions and engagement (Benkler & Nissenbaum, 2006, p. 403).

One might find that engaging in al-Qaeda activities, online or in real life, cannot be referred to as virtuous. Nevertheless, it is a central discussion in virtue ethics, whether or not we are to consider a terrorist as being a virtuous agent, since she or he shows courage in carrying out her or his mission (Foot, 1978). But, in emphasizing the shortcomings of the al-Qaeda practice, which is characterized by not being open to criticism; I seek to demonstrate why it does not make sense to speak of a virtuous terrorist.

Virtue Ethics

It is a general characteristic of virtue ethics that it, contrary to Kantian and utilitarian moral philosophy, is concerned with the agent behind the action, rather than the action in itself. Act morality discusses moral rules or obligation in establishing what constitutes a morally right or wrong action. The decisive feature of the moral value of an action is considered to be whether it is consistent with certain rules or principles. On the other hand, agent morality focuses on the person behind the action, and discusses what makes a person a good person? Thus, the moral value of an action is the character of the person behind that action – good actions hold no moral values by themselves. Of course, action centered ethics can explain what it takes to be a good person, as well as agent centered ethics can explain what constitutes a morally good action. But the definitions are derived from their respective starting points, which are inherent in the good action and the good person. Consequently, virtue ethics further presupposes a conception of psychological concepts, such as intention, happiness, and action (Anscombe, 1958).

Modern virtue ethics does not appear as a well-defined ethical theory; instead it covers a variety of different positions. Also, there is no exhaustive catalogue of virtues to be found anywhere. We have of course the four cardinal virtues; courage, justice, temperance and wisdom, and the theological virtues belief, hope and love. The list could be further extended to include for instance; loyalty, benevolence, empathy, honesty, tolerance and so on. In the writings of Alisdair MacIntyre, a virtue is considered to be a quality, which enables individuals to exercise exactly those actions required by a given social role, and to do it well. A virtue is "an acquired human quality the possession and exercise of which tends to enable us to achieve those goods which are internal to practices and the lack of which effectively prevents us from achieving any such goods" (MacIntyre, 2000, p.191). Our activities are embedded in, and understood through the light of tradition and narratives, and it is by means of the virtues and through participation in a practice, that we achieve those internal goods and standards of excellence inherent to a particular practice. A practice is a socially established cooperative human activity, which enables its participants to realize internal goods characteristic to that practice. As examples of different kinds of practices, MacIntyre mentions art, the game of playing football, the game of playing chess, policy, family life, farming, science. Common for all of these are the fact that, in participating in them, we seek to achieve those standards of excellence inherent to these practices (MacIntyre, 2000, p. 187). The history of a given practice provides it with a certain authority to which we must subject ourselves in the first place. All though the standards of excellence are by no means resistant to criticism, one cannot enter a practice not accepting the authority of the best standards evolved in that practice (MacIntyre, 2000, p. 190). In the practice of for instance chess playing, the internal goods that we strive for are; analytical skills, strategic imagination and competitiveness. In participating in a specific practice external and contingent goods too can of course be gained - that is, goods, such as money, prestige and social status: These are all goods, which can be achieved independent of a given practice, whereas internal goods cannot be obtained in any other way than participating in the practice that fosters them (MacIntyre, 2000, p. 188). Furthermore, whereas external goods are possessed by individuals, such as the more one have, the less there is for others, internal goods represent goods for the whole community of practice.

A whole range of key virtues are important for the flourishing of our life, and we cannot do without them if we are to achieve those goods internal to a given practice. Any practice, with internal goods and standards of excellence, depends on the virtues of justice, courage and honesty – "we have to learn to recognize what is due to whom; we have to be prepared to take whatever self-endangering risks are demanded along the way; and we have to listen carefully to what we are told about our own inadequacies and to reply with the same carefulness for the fact" (MacIntyre, 2000, p. 191).

Online Jihadism and Virtues

Virtues are not defined in relation to a right or wrong sound practice; instead the definition rests on a neutral concept of practice. All though counter intuitive, it seems that we are to consider al-Qaeda activities as virtuous, as part of a practice with its own internal goods and standards of excellence. It is probably also the case that online jihobbyists think of their activities as virtuous, and bearing in mind the points of Benkler and Nissenbaum, this might count as a possible explanation of why online collaboration serving the cause of jihadism is able to foster ongoing engagement among participants. As such, the virtues might support a seemingly wrong ethical practice, for instance loyalty might strengthen al-Qaeda and related extremist Muslim movements. From this perspective, the 9/11 terror attack and the 7/7 London bombing are to be considered as courageous acts, and these actions are also honored in the al-Qaeda community as acts of great bravery carried out by virtuous heroes of al-Qaeda. Thus, the online community pays its tribute to terrorists, as an example of this, a matyr-promoting video targeted at the English and American Muslim market was released on the first anniversary of the 7/7 London bombing. The video featured Osama bin Laden, Zawahiri and one of the suicide bombers, Tanweer, who gave his final testament

in English, assuring his commitment to die for the cause of Islam. The video also described war crimes committed in Iraq by U.S. soldiers (Seib, 2008, p. 78). Here the tradition of the practice for violent action in the name of Islam is being reinforced by introducing a narrative. But, in the view of the fact that Islam prohibits violence, al-Qaeda is faced with the challenge of legitimating violent actions and killings in a political as well as a religious perspective. This is done by promoting their special interpretation of the Quran combined with narratives about the heroic fight against the American forces and Western imperialism. Thus, our stories and traditions matter for our conception of what is right and wrong.

"I can only answer the question 'What am I to do?' if I can answer the prior question 'Of what story or stories do I find myself a part?' We enter human society, that is, with one or more imputed characters – roles into which we have been drafted – and we have to learn what they are in order to be able to understand how others respond to us and how our responses to them are apt to be construed (..) Hence, there is no way to give us an understanding of any society, including our own, except through the stock of stories which constitute its initial dramatic resources. Mythology, in its original sense, is at the heart of things. Vico was right and so was Joyce. And so too of course is that moral tradition from heroic society to its medieval heirs according to which the telling of stories has a key part in education us into the virtues" (MacIntyre, 2000, p. 216).

One could argue that terrorists are not terrorists but part of a resistance movement fighting for justice, and one should of course bear in mind that Muslims have in fact plentiful good political reasons for claiming justice. But it is also important to dissociate from violence as an explicit mean brought to use in order to obtain good ends. As a comparison, it could be argued that the Danish resistance movement under the Second World War was also a terrorist movement; and considering a counterfactual cause of history, implying that the Nazis had won the war, it is a plausible outcome that the movement would indeed have been considered a terrorist organization. Consequently one might argue that the whole conception of whether we are to talk about terrorists or fighters of resistance stands or falls with the actual political consensus. Nevertheless, one has to pay attention to the fact that the Danish resistance movement, all though their actions caused people to die, did not operate with the specific intent to kill civilians in order to reach their ends.

But we are still faced with the issue regarding whether or not it is reasonable to speak of a virtuous terrorist? Thomas Aquinas suggested that virtues can bring about only good actions; they are dispositions, which we cannot use for bad purposes. Nowadays, opinions on that matter differ: for instance, Von Wright find it in order to speak of the "courage of the villain", whereas Foot makes a distinction, which enables us to avoid having virtues displayed in relation to bad actions. Consequently, the seemingly courageous act of a terrorist can be rejected in arguing that "courage" is not operating as a virtue when it is turned into bad ends, such as killing hostages or becoming a suicide bomber. Foot elaborates on this point with reference to an analogy, by which she brings attention to the fact that poison, like arsenic or Botox, is not a poison in all occurrences of it. For instance low dosage of Botox injections are used for cosmetic purposes, and likewise arsenic is prescribed as heart medicine. In a similar vein, courage is not operating as a virtue when a terrorist turns his courage, which is a virtue, into bad ends (Foot, 1978, p. 116 - 119). Moreover, one could add that the terrorist is not acting like a virtuous individual would act, since it does not make sense to ask how the virtuous person would carry out actions of terror, because the virtuous person would never do that in the first place. In fact, the virtuous is an individual, who understands reasons for moral action, which implies that the

virtues shape our practical reason in specific ways. Thus, to be honest is not simply to respond with honesty in situations where one could be tempted to lie, instead the virtue in general allows for a pertinent understanding of the value of honesty, and in practice this understanding lets reasons for acting with honesty guide ones actions. As such, situated reasoning in the sense of practical wisdom – *phronesis* – is needed in order to know good means to bring about good ends (Aristotle, 1909).

As persons, we develop into *independent practical reasoners* and practice practical sense through life experience and through the learning we get from care persons in our upbringing, and thus we become able to make our values and ideas explicit socially. Through rational critical reflection we can thus cement or reject values, ideas and prejudices by examining them and ask for their justification (MacIntyre, 1999, p.158-59). A practice that flourishes, in being morally robust and sound, is a practice which is challenged by morally criticism, passed on in the form of formally legislative power as well as by independent practical reasoners.

As before mentioned, when it comes to al-Qaeda, critical reflection and self-selection of goals is only allowed for as long as participants do not question the religious interpretation contained in global jihadism. Thus actual self-articulation of goals is not offered as an opportunity within the jihadist movement, and in the future, the suppressing of critical reflection might bring about the fall of al-Qaeda. Actually, moderate Muslims have begun to form counter al-Qaeda online communities. Likewise, leading clerics raise their voices against al-Qaeda, claiming that terror actions against civilians contradict with the teachings of the Prophet Mohammed.

The notion of critical reflection and the importance of self-articulation of goals can be further clarified by introducing the work of Hannah Arendt (1964, 1971), in which she seeks to explain for the counter intuitive fact that seemingly caring individuals can be seduced by extreme movements, in her case, the Nazis. In seeking to understand the Holocaust in general, and the motives of Eichmann, as representative of the individual, who participated in Holocaust, she asks whether the ability to think as such prevents us from doing evil (Arendt, 1971, p. 418)? And she answers affirmative. Thus, she presents a phenomenological investigation of the experience of thinking with reference to Socratic thinking and the Kantian distinction between knowledge (*Verstand*) and thought (*Vernuft*), the former of which deals with the intellect, which strives for verifiable knowledge often in the seek for tangible results, whereas thinking displays the quest for meaning obtained by pondering reflection (Arendt, 1971, p. 422).

The Socratic dialogues are characterized by being aporetic, which implies that Socrates is always able to bring his interlocutor in aporia about the nature of the subject matter in question. Thus, during the conversation with Socrates, the interlocutor comes to realize that what he thought he knew, he, in fact, did not know. And Socrates himself does not hold the truth, but instead inspires the person to further investigate the nature of the concept under discussion. The kind of thinking reflected in the Socratic dialogues "unfreezes frozen thoughts" (Arendt, 1971, p. 431) and teaches people how to think, without being told what to think. Thus, Socrates described himself as a gadfly, a midwife and an electric ray: As a gadfly, he aroused people; being an electric ray, he was paralyzed himself by his own perplexity and this condition he transferred to people around him. The paralysis of thought also implies an interruption, forcing people to question assumptions held while being "unthinkingly engaged in whatever you were doing" (Arendt, 1971, p. 434). Finally, as a midwife he delivered others of their thought and decided whether the child was fit for life or just a "windegg" that the bearer had to be freed from – in all cases, the thoughts ended as windeggs, and thus people were purged from their assumptions and prejudgments. Furthermore, as a midwife, Socrates was sterile (as was the case

with midwifes in ancient Greece, since they had passed the age of being fertile), symbolizing that he had nothing to teach people, no truth to sell (Arendt, 1971, p. 432).

"However, non-thinking, which seems so recommendable a state for political and moral affairs, also has its dangers. By shielding people against the dangers of examination, it teaches them to hold fast to whatever the prescribed rules of conduct may be at a given time in a given society. What people then get used to is not so much the content of the rules, a close examination of which would always lead them into perplexity, as the possession of rules under which to subsume particulars. In other words, they get used to never making up their minds" (Arendt. 1971, p. 436).

For Arendt, good judgment does not equal either objective knowledge or subjective opinion, it is related to inter-subjectivity. Consequently, one has to develop a visiting imagination allowing one to imaging the variety of relevant perspectives that come into play when judging a situation – "to visit, in other words, you just travel to a new location, leave behind what is familiar, and resist the temptation to make yourself at home where you are not" (Arendt, 1973, p. 159). Characteristically of Eichmann, was the fact that he was unable to take the perspective of the unique other into consideration and his lack of imagination blocked for his understanding of the other (Arendt, 1964, p 48). Above all, Arendt concluded that Eichmann was unable to judge because he did not bother to think:

"Inability to think is not stupidity; it can be found in highly intelligent people, and wickedness is hardly its cause, if only because thoughtlessness as well as stupidity are much more frequent phenomena than wickedness. The trouble is precisely that no wicked heart, a relatively rare phenomenon, is necessary to cause great evil" (Arendt, 1971, p. 423).

In the jihobbyistic online communities, one cannot take the perspective of the other into account when deliberating about a matter, thus only one-sided judgments can be passed and no room for constructive action is given - the repeated argument runs; either you are with us or you are against us, which unfortunately has also been a well known rhetorical phrase in the American and European formulations concerned with "the war on terror".

Solutions and Recommendations

The solution to the complex problems surrounding the use of the Web as a tool of radicalization is probably going to be found in the participatory oriented Web 2.0 practice, which affords many-with-many bottom-up interactions and creation of user-driven content. Alas, for the moment being this is also what allows for the fostering of online engagement among jihobbyists, who through self-selection of goals feel motivated to participate in online activities at all levels.

In trying to predict the future, one should always be cautious, but in the long run al-Qaeda's online efforts is going to face a difficult future, since the dynamics of online social networking activities is hard to control. Besides, more moderate voices are forming online counter movements, who by means of videos, message posts and Facebook groups seek to flood the violent rhetoric of jihobbyists. Thus, ironically speaking, the Web 2.0 empowered version of global jihadism presumably bears the seed to its own destruction.

FUTURE RESEARCH DIRECTIONS

In this chapter, I have outlined ways in which the official al-Qaeda media and Web strategy plays a pivotal role in the radicalization of young Muslims by setting the agenda for jihobbyists' activities on Web forums and on global social networking platforms, such as Facebook and YouTube.

But I have mainly approached the topic from an analytical and descriptive perspective. Thus, this contribution has dealt with a little fragment of a multi facetted problem and primarily done so without reaching beyond the Web. Accordingly, the whole area needs further investigation. First of all, a broader socio-cultural conception of how to break the cycle of radicalization is called for. From the angle of it-ethics, this sociological endeavor could be supplemented by empirical based investigations; in particular there is a need for case based ethnographic studies, in seeking to comprehend mechanisms behind online- radicalization. Also, one should pay attention to the role played by the growing movement consisting of moderate Muslims and other individuals, who establish counter jihadist forums and Facebook groups.

From a quite different perspective, it is crucial to address issues of privacy and free speech. After 9/11, the number of counterterrorism research labs has increased massively (for an example, see the homepage of the Danish Counterterrorism Research Lab). As a result, scientific achievements within the fields of applied mathematics and computer science have led to the development of advanced search engines, which enables intelligent services to monitor online activities with the purpose of analyzing terror networks and prevent terror attacks. This is without doubt a noble goal, but with the development of this kind of surveillance technology follows a demand to take care that the privacy of ordinary individuals is not endangered.

CONCLUSION

It is hard not to admire the professionalism surrounding the al-Qaeda media machine: Video releases featuring leading al-Qaeda members, who address jihadist ideological important issues combined with clever use of Web 2.0 tools for radicalization, recruitment and training.

The notion of Web 2.0 can be looked upon from a technical perspective, but here, in referring to Web 2.0 from a practice perspective, the main focus has been on the prototypical use modes related to Web 2.0. The practices surrounding Web 2.0 are characterized by collaboration and a participatory-oriented approach to Web activities. Consequently, interaction on the Web has gradually shifted from one-to-many display of information on homepages to many-to-many bottom-up user driven interaction. So far, Al-Qaeda has been proficient in utilizing the shift from Web 1.0 to Web 2.0 for purposes of radicalization. Thus, through the use of persuasive Web design, the al-Qaeda leaders set the agenda for topics to be discussed in grass root jihadist online communities. Furthermore most online communities provide opportunities for user participation on different levels, whereby it becomes possible to gradually build up and foster long lasting engagement. Besides Web communities of sworn jihobbyists, the social affordance of the Facebook platform is by itself a base for large scale interpersonal persuasion, which allows jihobbyists to reach out to a broad audience including moderate Muslims and others sympathetic to their case.

From a virtue ethical approach it can be argued that the above mentioned Web 2.0 tools allows for participation in practices in which volunteerism and self-articulation of goals are important preconditions for forming user-driven online communities. Also, it is without doubt the case that jihobbyists think of their enterprise as virtuous, where in fact only pseudo virtues go into the formation of engagement in the jihadist practice, since a practice can only flourish and become morally mature as long as it is receptive to morally criticism by independent practical reasoners. Currently, moderate Muslims have begun to form communities in which they seek to enter into dialogue and question the dogmas of jihadism. Thus, they can be viewed as representing Socratic gadflies, who pass by jihobbyists in trying to force them to wake up and think and act as independent practical reasoners instead of reproducing "windeggs".

REFERENCES

Ansar Al-Mujahideen Network. (2010). *Info.* Retrieved August 16, 2010, from http://www.ansar1.info/

Anscombe, E. (1958). Modern moral philosophy. *Philosophy (London, England)*, *33*, 1–19. doi:10.1017/S0031819100037943

Arendt, H. (1964). *Eichmann in Jerusalem: A report on the banality of evil*. New York, NY: Penguin Books.

Arendt, H. (1971). Thinking and moral consideration: A lecture. *Social Research*, *38*(3), 417–446.

Aristotle,. (1909). *Nicomachean ethics* (Greenwood, L. H. G., Trans.). Cambridge, UK: University Press.

Benkler, Y., & Nissenbaum, H. (2006). Commons-based peer production and virtue. *Journal of Political Philosophy*, *14*(4), 394–419. doi:10.1111/j.1467-9760.2006.00235.x

Bermingham, A., Conway, M., McInerney, L., O'Hare, N., & Smeaton, A. F. (2009). *Combining social network analysis and sentiment analysis to explore the potential for online radicalisation*. Retrieved August 16, 2010, from http://doras.dcu.ie/4554/

Brachman, J. (2008). *Global jihadism: Theory and practice*. Routledge Press.

Conway, M., & McInerney, L. (2008). *Jihadi video & auto-radicalisation: Evidence from an exploratory YouTube study*. Retrieved August 16, 2010, from http://doras.dcu.ie/2253/

Cool, S., & Glasser, S. B. (2005, August 7). Terrorists turn to the Web as a base of operation. *Washington Post*.

CTA. Center for Terror Analysis. The Danish Security Intelligence Service. (2010). *Youtube. com og Facebook.com – de nye radikaliseringsværktøjer?* PET, Center for Terroranalyse. Retrieved August 16, 2010, from http: //www. pet. dk/upload/ youtube_og_ facebook_-_de_nye_ radikaliseringsvaerktoejer.pdf

Fogg, B. J. (2003). *Persuasive technology – Using computers to change what we think and do.* San Francisco, CA: Morgan Kaufmann.

Fogg, B. J. (2008). Mass interpersonal persuasion: An early view of a new phenomenon. In H. O. Kukkonen, P. Hasle, M. H. K. Segerståhl, & P. Øhrstrøm (Eds.), *Proceedings of the 3rd International Conference on Persuasive Technology* (pp. 23-35). Oulu, Finland. Berlin, Germany: Springer-Verlag.

Foot, P. (1978). Virtues and vices. In Darwall, S. (Ed.), *Virtue ethics.* Oxford, UK: Blackwell.

MI5 Security Service. (2010). *Al Qaida's structure.* Retrieved August 16, 2010, from https: //www. mi5.gov. uk/output/ al-qaidas-structure.html

MacIntyre, A. (1999). *Dependent rational animals – Why human beings need the virtues.* Illinois: Carus Publishing Company.

MacIntyre, A. (2000). *After virtue.* London, UK: Duckworth.

O'Reilly, T. (2005). *What is Web 2.0? Design patterns and business models for the next generation of software.* Retrieved August 16, 2010, from http: //oreilly. com/Web2/ archive/what-is-web- 20.html

Seib, P. H. (2008). The Al-Qaeda media machine. *Military Review*, 74–80.

Shactman, N. (2008). *Online Jihadists plan to invade Facebook.* Retrieved August 16, 2010, from, http://current.com/1r3i84c

The Danish Counterterrorism Research Lab. (2010). *CTRLab*. Retrieved August 16, 2010 from, http://www.ctrlab.dk/

Weingberg, L., & Perliger, A. (2010). How terrorist groups end. *CTC Sentinel, 3*(2), 16–18.

WikiLeaks. (2010). *About WikiLeaks.* Retrieved August 16, 2010, from http: //wikileaks. org/wiki/ WikiLeaks:About

WikiLeaks. (2010). *Collateral murder.* Retrieved August 16, 2010, from http://www.collateralmurder.com/

ADDITIONAL READING

Andersen, L. E. (2007). *Innocence Lost – Islamism and the battle over values and world order.* Odense: University Press of Southern Denmark.

Annas, J. (1992). Ancient Ethics and Modern Morality. *Philosophical Perspectives, 6,* 119–136. doi:10.2307/2214241

Arendt, H. (1968). *Between past and Future: Eight exercises in political thought.* New York: Penguin Books.

Arendt, H. (1973). *The Origins of totalitarianism.* New York: Harcourt Brace & Company.

Arendt, H. (1978). *The Life of the Mind.* New York: Harcourt Brace & Company.

Cheong, P. H. (2009) *A Broader View of Internet Radicalization.* Retrieved August 16, 2010 from http: //comops. org/journal/2009/03 /26/a-broader-view-of- internet-radicalization/

Corlett, J. A. (2003). *Terrorism – A Philosophical Analysis. Dorcdrecht.* Kluwer Academic Publishers.

Corman, S. R., & Schiefelbein, J. S. (2006). *Communication and Media Strategy in the Jihadi War of Ideas*. Arizona: Arizona Board of Regents. Retrieved August 16, 2010, from http://comops. org/publications/ CSC_report_0601-jihad_comm_media.pdf

Corman, S. R., Trethewey, A., & Goodall, H. L. Jr., (Eds.). (2008). *Weapons of mass persuasion: strategic communication to combat violent extremism*. New York: Peter Lang Publishing Inc.

Foot, P. (2001). *Natural Goodness*. Oxford: Clarendon Press. doi:10.1093/0198235089.001.0001

Fukuyama, F. (1992). *The End of History and the Last Man*. New York: Avon Books.

Gartenstein-Ross, D., & Grossman, L. (2009). *Homegrown Terrorists in the U.S. And U.K – An Emperical Examination of the Radicalisation Process*. Washington: FDD Press. Retrieved August 16, 2010, from http://www.defenddemocracy. org/downloads/HomegrownTerrorists_USandUK.pdf

Geach, P. (1977). The Virtues. [ambridge University Press.]. *The Stanton Lectures, 1973-4*, C.

Kepel, G. (1993). *Muslims Extremism in Egypt: The Prophet and Pharaoh. Berkely*. University of California Press.

Khatchadourian, R. (2007). The making of an Al Qaeda Homegrown. *New Yorker (New York, N.Y.)*, (Jan): 22.

Kruschwitz, R., & Roberts, R. (Eds.). (1987). *The Virtues: Contemporary Essays on Moral Character*. Belmont: Wadsworth.

Lutz, J. M., & Lutz, J. B. (2005). *Terrorism: Origins and Evolution*. New York: Palgrave.

O'Reilly, T. (2006). *Web 2.0 Compact Definition: Trying again*. Retrieved August 4, 2010, from http://radar.oreilly. com/2006/12/web-20- compact-definition-tryi.html.

Roberts, R. C. (1989). Aristotle on Virtues and Emotions. *Philosophical Studies*, *56*(3), 293–306. doi:10.1007/BF00354366

Schmid, A. P. (2010). *Perspectives on Terrorism – a Journal of the Terrorism Research Initiative*. Retrieved August 16, 2010, from http://www. terrorismanalysts.com/pt/

Singer, P. (2002). *A Companion to Ethics. Cornwall*. Blackwell.

Tavani, H. T. (2007). *Ethics & Technology – Ethical Issues in an Age of Information and Communication Technology*. Danvers, MA: John Wiley & Sons, Inc.

Trianosky, G. (1997). What is Virtue Ethics all About. D. Statman (ed.). *Virtue Ethics. A critical Reader*. Edinburgh: Edinburgh University Press.

Von Wright, G. H. (1963). *Varieties of Goodness*. New York: Humanities Press.

Watson, G. (1997). On the Primacy of Character. D. Statman (ed.). *Virtue Ethics. A critical Reader*. Edinburgh: Edinburgh University Press.

Williams, B. (1993). *Ethics and the Limits of Philosophy*. London: Fontana Press.

KEY TERMS AND DEFINITIONS

Jihobbyist: A term coined by Jarret Brachman to describe a person who sympathizes with the religious ideology of global jihadism. A jihobbyist is a self starter, an individual or a small group of people, who emerge without direct support from any official al-Qaeda factor. A jihobbyist drives his own radicalisation and is an active participant on the Web.

Mass Interpersonal Persuasion (MIP): A new form of persuasion introduced by B.J. Fogg. MIP is fostered by the use of Web 2.0 technologies, such as Facebook Platform. The advance of Web 2.0 technologies affords mass interpersonal persuasion by which it becomes possible to make individuals change attitudes and behaviors on a mass scale; also ordinary people can reach a broad audience in seeking resonance for their message.

Practice: A practice is a socially established cooperative human activity, which enables its participants to realize internal goods characteristic to that practice. A practice that flourishes and is morally robust and sound is a practice which is challenged by morally critic.

Thinking Experience: Hannah Arendt's phenomenological investigation of the experience of thinking with reference to Socratic thinking and the Kantian distinction between knowledge (*Verstand*) and thought (*Vernuft*), the former of which deals with the intellect, which strives for verifiable knowledge often in the seek for tangible results, whereas thinking display the meaning gained by a wondering open minded kind of reflection. Hence, Arendt describes the thinking faculty with reference to *Vernuft*, and illustrates that it is always tentative, unverifiable and self-destructive. She takes Socratic thinking as a standard, since through his dialogues, Socrates was able to show his interlocutor that what he thought he knew he did in fact not know. Consequently, Arendt refers to "frozen thoughts" that must unfreeze in her attempts to illustrate how we through thinking activities can avoid acting morally wrong.

Virtue: A virtue is a character trait of a certain kind, it is a disposition which is deeply rooted in the virtuous person, not just a habit but a fundamental trait which guide us in our lives and makes us capable of achieve goods which are internal to the practices which we are participating in.

Virtue Ethics: Modern virtue ethics does not appear as a well defined theory, but covers a variety of positions. Virtue ethics place focus on the agent in emphasizing character traits of the moral agent as well as seeking to describe how human flourishing can be achieved. Thus, of the three major approaches in normative ethics - the other two being: deontology, which places focus on rules or duties as criterions for judging whether an action is morally right or wrong; and consequentialism, which highlights the consequences of actions in the moral judgment – virtue ethics can be described as an agent centered form of ethics (agent morality) as opposed to action centered ethics (act morality). Central concepts within virtue ethics are *virtue*, *phronesis* (practical wisdom) and *eudaimonia* (tentatively translated: happiness, flourishing, well-being).

Web 2.0: The notion of Web 2.0 stresses many-to-many interaction in the production of content, whereby users are turned into active participants. Web 2.0 has evolved from and can be contrasted to Web 1.0, which emphasizes content delivery and one-to-many communication via homepages only allowing users to be passive browsers. Typically Web 2.0 technologies are: Facebook, Wikipedia, YouTube, Blogs, Twitter.

Chapter 11
Google in China:
Corporate Responsibility on a Censored Internet

Richard A. Spinello
Boston College, USA

ABSTRACT

This chapter, focusing primarily on the search engine company Google, treats the normative issue of how U.S. or European companies should respond when asked to abet the efforts of countries like China or Iran in their efforts to censor the Web. Should there be international laws to prevent these technology companies from yielding to the demands of totalitarian regimes? We argue that such laws would be reactive and ineffectual and that the optimal solution is proactive corporate self-regulation that gives careful prominence to moral reasoning. Our moral analysis concludes that a socially responsible company must not cooperate with implementing the censorship regimes of these repressive sovereignties. This conclusion is based on natural law reasoning and on the moral salience that must be given to the ideal of universal human rights, including the natural right of free expression.

INTRODUCTION

Since the 1990's the technology landscape has been dominated by Internet gatekeepers which provide tools like search engines and portals that help users access and navigate the Internet. As Yahoo, Microsoft, and Google have expanded into markets like China or Saudi Arabia they have been asked to support various censorship laws and other online restrictions. Yahoo, for example, signed a self-discipline pledge when it entered the Chinese market, promising to abide by Chinese censorship law. Social media sites like Facebook are likely to face similar censorship requirements in the near future.

DOI: 10.4018/978-1-61350-132-0.ch011

Despite the Internet's great promise as a borderless global technology and a free marketplace of ideas, there has been considerable friction between the speech enabled by Internet technologies and the laws of authoritarian countries which define their culture in a more paternalistic fashion. Cyberspace was supposed to be an open environment where anyone could express their opinions, start a new business, or create a web site. Its end-to-end design created an environment conducive to liberty and democracy, with unfettered access to information. As the U.S. Supreme Court eloquently wrote in its *Reno v. ACLU* (1997, p. 857) decision, the Internet enables an ordinary citizen to become "a pamphleteer,...a town crier with a voice that resonates farther than it could from any soapbox". But a lethal combination of stringent law and software code in the form of filtering programs has enabled authoritarian societies to effectively undermine the Internet's libertarian ethos.

Many Western companies have been forced by these foreign governments to help regulate activities in cyberspace as a condition of doing business within that country. This regulation most often comes in the form of code, filtering software which allows a sovereign nation to restrict its citizens from accessing or disseminating certain information on the Internet. In China, data is transmitted over the Internet through fiber-optic networks controlled by routers, and those routers controlling the flow that data are configured to filter out certain web sites that have blacklisted terms. This system has been called the "great firewall of China". Internet gatekeepers, which provide a service such as online access or search results, cannot subvert this firewall if they expect to do business in China. Countries like Iran and Saudi Arabia deploy similar techniques. The gatekeepers along with other technology and social media companies are caught in a vice between countries exercising their legitimate sovereignty and individual citizens seeking to exercise their basic speech rights. It was once thought that states would have a difficult time enforcing their

sovereignty in cyberspace but, thanks to code such as filtering software, freedom of expression is threatened by state power often assisted by private companies. But states are re-asserting their authority and demanding compliance with local law. As a result, the Internet loses some of its "generative" potential as a viable force for semiotic democracy (Zittrain, 2003).

The Internet gatekeepers are especially vulnerable and must find ways to responsibly navigate this perilous virtual terrain. Their corporate strategies, oriented to rapid global expansion, cannot ignore the question of the Internet's role in authoritarian societies like China, Iran, and Cuba. The problem is exacerbated by the lack of international laws that govern cyberspace along with the policy disputes that prevent the dissemination of anti-censorship technologies. Without the guidance of law, companies must determine whether to side with the host government or with many of their citizens who have a different conception about free speech.

Google's unfortunate experience in China will be the main springboard for our discussion, but we will also take into account the practices of companies like Microsoft and Yahoo. After briefly reviewing some background on Google, which is attracted to foreign markets by the need to sustain its economic growth, we will turn to the legal issues and the prospects that there may be some legal resolution on the horizon. We conclude that those prospects are dim and that corporate self-regulation is essential in the face of this policy vacuum. *Ethical self-regulation* subjugates rational self interest to the legitimate needs and rights of others and, above all, respect for the common good of the Internet community.

We then turn to a moral analysis of Google's strategy, which revolves around an apparently irresolvable polarity: either the company can initiate cultural and normative changes in China *or* compromise its core values and adapt to China's norms and law. This analysis pursues several key questions. If it chooses the latter alternative, can

Google's conduct in China be morally justified according to the pragmatic and utilitarian reasoning adopted by the company to defend its decision? Or should companies like Google and Yahoo refrain from participating in online censorship or surveillance as a cost of doing business in certain states? We argue that Google cannot responsibly cooperate with China's systematic repression of free speech rights. The right to free expression is universal and cannot be relativized away despite the persuasive claims of some ethicists to the contrary. In reaching this conclusion we must explore the philosophical grounding for this right and address the valid concerns of the pluralists. We begin all this with a look at Google and the search engine business.

BACKGROUND ISSUES: THE TROUBLED HISTORY OF GOOGLE IN CHINA

Google, the ubiquitous U.S. Internet search engine company, was founded in 1998 by two Stanford graduate students, Sergey Brin and Larry Page. Their ambitious goal was to create software that facilitated the searching and organizing of the world's information. Thanks to its PageRank algorithm the Google search engine delivered more reliable search results than its rivals by giving priority to web pages that were referenced or "linked to" by other web pages. The company continues to refine its search algorithm so that it can better respond to obscure and complicated queries. Google monetized its technology by licensing its search engine and by paid listings, or "sponsored links," that appeared next to web search results.

Google is the most popular search engine on the Web and still powers the search technology of most major portals and related sites. In 2010 Google enjoyed a 65% share of the global search engine market with rival search engines like Microsoft's Bing falling far behind; 86% of all Internet searches in the U.S. are now done on Google (Miller, 2010). Searches on Google's site generated about $55 billion in economic activity in the United States, giving the search engine giant considerable power over companies that rely on Google for their traffic.

Early in Google's history its founders insisted that the company must be centered upon several distinctive corporate values: "technology matters," "we make our own rules," and "don't be evil." In accord with its first two principles, Google is committed to technology innovation and to sustaining a creative leadership role in the industry. The "don't be evil" principle is realized primarily through the company's commitment not to compromise the integrity of its search results, but it has been given a broader meaning over the years. This core value, however, has been a source of continual controversy for Google whenever it is perceived to have violated social norms or transgressed ethical boundaries.

Google introduced a version of its search engine for the Chinese market in early 2006, google.cn.[1] Google's biggest rival in China is Baidu.com, Inc., which has a 60% share of the China Internet search-engine market. Given the size of the market and its future potential, the company admitted at the time that China was "strategically important" (Dean, 2005, p. A12). In order to comply with China's strict censorship laws, Google agreed to purge its search engine results of any links to politically sensitive web sites disapproved by the Chinese government. These include web sites supporting the Falun Gong cult or the independence movement in Tibet. As one reporter indicated:

"If you search for 'Tibet' or 'Falun Gong' most anywhere in the world on google.com, you'll find thousands of blog entries, news items and chat rooms on Chinese repression. Do the same search inside China on google.cn and most, if not all, of these links will be gone. Google will have erased them completely" (Thompson, 2006, p. 37).

In order to avoid further complications, the company does not host user-generated content such as blogs or e-mail on its computer servers in China for fear of the government's role in restricting their content. Unlike its competitors, Google alerted users to censored material by putting a disclaimer at the top of the search results indicating that certain links have been removed in accordance with Chinese law. Also, Chinese users could still access Google.com with its uncensored search results (though links to controversial sites would not work thanks to the firewall).

Google's cooperation with the Chinese government was met with considerable consternation by a plethora of human rights groups such as Human Rights Watch. These groups and many other critics chastised Google for so blatantly violating its high-minded corporate ethos. The company was reprimanded by several U.S. Congressmen who sought to craft legislation aimed at stopping Google and other companies from abetting the Chinese government and forcing them to comply with the United Nation's Universal Declaration of Human Rights.

In defense of its corporate policies, the company argued that its presence in China created abundant opportunities for Chinese citizens to have greater access to information. Most technical experts agree that Baidu's search results are not nearly as comprehensive or unbiased as Google's. According to a Google spokesperson, "While removing search results is inconsistent with Google's mission, providing no information (or a heavily degraded user experience that amounts to no information) is more inconsistent with our mission" (Google in China, 2006, p. A23). Google believes that its presence in China contributes to the country's modernization, and that this consideration must be balanced with the legal requirements imposed by the Chinese government.

The corporate hierarchy has been ambivalent about the moral ramifications of the company's controversial foray into the China market. One of the Google's founders, Sergey Brin, explained that his company was grappling with difficult questions and challenges: "Sometimes the 'Don't be evil' policy leads to many discussions about what exactly is evil" (Dean, 2005, p. A12). Google has apparently assumed that by improving access to information in a repressive country like China the company is bringing about sufficient benefits that outweigh the costs of abetting censorship. Despite its censorship of some information sources, Google still provides Chinese citizens with an opportunity to learn about AIDS and other health related issues, environmental concerns, world economic markets, and political developments in other parts of the world.

After a few tumultuous years and several notorious security breaches, Google decided to stop censoring its Web search and news services in China. In March, 2010 the company announced that it would redirect people who come to google. cn to an uncensored site hosted in Hong Kong. Of course, the government still has the ability to block Google searches by mainland Chinese on the Hong Kong site. Google's defiance of the Chinese government will undoubtedly damage its efforts to compete successfully with Baidu, China's own Internet search engine. While moral issues were part of the company's overall calculus, its decision to confront Chinese authorities reflected a more realistic view about its "limited business prospects" in this country (Waters, 2010, p. B1).

Google is not the only company accused of yielding to the pressures of authoritarian governments. In 2006 Microsoft shut down a popular Chinese language blog hosted on MSN, worried that some of the content was offensive to the Chinese government. The site criticized the firing of editors at a progressive Beijing newspaper called the Beijing News. In a statement defending its actions, Microsoft simply said that "MSN is committed to ensuring that products and services comply with global and local laws, norms, and industry practices in China" (Chen, 2006, p. A9). Yahoo has also run into problems in China. In 2001 Wang

Xiaoning posted comments calling for democratic reform in China to a listserv called Yahoo Group where users could send and receive emails with their identities kept anonymous. In one posting Wang said that "we should never forget that China is still a totalitarian and despotic country." The Chinese government forced Yahoo to remove the content and sought the culprit's identity which it was able to do thanks to information Yahoo Hong Kong provided to the Chinese police. Wang was convicted of "incitement to subvert state power" and sentenced to ten years in state prison where he was allegedly tortured into signing a confession about his "seditious" activities (Bryne, 2008, pp. 159-60).

There have been similar incidents in other countries, but these examples will suffice to illustrate the nature of this problem, which has vexed American technology companies for almost a decade. How can this dilemma be effectively resolved? Does the resolution lie in law and policy implemented at the national or international level, or does it lie deep within the recesses of corporate conscience?

LEGAL ISSUES

U.S. law does not directly address Google's indirect participation in China's censorship regime nor does it deal with Yahoo's apparent willingness to aid the Chinese government in tracking down dissident journalists. There are, however, several laws under which U.S. companies abetting censorship or surveillance might be held accountable, including the Alien Tort Claims Act (ATCA), enacted as part of the Judiciary Act in 1789. The ATCA (2000) gives US federal courts jurisdiction over torts filed by aliens against US companies which have acted "in violation of the law of nations or a treaty of the United States." There has been a contentious debate about the scope of this Act. Some have argued that the scope is quite narrow, confined to violations of law of nations at the time the law was written such as piracy. But in *Filartiga*

v. Pena-Irala (1980, p.878) the Second Circuit ruled the ATCA provides a broad jurisdiction for violations of "universally accepted norms of the international law of human rights, regardless of the nationality of the parties." This and related rulings have opened the door for corporations to be found liable for specific violations of international law by direct actions or by simply aiding and abetting the violations of foreign governments. Courts have not specifically delineated what constitutes the law of nations. Nonetheless they have affirmed that "certain forms of conduct violate the law of nations whether undertaken by those acting under the auspices of the state or only as private individuals" (*Kadic v. Karadzic*, 1995, p. 239).

In the case of Google, a Chinese citizen could file a claim under ATCA alleging that the search engine company was complicit in the infringement of his or her free speech rights. In most cases, however, it would be difficult to argue that this infringement constituted a tort violation. Violations actionable under the ATCA include crimes against humanity such as torture, racial discrimination, or enslavement. Hence it is far from clear that the ATCA would be an effective mechanism for Chinese citizens looking for legal redress for Google's complicity in censoring free speech unless Google's actions abetted other crimes on the government's part.

On the other hand, it would appear that Wang Xiaoning has a stronger case, given his imprisonment and treatment in Chinese jails. Wang filed suit against Yahoo in 2007 under the auspices of ATCA. Wang's lawyer contended that Yahoo aided and abetted China as it violated the law of nations through its torture of Wang and its infliction of cruel and inhuman punishment. Yahoo settled with Wang for an undisclosed amount so this case does not tell us anything about the applicability of ATCA in other cases involving Internet gatekeepers nor does it set any precedent for future litigation.

Despite its ambiguities, the ATCA remains a disputed avenue for aggrieved parties in authoritarian cultures, and corporations must be wary of its application. Nonetheless, this legislation offers no guidance for corporate policy. It's remotely possible that the US will develop new laws to cover the complicity of companies like Google and Yahoo. In 2007 several members of Congress proposed legislation called the Global Online Freedom Act that was designed to prescribe minimum standards for online freedom of expression. Title II of this act would eliminate jurisdiction of foreign countries for information housed on their servers and it would prohibit businesses from modifying the functionality of their search engines to produce different results compatible with a censorship regime like China's. Other federal legislators have called for a global first amendment that would constrain censorship activities in Internet restricting countries.

It's not evident that the U.S. Congress has the wherewithal to pass such legislation. Efforts have received some impetus from the State Department which now says that Internet freedom should be a cornerstone of American foreign policy. There is a spirit of "techno-utopianism" in Washington inspired by the sentiment that democratization throughout the world will happen more quickly once the Internet becomes liberated from the bonds of online censorship. The U.S. State Department, however, offered no help for Google claiming that the issue was strictly between Google and China.

But is such legislation aimed at US companies a feasible solution to this problem or will it simply put gatekeepers like Google and Microsoft at a competitive disadvantage around the globe? Will these laws really enable Chinese or Iranian citizens greater access to the Internet or will they just complicate the efforts of US companies to compete in these markets? There are few legal issues as complex and sensitive as state sovereignty and so any legislation must be carefully crafted to avoid unintended consequences. While the intentions of the U.S. government are laudable, there are at least three problems with such legislation. While these laws apply to US firms, some companies like Yahoo operate through local ventures in which they have an ownership stake, and those companies would be immune from the legislation. Yahoo now runs its Chinese operations through Alibaba.com, which it controls but does not own. In this era of global cooperative capitalism, businesses are no longer centralized vertically-integrated entities, but decentralized networks. If a new law is to be effective it must somehow deal with complicated jurisdictional and ownership issues where accountability is often murky. Second, it's hard to conceive that China would terminate its filtering system and tear down its great firewall just because companies like Google or Microsoft were forced out. Filtering technologies are widely available, and China has its own search engine company, Baidu, whose services are improving as it gains experience with this technology. Third, this legislation has been characterized as "an arrogant attempt for the United States to serve as a world police," and there is some merit to this claim, since the U.S. would be seeking to impose its will on the Internet (Eastwood 2008, p. 310). Fresh efforts to promote free speech throughout the world will likely be treated in the same way. Those efforts, however well-intended, could be counterproductive and only risk a backlash against the United States.

AN ETHICAL PERSPECTIVE AND RESOLUTION

If the law offers little direction, and there are scant prospects for a significant change, we have a policy vacuum which means that a responsible company can only discern the right course of action through moral and social analysis. Philosophers have been constructing the field of Information and Computer Ethics (ICE) for decades, so what does it have to say about Google's conundrum? While much has been written about the Western ideal of speech and the need to curb digital content controls (Spinello, 2010, pp. 58-72), little has been said about the more complex problem of intercultural ethical disputes with free speech as the focal point. Analysis has been focused on the problem of pornography and what some see as misguided efforts to limit its diffusion in cyberspace either through federal law or through filtering programs. Many ICE scholars are wary of restricting Internet speech, and especially concerned about the deployment of filtering technologies given that these technologies are so imprecise and opaque. The trend has been to argue for broad free speech rights on the Internet even for children. Yet at the same time these scholars embrace the notion of cultural pluralism, and, in this case, these two divergent objectives cannot be easily reconciled.

Hence the need for some original analysis which must begin with whether or not China is doing anything wrong when it engages in systematic censorship of political speech on the Internet. One argument in China's favor centers on the cultural moral imperialism of its critics who are intolerant of China's different standard for free speech. Accordingly, in response to calls for "Internet freedom," Chinese officials have accused the United States of "information imperialism." They have consistently maintained that China's Internet regulations are compatible with the country's "national conditions and cultural traditions" (Buruma, 2010, p. W1).

Moreover, computer ethicists like Hausmanniger (2007) have staunchly defended the ethical obligation to respect different moral belief systems, however discordant they are with traditional Western norms. Correlative with the turn to subjectivity, which began with Descartes' grounding of certitude in the *cogito*, is the post-Cartesian "turn to contingency" which gives primacy to difference and plurality, instead of cultural or social uniformity (p. 45). As a logical consequence, there must be respect towards "the free actions that create difference and plurality" (p. 56). Similarly, Ess and Thorseth (2010) have argued that we must be more sensitive to the reality of ethical pluralism. They claim that many

Western philosophers such as Plato and Aristotle are really pluralists at heart because they support general or formal moral norms (such as community well-being or privacy) that are applied differently depending on the cultural context. Discrepant free speech norms represent another instance of ethical pluralism, and should not really surprise us. Despite the reality of moral and cultural diversity, Ess and Thorseth hope for some sort of global ICE and a harmonization of policies.

Defenders of China's policy also point out that it has a different conception of the person and a more collectivist view of human rights which may justify the country's overall approach to censorship. The Chinese government respects in broad terms the value of free expression but interprets the scope of that value differently than its counterparts in the West. The Confucian tradition sees the purpose of law as the protection of social harmony, which is inconsistent with the normative individualism of the Western liberal tradition. Confucianism stresses obedience to authority which is part of Chinese culture. Deference to authority is an essential aspect of being Chinese and implies the need for severe limits on political dissent (Buruma, 2010, W1).

Since the days of Chairman Mao's cultural revolution, the country has sought to control knowledge and restrict expression in order to propagate the state's uniform message unencumbered by the dissonant voices of dissenters. This restriction is consistent with China's nationalist strategy which sees unequivocal support for the state as the only way for China to regain its long lost greatness and avoid the humiliation the country has repeatedly suffered at the hands of the West. According to Vincent (1988, p. 42), "The fundamental rights and duties of citizens are to support the leadership of the Communist Party of China, support the Socialist system, and abide by the Constitution and the laws of the People's Republic of China".

Given these cultural anomalies and different human rights standards, it is no surprise that China adopts a divergent view of free speech "rights" which are construed with such a narrow scope. The general norm of free expression is being interpreted according to a different set of particularities and cultural imperatives. The Chinese standard, which heavily limits freedom of information for the sake of the collective good, represents the concrete reality of ethical pluralism, which must be factored into moral decision making by those doing business in China. In their defense of pluralism, Ess and Thorseth (2010) argue that "As global citizens...we must learn and respect the values practices, beliefs, communication styles and language of 'the Other'" (p. 168). Failure to do so, they contend, "makes us complicit in forms of computer-mediated imperialism and colonialism" (p. 168). Pluralism, therefore, amounts to a strong version of cultural moral relativism where each culture's moral values are equally valid and deserving of our respect.

Rawls, who is also sympathetic with ethical pluralism, offers a more nuanced perspective that calls for recognition of a few basic rights that set a few limits to pluralism. According to this "thin" theory of rights, all persons do not have equal basic rights or entitlements grounded in a philosophical or moral conception of the person. Rather, there is a special class of "urgent rights" such as freedom from slavery and serfdom and security against genocide, whose violation should be condemned by all peoples (Rawls, 2001, p. 79). Free expression, however, does not qualify as one of these "urgent" rights.

This pluralistic understanding of ethics is implied in the public responses of Google, Yahoo, and Microsoft to criticism about their policies. All three companies have argued at one point that their policies reflect the moral flexibility mandated by cultural moral relativism. According to Microsoft, "Like other global organizations we must abide by the laws, regulations, and norms of each country in which we operate" (BBC News 2005). Implicit in this argument defending a "when in Rome" approach to morality is the notion that ethical

norms, like customs, have only local validity because they are prescriptive or action-guiding. The social norms and civil liberties in China and Iran are simply different from the norms and liberties enjoyed by U.S. citizens, and it's imperialistic to maintain that U.S. norms are superior. This moral perspective, if tenable, would seem to validate the behavior of the Internet gatekeepers like Google. In this context, despite the vociferousness of their critics, the companies are doing nothing morally wrong when they cooperate in China's extensive censorship regime. In an age of ethical relativism, where the definition of right and wrong is so indeterminate, and where cultural differences demand their due, how can we criticize Google's malleable ethical policy or Yahoo's cooperation with the Chinese government?

The problem with cultural moral relativism, however, is that it offers virtually no standards for judging, evaluating, or ranking particular cultures. It assumes that all cultures are equal and all cultural differences normatively acceptable. Also, how does the cultural relativist account for the source of a culture's moral norms? If not some transcendent standard, then it must be consensus of the majority or the will of the sovereign. But how can non-democratic countries determine the will of the people? Do the majority of citizens in China still accept the dogma of Confucianism as interpreted by the state autocracy? Grounding rights in sheer consensus or sovereign preference ignores the possibility that those rights are intrinsic to the human condition. Basic human rights become contingent on the whim of cultural consensus, which is often shaped by those in power. If pluralism is pressed too far, values like free expression, due process, or even human life itself could become feeble and shallow and lose any semblance of objectivity.

On the other hand, many philosophers ranging from Aristotle and Aquinas to contemporary thinkers like Phillipa Foot and Elizabeth Anscombe accept the thesis that we possess a common human nature. Despite our ethnic diversity, there are essential features we all share in common such as rationality and free will. According to Foot (1979, p. 6),

"Granted that it may be wrong to assume identity of aim between people of different cultures; nevertheless there is a great deal all men have in common. All need affection, the cooperation of others, a place in community, and help in trouble. It isn't true to suppose that human beings can flourish without these things -- being isolated, despised or embattled, or without courage or hope. We are not, therefore, simply expressing values that we happen to have if we think of some moral systems as good moral systems and others as bad".

Rejection of a common human nature is also a rejection of the equality of persons which is the foundation of human rights and justice. If we assume that all humans share in some essential common features, it follows that there must be intrinsic human values expressed in *transcultural norms* that are more specific and less culturally contingent than Ess and Thorseth are willing to admit. To be sure, even these specific norms must be applied with some cultural flexibility and sensitivity. Reasonable people can discern whether or not a particular norm is being flouted in a given culture or properly applied in a way that accounts for a culture's particular circumstances.

What is the basis for discovering these transcultural norms? As Plato first theorized, they must be grounded in a coherent notion of the Good (τό ἀγάθόν), the ultimate source of all efficacy and normativity. Plato (1935, VII 516b) believed that our actions must be in conformity with the Good, "cause of all that is correct and beautiful in anything." Almost every moral philosophy since Plato endorses some notion of the good. Even deontologists such as Rawls, who give priority to the concept of right over the concept of good, concede the need for a "thin" theory of the good. Rawls (1971) contends that there are certain primary goods, "liberty and opportunity, income

and wealth, and above all self-respect," which are necessary for the "framing and execution of a rational plan of life" (pp. 433-34).

More robust or "thicker" theories of the good are offered in teleological ethical frameworks, such as the new natural law, an updated and secularized version of the natural law theory found in the writings of St. Thomas Aquinas. According to this framework, practical reasoning about morality begins with the intelligible reasons people have for their choices and actions. Some of those reasons are based on ends that are intelligible only as a means to other ends. Tangible goods like money have only instrumental value, since they possess no intrinsic worth. Other goods are intrinsic, that is, they are valued and sought after for their own sake. These intrinsic or "basic" human goods provide reasons to consider some possibilities as worthwhile and choiceworthy for their own sake. These goods are "basic" not for survival but for human flourishing.

What then are these intrinsic human goods valued for their own sake as constitutive aspects of human flourishing? According to natural law theorists like Finnis (1980) and George (2007) it is reasonable to conclude that a list of basic goods should include the following: bodily life and health; knowledge of the truth; aesthetic appreciation; sociability or harmony with others; skillful performance in work and play. These intelligible goods are all distinct aspects of basic well-being, intrinsically valuable and sought after for their own sake because they are perfective of the human person. Knowledge of what is true, for example, is a beneficial possibility, because its possession represents a mode of existence superior to the mode of ignorance. Hence, knowledge is not just instrumentally valuable but is worthy of being pursued as an end-in-itself. These substantive goods constitute the foundation of normativity and provide a secure grounding for moral judgments about justice and human rights.

Where does free expression fit into this paradigm? Free expression is not a basic good, since it does not directly contribute to human flourishing. It is difficult to see how free speech would be valued in itself apart from the relational goods it supports. On its own, it doesn't really fulfill or perfect us, but it does allow us to pursue other forms of personal fulfillment. Thus, it is desired as a means to another end, that is, as instrumental to certain intrinsic goods that directly provide personal fulfillment. For example, speech or communication is essential for the harmonious cooperation necessary to build community and create bonds of fellowship. Miscommunication or misunderstanding among people is common, but this reality means that communication efforts must be refined or revised, but certainly not suppressed. Dissenting political speech often brings to light problems and conflicts that must be resolved if a political community is to overcome differences and evolve into a more authentic communion of persons based on the common good. Thus, a strong case can be made that the right to free expression is justified as an instrumental good promoting our intrinsic sociability.

Speech is also essential to support and preserve the intrinsic goods of knowledge and reflective understanding. People cannot be coerced in matters of speech and communication in a way that interferes with their capacity to inform others of the truth. The acquisition of objective, true knowledge by people in a community is contingent on the ability of teachers and others within that community to disseminate that truth without fear of retribution of punishment. Censorship and suppression of certain information is typically motivated by a desire to keep the truth from citizens and to prevent them from overcoming ignorance and error. Censors aim to achieve conformity of thought rather than propagation of the truth.

From this analysis we can deduce that there is at least a moral presumption in favor of free speech rights because free speech is a vital instrumental good (or value). These rights are necessary to protect individuals in their efforts to appropriate and share several intrinsic human goods that constitute the basis of human flourishing. These goods (objective knowledge and sociability) are not confined to the West or to liberal societies, but are sought by all rational human persons as intrinsic to their personal fulfillment, and therefore it is plausible to argue for the universality of this right. Basic human rights are not grounded on the basis of utility. Rather, they are rooted in necessity, in what human persons need and rationally desire "for the exercise and development of distinctive human powers" (Hart, 1983, p.17). The right to free expression, therefore, is necessary for the pursuit of several intrinsic goods common to all persons. Human beings need free expression to build authentic community and grow in fellowship and to advance in knowledge of the truth. Like all rights, the right to free speech must be limited in different ways that are consistent with the common good. Most sovereignties do not protect perverted forms of speech such as obscenity nor hate speech that incites violence.

Further support for the universality and intrinsic value of this right to free expression is its endorsement by the United Nations in its famous Universal Declaration of Human Rights first promulgated in 1948. This declaration, which represents a moral and political consensus among United Nations member nations, still carries great weight throughout the world. The U.N. has never disavowed this declaration nor qualified its support for these rights. Article 19 of the U.N.'s Universal Declaration (2007) states: "Everyone has the right to freedom of opinion and expression; this right includes freedom to hold opinions without interference and to seek, receive and impart information and ideas through any media and regardless of frontiers". The United Nations is certainly sensitive to cultural issues but it also recognizes that some rights transcend those cultural differences. The U.N document clearly favors the universalism suggested by Plato and natural law theorists instead of the radical ethical pluralism of more contemporary philosophers. Implicit in its endorsement of these rights is the assumption that people possess them not by some government's fiat or cultural consensus but as a matter of natural justice. This declaration also assumes that some cultures can be morally deficient and blind to the truth about particular rights such as free speech.

If we assume that there is such a natural, universal right to free speech, properly configured to take into account morally justified privacy, confidentiality, and security concerns, the Chinese government infringes on this right by ruthlessly imposing orthodox political beliefs on the entire community and providing no basis of dissent, good faith disagreement, or attempts to correct the historical record so that future generations will know the truth about events such as Tiananmen Square. As we have seen, China relies on culture and its history as an oppressed state as a pretext to support the government's authoritarian regime. However, China is guilty of a moral failing by not respecting this right to free political expression, which many of its citizens have demanded for decades. China's nationalism is excessive and unhealthy, since it involves the pursuit of the nation's social welfare without proper regard for the needs and natural rights of all its citizens. If China is willfully infringing on the rights of its citizens by blocking speech and keeping important information from its people, its actions are unjust and immoral.

If this analysis is sound, Google's moral culpability logically follows, since the company willingly cooperated in perpetuating restrictions on this basic right. For a sincere company committed to corporate responsibility, the "don't be evil" principle must preclude cooperation in evil. Instead of defying the Chinese government, Google facilitated and supported the perpetuation of its censorship regime until its change of policy in 2010.

The basic moral imperative at stake in the Google case is that a moral agent should not cooperate in or become involved in the wrongdoing initiated by another. This simple moral principle seems axiomatic. If someone intentionally helps another individual carry out an objectively wrong choice, that person shares in the wrong intention and bad will of the person who is executing such a choice and is guilty of formal cooperation. In this context, what one chooses to do coincides with or includes what is objectively wrong in the other's choice. For example, a scientist provides his laboratory and thereby willingly assists in harmful medical experiments conducted on human beings by a group of unscrupulous medical doctors because he is interested in the results for his own research. Although this scientist did not conduct the experiments, he shares in the wrongful intentions and actions of the doctors who did. In the domain of criminal law, if a person helps his friend commit or conceal a crime, that person can be charged as an accessory. Hence, it is part of moral common sense that a person who willingly helps or cooperates with the actions initiated by a wrongdoer deserves part of the blame for the evil that has been perpetrated. There are also various forms of material cooperation whereby the acts of the cooperator and wrongdoer are distinct and share no bad intention (Grisez, 1991, pp. 871-74).

Google is accountable for its formal (not merely material) cooperation, since it intentionally participated in the wrongdoing (censorship) initiated by Chinese government officials. Google does not share completely in the bad will of the Chinese censors since it disagrees with their ends. Nonetheless, it intended the chosen means of abetting those censors in order to have a presence in the world's second largest market. However reluctantly, Google intended to censor its search results and further the aims of China's censorship regime as a condition of doing business in China. Neither this ulterior motive nor any extenuating factors mitigate its responsibility. It makes no difference that Google disapproves of China's policy and its reasons or motives for censoring search results does not coincide with the reasons of the Chinese government. It was guilty of formal cooperation by virtue of choosing the wrong means to achieve its valid business objectives. Responsible companies, which function as moral agents in society, must eschew both formal cooperation and those forms of material cooperation deemed ethically unacceptable according to traditional standards.

To sum up: in the absence of clear international laws, corporations like Google must rely on ethical self-regulation. We maintain that proper self-regulation should lead companies to preserve their core values by respect for universal rights and avoidance of formal cooperation with host governments willing to infringe those rights.

FUTURE DIRECTIONS

Given the other priorities of the U.S. government it is unlikely that there will be major legislation to address the issues delineated here. It's highly probable that companies will continue to be sued under ATCA for their alleged misdeeds abroad, but these suits will not resolve anything. We may hear more rhetoric from the West about "Internet freedom" but it will probably fall on deaf ears within the halls of the Chinese government. This will leave the corporate Internet gatekeepers and social media sites still caught in the crosshairs, perplexed about how to navigate this difficult terrain. Should companies like Google be forced into the *de facto* role of "policy maker" dictating the terms of its engagement in totalitarian countries like China? Should they resist helping China or Iran to enforce their laws in cyberspace? Finally, what would be the long term social and policy implications of helping these countries erect borders in cyberspace?

What also needs consideration and further in depth research is the normative issue of the scope and nature of free speech rights. Much has been written about problems like cyberporn, spam, and hate speech along with the use of content controls (see Spinello and Tavani, 2004; Spinello, 2010). But very little has been written about free speech and communication as an intercultural issue. Those who advocate for ethical pluralism typically avoid addressing specific thorny issues like speech let alone review the moral liability of gatekeepers who directly cooperate with authoritarian governments. On the other hand, they write at length about the need to bridge cultural differences to create more harmony in the infoshpere. One might contend, however, that the proliferation of censorship regimes and the intractability of many sovereign states on this issue does not augur well for "fostering a *shared* ICE that 'works' across the globe" (Ess and Torseth, 2010, p. 164). While working to promote this shared global ethos, ethicists must consider whether this right to free expression is contingent on culture and history or is a universal right. Is there a philosophical grounding for the United Nations claim that *everyone* has the right to freedom of opinion and expression? We have argued that this is so but recognize that this debate is far from settled. There is no doubt that public and corporate policy should turn on how that vital question is resolved.

CONCLUSION

Many governments have reasserted their sovereignty in cyberspace, and as a result, the Web's openness and universal character has been diminished. This has created problems for corporations like Google attempting to balance their core values with restrictions imposed by China and other countries. We have looked at the related issues of free expression and corporate liability through the prism of law and ethics. Thanks to jurisdictional constraints, the law offers little guidance for corporations who aspire to be morally responsible and to cooperate at least implicitly with the U.S. policy to maximize the free flow of information over the Internet. Given this policy vacuum, these corporations must fall back on moral reasoning as Google did, grappling with what "do no evil" really means in a context of moral and cultural diversity. We have argued in this paper that despite this diversity and even the so-called "turn to contingency," free expression is a fixed and universal value rather than a merely contingent one. We have based this analysis on natural law reasoning along with the argument that speech is an instrumental good necessary for instantiating intrinsic goods such as community and knowledge. Because of its status as a necessary instrumental good, it follows that people have a right to free speech since rights are based on what persons need and rationally desire. It also follows that companies like Google behave irresponsibly if they actively cooperate in the undermining of this right. In making this case we have suggested the propriety of a thick theory of rights as a matter of universal justice. This position is compatible with the UN's 1948 consensus on universal rights and stands in opposition to the thin theory proposed by Rawls who recognizes only a small set of "urgent" rights.

As a practical matter, this ethical analysis will probably not make corporate decision making any easier. Private companies must still struggle with how to respond when they are asked to participate in a censorship or surveillance regime like those in Iran or Saudi Arabia. As this paper has demonstrated, companies are caught in a vice between universal moral values like free expression and pressure to conform to local norms. The problem of online censorship will probably intensify as some countries continue to resist the Internet's open technology. As a result, gatekeepers and other Internet companies will be forced to give this issue the cogent moral reflection it deserves.

REFERENCES

Alien Tort Claims Act. (2000). 28 U.S.C. § 1350.

Buruma, I. (2010, January 30). Battling the information barbarians. *The Wall Street Journal*, W1-2.

Byrne, M. (2008). When in Rome: Aiding and abetting in Wang Xiaoning v. Yahoo. *Brooklyn Journal of International Law, 34*, 151.

Chen, K. (2006, January 6). Microsoft defends censoring a dissident's blog in China. *The Wall Street Journal*, A9.

Dean, J. (2005, December 16). As Google pushes into China, it faces clashes with censors. *The Wall Street Journal*, A12.

Eastwood, L. (2008). Google faces the Chinese Internet market and the Global Online Freedom Act. *Minnesota Journal of Law, Science, &. Technology (Elmsford, N.Y.), 9*, 287.

Ess, C., & Thorseth, M. (2010). Global information and computer ethics. In Floridi, L. (Ed.), *The Cambridge handbook of information and computer ethics* (pp. 163–180). Cambridge, UK: Cambridge University Press.

Filartiga v. Pena-Irala (630 F. 2d 876, 2d Cir.) (1980).

Finnis, J. (1980). *Natural law and natural rights*. Oxford, UK: Oxford University Press.

Foot, P. (1979, June). *Moral relativism*. Paper presented for Lindley Lecture, Department of Philosophy, University of Kansas.

George, R. P. (2007). Natural law. *The American Journal of Jurisprudence, 52*, 55.

Google in China. (2006, January 30). *The Wall Street Journal*, A18.

Grisez, G. (1991). *Difficult moral questions*. Chicago, IL: Franciscan Herald Press.

Hart, H. L. (1983). *Essays in jurisprudence and philosophy*. Oxford, UK: Oxford University Press.

Hausmanninger, T. (2007). Allowing for difference: Some preliminary remarks concerning intercultural information ethics. In R. Capurro, Frühbauer, J., & Hausmanninger, T. (Eds.), *Localizing the Internet. Ethical issues in intercultural perspective*. (pp. 39-56). Schriftenreihe des ICIE, Band 4. Munich, Germany: Wilhelm Fink Verlag.

Kadic v. Karadzic (70 F.3d 232, 2d Cir.) (1995).

Miller, C. (2010, August 2). A race for smarter search. *New York Times*, B1, B5.

News, B. B. C. (2005, September 7). Yahoo helped jail China writer. *BBC Online*. Retrieved July 31, 2010 from http://www.news.bbc.co.uk/1/hi/world/4221538.stm

Plato,. (1935). *The republic*. Cambridge, MA: Harvard University Press.

Rawls, J. (1971). *A theory of justice*. Cambridge, MA: Harvard University Press.

Rawls, J. (2001). *The law of peoples*. Cambridge, MA: Harvard University Press.

Reno v. ACLU. (521 U.S. 844). (1997).

Spinello, R. A. (2010). *Cyberethics: Morality and law in cyberspace* (4th ed.). Sudbury, MA: Jones & Bartlett.

Spinello, R. A., & Tavani, H. (2004). *Readings in cyberethics* (2nd ed.). Sudbury, MA: Jones & Bartlett.

Thompson, C. (2006, April 23). China's Google problem. *New York Times Magazine*, 36-41; 73-76.

United Nations Charter. (2007). The Universal Declaration of Human Rights. In Spinello, R. A. (Ed.), *Moral philosophy for managers* (5th ed., pp. 293–297). New York, NY: McGraw-Hill.

Vincent, R. J. (1988). *Human rights and international relations*. New York, NY: Cambridge University Press.

Waters, R. (2010, March 24). Realism lies behind decision to quit. *Financial Times*, B1.

Zittrain, J. (2003). Internet points of control. *Boston College Law Review. Boston College. Law School, 44*, 653.

ADDITIONAL READING

Buruma, I. Battling the information barbarians. *The Wall Street Journal*, January 30, 2010 W1-2.

Chen, K. Microsoft defends censoring a dissident's blog in China. *The Wall Street Journal*, January 6, 2006, A9.

Dean, J. As Google pushes into China, it faces clashes with censors. *The Wall Street Journal*, December 16, 2005, A12.

Eastwood, L. (2008). Google Faces the Chinese Internet Market and the Global Online Freedom Act. *Minnesota Journal of Law, Science, &. Technology (Elmsford, N.Y.), 9*, 287.

Ess, C., & Thorseth, M. (2010). Global information and computer ethics. In Floridi, L. (Ed.), *The Cambridge handbook of information and computer ethics* (pp. 163–180). Cambridge: Cambridge University Press.

Finnis, J. (1980). *Natural law and natural rights*. Oxford: Oxford University Press.

Hausmanninger, T. Allowing for difference: Some preliminary remarks concerning intercultural information ethics. In R. Capurro, Frühbauer, J., & Hausmanninger, T. *Localizing the Internet. Ethical issues in intercultural perspective*. (pp. 39-56). Schriftenreihe des ICIE, Band 4, Munich: Wilhelm Fink Verlag, 2007.

Rawls, J. (2001). *The law of peoples*. Cambridge, MA: Harvard University Press.

Smith, K. (2008). A global first amendment? *Journal on Telecommunications & High Technology Law, 6*, 509.

Spinello, R. A. (2010). *Cyberethics: Morality and law in cyberspace* (4th ed.). Sudbury, MA: Jones & Bartlett.

Spinello, R. A., & Tavani, H. (2004). *Readings in cyberethics* (2nd ed.). Sudbury, MA: Jones & Bartlett.

Thompson, C. China's Google problem. *New York Times Magazine*, April 23, 2006, 36-41; 74-76.

Vincent, R. J. (1988). *Human rights and international relations*. New York: Cambridge University Press.

Zittrain, J. (2003). Internet points of control. *Boston College Law Review. Boston College. Law School, 44*, 653.

Zittrain, J. *The future of the Internet--and how to stop it*. New Haven, CN: Yale University Press, 2009.

Zittrain, J., & Edelman, B. (2003). *Empirical Analysis of Internet Filtering in China*. Research Publications of Berkman Center for Internet and Society, Harvard Law School.

KEY TERMS AND DEFINITIONS

Censorship: The intentional suppression or regulation of expression based on its content.

Code: Hardware and software applications that use Internet protocols and can function as a regulatory constraint.

Content Filtering: Software that restricts access to Internet content by scanning that content based on keyword searches.

Firewall: An electronic barrier restricting communications between two points of control on the Internet.

Formal Cooperation: Intentionally sharing in another person's or group's wrongdoing.

Internet filtering: Technologies that prevent users from accessing or disseminating information on the Internet.

Pluralism: Different ethical responses to a moral problem, usually based on cultural diversity.

Search Engine: Navigation tool for searching web sites usually based on proprietary algorithms.

ENDNOTE

[1] In 2000 Google began providing a Chinese language version of its search engine from the U.S., but it had to deal with sluggish performance thanks to the firewall along with occasional blockades by the Chinese government. By moving its servers to China, Google could provide faster service, since it wasn't subject to the firewall and, but it would have to deal with China's censorship law. See Thompson, "China's Google Problem."

Chapter 12
All's WELL that Ends WELL:
A Comparative Analysis of the Constitutional and Administrative Frameworks of Cyberspace and the United Kingdom

Jonathan Bishop
Swansea University, UK

ABSTRACT

Constitutional and Administrative Law is a core component of legal studies throughout the world, but to date little has been written about how this might exist on the Internet, which is like a world without frontiers. John Perry Barlow's "Declaration of the Independence of Cyberspace" served to start the debate about the legitimacy of nation-states to impose laws on such a virtual space. It has been argued that the nation-states won as there are now a significant number of laws regulating the Internet on national and international levels. It can however be seen that there are commonalities between the two entities. For example, there are commonalities in the way they function. There are also commonalities in the way civil rights exist, and the existence of civil remedies and law enforcement. These are all explored in the chapter, which also presents two concepts about the authority of the state in regulating behaviour in online communities. One of them, "sysop prerogative," says that owners of website can do whatever they want so long as they have not had it taken away by law or given it away by contract. The second, 'The Preece Gap', says that there is a distance between the ideal usable and sociable website that the

DOI: 10.4018/978-1-61350-132-0.ch012

users want and that which the owners of the website provide in practice. Two other concepts are also introduced, "the Figallo effect" and the "Jimbo effect." The former describes an online community where users use their actual identities and sysop prerogative is delegated to them. The latter describes those where sysop prerogative is exercised by one or more enforcers to control users who use pseudonyms. The chapter concludes that less anonymity and a more professionalised society are needed to bridge the gap between online and offline regulation of behavior.

INTRODUCTION

At the dawn of the Worldwide Web when there was a heating up of imposition of laws by nation states on the international communications networks, one isolated voice spoke out and was cross-posted more times than the author could imagine. In March 1999, the strategy for regulating government exploitation of the Internet in the UK was set out for the first time in the Modernising Government White Paper. Until late 2005 the focus of policy development in respect of interactive and transactional services online had been based upon consideration of how to drive up access and demand (Saxby, 2006). However, government intervention with regard to the Internet has to some people been unwanted, as was voiced quiet vehemently by John Perry Barlow (see Figure 1) in his 'Declaration of the Independence of Cyberspace' (Barlow, 1996). He openly declared in this document, "*Governments of the Industrial World, you weary giants of flesh and steel, I come from Cyberspace, the new home of Mind. On behalf of the future, I ask you of the past to leave us alone. You are not welcome among us. You have no sovereignty where we gather.*" This text is now one of the cornerstones in the history of the Internet. Barlow's concept of cyberspace as a homeland without and beyond frontiers is somewhat challenging to the concept of a nation state put forward by Adam Smith (Smith, 1966) but perhaps more consistent with the view of a nation as an 'imagined community' put forward by Benedict Anderson (Anderson, 1991).

Barlow's separation between the virtual world and the "real world" has been overturned by legislation and legal cases as soon as analysts began to worry about "spill over" from problems in cyberspace to problems in the real world (Manjikian, 2010). However, as Manjikian suggests, the legal and political systems are only one part of the story. Legitimate questions on the authority of websites in Cyberspace and its users as opposed to whether it can be considered a sovereign body can still be asked. Cyberspace may still exist as a cultural society, where its users share the same technologies and share similar networks of mental artefacts, such as beliefs, values and experiences (Bishop, 2010a). A question that might arise is whether Barlow's document could be considered a constitution for the Internet. If so what impact does it have on the way we think about the constitutional and administrative laws that make up 'the British Constitution'. Definitions abound as to what a constitution is. It has been pointed out that a source that can be used to find information on such a definition would be the WELL (Whole Earth 'Lectronic Link), a California-based online community (Rheingold, 2000). It has also been argued that our current understanding of what a constitution is largely depends on the constructions which nineteenth-century constitutionalism placed upon it, locking the constitution into a series of complex relationships with liberal views of the modern nation state (Castiglione, 1996). A current understanding of constitution is that it is a set of principles which determine the way a country will be governed, and a description of the order in which the principles should be invoked (Hey & Pasca, 2010). Others have defined a constitution as something to which people subscribe to which sets out rules they agree to abide by. Based on these definitions, John Perry Barlow's document could be consid-

ered a constitution for the Internet as it was at one point cross-posted by 40,000 websites who accepted the ethos of an ungoverned community called Cyberspace driven by a distinct order of statelessness. However, a constitution is not only a repository of values; it also has considerable legal and political consequences (Weiler, 2002). From this it can be seen that the United Kingdom's constitution, while not written, has a structure of institutions governed by a set of shared economic and legal frameworks subscribed to by all those subjects who are deemed British citizens. This suggests that while Barlow's document serves as a symbol of Internet users' wish to be untouched by State-like institutions and legal rules, the unwritten British constitution has shown there is more meaning to the term than a document that prescribes a set of common values and beliefs. Indeed, it has been argued that the British constitution is at a critical historical, political and institutional juncture in which a number of inter-linked emerging agendas are altering the relationship between parliament and the executive (Flinders, 2002). A constitution could perhaps therefore be defined as "*a common agreement between a network of actors as to how they agree to co-exist as a society*".

COMPARING THE CONSTITUTIONAL AND ADMINISTRATIVE FRAMEWORKS OF THE UNITED KINGDOM WITH CYBERSPACE

Using this definition it could perhaps be possible to consider that Cyberspace has a constitution. Actors have agreed to use common means of communicating and sharing knowledge. They have agreed that contracts govern how they interact with each site. And they have agreed that traditional financial institution can be the bridge between the vendor and the customer.

Also, there appears to be clearly commonalities between the independent websites that exist within Cyberspace and the United Kingdom and its various constitution entities and administrative procedures. These include with regard to functional issues, civil rights, and civil remedies and law enforcement.

Functional Issues

Barlow in his declaration said, "We have no elected government, nor are we likely to have one, so I address you with no greater authority than that with which liberty itself always speaks". While it still appears to be true that there is no authority directly elected by the citizens of the world who use the Internet, referred to as 'Netizens', there are still comparisons that can be drawn between the UK's elected government and Cyberspace. The United Kingdom constitution consists of the Monarch, the Executive, Parliament, the Judiciary, and other instruments of the state such as the Civil Service, devolved bodies and tribunals. The Monarch is responsible for various tasks including settling such issues as the selection of a prime minister, the dismissal of a parliament and the operation of the judicial system (Hames & Leonard, 1998). The main difference between a monarchy and a republic is that with the former sovereignty lies with the monarch and with the latter it is shared among citizens (Bentele & Nothhaft, 2010). The main difference between a monarchy and despotism is that in the former sovereignty is conferred above and below the monarch and in the latter it is exercised by one individual in a tyrannical manner (Long, 2010). In all cases the sovereignty lies within a particular nation state or in the case of a monarchy or republic it can be conferred to wider polity, as the UK does with the European Union for example. Based on this, 'Cyberspace' can be seen to be a web of independent communities all connected by 'the Information Superhighway'. Online communities like Wikipedia perhaps resemble a monarchy, in that its founder Jimmy Wales has conferred power to 'Administrators' and 'Editors' yet supreme authority lies with his organisation. Most independent bulletin boards can be seen to more so resemble despotism in that they are usually controlled by one man who enforces his will on the other members who wishing to use the forum, in that he can remove anyone he wishes from the forum. This supports Barlow's assertion to world governments that 'Governments derive their just powers from the consent of the governed. You have neither solicited nor received ours. We did not invite you. You do not know us, nor do you know our world.' It can therefore be seen that in terms of the 'Cyberspace' metaphor as nearly all websites have terms and conditions they are self-governing units, but of course in reality are subject to the laws of the nation state in which they are established.

The Executive in the UK is responsible for the day-to-day operation of the state, which must be achieved within the accepted laws and constitutional principles (Johnston, 1983). Burmah Oil v Lord Advocate [1965] A.C. 75 established that the Executive has a 'royal prerogative' over any competency which Parliament has not exercised authority over unless the Courts decide otherwise. After the judgement Parliament did exercise authority over the specifics of the case by passing the War Damage Act 1965, but other judgements on royal prerogative mean that where the state (i.e.

the Crown) has obligations by statute it cannot use royal prerogative to exercise them such as in *Attorney-General v de Keyser's Royal Hotel Ltd* [1920] A.C. 508. In Cyberspace an equivalent of 'sysop prerogative' appears to exist where the Sysop (systems operator), who is the owner of a website, has the right to decide whether a particular policy is adopted or the outcome of a particular conflict (Bishop, 2011). In the case of the WELL, its Sysop, Cliff Figallo, resisted the temptation to control (Rheingold, 2000) and instead delegated his prerogative to the members in a way resembling that of a republic. Jimmy Wales (see Figure 2), Sysop of Wikipedia, on the other hand delegated his sysop prerogative to a series of 'Administrators' who without reference to standards of consistency and precedent seen in the British constitution make decisions on an ad-hoc basis based on their individual whims.

Civil Rights

Jenny Preece, in her influential book, 'Online Communities: Designing for Usability and Supporting Sociability', sets out what users should expect online communities to provide in terms of policies and practices that should mean that users and both able to use the online community and be sociable within it (Preece, 2001). These 'Netizen rights' to a supportive environment of freedom of expression, were also advocated by Barlow in his declaration, which stated:

"We are creating a world that all may enter without privilege or prejudice accorded by race, economic power, military force, or station of birth. We are creating a world where anyone, anywhere may express his or her beliefs, no matter how singular, without fear of being coerced into silence or conformity. Your legal concepts of property, expression, identity, movement, and context do not apply to us. They are all based on matter, and there is no matter here" (Preece, 2001).

Figure 2. Jimmy Wales (from http://wikipedia. org, Creative Commons Attribution Share-Alike license)

This concept of Netizen rights resembles the civil rights that exist in democratic societies, where they may only be partially codified, as in the case of the British constitution. One recent attempt to codify and enforce civil rights was the Human Rights Act 1998 introduced by the New Labour Government that came to power in 1997. Since 1998, the impact of the Human Rights Act has reached far beyond constitutional matters, into statutory interpretation, counter-terrorism legislation, general criminal law and the horizontal effect of rights in private law disputes (Townsend, 2009). The Act also opened up a number of potential points of conflict with regards to the rights of people to use the Internet and online communities that are part of it. For instance it gives effect to Article 11 of the convention, which while not being interpreted as imposing an obligation on associations or organisations to admit everyone wishing to join, says people do have a right to apply to join them in order to further the expression of their views and practices as set out in Associated Society of Locomotive Engineers & Firemen v United Kingdom (ECHR, App no 11002/05). An organization is an undertaking within the meaning of the EU Treaty, and the term undertaking has a broad meaning in EU Law, which can include someone who hosts a bulletin board. This means that someone should have a human right to be able to apply to join an online community, but they have no right to be a member if the administrators choose not to accept them. This case suggests that Barlow's suggestion that the government should have no say in the make-up of Cyberspace may be partly implemented, as the Human Rights Act means that the government has no right to impede 'sysop prerogative' in relation to whether or not someone is allowed to be a member of their website. Sysop prerogative does appear to be limited with regards to snooping on their member's emails on the grounds of privacy. However this can be restored through contract law, where for instance employers can assume the consent of employees for the reading of their e-mails (Taylor, Haggerty & Gresty, 2009).

All this suggests that there is a distance between what the users of an online community expect the sysop to allow and what is actually enforceable through properly developed policy systems. This could perhaps be called the 'Preece Gap' after Jenny Preece who in Preece (2001) advocated online communities with policies that promoted good usability and sociability. An example where the Preece Gap may be wider exists in the case of the Café Moms website. A mother dedicated to raising her children may join the website and later be dismayed to find her membership suspended and accounted deleted after failing to log-in for a specific amount of time. The mother may naturally feel betrayed by a site designed to support her is using their sysop prerogative to decide who can and can't be a member and the terms on which that membership is governed. Facebook may be an example of a low Preece Gap, as its ease of use enables people to easily connect with each other, and most of the sysop prerogative over which content stays and goes has been delegated to those affected by it.

Civil Remedies and Law Enforcement

It has been backed up through case law that the UK Parliament has complete authority over its own affairs and the Courts cannot rule over whether it has followed its own procedures, as shown in *R. v Graham-Campbell, Ex p. Herbert* (HC, 1935). It has also been shown that the UK Parliament has the right to legislate in any area, even where it has little or no power to enforce it beyond its own Courts, as demonstrated by the passing of the Hijacking Act 1967, which applied to non-UK Nationals in non-UK territories. Barlow (1996) declared to world governments that he wanted the same authority for Cyberspace;

"You claim there are problems among us that you need to solve. You use this claim as an excuse to invade our precincts. Many of these problems don't exist. Where there are real conflicts, where there are wrongs, we will identify them and address them by our means. We are forming our own Social Contract. This governance will arise according to the conditions of our world, not yours. Our world is different".

This is almost essentially what has happened in cyberspace with its network of self-governing websites. In most cases in the UK the right of the state to investigate a misdemeanours is exercised by the police, where there is 'reasonable suspicion' a crime has been committed *Hough v Chief Constable of Staffordshire* as found in [2001] EWCA Civ 39. Individual website's policies differ on investigatory powers. For instance eBay's says:

"The eBay Investigations team tries to resolve reported cases of inappropriate trading behaviour. We will consider the circumstances of an alleged offence and the user's trading record before taking action. Disciplinary action may range from a formal warning up to indefinite suspension of a user's account. However, to be fair to all members, if a complaint cannot be proven with certainty, eBay will not take action" (eBay, 2010).

The British constitution gives UK subjects the right to challenge the powers exercised by the state through judicial review, where after an application for permission they may be entitled to a hearing. This has been reflected in similar ways in some online communities in Cyberspace. Wikipedia for instance allows for a referendum on removing articles from the site called AfD (Articles for Deletion), which calls on someone exercising sysop prerogative to make a decision on whether to keep the article or remove them. Sysop prerogative in this context appears to resemble judicial procedures where it has to be decided whether the claims are 'held' to be true or 'dismissed' as false so that the status quo is maintained. The remedies of judicial review in UK law are more complex and include prerogative orders, which are 'quashing', 'prohibiting' and 'mandatory orders' as well as declarations and injunctions, the latter two not being based on prerogative. Social networking site Facebook has come under a barrage of attacks for changing its terms and conditions and members have sought to regain the initiative by challenging them through the media and threatening to get state authorities to enforce human rights laws against them (Mesure & Griggs, 2007). This suggests that despite the self-governing nature of websites in Cyberspace there will always be recourse to state institutions.

The prerogative orders available under judicial review resemble the exercise of sysop prerogative by some websites in Cyberspace. A quashing order is used to quash the decisions of emanations of the state at an inferior level of authority where they act illegally, irrationally, or procedurally improperly, or where they interpret the law incorrectly. This happens regularly in Cyberspace, where the sysop of a website will overrule their moderators on a contentious issue by exercising their sysop prerogative. A prohibiting order is used by a superior court to restrain an inferior authority, such as a government minister, from acting outside their authority. Such actions are seen on websites like

Wikipedia, where those persons who are exercising sysop prerogative will instruct editors not to edit an article where there is a dispute, such as by trying to enforce the 'three-revert-rule'. In a mandatory order the court instructs an inferior authority to perform a particular duty ascribed to them. It is not possible as a result to instruct the Crown, as the Crown is not commandable, but it is possible to instruct it against a servant of the Crown who has an independent public duty to perform a specific action, such as a local authority being required to fulfil its obligations to people with special educational needs who need access to specialist equipment and services.

Most online communities have only themselves to blame for the need for recourse to the state due poor behaviour management and lack internal complaints and dispute resolution procedures. Many have enshrined in their set-up the opportunity for its users to be anonymous and therefore unaccountable for their actions, in keeping with the claim of Barlow (1996) that identity is not an issue in Cyberspace. This has not always been the case, as Rheingold (2000) points out that the WELL had a requirement that users identify themselves by their real names, making it one of the most civil online communities in Cyberspace. In online communities where anonymity has been use the uncontrolled abuse typical of Cyberspace's pariahs, the Snerts (Bishop, 2009), goes on without limits. (Carr-Gregg, 2006) reported on the case of Robert, 17, who using World of Warcraft, a virtual world that was based on anonymity, developed psychiatric problems including suicidal ideation. Since then the makers of World of Warcraft announced that they would "remove the veil of anonymity typical to online dialogue" with a view to creating "a more positive environment that promotes constructive criticism", as well as giving gamers the chance to get to know who their virtual opponents are in real life (Armstrong, 2010).

TOWARDS A PROFESSIONALISED SOCIETY AND INTERNET OMBUDSMAN

It is not entirely necessary to remove anonymity from Cyberspace in order to reduce rogue behaviour, as with the correct disciplinary procedures users may be less willing to act inappropriately. However, it may be no error that World of Warcraft should seek to aspire to the civil nature of the WELL by removing the ability of users to hide their true identities. However, there is still no guarantee that 'flames' such as aggressive and threatening comments posted by Snerts and E-Vengers can be avoided (Bishop, 2009).

Indeed, at the dawn of the Worldwide Web and realisation of Cyberspace, Johnson (1994) spoke out the conflicts in Cyberspace, which while not 'fist-fights', would need to be resolved. Two years before Barlow's constitution-like declaration he said:

"Suppose we created a new portion of the "law of cyberspace" to deal with the means by which disputes arising in this new domain could be authoritatively settled. Such a doctrine would map nicely against the topics covered by our existing jurisprudence -- but might incorporate novel rules. It would govern such matters as (1) when a formal dispute is to be viewed as having been initiated; (2) what "jurisdiction" (e.g., local sysop or international arbitration panel), is entitled to resolve particular types of disputes; (3) who may argue a case; (4) what kinds of evidence will be accepted; (5) what sources of law will be consulted; (6) what procedures provide the equivalent of due process; (7) what appeals are available; (8) what types of "persons" will be permitted to appear and seek rights in their own name; (9) what time limits will bar actions; and (10) what means are available to enforce final decisions" Johnson (1994).

Many of these questions have now been answered as (Manjikian, 2010) points out. In the British Constitution it has been established since the Middle Ages that keeping the peace is reserved by royal prerogative, as was made clear by the judiciary in *R. v Secretary of State for the Home Department Ex P. Northumbria Police Authority* [1989] 1 Q.B. 26. At present 'sysop prerogative' gives online community managers the right to decide whether or not they involve themselves with or seek to resolve a dispute between its users. Bishop (2009) draws attention to the practice of some systems operators cancelling the accounts of those in a dispute, in a similar way to other practices in the Middle Ages where those involved in a dispute could be sentenced without trial. Where a public authority in the UK is involved things are slightly different, however. Shipton (2010) reported on a case involving a Welsh councillor who posted such flames in e-mails to one of his constituents. The key difference between Cllr Paul Baccara and the many anonymous rogues that plague Cyberspace is that he was held accountable for his actions. The model used in Wales of a complainant being able to bring a complaint to the organisation that represents the accused, with the option of going to an Ombudsman is one that should be seen as best practice for disputes involving Cyberspace. If everyone in the UK had to be member of a professional body and sign-up to a code of conduct and practice it would be possible for them to be the second point if one of their members acts inappropriately online, because the complaint is not handled properly by the website the questionable action occurred on. The next point of call could be an Ombudsman. In the case of actions involving councillors, as was highlighted in Shipton (2010), is handled by the Public Services Ombudsman, though online disputes could also be handled by the Office of Communications Ombudsman if the complaint is against the website, something which may become more common if the practices set out in the *Digital Economy Act 2010* are to be built on by successive governments (Bishop, 2010b).

CONCLUSION

At the dawn of the Worldwide Web when there was a heating up of imposition of laws by nation states on the international communications networks, one isolated voice spoke out and was cross-posted more times than the author could imagine. John Perry Barlow's 'Declaration of the Independence of Cyberspace' served to start the debate about the legitimacy of nation states to impose laws on a virtual space that crossed frontiers. While it has been argued that the nation states won as there are now a significant number of laws regulating the Internet on national and international levels, there are still questions on the authority of the state in regulating behaviour in online communities.

This paper has discussed the constitutional and administrative arrangements of the United Kingdom and how these contrast with 'Cyberspace', as portrayed by Barlow (1996). From this a number of similarities and differences have been drawn. It is apparent that like in the British constitution there is royal prerogative, in online communities there is 'sysop prerogative'. The former governs powers held by the UK Monarch which have been delegated to ministers for which not Act of Parliament has taken the powers away from the monarch. In the case of the latter it is all the powers which an online community systems operator (i.e. 'sysop') has as a result of not having them taken away by statute or given away by contract.

It can be seen that in online communities such as Wikipedia where sysop prerogative is assigned to faceless enforcers who impose their will on a anonymous group of posters then there will be an eventual downturn in the number of members of the community, as those driven by recognition and community become marginalised by those who cloak their self-interest in a pseudonymous deceptive identities. This could perhaps be called the 'Jimbo effect', after Jimmy " Jimbo" Wales, and contrasted with the 'Figallo effect', named after Cliff Figallo, the sysop of the WELL. It the WELL authority has been delegated to the members whose actual identities are used, making the community grown organically with trust and comradeship among the members. It could be argued that the sysops of World of Warcraft are trying to give their community the Figallo effect as a result of them suffering the Jimbo effect with members hiding their behind their fictitious identities.

Limitations and Directions for Future Research

This chapter has explored a range of existing principles that make up the constitutional and administrative arrangements of the United Kingdom as compared to those envisaged in Cyberspace by John Perry Barlow in 1996. There is currently a shortfall in the amount of research looking at how existing constitutional law, such as that relating to human and civil rights apply to contemporary concepts such as Network Neutrality. This chapter can go some way to understanding the constitutional arrangements that exist in the UK and the basis on which such policies can exist within the current legal framework without massive changes needed to primary legislation.

REFERENCES

Anderson, B. (1991). *Imagined communities: Reflections on the origin and spread of nationalism*. London, UK: Verso.

Armstrong, R. (2010). *Naming and shaming gaming commenters* (p. 42). The Independent.

Barlow, J. P. (1996). *A declaration of the independence of cyberspace*. Retrieved July 10, 2010, from https://projects.eff.org/ ~barlow/ Declaration-Final.html

Bentele, G., & Nothhaft, H. (2010). Strategic communication and the public sphere from a European perspective. *International Journal of Strategic Communication, 4*(2), 93–116. doi:10.1080/15531181003701954

Bishop, J. (2009). Increasing capital revenue in social networking communities: Building social and economic relationships through avatars and characters. In Dasgupta, S. (Ed.), *Social computing: Concepts, methodologies, tools, and applications* (pp. 1987–2004). Hershey, PA: IGI Global. doi:10.4018/978-1-60566-984-7.ch131

Bishop, J. (2010a). *Multiculturalism in intergenerational contexts: Implications for the design of virtual worlds*. Paper Presented to the Reconstructing Multiculturalism Conference, Cardiff, UK.

Bishop, J. (2010b). Tough on data misuse, tough on the causes of data misuse: A review of New Labour's approach to information security and regulating the misuse of digital information (1997–2010). *International Review of Law Computers & Technology, 24*(3), 299–303. doi:10.1080/13600869.2010.522336

Bishop, J. (2011). *The equatrics of intergenerational knowledge transformation in techno-cultures: Towards a model for enhancing information management in virtual worlds. (Unpublished MScEcon)*. Aberystwyth, UK: Aberystwyth University.

Carr-Gregg, M. (2006). *Australian doctor, 2006.*

Castiglione, D. (1996). The political theory of the constitution. *Political Studies, 44*(3), 417–435. doi:10.1111/j.1467-9248.1996.tb00592.x

eBay. (2010). *Reporting inappropriate trading behaviour*. Retrieved July 10, 2010, from http:// pages.ebay.co.uk/ help/buy/ report-trading.html

Flinders, M. (2002). Shifting the balance? Parliament, the executive and the British Constitution. *Political Studies, 50*(1), 23–42. doi:10.1111/1467-9248.00357

Hames, T., & Leonard, M. (1998). *Modernising the monarchy*. London, UK: Demos Medical Publishing.

Hey, J. D., & Pasca, C. (2010). (in press). On choosing a constitution (at least the part relating to the distribution of income). *Economics Letters*.

Johnson, D. R. (1994). *Dispute resolution in cyberspace*. Retrieved July 10, 2010, from http://w2.eff.org/legal/ Arbitration/ online_dispute_resolution_johnson.article

Johnston, R. J. (1983). Texts, actors and higher managers: Judges, bureaucrats and the political organization of space. *Political Geography Quarterly, 2*(1), 3–19. doi:10.1016/0260-9827(83)90003-4

Long, K. (2010). Civilising international politics: Republicanism and the world outside. *Millenium: Journal of International Studies, 38*(3), 773. doi:10.1177/0305829810364195

Manjikian, M. M. E. (2010). From global village to virtual battlespace: The colonizing of the Internet and the extension of realpolitik. *International Studies Quarterly, 54*(2), 381–401. doi:10.1111/j.1468-2478.2010.00592.x

Mesure, S., & Griggs, I. (2007). *The facebook betrayal - Users revolt over advertising sell-out: Networking site to put members' mugshots on ads* (p. 3). The Independent on Sunday.

Preece, J. (2001). *Online communities: Designing usability, supporting sociability*. Chichester, UK: John Wiley & Sons.

Rheingold, H. (2000). *The virtual community: Homesteading on the electronic frontier* (2nd ed.). London, UK: MIT Press.

Saxby, S. (2006). A critical analysis of the synergy between e-government information and related UK policies. *Computer and Telecommunications Law Review, 12*(6), 179–215.

Shipton, M. (2010). *Councillor suspended over e-mail outburst* (p. 14). The South Wales Echo.

Smith, A. (1966). *The wealth of nations*. Raleigh, NC: Hayes Barton Press.

Taylor, M., Haggerty, J., & Gresty, D. (2009). The legal aspects of corporate email investigations. *Computer Law & Security Report, 25*(4), 372–376. doi:10.1016/j.clsr.2009.05.006

Weiler, J. H. H. (2002). A constitution for Europe? Some hard choices. *Journal of Common Market Studies, 40*(4), 563–580. doi:10.1111/1468-5965.00388

Chapter 13
A UK Law Perspective:
Defamation Law as it Applies on the Internet

Sam De Silva
Manches LLP, UK

ABSTRACT

The development of the Internet raises challenges in the application of defamation, given that the click of a mouse can communicate a defamatory statement instantly to thousands of people throughout the world. This can pose a serious threat to the reputation of an individual or company. This chapter considers: (1) the laws of defamation applicable to the Internet, including analysis of the Defamation Acts 1952 and 1996 and the E-Commerce Directive; (2) the way UK law is currently being applied in practice, including discussion of the key UK cases in this area; (3) the Internet defence in the Defamation Act 1996, which can protect innocent disseminators of defamatory material over the Internet; and (4) future reform of defamation law in the UK.

INTRODUCTION

Defamation involves the protection of the personal brand (in terms of a person's reputation), and the corporate brand (in respect of goodwill and reputation). Defamation occurs when there is publication to a third party of words or matters containing an untrue imputation against the reputation of individuals, companies or firms which serves to undermine that reputation in the eyes of right thinking members of society generally.

The development of the Internet raises challenges in the application of defamation, given that the click of a mouse can communicate a defamatory statement instantly to thousands of people throughout the world. This can pose a

DOI: 10.4018/978-1-61350-132-0.ch013

serious threat to the reputation of an individual or company. To-date, Internet service providers (ISPs) have been the subject of defamation actions from those who claim they have been libelled on the Internet. However, the risks apply to all players on the Internet, including search engines, usenet hosts, website design companies and companies who use the Internet for sales or marketing purposes.

This chapter considers: (1) the laws of defamation applicable to the Internet, including analysis of the Defamation Acts 1952 and 1996 and the E-Commerce Directive; (2) the way UK law is currently being applied in practice, including discussion of the key UK cases in this area; (3) the Internet defence in the Defamation Act 1996, which can protect innocent disseminators of defamatory material over the Internet; and (4) future reform of defamation law in the UK.

This chapter is based on the law as at 15 September 2010.

GENERAL PRINCIPLES

Definition of Defamation

A defamatory statement is one which tends to lower the claimant in the estimation of right-thinking members of society generally (*Sim v Stretch* [1936] 2 All ER 1237). For a plaintiff to have an action for defamation, the plaintiff must show that the words complained of:

- Are defamatory;
- Identify or refer to the plaintiff; and
- Are published by the defendant to a third party.

Once the plaintiff has established the points above, the defendant will need to prove the truth of the statement or establish that he can benefit from one of the other defamation defences, such as fair comment or privilege. The plaintiff is not usually required to prove that he has suffered damage to his reputation or even that he had a good reputation in the first place. However, if he has a generally bad reputation, which can be proved, his damages will be reduced.

The rules as to:

- When a statement is defamatory;
- Who may sue;
- When publication has occurred; and
- Whether a defence applies,

are laid down in centuries' of English case law. This case law is also supplemented by:

- The Defamation Act 1952;
- The Defamation Act 1996 (the "Defamation Act"); and
- The EC Directive on electronic commerce (Directive 2000/31/EC) (the "E-Commerce Directive") The E-Commerce Directive is given effect in the UK by the Electronic Commerce (EC Directive) Regulations 2002 (SI 2002/2013) (the "E-Commerce Regulations").

Defamation and the E-Commerce Directive

Despite lobbying by ISPs, the E-Commerce Directive does not change the law of Internet defamation in the UK. The provisions in the E-Commerce Directive are broadly consistent with the Defamation Act, and can be summarised as set out below.

ISPs providing hosting services (i.e. the hosting of newsgroups and websites) receive partial immunity from libel actions (Article 14 of the E-Commerce Directive). An ISP will be immune if it does not have:

- Actual knowledge of illegal activity or information; or

- Knowledge of facts or circumstances from which it is apparent that the activity or information is illegal.

However, an ISP will lose immunity if, on obtaining knowledge of the illegal activity, it fails to act expeditiously to remove or to disable access to the information. It is not entirely clear as to how expeditious an ISP needs to be to avoid liability. The requirement to act expeditiously is the equivalent to (and just as vague as) the reasonable care requirement of the section 1 defence under the Defamation Act (see under the heading "Defence raised by intermediaries").

Countries adopting the E-Commerce Directive:

- Must not place any general obligation on ISPs to screen or actively monitor third party content (Article 15 of the E-Commerce Directive). This recognises, as is now widely accepted, that it is impossible for ISPs effectively to monitor their systems; and
- Must encourage industry self-regulation, including the establishment of codes of conduct and hotline mechanisms (Article 16 of the E-Commerce Directive).

It appears likely that the meanings of reasonable care and contribution to publication in the section 1 defence of the Defamation Act will be construed in light of the code or codes of conduct which ISPs adopt (see under the heading "Future Developments and Reform").

In a case involving the BBC, the interplay of related hypertext links was found to affect whether words had a defamatory meaning. The High Court struck out a claim for libel brought against the BBC in respect of three articles in its online archive. Only the second and third articles came up on Internet searches, but these included hyperlinks to the first article. The court found that the first article would only be accessed via the second and third articles and, read in the context of those articles, the first article was not defamatory. The courts also found that the second and third articles were not defamatory (*Samuel Kingsford Budu v BBC* [2010] EWHC 616 (QB)).

The High Court also considered the role of hyperlinks in aggregating information on linked web pages in *Islam Expo Ltd v The Spectator (1828) Ltd and another* [2010] EWHC 2011 (QB). The judge, Tugendhat J, said that the principles to be applied were the same as those where the issue was whether words were capable of bearing a defamatory meaning. Case law established that, in order to determine the meaning of words complained of, account had to be taken of the context in which the words were used. In deciding that the words of the article complained of were capable of referring to the claimant, Tugendhat J took into account the text on the web pages linked to from that article. However, he did emphasise that he did this without intending to imply any ruling as to whether that approach was right in law.

Meaning of Libel and Slander and Their Relationship with the Law of Defamation

Libel and slander are the two limbs of the tort of defamation. There has been some debate as to whether postings on the Internet amount to libel or slander. Libel is the publication in permanent form of a defamatory statement. Slander is its publication in transitory form. It is generally accepted that defamatory statements on web pages are to be regarded as libel, whereas, in the case of *Smith v ADVFN Plc and others* [2008] EWHC 1797 (QB) the High Court classified chat on an Internet bulletin board as more akin to slander than to libel. An important difference between the two is that for slander the claimant will often have to prove that he has suffered some actual financial loss, but this is not necessary in the case of libel.

Primary Publishers vs. Secondary Publishers

For a defendant to be liable for defamation, he must be a publisher of the defamatory statement. The definition of publisher at common law includes anyone who participated in the publication of a defamatory statement. This is very wide, encompassing both primary and secondary publishers.

A primary publisher of defamatory material is one who exercises direct editorial control over the published statements. This is defined in section 1(2) of the Defamation Act (and will include authors, editors and publishing houses).

Secondary publishers do not take an active editorial role but still make the defamatory comments available to third parties. Examples of activities which can be undertaken without making the person a primary publisher are set out in section 1(3) of the Defamation Act (these include libraries, news-stands, bookshops and ISPs). Secondary publishers can still be liable for defamatory material communicated to a third party, even in the absence of proof of fault.

The distinction between primary and secondary publishers is of particular importance in relation to the Internet. In many cases, the originator of a defamatory statement cannot always be identified and is rarely worth suing. It may therefore be necessary to pursue a secondary publisher. Where a defamatory statement is made on a company website, for example, the plaintiff has a choice of who to sue. He could choose the owner of the website, as the primary publisher, or pursue the operator of the website, the ISP, as a secondary publisher. The lack of protection given to secondary publishers means that, in practice, ISPs are often the first target of plaintiffs wishing to remove a defamatory statement from the Internet (see under the heading "Practical Application of the Law of Internet Defamation and the Internet").

The distinction between primary and secondary publishers can become blurred in Internet cases. For example, a company providing an online news service may be a secondary publisher if all it does is collect news articles and print them in the same form on the Internet. However, if the company decides to exert some form of editorial control by editing the articles or providing summary extracts, it may become a primary publisher. This can cause considerable difficulties for ISPs (see under the headings "The intermediaries' defence" and "Notice-and-take-down procedures").

There is also some doubt as to whether providers of hyperlinks are publishers. In *Hird v Wood* ([1894] 38 SJ 234), a man sitting in a chair pointed out to passers-by a defamatory sign erected over the road. He was held to be a publisher. By pointing out the sign, he had contributed to its publication. By analogy, the same principle could apply to the provider of a hypertext link. However, this will depend on the facts. For instance, if the link is to a website as a whole, as opposed to a particular article on it, there is a stronger argument that no act of publication takes place. There has, as yet, been no definitive court decision on this point.

The liability of search-engine operators was considered in *Metropolitan International Schools Limited v (1) Designtechnica Corporation, (2) Google UK Limited, (3) Google Inc* [2009] EWHC 1765 (QB), in which Google Inc was held not to have "published" a defamatory statement that appeared when users input certain words into its search engine. The High Court ruled that, as Google had no role in deciding the search terms, it had not authorised or caused the statement to appear on the user's screen in any meaningful sense; it had merely, by the provision of its search service, played the role of a facilitator. Although the law recognised that a person could become liable for the publication of a libel by acquiescence, a search engine operator could not control the search terms input by users, and so (unlike someone who was merely hosting a website from which it could easily remove offending material) it had no easy way of ensuring that the offending words would not appear in its search results. In this particular case, the evidence showed that Google had taken steps to ensure that certain identified Uniform Resource Locators (URLs) were blocked, so that the content of such URLs would not be displayed in response to Google searches. However, it needed to have specific URLs identified in order to be able to block them and was not in a position to put in place a more effective block on the specific words complained of without, at the same time, blocking a huge amount of other material which might contain some of the individual words comprising the offending statement. In such circumstances, it could not be said to have acquiesced in the continued publication of the libellous statement.

The effect of search engines was also considered in *Samuel v BBC* (cited above), but this time from the point of view of the original publisher of material listed in the results rather than that of the search engine operator. The judge ruled that, where a Google search against the claimant's name brought up a "snippet" of a BBC article which divorced it from its context so as to render it libellous, the BBC could not be held responsible for the libel. He therefore struck out the claim.

Limitation Period for Making a Claim of Defamation

Under section 4(a) of the Limitation Act 1980, a plaintiff has only one year from the date of publication of a defamatory statement to sue for defamation. This rule is subject to the court's broad discretion to extend the limitation period in circumstances where it is equitable to do so. The court will have regard to a number of prescribed factors, such as the reasons for the delay and the effect of the delay on the reliability of evidence.

A fresh cause of action for defamation arises each time a defamatory statement is published (*Duke of Brunswick v Harmer* (1849) 14 QB 185). This means that the limitation period for bringing an action is extended each time the original defamatory comments are republished. This rule is particularly relevant to the Internet due to the existence of online archives and the ease with which defamatory statements can be stored and republished.

This issue was specifically considered in *Loutchansky v Times Newspapers Limited* ([2001] EWCA Civ 1805). The case concerned a series of articles in *The Times* which accused a Russian businessman of being the head of a major Russian criminal organisation, with involvement in money laundering and the smuggling of nuclear weapons. The articles in question had been posted and archived on *The Times* website.

The newspaper argued that the limitation period in relation to the online version of the articles began when the articles were first posted on *The Times* website. The Court of Appeal upheld the first instance decision, holding that publication occurs each time the defamatory comments are accessed on the website, not just when the articles are first posted on the website. Each hit therefore constitutes a fresh publication with a fresh limitation period.

The court rejected the single publication rule which exists in the US, whereby the publication of a defamatory statement occurs only once, when the statement is first published, and a subsequent publication, does not give rise to a fresh cause of action.

The rule in *Duke of Brunswick* has been held by the European Court of Human Rights ("ECHR") to be consistent with Article 10 of the European Convention on Human Rights, which guarantees freedom of expression. However, the ECHR did add that libel proceedings brought against a publisher after a significant lapse of time might well, in the absence of exceptional circumstances, give rise to a disproportionate interference with press freedom under Article 10.

The unfortunate consequence of the rule is that the operator of an online archive may be held liable for defamation several years after the statements were first published. This result has been criticised and has led the Law Commission and a House of Lords Select Committee to recommend reform in this area (see under the heading "Future Developments and Reform").

To manage risk, operators of online archives, particularly newspapers and other news services, must take care in deciding which articles to keep on their websites, particularly if an article has been the subject of a complaint. Where the operator of an online archive knows that a particular article may be defamatory, it should either remove the article or attach a notice warning readers not to rely on the truth of the material. Such action would, in the opinion of the court in *Loutchansky*, normally remove the sting from the material published.

Defence Raised by Intermediaries

Section 1 of the Defamation Act provides a defence to protect intermediaries who could otherwise be liable for publishing a defamatory statement on the Internet. This codifies what had previously been described at common law as the "innocent dissemination" defence.

Under section 1(1)(a), (b) and (c) of the Defamation Act, a person has a defence to an action for defamation if he shows that he:

- Was not the author, editor or publisher of the statement complained of;
- Took reasonable care in relation to its publication; and
- Did not know, and had no reason to believe, that what he did caused or contributed to the publication of a defamatory statement.

The meanings of author, editor and publisher are defined in section 1(2) of the Defamation Act:

- "Author" means the originator of the statement.
- "Editor" means a person having editorial or equivalent responsibility for the content of the statement or the decision to publish it.

- "Publisher" means a commercial publisher. That is, a person whose business is issuing material to the public, or a section of the public, who issues material containing the statement in the course of that business. It does not mean publisher in the common law sense.
- However, under section 1(3) of the Defamation Act a person will not be considered the author, editor or publisher of a statement if he is involved only:
- In processing, making copies of, distributing or selling any electronic medium in or on which the statement is recorded;
- As an operator or provider of a system or service by means of which a statement is made available in electronic form; or
- As the operator of or provider of access to a communications system by means of which the statement is transmitted, or made available, by a person over whom he has no effective control.

It is clear that ISPs and other intermediaries are intended to benefit from the section 1 defence by falling into one of the above categories (the last two of which being the most relevant to ISPs) but, in practice the requirements referred to above under section 1(1)(b) and (c) of the Defamation Act to show reasonable care and lack of knowledge represent considerable barriers to its application (see under the heading "The intermediaries' defence").

PRACTICAL APPLICATION OF THE LAW OF DEFAMATION AND THE INTERNET

The Intermediaries' Defence

The section 1 defence under the Defamation Act was first considered in the case *Laurence Godfrey v Demon Internet Limited* ([1999] 4 All ER 342). This case arose from a defamatory statement posted on a usenet newsgroup which Demon Internet (the defendant) carried and stored as part of its ISP services. A critical feature of the case was that Professor Godfrey sent Demon a fax informing it of the defamatory statement and requesting its removal. Despite having the facilities to remove the statement, Demon chose to ignore the complaint and allowed the statement to remain on its server for a further ten days.

At a pre-trial ruling Morland J held, rejecting the US authorities, that Demon was a common law publisher of the material and that because it knew of the offending statement but chose not to remove it, it placed itself in an "insuperable difficulty" (under sections 1(1)(b) and (c) of the Defamation Act) and could not, therefore, avail itself of the section 1 defence.

The decision received considerable attention and was criticised as imposing too great a restraint on free speech on the Internet. However, the decision is a correct interpretation of UK law as it stands. Once it was established that Demon was a publisher at common law, Demon could not successfully argue that it did not know, and had no reason to believe, that what it did caused or contributed to the publication of a defamatory statement (as would be required under section 1(1)(c) of the Defamation Act).

By choosing to ignore the defamatory statement, Demon unquestionably contributed to its continuing publication. By contrast, defendant ISPs who act as mere conduits of defamatory information rather than hosting it, and have no involvement in initiating its transmission, selecting or modifying it, or choosing who would receive it, should have defences under the Defamation Act and the E-Commerce Regulations (*John Bunt v David Tilley and others* [2006] EWCH 407 (QB)). Alternatively, it could be held that they did not qualify as "publishers" of the material in the first place (as occurred in the *Google* case discussed above).

Orders to Disclose Identity of Those Responsible for Defamatory Statements

In October 2007 the High Court ordered the operator of a football club fan website to disclose the identity of five users of the site in relation to the posting of allegedly defamatory messages concerning the club's management (*Sheffield Wednesday Football Club Limited and others v Neil Hargreaves* [2007] EWHC 2375 (QB), 18 October 2007). However, the court refused to disclose the identity of nine other users, finding that their messages were of a more trivial nature. The court set out some clear guidelines as to when a court can require a website operator to disclose the source of defamatory material by way of a *Norwich Pharmacal* order, which build on the principles first set out in the case of *Totalise PLC v The Motley Fool Limited* [2001] EMLR 750 (the "*Motley Fool*" case).

Background

The court has jurisdiction to make an order for the disclosure of the identity of a wrongdoer against anyone who, albeit innocently, becomes involved in the wrongful act of another (*Norwich Pharmacal Co. v Customs and Excise Commissioners* [1974] AC 133).

In the *Motley Fool* case, the High Court granted *Norwich Pharmacal* relief to the claimant, holding that the website operators should disclose the identity of the source of defamatory material posted anonymously to their discussion boards.

The Data Protection Act 1998 ("DPA"), imposes broad obligations on those who collect personal data (data controllers), as well as conferring broad rights on individuals about whom data is collected (data subjects). In addition to the general fairness requirement, a data controller must meet at least one of the conditions in Schedule 2 to the DPA, including that:

"The processing is necessary for the legitimate interests of the data controller or a third party to whom the data is disclosed, except where the processing is unwarranted because it is prejudicial to the rights and freedoms or legitimate interests of the individual concerned" (Schedule 2, Paragraph 6(1) of the DPA).

Facts

The eight plaintiffs comprised Sheffield Wednesday Football Club Limited (the "Club"), its chief executive and directors, and the chairman of Sheffield Wednesday PLC (which owned all the shares in the Club).

The claimants sought *Norwich Pharmacal* relief against the defendant, Neil Hargreaves. Mr Hargreaves owned and operated a website, www.owlstalk.co.uk, on which fans of Sheffield Wednesday football club posted messages on matters relating to their club.

The website was freely accessible to anyone with Internet access. Users registered as members by providing an e-mail address and password, and then giving a user name (invariably a pseudonym) by which they identified themselves when making a posting. When a member registered for the website, he agreed not to use the bulletin board to post any material which was, among other things, knowingly false or defamatory.

The plaintiffs wanted to bring libel proceedings against eleven members of Mr Hargreaves' website in relation to fourteen messages which they had posted between 24 July 2007 and 3 August 2007. The claimants alleged that the postings, which largely concerned the claimants' management of the Club, were defamatory.

The defendant did not oppose the plaintiffs' application for *Norwich Pharmacal* relief and disclosure of the identity of the eleven members, but was not prepared to consent to it.

Decision of the Judge

Richard Parkes QC, sitting as a deputy High Court judge, ordered the website operator to disclose the identity of five of the members of his website, but not the other seven requested by the plaintiffs.

The deputy judge's reasoning is summarised below.

Referring to the Court of Appeal's decision in the *Motley Fool* case (see above), the deputy judge said that a court must be careful not to make a *Norwich Pharmacal* order which unjustifiably invaded the right of an individual to respect for his private life, especially when he was not a party to the proceedings.

The deputy judge held that equally an order should not be made for the disclosure of the identity of a data subject (whether under the *Norwich Pharmacal* doctrine or otherwise) unless the court had first considered whether the disclosure was justified having regard to the rights and freedoms or the legitimate interests of the data subject (Schedule 2, paragraph 6(1), DPA).

According to Lightman J in *Mitsui Limited v Nexen Petroleum UK Limited* [2005] EWHC 625 (Ch), there were three conditions which had to be satisfied before the court could grant *Norwich Pharmacal* relief:

- A wrong must have been carried out or arguably carried out by an ultimate wrongdoer;
- There must be the need for an order to enable action to be brought against the ultimate wrongdoer; and
- The person against whom the order was sought must be mixed up in the wrongdoing so as to have facilitated it, and must be able or likely to be able to provide the information necessary to enable the ultimate wrongdoer to be sued.

The deputy judge explained that even if these conditions were met, the court retained a discretion whether or not to make an order. Matters relevant to the exercise of this discretion (as set out in *Motley Fool*) included the strength of the claimant's case; the gravity of the defamatory allegations; whether it was part of a concerted campaign; and whether the defendant had a confidentiality policy for website users.

Applying the above principles to the facts, the deputy judge said that he accepted that Lightman J's second and third conditions were met (the claimants had no other way of finding out the authors' identity, and Mr Hargreaves had facilitated the alleged wrongdoing by giving users the means to address other users), but the deputy judge was more hesitant about the first condition. However, he concluded that the words in the postings met the threshold tests of being arguably defamatory and at least arguably false.

The claimants argued that the court should exercise its discretion and grant relief as there was a strong prima facie case against all the eleven members. However, the deputy judge held that nine of the postings bordered on the trivial and it would not be right to make an order for disclosure where the messages were barely defamatory, little more than abusive or likely to be understood as jokes: that would be disproportionate and unjustifiably intrusive.

The deputy judge found that the remaining five postings were more serious as they could reasonably be understood to allege greed, selfishness, untrustworthiness and dishonest behaviour by the plaintiffs. Consequently, the plaintiffs' entitlement to take action to protect their reputation outweighed the authors' rights to maintain their anonymity and to express themselves freely. In reaching this decision, the deputy judge took into account the website restrictions on the use of defamatory language and the absence of any confidentiality policy for users.

Practical Implications

The deputy judge has provided some clear guidelines as to when a court can require a website operator to disclose the source of defamatory material by way of a *Norwich Pharmacal* order, which build upon the principles first set out in the *Motley Fool* case. As this case illustrates, a court will not reach a decision to require disclosure lightly, as it will have an impact upon an individual's rights of privacy and freedom of expression.

The website operator did not oppose the claimants' application for *Norwich Pharmacal* relief in this case, but he was not prepared to go as far as consenting to it, as he regarded it as inappropriate for him to do so. Although there was no formal confidentiality policy in place for users, Mr Hargreaves considered that users could reasonably expect that their personal details would not be disclosed by him without a court order.

The position taken by the website operator is similar to that taken by Google in a request to disclose the identity of an advertiser in a potential copyright infringement case (*Helen Grant v Google UK Limited* [2005] EWHC 3444 (Ch), 17 May 2005).

It is not clear from the judgment whether the website operator has details of the users' postal addresses or just their e-mail addresses. If he can only provide e-mail addresses to the claimants, they may have to make a further *Norwich Pharmacal* application against the ISPs to establish the users' identities so that the claimants can bring libel proceedings against them.

Notice and Take-Down Procedures

The result of the *Godfrey* ruling is that, in order to rely on the section 1 defence under the Defamation Act, ISPs and other intermediaries now have to remove allegedly defamatory postings as soon as they are put on notice of their existence. This removal process is called a notice-and-take-down procedure. The ISP would not be entitled first to investigate the merits of the allegations nor to assess the availability of other libel defences, unless it suspends access to the posting while it does so.

As explained above, to qualify for the defence, an ISP has to show that it was not the author, editor or publisher of the defamatory statement, and section 1(3) of the Defamation Act sets out the categories of intermediaries who fall outside these definitions (see under the heading "Defence raised by intermediaries").

An ISP or other intermediary which decides to exert some kind of editorial control over the content of its server or statements made by its users may therefore become classified as an author, editor or publisher under the Defamation Act and so lose the benefit of the section 1 defence. On the other hand, an ISP which decides not to monitor its server or respond to complaints, as in the *Godfrey* case, is likely to clear the first hurdle of not being an author, editor or publisher, but will fall foul of the requirement of section 1(1)(b) of the Defamation Act to take reasonable care in relation to the publication of the statement complained of. In this context, the High Court has ruled that the fact that a website operator moderates some parts of its content, but not other parts, does not automatically make it the author, editor or publisher of its entire content (*Kaschke v (1) Gray (2) Hilton* [2010] EWHC 690 (QB)).

The practical result is that whether the ISP believes that a statement complained of is libellous or not, it is now simply not worth risking the consequences of allowing it to remain on its server. It is thought that, although some ISPs may use electronic-monitoring devices, most will not spend large sums of money and time attempting to track down defamatory comments. Given the vast amounts of material on their servers and the present state of the law, it is impossible for ISPs to monitor content in this way. Instead, they will simply operate as efficient a notice-and-take-down procedure as possible.

If the owner of the website in question is financially secure, the ISP may be willing to accept an indemnity from the owner in respect of any litigation resulting from the defamatory material. In such circumstances, the ISP may take the risk of allowing the defamatory material to remain on its server. However, indemnities are difficult to obtain and may be difficult to enforce against an individual or small company, so in most cases an ISP will not take this risk.

Another problem facing ISPs is that taking material down from their servers may put them in breach of their subscriber contracts, particularly in the case of consumers. In the case of consumers, a clause allowing the ISP to remove material will be subject to the test of reasonableness (see under the heading "Recommendations for ISPs"). Simply removing material without any investigation at all may therefore leave an ISP open to claims for breach of contract from its subscribers.

Case Law Demonstrating Notice and Take-Down Procedures

Although most notice-and-take-down situations will not even reach the press, let alone the courts, two post-*Godfrey* incidents provide good examples of the kind of problems that ISPs are facing.

Demon Internet

The first incident related to the *Godfrey* case itself. Professor Godfrey had complained about further newsgroup postings, which quoted the original words complained of in his action against Demon before the case had been tried. Demon responded to his complaint by not only removing the comments complained of, but also suspending newsgroup access to certain members until they signed a form of indemnity so that they, and not Demon, would be liable for any further defamatory postings.

This secondary action was taken because the previous conduct of the author, editor or publisher is one of the factors to be taken into account in determining whether reasonable care has been taken (section 1(5)(c), Defamation Act) (see under the heading "Practical steps for an ISP"). Demon was concerned that if the same user repeated any of the comments in subsequent postings, it would not be able to claim the benefit of the section 1 defence.

Although the removal of the postings was necessary to avoid any possible future liability, it is arguable that suspension of newsgroup access was not necessary for first-time offenders, who may not even have realised that what they were doing amounted to publication of defamatory material. However, from a commercial perspective, Demon cannot be blamed for taking this action given the uncertainty as to what amounts to "reasonable care". The dissatisfaction of a small number of subscribers is a small price to pay for avoiding the high cost of an unsuccessful defamation defence.

Kingston Internet

The second example concerned a so-called "anti-judge website" constructed by a Mr Hulbert, who claimed in a series of open letters to the Lord Chancellor on the website, alleging that he had been denied justice at the hands of a number of identified judges. In response to the letters, the Lord Chancellor's department wrote to the ISP involved, Kingston Internet Limited, describing the statements by Mr Hulbert as offensive and asking the company to remove them. Kingston Internet promptly did so, stating in a letter to Mr Hulbert that he had breached their terms and conditions.

Not only did Kingston Internet remove the comments complained of, but it also closed down the whole website. Mr. Hulbert might have had a valid defence to a libel action but, understandably, this was not the concern of the ISP. As mentioned above, under the section 1 defence, an ISP is not entitled to investigate the merits of a claim before taking action. Like Demon, Kingston Internet was merely taking the precautions it felt necessary to avoid any liability.

Practical Steps for an ISP

What does an ISP need to do to show that it took reasonable care and that it did not know or have reason to believe that what it did contributed to the publication of a defamatory statement (as it must do in order to satisfy the requirements of section 1(1)(b) and (c) of the Defamation Act)? This will depend on whether the ISP is on notice of the defamatory statement.

Before Notice Has Been Given

As mentioned above, if an ISP chooses to have editorial control over the content of its server or to impose effective control over statements made by its users, it may fall outside the scope of the section 1 defence on the basis that it falls within the definition of an editor in section 1(1)(a) of the Defamation Act. Because of this anomaly and the high costs of exerting editorial control, ISPs are unlikely to exert sufficient control so as to lose the section 1 defence. The key question in most cases will be whether the ISP exercised reasonable care and did not know, or have reason to believe, that what it did contributed to the publication of a defamatory statement.

The Defamation Act gives only limited guidance as to what constitutes reasonable care or knowledge, or reason to believe, that what a person did caused or contributed to publication. Under section 1(5) of the Defamation Act, factors to consider include:

- The extent of his responsibility for the content of the statement or the decision to publish it;
- The nature or circumstances of the publication; and
- The previous conduct or character of the author, editor or publisher.

After Notice Has Been Given

Usually, an intermediary will not be expected to actively seek out potentially defamatory material. What, therefore, does reasonable care mean once an intermediary has been notified of a defamatory comment, and when might an intermediary contribute to its publication? The answer will remain uncertain until such time as the following issues are clarified:

What constitutes notice? Is a single fax or e-mail sufficient? If so, does that fax or e-mail have to be read or simply received? Again, the Defamation Act and *Godfrey* offer little guidance. As with the application of technology to the offer and acceptance rules in contract law, a whole variety of scenarios can be thought of where notice might be in dispute. For example, if a fax is sent but remains unread for 24 hours, does this constitute notice from the time the fax was received by the fax machine, or will only actual notice suffice?

Of what does notice need to be given? Is it necessary for the complainant to ask for the defamatory comment to be removed or would a general complaint about a whole newsgroup or website suffice? In *Godfrey*, the complaint related to specific comments and the claimant expressly asked for those comments to be removed. However, it is clear from the *Kingston Internet* case that general complaints about the content of a whole website can be enough for an ISP to close down the site.

Once an intermediary is put on notice, how quickly must it react? The nature of the Internet is such that by the time an ISP reacts, even if it does so quickly and efficiently, enormous damage may have already been done. Clearly, an ISP which reacts quickly and is in no way at fault should not be fixed with liability. But what of the ISP which is on notice of the defamatory comment but fails to remove it for a further two days? In *Godfrey*, damages were only sought for the period of ten days over which the defamatory comment was displayed after notice had been given. The compensatory damages agreed were, therefore, not very high. The damages may be much higher for a person whose livelihood is especially dependent on his reputation. For example, the claimant in *Keith-Smith v Williams* ([2006] EWHC 860 (QB)) was a UK Independence Party member whose reputation suffered as a result of abusive postings on an Internet bulletin board. The court awarded a high level of damages despite the fact that the statements had not reached a wide audience. It took into account the malicious nature of the allegations, and the unrepentant behaviour of the defendant. In *Flood v Times Newspapers Ltd* [2010] EWCA Civ 804 the Court of Appeal made it clear that where, during the course of negotiations with a complainant, a newspaper knowingly maintains a defamatory article in its archive without qualifying it with a warning message, it will not be able to benefit from Reynolds privilege (which provides protection for responsible journalism when reporting matters of public concern).

The court will also take into account the likelihood of a high level of "hits" on the webpage that carried the defamatory statements. A prime example of this was the award of £22,000 in damages against the individual defendant in the Facebook libel case of *Firsht v Raphael* [2008] EWHC 1781 (QB). In that case the damages took into account the fact that the defamatory pages set up by the defendant could be accessed by the Facebook "London" group, which had around 850,000 members at the relevant time.

To what extent will the previous conduct or character of a particular person, website or newsgroup be influential in determining "reasonable care"? There will doubtless be some newsgroups and websites which develop a reputation for producing defamatory material. Does this mean that an ISP will have to monitor or close down consistently offending websites and suspend the accounts of frequent offenders, or otherwise risk losing the section 1 defence?

The answers to the above questions will inevitably depend on the facts of each individual case. The extent of the intermediary's responsibility, the nature and circumstances of the publication and the previous conduct or character of the originator will all vary from case to case. As in the law of torts generally, the concept of reasonableness will have to be adopted. However, without a developed body of case law, intermediaries are left with little guidance as to how a judge or jury will interpret a given set of facts and what is perceived to be "reasonable".

FUTURE DEVELOPMENTS AND REFORM

The problems highlighted above have led many, including the Law Commission, to put forward a case for reform. The Law Commission has suggested a number of ways to ease the current problems, including:

- Introducing an industry code of conduct;
- Adopting the US approach by giving immunity to ISPs; and
- Extending the innocent dissemination defence.

The adoption of a code of conduct and/or the extension of the innocent dissemination defence are the more likely solutions in the UK. In February 2010 a House of Commons Select Committee recommended a one-year limitation period for bringing proceedings for Internet libel, saying that it should be capable of extension if the plaintiff can satisfy the court that he could not reasonably have been aware of the existence of the publication. However, it also recommended that a plaintiff should be entitled to obtain a Court Order to correct a defamatory statement after expiry of the limitation period (Select Committee report on press standards, privacy and libel 2010).

In July 2010 the Ministry of Justice announced that it intended to publish in 2011 a draft Defama-

tion Bill for consultation purposes (Ministry of Justice Press Release, 2010).

In the meantime, there are a number of precautions which ISPs can take to help avoid liability for defamation (see below).

Code of Conduct

Many are now calling for an industry code of conduct for dealing with defamation-related complaints, to ensure consistency across the industry. Although a general code of conduct is likely to be agreed between ISPs, it would require a substantial amount of flexibility to take into account the different sizes, terms and conditions, resources, and commercial objectives of ISPs. Consideration would also need to be given to the scope of the code. Should it apply just to ISPs or should it include search engines and other online intermediaries? Any industry code would also need to be approved as reasonable by the courts.

US Approach

ISPs in the US are immune from defamation actions resulting from the comments of third parties. Legislation provides that no provider or user of an interactive computer service shall be treated as the publisher or speaker of any information provided by another information content provider (section 230(c) of the Communications Decency Act 1996).

US Case law has since held that this provision, by its plain language, created a federal immunity to any cause of action that would make ISPs liable for information originating from a third party user of the service (*Zeran v America On-line Inc.* (129 F 3d 327 (1997), Cert. den. 48 S Ct 2341 (1998)).

However, when comparing the US defamation laws with those of the UK, it is crucial to bear in mind the impact in the US of the First Amendment to the American Constitution on freedom of speech, which ensures that courts are very reluctant to prohibit free speech, particularly concerning public figures.

The effect of the Communications Decency Act has been to strip American ISPs of their responsibility to police the Internet. This was held to be an undesirable effect in *Blumenthal v Drudge and America On-line (AOL)* (992 F Supp 44 (US District Ct, DC 1998)), which applied section 230 of the Communications Decency Act with some reluctance. Such an effect also makes it unlikely that UK law will follow the US approach.

Legislative Reform

Some argue that the only real way to improve the position of intermediaries is to amend the section 1 defence under the Defamation Act. The difficulty is finding a balance that will encourage ISPs actively to respond to legitimate complaints, but without incurring unfair liability in doing so. One possibility is to amend the Defamation Act so as to provide intermediaries with immunity when they have investigated a complaint and reasonably concluded that there is a valid defence to defamation proceedings. In applying this test, regard could be had to any relevant code of conduct.

If section 1 of the Defamation Act were amended in this way, an ISP would be likely to adopt different approaches depending on the nature of each case rather than pursuing a policy of the blanket removal of all potentially defamatory statements. In the case of small-scale complaints concerning newsgroup postings, such as the initial complaint by Professor Godfrey in the *Godfrey* case, ISPs would still be likely to remove the offending comments. As the *Godfrey* case has shown, there is little to be gained from allowing them to remain and little to be lost by removing them. Where, however, more high-profile complaints are made, involving competing commercial interests or matters of public interest, the ISP would be likely to consider the merits of a complaint as the consequences of removal could be severe. Any future code of conduct should provide guidance as to when it would not be appropriate to allow a comment to remain.

Recommendations for ISPs

ISPs can help themselves to avoid liability for Internet defamation by incorporating appropriate provisions in subscriber contracts and adopting suitable procedures:

In subscriber contracts with businesses, ISPs may reserve the right to remove material in any circumstances (although over-restrictive clauses could encourage informed businesses to go to another ISP). In subscriber contracts with consumers, however, regard must be had to the application of consumer protection rules such as those contained in the Unfair Contract Terms Act 1977 and the Unfair Terms in Consumer Contracts Regulations 1999. The ISP's right to remove material should therefore be formulated so that it only arises if "in its reasonable opinion" or "[having received notice of a complaint] it reasonably believes that" the material is defamatory of any person.

ISPs and other online intermediaries should ensure that detailed procedures are in place for dealing with defamation-related complaints, including setting response times for examining complaints and removing material if necessary; maintaining detailed records of complaints received and the action taken; and making clear to subscribers the limits of acceptable content.

CONCLUSION

There are some challenges when defamation law is applied to the Internet. Whilst the Defamation Act and E-Commerce Regulations was intended to address such challenges, they do not substantially change the law of defamation in the UK. Although section 1 of the Defamation Act provides a defence to protect intermediaries (such as ISPs), who could otherwise be liable for publishing a defamatory statement on the Internet, there are difficulties for that intermediary to establish that it took reasonable care in relation to its publication and did not know, and had no reason to believe, that what it did caused or contributed to the publication of a defamatory statement. As mentioned above, the Law Commission has suggested a number of ways to ease the current problems, including:

- Introducing an industry code of conduct;
- Adopting the US approach by giving immunity to ISPs; and
- Extending the innocent dissemination defence.

It remains to be seen if any of these proposals will be implemented.

REFERENCES

Blumenthal v Drudge and America On-line (AOL) (1998). (992 F Supp 44 (US District Ct, DC 1998)).

Communications Decency Act. (1996). Retrieved 15 September 2010, from http://www.law.cornell.edu/ uscode/html/uscode47/ usc_sec_47_00000230----000-.html

Culture, Media and Sport Committee. (2010). *Second report: Press standards, privacy and libel*. Retrieved 15 September, 2010, from http://www.publications.parliament.uk/ pa/cm200910/ cmselect/ cmcumeds/ 362/36202.htm

Data Protection Act. (1998). Retrieved 15 September, 2010, from http://www.bailii.org/

Defamation Act. (1952) Retrieved 15 September, 2010, from http://www.bailii.org/

Defamation Act. (1996). Retrieved 15 September, 2010, from http://www.bailii.org/

Duke of Brunswick v Harmer (1849) 14 QB 185.

EC. (2000). *Directive on electronic commerce* (Directive 2000/31/EC). Retrieved 15 September, 2010, from: http://eur-lex.europa.eu/ LexUriServ/ LexUriServ.do? uri=CELEX:32000L0031:en:NOT

EC. (2002). *EC Directive regulations 2002* (SI 2002/2013). Retrieved 15 September, 2010, from http://www.bailii.org/

Firsht v Raphael [2008] EWHC 1781 (QB).

Flood v Times Newspapers Ltd [2010] EWCA Civ 804.

Helen Grant v Google UK Limited [2005] EWHC 3444 (Ch), 17 May 2005.

Hird v Wood ([1894] 38 SJ 234).

Islam Expo Ltd v The Spectator (1828) Ltd and another [2010] EWHC 2011 (QB).

John Bunt v David Tilley and others [2006] EWCH 407 (QB).

Kaschke v (1) Gray (2) Hilton [2010] EWHC 690 (QB).

Keith-Smith v Williams ([2006] EWHC 860 (QB).

Laurence Godfrey v Demon Internet Limited ([1999] 4 All ER 342).

Limitation Act. (1980). Retrieved 15 September, 2010, from http://www.bailii.org/

Loutchansky v Times Newspapers Limited [2001] EWCA Civ 1805.

Metropolitan International Schools Limited v (1) Designtechnica Corporation, (2) Google UK Limited, (3) Google Inc *(2009) EWHC 1765 (QB)*.

Ministry of Justice. (July 2010). *Press release: Plans to reform defamation law announced*. Retrieved 15 September, 2010, from http://www.justice.gov.uk/ news/newsrelease090710a.htm

Mitsui Limited v Nexen Petroleum UK Limited [2005] EWHC 625 (Ch).

Norwich Pharmacal Co. v Customs and Excise Commissioners [1974] AC 133.

Samuel Kingsford Budu v BBC, [2010] EWHC 616 (QB).

Sheffield Wednesday Football Club Limited and others v Neil Hargreaves [2007] EWHC 2375 (QB), 18 October 2007.

Sim v Stretch [1936] 2 All ER 1237.

Smith v ADVFN Plc and others [2008] EWHC 1797 (QB).

Totalise PLC v The Motley Fool Limited [2001] EMLR 750.

Unfair Contract Terms Act. (1977). Retrieved 15 September, 2010, from http://www.bailii.org/

Unfair Terms in Consumer Contracts Regulations. (1999). Retrieved 15 September, 2010, from http://www.bailii.org/

Zeran v America On-line Inc. (129 F 3d 327 (1997), Cert. den. 48 S Ct 2341 (1998)).

ADDITIONAL READING

Duncan, C., Neill, B., & Rampton, R. (2009). *Duncan and Neill on defamation* (3rd ed.). Butterworths LexisNexis.

Gatley, J. C. C., Milmo, P., & Rogers, V. W. H. (2008). *Libel and slander* (11th rev ed). Sweet and Maxwell.

Lloyd, I. J. (2008). *Information technology law* (5th ed.). Oxford University Press.

Price, D., Duodu, K., & Cain, N. (2009). *Defamation: law procedure and practice* (4th ed.). Sweet and Maxwell.

Singleton, S. (2007). *Business, the Internet and the law* (2nd ed.). Tottel.

Smith, G. Chalton, S et al (2007). Internet law and regulation (4th ed), Sweet and Maxwell.

Tugendhat, M., & Christie, I. (2011). *The law of privacy and the media* (2nd ed.). Oxford University Press.

KEY TERMS AND DEFINITIONS

Defamation: The publishing of a statement which lowers the individual or the company in the estimation of right-thinking members of society generally. Broadly, the test is whether a statement would cause one to think less of the person or company to whom it refers. Defences may be based on justification, privilege and fair comment.

Defendant: The party who defends the action.

Intermediary: An operator of a computer system which provides the technical link between Internet content providers and Internet users, whether by hosting, caching or distributing information.

Internet Service Provider (ISP): The operator of a network of interconnected computers, which allow information to be stored, accessed and transferred by Internet users via the worldwide web, usenet and e-mail.

Norwich Pharmacal Order: A Court Order which requires a defendant to disclose certain documents or information to the plaintiff. The defendant must be a party who is involved or mixed up in a wrongdoing, whether innocently or not, and is unlikely to be a party to the potential proceedings.

Plaintiff: The party who brings a court action.

Chapter 14
The Hellenic Framework for Computer Program Copyright Protection Following the Implementation of the Relative European Union Directives

Eugenia Alexandropoulou-Egyptiadou
University of Macedonia, Greece

ABSTRACT

The huge financial rewards that may be gained from software sales have resulted in computer piracy, an increasing worldwide phenomenon. This situation has posed a challenge to the legislator, who has imposed regulations concerning the protection of software, both at national and international level. The following chapter focuses on the presentation of the current Hellenic legal framework on computer program copyright protection following the implementation of the relative E.U. Directives (Law 2121/1993, as amended). The chapter consists of an introduction focusing on software piracy rates and on the international legal framework of the protection; there is a unit on the right holder, being the subject of software copyright protection; a unit on the field of the protection; a unit on the rights of the author (the moral right, the property right and the resulting powers thereof), focusing on the power of software reproduction and specific cases where the lawful user can carry out acts without the author's consent; a unit on the consequences of copyright infringement (sanctions at civil, criminal, and administrative level); a unit on the duration of the protection; and finally concluding with final remarks and recommendations.

DOI: 10.4018/978-1-61350-132-0.ch014

INTRODUCTION

The huge economic gains of computer programs are known worldwide. The enormous financial rewards of the software market have resulted in computer piracy, i.e. the illegal use, including reproduction and distribution, of software.

Software piracy is indeed a worldwide phenomenon. According to the "BSA 7th annual global software piracy study" (B.S.A., 2010), world piracy rate increased from 35% in 2005 to 38% in 2007, to 41% in 2008, to 43% in 2009. The increase of the above rate is largely due to the rapid growth of software sales in markets with the higher piracy rates, such as Brazil, India and China. The countries with the highest piracy rates (over 90%) are Georgia, Zimbabwe and Moldavia. The countries with the lowest piracy rates are the U.S.A. (20%), Japan (21%) and Luxembourg (21%). In the European Union, software piracy has remained on average at 35% since 2007, although in a number of E.U. countries, such as Austria, Germany, Greece and Italy, it has increased. In Greece the above rate fell from 64% in 2005 to 61% in 2006, to 58% in 2007 and to 57% in 2008. In 2009, however, it rose to 58% again, making it the highest piracy rate in the E.U. in 2005 and the third highest rate from 2007 to 2009. Since 2007 Bulgaria and Romania, newcomers in the E.U., have held the highest piracy rates (67% for Bulgaria and 65% for Romania).

The vast problem of software piracy has posed a challenge to the legislator, who has imposed regulations on the protection of software, both at national and international level.

It is worth noting that international treaties have been signed to protect copyright in general. Among these are the Berne Convention for the Protection of Literary and Artistic Works (1886 – as subsequently amended, ratified by Greece – law 100/1975), the Agreement on Trade-Related Aspects of Intellectual Property Rights, Including Trade in Counterfeit Goods (Trip's Agreement, 1994, ratified by Greece – law 2290/1995), the

WIPO Copyright Treaty (WCT, 1996, ratified by Greece – law 3184/2003).

In the E.U. the specific legal protection of computer programs has been harmonized by the Directive 91/250/EEC of 14 May 1991 "on the legal protection of computer programs", called "Software Directive", Official Journal (O.J.) L 122/42, 17/05/1991 (Lloyd, 2004; Millard, 1996; Lucas, A., Devèze, J.& Frayssinet, J., 2001). The Software Directive has been amended by the Directive 93/98/EEC of 29 October 1993 harmonizing the term of protection of copyright and certain related rights, O.J. 290/9, 24/11/1993. The Directive 93/98/EEC was repealed by the Directive 2006/116/EC on the duration of the protection of copyright and related rights (codified version), O.J. L 372/12, 27/12/2006. Recently Directive 91/250, as amended, has been codified (and thus repealed) by the Directive 2009/24/EC of 23 April 2009 of the European Parliament and the Council "on the legal protection of computer programs-codified version" (O.J. 111/16, 5.5.2009).

The Software Directive is one of the most significant in the area of Intellectual Property Legislation. Other significant Directives, which reinforced the copyright protection of works in general, including that of computer programs, are the Directive 2001/29/EC of the European Parliament and of the Council of 22 May 2001 on the harmonization of certain aspects of copyright and related rights in the information society (O.J. L 167/10, 22/6/2001), also known as the "Copyright Directive" and the Directive 2004/48/EC of the European Parliament and of the Council of 29 April 2004 on the enforcement of intellectual property rights (O.J. L 157/45, 30/4/2004, O.J. 195/16, 2/6/2004), also known as "IPR Enforcement Directive" or "IPRED"). Directive 2001/29/EC aims to adapt national legislations concerning the copyright in the digital environment. One of the most important regulations of this Directive concerns the legal protection of technological measures which aim to protect a work against infringements, as well as the legal protection of electronic copyright-management information. On the other hand, Directive 2004/48/EC provides for the measures, procedures and remedies, which shall apply to any infringement of intellectual property rights.

Computer programs are legally protected as literary works (L. 2121/1993, art. 2 par. 3a, Software Directive, art. 1). The protection of computer programs by the copyright law rather than the industrial property law or the law of free competition was chosen after extended legal debate. Industrial property law and the law of free competition are applied on a complementary basis.

This paper focuses on the presentation of the current Hellenic legal framework on copyright protection in the area of computer programs, after the implementation of the relative E.U. directives in Hellenic law.

The main domestic statute in Greece is the law 2121/1993 on "Intellectual Property, Related Rights and Cultural Issues", as subsequently amended (last amendment by Law 3524/2007). Through this law the "Software Directive" and the relative E.U. Directives have been implemented in Hellenic legislation. The above Hellenic law contains general provisions which apply to all works, including computer programs, as well as special provisions for the protection of computer programs (articles 40-43 & 45).

THE RIGHT HOLDER

Copyright Law protects the author (creator) of the software or the person to whom the author has assigned his rights. Copyright is acquired automatically (ipso jure) with the creation of the program, without any formal procedure such as the submission of the work to a public institution, its registration to a special registry, the payment of a specific fee, etc. (as it is with industrial property law). In cases where authorship is in doubt, the practices below are used to prove authorship by certifying the date on which the program was developed. This certification may be achieved in two ways: (a) by submitting the program to a notary or (b) by including it in a registered letter addressed to either themselves or to a third person, retaining the post office receipt and the letter unopened. This may be used as proof of authorship before court if necessary (Hellenic Copyright Organisation, 2007).

According to Hellenic Law 2121/1993, the author is always one or more natural persons (never a legal person). The author can transfer his property rights to a second (natural or legal) person, who then becomes the right holder.

According to article 2 par. 2 of the Software Directive, in cases where a computer program is jointly created by a group of natural persons, the exclusive rights are obtained jointly. Since the programs are in many cases collaborative works, with each contribution geared towards the final outcome, they are jointly owned by the co-authors, unless otherwise agreed. If however during the development of a program, a natural person is responsible for coordinating and mentoring the developers involved, the above person becomes the legal owner of the copyright. Individual components belong to individual developers where this is feasible.

According to article 40 of Law 2121/1993, where a computer program is created by an employee in the course of his duties or following an employer's instructions, the employer becomes the right holder of all property rights, unless otherwise agreed by contract (Sinodinou, 2009). The author-employee is not entitled to added remuneration for a creation (Lucas et al., 2001). This provision in the above article gives the employer unrestricted use, since the development of computer programs is usually funded by companies which invest large sums for this purpose. Taking the above into consideration, it is necessary for an employee's duties to be clearly set out in his employment contract. In the absence of a relevant contract clause, the two parties should come to an agreement after the development of the program.

It is worth noting that the above mentioned rule of art. 40 of Law 2121/1993 concerns only the property rights of an employee and not his moral rights to a computer program developed by himself. The same rule applies to the computer programs developed during the term of employment (not before its beginning or after its end).

Unless proven otherwise, the author is the person whose name appears on the material body of the computer program in the manner normally used to indicate the author.

The above presumption facilitates proof of authorship, since the development does not normally take place in a public place. A similar presumption applies to the right holder, if different from the author. So the copyright holder of a computer program is the natural or legal person whose name appears on the material body of the work in the manner normally used to indicate the right holder.

THE FIELD OF PROTECTION

Neither Hellenic law nor the Software Directive provide for a definition of a computer program, in order to adapt to both current and future technological advancements.

Legal protection extends to programs of every form and kind (e.g. source code, objective code, Microsoft Office, excel, word, adobe acrobat, antivirus programs, search engines, links), including those which are incorporated into hardware (Stamatoudi, 2009). It also extends to their preparatory design material which leads to the development of a computer program, on condition that the nature of the preparatory work is such that a computer program can result from it at a later stage.

Hellenic case-law accepts that the general concept of software includes: (a) a computer program, (b) a description of the program (preparatory material) and (c) the accompanying material. According to Hellenic courts, the description

of a program includes (a) the preparation stage which is part of the general idea of the software and is defined by the standard instructions, as a complete presentation of procedure, in speech, graphic or other form, (b) a series of commands, which constitute the final program. The accompanying material or documentation of application includes user instructions, comments, remarks and notes explaining the handling of the program (Multimember Court of First Instance of Athens 18201/1998, Board of Court of Appeals of Athens 2949/2003). Typical cases of preparatory material are the list of commands and the flowchart (Hellenic Copyright Organization, 2007).

In accordance with a basic principle of copyright, it is the expression of an idea which is protected and not the idea itself. Therefore, in the field of computer programs, only the expression of a computer program (e.g. written down or stored in computer memory) is protected. That means that ideas and principles which underlie any element of a program, including those which underlie its interfaces, are not protected by copyright. Neither the algorithms nor the programming languages are protected. These ideas may be protected by the industrial property law.

According to Law 2121/1993, art. 2 par. 1, the originality of a work is *condition sine qua non* for its legal protection. Art. 2 par. 3d gives the definition of a program's originality: A program is considered to be original if it is "the author's own intellectual creation." Additionally, according to art. 1 par. 3b of the above mentioned Software Directive, legal protection "is not dependent on the application of any other criterion". For the complete definition of originality provided by the Directive, one should also include the recital 8 of its preamble where guidelines for interpretation are given: "In respect of the criteria to be applied in determining whether or not a computer program is an original work, no tests as to the qualitative or aesthetic merits of the program should be applied".

We are of the opinion that the above mentioned regulation is such that there is no need for the application of any known criterion of originality (e.g. high standard of creativity, statistic uniqueness e.t.c.: Karakostas, 2001; Kotsiris, 2005; Koumantos, 2002; Marinos, 2004; Nouskalis, 2003). This originality does not require strict conditions. It suffices that the software is not a copy of software (Alexandropoulou–Egyptiadou, 2007; Kallinikou, 2000; Koumantos, 2002; Nouskalis, 2003). No other criteria need to be applied to determine its eligibility for protection.

THE RIGHTS OF THE RIGHT HOLDER

According to Law, the author of a program, as any author, has two rights: A property one (the right to the economic exploitation of the program and a moral one (the right to protect his personal tie with the program). Both these rights provide the author with relative powers.

The Property Right

The property right consists of the powers of the author to permit, to forbid or to do the recording of a program, its reproduction, translation, adaptation or any other alteration, its circulation, distribution (e.g. assignment or licensing) or, more generally, its financial exploitation.

Powers Accruing from the Property Right

Although Law 2121/1993 does not make any reference to the rights of the right holder in the area of computer programs, except for the provision of art. 41 (Sinodinou, 2009), which regards the exhaustion of the distribution right within the European Union), the software Directive does. According to our opinion, Hellenic law should have included a similar regulation.

According to article 4 of the Software Directive, the exclusive rights of the right holder include the right to do, to authorize or to forbid:

a. the permanent or temporary reproduction of a computerprogram by any means and in any form, in part or in whole; in so far as loading, displaying, running, transmission or storage of the computer program necessitate such reproduction, such acts shall be subject to authorisation by the rightholder;

b. the translation, adaptation, arrangement and any other alteration of a computer program and the reproduction of the results thereof, without prejudice to the rights of the person who alters the program;

c. any form of distribution to the public, including the rental, of the original computer program or of copies thereof.

Acts Which May Be Carried out by the Lawful User without the Right Holder's Authorization

The person having the right to use a program ("lawful user') is entitled to carry out some acts, referred to in art. 42 and 43 of Law 2121/1993, without the right holder's authorization ("free acts"). For instance, the lawful user is allowed to reproduce, translate, adapt or make any other alteration which is necessary (a) to utilise the program in accordance with its designated use ("intended purpose"), (b) to achieve the interoperability of an independently created program with other programs, (c) to observe, study or test the functioning of the program in order to determine the ideas and principles which underlie any element of the program, (d) to make a back-up copy, under legall conditions. Reproduction during a process of decompilation is allowed in order to obtain information necessary to achieve the interoperability with other programs of an independently created program. This reproduction is permitted under strict conditions, described in art. 43 of Law 2121/1993 (Sinodinou, 2008).

Recently, Law 3328/2005 introduced an additional case of free reproduction concerning educational software. This has been approved and distributed free of charge by the Hellenic Ministry of Education. According to our opinion the above mentioned exception to the rule of authorized reproduction should be incorporated in law 2121/1993.

The abovementioned cases of free reproduction in the area of computer programs (art. 42-43 of Law 2121/1993) are fewer than the cases of free reproduction in areas of other protected works (art. 18 et seq. of Law 2121/1993). This regulation provides more protection against software piracy than against the infringement of other protected works. This is due to easier infringement of computer programs through the wide use of internet.

The Moral Right

The specific powers resulting from the moral right in every protected work are the right of divulgation, paternity, integrity, the right to access work and the right of withdrawal. The moral right of a program's author is quite limited because of the nature of the program. Nevertheless one can support the view that the moral right is the author's right to be indentified as the author of a particular program (Liakopoulos, 1999).

CONSEQUENCES OF COPYRIGHT INFRINGEMENT (SANCTIONS)

Copyright infringement (exploitation without the author's consent) may have civil, criminal and administrative consequences (Alexandropoulo–Egyptiadou, 2007; Vagena, E., 2009). These legal consequences, which concern all sorts of protected works, including computer programs, are provided in art. 64 et seq. of Law 2121/1993, which were

amended by Laws 3057/2002 and 3524/2007 ((by which the Directives 2001/29/EC and 2004/48/EC were implemented in Greece). It is worth noting that Hellenic Law does not include the specific regulations on the infringements of computer programs in its special chapter (no 7) concerning computer programs (art. 40-45), but in the general articles regarding the copyright protection of any kind of protected work (art. 63A et seq.)

Civil Protection (art. 64, 64A, 65 of Law 2121/1993)

In cases of copyright infringement, the right holder may claim recognition of his right, as well as the termination of the infringement (e.g. destruction or withdrawal of piracy programs from the market) and its reoccurrence in the future. The infringing party is obliged to pay both property and moral damages according to the general provisions of the Civil Code (art. 297-298). Moreover, it is provided that the payment of damages shall not be less than twice the sum the infringing party has earned from the illegal exploitation. Instead of seeking damages, the right holder has the right to demand either the payment of the sum accrued or any other profit gained by the infringing party from the unlicensed exploitation.

Finally, civil protection includes provisional remedies such as the (provisional) seizure of programs which were marketed in violation of the law and their detailed description. Additionally, the right holders have the right to apply for an injunction against intermediaries whose services are used by a third party to infringe a copyright.

Criminal Protection (art. 66 of law 2121/1993)

Illegal use or/and illegal distribution of software is punished with 1-10 years imprisonment and a fine of 2.900-60.000 €.

Of particular importance to the right holder is the legal protection of the technological protective measures, the infringement (e.g. removal or circumvention) of which is punished with 1-5 years imprisonment and a fine of 2.900-15.000 €.

Administrative Protection (art. 65A of Law 2121/1993)

In addition to the above mentioned civil and criminal consequences, the recent law 3524/2007, which has added the new article 65A to law 2121/1993, provides for an administrative fine of 1000 € for every program infringed (by illegal reproduction, selling or other illegal manner of distribution). It is believed that this regulation will assist enormously in the fight against software piracy.

Civil and Criminal Protection of Electronic Copyright: Management Information (art. 66B of Law 2121/1993)

The removal or alteration of an electronic copyright - management information, attached to a computer program, has both civil and criminal consequences, according to the provisions of art. 66B of law 2121/1993, as amended by law 3057/2002.

DURATION OF PROTECTION

Copyright protection is granted for life and for seventy years after death. In cases of joint copyright, the seventy years are calculated from the first of January of the year following the last survivor's death. This regulation is based on art. 29 of Law 2121/1993 in conjunction with the abolishment of art. 44 of the same Law. The abolished article provided that in the area of computer programs the duration of legal protection was fifty years.

FINAL THOUGHTS: RECOMMENDATIONS

According to our opinion, the Hellenic regulatory framework on software copyright protection after the implementation of the relative E.U. Directives is quite adequate.

Moreover, the technological reinforcement regarding protective measures is also of great importance and related to the effectiveness of the legislation in force. According to Directive 2001/29/EC (recital 13 of the preamble), the aim of the technological protective measures is to give effect to the principles and guarantees laid down in law.

Another very important weapon against software piracy is the necessity of change of attitude of the end user. This can only be achieved through appropriately informing and educating him on his rights and obligations. This education should start from childhood.

Finally it is worth noting that in the area of copyright the legislator has to balance between the author's rights to his own work and the rights of others to have access to it, exercising the right to information and e-participation. This is most important in the field of software, where technological development may depend on the work of more than one person and requires not only unrestricted information between the parties, but also access to any previous relevant information. With the above mentioned balance in mind, one could support that the protection of the financial interests of the right holders should not be allowed to act as an obstacle to the overall technological progress of humanity and the expansion of knowledge.

REFERENCES

Alexandropoulou–Egyptiadou, E. (2007). Software piracy and protection of the right of reproduction. *Hellenic Justice, 48*, 1315–1327.

Business Software Alliance (BSA). (2010). *7th annual global software piracy study*. Retrieved September 10, 2010, from http://portal.bsa.org/global-piracy2009 /studies/globalpiracystudy2009.pdf

Hellenic Copyright Organisation. (2007). *Website*. Retrieved September 10, 2010, from http://www.opi.gr

Kallinikou, D. (2000). *Intellectual property and related right*. Athens, Greece: P. Sakkoulas.

Karakostas, I. (2003). *Law and Internet – Legal issues of the Internet* (2nd ed.). Athens, Greece: P. N. Sakkoulas.

Kotsiris, L. (2005). *Intellectual property law* (4th ed.). Athens-Thessaloniki, Greece: Sakkoula.

Koumantos, G. (2002). *Intellectual property* (8th ed.). Athens-Komotini, Greece: Ant. N. Sakkoulas.

Liakopoulos, A. (1999). *Intellectual property law in Greece*. Athens, Greece: Kluwer – Sakkoulas.

Lloyd, I. (2004). *Information Technology law* (4th ed.). Oxford University Press.

Lucas, A., Devèze, J., & Frayssinet, J. (2001). *Droit de l'Informatique et de l'Internet*. Paris, France: P.U.F. Thémis.

Marinos, M.-T. (2004). *Intellectual property* (2nd ed.). Athens-Komotini, Greece: Ant. N. Sakkoulas.

Millard, C. (1996). Copyright. In Reed, C. (Ed.), *Computer law*. Blackstone Press Ltd.

Nouskalis, G. (2003). *Criminal protection of a computer program according to Law 2121/1993*. Athens – Thessaloniki, Greece: Sakkoula.

Sinodinou, T.-E. (2008). *Copyright and new technologies: The relationship between the user and the author*. Athens – Thessaloniki, Greece: Sakkoula.

Sinodinou, T.-E. (2009). Interpretation of art. 40 et seq. of Law 2121/1993. In Kotsiris, L., & Stamatoudi, I. (Eds.), *Law on the intellectual property (interpretation)*. Athens – Thessaloniki, Greece: Sakkoula.

Stamatoudi, E. (2009). Interpretation of art. 2 of Law 2121/1993. In Kotsiris, L., & Stamatoudi, I. (Eds.), *Law on the intellectual property (interpretation)*. Athens – Thessaloniki, Greece: Sakkoula.

Vagena, E. (2009). Interpretation of art. 63 Aff of Law 2121/1993. In Kotsiris, L., & Stamatoudi, I. (Eds.), *Law on the intellectual property (interpretation)*. Athens – Thessaloniki, Greece: Sakkoula.

Chapter 15
Internet Advertising:
Legal Aspects in the European Union

Radomír Jakab
University of P. J. Safarik, Slovakia

ABSTRACT

As can be derived from its name, Internet advertising means any form of promoting products or services through the Internet. This form of advertising can be distinguished into more forms such as e-mail advertising, on-line advertisements, corporate and marketing websites. Such differentiation is important from a legal point of view as well. Besides the definition and classification of Internet advertising, this chapter is mainly aimed at an analysis of the applicable European law regulating this area: such as general requirements for advertising, including its Internet form or rules relating to unsolicited commercial communications (spam). Further, when advertising through the Internet, rules designed for the protection against unfair commercial practices or prohibited comparative advertisements may be challenged. The objective of this chapter is not only to analyze some relevant provision of the European law but also to submit proposals for its improvement if needed.

INTRODUCTION

The substance of doing business in any entrepreneurial area is to sell as many of products as possible, eventually to provide a large quantum of services in order to gain profit. For this purpose, promoting of products or services is essential.

DOI: 10.4018/978-1-61350-132-0.ch015

There are many marketing activities aimed at reaching this objective, advertising being one of them.

Advertisement has been an integral part of business life for a relatively long time. It is a very effective tool used by marketing competitors in the open competition for consumers´ wallets. When considering advertising strategy, the type of media used for this purpose must be taken into consideration. Marketing theory recognizes many types of media suitable for advertising purposes such as TV or radio broadcasting, magazines or newspapers, direct mail, outdoor advertisement, the Internet, etc. It must be noted that the significance of the latter one is constantly increasing.

As the advertising carried out through the Internet is becoming a very popular and frequently used tool, legal regulation thereof appears to be very desirable; in other words the Internet advertising needs to fall under some legal regulation in order to protect consumers, other competitors, as well as public interest. Before analyzing the legal regulation of the Internet advertisement, two very important facts must be taken into account. Firstly, law is locally determined; law is applied only on the territory of the relevant state within its borders. Secondly, the Internet is a worldwide network regardless of the jurisdiction of a particular state. So how do we regulate activities spreading through the Internet including Internet advertising? Perhaps the only way is through harmonization of law on the international level or at least within larger organizations such as the European Union.

The objective of this chapter is to analyze the existing legal regulation of Internet advertisement applied in the European Union (partially in its Member states). As the result of the analysis, proposals de *lege ferenda* are going to be suggested. In order to reach this conclusion a deductive method is chosen; this is reflected in the structure of this chapter too. First of all, it is necessary to specify "Internet advertising". Its position is found in the intersection of two terms: Internet and advertising. Internet advertising can have several forms having sometimes a different legal status. Therefore, its forms must be determined as well. The law pays special attention to advertising disseminated per electronic mail; it is connected with the problem known as spam that is annoying its recipients. Further, there are legal restrictions relating to the content of the advertisement, incl. its Internet

type. For instance, advertising cannot be neither misleading, misusing credulity of minors nor being unfair commercial practice, etc. The analysis of the above mentioned issues is the subject-matter of this chapter.

BACKGROUND

The Internet is relatively a new phenomenon that has, perhaps, affected each type of human activity. During its approximately vicennial history it has changed how people spend their leisure time, how they work and communicate with each other, how they are being entertained and mostly how people think. The Internet has changed almost everything including ways of doing business and practices used for this purpose.

"What is the Internet? It is a network of networks" that operates on a set of technical protocols that enables people from around the world to access and exchange information using tools such as World Wide Web, e-mail, chat rooms, etc." (Schumann & Thorson, 2007, p. 15). *"It is a system of linked computer networks, international in scope, that facilitates data transfer and communication services, such as remote login, file transfer (FTP), electronic mail (e-mail), newsgroups, and the World Wide Web."* (Jansen, 2002, p. 218-219).

"One of the fastest growing internet-based applications is electronic-commerce (e-commerce); the use of the internet as a system to facilitate the exchange of commercial information (e.g. advertising and marketing material) and the execution of commercial transactions (e.g. processing of orders and payments)" (Delta & Matsuura, 2002, p. 12). *"The emerging e-commerce market gave rise to a multitude of legal questions ranging from such areas as on-line contracting to digital signatures to copyright"* (Vogel, 2003, p. 29).

E-commerce can be defined as the process of purchasing and selling products supported by electronic means, mainly via the Internet. E-commerce comprises e-marketing and e-purchasing (e-procurement). E-purchasing covers activities connected with buying products and services via electronic ways, especially through the Internet. "E-marketing (Internet marketing) denotes a marketing site of e-commerce. It presents effort of the trader to inform on products and services offered, promote them and sell via the Internet (Kotler, 2007, p. 182). Over the course of time the Internet has become a very popular tool for promoting different types of products or services. Such campaigns have used to appear highly effective. There are different forms of e-marketing; Internet advertising being one of them.

As has been suggested, Internet advertising is an interdisciplinary category; that means not only a legal approach to this issue is relevant. It is a research target of more disciplines including legal science, marketing science as well as IT science. On the other hand, no approach can be applied separately because research in each of the above mentioned areas is inevitably interconnected with another one. Even if this work is aimed at the legal side of Internet advertising, results of research achieved in the other disciplines must be also taken into consideration and vice versa.

There is a broader spectrum of publications dealing with Internet advertising from a marketing point of view. From this variety, the research activities of David W. Schumann and Esther Thorson (e.g. Schumann & Thorson, 2007; Schumann & Thorson, 1999) as well as Steven Armstrong (e.g. Armstrong, 2001) warrant attention. Research of Internet advertising from a legal view is determined by the jurisdiction of the relevant state. Therefore, it is not generally applicable. In the European Union there is a lack of complex research outcomes concerning this topic. Internet advertisement is analyzed usually as a part of the issue not in its complexity (e.g. Reed, 2004). That is why the legal research of Internet advertising is

of higher importance. On the contrary, research in the IT science is not limited by a certain territory; its results are widely used. So there is a larger scope of published outputs (e.g. Fielden, 2001; Barker & Terry, 2008).

INTERNET ADVERTISING AND LAW

Internet Advertising and Its Forms

As mentioned above, the Internet advertising lies in the intersection of two terms: Internet and advertising. A broad definition of the Internet was introduced in the previous part of the chapter. Of course, this definition is sufficient only for the purpose of that work aimed at the legal side of the matter. What is the advertisement? This is the question that has not been answered yet.

According to Lee and Johnson "advertising is paid, non-personal communication about an organization and its products that is transmitted to the target audience through a mass medium such as television, radio, newspapers, magazines, direct mail, outdoor displays, or mass transit vehicles. In the new global community, advertising messages can be transmitted via new media, especially the internet" (1999, p. 3). In this definition two features are missing. Firstly, advertising is a human activity carried out either directly or on behalf of the competitive trader. Furthermore, the purpose of advertising is not included therein, i.e. to persuade the target audience of expedience and need for the advertised products. (Similarly Vysekalova & Mikes, 2007, p. 14). According to Janoshka (2004, p. 16) "advertising needs to be more than just informative. It needs to be persuasive which is one of its most important functions." Having added these features, advertising can be defined as a communication process usually paid for; carried out either directly by the competitive trader or by someone else on his/her behalf; designed to persuade receivers of expedience and need for the promoted products or services through various media.

The legal definition of advertising can be found in the European legislation; for instance pursuant to Article 2(a) of the Directive on misleading and comparative advertising[1] "advertising means the making of a representation in any form in connection with a trade, business, craft or profession in order to promote the supply of goods or services, including immovable property, rights and obligations." A similar specification of advertising is contained in the Directive on advertising and sponsorship of tobacco products[2] but with a limitation to tobacco products. According to Article 2(b) advertising "means any form of commercial communications with the aim or direct or indirect effect of promoting a tobacco product. Both legal definitions shall be applied only for the purpose of the particular directive; either for the purpose of misleading or comparative advertising or in relation to the tobacco products. European legislation therefore lacks some generally used specification of advertising applicable to each type thereof.

Internet advertising is a special type of advertising itself. In this case, a type of medium used for dissemination of the advertised information is the relevant classification criterion. As it can be derived from its name, Internet advertising is communicated through the Internet. When taking into consideration the above mentioned definition of advertising used in the marketing theory, it can be concluded that Internet advertising is a communication process usually paid for; carried out either directly by the competitive trader or by someone else on his/her behalf; designed to persuade receivers of expedience and need for the promoted products or services through the Internet.

The legal definition thereof cannot be found in the European legislation. Again, it must be derived from the legal definition of advertising in the relevant directives while being specialized for the Internet communication process. I suppose that the term of Internet advertising and its basic rules should be regulated by law on the European level in order to unify a legal status at least in the Member states of the European Union. Advertising communicated via the Internet crosses the borders of a particular state, i.e. it is not only the issue of a single state. To achieve effective protection of consumers, other competitors and public interest, the same or eventually similar rules for such a cross-border activity must apply.

It has been already stated that Internet advertising is a special type of advertising itself; it is advertising communicated through the Internet. The internet provides different ways how to communicate some advertised message to its recipients. For example, an advertisement can be placed on a website or sent by electronic mail (e-mail) or may automatically appear when browsing the Internet. That means that Internet advertising can be internally classified into more forms. Such differentiation is important from a legal point of view as well; the law regulates each form differently starting from detailed regulation (e.g. e-mail advertising) to some very weak enactment (e.g. corporate websites). Which forms of Internet advertising can be recognized?

1. **Corporate websites.** Corporate websites are informational websites operated usually by companies, other entrepreneurial entities or eventually by other subjects (e.g. non-profit organizations, foundations). A corporate website "carries information about the company and other features designed to answer customer questions, build customer relationships and generate excitement about the company." (Kotler, 2008, p. 850). So, the main purpose of such websites is to inform the public about its operator, its history or philosophy, about its products or services, etc. They are not primarily aimed at selling its products but at improving its goodwill and reputation. Corporate websites serve as an instrument for supporting interactive communication between the trader and its

customers that is initiated by customers themselves.

2. **Marketing websites.** Marketing websites are intended to motivate a customer to buy products, or are of any other marketing objective. In case of marketing websites, communication and interaction is ensured by a marketer. These websites may contain catalogs, shopping tips, promotional items such as vouchers, special offers or consumer contests. Traders are seeking to propagate these websites aggressively by means of the traditional off-line advertising either in a printed form or through broadcasting or by banners located on foreign websites (Kotler, 2007, p. 194).

3. **On-line advertisement.** Online advertisement appears to customers when browsing the web as banners (advertising strips), tickers (moving strips containing advertising message), skyscrapers (tall and tight strips located on the side of the website), interstitials (advertising appearing when passing websites), microwebs (the minimized website of an entrepreneur located on the corporate or marketing website of another enterprise), etc. (See details in Janoshka, 2004, p. 51-53).

4. **E-mail advertising.** E-mail advertising rests on spreading marketing messages through electronic mail. Producers of some advertised products, eventually providers of advertised services, or any other persons acting on their behalf (e.g. PR agency, advertising agency) are mostly senders of such e-mails. The so-called "viral e-mail advertising" presents a special form thereof. Such a campaign is based on spontaneous dissemination of advertising messages by customers alone through e-mails. The customers are motivated in some ways to forward marketing e-mails to their friends in order to establish a chain of reactions. E-mail advertising can be very annoying in practice; it is connected with the general problem named as "unsolicited commercial communications (spam)". Therefore it is subject to increased legal restrictions.

Inasmuch as the Internet is a very rapidly developing system, any other forms of the Internet advertising cannot be excluded. Smart marketers are permanently trying to find new ways how to make advertising more effective and interesting for potential customers. While the Internet always provides new challenges to reach this objective. Anyway, marketers are required to find a compromise between their creativity and rules stipulated by the law as such.

General Legal Rules of Internet Advertising

Internet advertising is a very effective instrument for promoting products or services on the relevant market. Marketers have already developed many forms how to use the Internet for advertising purposes. But some of those forms are annoying or even dangerous, impairing other competitors and customers. For example, sending unsolicited commercial e-mails forces their recipients to invest a lot of money in the countermeasures (e.g. to buy additional software), wastes their time when deleting all those e-mails etc. Therefore Internet advertising needs clearly defined rules specifying the limits of marketers` freedom.

On the territory of the European Union (the territory of its 27 Member states) these limits are stipulated either by European law or by the law of the Member states. In this chapter especially the first one is analyzed. However, the law of each Member state is affected by the European law regulating this area. Only areas not covered by European law can be independently governed by the Member states providing that the principles of the European cooperation are not breached.

European law regulates advertising, including Internet advertising mostly in the form of directives. "A directive sets out the result to be achieved, but leaves some choice to each Member state as to the form and method of achieving the end result. A directive will quite often provide a Member state with the range of option it can choose from when implementing the measure. A directive is not directly applicable. It requires each Member state to incorporate directive in order for it to be given effect in the national legal system." (Fairhurst, 2007, p. 62). "Even if there is no direct applicability of directives, the legal system of each Member state must be interpreted with regard to the diction and purpose of a particular directive." (Vernarsky, 2008, p. 23). Implementation of directives can be made either by national legislation or by some administrative action of the Member state. "Basically there are two requirements, which have to be complied with when implementing European Union law indirectly: firstly, prohibition of discrimination and secondly, principle of efficiency" (Fabian, 2009, p. 3).

On the other hand, direct implementation of the European law is carried out by regulations. "Regulations have general application; after being issued they are binding for all Member states. Moreover, regulations are directly applicable in all Member states." (Krunkova, 2005, p. 32). I suppose that the direct form of implementation of the European law regulating Internet advertising would be more appropriate.

General requirements applying to advertising (including Internet advertising) can be deduced from the legislation of the Member states. Of course, a detailed analysis of the relevant legislation of each Member state would not be essential for the purpose of this chapter. After making it generalized, advertising including its Internet form must be polite, honest and truthful. Responsibility towards customers must be taken into consideration when preparing it.

Advertising can be considered as polite if it does not contain statements or a visual presentation breaching general ethical standards in a serious way. Furthermore, advertising on the whole or any of its parts may not attack human dignity; in particular when presenting the human body (for example, as impolite can be deemed demonstration of how erotic toys work). Thus the effect on the target group of customers must be considered. Broadly speaking, the politeness of the advertisement is measured with regard to its general impression, target group of customers, used media or relation of the advertising to the advertised products.

Moreover, advertising requires being honest. That means that advertising may not be used as the instrument for abusing customers' credulity as well as lack of their experience or knowledge. Above all, abusing minors' credulity is prohibited. For example, minors are not allowed to be incited to such kind of activity that endangers their health, mental or moral formation, to be presented in the situation of danger or further to be encouraged to buy products inappropriate or forbidden for them. Advertising also cannot contain a call for persuading parents to buy advertised products. Finally, advertising shall not exploit the special trust minors place in parents, teachers or other persons. As Internet advertising is based on impersonal communication, as a result, any form of abusing minors' credulity or inexperience is thus much easier.

Subjects involved in preparing the advertisement (sponsors, advertising agencies, media operators) have to consider the public good in the course of their activity. Primarily, advertising is prohibited to misuse customer's fear without any justified reason or even to form such a feeling (for example, persuading customers that only using certain herbal product can prevent them from cancer). The same shall apply in relation to superstition or prejudice. Advertising is also proscribed when encouraging people to act violently. The content of advertising may not contain information or presentations that are attacking race, political, religious or national status of customers in a gross manner. Furthermore, information challenging people to act against the law or accepting illegal behavior is prohibited as well. Generally speaking, advertising may not jeopardize the goodwill of the advertising itself. Therefore, the creators of a shocking advertising must be very careful. For instance, advertising of the jumps without a parachute can be risky as well, even if the purpose of the advertisement rest only on attracting people to click on the ad-banner. Its purpose is not to sell and provide such type of services.

Additional requirements relating only to Internet advertising are specified in the Directive on electronic commerce[3]. According to its Article 1(1), this directive seeks to contribute to the proper functioning of the internal market by ensuring the free movement of information society services between the Member states. In other words, this directive regulates, *inter alia*, "commercial communication" carried out through information society services.

For the purposes of this directive, commercial communication is defined as any form of communication designed to promote, directly or indirectly, the goods, services or image of a company, organization or person pursuing a commercial, industrial or craft activity or exercising a regulated profession. On the contrary, information allowing direct access to the activity of the company, organization or person, in particular a domain name or an electronic-mail address, do not constitute commercial communications within themselves. The same shall apply towards communications relating to the goods, services or image of the company, organization or person compiled in an independent manner, particularly when this is without financial consideration (Article 2(f)). For example, disclosed results of a commodity test carried out by an independent testing organization do not constitute a commercial communication for the purposes of the Directive on electronic commerce.

Arising out from the definition of commercial communication, it can be concluded that commercial communication under the meaning of the directive incorporates Internet advertising

as mentioned above. Therefore rules regulating commercial communication also apply to Internet advertising. Which rules can be inferred from the Directive on electronic commerce?

Firstly, Internet advertising must be clearly identifiable as such (Article 6(a)). It comes to this that recipients of the advertised message must be able to recognize the nature thereof; especially that information provided is of a commercial character being motivated with the effort to sell advertised products. Such information cannot be introduced, for instance, as the article inside the e-news or as the independent report having some objective character.

Secondly, the natural or legal person on whose behalf Internet advertising is made shall be clearly identifiable (Article 6(b)). In other words, recipients of Internet advertising or other competitors must be able to find out who the sponsor of the advertising is or eventually whose products are promoted by the advertisement. In comparison with the other media used for the advertising purposes the Internet provides more instruments for acting anonymously. If doing so, injured persons do not have remedies to fight against unjustified activities as the law-breaker is not known (or very difficult to trace). That is the critical problem mostly in case of e-mail advertisement sent by an undisclosed sender.

Further, when advertising through the Internet promotional offers such as discounts, premiums and gifts shall be clearly identifiable as such, and the conditions which are to be met to qualify for them shall be easily accessible and be presented clearly and unambiguously (Article 6(c)). This provision of the directive relates to the content of Internet advertising, particularly to the benefits offered to the customer when buying advertised products. In addition, conditions to qualify for these benefits must be accessible for recipients either directly on the advertisement field, on the ad-banner or on the stated webpage. The conditions must be clear and unequivocal in order to be understandable for the target recipients of the advertising.

Finally, Internet advertising may contain calls for any promotional competitions or games; of course, with the intention to increase sales of advertised products. If so, promotional competitions or games shall be clearly identifiable as such, and the conditions for participation shall be easily accessible and be presented clearly and unambiguously (Article 6(d)). Concerning accessibility and exactness of such a method of Internet advertising the same shall apply as described in the latter paragraph.

General requirements, as described above, relate to each form of Internet advertising. But some of its forms or types are subject to special legal requirements considering the special nature thereof. In particular, special requirements apply to the e-mail advertising aimed at preventing from unsolicited commercial communication (spam), further to advertising of special types of products (tobacco, medicaments) as well as to special methods used for advertising through the Internet (comparison or unfair commercial practices).

E-Mail Advertising and Spam

One of the most popular forms of Internet advertising is an e-mail advertisement. The main advantage of using this form rests on low costs required to carry out such an advertising campaign. Moreover, e-mail advertising seems to be a very effective instrument of marketers for promoting products. It allows marketers to address the marketing message directly to the customers who are likely interested in buying the advertised products. However, the marketers have to be very careful when acting so. This advertising has its dark side named as spam or unsolicited commercial communication.

"Unsolicited commercial communications by electronic mail ("spam") are considered to be one of the most significant issue facing the Internet today. Spam has reached worrying proportions for various reasons, such as privacy, deception

of consumers, protection of minors and human dignity, extra costs for businesses, lost of productivity." (Nikolinakos, 2006, p. 353). "The motivation behind spam is to have information delivered to the recipient that contains a payload such as advertising for a (likely worthless, illegal or non-existent) product, bait for a fraud scheme, promotion of a cause, or computer malware designed to hijack the recipient`s computer." (Cormack, 2008, p. 2). However, spam usually follows a commercial intention; therefore it is denoted as unsolicited commercial communication. Mostly, unsolicited commercial communication is a kind of direct marketing and is viewed by companies as an important tool to approach (potential) customers, because email provides a cheap and easy way to contact a large group of customers." (Schryen, 2007, p. 13). Because the costs of sending spam are so low, spammers can make a profit despite extremely low response rates.

In order to face this permanently increasing problem new European legislation has been adopted, i.e. the Directive on privacy and electronic communications[4]. Pursuant to the Article 13(1) of this directive the use of electronic mail[5] for the purposes of direct marketing may be allowed only in respect of subscribers or users who have given their prior consent. This is referred to as "opt-in" consent. This consent can be described as some freely given specific and informed indication of subscribers` or users` wishes by which they signify their interest to receive electronic mails containing advertisement. "An opt-in is usually arranged by the act of ticking a box or clicking an icon when registering for a mailing list, or following an e-mail request for specific information" (Michael & Salter, 2006, p. 97).

However, the general rule requiring opt-in consent for e-mail direct marketing does not apply to established customer relationships. Within such an existing customer relationship the company who obtained the data may use them for the marketing of similar products or services as those it has already sold to the customer. Nevertheless, even then the company has to make clear from the first time of collecting the data, that they may be used for direct marketing and should offer the right to object. Moreover, each subsequent marketing message should include an easy way for the customer to stop further messages (opt-out). "The theory behind this provision is that the customer`s prior purchase and provision of an e-mail address creates a consensual business relationship that the seller may legitimately maintain via e-mail unless and until the customer opts out of further communications." (Plotkin, Wells & Wimmer, 2003, p. 99-100).

The opt-in system, as described above, must inevitably relate to the e-mail advertising sent to the customers – natural persons. Concerning other subjects than natural persons (mainly legal entities), the Member states were not bound to implement the same regime. However, the Member states should also have ensured that the legitimate interests of subscribers other than natural persons with regard to unsolicited communications were sufficiently protected. In other words, the Member states were allowed to adopt other rules regulating unsolicited commercial communications in case when other than natural persons were thus affected hereby. But these rules must have ensured sufficient protection of such persons. Indeed, the Member states either applied the same rules for these subjects or constituted the opt-out system for them (allowing them to opt out receiving further marketing e-mails). For example, in the Slovak Republic the e-mail advertising for the purposes of direct marketing is allowed only under the prior consent of the user concerned either a natural person or a legal entity. That means the same regime applies to each type of persons.[6] Similar rules apply in the Czech Republic.[7] Further, sending e-mail advertisements to either natural or legal persons is in Germany considered as unpleasant annoyance that is also prohibited.[8] As seen, the Member states prefer the same rules applying to both natural or legal entities.

Moreover, European legislation is much more radical in relation to the practices of sending electronic mails for the purposes of direct marketing which disguise or conceal the identity of the sender on whose behalf the communication is made. Such practices are *a priori* prohibited regardless of the type of subject being affected hereby (natural person, legal entity or other subject). The same applies to e-mail advertising which does not have a valid address to which the recipient may send a request that such communication should cease. If e-mail advertising does not fit the conditions stipulated in the Directive on electronic commerce as described above (general requirements applying to Internet advertising), it must also be considered as prohibited. This destiny relates not only to electronic mails incorporating some advertisement in its body but also to electronic mails containing only some marketing website address while encouraging recipients to visit this website.

Under Article 17 of the Directive on privacy and electronic communications, the Member states of the European Union were obliged to implement these rules into their national legislation before 31 October 2003. New Member states had been obliged to adopt these rules before their membership in the European Union became effective. As a result, there are the same or similar rules regulating e-mail advertising in the European Union.

It can be concluded that this form of Internet advertising is quite well adjusted from the legal point of view. It helps to mitigate negative impact of misusing e-mails for commercial purposes. But it does not mean that this problem can be totally eliminated. The Internet provides plenty of possibilities facilitating evasion of legislation while not being caught in flagrante. There will always be unfair traders trying to take advantage of e-mail advertisement carried out in an illegal way. As it is not possible to be eliminated, the law should primarily motivate a relevant person to obey legal rules, i.e. to act as a preventive tool. For that purpose, the fear of sanctions for breaching these rules has to be effective, i.e. sanctions must be serious enough in order to reach this objective. Further, protection from unjustified forms of e-mail advertising cannot be only in the hands of customers or other competitors. It must be as well the task of state authorities entitled to act independently and immediately in the administrative proceedings. European legislation does not state exact procedural forms how to protect customers, competitors or public interest when the law is breached. It should be in the competence of the Member states. It is up to their decision which way of protection will be chosen either in the administrative proceedings or at courts or its combination. Therefore, in each Member state a different way of protection to unjustified e-mail advertising can be enacted. I suppose there should be the same legal ways of protection in the whole European Union; otherwise this system lacks effectiveness.

Viral Internet Advertising

As it was mentioned above, e-mail advertising is required to fulfill all the criteria stipulated in the Directive on privacy and electronic communications; especially to comply with the opt-in system introduced thereby. In order to avoid this very strict rule, inventive marketers have developed a special form of Internet advertising – the so-called viral advertising. "Viral advertising refers to the idea that people will pass on and share interesting and entertaining content; this is often sponsored by a brand, which is looking to build awareness of a product or service." (Gupta, 2009, p. 299). It also involves a method of customer referral, i.e. customers alone are recommending their friends as suitable persons for obtaining some e-mail advertising or as potential customers. Such information or introductions are then spread as a virus. Of course, marketers must be very careful when doing so as it can result in the breach of the law.

For example, an Internet shopping portal has recently started a campaign based on the viral advertising. When a customer has made purchase,

he has been sent an opportunity to receive future discounts by introducing a friend. The customer has been given a code to forward it to his friends or family. If they have shopped with the Internet shopping portal and inserted the code in the appropriate place in the order form they would receive some discount on that order. The code has been recognized by the portal`s system and, as a result of this, it has known that this new customer had been introduced by the former customer. The former customer has been rewarded with a voucher for a discount off his next purchase. That has been one of the successful uses of the viral advertising while being in compliance with the law. It is the customer who has started communication with the trader (portal provider) and thus has established an exception from the opt-in system as stipulated in the Article 13(2) of the Directive on privacy and electronic communications (genuine business connection already being in existence).

On the other hand, an example of illicit use of viral advertising can be seen in the marketing activity of one unnamed airline company. This company has offered customers a 10 EUR discount for buying any flight ticket provided that they put four e-mail addresses of friends or family members into its mailing list for sending commercial e-mails with special offers. Afterwards, these persons have been attacked with a huge number of commercial e-mails of this airline company without having given their prior consent. Therefore, such type of viral advertising has been to the contrary with Article 13(1) of the Directive on privacy and electronic communications.

Similarly, contrary to this provision is as well viral advertising based on inducing customers "to input" not only their addresses but also that of their friend/s or other third parties. The friend in question is then targeted and will receive an e-mail that looks like it was sent by the person making the recommendation (looking like it comes from a trusted person is often the main driver so it is more likely to be opened rather than deleted)" (Brock & Azim-Khan, 2008, p. 154).

In order to prevent viral advertising from being illegal, the following recommendation of the EU Information Commissioner should be taken into consideration: Firstly, it is useful to avoid incentivising customers to recommend marketing messages to their friends or other third parties. Secondly, a suppression list must be permanently checked if the recipient has not already asked to suppress his details. Further, it must be taken into account that sending commercial e-mails is possible only with a prior consent of the recipient. Therefore, the customer putting another person`s contact details must declare that he/she has the consent of the person whose details he/she is supplying. Finally, it is recommended to let the recipient know how his/her e-mail address or further details appear in the distribution list.

Internet Advertising and Unfair Competition

The off-line advertising facilitates dissemination of information on advertised products or services through different traditional media such as TV, magazines, posters and so on. After a customer receives sufficient information, process of selling advertised products or services may start. For this purpose, visiting traditional shops is required. That means the advertising process is running independently from the selling process. In case of Internet advertising, the advertising stage and the selling stage are interconnected; the customer can buy advertised products or services immediately by clicking on an icon launching some e-shop. As the result, advertising and selling through the Internet are considered as a more customer-friendly and less time-consuming procedure. On the other hand, impersonal communication is a good breeding ground for unfair or misleading commercial practices. "Although the advertising will contain an address and telephone number, it is probable that the company will disappear before even a law enforcement agency will have time to

investigate misleading character of the respective communication" (Coteanu, 2005, p. 140).

In order to protect consumers against unfair commercial practices of traders the so-called Unfair Commercial Practices Directive[9] has been adopted. This directive relates as well to unfair commercial practices when advertising through the Internet.

The protection ensured by the directive is threefold. Firstly, in the Article 5 of the directive general clause prohibiting any kind of unfair commercial practices is determined. For this purpose, the commercial practice is found as unfair if it is to the contrary to the requirements of professional diligence and it materially distorts or is likely to materially distort the economic behavior with regard to the product of the average consumer whom it reaches or to whom it is addressed to or of the average member of the group when a commercial practice is directed to a particular group of consumers. The requirements must be satisfied cumulatively in order to justify unfairness.

On the second level, the directive deals with those advertising practices which are particularly unfair. According to Article 5(3), those commercial practices in particular which are unfair are misleading in terms of Article 6 (misleading actions) and Article 7 (misleading omissions) or aggressive in terms of Article 8 (aggressive commercial practices) and Article 9 (harassment, coercion and undue influence). (Micklitz, 2006, p. 85).

In accordance with the Directive, a commercial practice shall be regarded as misleading if it contains false information and is therefore untruthful or in any way, including an overall presentation, deceives or is likely to deceive the average consumer even if the information is factually correct and in either case causes or is likely to cause him/her to take a transactional decision that he/she would not have taken otherwise. According to Henning-Bodewig "average consumer" means the consumer who is reasonably well-informed and reasonably observant and circumspect." (2006, p. 61). Being misleading is one of the most frequent infringement in case of Internet advertising; the Internet provides plenty of technical tools allowing dishonest traders to act misleadingly (temporal pop-up websites, untraced activity, etc.).

In addition, not only the activity of the trader can be considered as misleading but also the omission of material information that the average consumer needs to take an informed transactional decision and thus causes or is likely to cause the average consumer to take a transactional decision that he/she would not have taken otherwise. That is referred to as misleading omission. It must be considered in its factual context taking all of its features and circumstances and limitations of the communication medium into account. Moreover, misleading omission includes, as well, hiding and providing material information in an unclear, unintelligible, ambiguous or untimely manner or failing to identify the commercial intent of the commercial practice if not being already apparent from the context provided that it is a substantial reason for the consumer to take a transactional decision.

Finally, unfair commercial practices can be aggressive, too. Under the directive, a commercial practice shall be regarded as aggressive if, in its factual context and taking account of all its features and circumstances, by harassment, coercion including the use of physical force or undue influence, it significantly impairs or is likely to significantly impair the average consumer's freedom of choice or conduct with regard to the product and thereby causes him/her or is likely to cause him/her to take a transactional decision that he/she would not have taken otherwise. For example, making persistent and unwanted solicitations by e-mail to enforce a contractual obligation is a typical instance of aggressive commercial practice. Further, automatic opening of plenty of marketing pop-ups when browsing different websites can be found as aggressive as well.

As the third level of protection against unfair commercial practices, the directive specifies the list of those commercial practices which are in all circumstances regarded as unfair. Those activities are listed in the Annex 1 of the directive while being always considered as unfair. "These are the only commercial practices that can be deemed to be unfair without a case-by-case assessment." (Ratai, Homoki & Polyk, 2010, p. 210). For instance, if an advertisement encompasses inclusion of a direct exhortation to children to buy advertised products for them or falsely claiming that a product is able to cure illness, dysfunction or malformations and so on.

The unfair Commercial Practices Directive is mainly aimed at the protection of consumers who are natural persons acting for purposes which are outside their trade, business, craft or protection. A contrario, this directive protects neither legal entities nor natural persons acting in an entrepreneurial way. Their protection can be partially assured by the Directive on misleading and comparative advertising[10] that defines misleading advertising. But it does not regulate other forms of unfair commercial practices (misleading omission, aggressive commercial practices). I suppose that the definition of the "consumer" should not be based only on the formal but on the material criterion. Therefore, the term "consumer" for the purposes of this directive should by defined as any natural or legal person who is procuring products or services for its individual or household need. As the result, a legal person can be deemed as the consumer if being the end-consumer of products or services. (Similarly Corba, 2006, p. 796). If purchased products or services are intended for further sale, then this person cannot be considered as the consumer requiring protection under the directive.

Comparative Internet Advertising

The Internet facilitates the use of many on-line applications allowing comparing any products or services or even competitors themselves. As Internet advertising is performed through the Internet, it provides many more challenges for the traders to start a marketing campaign based on comparison than other types of an off-line advertisement; when advertising on-line it is easier for the trader to point out that his/her products or services are of better quality or price than those offered by the other competitors. As suggested, the intent of Internet advertising may rest on comparing products, services or competitors.

A comparative advertisement became part of European legislation in 1997 after the Directive 97/55/ES [11] had been adopted. Before 1997, its regulation had differentiated in each Member state. Some Member states had allowed comparative advertising (Great Britain), some had prohibited any kind of comparative practices in the advertising (Germany, France, Italy). As the result of this directive, each Member state was obliged to implement legal rules allowing comparative advertising into their national legislation within a 30-month time limit. Today, comparative advertising is regulated on the European level by the Directive on misleading and comparative advertising (2006/114/EC).

According to Article 2(c) of the latter Directive "comparative advertising" means any advertising which explicitly or by implication identifies a competitor or goods or services offered by a competitor. But it does not mean that all comparative advertisements are allowed. In order to be permitted the requirements stipulated in Article 4 of the directive must be met.

The comparative advertising shall, as far as the comparison is concerned, be permitted when the following conditions are met: it is not misleading, it compares goods or services meeting the same needs or intended for the same purpose; it objectively compares one or more material, relevant, verifiable and representative features of those goods and services which may include the price; it does not discredit or denigrate trademarks, trade names, other distinguishing marks,

goods, services, activities or circumstances of a competitor; for products with designation of origin it relates in each case to products with the same designation; it does not take an unfair advantage of the reputation of a trade mark, trade name or other distinguishing marks of a competitor or of the designation of origin of competing products; it does not present goods or services as imitations or replicas of goods or services bearing a protected trade mark or trade name; it does not create confusion among traders, between the advertiser and the competitor or between the advertiser's trademarks, trade names, other distinguishing marks, goods or services and those of the competitor.[12]

The same rules, as described above, must be met as well if there is comparing in the advertisement through the Internet, i.e. if a trader compares himself with the other competitor, event. his/her products or services with those produced or provided by another one. It is unimportant, whether a comparison is done directly or indirectly provided that the average customer could have understood the advertising message as comparing between the competitors or products/services (for example if Pepsi-cola states that its beverages are more tasty than similar beverages produced by the other unnamed competitor, the average customer can easily identify him.). For the comparative advertising being established, a direct link to the competitor's web-site containing information allowing the comparison is sufficient to be stated.

The truth is that the legal requirements for the comparative advertising being permitted are very strict and restrictive. Moreover, their wording is ambiguous and vague. That is why the traders are afraid of using comparing in their advertising activities. (opp. Kubinec, 2005, p. 1079). In addition, the Member states have chosen distinct ways of its implementation; some have incorporated it into administrative acts, the others have constituted a special type of unfair competition. It results in different remedies available to the injured persons when those rules are breached.

Internet Advertising of Certain Products

In the previous text general legal requirements relating to the advertising, including its Internet form, were described and analyzed. But European legislation comprises as well special rules applying only to advertising of a certain type of products or services. In order to provide complex information on the relevant legislation governing the Internet advertising, a reference to these legal acts cannot be omitted. On the other hand, a very detailed analysis would not contribute to achievement of the stated objective.

Special rules are regulating mainly the advertising and sponsorship of tobacco products, i.e. all products intended to be smoked, sniffed, sucked or chewed inasmuch as they are made, even partly, of tobacco. According to the Directive on advertising and sponsorship of the tobacco products[13], advertising of these products is prohibited except for the advertising intended exclusively for professionals in the tobacco trade and the advertising published in third countries where those publications are not principally intended for the European market. The same shall apply concerning advertising published through the Internet. However, it is hardly to eliminate marketing websites containing tobacco advertising intended for the European market while being registered in the third countries. Thus, that rule is very easy not to be obeyed.

Further, some special restrictions are applied to the advertising of medical products for human use. These products may be understood as substances or a combination of substances presented for treating or preventing diseases in human beings. Any substance or combination of substances which may be administered to human beings with a view to make a medical diagnosis or to restoring, correcting or modifying physiological functions in human beings is likewise considered a medicinal product. The advertising regulation thereof can be found in Article 86 to 100 of the Directive on Community code relating to medicinal products for human use.[14] For example, advertising of a medicinal product shall encourage the rational use of the medicinal product by presenting it objectively and without exaggerating its properties; further, advertising of medicinal products is prohibited to the general public if are available upon a medical prescription only or if containing psychotropic or narcotic substances, etc.

In addition, advertising is specially regulated when the following products are promoted: package travel, package holidays and package tours[15], consumer financial services[16], consumer credit[17], collective investment in transferable securities[18], insurance (including life insurance and non-life insurance)[19], financial instruments[20] or securities[21]. Moreover, most of the Member states have enacted special rules when advertising, for instance, alcoholic beverages, weapons and munition, nursing supplies, etc. Of course, Internet advertising must reflect all these requirements applying to those special types of products.

As can be seen, the legal regulation of the Internet advertising in the European Union is widely dispelled, regulated by many legal acts. Therefore, it is very difficult for a layman to find the answer to the question, whether the Internet advertising is in compliance with the European law. I suppose that concentrated legal regulation of the Internet advertising would be desirable; especially when taking into consideration permanently increasing number of acts trying to regulate this area. If not on the European level, then at least on the level of the Member states.

SOLUTIONS AND RECOMMENDATIONS

The Internet advertising is a very effective tool for promoting products or services on the market. If it is persuasive enough, it will make consumers to buy those products or services by clicking on an icon launching some online shop. But there are as well negatives connected with such type of advertisement. As there is impersonal communication between a trader and a customer when buying on-line, certain limits must be determined, including limits for Internet advertising. That is the role of law to regulate fair use of this marketing instrument in order to protect consumers, other competitors or public interest.

Legal limits for Internet advertising are on the territory of the European Union stipulated primarily by the European law. It is regulating this area in the form of directives which require further implementation into national law of each Member state. Of course, each Member state performs implementation in its own way provided that the purpose of the directive is met; therefore there can be seen differences in the adopted national legislation to implement the directive. To avoid these discrepancies the form of regulation in European legislation would be more appropriate. In comparison with the directive, a regulation is binding directly to natural persons or legal entities in each Member state without being required to be implemented into national legislation. Afterwards, the same legal regime of Internet advertising in the European Union can be fully ensured.

In addition, European legislation is regulating only particular issues relating to Internet advertising, such as unsolicited commercial communication, unfair commercial practices, etc. Applicable provisions are to be found in plenty of directives. There is no directive or other act aimed at complex regulation of Internet advertising; for instance containing some specification of the term, its basic rules, prohibition of annoying or impairing forms (spam, forms attacking minors` credulity, etc.), guarantees of consumers` protection and finally methods for prevention of breaking the law (e.g. sanctions). As mentioned in the last paragraph, the form of the regulation would be more suitable.

The Internet advertising can violate law when being one of the unfair commercial practices as described in the Directive on unfair commercial practices. Unfortunately, this directive protects only consumers who are natural persons (individuals). Legal entities are excluded even if they can be end-consumers as well. I am of opinion that this directive should protect all subjects who are in the position of end-consumers regardless of an individual or legal entity being affected.

Finally, when advertising through the Internet, a comparison of competitors, their products or services may take place. The Internet provides many opportunities to facilitate such comparison, either in a direct way or by implication. If doing so, very strict rules must be obeyed. Moreover, those rules applying to comparative advertising are not very clear and unambiguous. As the result, the traders must be very careful when running a marketing campaign based on comparison.

The utilization of the Internet is rapidly increasing; it is simplifying day-to-day human activities. On the other hand, growth of malicious Internet practices can be noticed, too. As those practices can be significantly detrimental, the Internet cannot stay out of the law influence. Law must be a reasonable guarantee of the Internet being fairly used.

FUTURE RESEARCH DIRECTIONS

The objective of this chapter was to analyze Internet advertising from the European law point of view, i.e. how it is regulated in the European law. As it has been mentioned, the European law uses directives as the form of regulation. The directives are not directly binding for individuals or legal entities; for this purpose, their implementation into national law is required. The Members states are obliged to implement the purpose of the directives; ways and methods how to reach it are up to their decision. Therefore, the final version of relevant national legislation concerning Internet advertising in each Member state would be worth further research activity. As the result of the comparison, positives and negatives of particular ways of implementation ought to be analyzed.

If Internet advertising is not in compliance with the legal rules, several remedies aimed at protection of affected interest will be activated. Each Member state was free in choice of remedies available to fight illicit forms of Internet advertising. Some of them have chosen administrative remedies that rest on activity of the public authorities when investigating and punishing illicit forms thereof. The other applied private-law remedies allowing the injured persons to start actions at courts in order to eliminate or prevent unjustified Internet advertisements. Which is the optimal method of protection against illegal Internet advertising? That would be the objective of the further research as well.

CONCLUSION

Marketing theory recognizes a large variety of practices aimed at promoting products or services on the relevant market; of course, advertising being one of them. The advertising can be specified as a communication process usually paid for, carried out either directly by a competitive trader or by someone else on his/her behalf designed to persuade receivers of expedience and need for the promoted products or services through various media. For example, television, radio, newspapers, magazines, direct mail, outdoor displays or mass transit vehicles are the most popular media used for the advertising purposes. But in the list of relevant media especially the Internet cannot be omitted. Advertisement disseminated through the Internet is known as Internet advertising.

There are more forms of Internet advertising such as corporate websites, marketing websites, on-line advertising, e-mail advertising including a viral type. As the Internet is always developing, a catalogue of advertising forms can be expended as well. Those forms differ not only on the basis of the applied Internet tools but also regarding their legal regulation.

The objective of this chapter was to analyze the Internet advertising as it was governed by the European Law. As the first step, general rules applying to this type of advertising were required to be considered. It has been mentioned, that the European law does not legislate general principles of advertising itself. Therefore, those principles must have been derived from the legislation of the Member states. While taking it into consideration, advertising, including its Internet form, must be polite, honest and truthful. Responsibility towards customers must be taken into account when preparing it. Certain legal principles relating to Internet advertising could be found in the European legislation as well. For instance, according to the European directive the Internet advertising must be clearly identifiable as such, then a person on whose behalf Internet advertising is made shall be clearly identifiable and, finally, promotional competitions or games, event. promotional offers such as discounts, premiums and gifts, shall be clearly identifiable as such and the conditions which are to be met to qualify for them shall be easily accessible and presented clearly and unambiguously. I suppose that complex regulation of Internet advertising as such, including its basic rules, should be legislated by the European law; not only its particular issues.

Special attention is paid by the European law to e-mail advertising in order to prohibit unsolicited commercial communication (spam). According to relevant law, sending advertisement messages through e-mails is permitted only if a prior consent of the recipient is given. The European law is more radical when e-mail advertising is sent by an unknown sender or even if the recipient is deprived of the possibility to cease this unwanted communication (valid address is not provided). Such forms are *a priori* prohibited. Even if European legislation concerning e-mail advertising is quite well adjusted, the Internet provides plenty of possibilities facilitating evasion of this legislation. Therefore, it is necessary to implement a sufficient system of prevention of evasion or even breaching the law. To do so, protection from unjustified e-mail advertisements cannot be only in the hand of customers or other competitors; it must be as well the task of the public authorities investigating and punishing illicit forms *ex officio*. A particular type of e-mail advertising is so-called viral advertisement. It rests on the spontaneous dissemination of advertising messages by customers alone through e-mails in order to establish a chain of reactions. Viral advertising is subject to the same rules as are applied to e-mail advertisements.

When advertising through the Internet, rules designed for protection against unfair commercial practices may be challenged. Unfair commercial practices include misleading advertising, misleading omission and aggressive commercial practices. As the negative can be considered that those rules are protecting only natural persons (individuals). Legal entities are excluded even though they can be in the position of the end-consumer, too. I am of opinion that such protection should be available to all persons who are the end-consumers regardless of the fact if a natural or legal person is affected hereby.

Moreover, Internet advertising may involve a comparison of traders, their products or services. In this case, Internet advertisement must be in compliance with the rules relating to the comparative advertising as well. These rules are very strict. In addition, their wording is vague and unambiguous. Therefore, marketers must be careful when comparing with the other traders or with their products/services.

Finally, particular issues of Internet advertising are in the European law regulated in the form of directive. On one hand, this form allows the Member states to implement some desired purpose of the directive into the national law in a way they consider to be a suitable one. On the other hand, due to a possibility of "independent" implementation by each Member state, certain legal regulations may more or less differ in each Member state. As the advertising through the Internet crosses the borders of a state, a higher degree of uniformity would be desirable at least in the European Union. I suppose that the form of regulation could be able to achieve this objective.

Further research activities concerning Internet advertising should be focused on the comparison of the Member states' national legislation adopted for implementation of the European law, esp. on the positives and negatives of a particular approach chosen by each Member state. Moreover, remedies adopted by each Member state for protection of customers, other competitors and public interest should be the objective of further research as well.

REFERENCES

Armstrong, S. (2001). *Advertising on the Internet* (2nd ed.). London, UK: Kogan Page Publishers.

Barker, D. I., & Terry, C. D. (2008). *Internet research* (4th ed.). Boston, MA: Cengage Learning.

Brock, A. C., & Azim-Khan, R. (2008). *E-business: The practical guide to the laws* (2nd ed.). Great Britain: Spiramus Press Ltd.

Brown, B. C. (2006). *How to use the Internet to advertise, promote and market your business or website-- With little or no money.* Ocala, FL: Atlantic Publishing Company.

Corba, J. (2008). Aktivna a pasivna legitimacia v sporoch z nekalej sutaze. *Justicna Revue, 58*(5), 793–801.

Cormack, G. V. (2008). *Email spam filtering: A systematic review.* Hanover, MA: Publishers Inc.

Coteanu, C. (2005). *Cyber consume law and unfair trading practices.* Hampshire, UK: Ashgate Publishing Ltd.

Fabian, A. (2009). The linking points of EU law and the member state's administrative procedure. *Curentul Juridic, 3*(3), 1-6. Retrieved December 30, 2010, http://revcurentjur.ro/ arhiva/ attachments_ 200903/ recjurid093_1F.pdf

Fairhurst, J. (2007). *Law of the European Union* (6th ed.). Edinburgh, UK: Pearson Education.

Fielden, N. L. (2001). *Internet research: Theory and practice* (2nd ed.). Jefferson, NC: McFarland & Company Inc.

Gupta, S. (2009). *Branding and advertising.* New Delhi, India: Global India Publications PVT Ltd.

Henning-Bodewig, F. (2006). *Unfair competition law. European Union and member states.* Netherlands: Kluwer Law International.

Janoshka, A. (2004). *Web advertising.* Amsterdam, The Netherlands: John Benjamins B.V.

Jansen, E. (2002). *NETLINGO: The Internet dictionary.* California: NetLingo, Inc.

Kotler, P., & col. (2007). *Moderni marketing.* 4. evropske vydani. Prague, Czech Republic: Grada Publishing, a.s.

Kotler, P., & col. (2008). *Principles of marketing,* 5th European edition. Essex, UK: Pearson Education Limited.

Krunkova, A. (2005). *Zaklady europskeho prava a prava Europskej unie.* Kosice, Slovakia: University of P.J. Safarik.

Kubinec, M. (2005). Este raz k problemom pravnej regulacie porovnavacej reklamy. *Justicna Revue.,* *57*(8-9), 1077–1083.

Lee, M., & Johnson, C. (1999). *Principles of advertising: A global perspective.* Binghamton, NY: The Haworth Press, Inc.

Michael, A., & Salter, B. (2006). *Mobile marketing: Achieving competitive advantage through wireless technology.* Oxford, UK: Butterworth-Heinemann.

Micklitz, H. W. (2006). The general clause on unfair practices. In Howells, G. G., Micklitz, H. W., & Wilhelmsson, T. (Eds.), *European fair trading law: The unfair commercial practices directive* (pp. 83–123). Hampshire, UK: Ashgate Publishing Ltd.

Nikolinakos, N. T. (2006). *EU competition law and regulation in the converging telecommunications, media and IT sectors.* Netherlands: Kluwer Law International.

Plotkin, E. M., Wells, B., & Wimmer, A. K. (2003). *E-commerce law and business.* New York, NY: Aspen Publishers Online.

Ratai, B., Homoki, P., & Polyk, G. (2010). *Cyber law in Hungary.* Netherlands: Kluwer Law International.

Reed, Ch. (2004). *Internet law: Text and materials* (2nd ed.). Cambridge, UK: University Press.

Schryen, G. (2007). *Anti-spam measures: Analysis and design.* Heidelberg, Germany: Springer.

Schumann, D. W., & Thorson, E. (1999). *Advertising and the World Wide Web.* Mahwah, NJ: Lawrence Erlabaum Associates, Inc.

Schumann, D. W., & Thorson, E. (2007). *Internet advertising: Theory and practice.* Mahwah, NJ: Lawrence Erlabaum Associates, Inc.

Vernarsky, M., & Molitoris, P. (2008). *Danove pravo.* Kosice, Slovakia: Univerzita P. J. Safarika – Fakulta verejnej spravy.

Vogel, H.-J. (2003). *E-commerce: Directives of the European Union and implementation in German law. Law and jurisdiction* (pp. 29–78). Hague, The Netherlands: Kluver Law International.

Vysekalova, J., & Mikes, J. (2007). *Reklama: Jak delat reklamu.* 2. aktualizovane a doplnene vydani. Prague, Czech Republic: Grada Publishing, a.s.

ADDITIONAL READING

Areni, C. (1991). *Differential effects of comparative advertising for an unfamiliar brand – The moderating role of audience elaboration.* Gainesville, FL: University of Florida.

Armstrong, S. (2001). *Advertising on the Internet* (2nd ed.). London, UK: Kogan Page Publishers.

Barker, D. I., & Terry, C. D. (2008). *Internet research* (4th ed.). Boston, MA: Cengage Learning.

Bodewig, F. H. (2006). *Unfair competition law. European Union and memeber states.* The Netherlands: Kluwer law International.

Brock, A. C., & Azim-Khan, R. (2008). *E-business: The practical guide to the laws* (2nd ed.). Great Britain: Spiramus Press Ltd.

Brown, B. C. (2006). *How to use the internet to advertise, promote and market your business or website-- With little or no money.* Ocala, FL: Atlantic Publishing Company.

Corba, J. (2008). Aktivna a pasivna legitimacia v sporoch z nekalej sutaze. *Justicna Revue, 58*(5), 793–801.

Cormack, G. V. (2008). *Email spam filtering: A systematic review.* Hanover, MA: Publishers Inc.

Coteanu, C. (2005). *Cyber consume law and unfair trading practices.* Hampshire, UK: Ashgate Publishing Ltd.

Dunne, R. (2009). *Computers and the law: an introduction to basic legal principles and their application in cyberspace.* Cambridge, UK: Cambridge University Press.

Edwards, L., & Waelde, Ch. (2000). *Law and the Internet: a framework for electronic commerce* (2nd ed.). USA: Hart.

Emmerich, V. (2002). *Unlauterer Wettbewerb.* Munich, Germany: C. H. BECK.

Fabian, A. (2009). The linking points of EU law and the member state`s administrative procedure. *Curentul Juridic, 3*(3), 1-6. Retrieved December 30, 2010, http://revcurentjur.ro/ arhiva/ attachments_ 200903/ recjurid093_ 1F.pdf

Fairhurst, J. (2007). *Law of the European Union* (6th ed.). Edinburgh, UK: Pearson Education.

Fielden, N. L. (2001). *Internet research: Theory and practice* (2nd ed.). Jefferson, NC: McFarland & Company Inc.

Girasa, R. J. (2008). *Cyber law: national and international perspectives.* USA: Michigan University.

Gupta, S. (2009). *Branding and advertising.* New Delhi, India: Global India Publications PVT Ltd.

Hajn, P. (1994). *Pravo nekale souteze.* Brno, Czech republic: Masarykova universita

Henning-Bodewig, F. (2006). *Unfair competition law. European Union and member states.* The Netherlands: Kluwer Law International.

Jakab, R. (2004). Pojmove vymedzenie porovnavacej reklamy. *Justicna revue.* 56(12). 1339-1351

Jakab, R. (2005). Problemy pravnej regulacie porovnavacej reklamy. *Justicna revue.* 57(4). 517-525

Jakab, R. (2006). Pravne prostriedky ochrany pred neopravnenou porovnavacou reklamou. *Justicna revue.* 58(12). 1852-1865

Jakab. R. (2010). *Porovnavacia reklama z pohladu prava (Comparative advertising from legal point of view).* Kosice, Slovakia: Univerzita P.J. Safarika, Fakulta verejnej spravy

Janoshka, A. (2004). *Web advertising.* Amsterdam, The Netherlands: John Benjamins B.V.

Jansen, E. (2002). *NETLINGO: The Internet dictionary.* California: NetLingo, Inc.

Kotler, P., & col. (2007). *Moderni marketing*. 4. evropske vydani. Prague, Czech Republic: Grada Publishing, a.s.

Kotler, P., & col. (2008). *Principles of marketing*, 5th European edition. Essex, UK: Pearson Education Limited.

Krunkova, A. (2005). *Zaklady europskeho prava a prava Europskej unie*. Kosice, Slovakia: University of P.J. Safarik.

Kubinec, M. (2005). Este raz k problemom pravnej regulacie porovnavacej reklamy. *Justicna Revue.*, *57*(8-9), 1077–1083.

Lee, M., & Johnson, C. (1999). *Principles of advertising: A global perspective*. Binghamton, NY: The Haworth Press, Inc.

Mexa, P. G. (2009). *European internet law*. Spain: Netbiblo S.L.

Michael, A., & Salter, B. (2006). *Mobile marketing: Achieving competitive advantage through wireless technology*. Oxford, UK: Butterworth-Heinemann.

Micklitz, H. W. (2006). The general clause on unfair practices. In Howells, G. G., Micklitz, H. W., & Wilhelmsson, T. (Eds.), *European fair trading law: The unfair commercial practices directive* (pp. 83–123). Hampshire, UK: Ashgate Publishing Ltd.

Monti, G. (2007). *EC competition law. Law in context*. Cambridge, UK: Cambridge University Press.

Morasch, M. (2005). *Comparative advertising: a comparative study of trade-mark laws and competition laws in Canada and the European Union*. Toronto, Canada: University of Toronto.

Munková, J. (1996). *Pravo proti nekale soutezi*. Prague, Czech republic: C.H.BECK

Nikolinakos, N. T. (2006). *EU competition law and regulation in the converging telecommunications, media and IT sectors*. Netherlands: Kluwer Law International.

Plotkin, E. M., Wells, B., & Wimmer, A. K. (2003). *E-commerce law and business*. New York, NY: Aspen Publishers Online.

Ratai, B., Homoki, P., & Polyk, G. (2010). *Cyber law in Hungary*. The Netherlands: Kluwer Law International.

Reed, Ch. (2004). *Internet law: Text and materials* (2nd ed.). Cambridge, UK: University Press.

Rosenoer, J. (1997). *Cyber law. The law of the internet*. San Francisco, CL: Springer-Verlag New York, Inc.

Schryen, G. (2007). *Anti-spam measures: Analysis and design*. Heidelberg, Germany: Springer.

Schumann, D. W., & Thorson, E. (1999). *Advertising and the World Wide Web*. Mahwah, NJ: Lawrence Erlabaum Associates, Inc.

Schumann, D. W., & Thorson, E. (2007). *Internet advertising: Theory and practice*. Mahwah, NJ: Lawrence Erlabaum Associates, Inc.

Vernarsky, M., & Molitoris, P. (2008). *Danove pravo*. Kosice, Slovakia: Univerzita P. J. Safarika – Fakulta verejnej spravy.

Vogel, H.-J. (2003). *E-commerce: Directives of the European Union and implementation in German law. Law and jurisdiction* (pp. 29–78). Hague, The Netherlands: Kluver Law International.

Vysekalova, J., & Mikes, J. (2007). *Reklama: Jak delat reklamu*. 2. aktualizovane a doplnene vydani. Prague, Czech Republic: Grada Publishing, a.s.

Waelbroeck, M., & Frignani, A. (1999). *European competition law*. USA: Transnational Publishers.

KEY TERMS AND DEFINITIONS

Advertising: Any form of commercial communications with the aim or direct or indirect effect of promoting products or services.

Commercial Practices: Any act, omission, course of conduct or representation, commercial communication including advertising and marketing, by a trader, directly connected with the promotion, sale or supply of a product to consumers.

Comparative Advertising: Any advertising which explicitly or by implication identifies a competitor or goods or services offered by a competitor.

Competitor: Any natural person or legal entity participating in commercial contest.

Electronic Mail: Any text, voice, sound or image message sent over a public communications network which can be stored in the network or in the recipient's terminal equipment until it is collected by the recipient.

Internet Advertising: Any form of promoting products or services through the internet.

Misleading Advertising: Any advertising which in any way, including its presentation, deceives or is likely to deceive the persons to whom it is addressed or whom it reaches and which, by reason of its deceptive nature, is likely to affect their economic behaviour or which, for those reasons, injures or is likely to injure a competitor.

Trader: Any natural or legal person who, in commercial practices, is acting for purposes relating to his trade, business, craft or profession.

Unsolicited Commercial Communication: Any message sent to numerous recipients by electronic mail with commercial content.

ENDNOTES

[1] Directive 2006/114/EC of the European Parliament and of the Council of 12 December 2006 concerning misleading and comparative advertising (codified version), Official Journal of the European Union, L 376, 27.12.2006, p. 21-27

[2] Directive 2003/33/EC of the European Parliament and of the Council of 26 May 2003 on the approximation of the laws, regulations and administrative provisions of the Member States relating to the advertising and sponsorship of tobacco products, Official Journal of the European Union, L 152, 20.6.2003, p. 16-19

[3] Directive 2000/31/EC of the European Parliament and of the Council of 8 June 2000 on certain legal aspects of information society services, in particular electronic commerce, in the Internal Market, Official Journal of the European Union, L 178, 17.7.2000, p. 1–16

[4] Directive 2002/58/EC of the European Parliament and the Council of 12 July 2002 concerning the processing of personal data and the protection of privacy in the electronic communications sector, Official Journal of the European Union, L 201, 31.7.2002, p. 37–47

[5] For the purposes of the Directive on privacy and electronic communications, „electronic mail" means any text, voice, sound or image message sent over a public communications network which can be stored in the network or in the recipient's terminal equipment until it is collected by the recipient.

[6] § 65 of the Act No. 610/2003 Coll., on electronic communications as amended by further regulations

[7] § 7 of the Act. No. 480/2004 Coll., on certain services of information society and on amendment of certain acts, as amended by further regulations

[8] § 7 of the Act on unfair competition (BGBl. I S. 254)

[9] Directive 2005/29/EC of the European parliament and Council of 11 May 2005 concerning unfair business-to-consumer commercial practices in the internal market

and amending Council Directive 84/450/EEC, Directives 97/7/EC and 2002/65/EC of the European Parliament and of the Council and Regulation (EC) No 2006/2004 of the European Parliament and of the Council, Official Journal of the European Union, L 149, 11.6.2005, p. 22-37

10   Directive 2006/114/EC of the European Parliament and of the Council of 12 December 2006 concerning misleading and comparative advertising (codified version) (Text with EEA relevance), Official Journal of the European Union, L 376, 27.12.2006, p. 21 - 27

11   Directive 97/55/EC of European Parliament and of the Council of 6 October 1997 amending Directive 84/450/EEC concerning misleading advertising so as to include comparative advertising, Official Journal of the European Union, L 290, 23.10.1997, p. 18–23

12   Comparative advertising was analyzed in details by author of this chapter in the monograph: Jakab, R. (2010). *Porovnavacia reklama z pohladu práva (Comparative advertising from the legal point of view)*. Kosice: Univerzita P.J. Safarika. Fakulta verejnej spravy

13   Directive 2003/33/EC of the European Parliament and of the Council of 26 May 2003 on the approximation of the laws, regulations and administrative provisions of the Member States relating to the advertising and sponsorship of tobacco products, Official Journal of the European Union, L 152, 20.6.2003, p. 16-19

14   Directive 2001/83/EC of the European Parliament and of the Council of 6 November 2001 on the Community code relating to medicinal products for human use, Official Journal of the European Union, L 311, 28.11.2001, p. 67 - 128

15   Article 3 of Council Directive 90/314/EEC of 13 June 1990 on package travel, package holidays and package tours, Official Journal of the European Union, L 158, 23.06. 1990, p. 59 - 64

16   Article 3 to 4 of Directive 2002/65/EC of the European Parliament and of the Council of 23 September 2002 concerning the distance marketing of consumer financial services and amending Council Directive 90/619/EEC and Directives 97/7/EC and 98/27/EC, Official Journal of the European Union, L 271, 09.10. 2002, p. 16 - 24

17   Article 1(d) of Directive 98/7/EC of the European Parliament and of the Council of 16 February 1998 amending Directive 87/102/EEC for the approximation of the laws, regulations and administrative provisions of the Member States concerning consumer credit, Official Journal of the European Union, L 101, 01.04. 1998, p. 17 - 23

18   Article 1(9) of Directive 2001/107/EC of the European Parliament and of the Council of 21 January 2002 amending Council Directive 85/611/EEC on the coordination of laws, regulations and administrative provisions relating to undertakings for collective investment in transferable securities (UCITS) with a view to regulating management companies and simplified prospectuses, Official Journal of the European Union, L 41, 13.2.2002, p. 20–34

19   Article 12 and 13 of Directive 2002/92/EC of the European Parliament and of the Council of 9 December 2002 on insurance mediation, Official Journal of the European Union, L 9, 15.1.2003, p. 3–10; Article 36 of Directive 2002/83/EC of the European Parliament and of the Council of 5 November 2002 concerning life assurance, Official Journal of the European Union, L 345, 19.12.2002, p. 1–51; Article 31 and 43 of Council Directive 92/49/EEC of 18 June 1992 on the coordination of laws, regulations and administrative provisions relating to direct insurance other than life assurance and amending Directives

73/239/EEC and 88/357/EEC (third non-life insurance Directive), Official Journal of the European Union, L 228, 11.8.1992, p. 1–23

[20] Article 19 of Directive 2004/39/EC of the European Parliament and of the Council of 21 April 2004 on markets in financial instruments amending Council Directives 85/611/EEC and 93/6/EEC and Directive 2000/12/EC of the European Parliament and of the Council and repealing Council Directive 93/22/EEC, Official Journal of the European Union, L 145, 30.4.2004, p. 1–44

[21] Article 5, 7 and 8 of Directive 2003/71/EC of the European Parliament and of the Council of 4 November 2003 on the prospectus to be published when securities are offered to the public or admitted to trading and amending Directive 2001/34/EC (Text with EEA relevance), Official Journal of the European Union, L 345, 31.12.2003, p. 64–89

About the Contributors

Alfreda Dudley is a Clinical Assistant Professor in the Department of Computer and Information Sciences at Towson University. She currently teaches the computer ethics, cyberlaw, database and Information Technology courses in the department. Dr. Dudley's research areas include: Information Technology, computer ethics, computer security, virtual technologies, and computer education with an emphasis on the application of ethics in augmented reality and virtual worlds. Dr. Dudley has published numerous journal articles, book chapters, and conference proceedings related to the application ethics in computing environments. Her other interests and pursuits include research involving underrepresented populations in the STEM area (specifically in the computing areas).

James Braman is a Lecturer in the Department of Computer and Information Sciences at Towson University. He earned a M.S. in Computer Science in 2006 and is pursuing a D.Sc. in Information Technology. James serves as joint editor-in-chief for the Institute for Computer Sciences, Social Informatics and Telecommunications Engineering (ICST) Transactions on E-Education and E-Learning along with Dr. Vincenti. He has published several edited books, the most recent, *Multi-User Virtual Environments for the Classroom: Practical Approaches to Teaching in Virtual Worlds*. He has been involved in virtual world research for several years, along with providing consulting and research services for businesses and organizations utilizing virtual worlds and augmented reality. He has also published numerous research articles related to affective computing, intelligent agents, computer ethics, and education in virtual and immersive environments.

Giovanni Vincenti is a Lecturer for the Department of Computer and Information Sciences at Towson University, in Towson, MD. He received his Doctorate of Science in Applied Information Technology from Towson University in 2007. He has been teaching undergraduate and graduate courses for several years, letting him develop his interest in instructional technologies that range from simple learning objects as a supplement to in-person instruction, all the way to the utilization of virtual worlds in the classroom. He has been collaborating for years with James Braman, co-authoring several published works including the edited volume titled "Multi-User Virtual Environments for the Classroom: Practical Approaches to Teaching in Virtual Worlds." Vincenti and Braman are also leading e-learning projects for the Institute of Computer Sciences, Social Informatics, and Telecommunications Engineering (ICST). In addition, Dr. Vincenti also serves as a consultant to companies and universities that focus on online learning.

* * *

Eugenia Alexandropoulou-Egyptiadou is an Associate Professor in Computer Law at the Department of Applied Informatics, University of Macedonia – Thessaloniki – Greece, where she's teaching I.T. Law in under-graduate and post-graduate level. She is also an attorney at law at the Supreme Court (Bar of Thessaloniki). She used to be, for several years, head of the legal department of a Greek bank (Egnatia Bank) and member of the editorial board of the Law Review Harmenopoulos (edited by the Bar of Thessaloniki). She has written many scientific articles and books in the area of civil, banking, labour, international, and IT law. In the last few years her interests focus on personal data protection, human rights, and intellectual software property.

Anteneh Ayanso is an Associate Professor of Information Systems at Brock University at St. Catharines, Canada. He received his Ph.D. in Information Systems from the University of Connecticut and an MBA from Syracuse University. His research interests are in data management, electronic business, quantitative modeling, and simulation in Information Systems and supply chains. He has published in journals such as *Communications of the AIS, Decision Support Systems, European Journal of Operational Research, Journal of Computer Information Systems, Journal of Database Management, International Journal of Electronic Commerce, Information Technology for Development, International Journal of Healthcare Delivery Reform Initiatives*, as well as in proceedings of major international conferences in Information Systems and related fields. His research in data management has been funded by the Natural Sciences and Engineering Research Council of Canada (NSERC).

Jonathan Bishop (Councillor) is the Chair of the Centre for Research into Online Communities and E-Learning Systems. A Chartered IT Professional Fellow of BCS – The Chartered Institute for IT, and a member of its Law Specialist Group, Cllr Bishop graduated from the Glamorgan Law School with a Master of Laws degree in 2007. Since then he has contributed articles to journals and websites and made a number of speeches about the interactions between IT and law and the impacts of governmental frameworks on the IT sector, with particular focus on the e-learning industry. In his spare time he enjoys listening to music, taking part in public speaking competitions, and model building.

Sam De Silva is a Partner and the Head of Technology and Outsourcing at a leading UK law firm, Manches LLP. His main areas of practice are technology and business process outsourcing and technology projects, such as software licensing and support, system development and systems integration. He has been published widely, speaks regularly on outsourcing and technology law topics and is on the Law Society's Technology and Law Committee. In addition to his LLB and Masters in Business Law, Sam has post-graduate degrees in information technology and business administration so is well aware of the commercial, business and technical issues facing both users and suppliers of technology. Sam is also one of very few UK solicitors who is a Member of the Chartered Institute of Purchasing and Supply (MCIPS), Fellow of the British Computer Society (FBCS) and a Chartered IT Professional (CITP). Sam also has in-house industry legal experience having been seconded to Accenture UK as a senior legal counsel. Dr De Silva is a Barrister and Solicitor of the High Court of New Zealand, a Solicitor of the Supreme Court of England and Wales and a Solicitor of the Supreme Court of New South Wales, Australia.

Miguel A. Garcia-Ruiz graduated in Computer Systems engineering and obtained his MSc in Computer Science from the University of Colima, Mexico. He received his PhD in Computer Science and

Artificial Intelligence at the University of Sussex, UK. He took a virtual reality course at Salford University, UK, and a graphics techniques internship at the Madrid Polytechnic University, Spain. Miguel is a Professor of Computer Science with the College of Telematics of the University of Colima. He has published three books and more than sixty peer-reviewed scientific papers and book chapters, and directed a video documentary on virtual reality. His research interests include virtual reality and usability of multimodal human-computer interfaces. Currently, Miguel is a Visiting Professor at the University of Ontario Institute of Technology, Canada.

Anne Gerdes (MA, Ph.D.) is Associate Professor in Humanistic Information Science at Institute of Business, Communication and Information Science, University of Southern Denmark. Her principal research interests are in the area of IT Ethics, Persuasive Technology and Learning studies. Anne Gerdes is the leader of the Danish Research Network on IT Ethics, which provides an interdisciplinary forum for investigating ethical issues associated with the development and application of Information and Communication Technology.

Lee Gillam, is a Chartered IT Professional Fellow of the British Computer Society (FBCS CITP). Currently, he is a Lecturer in the Department of Computing at the University of Surrey and Senior Tutor for Professional Training. Previous publications and research has been in the areas of knowledge acquisition and Grid and cloud computing systems. He has worked in and been responsible as PI or lead researcher for a number of research projects supported by the EU's IT Research and Development programmes and UK research programmes under EPSRC and ESRC. He has contributed a number of international standards through ISO, and to a national review of Cloud Computing, which formed a basis for an EPSRC/JISC research call. He has been running a knowledge transfer partnership with a London-based Financial Services provider, and is due to being an EPSRC/JISC funded activity on cloud computing benchmarking.

Tejaswini Herath is an Assistant Professor in the Faculty of Business at Brock University, Canada. She received her Ph.D. from the Department of Management Science and Systems at State University of New York, Buffalo (UB). She holds MMIS, MSCE from Auburn University, USA and BE from Pune University, India. Previously she worked as a systems analyst and a part time lecturer at University of Northern British Columbia, Canada. Her research interests are in information assurance and include topics such as information security and privacy, diffusion of information assurance practices, economics of information security, and risk management. Her work has been published in leading journals and conferences. Her work has appeared in the *Journal of Management Information Systems, Decision Support Systems, European Journal of Information Systems, Information Systems Management, International Journal of Business Governance and Ethics,* and *International Journal of E-Government Research.* In addition she has contributed several book chapters.

Radomir Jakab received his Master of Law from University of P. J. Safarik in 2004. In 2005 he received Doctor of Law (JUDr.) from the same university with his thesis entitled "Comparative Advertising." In 2010 he completed doctoral study (PhD) in the study field of administrative law at University of P. J. Safarik in Kosice. From 2004 to 2009 he worked as an in-house lawyer for the international industry company RWE. Since 2009 he has been working as a legal counsel for a local law firm. He is as well employed as a scholar and lecturer at University of P. J. Safarik in Kosice. His research activities are aimed at legal regulation of advertising. Moreover, he is dealing with the research of the administrative process in the public administration.

Gráinne Kirwan is the programme co-ordinator of the MSc in Cyberpsychology in Dun Laoghaire Institute of Art, Design and Technology, Ireland. She has seven years' experience of lecturing, and her primary areas of research are forensic psychology, virtual reality, and cyberpsychology. Most recently she has completed research identifying potential juror's attitudes towards cybercriminals and their victims. She has been interviewed by several major publications about her expertise in the field of cyberpsychology, as well as providing interviews for both regional and national radio stations. She regularly presents work at international psychological conferences and reviews articles for *Cyberpsychology and Behaviour* and *Computers in Human Behaviour*.

Ananda Mitra is the Chair and Professor of Communication at Wake Forest University. He teaches in the area of communication, technology, and culture and is the author of the six-volume encyclopedic series called Digital World (2010) and has also published a book called Alien Technologies: Coping with Modern Mysteries (2010). His primary area of research is exploring the ways in which new digital technologies are reshaping the way we live. With a Bachelor's degree in Chemical Engineering from the Indian Institutes of Technology at Kharagpur, and a doctoral degree in Communication from the University of Illinois at Urbana-Champaign, he offers a unique look at the role of technology in everyday life.

Jean-Philippe Moiny is a graduate of Law (University of Liège, Belgium, June 2008). In September 2008, he joined the Privacy department of the Research Centre in IT and Law [CRID] in Namur, as a researcher. He began the study of data protection, privacy, contract law, and private international law in the context of social network sites and cloud computing. And he also examined the legal rules related to access to and re-use of public sector information. In this respect, he was appointed in January 2009, by Royal Decree to the Commission on Access to and Reuse of Administrative Documents (Belgium Appeal Committee), Reuse section. Since October 1st, 2009, he is research fellow for the Belgian National Fund for the Scientific Research (F.R.S.-FNRS), and now carries out PhD research related to the spatial applicability of privacy and related rights in the context of Internet and cloud computing.

Patrik Olsson is an Assistant Professor of Criminology, Justice, and Policy Studies at the University of Ontario Institute of Technology (UOIT). His research agenda concerns the rights of children and youth as well as socio-legal aspects of Information Technology and social change. A more predominant focus has been on the rights of children and adolescents, e.g. child labor, human trafficking, children in conflict with the law, children in prison, the right to education, the principles of non discrimination, and child participation. Dr. Olsson has since the 1990s conducted extensive research in relation to the socio-legal situation for exposed children in the MERCOSUR countries in South America, as well as in Central America and South East Asia.

Ugo Pagallo is a Full Professor in Philosophy of Law at the University of Torino, Law School, and Faculty at the Center for Transnational Legal Studies (CTLS) in London, U.K. He is editor of the *Digitalica* series published by Giappichelli in Turin, co-editor of the AICOL series by Springer, and member of the Programme Committee of ETHICOMP since 2008. In addition to numerous essays in scholarly journals like *Journal of Business Ethics, AI & Society, Journal of Information, Communication and Ethics in Society, Hobbes Studies, Journal of Chinese Philosophy, Apuntes filosóficos, Knowledge, Technology & Policy,* and so forth, he is the author of eight monographs. His main interests are AI & law, network theory, robotics, and Information Technology law (specially data protection law and copyright).

Andrew Power is the Head of School of Creative Technologies at the Institute of Art, Design and Technology, Ireland. Prior to his academic career Andrew worked for sixteen years in industry, initially working for multinationals such as Digital Equipment Corporation and Intel, later for the Irish e-learning company SmartForce. Andrew serves on the board of directors of a number of not for profit organisations in Ireland and is pursuing Doctoral studies at the Institute of Governance, Queens University Belfast. Andrew regularly writes in the fields of e-governance, cyberlaw, online democracy, and social networking.

Richard A. Spinello is an Associate Research Professor in the Carroll School of Management at Boston College where he teaches courses on ethics, social issues in management, and corporate strategy. Prior to joining the faculty of Boston College he worked as a consultant and product manager in the software industry. He has written and edited nine books on applied ethics and related areas, including "CyberEthics: Morality and Law in Cyberspace" and "A Defense of Intellectual Property Rights" (with Maria Bottis). He has also written numerous articles and scholarly papers on ethics and public policy that have appeared in journals such as *Business Ethics Quarterly, Ethics and Information Technology,* and *The Journal of Information Ethics.*

Gurvirender Tejay is an Assistant Professor at the Graduate School of Computer and Information Sciences, Nova Southeastern University. His research interests include Information System security, Information Technology strategy, and information quality. His research work has been presented at various conferences including the Americas Conference on Information Systems, Hawaii International Conference on System Sciences, IEEE Intelligence and Security Informatics, and Annual Meeting of the Decision Sciences Institute. His academic interests led him to pursue graduate studies in the field of economics (University of Wisconsin, Milwaukee) and computer science (University of Chicago). He completed his doctoral studies with focus in Information Systems from Virginia Commonwealth University.

Miguel Vargas Martin is an Associate Professor at the University of Ontario Institute of Technology (Oshawa, Canada). Before joining UOIT, he was a post-doctoral researcher at Carleton University and Alcatel Canada. He holds a Ph.D. in Computer Science (Carleton University), a Master's degree in Electrical Engineering (CINVESTAV, Mexico), and a Bachelor's of Computer Science (Universidad Autónoma de Aguascalientes, Mexico). His main research interests are computer security, public safety, and optimization of websites for online healthcare education.

Anna Vartapetiance is a PhD student in the Department of Computing at the University of Surrey. Her research is mainly focused on the ethical and legal side of computing and artificial intelligence and their effects on society, and she is currently investigating the nature of deception. She has an interest in multi-user virtual environments and how they can be used to support real life projects and, since 2007, has had an active presence in Second Life. In 2008 she led the design and development of Surrey Island and has taken part in many educational projects including collaborating with the University of Idaho and being part of MUVEnation (Teaching and Learning with Multi-Use Virtual Environments). She also works as a Developer and Consultant in Second Life.

Sean Zadig is a federal law enforcement officer employed by the US Government and has conducted cybercrime investigations for over five years for a major federal agency. His areas of expertise include investigations involving botnets, network intrusions, and child exploitation. These cases have resulted in numerous arrests and prosecutions both in the United States and internationally. He holds a Master's in Criminal Justice from Boston University and is currently enrolled as a doctoral student at Nova Southeastern University focusing upon Information Systems security. His research interests include hacker deterrence, organized cybercrime, and botnets. His work has been presented at numerous conferences, including the Annual Meeting of the Decision Sciences Institute and the IEEE eCrime Researchers Summit.

Index